PATTON'S VANGUARD

Patton's Vanguard

The United States Army Fourth Armored Division

Don M. Fox

FOREWORD BY MARTIN BLUMENSON

McFarland & Company, Inc., Publishers
Jefferson, North Carolina, and London

LIBRARY OF CONGRESS CATALOGUING-IN-PUBLICATION DATA

Fox, Don M., 1958–
Patton's vanguard : the United States Army Fourth
Armored Division / Don M. Fox ; foreword by Martin Blumenson.
p.   cm.
Includes bibliographical references and index.

ISBN 0-7864-1582-7 (illustrated case binding : 50# alkaline paper) ∞

1. United States. Army. Armored Division, 4th — History.
2. World War, 1939–1945 — Campaigns — Western Front.
3. World War, 1939–1945 — Regimental histories — United States.
4. World War, 1939–1945 — Tank warfare.   I. Title.
D769.30534th.F69   2003   940.54'1273 — dc22   2003016495

British Library cataloguing data are available

Cover photograph: The final assembly of the
8th Tank Battalion, January 1946 (courtesy Al Irzyk)

Manufactured in the United States of America

*McFarland & Company, Inc., Publishers
Box 611, Jefferson, North Carolina 28640
www.mcfarlandpub.com*

Acknowledgments

Of all the resources utilized in the preparation of this work, none is more important than the men of the Fourth Armored Division. While conducting my research, I came in contact with several veterans, either face-to-face, via the telephone, or through written correspondence. I would like to thank the following men who took time out of the twilight of their lives to share their experiences:

Abraham Baum	10th Armored Infantry Battalion
Edward Bautz	37th Tank Battalion
John Colangelo	704th Tank Destroyer Battalion
Harry Feinberg	37th Tank Battalion
Anthony Giallanza	8th Tank Battalion
Donald E. Guild	94th Armored Field Artillery Battalion
Albin F. Irzyk	8th Tank Battalion
James H. Leach	37th Tank Battalion
Sam Ridley	35th Tank Battalion
John Whitehill	37th Tank Battalion

There are several other people who deserve special recognition for their contributions. First, I would like to extend my warmest thanks to Evelyn Irzyk and Marion Leach. Both of these women welcomed me into their homes and were kind enough to let me steal their husbands away from them for many hours of conversation.

Thanks are also given to Kay Besedick, who made available the art of her late husband, Frank. He served on the operations staff of the Fourth Armored during the war and created most of the illustrations for the division's official history. Kay's daughter-in-law, Susan, went the extra mile to make Frank's art a part of this project.

I have long admired the writing of Martin Blumenson. The quality of his life's work has earned him a spot among a very select group of military historians. His foreword is an invaluable addition to this work, not only because of his stature, but also because of his incredible knowledge of the subject. I am extremely grateful to him.

Colonel John S. Wood, Jr., provided a valuable and unique perspective from the vantage point of both soldier and son, and I greatly appreciate his help.

To David Wissolik, Ph.D., my thanks for his invitation to quote from *Men of the 704th* (Buchanan, Richard R., et al., eds.), for which he was an editor.

The reader of a unit history of this sort can have a tough time following the action without the aid of quality maps, and I am thankful that I had the opportunity to work with Jason Petho. His maps will no doubt enable the reader to navigate their way across Europe with the Fourth Armored Division.

Many of the veterans mentioned above reviewed portions of the manuscript at various stages of its development, and I extend my thanks to each of them. But none performed the task as exhaustively as Al Irzyk and Jimmie Leach. I owe both of these men a great debt for their edits, corrections, commentary, and encouragement.

Jamie Leach played a critical role. Had he not taken the time to pass on my initial correspondence to his father, I might have stumbled coming out of the blocks, and never recovered. Thank you, Jamie, for embracing a request from a total stranger.

I owe a special expression of thanks to James Kelly, whose father, Lt. Earl J. Kelly, served with the 10th Armored Infantry Battalion. His contribution regarding Lt. Charles Gniot provided a poignant ribbon with which to wrap the history of the Fourth Armored Division.

Nelson Wertz is the nephew of Corporal Lester Cussins, a member of the 51st Armored Infantry Battalion killed in action on November 9, 1944, at the town of Fonteny. Nelson was kind enough to hunt down several documents for me at Carlisle Barracks.

I would also like to acknowledge the professional work of Jim Parker at Double Delta Industries, Inc., who conducted a search of the National Archives for many of the photographs in the book.

To help ensure that my narrative was hitting the mark with a broad audience, I enlisted several friends to read early versions of the manuscript. I would like to thank David Parks, Steven Wyckmans, Todd Willoughby, and Jim Puff for their feedback and encouragement. In a similar vein, my appreciation goes out to many members of the Blitzkrieg Wargaming Club (too many to mention here) who offered words of support during the project.

Last, but absolutely not least, I must give immense thanks to my wife, Stephanie, and my sons, Alex and Andrew. During the two years I spent working on this project, I was often "missing in action" under my own roof. It wasn't always easy, but the fact that I was able to finish this work stands as testimony to their patience and support.

Contents

List of Terms
and Abbreviations

24/7 . . . . Twenty-four hours a day, seven days a week
A/37 . . . . Shorthand for identification of a Company (e.g., A Company, 37th Battalion)
AA . . . . Anti-Aircraft
AAA . . . . Anti-Aircraft Artillery
AD . . . . Armored Division
AFAB . . . . Armored Field Artillery Battalion
AG . . . . Assault gun
AIB . . . . Armored Infantry Battalion
Airborne . . . . Specialized troops trained for deployment by air (parachute)
AP . . . . Armor piercing
Armd . . . . Armored
Army . . . . Military unit, composed of two or more corps
Arty . . . . Artillery
AT . . . . Anti-tank
BAR . . . . Browning Automatic Rifle
Battalion . . . . Military unit, typically consists of three companies plus support
Bazooka. . . . . Shoulder fired rocket launcher
Bn . . . . Battalion
BOG . . . . Tank Bow Gunner/Assistant Driver
Bois . . . . Woods (French)
Bty . . . . Battery
Burp Gun . . . . German submachine gun
Capt . . . . Captain
Cav . . . . Cavalry
CCA . . . . Combat Command A
CCB . . . . Combat Command B
CCR. . . . . Combat Command Reserve

Company . . . . Military unit, typically composed of three platoons
Corps . . . . Military unit composed of two to five divisions
CP . . . . Command Post
Cpl . . . . Corporal
Col . . . . Colonel
Dom. . . . . Estate
DSC. . . . . Distinguished Service Cross
DSM. . . . . Distinguished Service Medal
Easy 8. . . . . M4A3E8 Sherman tank
Eng . . . . Engineer
Etang . . . . Lake (French)
ETO . . . . European Theater of Operations
FA . . . . Field Artillery
Fallschirmjager. . . . . Paratrooper (German)
Forêt. . . . . Forest (French)
G-1 . . . . Personnel Officer (Division level and above)
G-2 . . . . Intelligence Officer (Division level and above)
G-3 . . . . Operations Officer (Division level and above)
G-4. . . . . Supply Officer (Division level and above)
GI . . . . General Issue; also slang for an American Soldier
Grease Gun. . . . . American M3 submachine gun
Halftrack . . . . Armored vehicle with wheels up front, and tank-like tracks in rear
Haut. . . . . Heights (French)
Hellcat . . . . M18 tank destroyer
HMG. . . . . Heavy machine gun
HT. . . . . Half track
ID . . . . Infantry Division
Inf. . . . . Infantry
JagdTiger . . . . German heavy tank destroyer
Jumbo . . . . M4A3E2 Sherman tank
Kampfgruppe . . . . Battle Group (i.e., Task Force)
LCT . . . . Landing craft — tank
LD. . . . . Line of departure
LMG. . . . . Light machine gun
LST. . . . . Landing ship — tank
Lt . . . . Lieutenant
Lt Col . . . . Lieutenant Colonel
M1. . . . . Garand semi-automatic rifle
M4 . . . . Sherman tank
M4A3E2 . . . . Heavily armored variant of the Sherman tank
M4A3E8 . . . . Sherman tank w/76mm gun and improved suspension system
M5 . . . . Light tank
M7. . . . . 105mm Howitzer mounted on a tank chassis
M10. . . . . American self-propelled tank destroyer with 3-inch gun

M16 . . . . HT with four .50 caliber AA machine guns
M18 . . . . Tank destroyer with 76mm gun (aka "Hellcat")
M24 . . . . Chaffee light tank
M36 . . . . American self-propelled tank destroyer with 90mm gun
Mark IV . . . . German medium tank
Mark V . . . . German Panther tank
Mark VI . . . . German Tiger tank
Mer. . . . . Sea (French)
MG . . . . Machine gun
MP . . . . Military police
NCO . . . . Non Commissioned Officer
Ordnance. Supply (esp. weapons and ammunition)
P-47. . . . . American fighter-bomber (aka Thunderbolt)
P-51 . . . . American fighter plane (aka Mustang)
Panther . . . . German medium tank, model Mark V
Panzer. . . . . Tank (German)
Pfc . . . . Private First Class
PG. . . . . Panzer Grenadier
Pioneer. . . . . German engineer
Pl. . . . . Platoon
Platoon . . . . Military unit; in infantry, typically consists of three squads
Pvt . . . . Private
Pz . . . . Panzer
Recon . . . . Reconnaissance
RCT . . . . Regimental Combat Team (aka Infantry Regiment)
ROTC . . . . Reserve officers Training Corps
S-1 . . . . Personnel officer (below Division level)
S-2 . . . . Intelligence officer (below Division level)
S-3. . . . . Operations officer (below Division level)
S-4. . . . . Supply officer (below Division level)
Section . . . . Typically, half of a tank platoon
Sgt . . . . Sergeant
SNAFU . . . . Situation Normal All F — —-Up
SP. . . . . Self-propelled
Squad . . . . The smallest infantry unit, usually consisting of 10–12 men
SS. . . . . Schutzstaffel (Hitler's Bodyguards)
StuG . . . . German self-propelled assault gun
T/3 . . . . Corporal with specialized skill
T/4 . . . . Sergeant with specialized skill
T/5 . . . . Staff Sergeant
T/Sgt . . . . Sergeant with specialized skill
TD . . . . Tank destroyer
TF. . . . . Task Force
Tiger. . . . . German heavy tank

Tommy Gun . . . . Thompson submachine gun
VG . . . . Volksgrenadier (German for "People's Soldier")
V1 . . . . German winged rocket
V2 . . . . German rocket powered missile

Foreword
by Martin Blumenson

Don M. Fox has written a stirring book about a superb armored division operating in the European Theater of Operations in World War II. He has shown how the various parts of the organization functioned and fought. He has enshrined the names of the heroes who made armored warfare work, in this case, with such precision and effect.

Tanks are relatively new instruments in the history of war. They came into existence in the First World War, and George S. Patton, Jr., was the initial officer assigned to the U.S. Tank Corps, newly formed in the American Expeditionary Force. Patton was the foremost American tank expert, and he led his tank brigade to distinctive success in the St. Mihiel and Meuse-Argonne offensives.

After the war, the Tank Corps lost its independence and became part of the Infantry branch. During the interwar years, a time of penurious budgets and public indifference, the military suffered, and tank warfare and mobility languished. The blitzkrieg victories of the Germans in Poland and France in 1939 and 1940 ushered in armored warfare and stunned the world.

To develop an organization able to stand up to and defeat the Germans, General George C. Marshall, the U.S. Army Chief of Staff, created the Armored Force, which activated and trained armored divisions. Patton once again became a key figure in the emergence of American armored warfare — that is, the combined force of tanks, infantry, self-propelled artillery, and close support aircraft.

The 2nd and 3rd Armored Division, as Don Fox makes clear, were heavy, meaning that they were larger than the 4th, 5th, 6th, and the others activated afterwards. The latter were smaller in both personnel and equipment and designed to be more flexible.

Patton, the Third Army commander, is regarded as the master of armored mobility. Although the First Army had more armored units, Patton's Third was the premier organization in its handling of troops, showing drive, audacity, and combat effectiveness.

1

One of Patton's favorite units in his marvelous campaigns was the 4th Armored Division. Its chief, John Shirley Wood, has been dubbed Patton's most intelligent apostle. Known as "P" for Professor because he tutored classmates at West Point, Wood was smart, loyal, and sometimes eccentric. During his studies at the Command and General Staff College at Fort Leavenworth, Kansas, Wood ostentatiously read a newspaper in class while the instructor lectured. In Brittany, he complained that the high command was "winning the war the wrong way."

Wood and Patton were the best of friends, so it is difficult to understand why Patton relieved Wood, the beloved darling of his division, from command.

The relief has always been a controversial matter and remains so to this day. Don Fox's account of the event is excellent, yet two additional factors need to be considered.

The first is Patton's place in the command structure of the European Theater of Operations. Dwight D. Eisenhower, the commander-in-chief, and Patton had been close friends since 1919. But that friendship was unraveling for a variety of reasons, including Patton's impulsive actions in Sicily (the slapping incidents) and in England, and Omar N. Bradley's rise. Bradley, who had been Patton's subordinate in Sicily, was his superior officer in Europe. The change in status, brought about by Eisenhower, made both Bradley and Patton uncomfortable. Although Eisenhower had called Patton indispensable for Allied victory, Patton was always concerned, even after his most brilliant coups, about whether Eisenhower and Bradley would retain him.

Thus, the second consideration: Eisenhower and Bradley were infantrymen, and so was Manton Eddy, the XII Corps commander and Wood's immediate superior officer. Today, differences in branch or service matter little, but at that time, loyalties to branch or service were strong. The training and outlook of one differed markedly from the training and outlook of others. In Wood's opinion, Eddy, brought up in the Infantry, failed to understand the operation of armored units. And Wood, always direct in his relationships, was probably insubordinate.

Patton was caught in the middle.

And so the 4th Armored Division lost its most cherished leader. Yet "P" Wood, along with Bruce Clarke, Creighton Abrams, Hal Pattison, and others, has attained legendary proportions as a great fighting man.

Don Fox's history of the division does it honor. His account, mainly small unit action, is the best description of combat I have ever read. He recognizes the troops, whose motto was "They have us surrounded again, the poor bastards," as individuals and as teammates in a glorious venture. He has kept his focus clearly on the division, but has included enough of the big picture and of German intentions and opposition to make his narrative understandable. He has described the fighting at Avranches, Troyes, and, of course, Bastogne, as prime examples of courage, competence, ardor, and not only the will but also the know-how to win.

Preface

During the fall of 2000, I embarked upon a research project on the Fourth Armored Division's role in the Battle of the Bulge. My focus was on one very specific date: December 23, 1944. It was on that day that the Fourth Armored became fully engaged in its drive to relieve the encircled 101st Airborne Division at Bastogne.

During the course of my research, I came across the e-mail addresses for several veterans who had served with the division during World War II. It had never occurred to me, until that moment, to contact some of the men who had actually lived through the experiences I was so interested in.

As I sat staring at the computer screen, questions raced through my mind. Will an unsolicited inquiry come as an unwelcome intrusion? Will I be conjuring up memories that bring with them pain and anguish? Given my respect for these men and what they had accomplished, I wrestled with the thought that my request for information might come across as uncaring, trivial, and insensitive to the sacrifices they and their fallen comrades had made. For several days, I thought about the pros and cons.

I then made my decision. I assumed that if these particular men from the Fourth Armored did not welcome being contacted, they would have never made their e-mail addresses so easily available in the first place. I also realized that, if I did not make the attempt, I would probably spend the rest of my life wondering "What if…"

So on January 19, 2001, I set out to test the waters, and sent e-mails introducing myself to James Leach and John Whitehill. This much I knew: During the Battle of the Bulge, they were both company commanders in Lt. Colonel Creighton Abrams' 37th Tank Battalion. Leach was a captain; Whitehill, a second lieutenant. Along with other units serving under the Fourth Armored's Combat Command Reserve, they spent December 23 launching an attack toward the town of Bigonville. Leach commanded the Sherman tanks of B Company; Whitehill, A Company. I would begin my search with these two men.

The questions I asked them were concise. Specifically, I wanted to know if they recalled the types of Sherman tanks that the battalion was composed of during the Battle of the Bulge. I was looking for the percentage of their medium tanks that were equipped with the new 76mm guns, versus the older, standard 75mm guns. I also wondered how many of the "Jumbo" Sherman variants they might have had available in the battalion. These were questions that I hoped could be answered without unnecessarily painful memories being brought into play. For a commanding officer of a medium tank company within "Abe" Abrams' famous 37th Tank Battalion, perhaps these were important considerations that day back in December 1944. And perhaps they would remember.

Several days went by, and I saw nothing but junk mail and spams in my e-mail in-box. In an e-mail-crazed world, where expectations for return correspondence are almost immediate, the wait for a reply seemed interminable. The lack of a quick response was easily interpreted on my end as a silent rebuff of my inquiry, and I began to feel as though I had made a serious error in judgment in trying to contact them.

On February 9, long after I had given up hope of hearing from either of the veterans, an e-mail appeared from one "jhleach." But to my surprise, this wasn't James Leach answering my message. It was his son, Jamie, who was picking up messages on behalf of his father. Jamie wrote to tell me that he had relayed my questions to his father, and was now sending me the answers. He cautioned me that the passage of time had kept his father from being as specific as I might have liked. He was wrong.

The information that Colonel Leach provided through his son exceeded my expectations. He went beyond the cold numbers I was looking for and provided some insight and characterizations that spoke to the human side of the day I was researching, not just the amount of steel present in the Ardennes.

No, he did not have any Jumbos in his company. He considered them to be too heavy, and "had to destroy several perfectly good tanks (non–Jumbos) that had gotten stuck on other occasions and that may have tempered" his feelings. He relayed a good-natured ribbing that Abrams once gave him: "Leach, I think you could get stuck in an expansion joint." He thought that Lt. Boggess was driving a Jumbo (Lt. Charles Boggess was the company commander whose tank was the first one to break into the Bastogne perimeter on December 26). Colonel Leach recalled that of his seven tanks on December 26, he organized them into two platoons of three tanks each, ensuring that each one had at least one tank with a 75mm gun, since they were capable of firing smoke rounds and the higher velocity 76mm guns were not. His own tank was armed with a 76mm, and one of the platoons had the 105mm Assault Gun Sherman variant attached. Along with some other comments, he closed with a final sentence that, from that day forward, made all the difference in the world as I continued my research: "Thanks for your interest. I would enjoy, as would my dad, knowing what you finally come up with."

My fears and concerns had apparently been for naught. With the acknowledgement that my correspondence was welcome, I breathed a sigh of relief, and started thinking about more questions to send to retired Colonel "Jimmie" Leach.

During the next three weeks, Jamie passed on my questions and returned his dad's answers. The picture was evolving, and I was gaining increasing insight into various aspects of the Fourth Armored Division during the Battle of the Bulge. And then, in an e-mail on March 4, Jamie wrote an even more fateful passage. But before I reveal his comment, some background is in order.

In Hugh Cole's *United States Army in World War II: European Theater of Operations, Ardennes, Battle of the Bulge*, there is a passage regarding the 8th Tank Battalion (along with the 37th and 35th, one of the three tank battalions of the Fourth Armored

Division), wherein Cole wrote that the 8th lost 33 tanks due to mechanical failure as it moved to the Ardennes on December 19, 1944. This struck me as being a most extraordinary event. If Cole's account were true, then the 8th would have been in an extremely weak state as it began its attack toward Bastogne (at full strength, the battalion was allocated 53 medium tanks). It would have hardly been in a position to accept the role it had been assigned, which was, as the tank component of CCB, to spearhead the division's drive to relieve the 101st Airborne Division at that vital Belgian town. There was also the fact that the numbers I had regarding the 8th Tank Battalion's strength in medium tanks, from Cole as well as other authors, just didn't add up when the supposed loss of 33 tanks was thrown into the equation.

Something was fishy, and I looked to Colonel Leach for insight. I figured that a maintenance disaster of this magnitude might have been common knowledge within the ranks of the division.

Jamie's response to my question about the 33 tanks struck like a lightning bolt. He wrote: "I spoke with General Irzyk today and he said he lost none on the 162 mile road march. He described the assertion that he lost 33 as 'absurd.' He has a book, *He Rode Up Front for Patton*. You might wish to check it out."

Retired Brigadier General Albin F. Irzyk, was, at the time of the Battle of the Bulge, the commanding officer of the 8th Tank Battalion. What a discovery! I had never imagined that one of the battalion commanders from the division might still be alive (I was a victim of my own faulty perception that the commanders at that level would have been much older).

I immediately purchased Irzyk's book and devoured it. It was a fascinating account of his involvement in the war, starting with Pearl Harbor, when he was a 24-year-old second lieutenant serving with the 3rd Cavalry Regiment, and continuing through to the end of the conflict in Europe on May 8, 1945. Reporting for duty with the Fourth Armored Division on August 17, 1942, he quickly rose through the ranks as the result of his dedication, discipline, and work ethic. By the time the Fourth Armored came ashore at Normandy, Irzyk had risen to the rank of major, and was the S-3 for the 8th Tank Battalion. He was awarded command of the 8th shortly before the Bulge, and just a month shy of his twenty-eighth birthday. He was later promoted to lieutenant colonel and led the battalion until the end of the war. Among his awards were the Distinguished Service Cross, the Distinguished Service Medal, two Silver Stars, four Bronze Stars, and two Purple Hearts.

I immediately resolved to contact Brigadier General Irzyk. I tracked down his address, and sent him a letter on March 24, 2001, wherein I introduced myself and posed a series of questions focused on his battalion's activities on December 23, 1944. I knew from his book that this was probably a very memorable day in his life, since CCB was on the receiving end of the sharpest counterattack it would encounter during the entire war.

Al Irzyk's three-page, typewritten response was more than I had hoped for or expected. In a letter dated April 2, he took extreme care to answer all of my questions. He examined all of the numbers I had presented to him, conducted his own thoughtful analysis, and offered his vivid recollection of the state of affairs that day. And then he closed with a passage that had a great impact on me:

December 23rd, the day around which your whole project centers, as you can well imagine, was an important day in my life. I think of it often. It was a most defining day. I toss around the "might have beens"—the good and bad. One thing that stands out is pride in my battalion. We were hit by a totally unexpected, devastating blow that easily could have been cataclysmic. After the first shock, my men did not panic, they performed professionally, reorganized, and were soon ready to go again. I said men. These were youths—in their early 20s. As you well know, it is boys and youths who fight and win wars.

My correspondence with Al Irzyk blossomed into a frequent exchange of letters. I went into increasing detail, and he seemed to savor the opportunity to share his experiences. I soon asked Al if he would like to meet, and his response was quick and affirmative.

During a warm, friendly, and most enjoyable meeting at Al's home, we were able to discuss in greater detail Al's experiences during the Battle of the Bulge. Lengthy as our letters had been, nothing could compare to the experience of him one-on-one. I had brought along a 1:50,000 scale topographic map of the battle area, and we compared notes using his own 1:100,000 scale U.S. Army map, originally published in 1943. It was remarkable just how little the landscape had changed over all these years (at least on a topographic map). Some of the villages were slightly larger, but most of the roads and terrain features appeared on my current era map just as they were shown over 50 years ago.

Al spoke on a more detailed level about his men, and the manner in which they fought during that great battle. As the conversation continued, I realized that there was a great story to be told about the deeds of the Fourth Armored Division. Popular literature had barely scratched the surface of the accomplishments of this great unit.

After our meeting, I began to reflect on the volume of information that I had come across about the Fourth Armored Division and its battle in the Ardennes. The quantity and nature of the information I had collected, through Al Irzyk, Jimmie Leach, and John Whitehill, along with all of the published materials available, had grown to become a significant collection of documents and interview notes.

The information I possessed was well beyond the scope of my original project. The question now was, *What on earth are you going to do with it? Put all this away in a box that will never be seen by anyone else?* It was clear to me that there was a fascinating story to be told about a brave group of young warriors, who at heart were ordinary men asked to do extraordinary things. They did the hard part, by fighting and winning the greatest conflict between good and evil that the world has ever known. Telling their story would be the easy part.

It wasn't long before I decided to write the book that you now hold. The focus would be on the time period ranging from the activation of the division in 1941, up through and including its greatest battle: the drive to Bastogne. Once I announced my decision to Al Irzyk, I felt obligated, to him and to every veteran of the division, to see the project through to completion, no matter what obstacles or challenges I might face in the process. What you are about to read is the fulfillment of my vow to the members of United States Fourth Armored Division.

But enough about my own journey. It is now time for me to take *you* on a journey I began many months ago. Let's step back into a world at war, in search of heroes. I think we will find a few.

Introduction: Name Enough

George S. Patton, Jr., was arguably the most recognized American personality of the Second World War, having earned his reputation by virtue of both famous and infamous deeds. His name conjures up images of a star-studded, pistol-packing, hell-raising general. And unlike many other historical figures that have been subjected to the torture of revisionism, the public impression of Patton is still to this day very close to what it was more than 57 years ago.

The late actor George C. Scott did Patton a great service when he offered such a dynamic portrayal of the general on film. Scott's riveting performance made the 1970 movie *Patton* an unqualified success, ensuring that millions of people from the generations that followed World War II would have a glimpse of Patton's character and accomplishments. The film has served to immortalize Patton to a far greater extent than any of his contemporaries, and has surely inspired many people to learn more about him.

In the movie *Patton*, the identities of most of the men and units who actually executed the famous general's military vision are not revealed. The movie is painted with too broad a brush for that. And as a result, recognition of the bravest men — the ones who fought, bled, and died on the soil of countries that were not their own — is often something that slips through the cracks.

Within the pages of this book, readers will find many details about the men who carried out the military will of one of our nation's greatest generals — details that are often overlooked or glossed over in other accounts. Readers will also learn about the accomplishments of the best armored division to serve during the Second World War: the United States Fourth Armored Division. Without the courage and sacrifice of the men who made up the Fourth Armored, history might not have graced Patton in quite the same way.

Why did I call the Fourth Armored Division the best? Quite simply, because its record of achievement between July 1944, when it first joined the fight in Normandy, and the end of the war in Europe in May 1945, is hard to top in the annals of American combat divisions. The Fourth served as the premier armored division within the U.S. Third Army, and was out in front leading the way for Patton throughout most of the campaign in northwest Europe. In December of 1944, the Fourth embarked upon its most famous mission of the war, as it became Patton's spearhead against the German's south flank in what became popularly known as the Battle of the Bulge. In this, their greatest battle, they would drive a stake into the heart of Adolf Hitler at the Belgian crossroad town of Bastogne.

I am not alone in my high regard for the Fourth Armored Division. Perhaps one of the loftiest compliments the Fourth ever received came from Patton himself, who had this to say about his favorite division:

"The accomplishments of this division have never been equaled. And by that statement, I do not mean in this war, I mean in the history of warfare. There has never been such a superb fighting organization as the 4th Armored Division."

It was common knowledge that the division was Patton's favorite, as his own remarks clearly reveal. As a result, the Fourth earned the unofficial nickname "Patton's Best."

General Patton was not the only person who considered the Fourth Armored the best. The Fourth was one of only two divisions during the Second World War to be awarded the Presidential Distinguished Unit Citation, and the *only* armored division so recognized. This was indeed an honor of the highest order for the division, and served as validation of their great achievements.

Units of any size can earn the Presidential Distinguished Unit Citation; even individual platoons have been recognized. It is interesting to note that the Fourth Armored Division cannot count a single one of its units as a separate and distinct recipient of the award. Given their stellar track record as a division, one would think that some of the battalions comprising the division would have earned the honor along the way, based on the merits of their individual feats, as viewed apart from the division as a whole.

The reason for the void in recognition was simple: Major General John Shirley Wood, who led the division through the majority of its training and then into battle in France, had a strong conviction that no unit below the division level should be singled out for recognition. The team they fought for was the Fourth Armored. *All* of them would be recognized, or *none* of them would be recognized. That philosophy bound them together, and made the accolade of the Presidential Distinguished Unit Citation all the sweeter when it was bestowed upon the entire division. Because of Wood's foresight, every man in the division received the recognition that Wood knew he deserved.

Such an outstanding award is the result of great achievements on the battlefield, and in war, great achievements can often be quantified. Statistics can be very telling and, by the end of the war, after ten months of battle, the Fourth Armored Division had registered some amazing numbers:

Prisoners taken	90,364
Enemy killed	13,641
Enemy wounded	30,000 (est)
Enemy tanks destroyed	847
Vehicles destroyed	3,688
Artillery and anti-tank guns destroyed	603
Horse drawn wagons destroyed	1,192
Locomotives destroyed	103
Enemy planes shot down	128

Though the battalions and companies of the division were not recognized with citations for their actions, individual accomplishments were a different matter. Wood understood the critical importance of the individual soldier, and as a great motivator, he understood the value of recognizing superior individual performance. The performance of the men of the Fourth Armored is reflected in the awards earned by its members:

Medal of Honor	3
Distinguished Service Cross	34
Silver Star	802
Bronze Star	3,031
Air Medal	88
Soldiers Medals	11
Croix de Guerre	92
Purple Heart	6,000

The division total of 34 DSCs is the highest of any armored division to serve during the Second World War. In fact, none of the other armored divisions even came close (the next highest total was the 21 DSCs awarded to the 2nd Armored Division).

Unlike almost every other division in the United States Army, the men of the Fourth Armored Division did not carry an official nickname on their shoulder patch (the Second Armored Division, for example, was known as "Hell on Wheels," and the nickname was emblazoned below the standard armored division insignia). The lack of an official nickname was, once again, the handiwork of General Wood. When asked to provide one for the Fourth, Wood replied: "The 4th Armored Division does not need and will not have a nickname. They shall be known by their deeds alone."

Wood's statement became the division's motto. According to Wood, the title "Fourth Armored Division" was name enough. And henceforth, "Name Enough" became the most popular of the unofficial nicknames of the division.

Before we turn our story to the battlefields of Europe, there is one more statistic that deserves mention. In fact, it is the most meaningful, since it reveals the price that was paid on the road to victory.

One thousand, five hundred and nineteen men who wore the emblem of the fourth Armored Division on their sleeve lost their lives while serving their country. Readers will learn about some of those men in this book. But most of them will remain nameless, simply because there is not enough room between the covers to tell each of their stories. So, in essence, many of these brave souls will be known within these pages for their deeds alone. And in a sense, it will be fitting that "member of the Fourth Armored Division" will have to suffice as "name enough."

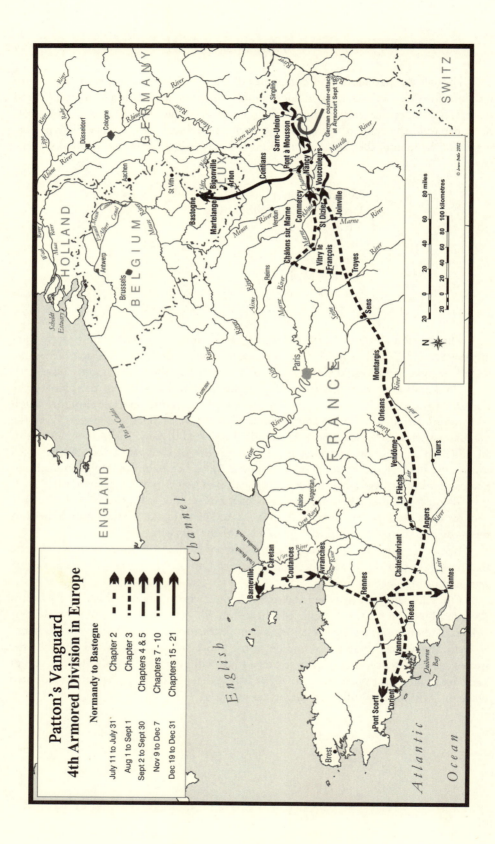

Patton's Vanguard
4th Armored Division in Europe

Normandy to Bastogne

July 11 to July 31   Chapter 2

Aug 1 to Sept 1   Chapter 3

Sept 2 to Sept 30   Chapters 4 & 5

Nov 9 to Dec 7   Chapters 7 - 10

Dec 19 to Dec 31   Chapters 15 - 21

1. Birth

Origins

At precisely 6:05 P.M. on April 15, 1941, a lone bugler, standing before some 3,800 troops, sent the crisp notes of "attention" soaring through the spring air at Pine Camp, New York. The trumpeted tones signaled the start of a milestone ceremony: the activation of the United States Fourth Armored Division. The general orders activating the division were read aloud to the men, and with that accomplished, Brigadier General Henry Welles Baird assumed command of America's newest armored division.

At the time of the Fourth's activation, America was still at peace. But ever since Hitler's invasion of Poland on September 1, 1939, it was increasingly clear that the United States military had to be strengthened. The years since the Great War saw a decline in America's readiness for war, and there was now a tremendous amount of work to be done to raise and equip an army that could counter a threat from the Axis powers.

None of the soldiers who stood in rank before the headquarters building at Pine Camp that day could have envisioned where the flow of world events would carry them. Slightly more than year and a half had passed since Hitler's act of naked aggression against Poland. And during those 19 months, the countries of Poland, Norway, Denmark, Belgium, Luxembourg, the Netherlands, and France had all fallen beneath the churning treads of German tanks. As he expanded his empire, Hitler used both common interests and coercion to build a stable of allies that included Japan, Italy, Romania, Bulgaria, and Hungary. Germany had also reached a peaceful state of coexistence with Russia (it was a totally self-serving and uneasy peace, however, for in reality, both sides deeply distrusted and harbored great contempt for one another). It had become clear to the entire world that Adolf Hitler had an insatiable appetite for power. At the very moment that the Fourth Armored Division was being activated, Hitler's panzer divisions were racing through the mountains of Yugoslavia, and Greece was on the verge of surrender. So while Americans prayed for continued peace for their country, the prudent step of preparing her military was under way. The fledgling Fourth Armored Division was a key part of the expansion of American military might.

Armored units were a relatively new concept for the U.S. Army. The infantry division formed the foundation of America's ground forces, and despite the appearance of the first tanks during the late stages of World War One, and the continued development of motorized vehicles, it was horse mounted cavalry that remained the Army's primary mobile force throughout the 1920's and even into the 30's.

The idea of replacing horses with fighting vehicles didn't take hold until 1930, and it was a tenuous hold at that, as old-school cavalry officers hesitated at the thought of giving up their steeds. The period between 1930 and 1940 became known as "the ten lean years" for the Mechanized Force, as they competed for financial and human resources with the other established branches of the armed forces.

As Hitler began demonstrating the power of armor in a fast moving offensive role, mechanization was given a higher priority. In 1940, the Armored Force was born. From its base at Fort Knox, Kentucky, the Armored Force would train the officers that would lead the various armored units, and its staff would develop the doctrine for employing armor in combat.

Staffing the armored divisions presented a different challenge than filling the ranks of the infantry divisions. As part of a long-standing tradition, most of the infantry divisions drew their enlisted personnel from a particular state or region of the country. As a result, the men often shared a common background and culture. The infantry division usually maintained a strong identification with its home state, and this provided a source of pride for the men of the unit and their families back home.

An armored division required more specialized skills than an infantry division, so when it came time to fill the enlisted ranks of the armored divisions, the idea of regional or state integrity was abandoned, since it was believed that the required number of enlisted men could not be culled from a specific geographic area. Thus, the enlisted men of the Fourth Armored came from all parts of the United States, and as a result, an eclectic mix of urban and rural types swelled the ranks of the division during the first six weeks after its activation.

Many of the members of the Fourth were transferred in from other units. The roots of the Fourth Armored can be traced back to units such as the 1st Armored Regiment, 1st Armored Brigade, 1st Reconnaissance Battalion, 27th Field Artillery Battalion, 68th Field Artillery Regiment (Armored), 16th Engineer Battalion, 47th Medical Battalion (Armored), 19th Ordnance Battalion, 47th Signal Company (Armored), and the 67th and 69th Armored regiments. Most of the Fourth Armored Division's officers came from Fort Knox and the 1st Armored Division, but others were culled from the Army's old horse cavalry units. While the cavalrymen had to adjust to the new technology and application of armor, they brought with them a heritage, culture, and sense of discipline that would serve them well with the new steeds of the 20th century.

As new officers came in, other officers went out. During their training period, the Fourth Armored was called upon to provide officers for other fledgling armored divisions (e.g., the 5th, 9th, and 16th Armored divisions). The cadre system became a means of continuously improving the talent pool of the division, since the lower performing commanders were typically the ones selected to seed the other divisions. While the basis for selecting the transferees was perhaps not in the spirit of the program, it nevertheless

"Sandbox" training being conducted at Pine Camp in the Autumn of 1941. Said Major Bautz: "With only one tank per company, we did a lot of this" (courtesy Ed Bautz).

helped the Fourth Armored develop a pool of talent that was unequalled in any of the other armored divisions.

By the final week of May 1941, the division's strength stood above 10,000 men. It was now time to begin their training regimen, which kicked off on May 26 with thirteen weeks of basic training at Pine Camp.

General Baird shepherded the Fourth Armored through its first year of training. It wasn't always an easy endeavor, since America was still not on a full war footing. Equipment was hard to come by, evidenced by the fact that the division's initial tank strength stood at only 20 vehicles. Edward Bautz, who would rise to the rank of major and serve on the staff of the 37th Tank Battalion throughout the ETO campaign of 1944/45, later recalled that his company in those days had to share one light tank, an armored scout car, a single 2½ ton truck, a ¾ ton reconnaissance car, and a jeep (or "peep," as it was known back then). It would be quite a while before the expanding capacity of American war production caught up with the needs of the swelling ranks of the military.

In the meantime, improvisation became a key attribute for units that wanted to improve their training regimen. As an example, the commander of the 704th TD Battalion, Major Douglas Cameron, placed 75mm artillery pieces in the backs of trucks as a substitute for the M3 tank destroyers that were yet to be received. Creighton W.

A cold winter at Pine Camp … training that would pay dividends during the Battle of the Bulge (courtesy J. Leach).

Abrams, then the regimental adjutant of the 37th Armored Regiment, took his tankers into the field armed only with their imaginations. He would have each crew cluster together as though inside their tank, hands on each other's shoulder to keep them moving together, and then had the whole lot of them practice their tank formations.

As the Fourth Armored Division honed its skills, world events continued to reinforce the need to bulk up the American military machine. On June 22, 1941, Hitler finally acted on his long-standing desire to invade the Soviet Union. As the world watched in awe, the Germans blitzed their way deep into the Russian interior, coming within 20 miles of Moscow (the onset of winter, and a surprisingly resilient Russian military, would stop Hitler short of the spires of the Kremlin).

The Fourth's training took on new urgency after the Japanese attack on Pearl Harbor on December 7, 1941. America, the "Sleeping Giant," immediately declared war against Japan. Obligated by his treaties with the Japanese, Hitler declared war on the United States, and the nature of the conflict changed dramatically as a result. The prospects of seeing combat were now very real, and it provided the men of the Fourth Armored with extra incentive to excel at their assigned tasks. They began to develop a work ethic that distinguished them from most of the other combat divisions.

The New Leader of the Fourth Armored

During the spring of 1942, 61-year-old General Baird retired from the military. His replacement was 54-year-old Brigadier General John Shirley Wood.

John Wood took an unorthodox route on his way to commanding the Fourth Armored Division. Endowed with both physical and mental faculties that set him apart from his peers, Wood entered the University of Arkansas as a sophomore when he was just 16 years old. Despite giving up at least two years of physical maturity to his classmates, he became the captain of the football team during his third and final year in 1907. After graduating with a degree in chemistry, he accepted a teaching position at his alma mater.

When an old college roommate gained an appointment to West Point, he tried to convince Wood to apply as well. Motivated by the chance to play some more football, Wood abruptly changed the direction of his life and pursued an appointment to the Academy. He took his entrance exams in 1908, passing them with ease. During his physical exam, however, he ran into a bottleneck: An eye defect — myopia — threatened to prevent his acceptance. That would have likely been the end of John Wood's military career, had not the head of the hospital, Colonel Gandy, walked by at a fortuitous moment. Presumably impressed with Wood's physical endowments, Gandy, a big fan of West Point's football program, asked Wood if he had ever played the game. Fate had split the clouds for John, and he shared with the colonel his playing experience as a quarterback at Arkansas. Impressed, and knowing that the Academy team desperately needed a quarterback, Gandy cleared the bottleneck by waiving the defect found during the eye exam.

When Wood entered the Academy that same year, he had a unique perspective relative to the other members of the freshman class. He was older than his peers by at least two years, had already earned a degree from a major university, and was earning his way in life. From the outset, his point of view was more sophisticated and worldly, and he stood out among his fellow cadets as an independent thinker who questioned what he believed to be some of the less desirable practices of the Academy (such as hazing). But he also gained respect for the positive traditions and disciplines of West Point.

Wood made the football team, not as a quarterback, but as an end. His main reason for attending the Academy had been fulfilled. The academic portion of his life posed no challenge, and he finished 12th in his class with only the most modest of effort. He would have perhaps finished higher still, if not for the fact that he simply found the academic program to be a "bore." His intellect stood out, and he was often asked to tutor those that were struggling with their studies. He had no hesitation in coaching them, and among the rewards he earned by doing so was the nickname that would remain with him for the rest of his life: "P," for Professor.

During his time at the academy, many of the students he crossed paths with would go on to positions of great importance. At one time or another, he shared the campus with Dwight D. Eisenhower, Omar Bradley, Jacob Devers, Carl Spaatz, and William Simpson. Wood knew all of these men, and they knew *him*. Also on the list was George S. Patton, who would play an integral role in Wood's future. Patton graduated with the class of 1909, so their overlap at the Academy was brief. But during that period, they struck up a friendship that would ultimately last the rest of their lives.

Wood graduated from the Academy in 1912. The onset of the Great War hastened his promotion, and before departing for France, he had risen to the rank of major. Upon his arrival in Europe, Wood served as the ordnance officer for the 3rd Division, and

Major General John S. Wood
(National Archives Photograph
SC193740).

then after a period of study at the staff college at Langres (where George Patton was once again a fellow class-
mate), he was reassigned as a staff officer for the 90th
Division. He returned to the United States for an assignment as the Assistant Chief of Staff, G-4, of the 18th
Division, which was training in San Antonio. Armistice
Day arrived while he and the division were still in Texas.

During the years in between the two World Wars,
Wood settled into a career within the slumbering Army.
Artillery was his specialty, and during part of that time,
he studied further at Leavenworth, where he once again
found himself side by side with Patton. The two men
continued to expand their friendship, spending many
hours together reading and debating matters of military
history and philosophy, strategy, and tactics.

Wood was greatly influenced by the static battles
he had witnessed during the Great War, and he was
determined not to see that style of warfare repeated.
Though his discipline was artillery, he easily adjusted to
the tenets of armored warfare. In fact, he played an
important role by developing new techniques and infus-
ing mobility into the artillery arm. He was a truly original thinker, and held few military figures in esteem,
either past or present. Robert E. Lee was the only general with attributes that "P" felt worthy of imitation,
which says something about Wood's approach to leadership and command.

Wood's greatest desire was to have the privilege of commanding troops. But the
severe scaling back of the military during the 1920's and 30's made his dream more
difficult to realize. He spent nearly ten of those years heading up ROTC programs,
with the time split evenly between Culver Military Academy and the University of
Wisconsin. As noted by his biographer, Hanson Baldwin, "This helped him materi-
ally, not only in developing his concepts of leadership but in aiding him to understand
the psychology of the citizen soldier…"

In 1936, Wood turned down an assignment at the Army War College in favor of
the role of Commanding Officer, 80th Field Artillery Regiment, Motorized. He par-
layed his philosophies on rapid movement into the development of the 80th FA Regiment as the only one of its kind. He implemented practices that were totally new and
unique, and which resulted in an unprecedented display of mobility for his howitzers.

At the time of Hitler's conquest of Poland in 1939, Lt. Colonel Wood was serving as the chief of staff for the Third Army. In April of 1941, he was promoted to the
rank of Colonel and placed in command of artillery for the Second Armored Division,
which was then under the command of his old friend George Patton. This assignment
did not last long, however, for in June 1941, he became the chief of staff for the Army's
first and only armored corps (the armored corps differed from a "regular" corps in that

it was to consist entirely of armored divisions, as opposed to a combination of infantry and armored divisions).

The demise of the armored corps concept later that same year did not stop John Wood's personal progress. Promoted to the rank of Brigadier General on October 31, 1941, Wood was assigned command of the 5th Armored Division's Combat Command A shortly thereafter. Seven months later, in May of 1942, "P" took over the reins of the Fourth Armored Division from the retiring General Baird, and the following month, ascended to the rank of Major General.

First Impressions

General Wood wasted no time in establishing a reputation within the ranks of the Fourth Armored Division. He had extremely high standards, to the point that he expected perfection (his philosophy being that, while perfection might not always be achieved, the pursuit of it is what makes one great). "Paper and Butts" was a moniker awarded by his men during the early days of his tenure; his high standards for cleaning and maintenance of the unit areas earned him the nickname.

There was an early perception among some of the men that the new commander was weak in character. One man summed up the concern, saying, "Well, we recently had a division review and after it, he made a speech and ended it by saying 'God bless you men.'" In retrospect, any veteran of the Fourth would be dumbfounded by the idea that such an expression could be equated with weakness. Retired Brigadier General Albin F. Irzyk put it best:

> Weakness? That man was to utter those words in his remarks to his troops endless times, so fervently, so emotionally that he sometimes brought tears to the eyes of his listeners.

Far from a weakness, the compassion that Wood displayed for his men was perhaps his greatest strength.

The Tennessee Maneuvers

Soon after his arrival, Wood brought the division to the autumn fields and meadows of Tennessee, where it engaged in training maneuvers from early September to mid–November, 1942. During these maneuvers, Wood began to demonstrate his philosophy regarding the application of armor. He knew that an armored division was best used as a weapon of exploitation, and he employed it as such in Tennessee. During the maneuvers, his rapid advances and the use of the element of surprise were unique to the Fourth. It is clear, especially in hindsight, that "P" Wood was far ahead of his time; the Tennessee maneuvers established that as a fact. The maneuvers would also reveal the mettle of which John S. Wood was made.

Each week of the maneuvers featured a new "problem" that would be worked via an exercise between two opposing forces. The exercises would begin on Monday, and were designed to last for a prescribed period, typically three days or more. Sunday was always spent reviewing and critiquing the prior week's exercise.

Almost from the start, Lieutenant General Ben Lear, who, as Commanding General of the Second Army, was in overall command of the exercises, began taking exception to the manner in which General Wood employed the division. Wood's methods were, in Lear's view, unrealistic and disruptive to the conduct of the exercises. The Fourth Armored was apparently making a habit of solving their problems quicker than any of the planners anticipated, which basically short-circuited the balance of the exercise schedule. Suffering from incredible tunnel vision, Lear could not see the forest through the trees, and failed to recognize that Wood was setting a new standard for the application of a mechanized force.

At one point during the maneuvers, Lear was called to Washington, D.C. He was to depart on a Sunday night, and was due to return late the following Wednesday. During the regularly scheduled critique held on the day of his departure, Lear emphasized his concerns about the practices of Wood's division, and further emphasized that the next exercise, slated to begin the following day, must run for a minimum of three days, "or the responsible individuals would suffer dire consequences." The exercise for that week involved the defense of a line in front of a river. An infantry division was defending, and the Fourth Armored Division was cast in the offensive role.

As the first day progressed, Wood's men were on their way toward routing the defenders. Apparently worried that Lear's edict was in danger of being violated, the umpires overseeing the action had to impose some "artificial decisions" in order to hold back the attackers and forestall the end of the exercise. At one point, the chief umpire ordered all of Wood's forward elements to halt their advance. Wood was determined to find a way to continue the attack. He saw a loophole in the umpire's instructions, and ordered his light tank battalion, which was in reserve and apparently not subject to the chief umpires ruling, to attack the boundary line between two of the defending infantry regiments. There was only one umpire traveling with the reserve battalion, and he was a young and inexperienced fellow. He apparently allowed the light tank battalion, command by Lt. Colonel Hal Pattison, to proceed unbridled.

Before any of the other umpires could intervene, Pattison's battalion had broken through the line. The light tanks overran the headquarters of both infantry regiments, some of the supporting artillery, and the bivouac of the enemy's supporting tank battalion. The attack continued through the night, and by morning, the battalion had seized the only two bridges available to the enemy division. One of the bridges was subsequently "destroyed," and the other was used by the Fourth Armored to establish a friendly bridgehead on the far side of the river. There was nothing the umpires could do to extend the exercise beyond that point. The Fourth Armored had solved the problem with amazing speed and agility ... and one day sooner than Lear wanted.

At the critique session held the Sunday following General Lear's return, the Commanding General of the Second Army was furious that Wood had continued to utilize tactics, which, in his view, could never be employed on a real battlefield. Lear made his feelings known before all who were assembled for the critique (this included General Wood and the officers of the Fourth Armored Division). He berated not only Wood, but also the men of the Fourth as a whole for using "poor judgment."

Wood could stand for no more of it. Perhaps the final straw came when Lear characterized the division as "an undisciplined rabble." Whatever the catalyst for reaching the breaking point, Wood charged onto the platform and interrupted General Lear as he was speaking. In front of everyone, he stood up for his men, and in so many words said that Lear didn't know a thing about the proper employment of armor, and that he knew even less about "the quality of the people of his division."

As Bruce Clarke, then Wood's Chief of Staff, recalled it, "He (Wood) said that he had sat through several of these Sunday sessions when he would be better off in church. He said he listened to enough incidents of stupid sergeants and lieutenants. He said they were just learning. He felt we should talk about stupid generals who should have learned better." Lear ordered Wood off the stage, but Wood refused to leave. It took Clarke's urging to get him down from the platform. As Wood stepped down, General Lear followed behind him, and the two men headed out a back door and continued their argument outside of the room.

With so many witnesses on hand, word of the encounter spread like wildfire throughout the division. This event created a dynamic bond between "P" Wood and his men, and served to wash away any negative impressions that may have formed during the early days of his tenure. This was classic Wood. He had little patience for officers above him who appeared to be intellectually bankrupt, and unlike most other officers, would not hesitate to challenge the status quo. His men loved his style. Many of his superiors hated it.

The Training Continues

Following the Tennessee maneuvers, the Fourth Armored shipped out from Camp Forest and headed for the California Desert Training Center, where Wood led the division through an exhaustive training period. The hot days and cold nights tested the men at both ends of the thermometer, and there were few creature comforts available at their encampments. The exercises were rigorous, and even included sessions where tanks in competing companies used their .30 caliber machine guns to fire live rounds at each other. Normally, a unit would conduct live fire exercises against dummy targets. But in order to help them prepare for combat, Wood took them as close to the real thing as possible.

As intense as the training was, it wasn't always a 24/7 ordeal. During early 1943, some of the members of the division were provided with an entertaining diversion when they were employed as extras during the filming of the Humphrey Bogart movie "Sahara." The War Department had given a nod of approval to Columbia Pictures to film on location where the Fourth Armored was training. The movie was one of many that helped boost the moral of the American citizenry when there were few successes yet achieved on the battlefield. The men were astonished, but no less willing to help, when they learned that they had been cast as Germans!

After several months, the Fourth Armored moved on to Camp Ibis, located about 20 miles north of Needles, California. The division participated in maneuvers at locations throughout the desert, and after a total of seven months, the Fourth's training experience in the region came to a close. They passed on their vehicles to the 9th Armored Division, and set out for Camp Bowie, Texas. They arrived there on June 14, 1943, and resumed their training.

Reorganization

In early September of 1943, the division was reorganized under the new "light" armored division structure (the 2nd and 3rd Armored divisions were the only units to retain the "heavy" table of organization throughout the entire war). Under the new structure, the division numbered 10,937 men when at full strength, as compared to the heavy organization strength of 14,500 men.

In order to achieve the new organizational structure, the existing 35th and 37th Tank regiments were broken up, and from their ranks were born the 35th, 37th and 8th Tank Battalions. These three tank battalions would serve as the steel foundation of the Fourth Armored Division, and as such, it is worth exploring their composition.

The core of the standard tank battalion consisted of three companies of medium tanks and one company of light tanks. At full strength, each company consisted of three platoons of 5 tanks each, plus two command tanks, for a total of 17. There were also two more medium tanks that served as command tanks at the battalion level, bringing the total number of mediums to 53 for the battalion. When at full strength, the tank battalion roster called for 729 men.

Captain Bautz, cleaning up after a sandstorm. December 1942 (courtesy Ed Bautz).

While training in the United States, the light tank companies of the Fourth Armored Division were initially equipped with the M3 light tank. The primary gun was only a 37mm, and it was of little use versus enemy tanks. But it was more than capable of wreaking havoc on "soft" targets, such as enemy infantry, towed guns, and non-armored vehicles. The original M3 was a no-frills affair. It was equipped with a manual transmission and manual turret traverse, and did not have an intercom system for communication between the four crewmembers (the tank commander would issue movement orders by using his foot to tap out a code on the driver's shoulders and

Staff sergeants Farese (left) and Fitzpatrick (right) of Co E, 37th Armored Regiment, in the Mohave Desert, 1943 (courtesy J. Leach).

back). Many of the shortcomings of the M3 light tank were remedied when the M5 and M5A1 were put into production. The automatic transmission was a real plus, and the intercom system a welcome enhancement. Small and lightly armored, the M5 light tank weighed in at just under 17 tons (about half the weight of Sherman tank). The top speed of the M5 was a blistering 40 mph, which made it an excellent vehicle for reconnaissance work or any situation where speed was of the essence. The Fourth Armored traded in its M3 light tanks for the M5 while it was still training in the United States. The M5 would continue as the division's primary light tank throughout 1944 and early 1945. After the Battle of the Bulge, the light tank companies began to receive the new M24, also know as the "Chaffee."

The medium tank companies were armed with the M4 "Sherman" tank. By the time the Fourth Armored Division arrived in Europe, the venerable M4 was the only medium tank in use (having replaced the M3 "Grant" tank). During the war, several variations of the Sherman tank were manufactured, and for practical purposes, they fell into five distinct types.

First and foremost was the "standard" M4, which was armed with a 75mm low velocity gun. Hull designs and motors varied by model, and each variation carried a different classification, such as M4A1, M4A3, etc. The Sherman weighed between 33 and 34 tons, and had a top road speed of 24 to 30 miles per hour (maximum speed

Camp Bowie, Texas
Summer 1943

The 37th Armored Regiment -- Staff and Command

Back Row

Lt Higgins - Commo; Capt Friedman -- CO Service Company;
Capt Rapp - CL Maintenance Company; Capt Wilson - Assistant
S3; Lt Donahue - Assistant S2.

Front Row

Maj Bautz - S1; Maj Kimsey - S2; Lt Col Abrams - Regt'l Exec O;
Col Withers - Regt'l CO; Maj Heid - S3; Maj Hunter - S4.

The staff and command officers of the 37th Armored Regiment. This photograph was taken at Camp Bowie, Texas, during the summer of 1943, just prior to the reorganization of the division (courtesy Ed Bautz).

varied by model, since each had a different engine, with different horsepower ratings). When the Fourth Armored went into action for the first time in France, the standard M4 was the only medium tank they had in inventory for the entire division (predominately the M4A1 model).

The first significant Sherman variant was the 105mm Assault Gun. This was basically a standard Sherman with a short 105mm howitzer in place of the 75mm gun. A disadvantage of the assault gun was that the turret could only be rotated manually (as opposed to the power traverse of the standard Sherman tank). Each tank battalion was equipped with 3 of the assault guns, and they were organized into a single platoon assigned to the Headquarters Company. At a later point in the war, one 105mm Assault Gun Sherman was assigned to each medium tank company in place of a standard 75mm Sherman, bringing the total number of 105mm AG's to six per battalion.

A third and very important variant of the M4 began to appear during the course of the campaign in northwest Europe. It was more or less a standard Sherman, but was equipped with a 76mm high velocity gun. The upgraded gun, along with its improved armor piercing shot, was needed in order for the American tankers to take on their German counterparts at longer ranges (though against a Panther or Tiger tank, getting a shot at the thinner side or rear armor was still a must, even with the 76mm). When the Fourth Armored entered the fray in France, none of the 76mm Shermans were in their inventory (they would gradually be added to the division in the form of replacement tanks). The 76mm gun wasn't without some disadvantages. For one thing, unlike the 75mm gun, it did not have the ability to fire smoke rounds. But there was an even more important drawback to the initial 76mm guns: they were shipped without a "muzzle brake."

The muzzle brake is a device that eliminates the smoke discharge from the end of the gun barrel. Without the brake, the smoke obscured the target from view at the very moment the shell would strike, thus making it difficult for the gunner to tell if his aim had been true. John Whitehill, who commanded Company A of the 37th Tank Battalion, described for me how he would have a commander from another tank spot his fire for him when he used the 76mm gun on his command tank. The spotter would tell him where the round hit, and to what degree the gunner had to adjust his aim. When the muzzle brakes were added, the gun become more effective.

Another important variant of the Sherman (but again, one that was not available to the Fourth when they first entered combat) was the M4A3E2. Popularly known as the "Jumbo," it was armed with the 75mm gun (some of these tanks were later upgraded in the field to include the 76mm gun). But what set the Jumbo apart was the substantial armor added to the turret and hull. Only 253 of the factory spec M4A3E2s rolled off the assembly line in the United States. But many more Shermans were converted in the field to the "Jumbo" standard by attaching extra armor plating to the hull and turret (this practice become especially popular within Patton's Third Army). The extra armor gave the Jumbo a level of protection that was even superior to the German Panther tank. It served as an excellent assault tank, and was the one vehicle that an American tank commander might have confidence in if forced to advance head-on against strong German anti-tank fire. The down side was that the weight of the tank ballooned to 42 tons, with a commensurate reduction in speed.

The final important variation of the Sherman was the M4A3E8, which featured the latest high velocity 76mm gun, an improved suspension system, higher horsepower engine, and wider tracks. Tankers rejoiced at the opportunity to climb into an "Easy Eight." It was the best American tank available, as it combined the best gun with the best suspension and drive system. Unfortunately, the first M4A3E8s did not start to arrive in the Fourth Armored's inventory in significant numbers until late December 1944.

As the war in Europe progressed, the Sherman tank became somewhat maligned. During its initial engagements in North Africa, it was arguably the best tank on the battlefield. The Panther was not yet in production, and in a tank versus tank duel, the M4 would usually be pitted against the German Mark III or Mark IV. Though the Mark IV held an advantage in firepower with its higher velocity 75mm gun, the M4 was superior in virtually every other category (e.g., road speed, rate of fire, rotational speed of the turret, mechanical reliability, and armor protection). The American tanker didn't have much to worry about until the appearance of the powerful Tiger tank during the late stages of the campaign in North Africa. With its thick armor and high velocity 88mm gun, the Tiger held a considerable advantage when engaging Shermans at long range in the desert (fortunately, there weren't that many Tigers available in North Africa). By the time the ground war had returned to Northwest Europe, the Germans had moved into production of the Mark V Panther. As far as a combination of armor protection, firepower, and speed, the Panther was probably the best tank manufactured during the war. But the success of a tank rests on far more than the merits of its gun and armor alone. If it is not mobile enough, if it is mechanically unreliable, or if it demands too much gas, then its other combat attributes might well be negated.

When all things were considered — not just the thickness of the armor and the power of the main gun — many American tankers (though certainly not all) felt the Sherman was actually the best tank on the battlefield. A well-trained crew knew how to work within the limitations of the Sherman, and knew how to take advantage of its strengths. That it could be produced and fielded in great numbers added to its value, and experienced American commanders knew how to exploit their numerical advantage when coming face to face with the heavier, lumbering German tanks.

While the tank battalions defined an armored division during World War Two, the armored infantry component was no less important. The tankers knew that they would have to depend on the armored infantry in a variety of situations. If they were to succeed on the battlefield, it would be done as a team, working hand in hand with their infantry support.

When the division was reorganized, the 51st Infantry Regiment was split into three independent Armored Infantry Battalions: the 10th, 51st, and 53rd. Each battalion numbered 1,001 men when at full strength. The core of the Armored Infantry Battalion consisted of three companies of infantry supplied with M3 halftracks for transport.

The armored infantry battalion was equipped to ensure greater mobility and striking power than its counterpart in the regular infantry division. One thing that distinguished it from a regular infantry outfit, other than the halftracks, was a higher allotment of automatic weapons and bazookas. The .45 caliber Thompson submachine gun and the M3 "Grease" gun were the primary personal automatic weapons. The division fielded an allowance of 465 .30 caliber machine guns, and another 404 .50 caliber heavy machine guns. When in full supply, the division carried more than 600 bazookas. The number of machine guns and bazookas were well in excess of what a standard infantry division had available (despite the fact that the total strength of an infantry division was 14,253 men). But even with the greater number of automatic weapons, the standard infantry weapon was still the M1 Garand semi-automatic rifle. Officers and support personnel were usually armed with the lighter M1 carbine.

In addition to the primary fighting battalions of tanks and armored infantry, the Fourth Armored Division also had an armored engineer battalion (the 24th), an armored cavalry reconnaissance squadron (the 25th), and three battalions (the 22nd, 66th, and 94th) of self-propelled howitzers (the M7, which was a 105mm howitzer mounted on a tank chassis). Each battalion of M7s consisted of 18 vehicles, giving the armored division a total complement of 54 highly mobile artillery pieces. Other supporting units were the 126th Armored Ordnance Maintenance Battalion, 46th Armored Medical Battalion, 144th Armored Signal Company, a Military Police Platoon, and the Division Band. There were also the headquarters and train (i.e., supply) units.

Though not an integral part of the division, a tank destroyer (TD) battalion was typically attached to each armored division. A TD battalion consisted of three companies of TDs, with each company consisting of three platoons of 4 TDs each.

Tank destroyers differed from tanks in a couple of key respects: They were armed with more powerful guns than the standard M4, and they were considerably lighter and faster. The lighter weight was achieved by having thinner armor and a turret that was completely open on top. Of course, these features made the TD more vulnerable to enemy fire. The open turret was a key weakness, since it exposed the crew to artillery and mortar fire from above, not to mention the occasional hand grenade that could be tossed in at close range.

The most common American tank destroyer produced during the war was the M-10. The open turret was mounted on a Sherman tank chassis, and carried a 3-inch high velocity gun. The hull was sloped on the sides and front in an attempt to offset, at least in part, the thinner armor. The M-10 saw action as early as North Africa, and remained in service until the end of the war.

As heavier German tanks took to the stage in greater numbers, the need for a more powerful anti-tank weapon became increasingly obvious. The U.S. already had in its arsenal a powerful 90mm anti-aircraft gun that could serve equally well in an anti-tank role (in the same way the Germans employed their famous 88mm anti-aircraft gun as an anti-tank weapon). Efforts were made to mount the 90mm in a self-propelled tank destroyer format, and the result was the M-36. As with the M-10, a Sherman tank chassis served as the foundation, and a custom hull and open turret were designed to accommodate the longer, heavier gun. The M-36, while not the fastest of the American tank destroyers, racked up an impressive number of kills with its powerful 90mm gun.

Both the M10 and M36 were improvised designs based upon the foundation of the Sherman tank. There was one design, the M18, which was designed from scratch.

The M18 (also known as the "Hellcat") was the fastest armored fighting vehicle of the war, with a top road speed in excess of 55 mph. This was unheard of for a tank, tank destroyer, or assault gun during World War II (in fact, the M18 remained the fastest armored fighting vehicle in the world until the introduction of the M1 Abrams tank during the 1980's). Armed with a 76mm high velocity gun, the M18 could use its speed to great advantage by maneuvering into position for favorable shots.

A common tactic for the tank destroyer was to assume a position behind the crest of a hill or ridge that would allow the TD commander to observe beyond the crest while standing in the turret (known as a hull-down or turret defilade position). When the enemy approached, the TD commander would have the gunner swivel the cannon in the approximate direction of the threat. The TD would then pull forward far enough to bring the gun over the crest in preparation for taking the shot. The vulnerable, thin-skinned hull of the TD would be protected behind the ridge (this was referred to as being in a hull defilade position). After firing at the enemy (the number of shots taken being dependent on how quickly the enemy might be able to get his own cross hairs on the exposed turret and gun of the TD), the TD would pull back into a full hull-down position. Rather than emerge again at the same location behind the ridge, the TD would scurry left or right, and emerge at a different location. This type of tactic took full advantage of the speed and agility of the M18. When carried out in concert with other TDs behind the same ridge, a constant rate of fire could be laid upon the enemy, often with devastating results. The fact that the M18 ended up with the highest kill to loss ratio of any tank or TD in the American arsenal stands as testimony to

both the quality of the design and the effectiveness of the tactics used when employing it.

There is a unique bond between the Fourth Armored Division and the M18 tank
destroyer. The 704th TD Battalion, which would serve with the Fourth throughout
most of the war, originally trained with the antiquated M3 TDs (basically, a half track
with a 75mm gun in the bed), and then upgraded to M10s while finishing its training
in the United States. After establishing a superlative training record, the battalion was
chosen to run tactical tests on the new T70 tank destroyers, which was the prototype
for the M18. The officers and men of the 704th were instrumental in fine-tuning the
design. When the battalion ultimately reached England, it was issued brand new Hellcats, and the men were delighted to find that many of their suggestions had been incor-
porated into the final production version. The M18 served as the 704th's sole tank
destroyer throughout the war in Europe.

Teamwork was an essential element of the new light armored division's structure.
Rather than a having a fixed, rigid organization, the light armored division scheme
called for a flexible command structure that lent itself toward the creation of mission-
specific task forces.

The task forces operated under one of three "Combat Command" headquarters,
designated Combat Command A, Combat Command B, and Combat Command R
(Reserve). Commands A and B usually contained the primary fighting elements of the
division; this was typically some combination of the three tank and three armored
infantry battalions assigned to the division.

According to doctrine, CCR would hold units in reserve status, either for tactical
purposes or for rest and refitting. Most of the armored divisions broke with this doctrine, however, and established CCR as a standard fighting unit, usually making it
comparable in strength to CCA and CCB. It was not unusual to find that each combat command contained one tank battalion, one armored infantry battalion, and one
field artillery battalion. The division's supporting engineer battalion, tank destroyer
battalion, anti-aircraft battalion, and armored cavalry squadron were usually divided
equally amongst the three combat commands.

The Fourth became a notable exception to the practice adopted by the other
armored divisions. Throughout the war, it retained the organizational flexibility called
for by the original doctrine. In some instances, the division commander would stack
the deck in favor of one combat command, so much so that that it might contain two
of the division's three tank or armored infantry battalions. It was rare for CCR/4 to
fight as a tactical combat command, as it held to the doctrine of functioning as a
reserve.

General Wood had prepared his division well, and had a firm grasp on how to use
the new light division organization. During the Fourth's extensive training, he endowed
the division with a fresh view on the use of armor. He understood that an aggressive
armored force can defeat the enemy by the combined shock effect of movement and
firepower, and he imbued his officers with his philosophy. As the Fourth would soon
discover, an enemy that finds itself surrounded by a mobile, powerful armored force
will often lose its desire to fight. Defeat and death becomes a prospect that gnaws at
the will to resist, and surrender becomes the best available option for all but the fanat-

ical. Led by the irrepressible Wood, the Fourth was ready, able, and willing to engage the enemy.

To England

The Fourth Armored began its departure from Camp Bowie on December 11, 1943. It took 22 trains to transport the division, and on December 18, the final elements pulled into their destination of Camp Myles Standish in Taunton, Massachusetts. Eleven days later, on December 29, the division would once again board trains and head for Boston.

On a day that could best be described as frigid (even by New England standards), the men of the Fourth Armored left their trains and marched up gangplanks to board one of the ships that awaited them (the *Santa Rosa*, SS *Oriente*, SS *Exchange*, HMS *Brittanic*, and *Queen Elizabeth* were among the ships that carried the Fourth Armored to England). The enlisted men and officers marched aboard with full combat gear; almost as though they were being sent directly into a fight, save for their musette bags stuffed with personal belongings. By nightfall, several of the ships, stuffed to the gills with troops, were underway.

During the first night at sea, the ships carrying the Fourth Armored joined a larger convoy headed across the Atlantic. Ships were visible as far as the eye could see, but spaced far apart as a defensive tactic against the threat of U-Boats. What began as a pleasant voyage became increasingly uncomfortable as the convoy headed further north. Huge swells rocked the ships, and seasickness took hold of more and more men. Reading, writing, and card games filled the early days, but participation in these pastimes dwindled as the increasingly bitter seas sent men scrambling to their hammocks for refuge. Fresh water was reserved for drinking and cooking, so showers had to be taken with salt water, which left the men feeling anything but clean. The officers had it a little bit better, since they had cabin accommodations that were less cramped than what the enlisted men had to endure. Still, with the ships filled three to four times their normal capacity, no one could claim to be sailing in the lap of luxury.

After an eleven-day journey, the ships finally drew within sight of the Irish coast. They continued around the northern coast of Ireland, and then headed south toward the Bristol Channel. They docked in ports in Wales and England, where they disgorged the men of the Fourth Armored Division.

As Wood's men entered Great Britain, they saw their first evidence of the war. The scarred, battered buildings of the cities and villages stood as testimony to the impact of the Luftwaffe. Warplanes were often overhead, while anti-aircraft guns dotted the landscape. The military presence was everywhere, as increasing numbers of American troops launched a friendly invasion of the British Isles. There was no escaping the fact that Britain was an armed camp.

Upon its arrival, the division's strength was enhanced by the attachment of the 704th Tank Destroyer Battalion and 489th Anti-Aircraft Artillery (AAA) Battalion (Self Propelled). The 704th had shipped over on the HMS *Britannic*; a journey made even more eventful when the ship collided with a Panamanian vessel while negotiating

RESULTS OF THE FIRING AT MINEHEAD RANGE

a Cavalry holdover
CC = CAR (Tank) COMMANDER

	Score Total	MG	75	
COMPANY "A"	133.1	98.4	6.8	
Co. Hq.				
Capt Spencer	146	95	10	Superior
Sgt. Morganti	108	73	6	Excellent
1st Platoon	124.6	88.6	7	
Lt. Turner	125	80	8	
S/Sgt Welters	110	85	5	Slow
Sgt. Griggs	88	58	6	
Sgt Gritzke	173	128	9	Superior
Sgt. Allison	127	92	7	Excellent
2nd Platoon	122.2	94.2	5.6	
Lt. De Creane	110	80	6	
S/Sgt Hickey	111	96	3	Poor Gunner
Sgt. Ealling	157	122	7	Superior
Sgt. Noe	132	82	7	Excellent
Sgt. DiSanto	101	91	2	Gunner poor—C.C.(?)
3rd Platoon	156	118	7.6	
Lt. Donnelly	179	134	9	Superior
S/Sgt Mc Nevey	114	89	5	
Sgt. Rowland	172	117	11	Superior
Sgt. Casmero	141	101	8	Excellent
Sgt. Rebovich	174	149	6	Slow
COMPANY "B"	144.7	105.9	7.7	
Co. Hq				
Capt. Tiega	161	111	10	
Sgt. Slifka	106	60	8	MG firing inaccurate
1st Platoon	138	107	6.2	
Lt. Leach	97	72	5	Gunner poor C.C Excellent
S/Sgt Fitzpatrick	185	155	6	Loader slow Many hits on AT.
Sgt. Kobela	141	96	9	
Sgt. Grady	87	62	5	Crew lack discipline
Sgt. Morphew	180	150	6	Superior
2nd Platoon	154.8	107.3	9.4	
Lt. Bohn	204	144	12	Superior
S/Sgt. Langmier	148	113	7	Slow
Sgt. Sowers	114	74	8	Excellent
Sgt. Del Vecchio	147	107	8	Superior
Sgt. Lewis	161	101	12	Superior
3rd Platoon	147.2	111.2	7.2	
Lt. Marston	160	120	8	Many hits on AT
S/Sgt Farese	164	114	10	Excellent
Sgt. Krasaner	273	133	8	Superior
Sgt. Whiteside	145	130	3	Gunner poor on moving target
Sgt. Heintz	94	59	7	Loader slow gunner poor
COMPANY "C"	112.8	84.0	7.1	
Co. Hq.				
Capt. Smith	130	85	9	Excellent
Sgt. Gutrell	127	112	5	
1st Platoon	125.8	89.8	7.2	
Lt. Anderson	131	101	6	
S/Sgt. H.L. Smith	137	77	12	Superior
Sgt. Echols	136	108	6	Excellent
Sgt. Moses	132	101	6	
Sgt. Townley	92	62	6	Poor on MG

– 1 –

Above and opposite: The tank gunnery scores for the 37th Tank Battalion, compiled during a test conducted on a firing range in England just prior to D-Day (courtesy J. Leach).

	Score Total	MG		
2nd Platoon	100.4	70.4	8	
Lt. Berard	89	74	3	Loader poor
S/Sgt. Hicks	80	55	5	Poor
Sgt. Dunn	106	66	8	
Sgt. Flaherty	110	85	5	Loader poor on MG orders poor
Sgt. K.J. Smith	117	72	9	Excellent
3rd Platoon	106	86	8	
Lt. Wrolson	105	70	7	Excellent
S/Sgt. Grubbs	131	96	7	Excellent
Sgt. Hangarak	85	50	7	Excellent
Sgt. Clepper	90	40	10	Superior
Sgt. Sole	119	74	9	Superior
COMPANY "D"				
	135.2	98.6	7.3	
Co. Hq				
Capt. McMahon	105	50	11	Superior
Sgt. Ballison	159	119	8	Excellent
Sgt. Schaefer	166	126	8	Excellent
1st Platoon	140	110	6	
Lt. Klingbeil	158	123	7	Superior
S/Sgt. Mallon	154	119	7	Excellent
Sgt. Miller	126	111	3	
Sgt. Worsnop	173	133	8	Needs better interphone language Gunner good
Sgt. Farr	89	64	5	
2nd Platoon	127.4	97.4	6	
Lt. Donahue	135	95	8	Superior
S/Sgt. Smith	147	107	8	
Sgt. Caleca	126	101	5	
Sgt. Vannett	124	114	2	Poor on moving target
Sgt. Hourn	105	70	7	
3rd Platoon	133.6	88.6	9	
Lt. Mueller	148	103	9	
S/Sgt. Lafferty	144	109	7	Excellent
Sgt. Cranford	85	45	8	Poor with MG
Sgt. Piechowski	102	62	8	
Sgt. Weiss	139	124	13	Superior

C. W. Abrams.
C. W. ABRAMS
Lt. Col., Cav.,
Commanding

the fog-shrouded waters of Liverpool Harbor (the men on board feared that they had struck a mine in the harbor, and it was a big relief when they realized that the collision was relatively harmless).

The tank destroyer battalion was no stranger to the Fourth Armored, since it was formed around a nucleus of 7 officers and 101 enlisted men from D Battery, 22nd Armored Field Artillery. The 704th was activated on December 15, 1941, and at full strength, numbered 669 men. It had trained alongside the Fourth ever since its activation, and while its official status was that of an "attached" unit, the division embraced it as one of its own.

Evidence of the bond between the 704th and Fourth Armored was seen very early in its history. Prior to the Fourth's departure for the Tennessee maneuvers, the 704th was detached and sent to the Tank Destroyer Center at Camp Hood, Texas. Upon its arrival, the CO of the 704th, Major Delk Oden, was instructed to have the battalion replace its approved Armored Force uniform with the new uniform style approved by the Tank Destroyer command. Being loyal to the Fourth, Oden informed the staff of the TDC that his battalion's assignment was temporary, and that he would only comply with such an order if it came directly from General Wood. This didn't exactly get the relationship between the 704th and TDC staff off to a glowing start.

When Oden shared with his men what had happened, it helped inspire them to a higher level of performance, as they figured they might be in for a tough go of it while stationed at the Center. When the battalion left Camp Hood in January 1943, they had broken all of the existing records for gunnery, tactics, maintenance, administration, and logistics.

The Fourth Armored establish three encampments in the county of Wiltshire, near the towns of Chippenham, Trowbridge, and Devizes, and the men of the Fourth soon began contributing to the local economy. The locals embraced the men from the United States and made their stay as pleasant as could be expected under the circumstances.

The Fourth's arrival in England did not signal an end to the division's training and preparation for battle. At first, the regimen included calisthenics and classroom training (the outdoor activities were none too pleasant due to the sunless, chilly, misty days typical of winter in England). Once they drew their vehicles and weapons from the stockpiles in Great Britain, they began familiarizing themselves with their new equipment. In some cases, the equipment was an improvement over what they had been training with in the States. But much to the tankers' disappointment, they were handed the older model M4A1, instead of the newer M4A3 version they used back home.

Over the weeks and months that followed, the Fourth Armored utilized the cramped English countryside to fine-tune its performance. Due to the limited real estate available for live-fire exercises, firing ranges were set up along the coast. Floating targets were set out on the water, and the tankers sharpened their skills from firing positions set along the shoreline. Time was also spent at the more ideal training area at Salisbury Plains, where there was sufficient room to practice small unit tactical maneuvers.

On February 1, the Fourth Armored was assigned to the United States Third

Army. On that same day, General Patton made his first visit to the division while in England. He addressed the officers and senior noncommissioned officers in spectacular fashion, bowling them over with his colorful language and forceful style. They had never heard anything like it, and those who attended the event would forever remember it as "the speech." To simply say that the men were motivated would be a gross understatement.

The assignment to the Third Army must have been a source of great satisfaction for both General Wood and General Patton. By this time in their lives, the two men had developed an extremely close personal relationship. They considered themselves to be the best of friends, and they loved each other like brothers (a fact established by Wood's own revelations). Fate had now brought them together for the most important mission of their lives.

As winter turned to spring, England continued to swell with American troops and equipment. It became increasingly difficult to reserve training space, as newly formed units with less time together than the Fourth were given priority. As a result, the prospect of having too much idle time on their hands was a growing concern. But fortunately, the improving springtime weather allowed for outdoor recreation, and baseball and football games were organized with increased frequency.

The lack of training space also provided the Americans with more time to take in the sights of England. Stonehenge was a very popular attraction, and some were fortunate enough to visit London. While enjoying the historic and social elements of the city, the sight of barrage balloons, enemy planes, buzz bombs, and destroyed buildings provided constant, lingering reminders of why they were there.

D-Day

The morning of June 6, 1944, was a busy day for the men of the Fourth Armored Division. The training facility at Salisbury Plain became available on short notice, and some of the units of the Fourth made hasty plans to utilize the facility that day. Other elements of the division were busy that morning waterproofing their vehicles and drawing basic loads of ammunition. The men knew that the real fighting would begin sooner rather than later, and every chance to fine-tune their performance was taken advantage of.

The tankers drove their Shermans relentlessly that morning across Salisbury Plain. As they prepared to make their final charge of the day, the drone of a large body of aircraft could be heard above the din of the exercise. The drumbeat of the aircraft engines grew in volume, signaling the fact that they were drawing closer to the tankers' positions. The sound and intensity echoed a similar flight that had passed overhead during the dark, early morning hours. But as the armada of planes approached, the men of the Fourth instantly recognized that this time, things were different. Even from a distance, the men could make out that the planes were a mix of fighters, bombers, and transports. And one very unusual thing stood out about the transport planes. Dangling in the wind behind their tails, the tankers could see tow cables ... with nothing attached! The same type of transport had been seen on other occasions towing gliders, and so it was immediately obvious that these planes were returning from a drop. Was it a drill, or the real thing?

The answer became glaringly obvious as the planes passed overhead. Scattered throughout the loose formation were battle-damaged aircraft. The scars of enemy fire were unmistakable, and offered the first evidence that the invasion was on!

The activities on Salisbury Plain came to a screeching halt. The men backslapped one another, shouted exuberantly to the heavens, and rejoiced in the knowledge that the mission they had trained so long and hard for was about to begin. It was now just a matter of time before their mettle would be tested on the battlefield.

The events unfolding across the English Channel were of epic proportions. In all, elements of seven Allied divisions hit the Normandy beaches that day, supported by three airborne divisions landing behind enemy lines. The strength of German opposition varied at each of the five beaches, but none was more intense than Omaha, where the outcome remained in doubt throughout much of the day. The Germans on that beach were so confident of their defensive effort that, at 1:35 p.m., they signaled their HQ with the news that they had pushed the invaders back into the sea. The Germans' optimism had led them to report a prediction, and not the facts, for eventually, the men of the 1st and 29th Infantry divisions overcame the fierce opposition offered by the German 352nd Infantry Division and pushed inland. The Wehrmacht mounted an immediate attempt to push the Americans and British back into the sea. But the effort never gained sufficient momentum, and the German's aspirations and effort eventually turned from counterattacks to containment.

During the weeks that followed, the Nazi effort was compromised by Hitler's belief that a second invasion was imminent in the Pas de Calais region. His belief was fueled by a carefully orchestrated deception that led him to believe that General Patton was to lead the "real" invasion. As a result, valuable German assets were held in the area of Pas de Calais that might have otherwise been utilized in Normandy.

Though deprived of the full utilization of their resources, the Germans nevertheless waged a tenacious defense. During the days and weeks that followed D-Day, a bitter struggle took place around the city of Caen, as SS panzer divisions were thrown into the breach to thwart the advancing armor of the British and Canadian armies. Meanwhile, the American First Army pursued two primary objectives: the port of Cherbourg, located at the northern tip of the Cotentin peninsula, and a southern expansion of the beachhead toward St. Lo.

On June 19, General Manton Eddy's 9th Infantry Division cut through to the Atlantic coast on the west side of the peninsula. The drive was made easier by Hitler's decision to pull his forces to the south, but nevertheless, it represented one of the more significant accomplishments during the early weeks of the campaign. The defenders caught on the north side of the incision pulled back toward Cherbourg, and on June 27, the last of the city's defenders were rounded up.

The advance toward St. Lo was a much more difficult affair, due to the excellent defensive positions afforded the Germans by virtue of the centuries-old hedgerows that defined the Norman landscape. As June turned into July, St. Lo was still in German hands, and the American advance to the south went forward at a snail's pace.

As the allies pushed deliberately forward against a staunch German foe, a constant flow of reinforcements entered Normandy via the invasion beaches. The Fourth Armored Division would soon be among the new arrivals on French soil. Three years of hard work and training were about to be put to the test. General Wood's division was ripe for action; it was time to pluck it from the tree and put it to work.

2. Baptism

To France

On July 9, elements of the Fourth Armored began boarding the ships that would take them on the cross-channel trip from England to France. The conditions in the Channel were extremely rough, and the degree of seasickness that occurred rivaled, and perhaps surpassed, what the men had experienced while crossing the Atlantic. It was a welcome relief when the transports finally discharged their metal and human cargo onto the beaches of Utah and Omaha.

Some of the men had to stay at sea longer than others. The LCT (Landing Craft — Tank) carrying Major Bautz and a platoon of Sherman tanks experienced engine trouble, and fell behind the rest of the convoy. The tankers had to spend three long days at sea. The only consolation for some of Bautz's men was that the skipper of the LCT had a liberal amount of rum on board, which he doled out to those who were inclined to keep it down. Bautz's arrival in Normandy was delayed even further when the skipper brought them to Omaha Beach by mistake (his orders were to disembark at Utah). Though prodded by the beach master to unload right then and there, the skipper backed away from the beach and made his way to Utah.

It would take several days for the division to unload and move into its assigned assembly areas (Major Bautz, who disembarked long after the rest of his battalion had moved inland, would roam the countryside with two platoons of Shermans for two days before finding the 37th's bivouac area). Even though the initial assault on Fortress Europe had taken place some five weeks prior to the arrival of the Fourth Armored Division, the debris of battle was still piled above the shoreline, and served as a vivid reminder of the struggle that had been waged between the sea and the bluffs overlooking the beach. The vestiges of the invasion, and of the battles fought inland, provided sobering moments for the men of the Fourth as they rolled over the beach and into the French countryside.

While in England, the Fourth had been assigned to Patton's still-secret U.S. Third Army, but upon its arrival in France, it was reassigned to Omar Bradley's First Army. It immediately became a part of Major General Troy Middleton's VIII Corps, which held the right flank of Bradley's line in Normandy. The Fourth was initially deployed in the rear of the VIII Corps' 79th Infantry Division, near the town of Barneville-Sur-Mer, which was a relatively safe distance from the enemy. The sounds of war could be heard in the distance, but the Fourth was far enough from the action that it could organize and prepare without too much interference from the enemy. The division wasn't completely outside the reach of danger, however, and this was put into evidence on its very first evening in France, when the 94th Armored Field Artillery Battalion received a visit from the Luftwaffe. That night, a plane dropped several bombs within a couple of hundred yards of the 94th's assembly area. It was clear to all concerned that the rehearsal was over. This was the real thing.

Normandy had been torn apart by war during the past few weeks. Many of the natives were reluctant to become refugees, however, and stayed in their farmhouses and villages, despite the inherent risks. Once liberated, the civilians were eager to return to normal life. Conditions for the local population were far from ideal, however, and the Americans began to enhance their reputation as ambassadors of good will by spontaneously offering provisions and medical care to the needy civilians. The villagers returned the generosity of their liberators by extending to them the comfort of their homes, potent cups of calvados (a cider-based concoction), hugs, kisses, and prayers for a safe return to their homes in America.

A quiet nervousness ran through the units as they went about their tasks on French soil. The exuberance exhibited on the Salisbury Plain on June 6 was now tempered a bit; the past five weeks had provided time for sobering thoughts. As the division settled in to the Norman landscape, the idiosyncrasies of military life managed to creep in and vie for the men's attention. To some, it was incredible that the nit-picky elements of stateside military life were still being enforced at the front. For example, on July 16, the topic of the day among the men of the 51st Armored Infantry Battalion was whether or not their shirts were to be buttoned at the neck. They actually received several orders regarding this topic, and the men were beside themselves that this could be on anyone's mind when the battlefield was just eight miles away!

The relative calm wouldn't last long for the Fourth Armored. On July 14, General Bradley asked Patton if he had any objection to placing Wood's division into defensive positions on the front line. Patton favored the move, and recorded in his diary, "the sooner we get troops blooded, the better." General Wood, however, abhorred the idea of "blooding" his division. He was confident in their training and talent, and trusted that when the time came for offensive operations, his men would be ready, and would perform quite well without having gone through Bradley's regimen for introducing new divisions to the front.

For this particular assignment, the three armored infantry battalions were all assigned to Brigadier General Dager's Combat Command B. The division's three armored field artillery battalions, the 704th Tank Destroyer Battalion, and two troops of the 25th Cavalry Reconnaissance Squadron would play a supporting role alongside the armored infantry. The three tank battalions would have to be content sitting on the sidelines for the time being.

At 11:30 P.M. on July 16, the 51st Armored Infantry Battalion, commanded by Lt. Colonel Alfred Maybach, received its orders for the following day. And this time, it

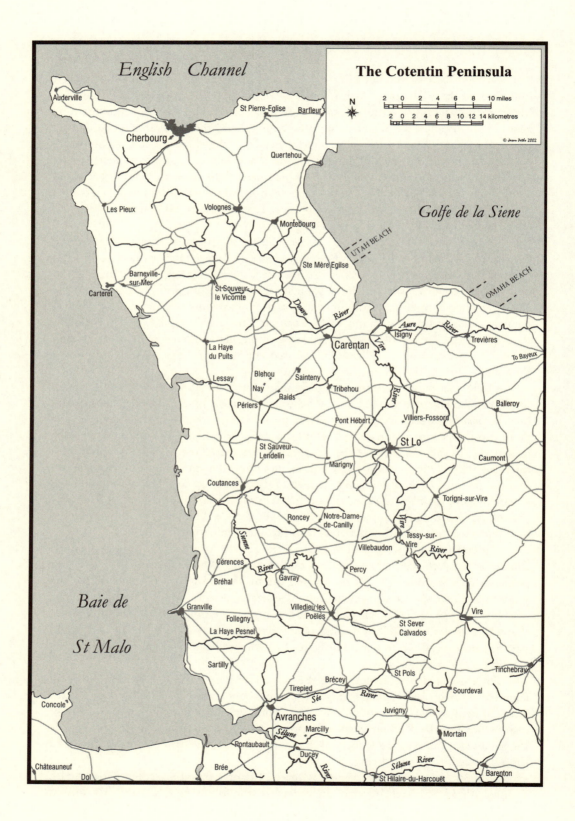

The Cotentin Peninsula

had nothing to do with the proper way to wear their uniform. They would be part of the force from the Fourth Armored that would take up positions on the front line, as Bradley had ordered. The other two armored infantry battalions received similar orders. The 51st was to be ready to move by 9 A.M. on July 17. The 53rd AIB, command by Lt. Colonel George L. Jaques, and the 10th AIB, commanded by Lt. Colonel Graham Kirkpatrick, would be moving during the morning as well.

This was an unexpected way for the division to cut its teeth. Rather than being engaged in a slashing, driving, offensive role, the armored infantry would soon find themselves in static positions serving as traditional doughboys. This wasn't exactly the mission they had trained and prepared for during the past three years.

Into the Line

The three armored infantry battalions were to take over positions previously held by the VIII Corps' 4th Infantry Division, just south of the town of Carentan. For this assignment, Company C of the 10th Armored Infantry Battalion would be attached to the 53rd AIB, and would serve as a local reserve for that battalion.

At 11:00 A.M. on July 17, the three armored infantry battalions set out toward their positions at the front. The third platoon of B/51 took the point as the column moved some 40 miles toward its assembly area near the village of Blehou. The armored infantry moved up to relieve the men of the 4th Infantry Division, and they immediately began improving their positions. Without a doubt, a degree of nervousness ran through the ranks as they prepared for their first night on the front line. After the long summer day came to a close, they settled down in their slit trenches and grabbed whatever amount of sleep the combination of jitters and hard ground would allow. Everyone wondered if the Germans would welcome them by shelling their positions, but the night passed without incident.

The daylight hours of July 18 were uneventful as well, and the men continued to improve their positions without any harassment from the enemy. Brigadier General Dager visited the 51st AIB's command post that day in order to see how they were coming along. He didn't have to give them much external motivation to make their trenches and foxholes deeper.

Sometime after the armored infantry went into the line, General Wood also came forward to inspect the positions of CCB. On the way, he decided to pay a visit to General Bradley's headquarters. Upon his arrival, he found Bradley and Major General Walton Walker conferring together in a trailer (Walker was a familiar figure to Wood, as they had been in the same graduating class at West Point; Wood did not think very highly of Walker during their days at the Academy, and his opinion had not changed over the course of the past thirty-two years). Wood struck up a conversation, seemingly with the intent of letting Bradley know that the Fourth Armored was "ready to move." Wood also expressed his concern regarding the length of time that his armored infantry might be required to remain in a static role. In his typical straightforward fashion, Wood told Bradley that he "hated to lose (his) armored infantry who had been trained to operate with tanks on the move." Bradley took the opportunity to reiterate his desire to "blood" new units as they arrived in Normandy. Wood's reaction is best told in his own words:

> This remark disgusted and infuriated me and I so expressed myself in no uncertain terms, saying that my people would do whatever they had to do without the need of any blood-bath. I knew my division, and its soldiers never failed me...

The Germans Attack

The scene south of Carentan changed abruptly after nightfall. At about 8 P.M., the positions of the 53rd AIB were hammered by a strong counterattack, courtesy of the 2nd SS "Das Reich" Panzer Division. The 2nd SS was a tough opponent to take on in their very first engagement, and the men of the 53rd were pushed back from their forward positions. Some of the positions were overrun, and several of the armored infantrymen were captured. Company A became scattered and disorganized, and it took one of the forward observers of the 94th Armored Field Artillery Battalion, which was directly supporting the 53rd, to help reorganize the infantry and lead them back to safe positions (the observer, Staff Sergeant Herman Orsbon, was awarded the Silver Star for his actions that night).

With the situation deteriorating along the 53rd AIB's front, Company C of the 10th AIB was moved up from reserve and inserted into the front in an effort to stem the tide of the German advance. The men of C/10 managed to hold their ground, but the rest of the 53rd AIB continued to fall back. In a further attempt to restore the situation, and ensure that C/10 was not engulfed, the balance of the 10th AIB was ordered to assist the 53rd AIB. The staff of the 53rd was relieved of command of the operation, and the staff of the 10th took temporary control of both battalions.

In order to free up the 10th AIB for their assignment, Company B of the 51st AIB slid into their positions. A/10 and B/10 then moved toward the front to take up the battle alongside C/10. The balance of the 51st AIB (A and C Companies) moved quickly toward a position about one mile west of the town of Sainteny, where they became the reserve force for the three battalions.

When A/51 and C/51 arrived at their positions near Sainteny, they came across men from the 53rd AIB who had fled from the front. The beleaguered armored infantrymen told wide-eyed stories of their unit being wiped out (in fact, the 53rd's casualties for the day were six killed and 25 wounded). Hearing these stories, and seeing the fear in the eyes of the men that had been forced to retreat, added to the nerves of everyone who had yet to see combat.

After a night of hard fighting, the 10th Armored Infantry Battalion was able to stabilize the front. It had been a rough night for the 53rd AIB, however. Their baptism of fire brought with it an element of fear that they had not known before. The armored infantry had indeed been "blooded," and they now knew first hand the sights, sounds, and smells of combat. Of all the human senses, perhaps none was impacted more than the sense of smell, as the stench of death was carried aloft by the warm summer breeze and permeated every fiber of their being.

Restoring the Line

July 19 was spent shuffling the infantry companies in the wake of the prior night's battle. As part of the day's operations, the 10th Armored Infantry Battalion utilized Companies A and B to launch a limited attack designed to take back some of the ground lost during the German attack. At 1 P.M., the size of the attacking force was expanded to include the entire 10th AIB, plus B/51. Their mission included a reconnaissance in force "into the forward area not to pass beyond line Nay-Raids."

The first offensive operation of the Fourth Armored Division was going well. Company C, under the command of Captain John Leighton, advanced as far as Raids. It was here that the attack ran into some difficulty. Upon reaching the village, the tempo of the battle increased. Leighton's men came under heavy fire, and the Germans began advancing against his positions. As Leighton was leading his men in battle, an enemy round struck him in the stomach. The wound was serious, but it did not deter him from staying at the front to direct his company.

The situation facing the 10th AIB began to deteriorate, and Leighton made the decision for the company to withdraw to better positions. Weakened by his wound and unable to move under his own power, he would need the assistance of his men if he were to evacuate along with his troops. Not wanting any of his men to risk being slowed down by having to carry him out, he told them to leave him behind. Those around him were reluctant to do so, but they finally acquiesced when he assured them that "friendly medics would pick him up shortly." This was probably an intentional, courageous ploy by Leighton to get his men moving to safety. Little did Leighton know, however, that at least one medic stood a chance of helping him.

That medic was Pfc. Thomas Rankin, who had gone forward during the battle to treat the wounded men of C Company. When the company finally withdrew at the insistence of Captain Leighton, Rankin stayed behind to tend to the wounded that could not be evacuated. After nightfall, once he felt certain that all the men had been treated, he snuck back to his own lines (he was awarded the Bronze Star for his actions at Raids). But if he came across Captain Leighton, he was unable to evacuate him. At the end of the day, the Captain would be reported as missing in action.

During the next several days, the armored infantry continued to bear the brunt of the fighting, with the division's artillery battalions and tank destroyers firing in support (the TD's were used in this instance to provide indirect fire). German artillery and mortar fire continued to hit their positions, and enemy aircraft made a few attempts at strafing runs.

The Bull's-eye

As the armored infantry battalions were receiving their baptism of fire, the tankers tried to put their time to good use. In addition to the cleaning and maintenance of their equipment, they conducted reconnaissance in order to gain a better understanding of the terrain that the tanks would have to negotiate once committed to action. While out scouring the battlefield for just that purpose, Major Albin F. Irzyk, then the

Major Albin F. Irzyk (courtesy Al Irzyk).

S-3 (Operations Officer) of the 8th Tank Battalion, stumbled upon a scene that would reward him with a bounty of insight.

During his reconnaissance, Irzyk came across a knocked out Panther tank that stood silently at the edge of a wooded area overlooking an open field. Irzyk climbed to the rear deck of the tank to examine it in greater detail. As he stood behind the turret, he glanced down the length of the Panther's long, sleek 75mm cannon. In the distance, he spotted five Sherman tanks, lined up neatly from left to right, in a tight grouping, heading straight for him across the field. But after a brief moment, he realized that the tanks were not moving. From his perch atop the Panther, the scene suddenly became very clear to him. The Shermans were *never* going to move. They had fallen victim to the Panther's deadly, high velocity gun.

Major Irzyk descended from the Panther and crossed the field to the final resting place of the M4s. The Shermans shared more than an identical design: each had a clean hole through its sloped frontal armor. Glancing back in the direction of the Panther, he could clearly see the barrel of the silent enemy tank pointing in his direction.

There was no doubt in his mind about what had transpired. The American tank crews had clearly violated some basic principles. They had bunched up too close together, and they had not staggered their formation. As a result, the German gunner had an identical range to each of the targets, which meant that he did not have to waste any time elevating or depressing the barrel to compensate for distance. Because of the tight grouping, he didn't have to traverse the turret very far from side to side. In Major Irzyk's words, "it was like the proverbial ducks in a row."

The tactical errors committed by the American tankers were obvious to Irzyk. The scene provided vivid reinforcement of the soundness of the tactics the Fourth Armored tankers had been taught during their three years of non-stop training. But there was a new, unexpected lesson he would carry back to his command post that day. Painted on the front armored slope of each Sherman tank was a large white star, which served as a means of identifying the tanks as American. Al came to the sickening realization that each star had served as a bull's-eye for the German gunner. And the Kraut hadn't missed a single one. All five shots had found their mark.

That same day, Major Irzyk reported his observations to his battalion commander, Lt. Col. Tom Conley. They agreed that the stars had to go, and immediately set about having them painted over. And it wasn't just on the front and side armor of the Shermans. Every vehicle in

The crew of the 8th TB S-3 tank. *Left to right:* John Keen, Al Irzyk, Husie Mauro, Carl Winkler (courtesy Al Irzyk).

the battalion received the same treatment, and in a hurry. By the end of the following day, there wasn't a star to be seen within the 8th Tank Battalion. The practice spread to some of the other units in the division as well. The war was going to be tough enough. There was no need to make it any easier for the enemy.

Another Counterattack

On July 20, the Germans continued to shell the Fourth Armored's forward positions. The discomfort of the armored infantry was multiplied when a heavy downpour of rain flooded their foxholes and trenches. The intensity of the German artillery picked up considerably at 6:40 P.M., and the Krauts followed up the barrage with another counterattack conducted under the cover of darkness.

This time, the 51st AIB was on the receiving end, with the brunt of the attack being directed at A/51 and B/51. The fighting was heavy and confused, and casualties ran high among the armored infantry. The fog of war permeated the command post of the 51st AIB. Exaggerated casualty reports and rumors created a great deal of confusion among the staff. Word came in to the field artillery supporting the 51st that the armored infantry had abandoned their forward positions. In response, the artillery commander brought down a barrage on top of that sector. But there was one major problem: The report that the 51st had retreated was not true. The men of the 51st were clinging valiantly to their positions, and had not yielded any ground. As a result, their own guns pounded them with "friendly" fire. Despite this setback, the 51st AIB repulsed the enemy throughout the night (the 704th TD Battalion's recon platoon also played a role in the fight). But it was an extremely costly effort, with the 51st suffering 134 casualties. Companies A and B were hit particularly hard, with 59 and 72 casualties, respectively. If the casualty reports had been exaggerated, it was not by much.

The early morning hours of July 21 were consumed with the treatment and evacuation of those wounded during the prior night's battle. There was also the grim task of retrieving the bodies of the men killed in action. Lt. Dorf led a detail forward to retrieve the dead, but misery begot misery, as the Germans shelled the area while the mission was underway, causing yet another American casualty.

Around midday, General Wood and General Dager visited the 51st AIB's command post. There was more than ample evidence at hand that the division was being "blooded." The armored infantry battalions collectively suffered 400 casualties during the time they held their static positions in Normandy. It was an expensive indoctrination.

The three days from July 22 though 24 were relatively calm. The Germans lobbed intermittent shells across the front and rear areas, and sniper fire punctuated the scene from time to time. The Americans responded with their own artillery and mortar rounds at a rate that exceeded what the Germans could muster on their side of the battlefield. During those relatively idle days, General Wood continued to make the rounds of his units to ensure they were fit and ready for the next phase of operations.

Operation Cobra

By late July, the Allies had built up enough force within Normandy to contemplate a strong and concerted effort to break through the German front. On the morning of July 25, General Bradley launched Operation Cobra, which was designed to break open the logjam that had been created among the hedgerows of Normandy. The Cobra plan called for the U.S. VII Corps to strike southwest, angling toward the west coast of the Cotentin peninsula. Once the VII Corps captured the city of Coutances, the VIII Corps, led by the 4th and 6th Armored divisions, would attack south. If everything went as planned, the Americans would trap any German units remaining between Coutances and the divisions of the U.S. VIII Corps to the north

The VII Corps' 3rd Armored Division was responsible for the capture of Coutances. The 3rd was a powerful unit, built according to the specifications for a "heavy" armored division (as was the 2nd Armored, with which the 3rd Armored was paired in VII Corps). Like the Fourth Armored, the campaign in Normandy was the 3rd Armored's first time in action. It arrived in Normandy before the end of June, and had already learned some expensive lessons: During its first offensive action on June 29 and 30, CCA/3 lost 31 tanks.

The opening gambit for Operation Cobra was a massive air bombardment designed to pulverize the German positions, thus opening the way for a quick breakthrough by the infantry and armored divisions of VII Corps. At 9:38 A.M., the lead fighter-bombers of the IX TAC began hitting their assigned targets in textbook fashion.

Wood's men were located about four miles to the west of the area being bombed. From that vantage point, they had a good view of what was happening in the skies above the front of VII Corps. First, they saw the fast-moving fighter-bombers make their steep dives toward targets hidden beyond the horizon. Next came wave after wave of medium and heavy bombers, marching in an endless parade punctuated by the release of their deadly payloads. The vibrations felt underneath the heels of the men of the Fourth

Armored served as powerful testimony to the raw, deadly power of the bombs falling to the east. After the bombers completed the most important part of their mission, they made a sweeping right turn that carried them south across the face of the Fourth's positions. They then turned gently to the northwest and formed a thick conveyor belt of aerial machines that disappeared over the horizon.

German AA gunners on the ground that survived the initial onslaught of the fighter-bombers were determined to put a dent in the aerial armada. Given the thick layer of targets they had to choose from, it is no surprise that they had occasional success. Here and there, a bomber would be sent into a death spiral that was clearly visible from where the men of the Fourth Armored sat. But the German response was nothing but a pinprick in the grand scheme of things. Surely, the aerial bombardment was ripping apart the German defenses.

But all was not right below the bellies of the American aircraft. As subsequent waves of Allied planes rolled across the sky, an increasing number of bombs fell short on the positions of the American troops poised to go on the attack as soon as the bombing had ceased. The forward positions of the 9th, 30th, and 4th Infantry divisions were a shambles after the miscue; four hundred and ninety men were wounded, and 111 Americans were dead, including Lt. General Lesley J. McNair, head of all U.S. ground forces (McNair had taken an ill-advised position close to the front in order to observe the attack). It was a disheartening start to the much-anticipated Operation Cobra.

Major General Wood's division was not scheduled to move that day. For now, it would remain deployed behind the positions of the 90th Infantry Division. But many of the men saw the bombing as a sure sign that their time to advance was close at hand. This was to be their first big show, and the butterflies were swarming.

The Fourth Armored would be left sitting idle longer than had been anticipated. The inaccurate delivery of the bombers' payload forced the attack of the VII Corps to stall right from the start. The forward American elements were dazed and confused, and there was the immediate task of caring for almost 500 wounded soldiers. The Germans were stunned as well, but to the chagrin of every GI that eventually took part in the advance, the Krauts managed to reestablish some of their positions and were ready to greet the Americans. As a result, the lead infantry divisions of VII Corps managed to scrape out a gain of only 1¼ miles on the first day of the attack. This was well short of the original game plan, and the VIII Corps was instructed to hold back until the VII Corps made more progress.

The following day (July 26), VII Corps committed its two armored divisions, but this was still not enough to force a clean breakthrough. VIII Corps got underway that same day, but in limited fashion. The 4th and 6th Armored divisions continued to stay back, while the 8th and 90th Infantry divisions began to press forward. Lending support to the advancing infantry were the Fourth Armored Division's own armored field artillery battalions (the 22nd, 94th, and 66th, under the command of Lt. Colonel Arthur C. Peterson, Lt. Colonel Alexander Graham, and Lt. Colonel Neil Wallace, respectively). The shells of their M7 self-propelled 105mm howitzers were added to the rain of steel falling on the German positions. Despite the extra support, the gains of the 8th and 90th were modest.

The Capture of Coutances

By midday on July 27, the tide had turned, and it appeared that German resistance was crumbling. Indeed, the enemy was falling back in significant numbers, as the weight of the attack had finally taken its toll. VII Corps began to surge, and it became apparent that the path in front of Middleton's VIII Corps was practically wide open (in fact, the enemy had slipped away during the previous night). The primary obstacle facing VIII Corps was an incredibly heavy concentration of mines that the fleeing Germans had left in their wake (General Middleton later described it as the worst minefields he had ever seen). With the enemy apparently on the run, the anvil was red hot, and it was time to strike a telling blow against the Germans. And that could mean only one thing: it was time for the master blacksmith to appear. General George S. Patton was about to burst on the scene.

For several months, Patton had been relegated to the role of a decoy. The Allies had attempted to fool German intelligence into thinking the flamboyant general would be in command of a second amphibious invasion force scheduled to strike at Pas de Calais. Hitler had always believed that the "real" Allied invasion would fall in that region, and the Allied deception involving Patton reinforced his suspicions. The ruse worked, and valuable resources were maintained in the area of Pas de Calais.

Patton paced like a caged lion as he played his role in the bluff. He finally arrived in France on July 6, and spent the 19 days prior to Cobra readying the headquarters of the Third Army.

The exact date for Patton's command to become operational was unknown. General Omar Bradley, who would soon take command of the newly formed 12th Army Group, would be the one to pull the trigger for the activation of the Third Army. The timing was completely at Bradley's discretion, but it was generally understood that it would take place when the divisions assigned to the Third Army were in position to exploit the success that was anticipated on the Allied right flank. Patton would then begin his assigned task of clearing out the Brittany region of France.

While not ready to activate the Third Army on July 27, Bradley knew that Patton could bring his considerable drive and energy to bear on the advance of VIII Corps. So that afternoon, he informed Patton that, effective the following day, he would be given oversight of VIII Corps (the corps was due to be assigned to the Third Army in any event). Patton and Middleton wasted no time before conferring, and they quickly agreed that the two armored divisions should be brought to the fore to lead VIII Corps to its rendezvous with VII Corps at Coutances (an objective which the struggling 3rd Armored had still not reached).

At 5:00 A.M. sharp on the morning of July 28, CCB spearheaded the Fourth Armored Division's drive through the positions of the 90th Infantry Division. The 8th Tank Battalion led the way, slicing through the battered German defenses and plunging toward Coutances.

The tankers met very scattered resistance as they moved south. The primary obstacles were the mines and roadblocks the Germans had left behind as parting gifts (there was a three hour delay near St. Sauveur-Lendelin while the engineers cleared a minefield that totally blocked the advance). By noon, the lead tanks of the "Rolling Eight Ball" had arrived at the doorstep of Coutances. But the enemy had not abandoned the town completely, and Brigadier General Dager's men would have to fight to clear it.

As the units trailing behind the 8th Tank Battalion began to move out, an advance party from the 10th AIB discovered the body of Captain Leighton, who had so bravely stayed behind after ordering his men to withdraw from the town of Raids. Leighton had been listed as MIA, and his men had held out hope that the enemy might have rescued him. But that was not to be. The sobering revelation that he died back on July 19 was a "hard blow" for the 10th AIB. He had served with the battalion since September of 1943, and was described by his men as "a capable, understanding, and courageous leader, well liked by those who served under him and worked with him."

General Wood wasn't content with directing the action from the rear. As CCB took on the enemy in Coutances, "P" came up to the front, and not satisfied with the pace of the advance, got to work playing a direct role in the action. Wood proceeded to enter the town on foot while under enemy fire, and then single-handedly captured a German soldier. He navigated his way through a minefield, and once safely through, used a pencil and paper to scrawl out a message, which he sent back to the commander of CCB. It read: "General Dager, send the Infantry through after me" (General Wood was awarded the Distinguished Service Cross for his actions at Coutances).

CCB continued to push through the city, taking out pockets of stubborn resistance along the way. In one instance, a deadly German 88mm gun, well positioned in an alley, had knocked out several vehicles and succeeded in stalling the advance. General Wood raced to the scene in his jeep. He ran up to a nearby Hellcat tank destroyer, and shouted to the crew, "Pull up in front of that damned alley and get rid of that gun!" After pushing one of the destroyed American half tracks out of the way, the TD of Harry Traynor traversed its turret 90 degrees, and then pulled up broadside across the opening of the alley. With the 76mm gun of the Hellcat now pointed straight toward the enemy position, the TD gunner quickly fired two rounds between the buildings, pulverizing the 88. Wood was still there to witness the accomplishment, and when the task was done, walked up to the front of Traynor's Hellcat, slammed his hand down on the sloped steel, and shouted, "Thanks! Those damned Heinies were holding up the war!" The men of the Fourth didn't soon forget their encounters with "P" Wood.

At the same time the town was being cleared, elements of CCB began pushing south. As the column advanced, it came across a string of mines blocking the bridge immediately south of the city. Captain Francis Pieri of the 24th Armored Engineer Battalion risked his life by deactivating the mines, thus enabling the advance to resume (he was posthumously awarded the Distinguished Service Cross). The 53rd Battalion, along with Company A of the 51st, was able to continue the advance, and took up positions for the night south of the town.

On that same evening of July 28, the 3rd Armored Division made contact with Wood's division at Coutances. Dager's CCB had planted the first of many feathers in the cap of the Fourth Armored by beating the 3rd Armored to their own objective. (The participants must have viewed it as a competitive affair, as VII Corps' own unit history speaks of losing "the race to Coutances.")

The coup of capturing Coutances was not achieved without cost. Among the casualties that day was Colonel Louis J. Storck, commander of Combat Command Reserve

(CCR). A mine claimed both Lou and his radio operator as their jeep traveled through the streets of Coutances. "Black Lou," as he was affectionately known, had been responsible for training the division's armored infantry battalions, and had commanded the 704th prior to Delk Oden taking command. To lose him so early in the Fourth Armored's first offensive engagement was a bitter note for those who knew him.

The very next day, another key figure within the Fourth Armored would be killed by yet another mine explosion: Major Alexander Newton, the S-2 for the division trains (the arm of the division responsible for supply). Early in their war, the men of the Fourth discovered that there was no safe haven, and no safe job. Death could reach out at any time, any place, and touch anyone.

The Great Race to Avranches

The next major objective was the city of Avranches. Control of this city was critical, since it served as the gateway out of the Cotentin peninsula. Once Avranches was in Americans hands, elements of both the Third and First armies could penetrate to

A Sherman tank from B/37 rumbles south toward Avranches. July 29, 1944 (National Archives Photograph SC192411).

A 4th AD patrol picks its way through the rubble of Coutances. July 29, 1944 (National Archives Photograph SC192109).

the west, south, or east, and break out of the restrictive hedgerow country that had defined the battlefield since D-Day.

The 6th Armored Division had been advancing on a parallel axis on the right flank of the Fourth Armored. It was the 6th Armored that had been given the assignment of capturing Avranches. Wood's less glamorous mission was to continue driving south on an axis that remained parallel with that of the 6th Armored, penetrate east of Avranches, and assume blocking positions that would prevent the enemy from counterattacking the left flank of VIII Corps. Other units would then spill through the city, and drive to the west, south, and southeast.

On July 29, the Fourth slashed its way south from Coutances in relentless fashion. The drive was so fast and furious that the two artillery battalions assigned to CCB, the 94th and 66th, had to play leapfrog in order to provide artillery support and keep the vanguard within range. One battalion would fulfill fire missions while the other moved south; then the battalion that had moved closer to the fighting would stop and take over the fire missions, while the trailing battalion pulled up stakes and drove to a position still closer to the front. By repeating the process, CCB ensured that at least a full battalion of 105mm howitzers would stay within supporting range of the main body of the combat command.

191888-S

German prisoners rounded up by the 4th AD near Coutances. July 29, 1944 (National Archives Photograph SC191888).

More often than not, the artillerymen set up their howitzers in firing positions toward the rear that afforded them relative safety. But in a swift, slashing advance like the one the Fourth was now engaged in, the front line is fluid, and the mobile artillery can find itself closer to the front than usual. This was the case during the drive south from Coutances, when men from one of the Fourth's artillery battalions found themselves face to face with the enemy. Near Sartilly, a half-track from the 94th was hit by a round from a German 88, killing two of the men on board, T/5 Joseph Shook and PFC George Adamson (these two men were the first combat fatalities of the war for the 94th).

As Wood's tanks plunged south, traffic control became a significant concern. The Second Armored Division, one of the few divisions in Normandy with pre-D-Day battle experience, had outpaced the Third Armored Division, and had cut a swathe to the southwest that intersected with the route being taken by elements of Colonel Bruce Clarke's CCA.

As the two divisions drew within close proximity of each other, elements of CCA opened fire on a unit from the "Hell on Wheels" Division. Once the Second Armored determined they were on the receiving end of friendly fire, Colonel Sidney Hinds, commanding officer of the 41st Armored Infantry Regiment, radioed the Fourth to inform them that they were firing on "Powerhouse" (the code name for the Second Armored). Suspecting that the voice over the radio was actually a German in disguise, the Fourth continued to lay fire on the suspected "enemy" positions. Hind finally rephrased his request, telling them that if they didn't cease fire, he would call their "P." Apparently, the use of Wood's nickname was enough to convince the men of CCA that the radio call was genuine, and they ceased fire.

As the day progressed, fate intervened in a way that dramatically changed the Fourth Armored Division's role in the offensive. The 6th Armored Division, despite having the most critical objective (Avranches), was progressing in a more tentative fashion than Wood's division. While visiting the "Super Sixth" that day, Patton found that the division had basically come to a halt. After hunting down the division command post, Patton found the commanding general, Bob Grow, surrounded by a large group of his officers, who in Patton's words, were "deeply engrossed in the study of maps" in search of a suitable location to ford the Sienne River. Patton was quick to point out his displeasure, and informed them that he had just personally waded across the Sienne and found the river to be no more than two feet deep at that spot. At Patton's urging — which included a threat to relieve Grow of his command — the 6th Armored Division eventually got it into gear. But in the meantime, seeing that Wood's division was in much better position to advance on the city, Patton reassigned the objective of Avranches to the Fourth Armored. General Wood immediately sent new instructions to Dager: "Present mission cancelled — using any roads [in zone] … move on Avranches … to capture it and secure crossings east thereof."

On Dager's orders, CCB struck out in two columns. The easternmost column was predominately composed of armored infantry, and screened the left flank of CCB's advance. The western column formed the main armored thrust of the advance, and was spearheaded by the 8th Tank Battalion.

The east column was brought to a halt when B Company of the 51st AIB ran into the enemy near the town of Loiretel. While advancing down a narrow road, the armored infantrymen were caught in an ambush, and quickly lost six halftracks to enemy fire, at least some of which came from some panzers. The battalion's towed 57mm anti-tank guns were brought forward to counter the enemy tanks, and actually managed to knock out one of the panzers (the 57mm towed guns weren't exactly renowned for their punch). After losing the tank, the Germans pulled back in apparent retreat. This was a ruse, however, and the Germans struck again with even heavier fire. The Germans took up positions on some high ground overlooking the Americans' route of advance. The position could not be bypassed, so substantial artillery and air support were called in to help eliminate the German position. In a battle that raged for most of the day, the men of B/51 managed to destroy several more enemy tanks, and eventually kicked the Germans off the high ground. But in the process, the 51st AIB suffered 43 casualties and lost an additional two halftracks. This was a heavy blow on top of the losses incurred back on July 20 (the 51st AIB had received 66 replacements on July 25, but this was not enough to fully replenish the battalion).

The western column, which was under the personal command of Brigadier General Dager, found the going much easier. They advanced south for 10 miles virtually unopposed, sweeping through the towns of La Haye-Pesnel and Sartilly. Unknown to the tankers, they passed within just a few hundred yards of the forward command post of the German 7th Army. Several top officers, including General Hausser and Generalmajor Rudolf Christeph, made their escape by dashing across the highway during regular intervals in the CCB column.

The advance resumed on July 30, and by late in the afternoon, Company A of the 8th Tank Battalion reached the edge of Avranches. As the lead tanks approached the city, a duel broke out between German and American tanks. Both sides took losses in the engagement, and A/8 broke off its attack in order to regroup. It was immediately clear that Avranches was not going to fall without a fight.

As the Shermans of A/8 faced off against the opposition, another company of tanks had advanced to positions located west of the city, overlooking a key bridge that spanned the See River. This was the route of the coastal highway, which fed into Avranches from Granville, a large coastal town northwest of Avranches (and an objective of the 6th Armored Division). The tankers were holding the position on their own, without the benefit of any supporting infantry.

At approximately 10 P.M., the tankers observed a column of German vehicles advancing toward the bridge. The enemy column could have easily been destroyed, but the Americans held their fire when they saw large red crosses adorning the lead vehicles. Figuring that the Germans were evacuating their wounded, they allowed the vehicles to continue down the road and across the bridge toward Avranches.

Several of the trucks passed without incident. Suddenly, rifle fire erupted from some of the German vehicles. The tankers responded immediately and fired on the column. Several of the vehicles were destroyed, which effectively blocked the road. German infantry spilled out of the trucks, but rather than take up the fight, they surrendered en masse. Several hundred Krauts threw their hands in the air and walked away from trucks loaded not with the wounded, but stuffed to the gills with ammunition and other non-medical supplies. They had almost succeeded in passing through the American positions. Had the Germans not opened fire, they would have probably continued on to the east without incident and made good their deceitful escape.

A quick interrogation of some of the prisoners revealed that another column was following behind this one. The next column was supposedly more heavily armed than the first. The prisoners' warnings were confirmed as truth when, shortly after midnight, the tankers' positions came under small arms fire once again. This time, an American ammo truck was hit and set ablaze. The leaping flames illuminated the positions of the American tanks, and the commander on the scene, believing his tanks were too exposed, ordered his force to withdraw to the east, to the See River Bridge on the Villedieu-les-Poëles road. The prisoners they had taken just a few hours before were released, since they could not be taken out on foot. Once the American tanks departed, the German force was able to head into Avranches unopposed.

It appears that Wood's main concern throughout the day was ensuring that the advance continued in an aggressive manner. Knowing that Dager was well forward and setting the tempo for the advance, Wood delegated control of CCA and an attached regiment of the 8th Infantry Division to the commander of CCB. Dager now had a tremendously powerful force at his disposal, and he made immediate plans to put it to work. He would use elements of CCB to screen the flanks, while CCA made the primary thrust into Avranches.

As General Dager plotted his next move, he was unaware of what was transpiring at the bridge over the See River. As far as he knew, the roads leading into Avranches from the west were outposted and secured, so no other plans were made to reinforce the tank company from the 8th that was supposedly holding down his right flank. The left flank was Dager's primary concern, and while retaining the weakened A/8 at CCB's HQ, he instructed the balance of the 8th Tank Battalion (C/8 and D/8) to drive east toward the town of Tirepeid. This would effectively secure the left flank, and allow CCA to drive south into Avranches with both flanks secure (Dager's decision to retain A Company at his HQ turned out to be a fortuitous development, as later that night, a column of German troops, attempting to flee south to avoid capture, stumbled directly into the area of the HQ; after a heated battle, the Germans were rounded up).

Darkness had already descended upon the battlefield when the task force from the 8th Tank Battalion started out toward Tirepeid. As it made its way down the road from Avranches, it stumbled upon a German column jammed together in a tight formation on the road ahead. The tankers proceeded slowly and deliberately down the dark road, raking the column with devastating fire as they went. Enemy infantry responded with scattered fire, but the tanks of CCB continued to press on. The fight continued until 2:00 A.M., with devastating results for the Germans. Still short of the objective of Tirepeid, the battalion halted for the night and set up defensive positions. Plans were made to continue the advance at first light.

As Dager put his plan into effect on the flanks, CCA pushed through the center into Avranches. As Bruce Clarke's men began advancing into the city, they found that stubborn resistance had cropped up. The Germans fully realized the importance of Avranches. If the Americans were to capture it, the German left flank would be in serious trouble, and the entire defensive line in Normandy would be in jeopardy. As a result, there was no shortage of enemy resistance within the town. The Luftwaffe even managed an appearance, as five Messerchmitts swooped down upon a group of American tanks. Fortunately, they flew off without inflicting any damage.

As the push into Avranches continued, the M18 Hellcat tank destroyers of Lt. Colonel Delk Oden's 704th TD Battalion engaged enemy tanks directly for the first time in the war. As A Company's 2nd Platoon, commanded by Lieutenant Addison, headed into the fray, the lead Hellcat, commanded by Sergeant Joe Shedevy, spotted a camouflaged panzer laying in wait. The driver, T/5 Beck, quickly brought the M18 into a good firing position, and the gunner, Corporal Treet, knocked out the panzer with one shot targeted on the Swastika that adorned the enemy steel. The 76mm armor-piercing round had barely left the Hellcat's gun when Treet spotted a second panzer hiding behind a hedgerow. The German gunner got off the next shot, but it sailed past Shedevy's Hellcat. Treet quickly aimed and squeezed off another round, which set the panzer ablaze. The quick destruction of the two panzers flushed out another pair of enemy tanks. The Kraut tanks tried to retreat, but the other M18s of the second platoon got off four more rounds that took out the balance of the panzers. While none of the M18s were hit, the engagement wasn't without cost: Lieutenant Addison was killed during the encounter.

The 25th Cavalry Reconnaissance Squadron helped lead the way deep into the interior of the city. Captain Murray W. Farmer, the commander of F Company, beefed up his unit's strength by commandeering the forward observer tank of the 66th Armored Field Artillery Battalion. The Sherman tank was leading the way when suddenly, Farmer found himself staring at a Panther tank just 30 yards away.

In a great display of heroism, Farmer ordered the driver to ram the enemy tank before his opponent could rotate his turret and take aim against the thinner-skinned M4. The Sherman struck the Panther broadside, and in the process blocked the traverse of the enemy gun, rendering the Panther helpless unless it managed to back away from the Sherman. Before it could budge, however, Sgt. Edward Rejrat turned the Sherman's 75mm cannon directly at the Panther, and let loose four rounds that rocked both tanks, but with the Panther obviously getting the worst of it.

The point-blank blows caused the German crew to bail out of their tank. Farmer brandished his submachine gun and mowed them down before they could escape. Though the tank was apparently abandoned and harmless, Farmer tried to do in the Panther for good by knocking it over with the Sherman. The effort backfired when the Sherman, straining against the heavier Panther, overturned into a nearby ditch, its treads reaching for the clouds. The Sherman began to burn, but Farmer and his crew managed to get out of the tank and raced to safety.

As the battle within Avranches continued on July 30, the 66th and 94th AFAB's established their firing positions about two miles north of the city. There was a concern that isolated groups of Germans trapped to the north would attempt to filter through their positions, so roadblocks were set up around a key intersection on the main highway leading toward Avranches. Sure enough, a steady stream of Germans came through, and many were taken prisoner. Not all of the Germans were eager to surrender, however. A group of Krauts traveling in a captured American scout car broke through one of the roadblocks, and set fire to one of the 66th's M7s. The fire burned for several hours, and as the on-board ammunition exploded, the camouflage netting covering an ammunition-laden four-ton prime mover belonging to the 969th FAB caught fire (the 969th was attached to the Fourth Armored at the time). With disaster looming, Captains Charles Temple and Robert Franks, along with T/S Carl Bergman and Pvt. John McGann, cleared the net from the vehicle. Meanwhile, Private Miles McClelland drove the truck to safety (he was wounded in the process). A wounded soldier owed his life to McClelland and the others, as he had been sleeping on top of the ammunition in the truck! McClelland, in turn, was awarded the Silver Star for his act of bravery.

Other rear elements of the Fourth Armored also ran into German units that evening. C Company of the 126th Armored Ordnance Maintenance Battalion was in search of CCB's HQ, and as it pulled into the town of Sartilly, its vehicles became entangled with some other vehicles occupying the village streets. An angry German voice shouted out in the night, apparently not aware that the source of the traffic jam was American, not German.

The GIs manning the 30 vehicles of C Company began to fight their way through the town. Many of the ordnance men dismounted from their vehicles and went head to head against the Germans in an attempt to clear the way for the battalion's vehicles.

Fortunately, at least one of the AAA halftracks of the 489th AAA Battalion was riding shotgun with the column, and its quad .50 caliber machine guns laid down a high volume of suppressive fire. The battalion was able to make it through intact and finally joined up with CCB.

While the 8th Tank Battalion was engaged on the flanks and the 35th Tank Battalion was pushing into Avranches, Lt. Colonel Abrams' 37th Tank Battalion was following up from the rear as a reserve element. The 37th had originally been ordered to pass through Coutances and then settle into a new assembly area, but Dager quickly changed its orders, and the 37th continued to move south all the way toward Avranches. En route, the tanks of the 37th came under small arms fire from a wooded area near the road. Companies D and C raked the enemy positions with their machine guns, and by the time the skirmish was over, the 37th had taken 162 Germans prisoner (they proceeded to turn them over to the Second Armored Division). That evening, the 37th set up a bivouac area near Follegny, and would resume the advance in the morning.

The morning of July 31 saw heavy fighting on both flanks. To the east, the tankers of D/8 were startled when the gathering light of day revealed they had set up their bivouac area on the opposite side of a field from the enemy. They quickly mounted up and pitted their M5 light tanks against the enemy positions. The Germans responded with small arms fire and salvos from some 88mm anti-tank guns. The situation was fluid and confused as other elements of the 8th Tank Battalion joined in the attack. During the heated engagement, Staff Sergeant Constance Klinga of C Company uttered what was to become a famous battle cry for the Fourth Armored: "They've got us surrounded again, the poor bastards!" Klinga's admonition rang true as the 8th Tank Battalion pushed forward and captured Tirepied. An additional bonus was achieved when a German prisoner (actually a citizen of Poland pressed into action for the Wehrmacht), serving as a willing guide, took members of C Company to the location of six 105mm German howitzers. The Sherman tanks descended upon the batteries, destroyed the guns, and took nearly 100 prisoners. After nightfall, elements of the 51st moved up to support the 8th in the area around Tirepied. The town was secured, and the infantry assumed outpost positions for the balance of the night to help protect the tanks from enemy raiding parties.

Fighting was just as heavy on the right flank. Before the arrival of daylight on July 31, the Germans who had been part of the fake Red Cross column, along with the second column that had followed behind them, stole into Avranches and weaved their way toward the south end of the city. Whether they were trying to mount a defense or were simply trying to escape to the east is unknown. But near the south edge of town, they ran head-on into elements of the 53rd and 10th Armored Infantry Battalions. It was here that Private William Whitson of the 53rd AIB came face to face with the advancing enemy column. Though staring into the teeth of an overwhelming number of Germans, he refused to abandon his .30 caliber machine gun. Firing relentlessly, he killed some 50 Germans and destroyed 25 trucks and other light vehicles before he was fatally struck by enemy fire. He was posthumously awarded the Distinguished Service Cross.

The armored infantry learned some costly lessons that summer day. After having secured an area of high ground south of Avranches, B/10, led by Captain Smith, noticed a white flag on display where some snipers had been known to be operating. Smith, along with one other man from his unit, advanced cautiously toward the building. "The snipers, in total disregard for the rules of war, started firing again." The Americans dashed for cover under the sudden and unexpected volley. Smith ordered his men to stay put, and then snared a soldier bearing a bazooka. They identified a spot from where they thought they could hit the sniper's nest with a bazooka round, and then took off in that direction.

Before they could reach their desired position, another sniper firing from a different location took aim and hit Captain Smith in the stomach and thigh. As he lay wounded, he relayed information back to his men about the sniper positions in the building. A tank from the 37th was brought forward, and used its main gun to wipe out the snipers.

Americans who witnessed this type of deceptive ambush obviously became wary when the enemy tried to surrender in the future. Who could blame them if they suffered from a nervous trigger finger?

Dager was now made aware that the tank company outposting the western approach to Avranches had retreated from its position the night before. He ordered elements of CCA to move west and reestablish the position.

As the American column approached, German artillery, which had taken up positions on a bluff overlooking the main road, opened fire on Colonel Clarke's men. The American tanks engaged the artillery, while the armored infantry crossed the river and scaled the bluff. They stormed the positions and captured the enemy guns. Once again, the western approaches were secure. And this time, it was for good.

Fighting continued in and around the city throughout the 31st of July. There was still mopping up to be done north of the city, as German units caught behind American lines tried to make their way to freedom by cutting across the rear of the Fourth Armored. By 1:00 P.M., the area north of the city was deemed secure.

There were important missions still to be completed to the south. The 37th Tank Battalion was dispatched to secure several bridges over the Selune River, the most prominent of which was the span at Pontaubault, located approximately four miles south of Avranches. Four small task forces were formed, each of which had a company of light or medium tanks as their foundation. All of the task forces pushed out through Avranches at 4:00 P.M., and though they encountered brisk resistance as they exited the city to the south — A/37's Captain Spencer and B/37's Lt. Bohn had their command tanks knocked out by enemy fire — they all succeeded in capturing their assigned objectives (the gunner in Lt. Bohn's tank was Corporal Peskar, who went on to finish the war as the "top gun" of B/37). D Company picked up an extra bonus with the capture of a German officer; Lt. Richard Donahue waded across the Selune at the village of Marcilly, and returned to his own lines with the prisoner.

The fourth task force, built around the tanks of C/37 and a portion of B/37, advanced toward the bridge over the Selune at the town of Ducey. A medium tank platoon led by 1st Lt. James Leach seized the bridge and outposted the crossing site. Their mission complete, the tankers assembled in a nearby field, and were joined for the night by Lt. Colonel Abrams. As he left the field the following morning, Abrams surprised an enemy panzer, destroying it with three armor piercing shells fired from the gun of his command tank, "Thunderbolt."

With the surrounding river crossings and critical roadways captured, and the enemy flushed out of the rear areas, Avranches was securely in American hands by the morning of August 1. It was a magnificent achievement in the short combat history of the Fourth Armored Division. In their first two weeks of action, they had already captured 3,000 prisoners (two thousand of them at Avranches alone), dealt severe losses to four enemy divisions (the 77th, 91st and 243rd Infantry divisions, plus the 5th Parachute Division), and wiped out the 6th Parachute Regiment. But most important of all, they managed to capture the vital Selune River bridges before the Germans could destroy them.

The early success of the Fourth Armored Division was the result of intense training and preparation, combined with excellent, inspired leadership. The guiding hand of General Wood was a fundamental contributing factor behind the effectiveness of the division. In a letter to his wife on July 31, Patton expressed his approval: "P ... has done well." Brigadier General Dager, a 51 year-old veteran of World War One, also proved himself as the commander of CCB, and was awarded the Distinguished Service Cross for his effort.

The accolades extended to the top brass of the Fourth Armored Division were well deserved. But the division's success ultimately rested on the performance of men like Whitson, Farmer, Rejrat, Shedevy, Klinga, Treet, and Pieri. Their names, and the names of many men just like them within the ranks of the Fourth Armored, were unheralded prior to July 31. If mentioned outside of the context of the Fourth Armored Division, they would be unremarkable figures to all but the men with whom they served, their family, and close friends. But due to their courage and aptitude under fire, by the end of the final day of July 1944, the city of Avranches was secured. The road into Brittany and the interior of France was open, courtesy of the Fourth Armored Division.

3. Breakout and Pursuit

The Mission

On August 1, it was clear that the German's left flank at Avranches had become unhinged. The time for exploitation had arrived. To that end, General Bradley activated the United States Third Army, with General Patton at the helm. The Fourth Armored Division now found itself out in front as Patton's spearhead. It was a role the men of the Fourth would grow accustomed to.

The original plan for Operation Overlord called for the capture of the ports located within the Brittany region, which lies west of Normandy. The build up in Normandy was supported by only two points of entry for supplies brought by sea: one was Cherbourg, at the northern tip of the Cotentin peninsula, and the other the artificial harbor facilities that had been constructed at the site of the invasion beaches. These two sources did not have the capacity to meet the long-term needs of both the 12th and 21st Army Groups. Thus the port cities of Brest, Lorient, and St. Nazaire were viewed as essential elements of the effort to supply the Allied Armies as they advanced methodically toward Germany. In the original Overlord plan, the U.S. Third Army was responsible for the capture of these ports, and it was anticipated that virtually all of Patton's divisions would be committed to the task.

There was a catch, however. The Allied command had feared that the Germans might render these ports virtually unusable before the Third Army could liberate them. Hitler's legions were notoriously adept at destroying assets as they retreated. And in this case, they could easily demolish and sabotage the port facilities so that it would take the Allies weeks or even months to put them in condition to receive supplies. As a result of the ports being at such high risk of sabotage, the most important objective assigned to the Third Army was Quiberon Bay. This natural harbor was nestled between the ports of Lorient and St. Nazaire on the south coast of Brittany. If needed, Quiberon Bay could be rapidly turned into a functional port (more rapidly than the time it would take to perform major repairs at the existing ports, should the Germans destroy them). But the sabotage of the ports was not a forgone conclusion, so they remained on the list of objectives for the Third Army, along with Quiberon Bay.

Most of the port cities of Brittany were far removed from the point of the Allied breakthrough. The closest was St. Malo, about 31 miles due west of Avranches. Brest was nearly 150 miles to the west, while Lorient lay approximately 112 miles to the south-west. St. Nazaire was located 106 miles to the south-southwest. Quiberon Bay, located between Lorient and St. Nazaire, was approximately 100 miles to the southwest. To capture the ports, the American forces, including the Fourth Armored Division, would actually be moving *away* from the German border. This originally wasn't viewed as an issue, due to the nature of the pre-invasion plan.

It was projected that the line of the Seine River would not be reached until approximately September 6 (D+90), and the Meuse River not until D+270 (March of 1945). This timetable allowed plenty of opportunity for the Third Army to capture the ports in Brittany, and then turn its divisions east to participate in the drive toward Germany.

It was never envisioned that the Allied advance would be so quick that it would render the ports almost useless before they could be captured. But that was exactly what happened (in fact, even when they finally fell into American hands, the ports in Brittany never contributed significantly to the Allied supply effort). Had this been foreseen, a smaller force could have been sent into Brittany to simply contain the German forces within the port cities. More American divisions could have been turned toward the east in an attempt to destroy the German forces west of the Seine River, and to race beyond it toward the German border before the enemy could gather itself.

To their credit, the Allied command did react to some degree. As mentioned above, the bulk of the Third Army was originally earmarked for action in Brittany. The plan was changed in early July, and Patton was informed on the seventh of that month that he was to use only one corps in Brittany (it is worth noting that Patton himself thought about using two corps for the Brittany venture as late as July 25). With only one corps committed in Brittany, the balance of his army would then be available to head south and east.

Middleton's VIII was the corps that would be dispatched into Brittany. Unfortunately, VIII Corps included two of the Third Army's most mobile divisions, the 6th and 4th Armored. These units were capable of exploiting the opportunities that now resided in the east, and would have been much better utilized if sent in that direction. Instead, they were dispatched to the west and southwest, respectively, where mobility and speed was no longer of the essence. It was a role suited for infantry, not armor.

The objectives of Lorient and Quiberon Bay were handed to the Fourth Armored Division. But before these objectives could be reached, there was a critical interim objective on the division's agenda. The immediate mission before General Wood was to drive south-southwest and secure the city of Rennes, located about 40 miles from Avranches. With a population of 80,000, it was the capital of Brittany and one of the larger cities in the region. It was also a vitally important road hub. For the most part, controlling Rennes meant you controlled access in and out of Brittany. After securing Rennes, Wood could begin his drive to the southwest, toward Lorient and Quiberion Bay. But Rennes had to fall first.

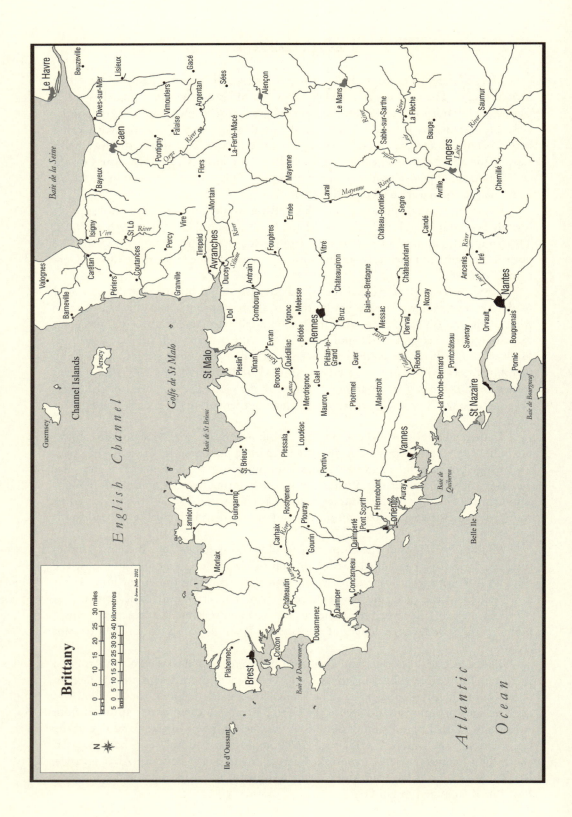

Brittany

The Drive Toward Rennes

On the morning of August 1, as Colonel Clarke's CCA prepared to advance toward Rennes, elements of General Dager's CCB were still working the division's left flank. Until other units of the Third Army could move south through the narrow corridor at Avranches, the Fourth Armored would have to provide its own flank protection.

To that end, the 51st AIB, supported by a platoon of tank destroyers, set out at 10:00 A.M. for the crossroads and bridges at Montviron. Company A took the lead and reached the objective at 2:30 that afternoon. After setting up their outposts, the 3rd Platoon of A Company received fire from several enemy tanks. Sgt. Young's anti-tank squad, equipped with towed 57mm anti-tank guns, knocked out one of the panzers. The enemy tanks in turn destroyed the platoon's command halftrack. The Hellcats came forward to engage the enemy tanks, and during the course of the next hour and a half or so, knocked out three more panzers and two enemy halftracks.

As A/51 engaged the enemy, B/51 began to assemble on a nearby section of high ground that was thought to be secure and shielded from the enemy's view. As their vehicles pulled into the assembly area, they soon discovered that the Germans had them in their sights. Several 88s laid into the parked halftracks, knocking out three of them. B Company quickly left the hill for a safer assembly area.

Toward the end of the day, the 51st AIB's recon platoon rejoined the battalion, and had an exciting story to tell upon their arrival. The day before, the 23-man unit had been sent on a mission to evacuate prisoners taken during the battalion's advance. After completing their assignment, they began making their way back to the 51st. But after passing through Avranches, they lost their way, and couldn't find the battalion. So they bedded down for the night, figuring they would get their bearings in the morning.

Their route took them through Tirepied, and while making their way through the town, they encountered—and captured—some 200 members of the German 896th Field Artillery Battalion, who had remained behind in a strongpoint after other elements of CCB had moved through the town. They turned their prisoners over to a unit from the 8th Infantry Division, which was following behind the Fourth Armored. Two hundred Germans captured by a team of 23 men! It had certainly been an exciting mission worth talking about.

The 8th Infantry Division was indeed on the move, and by noon on August 1, it had come forward to take over the positions held by the Fourth Armored near Avranches. The arrival of the 8th Infantry freed the tankers and armored infantry to move on to the next phase of their mission. Shortly after noon, a task force from CCA, consisting of B/37, D/37, A/53, and C/53, moved through Ducey, located about 6 miles southeast of Avranches. By 6:30 that evening, Colonel Clarke's CCA had charged south some 31 miles toward the northern approaches of Rennes. The task force moved into an assembly area approximately 9 miles north of the city.

The long drive toward Rennes was not a Sunday drive in the park. Though German resistance immediately south of Avranches had waned, there was no certainty regarding what would be encountered as the Fourth Armored drew closer to their next major objective. The 10th Armored Infantry Battalion would soon get a sample of what the Germans had in store at Rennes.

The 10th AIB's recon platoon, led by 1st Lt. Stan Lyons, was leading a column of tanks and armored infantry south toward Rennes. As he advanced, Lyons relied on the firepower of his jeep-mounted .30 caliber machine guns and the .50 cal on the half-track to clear out small pockets of enemy resistance encountered along the way. Rather than take prisoners, he left any surviving Germans to be cleaned up by the main body of the American column, which trailed him by about three minutes.

As the advance continued, German trucks would occasionally approach from the opposite direction. Lyons could have easily fired on the trucks and destroyed them, but he realized that, had he done so, the road might become choked with debris, and the advance would come to a grinding halt. So instead, Lyons let the enemy vehicles pass, and radioed back to Major West, who was back with the main body of the column, that an enemy truck was coming through. The only problem was that the rest of the column was then faced with the same dilemma!

To solve the problem, Lyons asked Major West for a platoon of tanks from B/37 to come forward and drive immediately behind the recon platoon. Then, as the German vehicles approached the column, the Shermans could force them off the road (the tankers would expertly "fishtail" the rear of their tank, and swat the lighter trucks right off the roadway).

The recon platoon continued to lead, with the five Sherman tanks trailing close behind. The road cut through an open field, with a lone house off to the right. The vulnerable jeeps and halftrack passed by without incident, but then inexplicably, a German machine gun opened fire on the tanks. The platoon leader, 1st Lt. Leach, directed his tank to head for the house. He crashed through a fence and rumbled right up to the corner of the house from whence the machine gun had fired. The gunner aimed the barrel of the 75mm main gun at the window and fired a devastating HE round point-blank into the house. A good chunk of the building collapsed, and the debris cascaded off the hull as the Sherman backed away from the ruins. Needless to say, the machine gun nest was silenced.

At a position approximately 20 miles north of Rennes, Lyons approached what might be a dangerous crossroad at the village of St. Aubin D' Aubigne. What made it dangerous was the fact that large, two-story buildings occupied the near corner lots of the intersection which, in combination with hedgerows and trees lining the road, prevented him from seeing if there were any enemy forces hiding around the corners. So rather than drive blindly into the intersection, Lyons dismounted and walked up to the crossroad to take a look around the corner. As he peered to the left, he saw the tail end of a double column of German infantry! By his estimation, the German force was some 400-men strong. Lyons huddled with his sergeants and Lt. Leach, and devised a plan to tackle the enemy battalion.

The road was flanked on both sides by ditches that were about two to three feet deep. Growing alongside of each ditch was a long strand of shallow woods perhaps some 12 feet in depth. Beyond the trees were wide-open fields on both sides of the road. Lyons' plan called for two of Leach's Shermans to move into position to cover the field on the right, while his other three Shermans covered the field on the left. Lyons would then approach the end of the column in his jeep and ask for their surrender. If they refused, the recon platoon would open fire with their machine guns, shooting right down

The tank crews of 1st Platoon, B/37. The CO, Lt. Leach, is perched atop the gun barrel. Platoon S/Sgt. Fitzpatrick is front and center (courtesy J. Leach).

the length of the road. If the Germans broke and ran into the open fields on either side, Leach's tanks would be in position to cut them to pieces.

Lyons drove forward with his gunner, who spoke German. The tail of the German column was now about 100 yards away, and Lyons was quickly within shouting distance. The Germans that were within earshot of the call to surrender tried to bring their weapons to bear, but Lyons' men immediately opened up on the vulnerable gray-clad troops. The firepower of nine jeep-mounted .30 caliber machine guns, plus the .50 caliber on the halftrack, "routed the enemy and pushed back what was left of a badly whipped enemy force." The 10th AIB took 60 prisoners, and estimated the German casualties at 200. None of Lyons' men were injured during the action.

Flush with their success on the road to Rennes, the 10th AIB continued south. The battalion's next orders for the day were "to seize and hold the high ground between St. Laurent and Lesboria." It fell on Companies A and B to secure the objective. The battalion commander, Lt. Colonel Kirkpatrick, and the CO of B/37, Captain Tiegs, accompanied A Company during the attack. As the infantry advanced toward St. Laurent, the primary German response came in the form of 88mm and artillery fire. Kirkpatrick and Tiegs were caught out in the open during the barrage, and a shell burst overhead, seriously wounding both officers. In Kirkpatrick's case, shrapnel cut through his side, searing the lining of his stomach. Both officers had to be evacuated, so Major West, who was standing close to Kirkpatrick when the shell hit, assumed command of the 10th AIB. 1st Lt. Leach was given command of B/37.

There were other casualties besides Kirkpatrick and Tiegs. Several American vehicles were hit and burning, and one of the medics, Tech 3rd Grade Vecchio, distinguished himself by removing casualties from one of the burning vehicles. One of the men had an extremely serious leg wound, and with shells bursting all around him, Vecchio conducted an amputation in the field. Though subsequently wounded himself, he continued to treat other casualties on the battlefield.

Inspired by Vecchio's relentless attempts to treat the wounded, another pair of medics, Staff Sergeant Wellman and Tech 5th Grade Kelliger, used a captured German vehicle to pick up casualties amidst the falling shells and machine gun bullets. Even when the vehicle was struck by enemy fire, they were not deterred from their mission (Kirkpatrick was among the men evacuated by the two medics).

By 6 P.M. that evening, both A and B Company reported that they had seized their objectives. The armored infantry dug in and weathered several artillery strikes during the night. While the infantrymen secured their positions, patrols were sent out around St. Laurent to determine the dispositions of the enemy. Now that the Fourth was plunging into unknown territory with such great speed, the gathering of intelligence was more important than ever.

There was one particular recon mission conducted that day by a member of A Company that was unrivaled for both its daring and success. Pfc. Wilfred Pelletier, as his name might suggest, was of French ancestry, and he spoke the language fluently. Using his linguistic skills to his unit's advantage, he volunteered to don civilian garb and pose as a French civilian in order to conduct a thorough reconnaissance of the enemy's positions. He strolled out into the French countryside, and was soon among the Germans without being challenged. He actually stayed with German troops that evening, and asked one of their guards to awaken him at 7 A.M. The German obliged! In the morning, Pelletier returned with a wealth of information regarding the enemy positions and the location of their supply dump. Armed with this invaluable intelligence, the 10th AIB easily destroyed the enemy strongpoints and depot.

The advance toward Rennes continued at first light on August 2. CCA encountered strong enemy resistance as it drove closer to the city. Elements of the 35th Tank Battalion, 10th Armored Infantry Battalion, 66th Armored Field Artillery Battalion, and 704th TD Battalion ran head-on into a strong enemy position built around eight 88mm AA guns deployed in an anti-tank role. Housed within concrete emplacements and ringed by trenches, the 88s formed an impenetrable position that dealt the advancing column a heavy blow. Company B of the 35th lost nine Sherman tanks in the engagement, and the advance came to a temporary halt.

In a twist of fate that would raise the hair on the back of the superstitious, the 704th lost their first Hellcat of the war along the approaches to Rennes: Tank Destroyer number 13 of A Company. The M18 took at least four armor-piercing shells flush on the frontal armor, all of which penetrated through to the driver and bow gunner positions. Three members of the crew were killed, but Sergeant Turcan survived and stayed at his position in the turret. He continued to load and fire the 76mm gun until he silenced the enemy fire that had taken the lives of his crew. He was awarded the Silver Star for his tenacious engagement of the enemy under dire circumstances.

It had become obvious that the Germans were going to make an issue out of Rennes. Resistance was starting to gel along the most obvious approaches from the north. It appeared as though there would be no easy way into the city.

The Encirclement of Rennes

General Wood knew that an assault on Rennes would result in the loss of two valuable resources: time and men. It was estimated that some 2,000 Germans were holed up in the city, and Wood figured that routing the enemy from their enclave was a job best suited for infantry, not tanks. He ordered elements of CCA and CCB to circle around the city to the west in order to cut the routes leading out of the town to the south. Another unit of the Third Army, the Second Cavalry Group, would cut the roads leading out of Rennes to the east.

When the breakout from Avranches began, Patton wanted Middleton to send an infantry division to Rennes along with the Fourth Armored. Middleton failed to do so, and Patton was none too happy with the fact that his wish had not been fulfilled. After more urging from Patton, Middleton finally got the 8th Infantry Division moving toward Rennes. The 8th was not fully mechanized, however, and would not be able to keep up with the pace being set by Wood's division. So Middleton used quartermaster trucks to motorize one of the Eighth's infantry regiments, which allowed it to follow up behind the Fourth with sufficient speed. Upon their arrival, the infantry would have the responsibility of capturing Rennes. But in the meantime, the Fourth Armored had a lot of work to do to ensure the German forces in the city were contained.

On August 3, CCB split into three task forces and swept in a wide arc around the west side of Rennes. Dager's command liberated the towns of St. Germain, Vignoc, Bedes, Plelan-le-Grand, and Guer, meeting only light resistance in the two latter villages. It then continued to sweep to the southeast, capturing the villages of St. Vincent and Chateaubriant, which were located about 30 miles south and southeast of Rennes.

By 6:30 on the evening of August 3, the task force commanded by Major Dan Alanis had passed through Carentoir. It continued to advance after sunset, and by midnight, the armored infantry of B/51 had entered Derval, also about 30 miles south of Rennes. Despite the late hour, the jubilant population of the town began spilling out of their homes to welcome their liberators. Fearing that the enemy might be too close for comfort, and that the villagers' celebration would alert them, Alanis had to plead with the crowd for quiet.

As dawn broke on the August 4, there was a great deal of confusion in Derval, as TF Alanis found itself unexpectedly sharing the village with the 696th Armored Field Artillery Battalion. As the day progressed, the units got untangled and moved into their assigned areas. The armored infantry dug in, and were warned that the Germans fleeing Rennes might try to advance through their blocking positions. Sure enough, German stragglers fell into the American trap throughout the day. But nothing equaled the excitement that took place early in the morning when four German ammunition trucks tried to drive through Derval, unaware that the Americans had occupied it. The HQ Company of the 51st AIB proceeded to fire on the trucks until all were blown up. Things quieted down after that, and the 8th Tank Battalion and B/51 took up positions at Derval for the night of August 4.

Meanwhile, CCA spent August 3 enhancing its containment of Rennes. The 37th Tank Battalion set up positions along several roads leading out of the city. D/37 took up a position at a road junction south of Chateagiron, and were soon alerted by members of the French Resistance that a column of about 500 infantry and a couple of towed 88mm guns were approaching down the road.

Lt. Mueller, who commanded one of D Company's light tank platoons, placed a 105mm Sherman assault gun into position with a line of fire toward the road. When the lead 88mm gun came crawling around the bend, the assault gun blasted the weapon and its crew. The Germans, who perhaps did not know which direction the Americans were firing from, seemed stunned, and hesitated for several minutes before dismounting to push the wreckage out of the way. After clearing the road, the Germans tried to push the second 88mm gun into position at the bend. When the 88 crept into view, it met the same fate as the first. Captain McMahon, the commanding officer of D Company, arrived during the action and called for an artillery concentration on the German positions. The 22nd Armored Field Artillery Battalion responded with a crushing barrage that sent the surviving Germans fleeing. It was clear that no man or weapon of German origin was going to make it in or out of Rennes using this particular road.

The 10th Armored Infantry Battalion and 94th Field Artillery Battalion were also left outside the city to contain the defenders. The Germans tried to break out in their sectors as well, but the effort was in vain.

The motorized elements of the 8th Infantry Division, which had been trailing behind the Fourth, arrived on August 3 and took an immediate stab at capturing the city. The attack was launched just before dark, and came up short of its objective. The spirit of the German 91st Division was apparently broken, however, and they decided to abandon the city. Later that night, in preparation for their evacuation, they began burning the supplies that they could not carry with them. At about 3 A.M. on the morning of August 4, the remaining Germans began filtering out of the city in small groups, moving cross-country and via secondary roads in an attempt to avoid the American roadblocks. Later in the day, the Eighth's 13th Infantry Regiment, supported by the howitzers of the 94th AFAB, moved into the city against light resistance (five days later, some of the survivors from the 91st would reach the city of St. Nazaire, at the mouth of the Loire River).

Rennes was a major objective that was captured at moderate cost. John Wood's division had demonstrated how the right combination of speed, maneuver, and firepower could outwit the enemy and save American lives. What would have been a costly frontal assault instead became a grand encirclement that cut off and demoralized the enemy. The Fourth Armored might not have been the unit that occupied Rennes, but they certainly were the unit that made the city a relatively easy prize for the 8th Infantry Division.

The Missed Opportunity

With Rennes in the bag, the road toward Germany appeared to be wide open. But rather than point the barrels of their 75mm guns to the east, CCA and CCB were given orders that would carry them southwest, toward the port cities of the Brittany region, which were still viewed as essential to the logistical support of the Allied armies. This was the original mission assigned to the Fourth, and even though the strategic situation now facing the Allies was nothing like the Overlord planners had envisioned, their orders remained unchanged. Granted, a widespread collapse of the German front had not been anticipated, and no one ever contemplated a scenario where the ports in Brittany would be rendered inconsequential. But that was exactly what was happening, and the Allied commanders were acting conservatively in the face of this unexpected situation. They were not reacting wisely to the new opportunity that had presented itself.

Not all of the commanders were mired in the tenets of the pre-invasion plan. General Wood spoke plainly to his superiors about his strong and urgent desire to turn his division toward the east. In fact, part of his rationale for encircling Rennes with a sweeping arc around the west side of the city was so that his forward columns would be facing to the southeast and east at the end of the maneuver, and thus be in a position to continue on toward Germany. He actually put this plan in motion by advancing as far as Chateaubriant, some 31 miles *southeast* of Rennes. To Middleton's credit, he seemed to sympathize with Wood's desire to head east, and offered only a muffled protest when he learned of Wood's improvisation.

Unfortunately, the reins were about to be pulled taut. Middleton began to receive some pressure from above regarding the need to push the Fourth Armored toward Lorient, and on August 3, he set out in a small convoy of two halftracks and a couple of jeeps for a treacherous trip to Wood's forward command post in order to have a face-to-face meeting with the brazen division commander. Upon his arrival, the commander of VIII Corps delivered the bad news: the higher-ups still wanted to proceed with the original plan for taking the ports in Brittany. As Middleton described it, "I had to get him back on the track and get him started toward Lorient — much to his disgust."

The "higher-up," of course, was Patton. And he was none too happy with the moves Wood had made. On August 4, he wrote in his diary:

> P. Wood got bull headed and turned east after passing Rennes, and we had to turn him back on his objectives, which are Vannes and Lorient, but his overenthusiasm wasted a day.

Patton's desires were reinforced two days later, when his chief of staff, Major General Hugh Gaffey, sent a direct message to Middleton informing him that Patton was working on the assumption that the bulk of the Fourth Armored Division was now headed toward Quiberon Bay, Vannes, and Lorient. Upon receipt of this communication, Middleton had clearly run out of wiggle room. And then for extra measure, Gaffey sent a message directly to Wood ordering him to have his division en route to Vannes and Lorient.

Wood had pressed his luck as far as he could. He was not compelled to flagrantly disobey orders that were coming directly from Patton's HQ. So with regret, CCA, which had remained poised to strike east, set out at 2:00 P.M. on August 5 from the town of Bain de Bretagne ... heading west.

Memories of this episode lingered within all of the parties involved. Later in the campaign, the topic came up in a discussion between Patton and Wood. Commenting on the improvised turn of the Fourth Armored to the east, Patton remarked, "You nearly got tried for that." Wood's reply was typical of both his dry sense of humor and the ease with which he could address his old friend, despite Patton's position as Commanding General of the Third Army: "Someone should have been tried, but it certainly was not I." After the war, Wood wrote about the initial exploitation after the breakout from Normandy, revealing just how deep the divide was between his vision and that of the higher command:

> There was no conception of far-reaching directions for armor in the minds of our top people, nor of supplying such thrusts. I was still under the First Army*, and it could not react fast enough. When it did react, its orders consisted of sending its two flank armored divisions back, 180 degrees away from the main enemy, to engage in siege operations against Lorient and Brest. August 4 was that black day. I protested long, loud, and violently — and pushed my tank columns into Chateaubriant (without orders) and my armored cavalry to the outskirts of Angers and along the Loire (river), ready to advance on Chartres (to the east). I could have been there, in the enemy vitals, in two days. But no! We were forced to adhere to the original plan — with the only armor available, and ready to cut the enemy to pieces. It was one of the colossally stupid decisions of the war.

The Drive into Brittany

Regardless of the direction they were headed, the men of the Fourth Armored Division smelled blood. The spirit with which they pursued the enemy is perhaps best

---

Wood was probably being generous to Patton when making this statement, since he was, in fact, under Patton's command at the time, not the U.S. First Army (the Third Army having been officially activated on August 1, 1944).

reflected by the August 3 entry in the combat journal of the 37th Tank Battalion. On that day, it was indelibly recorded that Lt. Colonel Abrams urged his men to "Kill every God Damned one of them."

Though the enemy was scattered and disorganized, they were still dangerous, especially since they could so readily appear behind the constantly moving front line. The S-3 of the 37th, Captain Dwight, found out first hand just how suddenly danger could arise. On the very day that his commanding officer was urging the unequivocal defeat of the enemy, a German soldier brandishing a Schmeiser submachine gun jumped into the road in front of Dwight's speeding jeep. The German got off a wild burst of fire, and Dwight answered with a burst from his own submachine gun. The evidence of his accuracy was left lying in the road for the trailing Battalion HQ staff to see when they passed by.

On August 5, with the support of the ever-present Thunderbolts and Mustangs of the XIX Tactical Air Command, CCA advanced 70 miles in seven hours. By 9:00 P.M., Colonel Clarke's men had moved into the port town of Vannes on the Atlantic coast. The Forces Françaises de l'Interieur (FFI) played an active role alongside CCA in liberating the French town. In fact, throughout the Fourth Armored's advance into Brittany, the resistance fighters of the FFI would help the Americans with vital information about enemy positions and troop movements. They helped disrupt enemy communications, and pitched in to deal with enemy pockets of resistance. They were willing and eager partners in helping to rid their native France of the enemy.

The following day (August 6), the FFI reported that the Germans had taken up positions not far from Vannes. Enemy anti-tank guns had been positioned about one mile outside the town along Route 165. It was also reported that a force of about 400 Germans were in the Champ de Tir, five miles to the north. Plans were made to assault both of the German positions.

Two task forces were formed. The first, led by Captain Dwight, consisted of the C Companies of the 37th Tank and 53rd Armored Infantry Battalions, supported by a platoon of mortars. The second, led by Major Bautz, consisted of B/37, A/53, and the 105mm Sherman Assault Guns of the 37th. Bautz's task force was assigned the mission of clearing the Champ de Tir, while Dwight's task force went after the anti-tank gun position along Route 165. TF Bautz did not encounter any resistance, as the enemy had apparently fled. The fate of Dwight's task force was quite another story.

The Shermans of TF Dwight went out in front, with the infantry following. The tank of platoon leader Lt. Jonathan Anderson was in the lead, and at about 10 A.M., he spotted a 20mm dual purpose AT/AA gun about 1500 yards down the road. At that point, a long row of tightly packed buildings flanked each side of the street, which prevented the tanks or supporting infantry from fanning out on either side. There was no choice at the moment other than to launch a frontal attack straight down the road.

As Anderson's tank started churning toward the enemy position, the German gun opened fire with high-explosive shells. The Krauts scored two hits on the tank: one knocked out the bow machine gun and the other destroyed the periscope. The Sherman was blinded by the loss of the scope, so the tank commander, S/Sgt. Howard Smith, opened the hatch and leaned out of the tank to observe for the crew. At that moment, another shell struck close by. Fragments from the shell struck his face, blinding him in one eye. Despite his wounds, Smith continued to provide directions for the driver, who continued to race the tank forward. Smith's gunner hit the enemy 20mm gun with direct fire, and then his driver sent the tank bolting forward, crushing the gun underneath the treads of the Sherman. With the enemy position silenced, the column proceeded up the road. It didn't go far before encountering two more 20mm guns and a 37mm weapon. These met the same fate as the first gun emplacement.

The column continued to roll through the village. At the end of the two rows of buildings, the flanks opened up, and it was at that point that the column came under small arms fire from Germans hiding behind nearby bushes and in ditches alongside the road. Automatic weapons, mounted on trucks, opened up from across nearby fields. The Shermans dealt with the opposition in the ditches, and then pushed forward toward an area where heavy concentrations of the enemy were observed. Apparently without an effective means of dealing with the American armor, the Germans hastily jumped into every vehicle they could and tried to flee.

Not content with seeing the Germans escape, Anderson's lead platoon of tanks pursued the fleeing vehicles. The Shermans hit several of the vehicles with direct fire, leaving them crippled on the road. The tanks continued to roar ahead and pushed the destroyed vehicles off the pavement so that the chase could continue. Lt. Anderson's platoon went after the enemy with a vengeance. His focus was so intense that Capt. Dwight's attempts to recall him on the radio went unanswered.

As Lt. Anderson continued the pursuit, the balance of Dwight's task force started cleaning up the enemy that remained behind. The Germans had taken cover in the woods, and the Shermans showered them with 75mm HE shells and raked them over with their machine guns. To Dwight's chagrin, his supporting infantry, which had taken up positions in the ditches alongside the road, failed to rise up and follow the tanks. The tankers went forward without them and overran the Germans along the line of the woods. But without infantry support to clean out the survivors and take prisoners, some of the enemy remained in place. The tankers repeated the exercise a second time, again without infantry support. Finally, the armored infantry left the protection of the ditches and moved up to support the tanks. The infantry's initial lack of resolve not withstanding, the mission up to that point was a resounding success.

Later that afternoon, after the enemy positions had been cleaned out and deemed secure, each of the three armored infantry platoons of C/53 were sent out to establish outposts along the roads leading into the area. Each infantry platoon was escorted to their position by one of the tank platoons. After the infantry secured their outposts, the tanks would retire to the assembly area.

Lt. Anderson, now back from his great chase, led the way once again as his tank platoon carried out its escort assignment. As Anderson's tank rounded a bend in the road, he encountered a German armored car, which had apparently escaped the scene earlier in the day. The armored car fired on Anderson's tank, killing the platoon leader who had showed such determination while in pursuit of the enemy. Sgt. Smith took over in the wake of Anderson's death, and responded by destroying the armored car and two other vehicles (Sgt. Smith was later commissioned as a second lieutenant, but unfortunately, he would be killed in action several weeks later near the city of Nancy).

As the day faded, Dwight took an accounting of his success. He registered 150 prisoners taken and as many as 70 enemy vehicles destroyed. The Germans had belonged to an anti-aircraft unit that was by and large bent on escape. The men of Dwight's task force, as exemplified by the actions of Anderson and Smith, were hell bent on not letting them get away.

The Fourth Armored Division had severed the Brittany Peninsula. The other divisions of VIII Corps could now pursue the ports to the west without significant concern for their backs. The Fourth's drive was a success, but Wood felt the mission was a grave mistake.

The German forces on the West Front were now in an absolutely critical situation. As the VIII Corps spilled into Brittany, other elements of Patton's army were starting to turn east in what had the potential of becoming a grand encirclement of the German divisions defending the balance of the front line in Normandy. Rather than attempt an organized withdrawal back to better defensive positions (such as the east bank of the Seine River), Hitler ordered a counterattack designed to cut off the funnel through which the forces of the American Third and First armies were spilling forth. While the following actions did not involve the Fourth Armored directly, they are worth exploring, since the actions of both the Germans and the Allies far to the rear of the Fourth Armored would ultimately influence the nature of Wood's mission.

Trouble to the Rear

On the night of August 6, the German 47th Panzer Corps launched a strong attack toward the coast. Their intent was to sever the lifeline stretching out to the Third Army through Avranches. The German assault penetrated the American front line, but a heroic stand by a single battalion of the 120th Infantry Regiment (30th Infantry Division) thwarted the German effort. The battalion had occupied a strategic hill located near the town of Mortain, and they refused to be kicked off. The position atop Hill 317 offered the Americans an excellent vantage point from whence to observe the German advance, and this enhanced the American's ability to turn back the enemy. After extremely heavy fighting, the Germans broke off the attack.

With the corridor through Avranches secured and expanded, and the Germans now committed to positions well to the west of the Seine River, the Allies attempted an envelopment that, if successful, would bag the great bulk of the German army facing them in the West. The envelopment hinged on the capture of two towns: Falaise and Argentan. The Canadian First Army would have the responsibility of capturing the former, while Patton's Third Army secured the latter.

Falaise and Argentan were about 30 miles apart. If the two armies stopped at their respective objectives, the retreating Germans would have to squeeze through the gap between the two cities (unless they chose to retreat by attacking though the Allied positions). If the Canadians and Americans pressed on beyond the towns, they would narrow the gap, making the escape that much more precarious (the narrower the funnel, the more vulnerable the retreating forces would be to artillery barrages and attacks from Allied planes). Should the Canadian Second and American Third armies actually forge a link-up, the escape route would be sealed off completely. This would result in either the complete surrender of the German divisions, or an attempt to fight their way out. Either way, it would be a devastating result for the German Army.

The Third Army reached the outskirts of Argentan on the night of August 13, and the Canadian First Army captured Falaise on August 16. While these two armies were tightening the noose behind the German forces, the British Second and American First armies were applying pressure against the north, south, and west portions of the German salient. As the pocket was compressed, it turned into a morbid, hellish killing zone, as Allied artillery and air power blasted the Germans within its borders.

Some of the Allied generals wanted to maintain the advance through Falaise and Argentan and completely cut off the German's route of retreat. To the chagrin of many of the field commanders, however, the forces at both of the towns were ordered to halt. There was a concern — some would say a greatly exaggerated one — that the two armies could not execute a link-up without a potentially catastrophic clash between friendly forces. This would supposedly be brought about by communication problems between the forward elements of the two armies. There was also a concern that the Germans, if robbed of their escape route, would lash out in violent desperation to break through the screen of forces that had moved into their path. This might result in an overrun of the American and Canadian units blocking the route to the east. After considering these risks, the top Allied commanders were content to leave the gap open. They would settle on pulverizing, as best they could, the German divisions that resided within what would become known as the Falaise Pocket.

In some respects, by making this decision, Eisenhower and his top generals returned the favor that Hitler had granted the British at Dunkirk in 1940. Even though the bulk of eight infantry and two panzer divisions were captured, and an extraordinary number of tanks and vehicles destroyed, a significant number of German troops managed to crawl back to the east. Those men, though battered and bruised, would later serve at the core of the hastily assembled divisions that would take up positions along the German border. The Fourth Armored would eventually find itself pitted against some of these very divisions. The failure to close the gap at Falaise would have far reaching consequences.

The Road to Lorient

CCA and CCB now turned toward their toughest challenge to date: the port city of Lorient, located some 30 miles west of Vannes.

The road to Lorient was not an easy one. It began at 6 A.M. on August 7, with the recon platoon and the light tanks of D/37 leading the way. After an hour and a half, the column approached the town of Auray, about 11 miles west of Vannes. There they came upon an outpost manned by two Germans who, at the sight of the approaching Americans, jumped onto a motorcycle and tried to beat a hasty retreat. They didn't get far, as 2nd Lt. Harris, leader of the recon platoon, cut them down with a burst from his .50 caliber machine gun. If their intent had been to warn their brothers in arms in Auray, then Harris' marksmanship had given the Americans the element of surprise.

The column continued along the narrow approach to the town. It was a precarious route, as the one and only road leading in was bordered by water and marsh on both sides for a distance of about a half-mile. As they advanced down the road (in effect, a causeway), they came across several manned anti-tank guns, but in each instance, the Americans got in the first shot. The enemy guns were silenced in rapid sequence, and it appeared that they had indeed caught the enemy by surprise. The leading elements charged into the town, and as the tanks sped down the narrow streets, they were upon the enemy positions before the Germans knew what hit them.

The Germans had barely been cast from Auray when the villagers began to emerge from the safety of their homes and basements to celebrate their liberation. A civilian band appeared and began playing triumphant tunes as the jubilant residents showered the Americans at the rear of the column with flowers and champagne.

Not all of the Americans had the luxury of being caught up in the celebration. The head of the column was now on the far edge of town, and came to an abrupt halt when one of the halftracks of the lead recon platoon sprung a leak in its radiator (the result of a German shell). A decision was made to halt for a brief period, so that the halftrack could be put back in order.

The scene changed with alarming abruptness. While the joyous celebration at the center of town was underway, dozens of Germans erupted from the houses. Their will to fight was not high, as they were emerging in flight, not resistance. The Americans drew no distinction, however, and rapidly opened fire on the enemy soldiers. The clatter of machine guns rose above the screams of the celebrants. A round from a tank slammed into a building near where the civilians had gathered, sending the musicians and their audience running for the cover of basements. Scores of Germans were killed, and as the American column departed, smoke and flames leapt into the sky behind them as sections of Auray burned in their wake. Though their celebration was ruined, the citizens of Auray were no less liberated.

The next objective for the task force was the bridge at Hennebont, located almost 19 miles northwest of Auray and about 6 miles northeast of Lorient. The approach was uneventful until the advance elements ran into the tail end of a horse cavalry unit, which was staffed with Russian POWs forced into service by the Germans. Hedgerows on both sides of the road confined the American column, and they could not maneuver off-road to engage the Russians, who managed to pull away. Though they eluded the Americans for the moment, this was not the last the Fourth Armored would see of their unusual opponents.

The advance continued until the column came to a hastily constructed roadblock just east of Hennebont. Fortunately for the Americans, a Frenchman who lived nearby turned out to be a member of the French Resistance. He warned the Americans about the location of some mines and booby traps the Germans had planted before their departure. So informed, the Americans were able to remove the roadblock and avoid the minefields.

D/37 continued its advance into Hennebont. As the light tanks and halftracks drew close to a bridge, they came under fire from German troops on the span. The tanks continued to move forward and closed to within ten yards of the end of the bridge. The German troops continued to fire at the M5 tanks as they closed in. Then, to the disappointment and amazement of the Americans, the Germans blew the bridge right in front of them, despite the fact that their own men were still on the structure.

No sooner had the dust cleared than the Germans opened up with anti-tank and machine gun fire from the opposite bank. There was a sharp exchange of fire between the Americans and Germans. A U.S. halftrack was hit with two rounds, and one of the light tanks managed to slam some 37mm rounds into one of the anti-tank gun positions in exchange. Captain McMahon and Lt. Mueller (commanding officer of D/37's 3rd platoon) dismounted from their vehicles and went on foot to establish an observation position on the high ground overlooking the bridge. Seeing that the span was beyond repair, they decided that assault boats would be needed to carry the infantry across.

Just as the decision had been made to call up the boats, the Germans brought down a tremendous artillery concentration on the American positions. Shells from 88mm, 105mm, and 150mm guns rained down on the tanks and recon vehicles. The barrage destroyed two jeeps, and most of the tanks lost their radio antennae. With the enemy bringing this sort of firepower to bear, it now appeared that a boat crossing would be a very hazardous affair.

Just when it seemed that the situation at the bridge was at a stalemate, good fortune struck for the Americans. The Maquis informed them of another bridge located about two or three miles north of Hennebont. The bridge did not appear on the 1:100,000 scale maps in use at the time, so this bit of intelligence was indeed a gift. With artillery shells still falling all around them, Captain McMahon began assembling a task force for the mission of capturing the secondary bridge. The job of organizing the force was made more difficult when two of his platoon leaders were wounded; Lt. Donahue was hit in the cheek with some shrapnel, and Lt. Mueller was knocked unconscious by an artillery blast that threw him against the side of a tank. Though their injuries caused a delay, D/37 and A/53 were eventually organized and set out on their mission to capture the secondary bridge.

The road to the bridge was arduous, as it ran atop a sheer 100-foot high cliff that traced the edge of the river. But what made it outright dangerous was the fact that, unknown to the Americans, the Germans had placed a number of anti-tank guns along the route. Some of the guns were located on the American side of the river in ambush positions, while others were placed across the river in concrete pillboxes and amidst the cover of a large factory.

The enemy guns on the American side of the river allowed the tanks of D/37 to pass and then opened up on them from the rear. The guns from across the river chimed in at the same time. The M5 light tanks responded quickly and deliberately. First, they engaged the enemy guns firing at them from across the river, and quickly silenced them with HE and AT rounds from their 37mm cannons. Getting to the enemy AT guns located to their rear was more problematic, as they could not leave the road to turn around and engage them. Fortunately, the supporting infantry was in a better position to respond. The infantrymen laid down 60mm mortar fire on the German positions, which forced the AT guns to retreat into a small village to the rear. The tanks were then able to knock out the guns, and a platoon of infantry was sent into the village to mop up. After the resistance had been eliminated, the tanks and infantry continued down the road and secured the bridge without further interference from the enemy.

As the fight along the riverbank raged, B/37 and C/37 were leading a flanking attack toward the same bridge, via the town of St. Giles. As they advanced, they ran smack into the 281st Ost Cavalry Battalion (elements of which the other task force had briefly encountered). Undoubtedly it was a strange scene, as the modern machines of war came face to face with the vestige of another era. The cavalry were guarding this approach to the bridge and dared to stand in between the Fourth Armored and its next objective. It was a fatal mistake for the Russians.

As the lead Shermans approached, some of the Mongolian soldiers dismounted and scurried up the six-foot high banks that rose from both sides of the road, returning fire as they sought positions on the high ground. Many of the horses were spooked and stampeded down the road directly towards the American tanks that blocked the way. Machine gun and high-explosive fire from the tanks ravaged man and animal alike. Horses that were not cut down by bullets galloped at full speed into the front of the lead tanks, and then lay crumpled beneath the shadow of the 75mm guns.

The 37th Tank Battalion cut a deadly swathe down the road to St. Giles, leaving in its wake a scene of absolute devastation. It was not without cost, however, as the commanding officer of C/37, Captain Dale Smith, was killed, along with his 1st Sgt., James Hagemeister. Sergeant Whiteside of B Company was also killed, and Lt. Bohn wounded.

As other units followed behind the 37th Tank Battalion, the remains of the men and horses that littered the road became less and less recognizable as the treads of tanks, halftracks, and self-propelled guns turned the road into a sea of trampled bone and flesh. The sides of the road streamed with the intermingled blood of the Russian soldiers and their steed. The history of the 94th FAB called it "one of the bloodiest scenes the battalion was ever to witness."

The two task forces now merged and set out over the bridge above Hennebont. By late afternoon, CCA reached the village of Caudan, where they encountered some AT guns and almost a battalion of German infantry. While the tanks of D/37 engaged them from the front, B/37 outflanked the enemy from the north. The Shermans knocked out the enemy anti-tank guns and destroyed a large enemy barracks found nearby. As they continued to mop up, they knocked out several German artillery pieces and some 88mm gun positions. It was then that CCA halted for the night.

A Bloody Day for CCB

While CCA was ravaging the enemy, CCB had drawn the assignment of making a direct approach toward Lorient. On August 7, Dager's command captured the village of Pont Scorff, located about 6 miles north of Lorient. From there, they turned south toward the port city. But before CCB reached Lorient, it was greeted with aggressive fire that scattered the lead elements from the road. Dager and Wood quickly discovered that the route to Lorient was heavily defended. As elements of CCB scouted the approaches, they discovered that anti-tank ditches and minefields added to the complexity and danger of the assignment ahead. It was clear that a well-coordinated plan of attack was needed in order to penetrate the outer defenses of Lorient.

The 51st AIB positioned two of its companies (B and C) on the high ground overlooking Lorient, while A/51 was retained near Dager's headquarters south of Pont Scorff to provide security. As the armored infantry were settling in around the command post, the commanding officer (Lt. Colonel Conley) and S-3 (Major Irzyk) of the 8th Tank Battalion met nearby to discuss their options for attacking Lorient.

Then it happened. Without warning, all hell broke loose as the HQ area was hit by intense artillery fire that rained down non-stop for two hours. The shells came down with great accuracy and remained concentrated in an area less than 500 yards square. There clearly was an enemy observer nearby directing and adjusting the fire. The men dove for cover wherever they could find it, but there were few places of refuge to be found.

Lt. Colonel Conley and Major Irzyk had just started their discussion when the first shells struck. They dropped to the ground and crawled under Conley's command tank, where they joined another man who had already seized upon the same idea. All three squeezed in underneath the Sherman and hugged the ground beneath them. As hot metal fragments clanged off the tracks and wheels of the tank, they prayed that the steel above them would keep them out of harm's way. Endless explosions pounded the earth, and some were of such power and intensity that the tank was actually lifted off the ground.

Compared to the plight of the many men caught in the open on the field, Conley, Irzyk, and their unnamed companion had found a safe haven. Or so they thought. For even the cover of 33 tons of steel couldn't provide complete immunity from the deadly shrapnel flying in all directions. Conley, who had been in the middle of the trio, suddenly realized he had been hit, struck in the buttocks by shrapnel that found its way under the tank. The men now grasped the fact that they were not exempt from the danger and horror that blanketed the open field. There was an unspoken feeling that death was inevitable.

Then, out of the blue, good fortune struck. Rising above the hellish din of the bombardment was the clanging of metal and the shout of a human voice. The despair that had taken hold of the men was broken when they realized that the tank commander had opened the escape hatch on the underbelly of the tank and was beckoning them in. One at a time, each man squeezed his way through the small opening. This was no easy task, since the escape hatch was designed for *exiting* the tank; no consideration had ever been given to anyone ever wanting to *enter* it that way. But each man had plenty of incentive to make it work, and all three of them were soon inside the tank. With eight men tightly clustered in a space normally reserved for a crew of five, the driver revved the engine and made his way out of the killing field.

The guns were finally silenced when the German artillery observers were found on a nearby hill and killed. But during that deadly barrage, twenty men of the Fourth lost their lives. Eighty-five were wounded. Five halftracks, two armored cars, six jeeps and two trucks were destroyed, and many other vehicles badly damaged.

The men of A/51 were widely scattered after the shelling. The unit was completely disorganized. With only two officers remaining, they struggled to reorganize in another field on the south edge of Pont Scorff. As the battalion journal describes it, "it was really a catastrophe for the company." As if all this wasn't enough, "Yank," the 51stAIB's mascot, was run over by a truck and killed. The twenty men that died on that bloody field were buried on the spot, and the local villagers lovingly and devotedly tended to their graves over the many months that followed.

Payback

Later that same day, following the devastating shelling at Pont Scorff, C Company of the 8th Tank Battalion had two opportunities to extract some revenge on behalf of the 51st AIB, and they took full advantage of both of them. For starters, a German truck convoy passed directly in front of the Sherman tanks, and the American tank gunners let them have it full-bore. The tankers decimated the trucks, which were loaded with German troops. Not long after that encounter, C/8 came upon a locomotive headed for Lorient pulling eight railroad cars loaded with German troops and supplies. They stopped the train dead in its tracks after wisely choosing the lead locomotive for their initial target. They then proceeded to decimate the cars behind it. Three hundred and fifty would-be defenders of Lorient were killed.

The carnage that C/8 wrought that day caused at least one member of the company to pause and reflect on the manner in which he engaged the train and its occupants. At the time, Sergeant Nat Frankel didn't see the sense of what he described as a "purely gratuitous" slaughter. In hindsight, he later wrote that his view was tainted by a lack of knowledge regarding the importance of Lorient and the necessity of ensuring that the bastion was not reinforced. When later armed with the broader knowledge of the situation, he appears to reconcile his actions against the military necessity; a necessity that he simply didn't understand when he had the train in his sights.

Frankel's reaction is noteworthy because it speaks to the mixed emotions that many soldiers harbor on and off the battlefield. In combat, there are reasons for killing that can be reconciled and justified. The warrior can gain a rightful and deserved measure of peace within himself, if he believes his cause is just in the eyes of God, his countrymen, and in his own conscience. But if he does not understand and respect the cause for which he is fighting, he will languish in self-doubt and misery over his actions. The men of the Fourth, as they reflect on their own contribution during the war, can count themselves among those who deserve to be at peace. The righteousness of the cause for which they fought, and for which many of their brothers-in-arms died, will never be in doubt. If there *were* any doubts, they would be removed during the waning weeks of the war, when the Fourth Armored became the first division to liberate a Nazi concentration camp. The experience at Ohrdruf was horrific, and offered the men proof that their sacrifices and actions had been for a just and noble cause.

The Containment of Lorient

As night approached, concern grew among some of the units that the German forces inside Lorient would attempt a counterattack. Continued shelling during the day fueled the American's suspicions, as it looked as though they were being softened up for a strike (the 51st AIB lost two M8 assault guns to the enemy artillery).

The infantry available to CCB was not abundant, and concerned that their lines were too thin, all of the personnel from the 51st AIB Headquarters and Headquarters Company were alerted that they would be occupying positions on the front line that night. Only a few men would be left behind to safeguard their vehicles. Before they moved out, however, it was decided that this wasn't necessary, and the men remained at the headquarters. That they had even considered bolstering the front line in this fashion, however, is testimony to the level of concern they had over their situation.

During the night, the 1st Platoon from C/51 sent a patrol out beyond the front line to establish a forward post where there was a better view of the surrounding terrain. The platoon wasn't heard from for the rest of the night, raising concerns about its fate. Fortunately, the 1st Platoon had made contact with B Company and decided to set up a defensive position in that area. Other than worrying about the fate of the 1st Platoon, the night was uneventful. The German counterattack never took place.

On the following day, action around the perimeter of Lorient continued to be heavy, with losses incurred on both sides. The defenders within the city outnumbered the Fourth Armored by a margin of five to one. The Germans also had sufficient time to fortify the city. An extensive system of minefields and anti-tank ditches had been put in place to deter an assault against their positions and they had ample artillery and anti-tank gun support, along with more than enough ammunition and other supplies stockpiled within the city. The strength of the German position was clear.

Wood realized that there was little value in wasting the mobility and firepower of the Fourth Armored Division in a time consuming, methodical assault against such well-prepared defenses. With the port surrounded, the enemy posed no danger beyond the perimeter of the city. (To venture out would be suicide on the part of the Germans, despite their advantage in numbers) So Wood and Dager were content to pull CCB back out of artillery range, where the men could take advantage of the lull to squeeze in some much needed repair, maintenance, and reorganization.

The subsequent rest period lasted longer than was originally anticipated. For five days, the men were able to rest and refit. They took care of their personal affairs, and the units absorbed replacement personnel.

The break in the action also gave the lead units a chance to enhance their supply situation. The dash across Brittany had already started to reveal some of the weaknesses in the logistical tether stretching back through Avranches to the Normandy Beaches and Cherbourg. The supply line was now over 125 miles long, and the division's supply vehicles were working around the clock to keep ammunition and gasoline coming forward.

Captured stocks helped relieve the pressure for some commodities, and also provided the men with some extra niceties. In one case, the 51st AIB came across a large supply of German stoves. These were distributed among the men so that they could enjoy some hot meals. Fresh meat, bread, and butter supplemented the normal rations. An extra bonus was gained when Tech 4th Grade William Cutrone and his service battery ration crew rescued a large supply of French champagne from a German warehouse that was engulfed in a raging fire. Every man in their battalion received three bottles of the bubbly with which to celebrate their successes since breaking out of Normandy (it was Wood's long-standing practice that captured goods, no matter the value, would go to the enlisted men first).

The perimeter around Lorient was not a sea of total tranquility, however. Patrols were sent out on a routine basis, often with the objective of capturing prisoners for the purpose of gathering intelligence. More prisoners were brought in as a result, but the patrols also led to more American casualties. Sometimes, the price was simply too high. On August 12, aggressive patrolling by all three companies of the 51st brought in 13 prisoners, but the battalion suffered 23 casualties in the process.

With his troops stationary at Lorient, General Wood took the opportunity to bring to a halt some bad habits that had been cropping up among the men. A memo sent from division cited several things that needed to change: No discarding of American weapons for German ones; uniform infractions; discarding insignia of rank; not using lemon extract that was included with the rations; pillaging; smoking while driving; lack of maintenance. It never seemed to fail that when things got quiet, military discipline was the first thing that filled the void.

The Dash East Begins

While the Fourth Armored Division was taking care of business in Brittany, elements of the 5th Infantry Division had advanced toward the city of Nantes, some 81 miles east of Lorient. Patton placed a call to General Middleton, and asked him to send a force to relieve a battalion of the 5th ID that had been containing the enemy garrison within the city.

Presumably, Patton had elements of the 8th Infantry Division in mind for the job. Middleton saw this as an opportunity, however, to satisfy "P" Wood's urges, and assigned the task to the Fourth Armored Division. When Middleton gave Wood the green light, very specific directions accompanied it: "Do not become involved in fight in city. Merely prevent any enemy movement north."

With Lorient surrounded and the decision reached to contain the German garrison rather than assault it, Wood had no problem freeing up part of his division for the task of relieving the 5th Infantry. While retaining CCB in the area around Lorient, Wood dispatched Clarke's CCA to the east. In preparation for the move, Major West issued the following instructions to his battalion:

> All officers and non-commissioned officers were to wear their insignia of rank and the division patch. All numbers and markings on vehicles were to be readable, no trash or paper was to be thrown over the sides of the vehicles or discarded during the march, every other vehicle was to have a gun pointing to the rear and an observer looking in that direction. Whenever firing is heard at the head of the column, the leading infantry company was to dismount and go to the head of the column. Vehicles under no circumstances were to travel at a greater speed than 30 miles per hour. Any German weapon in the possession of the troops or officers were not to be fired unless in self defense.

On August 10, Colonel Clarke's force left its bivouac near Vannes and proceeded to drive 80 miles in 7 hours, reaching the city of Nantes before the end of the day. At times, it hardly seemed like there was a war on. From the town of Bain de Bretagne all the way to the outskirts of Nantes, French villagers turned out along the roadside waving homemade American flags. Tears of joy streamed down the faces of some of the

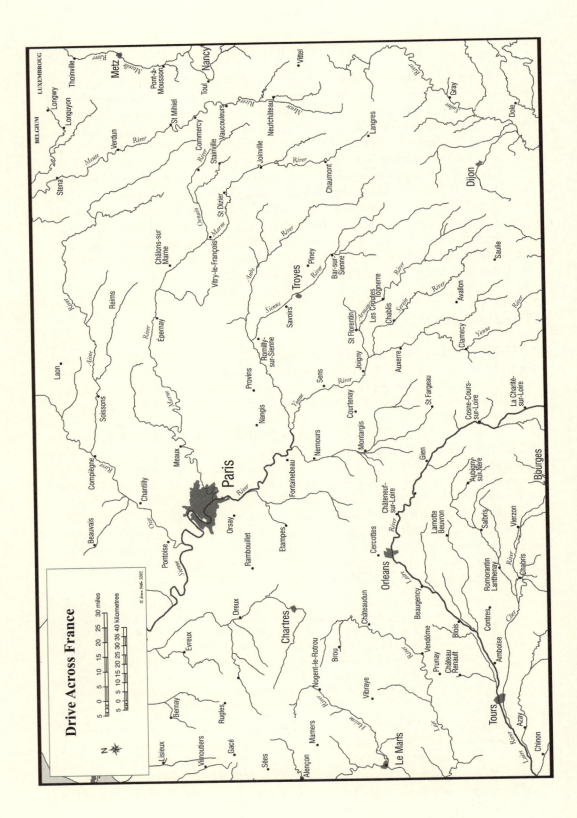

Drive Across France

N

5 0 5 10 15 20 25 30 miles
5 0 5 10 15 20 25 30 35 40 kilometres

© Anova Books 2002

BELGIUM
LUXEMBROUG

Longwy
Longuyon
Thoinville
Metz
Moselle River
Pont-à-Mousson
Toul
Nancy
Vittel

St Mihiel
Vaucouleurs
Commercy
Stainville
Neufchâteau
Joinville

Verdun
Meuse River
Langres
Gray
Saône River
Dole

Stenay
Ortrain River
St Dizier
Chaumont
Dijon

Reims
Châlons-sur-Marne
Vitry-le-François
Marne River
Piney
Bar-sur-Sienne
Saulie

Épernay
Aube River
Troyes
Les Croutes
Tognerre
Avallon
Serejn River
Clamecy
Yonne River

Laon
Aisne River
Sienne River
Savoirs
St Florentin
Chablis

Soissons
Marne River
Provins
Romilly-sur-Sienne
Joigny
Auxerre

Compiègne
Oise River
Nangis
Sens
Courtenay
St Fargeau

Chantilly
Meaux
Paris
Yonne River
Nemours
Montargis
Gien
Aubigny-sur-Nère
Bourges

Beauvais
Pontoise
Orsay
Fontainebleau
Châteauneuf-sur-Loire
Lamotte Beuvron
Salbris
Vierzon

Seine River
Rambouillet
Etampes
Cercottes
Orleans
Loire River
Romorantin Lanthenay
Chabris

Dreux
Châteaudun
Beaugency
Blois
Contres
Cher River

Evreux
Chartres
Brou
Vendôme
Prunay
Château Renault
Amboise
Tours
Azay
Chinon

Bernay
Rugles
Nogent-le-Rotrou
Loir River
Vibraye
Loir River

Lisieux
Vimoutiers
Gacé
Sées
Mamers
Alençon
Le Mans
Huisne River
Sarthe River
Loire River

most jubilant in the crowd. The French, who certainly had endured their share of hardship during the past four years and had little to spare, offered the passing GIs gifts of bread, butter and eggs. The scene was described in the 10th AIB diary: "It had all the appearance of a Victory parade and is undoubtedly prophetic of what will soon follow."

Upon the arrival of the lead elements of CCA, Clarke launched an attack against the German garrison at Nantes (in spite of Middleton's original directive). During the battle, the enemy blew up their ammunition stockpiles before they could fall into the hands of Clarke's force. After a full day and a half of fighting, Nantes was cleansed of German troops. The right flank of the Third Army was now nestled along the Loire River, and the Fourth was finally positioned for a forceful drive to the east.

On August 11, Wood received the surprising news that Patton was putting the Fourth Armored Division on alert for a possible move to the northeast, in order to support XV Corps' attempt to close the Argentan-Falaise Gap. Unfortunately, Wood was not in position to execute that mission, since CCB was still at Lorient, waiting to be relieved by the 6th Armored Division, and CCA was engaged at Nantes. Patton was quite angry that VIII Corps had not moved quickly enough to cut the Fourth Armored loose from its containment duties at Lorient. Patton was apparently now thinking more along the lines of Wood. Unfortunately, more than a week had been wasted before he had seen the light. The division had spent that time either moving west or sitting idle, instead of moving east toward more lucrative objectives.

On August 13, the Fourth Armored was shifted from Middleton's VIII Corps to the newly activated XII Corps, commanded by Major General Gilbert Cook. The XII Corps, of which the Fourth Armored was now the centerpiece, had two missions: pursue the enemy to the east, and secure the right flank of the Third Army, which ran parallel to the north bank of the Loire River.

CCA now began moving east in force as the spearhead for the Fourth Armored Division. From Nantes, Clarke's command advanced almost 125 miles to St. Calais, where it stopped to refuel. The command then continued to advance east for another six hours, until it arrived near the city of Orleans, which lies nestled along the banks of the Loire River. The distances covered were impressive by anyone's standards. The 10th Armored Infantry Battalion, for example, covered 164 miles in 22 hours. CCA, now just 62 miles south of Paris, had advanced further east than any division in the Allied Armies.

In terms of enemy resistance, the road from Nantes to Orleans had been a relatively easy one. Once CCA had gotten underway, it had encountered little organized opposition. The main obstacles were blown bridges that forced the column to seek out alternative routes. Still, a march of this sort, conducted through the night under blackout conditions, was a trying, tiring experience. It was no easy task to keep a column of this size moving this far, this fast. Clarke's men handled it magnificently.

The Battle of Orleans

CCA's dash to the east came to a temporary halt near Orleans. The Germans chose to defend the city, utilizing remnants of the 708th Division and mixed rearguard elements. The city was held in such strength that Wood could not consider bypassing it. A coordinated attack would be required to wrestle it away from the enemy.

On August 15, Colonel Clarke formed two task forces from elements of the 35th Tank Battalion (commanded by Lt. Colonel Bill Bailey), the 704th TD Battalion (commended by Colonel Delk Oden), the 10th Armored Infantry Battalion, and the 66th Armored Field Artillery Battalion. Clarke's plan called for TF Oden to descend on Orleans from the north, while TF Bailey circled clockwise around the city in order to strike from the east.

TF Bailey advanced to its position east of the city, but its attack toward Orleans was delayed when a severe thunderstorm struck. Once the weather cleared up, Bailey was informed that TF Oden had run behind schedule on its drive toward the northern part of the city. As a result, TF Bailey was held back from attacking the city that day. They would have to wait until TF Oden was in position.

TF Oden made contact with the enemy at the village of LePervay. As the lead elements drove into the center of the town, the column came under long-range fire from 20mm AA guns positioned southwest of the town. At the same time, small arms fire erupted at close range off to the column's immediate right.

The armored infantry of C/10 dismounted from their halftracks while Major West assessed the situation. After identifying the position of the 20mm fire, West arranged for a platoon of Shermans from C/35 to come forward. The tankers succeeded in silencing the enemy AA guns. Meanwhile, the Americans turned their heavy machine guns against the Germans on their right. They sent the enemy running for cover behind some haystacks, which were soon set aflame by the heat from tracer bullets. The Germans then tried to attack the right rear of the American column. Two trucks loaded with Krauts rushed forward (or perhaps the German trucks just stumbled into the American force). A .50 caliber machine gun mounted on one of the halftracks quickly eliminated this threat, and the surviving Germans were rounded up and taken prisoner.

It was late in the afternoon when the light tanks of D/35 approached the airport north of the city. They charged forward with their machine guns blazing, destroying several planes on the ground and wiping out the anti-aircraft and machine gun emplacements that were standing guard over the facility. German demolition parties had been preparing to sabotage the airfield, but the light tanks of D Company chased them off before they could do any damage. The airport was secured, and Oden prepared to renew the advance toward Orleans. But then the sudden, severe rainstorm mentioned earlier hit his area, causing a delay in TF Oden's advance as well. By the time the rain subsided, there was insufficient daylight remaining to carry the attack into Orleans. The night was spent maneuvering for position around the city in preparation for a morning assault.

By 11 A.M. on August 16, the two task forces were in position to attack. As planned, TF Oden pressed forward from the north. The spearhead of TF Oden, which consisted of B/51, B/35, and a platoon of engineers from A/24, was commanded by Major West. As the column proceeded, it passed an abundance of abandoned enemy vehicles and tanks. In the distance to the south, flames could be seen rising from Orleans. Apparently the Germans were bugging out and destroying what they couldn't take with them. As West's vanguard approached the outskirts of the city, it encountered a defended roadblock. Two tanks were brought forward, which quickly chased off the enemy. The Germans had laid an extensive minefield along the route, but a helpful civilian came forward and passed on valuable information to Major West regarding the location of the minefields and German emplacements. This greatly facilitated the work of the engineers, and TF Oden was soon on its way into the heart of the city.

Major West's immediate objective was City Hall, located near the center of Orleans. Company B/10, supported by two tanks, made steady progress toward the building. Fighting within the city streets was occasionally heavy, and consisted primarily of small arms fire. Perhaps the most dramatic moment of the battle occurred when a German armored car, escorted by about 30 infantrymen, advanced straight down a street toward the spot where Major West was standing. West called the two tanks forward, and they proceeded to knock out the armored car. Meanwhile, West brandished his own weapon and killed five of the enemy soldiers that were riding on the outside of the armored vehicle. The field artillery observer for the 66th AFAB, Lt. Hampton, also fired at the oncoming infantry, killing two of them.

As TF Oden moved in from the north, TF Bailey pressed into the city from the southeast. Apparently, Bailey's force caught the rear area of the German defenses by surprise and overran the enemy's artillery positions. The Germans did not have time to form a cohesive line of defense facing east, and TF Bailey pressed forward with "savage ferocity." Back near the city center, Oden's men came upon a contingent of SS officers and Gestapo agents, which they proceeded to kill or capture. The SS troops had apparently provided the backbone for the defense of the town, for without their fanatical leaders, the remaining defenders quickly collapsed.

Orleans was deemed secure by 3 P.M., save for some minor mopping-up. The civilian population wasted no time coming out to celebrate their liberation, but Clarke's men didn't have long to enjoy the party. Almost as quickly as they had taken it, CCA handed over Orleans to the 35th Infantry Division and proceeded to take up positions north of the city to prevent the enemy from advancing south against their left flank.

Clarke's blocking positions were tested when an enemy column of German staff cars ran smack into a roadblock established by the 704th at the village of Cercottes. Bill Minogue's platoon of M18s used their .50 caliber machine guns to shoot up the German vehicles, killing or wounding most of the occupants. Among the injured was a German Colonel, who received a very bad wound to his abdomen. Because of his high rank, the medical staff of the 704th was asked to apply extra urgency to save him, and then transport him to the rear for interrogation. The medics did their best, giving him plasma and morphine. But they were not about to use their valuable aid station truck "to transport a Kraut" when some of their own men were in need. So they did what they could, and sent him back to the rear in a captured German vehicle (the medics never knew what became of him).

Time to Regroup

On August 16, as CCA mopped up around Orleans, the 6th Armored Division relieved CCB/4 of their duties containing the German forces at Lorient. At the time

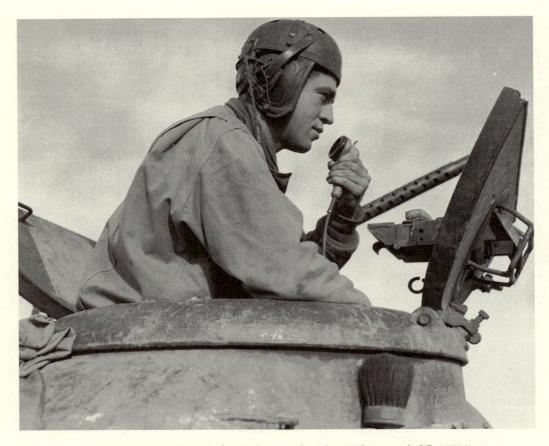

Captain J.F. Brady, CO of B/35 (National Archives Photograph SC195532).

of their departure from Lorient, CCB was separated from CCA by more than 200 miles, and had to make a swift drive to catch up with the balance of the division. Brigadier General Dager's men responded magnificently, conducting a 264-mile road march that carried them to the town of Prunay in only 34 hours. This advance was unprecedented for an armored force, and was made possible in large part by the discipline the tank and maintenance crews had shown during their five-day respite outside of Lorient. Had they not invested their time wisely by meticulously caring for their vehicles, the grueling road march would certainly not have gone as well as it did.

That same day, while basking in the glow of the successful assault on Orleans, General Wood visited with Patton at the Third Army HQ. Also present was the commander of the French 2nd Armored Division, Jacques Leclerc. The French general was lobbying hard with Patton for the honor of becoming the liberator of Paris. So hard, in fact, that Patton was inspired to say, "You see, Wood. He is a bigger pain in the neck than you are!" Wood had been pressing for the honor as well.

As the Fourth Armored moved further to the east, its southern flank became an increasing concern. General Wood's situation was eased a bit by the fact that the Loire River, which ran parallel with the right flank of the Fourth Armored's advance, provided a natural barrier against attacks originating from the south. Vehicles could not ford the river, so if the bridges were secured or destroyed, the enemy could be contained south of the Loire.

The mission of destroying the bridges was turned over to the Air Force. In addition, to reduce the chance of an attack coming from the south, the fighter-bombers of the XIX TAC aggressively patrolled the area along the river. After the Air Force hit the bridges between Tours and Blois, it was not entirely certain if the structures had been completely destroyed. So for an extra measure of security, plans were drawn up to have a task force run down to the line of the Loire River to inspect the damage and, if needed, complete the job.

Task Force Bautz

Major Edward Bautz was the S-3 of the 37th Tank Battalion. As the operations officer, it was standard procedure that, from time to time, he be given command of task forces drawn up for specific missions (the same was true in all three of the tank battalions). Just three days prior, on August 12, he led a task force built around C/37 on a mission to destroy the "enemy forces protecting the escape routes from the Quimperon Peninsula." On that mission, TF Bautz engaged the Germans at the towns of Flouharnel and Erdevan, leaving behind 65 dead Krauts and taking 107 prisoners.

Now, on August 15, Major Bautz was handed the assignment of sweeping the north bank of the Loire River in order to inspect the Air Force's work. The swath cut by his task force would also help ensure that the Germans had not tucked any troops away north of the river prior to the bridges being taken out. His group was a small one, consisting of 1st Lt. Leach's B/37, a company of engineers commanded by Captain Charlie Steel, and six M7 self-propelled howitzers. It set out on its mission on the same day it was created.

TF Bautz had to drive 102 miles to the south before reaching the banks of the Loire River. The only delay occurred when one of the tracks on Bautz's own tank broke, and the column had to stop and wait while the repairs were made (fortunately, he had enough spare track sections with him to do the job). Another glitch occurred that evening when they realized that they had not brought along enough gasoline to carry out their full mission, and still have enough fuel in their tanks to rejoin CCR to the north. Attempts were made to raise Abrams on the radio, in order to have some gasoline sent down to them, but the distance was too great for the transmission to be received.

In the morning, with the maximum range for the vehicles carefully calculated based on the amount of gasoline on hand, TF Bautz set out on its sweep along the Loire River. As the American column neared the town of Amboise, the vanguard sighted an enemy column marching east near the opposite bank of the river. Bautz ordered his men to attack, and the Germans suddenly found they were trapped along the low ground near the river. The Shermans of B/37 unloaded on them, inflicting heavy casualties. Sixty-five Germans were killed and 107 taken prisoner. The Americans lost two engineers.

The task force moved on with its mission of inspecting the three bridges in its path. The first two had indeed been destroyed by the Air Force. But before their departure for the third, Bautz checked his calculations again, and determined that he did not have enough gas to take the entire task force down to the site of the final bridge. Instead, he sent a single platoon of tanks and engineers to check it out. When they returned, they reported that this span had been blown as well.

The task force reassembled and began their trip back north. But by this time, things were moving so fast, and the situation was so fluid, that Bautz wasn't sure where the 37th had relocated during the time since his initial departure. When he got within 20 miles or so of where he thought they were most likely to be, he started trying to establish radio contact with the units of CCR. Finally, he made it back to the 37th Tank Battalion, where Abe Abrams gave him a warm greeting: "Where the hell have you been?"

Maintenance

With Orleans in the bag and its flanks secured, the division paused to gather itself. CCA and CCB now closed ranks, and the division settled into a more tightly concentrated area northwest of Orleans. CCA was temporarily attached to the 35th Infantry Division, which was now holding a line extending from Orleans to Viners and Chateau Dun (Clarke's command was released back to Wood on August 19). CCA's mission was to serve as a mobile reserve in the event of a German counterattack against the 35th Infantry. No such threat developed, so once again, the tankers took care of much needed maintenance and prepared for the next surge of movement. Their maintenance duties weren't just a matter of changing the oil and topping off the gas tanks. Tracks and even engines were replaced as needed.

The wear and tear of so many miles traveled in such a short time was beginning to tell. During a relatively short 22-mile road march on August 20, the 37th had several tanks fail due to engine problems and the breakage of worn tracks. Taking care of heavy maintenance out in the field was hard work, but as the tank battalions had already experienced, not resting on your laurels would pay great dividends when it came time to move on to the next assignment. There were certain maintenance items that the forward repair crews were not able to handle, in which case, the tank would be sent back to the rear for repairs. When a tank was passed back, the maintenance crews knew that the least they could do was bust their rumps at every opportunity to give the tankers the benefit of the best machines possible. In turn, the tankers knew that the maintenance crews were a vital part of the tank battalion's lifeline. And in the Fourth Armored, the tankers knew that they had the best men available supporting them.

XII Corps Changes Hands

On August 19, the command of XII Corps was passed on to Major General Manton Eddy. General Cook, who Patton held in high regard, fell very ill due to circulatory problems, leaving Patton little choice but to replace him.

Before his promotion, Eddy was the commander of the 9th Infantry Division. In that capacity, he established a solid reputation, having led the division through combat in Africa and Sicily, as well as the more recent campaign in Normandy. A wounded veteran of the First World War, he had recently been awarded the Distinguished Service Cross for his actions at Cherbourg.

One would think that General Wood might have been a contender for Cook's slot, especially if Patton was in his corner. But it appears that Wood was never seriously considered for the job. There is no doubt that Eisenhower favored Eddy, and the bond between them probably helped secure Eddy's ascension to the command of XII Corps. While some have criticized the decision to award Eddy the command, it must be said that Eddy's combat experience, at this point in the war, far exceeded Wood's (that isn't to say that Eddy was more capable; his resume was simply more impressive). Wood had been in combat with his division for only one month, while Eddy's experience extended all the way back to the campaign in North Africa. Eddy had certainly earned his shot at commanding a corps. It remained to be seen what he could do with the opportunity.

It didn't take long for some of Eddy's weaknesses to appear. One of his first concerns after taking command of XII Corps was his extended right flank. He asked Patton how much he needed to worry about it once he moved past Orleans. Patton later recounted: "I told him that depended on how nervous he was," adding, "He has been thinking a mile a day is good going. I told him fifty and he turned pale." General Wood certainly would not have needed that sort of coaching.

Through the Gap

The stage was now set for the Third Army to plunge through the "Orleans Gap" between Paris and the Loire River. All indications were that the Germans were still in disarray and that the advance should be conducted with as much speed as possible. Wood's division was once again called on to lead the charge.

The next set of orders were issued during the evening of August 20. The division, now amply restocked with ammo and rations, would hit the road at first light and resume its advance to the east. Wood's division was also beefed up by the attachment of the 137th Infantry Regiment (35th Infantry Division), which was in turn assigned to CCA. Clarke's artillery support was also increased to a total of four battalions: the 66th and 94th AFAB's, plus the 191st and 219th Field Artillery Battalions.

On the afternoon of a rainy August 21, CCA capped off a 12-hour, 90-mile advance by capturing Sens and securing a bridge over the Yonne River. The German troops at Sens did not pose much resistance. Most of the opposition came from snipers who had taken up positions in a schoolhouse. After one of CCA's tanks pumped five rounds of high explosive into the building, the armored infantry rushed the school, overwhelmed the enemy, and took 50 prisoners. The Free French forces also played a role at Sens, as they roamed the city taking out isolated pockets of German resistance. The continuous rain did not have an impact on the pace of the advance, nor did it deter the residents of Sens from coming out to celebrate the arrival of the Americans. Despite the weather, an enthusiastic crowd lined the streets to greet their liberators. The Fourth received an extra bonus when they captured a vast supply depot. Three hundred tons of food and 30 railroad cars of diesel fuel passed into the hands of the Americans.

The following day (August 22), a battalion of SS troops was spotted moving toward Sens for an apparent counterattack. But the Fourth lashed out at them with tanks, artillery from the 66th, and P-47s from the XIX Tactical Air Command. The German battalion was wiped out en route. Meanwhile, CCB had split off on its own route to the southeast, and by 3:00 P.M. on August 22, one of its task forces liberated the city of Courtenay. As had happened so often during the past three weeks, the civilians erupted from their homes to celebrate the arrival of the American tankers.

These spontaneous celebrations stood in stark contrast to the rigors of war. They seemed surreal to the men of the Fourth Armored Division. Combat, on the other hand, carried with it a stark, heart pounding reality; one is never more aware of the value of life then when faced with the immediate prospect of losing it. These glorious street demonstrations almost made the tankers forget about the foreboding future that lie ahead of them as they turned the corner towards the next objective. Almost, but never totally, and never for long.

While Courtenay was being taken, CCB sent a second task force, under the command of Lt. Col. Maybach, to swing south and then west in support of the 35th Infantry Division, which was driving east and preparing to attack the city of Montargis, some 38 miles east of Orleans. Maybach had the entire 51st Armored Infantry Battalion at his disposal, supported by Battery A of the 22nd Field Artillery Battalion, Company A of the 8th Tank Battalion, a platoon each of TD's, engineers, and armored cavalry, and the 179th Field Artillery Battalion (equipped with 155mm howitzers).

Company A of the 51st AIB led the column toward Montargis. The armored infantry passed through a heavily forested area, and then drew fire when they neared the village of Paucourt. The entire column pulled off the road at that point, and B/51 was brought forward to supplement the weight of A/51. The situation was tense, as the forest prevented Maybach from conducting any sort of quick reconnaissance in order to see what he might be facing. The artillery and mortar units were placed into firing positions, and barrages were launched against the enemy positions, suspected or real. Heavy exchanges of fire continued on into the night, and A and B Company used the cover of darkness to move into position for an early morning strike against the village.

On the morning of August 23, A/51 and B/51 launched their attack on Paucourt. B Company had the task of clearing out the houses, while A Company pressed a patrol all the way through to the far end of the village. The Germans suffered heavy casualties, and several prisoners were taken in town. The newly acquired POWs were identified as being from the 338th Infantry Division's 757th and 758th Grenadier regiments and the 338th Artillery Regiment. The Germans had apparently trekked more than 90 miles before taking up positions in the town, only to be hammered soon after their arrival.

By 3:30 P.M., Paucourt was declared clear, and the column resumed its advance southwest toward Montargis. C/51 was the rear guard for the column and ended up having quite a busy afternoon, as more pockets of Germans cropped up in the woods behind them. A platoon from C Company under the command of Lt. Lambert, accompanied by some of the tanks from A/8, accounted for the lion's share of some 250 prisoners that were flushed out of the woods that day. As the column drew closer to Montargis, it received word that the 35th Infantry Division had entered the town from the west and that the enemy was now withdrawing to the east and southeast. The 51st AIB set up positions north of Montargis, and established its command post at a local sports stadium. Shortly after sunset, "one of the worst downpours the battalion had ever experienced" served as a miserable punctuation at the end of what had been a very productive day.

Decisions at the Top

On August 23, a high-level conference took place far from the battlefields where the men of the Fourth Armored toiled. On that fateful day, Eisenhower met with Field Marshal Montgomery, with the intention of hashing out the manner in which the campaign would be conducted going forward.

Montgomery had a clear vision of how he wished to proceed: he wanted a concentrated thrust of forty divisions, punching to the northeast toward the Ruhr. Under his proposal, the axis of advance would be maintained north of the Ardennes region, and all other areas would become subservient to the main thrust. The direct consequences would be a halt to the advance of Patton's Third army, and a diversion of Patton's supplies (especially his gasoline ration) to Montgomery's force.

For a variety of reasons — some political, some military — Eisenhower did not accept Montgomery's proposal exactly as presented. But he did give Montgomery priority on supplies, so much so that it would have the net effect of stopping Patton's advance. Ike also ensured that the bulk of the First Army would indeed advance north of the Ardennes. So in the end, Montgomery received most of what he wanted.

Once informed of Eisenhower's decision, Patton was determined to make the most of what time and supplies he had left. At his reduced rate of supply, Patton could keep moving for perhaps a week. In the meantime, there would be no slowing of the pace or consolidation of positions. Patton was determined to continue the advance until his tanks ran out of gas. And then they would get out and walk. But his dogged determination was no substitute for petrol, so by September, he would be faced with the frustrating reality that Eisenhower had pulled the plug on his drive across France.

On August 23, XII Corps' responsibilities for guarding the long right flank of the Third Army were transferred to the VIII Corps, which was now heading east again after its mission in Brittany. This freed up XII Corps, and the Fourth Armored Division as its spearhead, to focus most of its resources in one direction, and that was toward Germany. On August 23, CCA/4 was almost 90 miles southeast of Paris (the French capital would fall to the French 2nd Armored Division the following day). On that day, the Fourth Armored Division was closer to Germany than any division in the West.

The Battle of Troyes

On August 25, Wood's division moved on to the city of Troyes, located on the banks of the Seine River some 88 miles southeast of the center of Paris. CCA's best estimate was that the Germans held Troyes with a force of about 500 men. A defensive force of this size could not be taken lightly, so a coordinated plan of attack was drawn up. Two task forces were formed for the assault: Major West commanded one, Colonel Oden the other.

TF Oden would pursue a crossing of the Seine River at a location seven miles northwest of Troyes, and then sweep around the Germans' right flank, cutting off their escape route to the east. Oden's force consisted of A/35, B/35/, D/35, C/10, 66th AFAB, one battery of 155mm howitzers, and A/24 (minus one platoon).

TF West would conduct a frontal assault on the city, attacking from the west. Major West had at his disposal two companies (A and B) of the 10th Armored Infantry Battalion, a company of Sherman tanks (C/35, commanded by Capt. Crosby "Dick" Miller), a platoon from the 24th Armored Engineer Battalion, the 94th AFAB, and the 191st FAB (minus one battery).

Task Force Oden jumped off at 7:00 A.M. as scheduled. The advance was uneventful until they reached the town of Saviors, where they found that all of the bridges over the Seine River had been destroyed. The engineers from the 24th came forward to put a temporary bridge in place, but it would be morning before TF Oden would resume its move to the area east of Troyes.

The burden for capturing the city now fell entirely on Task Force West, and they had a tough task on their hands. The terrain to the west of Troyes was wide open. The ground sloped gently down toward the city for a distance of over three miles. It was a long distance to cover in full view of the enemy, and the advancing vehicles would be extremely vulnerable if the Germans had sufficient firepower available to greet them.

As Major West began to consider his options for attacking the town, some of the American positions came under observation by the enemy. Almost immediately after the 94th AFAB set up its guns, it was hit with heavy counter-battery fire. Private Donald Ramey of Battery A was killed and another six men were wounded (three each from Batteries B and C). During the shelling, a loaded ammunition trailer caught fire and came dangerously close to exploding. If it had, it would have surely resulted in massive destruction within the gun positions. Tech 5th Grade George Wilds (C Battery) was awarded the Bronze Star for putting out the blaze before it caused more serious damage.

Despite the shelling, Art West prepared to launch his assault. Before he advanced in force, he sent out recon elements from the 10th AIB and 25th Cavalry to investigate the approaches to Troyes. Both of these forces departed at 1:20 P.M., and they were ordered to report back within one hour. The patrols returned safely and reported that they had drawn fire from the enemy positions at Troyes.

At 2:15 P.M., Colonel Clarke informed Major West that TF Oden had been hung up at Saviors and that he would have to shoulder the attack on Troyes alone. Shortly after 3:00 P.M., Colonel Clarke met with Lt. Col. Graham, Colonel Bixby, Major West, Captain Shea (S-3 for the 10th AIB), and the 10th AIB's Operations Sergeant. The group went to a position some 800 yards from the town, made a visual reconnaissance, and worked out the coordination of the supporting artillery. They discussed the method for the attack, and then Clarke asked West when he would be ready to go. West's response was 4:30 P.M., and with that, the battalion commanders returned to their respective units to prepare for the attack.

Prior to the attack, Major West issued comprehensive orders for the assault on Troyes:

> As you know, there is enemy artillery falling on this ground and to our left front. The artillery observers have been unable to determine the course of this enemy fire. Eight enemy personnel were observed running to the rear along that main highway to our front toward the city. The enemy occupies the roads and fields to our front, just in front of the city. Roads to the edge of the city are not mined. As stated this morning, enemy artillery pieces are located at various positions on the main road leading into the city itself, and the city is believed to be occupied by the main 300 to 500 enemy personnel. Explosions can be seen in Troyes, It is believed that the enemy are destroying ammunition dumps and equipment in preparation for leaving the city.
>
> You know the mission of CCB is to take the town to our right. Oden's column is now held up repairing a bridge across the Seine River at Severes (sic). The 94th and 191st are in position in that draw (pointing), They will support our attack on Troyes. A forward observer will go with each company to the attack. This task force attacks the town at 1630 — line of departure — this high ground we are now on — left boundary RR track (pointing) — right boundary that highway (pointing) leading into the city. We will attack in columns of companies, companies in line, deployed on a wide front. C/35 leading, 100 yards between vehicles, followed by A/10 plus assault gun platoon/10, Battalion headquarters with reconnaissance and mortar platoon followed by B/10 plus MG platoon. A detachment of engineers from a platoon of A/24 will ride with A/10 and carry mine detectors. The rest of the engineers will follow B/10 — they will be followed by our medical detachment. Service Company with maintenance section and trains will remain in present location.
>
> Our most dangerous ground is that open ground between here and the city, a distance of approximately 3½ miles. Our best security can be obtained by moving fast across that area to get into the protection of the town. The companies will follow each other in successive distance of 100 yards. The first phase line for reorganization will be about 500 to 600 yards inside the town proper (pointing). The second phase line will be the RR tracks at the RR station. We will then attack in column down the street until we reach the Seine Canal (pointing on map). At that time further orders will be issued. No town plans (maps) are available. You will have to feel your way after we get into the town. The Battalion CP will be in the rear of A/10.
>
> All companies of 10 turn on SCR 300 and 536 in addition to vehicular radios, now. When necessary to dismount, take them with you. The time is now 1600. Are there any questions?

In essence, West's orders had created a classic wide-desert formation. It was something that the Fourth had practiced in California, but had not had the occasion to use in combat. The main virtue of the formation was that, by spreading out wide, the advancing units would be less vulnerable to enemy fire. It was important that the vehicles not bunch up, in order to avoid being easy targets for the enemy gunners. It was a prudent approach, since there would be plenty of fire coming their way; for as it turned out, the assessment of 500 defenders was incorrect. In fact, there were more than 2,000

Germans in Troyes, including members of the 51st SS Brigade. West's disciplined, well thought out approach to the attack was about to pay great dividends.

Before the meeting broke up, one of the armored infantry company commanders, Lt. McDonald, asked West for a little more time to prepare. West granted his request and moved the start time to 5 P.M. All of the participating units moved efficiently into their positions, and at exactly 1700 hours, the tanks of C/35 began to roll.

The advancing horde of American armor and halftracks drew heavy artillery and small arms fire and a smattering of anti-tank fire. They initially moved at a deliberate, slow speed, but as the volume of enemy fire increased, all of the advancing units were urged to pick up the pace, starting with Captain Miller's Shermans. Despite the threat presented by the exploding shells and zinging bullets, Captain Miller never buttoned up his tank during the entire attack, in order to maintain the best observation possible during the advance (Miller would later be awarded the Silver Star for his role at Troyes).

The men of TF West drove on relentlessly across the open field. Recognizing the pattern of the artillery strikes, the halftrack drivers skillfully changed direction to avoid the likely location of the next incoming round. Much of the small arms fire was coming from an area of anti-tank ditches that covered the approach to Troyes. The volume of fire was particularly heavy on the right flank of the task force. As they closed in on the enemy positions, Major West took two tanks and Lt. Price's platoon from A/10 to deal with the threat coming from that direction. They quickly knocked out three or four machine gun nests. Major West himself wiped out the crew of one enemy machine gun with bursts from his own submachine gun.

As West tackled the enemy positions on the right, the balance of Miller's tanks approached the forward defensive line. Surely the Germans must have felt confident that the seven-foot wide anti-tank ditch would hold back the onrushing Shermans. The only problem for the Germans was that someone forgot to tell Miller that he had to stop. Without hesitation, the tankers gunned their engines and flew across the ditch, smashing into the opposite bank and breaking it down so that the halftracks and other vehicles could follow across. The tanks continued to advance toward Troyes while West's infantry platoon and pair of Shermans continued to mop up the Germans in the area of the trenches (two anti-tank guns, four machine guns, and 50 Germans were laid to waste in the German's forward defensive positions).

Task Force West was not able to cross the field without suffering losses. Some of the German guns started to find their mark, and when they did, there was no place to hide in the open field. The jeep carrying the forward observers for Battery A of the 94th was hit by machine gun fire, killing Lieutenant Lewis Dent and Private Victor Greenwalt, and wounding Staff Sergeant Orsborn (the same Sergeant Orsborn who had won the Silver Star for his actions back in Normandy). Lt. McDonald, who lost his own jeep just prior to this, was also riding in the observer's jeep, and was the only one of the four unscathed by the machine gun. He proceeded to assault the enemy position single-handedly, wiping it out with a hand grenade that he expertly tossed into the nest. After silencing the machine gun position, he made his way on foot toward one of his halftracks, but was wounded en route. His injury didn't stop him, however, and he rejoined his men as they advanced into the town. He refused to be evacuated during the entire night that followed (Lt. McDonald would be awarded the Silver Star for his action at Troyes).

Major West's jeep was also destroyed in the action. He climbed aboard the jeep of Lt. Hoffman from the 94th, and they sped forward into Troyes (Hoffman and Dent would also receive the Silver Star for their actions at Troyes, Dent's being awarded posthumously).

Up to this point, most of the action had been confined to the right flank of the attack. The left side of the assault force hit less resistance, and reached the edge of the city about 15 minutes ahead of the rest of the task force. There was initially some confusion as West tried to coordinate the drives being made by the forces on the left and right flanks. One of the problems was that the attack was launched without the benefit of detailed city street maps, and the units in front had to feel their way through the town. Eventually, adequate communications were established, and the two forces linked up.

As the task force pushed deeper into Troyes, a squad of armored infantry from the 1st Platoon, A/10 stumbled upon a large enemy headquarters, which included an elaborate communications center. When they searched the facility, they discovered a large quantity of detailed maps; just the very thing they needed. After confiscating the maps, the GIs destroyed the communications center. This single squad took more than 50 prisoners and seized some 500 rifles, carbines, and machine guns. Ten trucks and a motorcycle were also taken at the site of the enemy headquarters.

The Americans weren't the only ones taking prisoners, however. While tending to some of the wounded men on the front lines, Private Anthony Scarpa, a medic with the 10th AIB, suddenly found himself cut off from the unit he was supporting (the machine gun platoon of the 10th AIB's HQ Company). He was captured by the Germans and brought to an area hospital where some 100 armed Krauts had barricaded themselves in with the wounded. During the night that followed, he treated the wounded Germans while the battle raged outside the hospital walls. American tanks approached the building and began hammering its occupants into submission. With the help of an interpreter, Scarpa talked the Germans into surrendering (Scarpa would receive the Silver Star for gallantry in action).

Fighting raged in the city streets until nightfall. When darkness came, the task force consolidated its positions near the town square and made plans to resume the attack in the morning. By 11 P.M., Major West was given two critical pieces of intelligence: First, the Germans had blown up all of the bridges across the Seine River. Second, they were now facing some 3500 fresh SS troops.

But there was some good news thrown into the mix as well. A bridge leading to a vital island located in the middle of the Seine was saved from destruction when 1st Lt. Stanley Lyons, accompanied by Corporal Joe Ham, drove off a band of Germans guarding the approaches. The men then made their way to two bombs that had been planted for the destruction of the bridge. Lyons and Ham disarmed the bombs by literally tearing the burning fuses from the charges and throwing them into the water, whereupon they exploded. The balance of their recon platoon then crossed the bridge and established a perimeter on the far shore, where they defended against German counterattacks.

Later that night, Lyons was ordered to attack across the developed island in the hope of capturing an intact bridge that led to the east bank of the Seine. To add some weight to the attack, Lyons brought along an M8 assault gun for support (a light tank mounting a 75mm howitzer).

At about 2 A.M., Lyons' platoon began advancing down the dark city street without meeting any resistance. The buildings were about three to five stories high, and tucked in close to the street. As the Americans turned onto the street leading toward one of the bridges, many of the doors and windows suddenly sprang open, sending a cascade of blinding light into the faces of Lyons' men. Illuminated on the sidewalk were perhaps a dozen German soldiers standing with bicycles. Lyons' men immediately opened fire on the Germans as well as the silhouettes in the doors and windows. The Germans were caught by surprise and cut down. Unfortunately, the figures that had appeared in the windows and doorways were French civilians who had unwisely decided to welcome their liberators in the dead of night. Their untimely celebration had unwittingly unveiled the German troops, but it also, in all likelihood, resulted in some of the civilians being killed or wounded.

It was also unfortunate that the eruption of gunfire apparently alerted the Germans who were defending the bridge. When Lyons' platoon got within about 50 yards of the bridge, a "huge, green flash followed by a terrific blast" signaled its destruction. After a brief exchange of gunfire with the Germans on the opposite bank of the river, Lyons' platoon withdrew. He and his recon platoon would return just a few hours later with a group of engineers to assess the damage to the bridge in daylight; en route, they would encounter a column of five German 105mm howitzers and their supporting vehicles, which they proceeded to cut to shreds. Six of the recon platoon members were wounded during the action at Troyes; among them, Lt. Lyons, who was shot through the arm during this final encounter.

The Germans had made their own plans for the following day. At first light, before the American attack got underway, the SS unit formed a column of a dozen vehicles and attempted to drive their way out of the city. As they made their way down one of the side streets, a Sherman tank from C/35 blocked their path and destroyed the two leading vehicles, setting them ablaze. Meanwhile, an American halftrack snuck around to the back of the German column, blocking it from behind. The two trucks at the rear of the column were knocked out, and also started to burn.

The narrow street the Germans had chosen for their escape route now became an unforgiving killing ground, as there was no way for any of their vehicles to escape. The column was like a candle being burned at both ends. The other eight trucks were caught in the middle, and the flames started to eat their way toward them. Some of the trucks were loaded with ammunition, and the resulting explosions rocked the center of town. As bullets and high explosives continued to rip into the enemy column, an inferno engulfed the vehicles.

There was no sympathy for the SS soldiers caught in the maelstrom, as some of their Nazi brethren had intentionally shot and killed Captain Silverman (the 10th Battalion's surgeon), one of the medics, and their driver (apparently, the men had been executed at close range with gunshots to the head). Word of the atrocity had quickly spread among the men of the task force, and vengeance was swift and sure. Five hundred and thirty three Germans were killed, and another 557 captured (a high ranking officer, one General Major Hans George Schamm, being among the captured).

Some of the surviving Germans managed to flee the city, but they ran smack into TF Oden. With the assist of some Thunderbolts from the XIX TAC, Oden's men delivered the coup de grâce. The SS Brigade was wiped out. The town was secured at 11 A.M., and the 53rd AIB came in to relieve TF West.

Toward the end of the day, General Wood reported his success at Troyes to the headquarters of XII Corps. Patton was present, and heard the details first hand from General Wood. Patton would later describe the battle as "a very magnificent feat of arms." Bruce Clarke had clearly won the attention and respect of George Patton.

The Fourth Armored Division learned several valuable lessons at Troyes. These were itemized at the end of an account of the battle prepared by the 10th Armored Infantry Battalion (Col. Clarke had the battalion's excellent account of the battle submitted to CCA to serve as the official record of the engagement). There is one lesson in particular that stands out above all the rest, and as we shall see, was put to good use in subsequent battles:

> Once we have organized a small defense position in the rear of the enemy, we can strike in any direction. We have found that even Hitler's own SS troops are terrified by this type of operation and it makes the job of killing Germans much easier.

Clarke's CCA wasn't the only part of the Fourth Armored seeing action on August 25. After securing Courtenay and Montargis, General Dager's CCB continued moving east in support of the right flank of the division. Later that day, they secured a crossing over the Yonne River, and advanced to the next objective of Auxon. During the advance, a Task Force commanded by Major Irzyk doubled back to the southwest where scattered groups of Germans had been spotted near Les Croutes. The problem was quickly dispensed with, and the division continued to forge ahead.

The Marne River Crossings

The complexion of the Fourth Armored Division's advance now began to change a bit. Ahead of the Fourth lay a number of river obstacles that could impose a delay, should the enemy manage to either defend the crossings, or blow the bridges before they could be captured. A certain sense of urgency developed regarding the crossing sites, and the Fourth drove forward with great vigor during the days ahead.

After polishing off the Germans at Troyes, CCA, which now consisted primarily of the 37th Tank Battalion, 53rd Armored Infantry, and 94th AFAB, continued its drive on August 26. Task Force Jaques sped across the Marne River north of Vitry-le-Francois. A second task force, under the command of Lt. Colonel Abrams, planned on crossing further north at the town of Mairy, and then would continue the advance to St. Germain. The bridge at Mairy was blown, however, so D/37 and C/10 forded the river and advanced alone to St. Germain. As they moved toward the town, they spotted a column of six trucks loaded with German infantry. The M5 light tanks of D/37 quickly destroyed the enemy force, and the men of C/10 moved in and occupied the town. In the meantime, the balance of Abrams' task force took up positions on the west bank of the Marne and waited for the engineers to put a bridge in place. The Shermans of A/37 were sent about 1000 yards north of Mairy to outpost the approaches to the town. They encountered a small enemy force in that area, and had no problem dispatching them. Once the bridge was constructed, the balance of the task force crossed, and moved into an assembly area west of L'Epine.

On August 29, both task forces resumed their advance, and the towns of Vitry and Chalons-sur-Marne fell in rapid fashion. Interestingly, the 80th Infantry Division, which was still deployed on the west side of the Marne, had made elaborate plans to assault Chalons-sur-Marne with a strong force composed of an infantry battalion supported by a company each of tanks and tank destroyers. Their plans were for naught when TF Abrams raced into Chalons ahead of them with a much smaller force (A/37 and C/53). No resistance was met, and the staff of the 37th took some pleasure in beating the 80th to the punch.

On August 30, the recon platoon, light tanks of D/37, and the 37th's assault gun platoon of three 105mm Shermans advanced toward St. Dizier. Two 88mm guns were encountered on the outskirts of town, and the vanguard disposed of them. Before moving into St. Dizier, Jaques ordered Captain McMahon's D/37 to capture the airfield south of town, while Leach's B/37 was ordered to envelope the town to the north, with the objective of capturing the small village of Chancenay, and in the process, cutting highway N.35 and the rail line leading to St. Dizier. Jaques then planned on sending the 53rd AIB directly into St. Dizier, with C/35 (commanded by Dick Miller) and the 94th AFAB in support.

The light tanks made quick work of the airfield, overrunning the facility and destroying three planes while they were still on the ground.

Meanwhile, Leach's medium tanks advance through the Foret de Trois-Fontaines and emerged just west of Chancenay. While closing on the town, a towed German anti-tank gun opened fire, hitting platoon leader Lt. Mixon's command tank with a deadly blow. The shell entered the right-front side of the tank hull, killing the driver, Sgt. Leonard Blume, and the Bow Gunner, Pfc. Arthur Connelly. Undeterred, Leach ordered his tanks to plunge into Chancenay. By the time the melee was over, the Americans had taken thirty Germans prisoner and seized a number of AA guns, mortars, machine guns, and anti-tank guns. Some thirty Allied POWs being held in the town were liberated (each year since the end of the war, the citizens of Chancenay lay a memorial wreath at a monument they erected at the site where Blume and Connelly were killed).

While Leach's company was engaged at Chancenay, Jaques proceeded with the attack on St. Dizier. C/35 and the 53rd Armored Infantry Battalion liberated the town after heavy fighting.

The speed of the Fourth Armored's advance produced an unexpected reward when the reconnaissance platoon captured a stock of more than 100,000 gallons of German gasoline at a location northeast of Chalons-sur-Marne. Lt. Donald E. Guild, a forward observer for the 94th AFAB, was responsible for the discovery of the gasoline. Guild and the crew of his Sherman tank had been sitting atop a ridge looking down into a small town nestled within the valley below. As he descended toward the town, he noticed, off to the side of the road, clumps of tree branches that appeared to be covering something. Upon investigation, he found the containers of gasoline, ripe for the taking.

They didn't know at the time just how valuable a catch this was. Within a matter of days, however, they would discover that, for an army bent on destroying the enemy in the waning days of August 1944, gasoline was more valuable than gold.

The gasoline shortage hit home for George Patton on August 29. It was on that day that 140,000 gallons of gas failed to arrive on schedule at the depots of the Third Army. The very next day, Patton was hard at work lobbying for more gasoline, but to no avail. Upon returning to his command post, he discovered that Eddy had halted the XII Corps for fear of running out of gas. It was at this point that Patton told him, in his words, "to continue until the tanks stopped, and then get out and walk." He later wrote "…it was mandatory to get crossings over the Meuse. In the last war, I drained three-quarters of my tanks in order to advance the other quarter, and I felt Eddy could do the same."

As CCA forged ahead, CCB followed up behind them, and on August 28, traced CCA's footsteps over the Seine River. As the men of the 51st AIB traveled down the road near Troyes, they saw the carnage that CCA had wrought. It was noted in the battalion diary, "destroyed German vehicles were strewn all along the road. It looked as if an entire enemy column, including field artillery units, had been destroyed."

That evening, the 51st AIB and 8th Tank Battalion settled into positions near the village of Piney. The following morning, there were reports that the 15th Panzer Grenadier Division was moving toward their positions, but no threats materialized. As the Americans took over positions previously occupied by the Germans, they found a note, addressed to the Americans, warning them that they would be back in four weeks. Of course, the enemy would never set foot in Piney again. The German bravado was laughable.

On August 31, CCB met with strong enemy resistance right from the outset. The advance came to an abrupt halt when the Americans encountered a blown bridge at the Marne River. That afternoon, C/51 forded the river, and the engineers from the 24th Armored Engineer Battalion erected a temporary bridge before nightfall, which allowed the tanks of the 8th Tank Battalion to continue on after dusk toward the town of Chevillon. Heavy resistance was encountered, but CCB pushed through, and bivouacked for the balance of the night at a location east of the town. The Germans made an attempt to retaliate, mostly with indirect artillery shelling. During the period between 10:45 A.M. and 4:30 P.M., 364 enemy rounds landed in the area of the 37th Tank Battalion. Company C of the 10th AIB reported, "enemy shells poured in incessantly for three hours." The German's ability to put together this level of artillery support was an early sign that their defenses were starting to gel.

The Luftwaffe Strikes Back

Many popular accounts of the 1944 campaign in northwest Europe paint a picture of complete Allied dominance of the air, and would lead one to believe that Allied ground troops were virtually immune from harassment by the Luftwaffe. This charac-

A Sherman from the 8th Tank Battalion fires at German positions located across the Marne River. The men of the 8th frequently used foliage to camouflage their tanks. August 31, 1944 (National Archives Photograph SC193670).

terization is far from the truth, however. In the records of the Fourth Armored Division alone, there are numerous instances when German planes bombed, strafed, and harassed the men on the ground. The Fourth Armored was wary of the skies, and remained disciplined when it came to obeying blackout rules at night, and maintaining proper vehicle spacing while on a road march.

The need to exercise caution was never more evident than during the final days of August and early days of September. During that time frame, as the Fourth Armored approached the Meuse River, they seemed to become a magnet for German planes. The 94th AFAB, for example, was hit by a group of twelve ME-109 aircraft, followed by a heavy concentration of counter-battery fire from German artillery. One of the M7s caught fire, and the crew scattered. Some of the men were wounded, and one man, Technician 5th Grade Alexander Dubovy, was killed. As the ammunition on board the stricken M7 began to explode, Colonel Graham raced to the self-propelled howitzer, mounted the vehicle, and attacked the flames with a fire extinguisher. Motivated by his leadership, other men raced to help, and the gun was saved. On another day, the 94th recorded an attack by 40 to 50 planes. Fortunately, the Luftwaffe pilots failed to do any damage. Similarly, the 10th Armored Infantry Battalion recorded a strafing attack by 30 enemy planes on September 1. The armored infantry shared the luck of the 94th, as there were no casualties.

The 66th Armored Field Artillery Battalion wasn't as lucky. A force of 29 FW 190 and JU88 aircraft struck their positions, hitting them hard. Six Americans were killed, and 57 wounded. Nine of the enemy planes were shot down in return. As these same aircraft headed home from their strike against the American artillery, they passed back over the positions of the 37th, and attacked with bombs, rockets, and machine guns. The men of the 37th returned fire with their .50 caliber machine guns, and managed to shoot down three of the enemy aircraft.

When speaking of the Luftwaffe in the context of the Fourth Armored Division, it is a major oversight if one does not make a special mention of the 489th Anti Aircraft Artillery (AW) Battalion. Though not an integral part of the division, it was attached to the Fourth for the duration of the war; the men of the Fourth considered the 489th to be one of their own. During the course of the campaign in Europe, this unit established a record among all units in the European Theatre of Operations by shooting down 134 enemy planes. The battalion also holds the record for the number of planes shot down in a single 24-hour period (35). The men of the 489th were one more reason why the Fourth Armored Division could lay claim to being the best.

On to the Meuse

With both combat commands now in forward positions, Clarke and Dager were given more daring orders. On August 31, CCA would strike east in order to secure crossings over the Meuse River at Commercy. CCB, which was still crossing the Marne that day, would shoot for a crossing of the Meuse east of Vaucouleurs on September 1.

With the reconnaissance platoon and D/37 leading the way, CCA made a rapid advance and soon reached the intermediate objective of Stainville. After securing the town, a report came in from D Troop of the 25th Armored Cavalry Squadron that an enemy column was in the town of Ligny En Barrois, through which CCA would have to advance. The bridge at this location was mined, but rather than wait for engineers or infantry support, D/37 charged across the bridge and scattered the Germans before they could destroy the structure.

As the advance continued, a torrential rain began to fall, limiting the visibility of the column. D/37 led the way once again and raced ahead through the downpour into Commercy. The Germans were ready to defend the bridges with four deadly 88s, but Abrams' tankers beat the enemy gun crews to the punch. The 88s had been covered to protect them during the downpour, and before the breechblocks could be opened, the tanks of D Company blazed away with their .30 caliber machine guns and shot the defenders down in their tracks. Dead Germans and their weapons lay silent under the cascading sheets of water, crushed by a rain of steel delivered by the men of D/37. Once again, the right combination of speed, movement, and firepower had carried the day, as the bridge over the Meuse at Commercy was captured intact.

With the site of the bridge secured, A/37 moved toward the north end of town in order to guard the approaches against a possible enemy counterattack. En route, the tankers came across a railroad yard that was occupied by German troops. A fully loaded troop train sat idle on the tracks, while other Germans were assembled in a nearby courtyard for lunch. As the German soldiers ate outside, their commanding officers dined in the comfort of adjacent buildings. The tanks of A/37, under the command of 1st Lt. Turner, wreaked havoc on the unsuspecting enemy force. In addition to 100 prisoners and an uncounted number of dead Germans, A/37 destroyed two 88mm guns, three locomotives, and seven trucks. They also captured another large quantity of priceless gasoline. By nightfall, Commercy was secured, and the task force had advanced to the high ground about four miles east of town.

That evening, the 66th Armored Field Artillery Battalion, still feeling the sting of the 63 casualties they incurred during the air raid, had an opportunity to avenge their losses. A retreating enemy column was spotted, and the 66th was called upon for a fire mission. The 66th threw down a heavy barrage on top of the German troops and vehicles, inflicting tremendous losses. One hundred German soldiers were killed, and 150 wounded. Five tanks and a dozen other vehicles were destroyed. It was an awesome display of firepower by the men and guns of the 66th AFAB.

CCA was already across the Meuse when CCB tackled its respective crossing site. The 8th Tank Battalion set out early on September 1 with the objective of crossing the river at a site east of the town of Vaucouleurs. The level of resistance facing the tankers was on the wane, and the advance to Vaucouleurs was made against very light opposition. The town was captured early that afternoon, clearing the way for an advance to the bridge site. Sensing that the enemy had gone into retreat, CCB forged ahead and seized the bridge over the Meuse. The column pushed forward, and at 3:45 P.M., moved into and then through Sepvigny. The Americans then established a position on top of a large hill overlooking the Meuse River. CCB's progress that day on the right flank of the division was significant, as it registered an advance of a bit over 37 miles. With their bridgehead firmly established, CCB came to a halt, as had CCA at the Commercy crossing site.

The Advance Grinds to a Halt

The delay before resuming the advance would be longer than expected. The reason for the extended stop was totally unanticipated by the enlisted men of the Fourth: the Third Army had reached the end of its logistical tether, and was almost literally out of gas. The threat of empty fuel tanks accomplished what the Germans could not: with only 60 miles separating the Fourth Armored Division from the German border, the tanks were stopped in their tracks.

During its first six weeks of action, the Fourth Armored had established new benchmarks for the performance of American armor. They had achieved their assigned missions in brilliant fashion. Wood's men had given new meaning to the names of towns and cities like Coutances, Avranches, Rennes, Orleans, Troyes, and Commercy. Each of these cities would forever represent major victories for the Fourth Armored Division. And there were countless other victories along the way, many of them at

General Wood near Piney, France. August 27, 1944 (National Archives Photograph SC193741).

obscure villages and towns whose names would bring back memories of sacrifice and courage for decades to follow for the men who were there and lived through it.

Patton was quick to point out to all who would listen that his Third Army had advanced further and faster than any of his counterparts. He was also not ashamed to take credit for the feat, as evidenced by a letter to his wife on September 1, in which he noted "Really I am amazed at the amount of ground the Third Army has taken, and it is chiefly due to me alone." Patton probably could have found some men within the Fourth Armored Division who would have taken exception to that remark.

But now, with the Allies experiencing severe logistical problems, the bold dash across France had drawn to a close. The main war to be fought over the next few days was one of politics between nations and generals over the matter of where the main Allied thrust would take place. All that General Wood could do was consolidate his positions until adequate supplies could be brought forward.

It was during this time that Hitler's forces in the west managed to piece together enough troops to confront the advancing Allied forces. Though the Fourth Armored only remained idle for a week and a half, it was just the amount of time that Hitler's generals needed to pull off a minor miracle. With the front now so very close to their own border, there were able to rush new units into position. Also aiding them was the fact that increasingly poor weather and cloud cover helped shield the German columns from the threat of attack by American planes. This allowed them to reinforce the front faster than they could have, had they been on constant alert for the dreaded *jabos* of the XIX Tactical Air Command. From this point forward, the Fourth Armored Division would find itself in a whole new ballgame.

4. The Encirclement of Nancy

An Unwanted Respite

On September 2, Omar Bradley, Courtney Hodges, and George Patton met with General Eisenhower at Chartres, France. Eisenhower used the occasion to unveil his plan for the First and Third armies. To Patton's dismay, both of the American armies were to play a supporting role behind Montgomery's 21st Army Group. But the American generals had gone into the meeting with their own idea on how they should proceed, and managed to convince Eisenhower to allow them to push across the Moselle River. When supplies permitted, they would then press on from the Moselle bridgeheads to assault the Siegfried Line.

This was certainly not what Patton wanted. Given his druthers, he would have had his own Third Army leading the Allied charge to the Rhine and beyond. Instead, he was relegated to an advance made in opportunistic increments. But at least it was better than sitting on his hands while Monty was the only one attacking in force.

Patton left the meeting with some interesting thoughts swirling through his head. Later that day, he wrote in his diary, "Ike did not thank or congratulate any of us for what we had done." It is interesting that Patton felt slighted by what he seemed to consider a faux pas on Ike's part. One would think that his bombastic and braggadocios personality, coupled with his self-professed level of self-confidence, made him immune from that sort of sensitivity. Perhaps Patton's propensity for patting himself on the back was a factor behind Eisenhower's perceived oversight. Most would agree that there was no need to fuel Patton's ego, but his diary entry would seem to indicate that deep down, he was more fragile than some might suspect.

The day after the meeting at Chartres, Patton visited Manton Eddy in order to explain Eisenhower's new plan. During this visit, he was informed for the first time that substantial gasoline stocks had been captured. With extra fuel in hand, Patton now had the resources available to resume his attack in the sort of incremental fashion he had won approval for at Chartres. Even with the benefit of the captured gasoline, how-

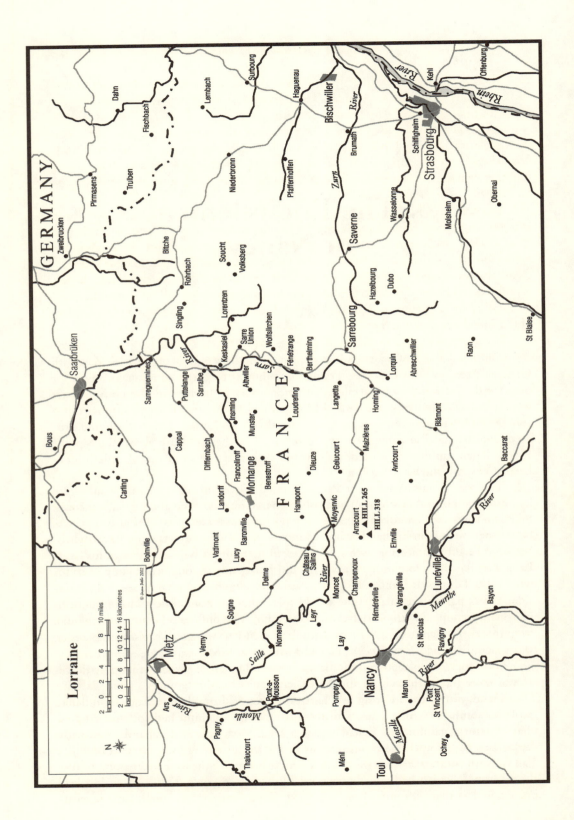

ever, there was not enough fuel available to make a strong attack involving all of Patton's divisions. Some elements of the Third Army began advancing again on September 5, but the effort was very limited in scope.

After Patton and Eddy finished their meeting, they departed together for a visit with the 80th Infantry Division. On his way back, Patton stopped to meet with Colonel Clarke. He was briefed on CCA's success at Vitry, which he later described as "another remarkable feat of arms." Bruce Clarke was making quite an impression on Patton.

During the lull imposed upon the Third Army, Montgomery's 21st Army Group kept moving forward, thanks in large part to the gasoline that had been diverted from Patton. They swept into Brussels on September 3, and the vital port city of Antwerp on the fourth. Unfortunately, Montgomery failed to have the foresight to clear and safeguard the waterways leading into Antwerp. It would be almost twelve weeks before supplies could be brought into the port (the first shipments arrived on November 26). The failure to immediately clear the Scheldt Estuary was one of the biggest blunders of the Allied campaign in northwest Europe.

During their imposed respite, XII Corps began making plans for the next phase of operations. Eddy's immediate objective would be the city of Nancy, which sat about 8 miles behind the line of the Moselle River and immediately west of the Meurthe River. Nancy was rivaled only by Metz as the most prominent objective in the Third Army's zone. The enemy would certainly make a concerted effort to keep the city from falling into Patton's hands.

Critical Decisions

Following the meeting at Chartres, the wrangling between the top Allied commanders continued. Montgomery was not happy about the fact that Patton had gained permission to continue his advance, and was even less happy that Ike had slightly increased Patton's supply of gasoline. After their meeting with Ike, Bradley and Patton did not leave well enough alone, and both men continued to lobby for more supplies and weight to be added to the 12th Army Group's axis of advance.

While all of this posturing was going on amongst his generals, Ike had yet to fully define the role of the 12th and 21st Army Groups. The Supreme Commander would have to make some critical decisions during the first two weeks of September in order to provide the Allied armies with their ultimate direction.

The disagreement between the generals was clear. Montgomery still argued for a strong, consolidated punch on the Allied left flank. In Montgomery's plan, Patton's Third Army and General Devers 6th Army Group would simply screen the right flank, as the balance of the Allied Armies drove through Belgium and Holland and erupted upon the open plains of northern Germany. This, Montgomery argued, would ensure the capture of the vital Ruhr industrial area, and pave the way for a drive to Berlin.

In stark contrast, Patton wanted the major thrust to be placed at the point of furthest advance, which had already been established by his own Third Army. His lead units were less than 100 miles from the Rhine River, and given enough supplies, Patton was confident that he could carry the river and create a situation that would undermine German resolve to salvage their positions on the West Front. Now that he was joined on his right by Allied forces advancing north after the invasion of the Mediterranean coast of France, he felt confident that he could execute a swift and decisive attack into the German interior; an attack which would include an over-run of the vital Saar industrial region.

Eisenhower settled for neither of these plans. Instead, he adopted a plan for a broad advance that failed to give the Allied armies a decisive concentration of force at any point along the front (he reiterated this plan in a written directive issued to his generals on September 4). He also made the critical decision of approving a plan by Montgomery — called Operation Market Garden — that would involve a parachute drop by three veteran airborne divisions (the American 82nd and 101st, and the British 1st). The plan was designed to secure the bridges over the Maas River in Holland and a bridge over the Rhine River at Arnhem. To make this happen, materials and supplies were dispensed with favor to the forces in the north, and Patton's operations came to a relative standstill as a result.

The German Situation

The timing of all this could not have been more fortunate for Hitler, since the Germans had yet to establish a truly cohesive defense in front of Patton's forces. The truth, as later acknowledged by the Germans themselves, was that a well-supplied Third Army could have been at the banks of the Rhine River in a matter of days. But the Allies' self-imposed delay gave the Germans the opportunity to rush hastily formed units into positions along their border. The cities of Aachen and Metz would become solidified defensive positions, and Hitler would even prove capable of raising Panzer formations that would seek to blunt the advance of Patton's forward elements. In a matter of one to two weeks, the great opportunity that had presented itself to General Eisenhower had evaporated, and the Germans were now in a position to defend their border. Aided by deteriorating weather, the prepared defenses of the Siegfried line, and the extra motivation of defending their native soil, the Germans were able to significantly reduce the pace of the Allied advance, and brought it to an outright halt along some sections of the front.

Reconstituting the line along Germany's western border wasn't the only grave concern facing Hitler. As the drama in the west was unfolding, the Soviets had been moving steadily forward in the east. On the Russian front, the Germans struggled to defend a line that stretched from the Baltic to the Aegean Seas. By September 1944, the Soviets had driven beyond their own borders, and had pushed troops into Poland, Romania, and Bulgaria. Seeing the writing on the wall, Romania, Bulgaria, and Finland came to terms with Stalin. The capitulation of Romania, in particular, left the German Army in a very precarious position, and the Soviets exploited it by punching through to Yugoslavia in short order. Hitler was losing his allies as well as his territory, and there seemed to be no realistic options for reversing the tide. Pressed from all sides, and still suffering both physically and mentally from the attempt on his life on July 20, Hitler was a desperate man searching for a way to avoid the complete collapse of his once expansive empire.

The German Plans

Hitler's focus in early September turned toward the debacle in the west, and one of his top priorities was stopping George S. Patton, who he saw as the biggest threat among the advancing Allied armies.

The Germans hastened to throw a defensive barrier before Patton's army. Three panzer grenadier divisions became the centerpiece of their effort to beef up the First Army, which was charged with the defense of this sector. Two of the three panzer grenadier divisions were brought up from Italy (the 3rd and the 15th), and were in good fighting condition, all things considered. The third was a reconstituted division that had been chewed up in Normandy (the 17th SS). All three of the divisions were under-strength to varying degrees, but very experienced. The deployment of the three panzer grenadier divisions was a critical development; before their arrival, the German First Army had only 9 battalions of infantry, a small handful of field and anti-tank guns, three Flak batteries, and a meager ten tanks with which to oppose the entire U.S. Third Army.

The 3rd Panzer Grenadier Division was assigned to guard the zone north of Nancy, while the 15th Panzer Grenadier Division occupied the area to the south. The 553rd Volksgrenadier Division, along with an attached regiment of Luftwaffe personnel, was responsible for the defense of Nancy itself. At Hitler's direction, the Germans used the time bought by the panzer grenadier divisions to begin gathering yet more force for offensive purposes (more about that development in the next chapter).

The American Plans

There was strong dissension within XII Corps regarding the best way to tackle Nancy. General Eddy's plan called for the 35th Infantry and 4th Armored divisions to attack south of the city. They would secure bridgeheads over the Moselle in that sector, and then cut off Nancy from behind by way of a thrust to the north. This plan was drawn up in the wake of a failed — and costly — series of attempts by the 80th Infantry Division to secure bridgeheads north of Nancy on September 5. Given the strong rebuff that the 80th had received at the hands of the aforementioned 3rd Panzer Grenadier Division, Eddy felt that the German positions along the river north of Nancy would be a tougher nut to crack, now that the defenders had the benefit of another week to shore up their defenses.

General Wood, however, favored another strike north of the city. His reasoning was simple: in that zone, only the Moselle had to be bridged. To the south of Nancy, there were a series of at least seven canals and tributaries that would have to be crossed, in addition to the Moselle. Wood was so disenchanted with Eddy's plan that he phoned the XII Corps' Chief of Staff, Colonel Ralph Canine, and informed him that, "My peo-

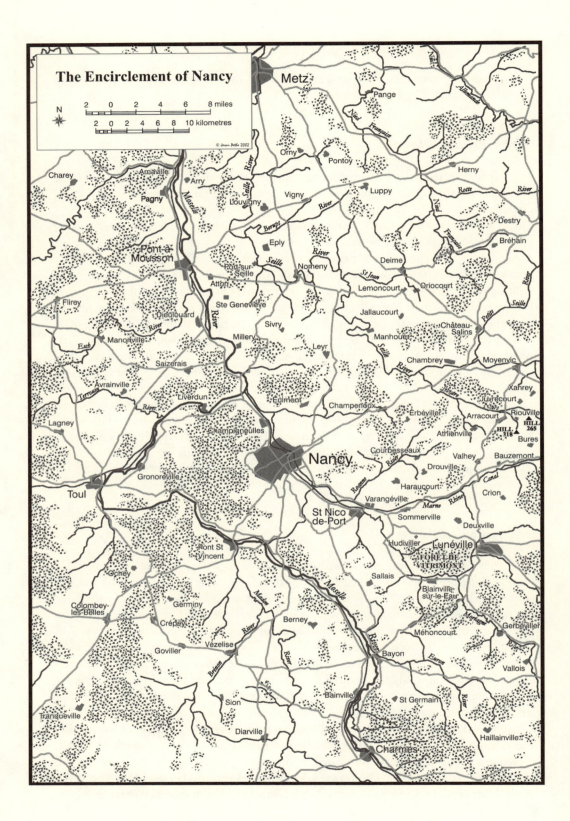

The Encirclement of Nancy

Metz

Pange

Orny

Pontoy

Herny

Charey

Arnaville

Arry

Vigny

Luppy

Rotte River

Pagny

L'ouvigny

River

Destry

Moselle

Eply

Seille River

Deime

Bréhain

Pont-à-Mousson

Port-sur-Seille

Nomeny

Lemoncourt

Oriocourt

Flirey

Atton

Sivry

Jallaucourt

Château-Salins

Dieulouard

Ste Geneviève

Seille

Manoncourt

Millery

Leyr

Chambrey

Moyenvic

Manonville

Saizerais

Champenoux

Xanrey

Avrainville

Liverdun

Eulmont

Érbéviller

Juvrecourt

Riouville

Arracourt

HILL 265

Lagney

Champigneulles

HILL 318

Bures

Courbesseaux

Athienville

Valhey

Bauzemont

Gronoreville

Nancy

Drouville

Toul

Haraucourt

Crion

Varangéville

Marne Rhine Canal

St Nico de-Port

Sommerville

Deuxville

Pont St Vincent

Hudiviller

Lunéville

Ochey

Sallais

FORÊT DE VITRIMONT

Colombey-les-Belles

Germiny

Blainville-sur-le-Eau

Gerbéviller

Crépey

Berney

Méhoncourt

Goviller

Vézelise

Bayon

Vallois

Sion

Bainville

St Germain

Diarville

Haillainville

Charmes

A Sherman of the 8th Tank Battalion fords a canal near Bayon. September 20, 1944 (National Archives Photograph SC19550).

ple are appalled at this thing." Wood had his staff draw up a plan that called for the entire Fourth Armored Division to strike across the Moselle north of Nancy, and then create an envelopment by attacking south, thus cutting across the rear of the 553rd VG Division.

Wood failed to sell his plan to Eddy, but his persistence earned him a compromise: Eddy would once again order the 80th Infantry Division to attack north of Nancy,

The countryside near Nancy, by S/Sgt. Frank Besedick (courtesy K. Besedick).

but only after the 35th Infantry Division and CCB/4 attacked south of the city, in order to draw the German's attention away from the 80th ID's crossing sites. CCA/4 would be held in XII Corps reserve, and would be used to exploit an opening on either the north or south zones, depending on when and where it occurred. The combined actions of the three divisions would result in a double envelopment of Nancy.

On September 8, prior to the start of the Nancy offensive, Patton and Eddy visited with General Wood. Patton later remarked that his friend's headquarters "was too close to the front." Enemy shells were literally dropping across the road from where they sat, and they could see and hear combat in the immediate area. While his comment seemed to indicate that he believed it more prudent if Wood had positioned his headquarters farther to the rear, he couldn't help but show his admiration for "P'"s leadership style when he noted, "it was very refreshing to find a man who got up that close."

CCB and the Fording of the Moselle

On September 11, Wood's Division was adequately re-supplied and ready to move. CCB's 8th Tank Battalion got the ball rolling as it advanced to positions near the town of Bayon, located along the Moselle some twenty miles south of Nancy. CCB was to attack in conjunction with the 35th Infantry Division, which had already closed in on the river.

The classic tank crossing of a major river unfolds with the infantry crossing the river first, in an effort to secure the opposite bank. The infantry has to either wade

A 76mm Sherman tank crosses a canal near Bayon. September 20, 1944 (National Archives Photograph SC195102).

across the river or use boats. Once across in force, they widen their territory on the opposite bank to give the engineers some breathing room to install a bridge. Once the bridge is in, the tanks and other supporting units cross the river, pass through the bridgehead held by the infantry on the far shore, and resume the offensive.

In this case, the 35th Infantry Division was assigned the task of securing the bridgehead. Unfortunately, they were coming up short. After putting a battalion of infantry across the river on September 10, they were forced to withdraw after their bridge was destroyed by German artillery fire. Renewed efforts on September 11 were more successful, but still, they only had a relatively small infantry force across the river, and it was under heavy fire from the Germans; there was little hope that the engineers would be able to start work on a bridge anytime soon. The tanks of the 8th Tank Battalion closed in on the river, expecting that they would be able to cross at the 35th's bridgehead. But instead, they discovered that they had no avenue of advance.

Rather than sit back and support the 35th from the west bank of the river, the 8th Tank Battalion, sensing it could break things loose in more dramatic fashion, pulled back from the 35th Division's crossing site and headed north, parallel to the river. After coming to a stop, Major Irzyk (the advance guard commander) and Lt. William C. "Bill" Marshall (the commander of the lead platoon of C/8), stared upon the river in front of them and took note of the fact that, at this point in its course, the nature of the Moselle was quite different than the site where the 35th was trying to establish its bridgehead. Rather than a single, swift moving river, the Moselle was now a series of three separate water obstacles, as canals branched off both sides of the river. In between the canal and the river were stretches of sandy ground covered with short underbrush.

The canal immediately in front of them was no minor obstacle by any means. The water was normally deep enough to allow for barge traffic. But as the tankers viewed the canal on this day, the water level was extremely low (the locks having been closed or perhaps damaged), and the steep, high banks were fully exposed. Though the water level was low, the bottom of the canal was filled with a deep, oozing sludge that could easily trap a tank attempting to cross. Conventional wisdom said that a bridge was a must-have if the 8th was going to continue its advance.

Anxious to cross, and faced with the fact that the Germans had blown every bridge in the sector, Major Irzyk turned to Marshall and asked, "Bill, can you do it?" With a look of determination, Marshall nodded and shot back, without hesitation, "We'll do our damnedest." With that, Marshall scouted the riverbank for the best spot to attempt a crossing.

Once he settled on a location, Marshall prepared for his dash across the canal in two steps: first by throwing logs into the area where his tank would enter the water, and second, by having his platoon of Shermans fire high explosive rounds into the steep east bank. The shells, which were set on a fuse delay, burrowed into the soft earth on the embankment and then exploded. The force of the explosion caused the earth walls of the canal to crumble, eventually reducing the grade that the tanks would have to climb when they reached the other side.

With the stage set, Marshall led the way in his own command tank. The Sherman raced down the log platform on the west bank and into the canal, its tracks fighting to gain a grip in the mud. The tank inched forward in low gear as it struggled to gain traction. But it never stopped advancing. Finally, the tank reached the opposite bank, and began to climb out of the canal. As the treads began to bite into increasingly drier ground, it pulled itself up to the rim of the canal wall. With a final roar of the engine, the tank surged up and over the crest of the embankment.

After emerging victorious on the opposite side, Marshall signaled for the rest of the platoon to follow. A tow cable was brought out and tied between Marshall's tank and the next tank in line to cross. The next Sherman went over the west bank on its own power, and then was given the assist of a tow to cross over and climb the opposite bank. The weight of the Shermans eventually collapsed the bank to the point where they no longer needed the assist to climb out, and the other tanks that followed came across completely under their own power.

Safely across the canal, Marshall's men now stared at the more imposing Moselle. Marshall selected a crossing point, dismounted from his tank, and waded into the swiftly flowing water to determine the depth. One thing was for sure: it was going to be close. The depth of the water didn't leave much room for error.

Once again, Marshall made his own tank the first one over the west bank. The Sherman moved forward deliberately, easing down the bank and into the muddy water of the Moselle. With every yard gained, the water rose steadily, first engulfing the tracks, and as it neared the midpoint of the river, rising to the sides of the tank. Fearing that the engine would be flooded if the water got any deeper, the driver, Corporal Ray Fisk, gunned his engine in the hope that his momentum would carry him through to shallower water past the mid point of the river. The tank gripped the bottom of the riverbed and, rather than stall, it quickly bolted forward into increasingly shallower depths. Without letting up speed, the tank hit the east bank, and with water cascading off the hull and spitting from the treads, it found dry land. Marshall's platoon followed suit, and then moved on to the third leg of the crossing. The canal east of the Moselle presented the same opportunity as the one to the west.

The balance of the 8th Tank Battalion followed Marshall's lead, and by nightfall, all three medium tank companies and the light tank company were across, and had secured the high ground east of the river. Tank destroyers from the 704th also forded the river to supplement the 8th's firepower.

Not all of the tanks made it across the Moselle without help, as some of the drivers failed to duplicate Fisk's timing for gunning through the deepest part of the river, and found themselves stalled and in need of a tow from the opposite bank. Phil Hosey, a member of the 704th TD Battalion, later provided a description of the crossing that illustrates just how touch and go it was for some of the armored vehicles during the crossing:

> ...we were told to go upstream and ford the river. The spot was chosen for us, but being of a suspicious nature, we buttoned up the driver and assistant, and the three of us in the turret sat on its upper edge. The book says fording maximum is four feet. This looked like more. We plunged in, and soon the water was coming down the gun barrel and pouring in around the turret top. I thought all was lost, for the driver and assistant were under one foot of water. So was the whole engine deck. Miraculously, the driver gunned the engine and it didn't stop. Luckily, this was the deepest spot of the crossing, but we made it. The book says that the height of the tank is seven-and-one-half feet. We must have forded at six-and-one-half!

While the crossing had been undertaken without much interference from the enemy, contact with the Germans would be made soon after the battalion established their positions on the east bank. Elements of the 553rd Volksgrenadier and 15th Panzer Grenadier divisions were committed to the battle for the purpose of pushing the Americans back across the river (the panzer grenadiers of the 15th were easily distinguished from other units the Fourth Armored had faced, since they were still adorned with the khaki uniforms they had worn in Italy). Before darkness came, D/8 pushed north of the new bridgehead, and proceeded to support the infantry of the 35th ID that had waded across the Moselle further down stream. The arrival of Lt. "Blackie" Blackburn's platoon of M5 light tanks was timely, and helped blunt the German counterattack in that sector.

The presence of the Shermans on the east bank provided the supporting engineers with some breathing room to work on installing a bridge, which was still a must if the other vehicles of CCB were to cross. The Germans tried to disrupt the engineers' effort all through the night of September 11 and into the morning of the 12th. They brought down heavy concentrations of artillery at the site where the bridge was being constructed, but it failed to stop the engineers. During the day on September 12, the engineers opened up their new 168-foot floating bridge to traffic. Thanks to the sheer will and determination of the 8th Tank Battalion to get across the river, a sound bridge-head was secured. Lt. Marshall was later awarded the Distinguished Service Cross for playing such a pivotal role in the crossing.

False Start at Bainville

While the 8th Tank Battalion was fording the river near Bayon, the 51st Armored Infantry Battalion was preparing to cross the Moselle at a point further south. At the proposed crossing site, there was a damaged bridge that could be repaired and put to use. The plan called for the infantry to move to the line of the river, cross in boats, and then expand the bridgehead in order to give the engineers room to work on repairing the bridge. A company of tanks, tank destroyers, artillery, and a platoon of engineers were attached for support during the operation.

Early on the morning of September 11, the 51st AIB assembled about two miles northwest of the enemy-held town of Bainville. There was a long delay as the armored infantry waited for the boats to arrive. During that time, a patrol from A/51 pressed up to the line of the river and located a ford. They reported their find, but remained on the west bank. As the day wore on and the boats failed to appear, a decision was made to put the battalion across at the ford, rather than continue to wait for the delivery of the boats.

A/51 forded the river at 3 P.M. against light resistance. Before any of the other units would cross, however, a decision was made to secure Bainville, which was on the west bank and could pose a threat to the rear of the bridgehead once the task force had crossed over. C/51was assigned the task of capturing the town.

As the armored infantrymen approached Bainville, they were met with mortars, artillery, and small arms fire. This did not deter their advance, and they attacked the town in routine fashion. Once the enemy resistance was neutralized and the town occupied and secured, C/51 moved up to the river and crossed at a spot to the left of A/51's positions on the east bank. In contrast to A/51's relatively easy occupation of the east bank, C Company ran into stiff resistance once they got across. After suffering 35 casualties, they retreated back across the river and took up positions in Bainville. Meanwhile, not knowing that C/51 had pulled back, A/51 started to patrol to their left in an attempt to make contact with C Company.

Once it became known that C/51 had run into trouble, B/51 was brought up from reserve to take over A Company's positions, so that A Company could shift left into the positions that C Company had vacated. When A Company pushed to their left in force, they encountered some of the enemy forces that had dealt C/51 such a heavy blow just a few hours before. After destroying an enemy machine gun position, A/51 dug in for the balance of the night, as did B/51 to their right. C/51 remained on the west side of the river at Bainville.

After sitting tight most of the following day, the entire 51st AIB was ordered to pull back and move toward the bridgehead gained by the 8th Tank Battalion. With C/51 covering, A/51 and B/51 withdrew across the river. By 6 P.M., the 51st AIB had assembled near the town of Villacourt, where they would remain for the night.

Meanwhile, the 8th Tank Battalion, along with other elements of CCB that had crossed over the new bridge, found themselves under increasing pressure from the enemy on September 12 and 13. The Shermans had established excellent firing positions on the east side of the river, and on September 12, A/8 destroyed three tanks, four half tracks, and several wheeled vehicles. Companies B and C were having success as well. By midday on September 13, the Americans had reinforced the Moselle bridgehead, and CCB was prepared to renew its advance.

The Advance of CCA

Buoyed by the news of a successful crossing of the Moselle by CCB/4 on September 11, Eddy instructed the 80th Infantry Division to renew its effort north of Nancy that very afternoon. The double envelopment was underway.

General Wood took advantage of the availability of CCA to exercise the attack that he longed for north of Nancy. Colonel Clarke originally hoped to pass CCA through a bridgehead to be secured by the 80th Infantry Division at Pont-a-Mousson. But the 80th had difficulty making the crossing, and CCA sat idle. Growing impatient, Clarke decided to use his attached battalion from the 318th Infantry Regiment to forge a crossing of his own near Pagny. With the 94th AFAB firing in support, the 318th and supporting engineers struggled on September 11 and 12 to secure a bridgehead. The difficulty of their task was compounded on the night of the eleventh when a bulldozer from the Fourth Armored "slid off the bank into the river in the dark and could not be recovered." A shortage of bridging equipment served as an additional source of frustration.

As they labored during the second day, Clarke and Wood became aware that the 80th Infantry Division had secured a bridgehead over the Moselle near the town of Dieulouard, located approximately 15 miles north of Nancy. Rather than continue to force a crossing at Pagny, Clarke decided to take advantage of the success at Dieulouard, where the engineers had already installed a series of three bridges, the last of which spanned the Moselle. On the afternoon of the twelfth, Colonel Clarke began to prepare CCA for the move over to the 80th ID's crossing site. His lead task force would set out at 4 A.M. on September 13. After crossing the river, the vanguard would head for Chateau Salins.

D Troop of the 25th Armored Cavalry Squadron, which was leading CCA, was the first unit to arrive at the bridge, but was not allowed to cross. Apparently, a control officer from XII Corps wanted to put all of the supporting artillery units on notice that friendly armor would be coming through the bridgehead, and was determined to hold back D Troop until the communication was made. While D Troop sat idle, the rest of CCA's lead task force had stopped at an assembly area west of the bridgehead in order to load up on gas before attacking through the bridgehead.

As D Troop sat at the foot of the first bridge, the situation on the east end of the third bridge had changed dramatically. At 1:00 A.M. on the thirteenth, the 3rd Panzer Grenadier Division launched a strong counterattack against the Dieulouard bridgehead. The enemy employed a battalion of panzer grenadiers from the 29th PG Regiment and ten StuG III assault guns in an attempt to dislodge the Americans. They were having success; the bridgehead was being compressed, and the men of the 80th Infantry Division appeared in danger of losing their grip on the east bank of the Moselle. They would have certainly lost their hold, were it not for the accurate fire delivered by the guns of the 702nd Tank Battalion, which forced the German armor to retreat. But as dawn approached, German infantry were on the verge of capturing the bridge furthest to the east, having drawn as close as 100 yards.

As the situation grew increasingly desperate, the control officer at the bridge finally relented and let D Troop pass during the waning moments of darkness. The M8 armored cars, under the command of Captain Charles Trover, raced across the first two spans, and upon reaching the third, spotted some of the German infantry on the bridge. Trover's men broke up the enemy attack and drove the Germans back toward the towns of Loisy and Ste. Genevieve. For the moment, some of the pressure on the bridgehead was relaxed (when Patton later learned of CCA's assist at the bridgehead, he would praise "the ubiquitous Colonel Bruce Clarke" for driving the Germans back. In this instance, Captain Trover was more worthy of the praise).

With their tanks and halftracks refueled, the balance of CCA, led by Lt. Colonel Abrams' 37th Tank Battalion, closed up to the crossing site. CCA's intent was to break out of the bridgehead and rush forward some 20 miles to the town of Chateau-Salins. But the situation at the bridgehead was still tenuous at best. In fact, the engineers were actually preparing the bridge for demolition, in the event the 80th couldn't hold its position on the east bank. Captain Trover was still holding his own with his light armored vehicles, but when the StuG III's appeared near Ste. Genevieve, he sent back a radio message: "That I can't handle." Trover pulled back onto "the reverse slope of the heights and reported to (Clarke) that he would hold his ground until the main body came through."

While D Troop was fighting valiantly to keep the bridge in American hands, a high level pow-wow took place on the west side of the river. Eddy, Wood, Clarke, Abrams, and McBride (the commanding general of the 80th Infantry Division) huddled to discuss their options. After some doubts were expressed about CCA's ability to pass safely into the bridgehead, Eddy asked Colonel Clarke, "Do you think you can make it?" Clarke's reply was confident. "Yes, General, I think that is the only thing to do. We can't fight the Germans on this side of the river." Eddy then left the decision in Clarke's hands: "Well, I will leave it up to you. If you think you can get through I'll let you go. If you think you can't make it no blame will be attached to you." Clarke then turned to the man who would ultimately have to execute the mission. He asked "Abe" Abrams, "What do you think?" As Abrams pointed to the east bank, he replied, "Colonel, that is the shortest way home." With that said, Clarke ordered Abrams to take his battalion across.

At 9:13 A.M., Lt. Colonel Abrams ordered D/37 and the 105mm Assault Guns across the river with the admonition to "dust off the shot." The light tanks of the 37th started rolling across the final bridge, followed by the armored infantry and self-propelled artillery. As they moved past the elements of the 80th, one of the infantrymen, obviously impacted by his experience defending the bridgehead during the past couple of days, sent them on their way with the warning, "you will be back." The infantryman couldn't have been more mistaken.

As the long column of vehicles comprising CCA followed the lead task force across the bridges, the Germans pelted them with artillery and heavy mortar fire from their positions near Pont-a-Mousson. Clarke's men were not to be denied, and continued to pour through the bridgehead.

The lead task force soon found itself engaged with the enemy after crossing over the final bridge. TF Abrams seized the high ground overlooking the bridgehead, and quickly secured the villages of Ste. Genevieve, Bezaumont, and Loisy. After organizing themselves south and east of Ste. Genevieve, the 37th Tank Battalion, along with the 66th AFAB and a company of armored infantry from the 53rd AIB, prepared to launch an attack against the Germans at Benicourt, located about 3 miles northeast of the bridgehead. The attack commenced at 10 A.M., and Abrams' tanks succeeded in driving out the Germans by noon. With Benicourt in hand, CCA controlled the primary route leading to Chateau-Salins.

As Abrams was fighting for control of the main highway, the balance of CCA continued to cross into the bridgehead. It took five hours in total to get all of the men and equipment across. Once on the east side of the river, Clarke organized his command into three task forces. The first task force was primarily composed of Abrams' tanks, while the second was built around the 53rd AIB. The third task force consisted of the engineers, the battalion from the 318th Regiment, and the supply trains.

It was not entirely certain what the Germans had in store at this point. Colonel Clarke, in a fashion customary for the division and combat commanders of the Fourth Armored, took to the air in a light reconnaissance aircraft. From his vantage point above the battlefield, he directed the movement of the task forces. Trover's D Troop spread out on the left flank, while Captain McMahon's D/37, reinforced with the 37th's assault gun platoon, screened the right flank. The bulk of CCA then rammed through the German positions, capturing one town after another as the tanks rolled non-stop. They penetrated into the German's rear area, shooting up roadblocks, anti-aircraft emplacements, and infantry formations.

At Lemoncourt, the tankers caught a large group of German infantry completely by surprise. The tanks rolled "through and over them without stopping and with all guns firing." Most of the Germans were killed, but among the handful of prisoners was a German officer, SS Standartenfuhrer Theodore Werner. An experienced and decorated veteran of the Russian Front (he had commanded a division there), he was quite impressed with the Fourth Armored Division's dismantling of his position. Once in captivity, he commented to his interrogators,

> I would be pleased to know the commander of this particular division, and I am sure that it must be part of General Patton's Third Army. General Patton is for the American Army, what Rommel stands for in the German Army, but to know the commander of this armored division would explain to me how this Army managed to achieve such speed of advance which in many instances caught us completely unprepared.

Shortly after 5 P.M., the primary combat elements reached the high ground west of Chateau-Salins, which afforded them a good view into the city. They formed a 360-degree perimeter and hunkered down for the night. The 94th Field Artillery Battalion set up their batteries near Fresnes-en-Saulnois, and spent the entire evening lobbing shells around the perimeter in an effort to discourage German counterattacks. The task force had the foresight of loading up heavily on supplies, and the trains that accompanied them were filled with about seven days worth of stocks.

The following morning, CCA's supply columns caught up with the combat units and replenished their fuel and ammunition. CCA had done plenty of shooting over the course of its 20-mile journey: 354 prisoners had been taken, 12 panzers destroyed, and another 85 vehicles put out of action. In short, the Fourth Armored was wreaking havoc in the rear areas of the German units defending Nancy and the line of the Moselle River.

After the supplies were delivered on that cold, rainy morning of September 14, CCA was ready to renew its attack. But rather than attempt a direct assault on the defenders' positions at Chateau-Salins, Wood ordered Clarke to strike south, toward the town of Arracourt. This would cut off Nancy from the rear and position CCA to link up with CCB, which had reached the line of the Marne-Rhine canal further south. As CCA drove south, CCB would continue to move north in order to close the trap. The two combat commands would form a solid wall to the east of Nancy, ensnaring the 553rd VG Division in the process.

CCA met only scattered resistance en route to Arracourt (primarily at the village of Chambrey). Bruce Clarke was once again flying overhead, spotting areas of German resistance and directing the course of the advance. When the leading task force of CCA arrived at Arracourt, they found a large assembly of German personnel and vehicles that they believed constituted a headquarters unit (reportedly a corps HQ and the rear echelon of the 15th Panzer Grenadier Division). Company A of the 37th, which was leading the advance, laid down a heavy volume of fire on the rich collection of targets. The tank gunners destroyed most of the enemy trucks and horse drawn artillery that sat assembled before them. While A/37 shot up the enemy camp, B/37 circled around the left flank of the town in order to cut off the German's route of retreat.

Battery C of the 94th went into position within view of Arracourt, and its men witnessed the armored assault carried out by Abrams' tankers. The M7s then moved through Arracourt, and took up positions south of the town. Private Larry Doyle, a machine gunner on one of the self-propelled howitzers, spotted a German vehicle fleeing the scene and asked permission to open fire, using a phrase that would become legendary within the battalion: "Should I give 'em a boist, Lootenant?" After the battle, the Americans discovered that the Germans had abandoned an entire division's train of vehicles at Arracourt.

Basking in the glow of Clarke's attack, General Wood decided to reinforce success by attaching an additional tank/infantry team to CCA. The team was composed of one company of Shermans from the 35th Tank Battalion and a company of armored infantry from the 10th AIB. As this task force closed in on CCA's positions at Arracourt, the commander in charge reported to Colonel Clarke that there had been no sign of the enemy between the Moselle bridgehead and CCA. With the supply route apparently clear, Captain Trover's D Troop was released from its duties guarding the flank and was brought forward to serve in a reconnaissance role for CCA.

After Arracourt was secured, some elements of the task force proceeded on to the town of Valhey (the story of which is told later in this chapter), while others (primarily B/37, commanded by Captain Leach) scouted for crossing sites over the Marne-

Rhine Canal, which they were to hold in anticipation of CCB's arrival from the south. Captain Leach had no luck finding a crossing, but he came close.

Leach's tanks were moving on the town of Bauzemont, which is nestled on the north bank of the canal, approximately one and a half miles southeast of Valhey. As the tanks rolled through the village streets, they saw the bridge ahead, and it appeared that they would have their crossing site in hand. Suddenly, an explosion tore the bridge apart, and prospects of crossing the canal vanished literally in a flash.

As Leach's men were moving toward the town, there had been no sign of the enemy. But right after the explosion, a platoon of about 30 Polish engineers emerged with their back to the destroyed bridge, ready to surrender themselves to the tankers. In fact, the Poles were rather happy to have the opportunity to surrender, and were chattering away, throwing praise toward their captors. Leach rendered some aid to some of the wounded Poles, and had his bow gunners dismount from the Shermans and round up the prisoners, who were dressed in the khaki uniforms of the 15th Panzer Grenadier Division. By the time Leach finished his sweep of the north bank of the canal, his men had made prisoners of some 100 enemy troops.

CCA's move to the south continued to cause great havoc behind the German lines. By 7 P.M., CCA had taken another 400 prisoners, killed 230 of the enemy, destroyed ten 88mm guns, 26 armored vehicles and 136 other vehicles. Even more important, they had thoroughly disrupted the plans of the 15th Panzer Grenadier Division, which had been preparing to launch a counterattack against CCB/4 to the south. The attack against the German's rear echelon at Arracourt had thrown the panzer grenadiers completely off balance and forced them to change their plans for the attack. For the second night in a row, Clarke's men formed a perimeter defense deep behind enemy lines. This time, the wagons were circled at Arracourt.

Unbeknownst to Wood, CCA's move into this zone had disrupted much more than the staging area for the 15th Panzer Grenadier Division. In fact, Colonel Clarke's force had upset the plans for the assembly of the bulk of the 5th Panzer Army, which had arrived on Hitler's orders to launch a counterattack against Patton's Third Army. The Fourth Armored's deep penetration east of the Moselle would have tremendous repercussions over the course of the next two weeks.

CCB Drives North

At midday on September 13, CCB punched its way out of the bridgehead on the Moselle River and began moving north in an effort to make contact with CCA. The projected location for the linkup of the two combat commands was Arracourt, which as we know, would fall to CCA the following day. CCB advanced for a little over a mile without incident. But then, just outside of the town of Mehancourt, two Mark IV panzers opened fire on the tanks of C/8. The Germans had taken up hiding places in the woods overlooking the road, and scored quick hits on two of the Shermans. Two crewmembers in the first tank were killed, and the tank commander in the second Sherman had his left arm blown off at the elbow by a high-explosive round. As he was taken back to the rear, he was heard to say, "Well, I won't have to sweat out that CBI deal with the rest of you guys." (China–Burma–India, i.e., the Pacific Theater).

Soon after the encounter with the panzers, the lead task force, which was under the command of Major Irzyk, was able to gain some revenge when they came upon a truckload of German infantry. The tanks of C Company's first platoon opened up on the vehicle with high-explosive shells. The survivors were taken prisoner.

The village of Bainville Sur L'Eau, nestled west of the Meurthe River, was the next objective on Irzyk's list. It soon became clear that the Germans had a strong contingent of infantry defending the town, with anti-tank guns deployed in a well laid out scheme guarding all of the approaches. Irzyk sent his light tank platoon, commanded by Lieutenant Erdmann, to sweep around and behind the town, so as to insert itself between the town and the river. Erdmann's tanks began shooting up the German's rear area, which created a diversion that allowed the Sherman tanks of C Company to come charging in the front door. The Germans were taken completely off guard, and all of the defenders were either killed or captured. Quite a few anti-tank guns were destroyed, including four dangerous self-propelled pieces. The road was now clear to the Meurthe River.

Bill Marshall, who had so capably led the fording of the Moselle, was assigned to the advance guard of Irzyk's task force. He proved to be equally skilled at tackling the Meurthe, and in short order found a spot where the tanks could ford the river. The engineers moved up in the wake of the tanks and erected a bridge for the other vehicles of the task force to cross. By nightfall, TF Irzyk had established yet another bridgehead. Under the threat of sporadic shelling, his force secured its position for the night, and would resume the attack toward Arracourt in the morning.

Irzyk's men got an early start on the morning of September 14. Their first obstacle was the densely wooded Foret de Vitrimont. The only way through was via the narrow, muddy logging trails that laced the forest. After picking its way through methodically for about two and a half miles, TF Irzyk emerged from the forest unscathed. Fortunately, the enemy had decided not to contest the Foret de Vitrimont. This came as a great relief to Irzyk, who had feared the worst when he started his journey through the narrow confines of the woods. The biggest aggravation he encountered was the mud, which was made even worse by the rain that continued to fall throughout the day.

The first confrontation with the enemy that day came at the town of Hudiviller, located on high ground a short distance north of the exit from the Foret de Vitrimont. The lead elements of Irzyk's force were shelled almost as soon as they came within view of the village. Sensing that this would require something bigger than his task force, Major Irzyk called up the bulk of CCB. The 22nd Armored Field Artillery Battalion brought its M7 howitzers into play, plastering the town and the high ground beyond it. As the artillery rounds were still falling, American armor and infantry plunged into Hudiviller, striking hard and fast at the defenders. It was a swift and brutal onslaught, resulting in the destruction of two Tiger tanks, eleven halftracks, and seven anti-tank guns and their transports. At least 100 Germans were killed, and forty survivors were rounded up and added to the Fourth Armored Division's ever-growing tally of POWs. CCB pushed on another six miles past Hudiviller before stopping for the night.

CCB's advance continued on the morning of September 15, but upon reaching the Marne-Rhine canal, they found the crossing sites to be heavily defended. They tried the familiar formula of a heavy artillery barrage to soften up the enemy, but this time, the Germans proved more resilient. Complicating matters was the fact that Bill Marshall would not be able to put his aquatic skills to work. The Marne-Rhine was simply unfordable by tanks, so the infantry would have no choice but to do the dirty work of establishing a bridgehead. This proved to be no easy task, and as nightfall came, they had not been able to get across the canal due to the relentless fire being poured into their positions. The tanks of the 8th answered with direct fire at the enemy on the opposite bank, but it wasn't enough to clear the way for the infantry.

While the infantry was certainly getting the worst of it, being on the near side of the canal didn't guarantee the safety of the tankers. Lt. Hugh McNally of B/8, an extremely extroverted and well-liked member of the battalion, who had a tendency to stick his head out of the turret more than most tankers (even by 4th Armored standards), was shot in the face as he directed his tanks in their supporting role. Fortunately, he survived, but he lost his left eye.

Just when things were looking their darkest, CCB got a break. A platoon of tanks from C Company, under the command of Lt. Gleason, had been backing up elements of the 35th Infantry Division, which had also been tackling the canal about two miles to the west at the town of Summerviller. The infantry had made it across, and it wasn't long before the engineers got busy and, under the cover of darkness, erected a bridge at the site. The balance of CCB stayed in position for the night, and prepared to advance over the new bridge in the morning.

The Trap Is Closed

On September 15, Colonel Clarke sent task forces from CCA out in several directions for the primary purpose of causing mayhem in the German rear areas. He also set up a screen of armored infantry from the 10th AIB facing back to the west, toward Nancy. This position would serve as a net to capture elements of the 553rd VG as they tried to escape from the jaws that were clamping down behind them from the north and south. The net had been cast just in time, for at 10 A.M., the 10th AIB was informed that a large enemy column was moving out of Nancy and was headed straight for the 10th AIB's outposts.

The enemy column came into view at 5 P.M., and the 10th unleashed a heavy barrage of fire against the convoy. The column was decimated, with 14 trucks destroyed, along with three staff cars and an armored car. Seventeen Germans were captured, while the rest of the survivors of the column retreated back toward Nancy.

The penetrations made by the Fourth Armored had created an untenable situation for the German defenders in Nancy. As a result, the 35th Infantry Division was able to capture the city later in the day with very little difficulty.

Before the day ended, General Patton and General Wood visited the positions of CCA in Arracourt. Among their stops was a small outpost consisting of one of the guns from B Battery of the 94th AFAB. Lt. Hoffman was in command of the outpost, and Sergeant Francis Maus commanded the M7. Lt. Hoffman briefed the generals on the situation at his outpost. He had plenty to talk about, since his men had killed 33 Germans during the course of the day.

There was good reason to celebrate during Patton's visit. General Wood's insistence on enveloping Nancy from the north as well as the south had paid off handsomely in one of the biggest catches of the campaign to date. The drive and enthusiasm displayed by the Fourth Armored during the crossing of the Moselle and envelopment of Nancy added to the luster of Wood's division. Patton also visited with Eddy that same day, and in contrast to the enthusiastic Wood, the corps commander appeared to Patton to be "quite nervous." Patton later wrote, "I told him to go to bed early and take a large drink, as I wished him to be in position to rush the Siegfried Line."

On the morning of September 16, CCB began attacking over the newly constructed bridge at Summerviller. At the same time, CCA dispatched a task force (A, C, and D Companies of the 37th, plus A and B Companies of the 53rd) to drive south along the opposite side of the river, clearing out opposition along the banks as it went. The CCA task force quickly moved through Athienville, Serres, and Doeville en route to their link-up with CCB. It was not a painless exercise, as the forward observer tank from the 94th was hit south of Valhey, proving once again that this was the most dangerous job to have if you were a member of one of the artillery battalions. Two of the crewmembers, Pvt. Robert Klenk and PFC Norman Dugan, were killed instantly, and a third man, Cpl. Kenneth Cossey was mortally wounded. Lt. Seaman and Sgt. Abram Fritts were both seriously wounded.

At 2:30 P.M., the 10th AIB received orders to attack and occupy the town of Luneville. Major West quickly moved his force into position ¼ mile south of Deusville, which was about 4 miles northeast of the objective. At 9 P.M., the recon platoon and a platoon of medium tanks led the charge into Luneville. C/10 was brought up to reinforce the attack, and they sent out patrols through the portions of Luneville that had not yet been cleared. With the sound of small arms fire ringing in the distance, C/10 outposted the town for the night.

While the attack on Luneville had been unfolding, other forces of CCB had captured the town of Haracourt. The advance guard, led by Major Irzyk, continued on toward the town of Courbesseaux. The column was shelled en route, and even though shrapnel was sent flying into some of the vehicles, they didn't stop. As the column neared Courbesseaux, the Germans met Irzyk's force with extremely heavy small arms and anti-tank fire. The advance guard was hit hard. Irzyk clearly didn't have the strength needed to take the town, so additional firepower was brought up from CCB. After a heavy artillery bombardment softened up the German positions, a strong tank and infantry team moved in and wrestled Courbesseaux from the enemy.

Late in the day on September 16, CCB and CCA forged their linkup. This was especially important for CCA, because the Germans had cut their supply lines leading back through the area near Chateau-Salins. Until the route through Ste. Genevieve could be reopened, CCA would have to rely on the corridor provided by CCB for their supplies.

Task Force Kimsey

The situation at Ste. Genevieve first became an issue on September 15. It was reported at 11:30 A.M. that day that the Germans were hitting the 80th Infantry Division quite hard in that sector. In response to the enemy counterattack, Colonel Clarke was ordered to return the 1st Battalion back to the 318th Regiment. C/35 was assigned the task of escorting the infantrymen back to their own division, and the executive officer of the 35th Tank Battalion, Major Charles Kimsey, was placed in command of the entire force. In addition to the tanks and infantry, the task force took along the supply vehicles of CCA. They were not filled with ammunition and gasoline, but rather 560 prisoners that had been rounded up during CCA's foray into the enemy's rear areas.

Sgt. Joseph Sadowski, awarded the Medal of Honor for his bravery and sacrifice at Valhey (National Archives Photograph SC-313760).

Kimsey's force departed that afternoon, and at 6:30 that evening, he sent back word to CCA that he had run into enemy tanks near the town of Nomény (the tanks belonged to the 106th Panzer Brigade). His task force had taken some losses in the encounter, but was still determined to press on toward Ste. Genevieve. At that point, radio contact was lost between Kimsey and CCA. Nothing was heard from the task force until noon on September 16. And when word arrived, it was from a very unexpected source. Captain Strong, who commanded the supply vehicles that accompanied TF Kimsey, suddenly appeared back at Arracourt. He was not alone, for in tow were all of his vehicles and all of the German prisoners he had departed with the day before, plus another 100 Germans they had captured during their trip. He reported to CCA that Kimsey's task force had remained continuously engaged since its contact with the enemy at Nomény. Kimsey had planned on making a strong attack toward Ste. Genevieve, and fearing that Strong's vehicles would be too much of a liability during a breakthrough attempt (especially when loaded with more than 600 prisoners), he sent them back to the relative safety of Arracourt.

Kimsey's attack came off as planned, and achieved the desired results. Ste. Genevieve was secured, and in the process, seven panzers were destroyed (C/35 lost three Shermans during the entire mission). As stated in the official history (*The Lorraine Campaign*), "This intervention by Kimsey's column gave results out of all proportion to the size of the force involved, for these fresh troops, by attacking from the east, were able to take the enemy completely by surprise." Afterwards, C/35 rejoined its parent battalion, which had moved into the area near Luneville.

A Test of Courage

CCA and CCB had ripped through the German defenses and inflicted heavy damage on the 15th and 3rd Panzer Grenadier divisions. The hard-charging 37th and 8th

Tank Battalions were responsible for the lion's share of damage inflicted during these engagements, and many a tank crew could count themselves among the ranks of the courageous that fought behind enemy lines for several days. But one of the men on this mission demonstrated courage of a different sort. His display of heroism didn't involve a charging tank, or a submachine gun spitting deadly fire in the face of enemy resistance. Instead, it involved an unselfish display of courage and camaraderie that would forever occupy an honored place within the collective memories of the Fourth.

During the mid afternoon of September 14, elements of the 37th Tank Battalion rolled toward the town of Valhey. They had been preceded by a small American patrol that had entered the town during the dead of night about twelve hours prior. The patrol had returned to Moncourt with a report that there were no Germans to be found in Valhey. But unknown to the Americans, about 250 Germans entered Valhey at about 4 A.M. that morning. They brought two 88mm AA guns with them and deployed them in the town.

The only hint the Americans had that Valhey might be occupied occurred when a Piper Cub reconnaissance plane flying overhead drew fire from at least one of the 88mm AA guns. The bursts from the enemy gun caught Lt. Colonel Abrams' attention, and he radioed Captain Spencer with the leading company of tanks to tell him, "Be careful. I think we might have something here." But as the tanks of the 37th approached the village, it otherwise had all the appearances of being just one more town that would be liberated by the men of the Fourth Armored Division.

At about 2:30 P.M., the Germans sent a motorcycle patrol down the road to Moncourt. They soon returned with a report that American tanks were heading toward Valhey from that same direction. The Germans shifted the position of one of the 88s so that it could guard the approach to the town. When the American tanks appeared, the 88 started shooting. The Germans disabled one of the Shermans with a shot that caused the tank to lose its track. The other Shermans left the road, and began moving cross-country toward the town.

With the tank of Captain William Spencer leading the way, the Sherman tanks of A Company headed straight for the center of the village. Spencer's tank passed through the square, turned around a corner, and started down another road. The German's second 88mm gun was positioned a short distance away (differing accounts state anywhere from 20 to 100 yards away), and its crew either wasn't alert enough to take on the first tank, or intentionally let it pass. But in anticipation of more tanks approaching, they set their gun sight directly toward the area where the first Sherman had entered the square.

The second tank in the column, commanded by Sergeant Joe Sadowski, came rumbling into the square, trailing behind the lead tank with the usual prudent spacing between them. In a flash, the routine scene became anything but, as an armor piercing shell tore into the side of the tank. The Sherman came to a stop with the crew shocked and dazed by the impact. As the tank started to burn, Sadowski quickly gathered himself, and hustled his men out through the hatches. As they exited they were greeted by a swarm of bullets from German infantry, and the tank crew darted for cover.

After taking shelter in a nearby building, Sadowski realized that his bow gunner,

Russel J. Hay, had never left the tank. In a display of courage that would earn him one of the three Congressional Medal of Honor awards received by members of the Fourth Armored Division during the war, Sergeant Sadowski braved the German small arms and machine gun fire and raced back to the burning tank. He scaled the front slope of the hull, and tried to open the hatch above the bow gunner's position. He tugged and pulled at it with all his might, but without success. All the while, the Krauts took aim at a man who could do them no harm at the moment, and whose intent was certainly obvious. Sadowski stood up above the hatch to gain better leverage, and in so doing, selflessly presented himself as an even easier target for the enemy. The bullets, which had up to that point only found steel in front of them, finally began to strike wool and flesh. A first bullet didn't deter Sadowski. Nor a second. In fact, there is no telling how many the Sergeant absorbed before his body buckled, and he slid from the tank onto the soft, muddy ground below.

The fighting continued in Valhey until it was finally cleared of the enemy. The 37th had to move on immediately toward Moncourt, and out of necessity, Sadowski's lifeless body was left beside his tank. Before the Americans could return, the citizens of Valhey respectfully and ceremoniously buried the brave men who had helped liberate their village. When the Americans returned to Valhey several days later, they discovered that the bodies of Sadowski and Hay had been taken from the scene. The villagers directed a party of GIs to where they had conducted the burial. When the Americans arrived at Sadowski's gravesite, they found it adorned with an abundance of flowers, which provided a sign of just how much the villagers appreciated the sacrifice of their liberators.

The following day, nearly all of the citizens of Valhey returned to the site of Sadowski's grave to pay solemn tribute as an American burial detail removed his body for transfer to a military cemetery. A downpour burst from the heavens and washed over the cemetery as Sadowski's casket was raised from the ground; the cascade of pelting drops of rain provided the soundtrack for the final scene in the courageous story of Joe Sadowski, a man who exemplified the courage and resolve of the Fourth Armored Division. His Congressional Medal of Honor was awarded posthumously to his parents.

Preparing for the Next Phase

With CCA and CCB now joined, there was a great debate over where the division should go next. Colonel Clarke, sensing that there was scant opposition remaining to the east, wanted to turn the division loose toward the city of Sarrebourg, 23 miles due east of Arracourt. But Major General Eddy had other plans in mind. His XII Corps had not yet managed to completely digest the German forces that were caught in the pocket west of the Fourth Armored. In fact, the going was still a bit sticky in some areas, even after the successful effort of Major Kimsey's task force to reopen the route to CCA.

Manton Eddy could not be swayed from his desire to tidy up the front before resuming the advance. Thus, before any further movement was made to the east, the Fourth Armored would have to turn still more of its resources back to the west to assist with the cleanup of the Germans remaining in their rear area. To that end, on September 17, CCB was ordered to move north and assume positions on the left flank of

CCA, where it would assist the 80th Infantry Division. Once CCB was firmly established, and the 80th Infantry Division had moved out of its bridgehead over the Moselle, Eddy planned on resuming the advance of XII Corps.

While CCB shifted to the north, CCR did some tidying up of its own on the division's right flank. The Reserve command had moved into Luneville on September 16 following a strong attack by the German 11th Panzer Division against the American 2nd Cavalry Group. On September 17, a fair number of prisoners were taken in the area of Luneville, and some of the captured Germans gave up a wealth of knowledge regarding their parent unit, the 15th Panzer Grenadier Division. General Wood visited Luneville at about 2:45 that afternoon, and he was briefed on the situation there. It was about this time that CCR ordered the armored infantry of C/10 to seize the high ground on the outskirts of Luneville. Supported by some TD's from the 704th, the company advanced and captured the heights without meeting any opposition. Once atop the hill, however, they began to receive enemy artillery fire. They held their positions nonetheless.

Chateau-Salins

The shift of CCB to the north would carry it toward Chateau-Salins, which CCA had bypassed earlier in favor of an advance to Arracourt. The city was still a key objec-

The ruins of Chateau-Salins (courtesy K. Besedick).

tive for the Fourth Armored. If captured, it would serve as an anchor for the left flank of the division.

For its march to the north, CCB formed two task forces, one of which was led by Colonel William P. Withers, the other by Colonel Tom Conley (CO of the 8th Tank Battalion). On the morning of September 17, in the midst of a drenching rain that continued unabated for most of the day, they advanced directly toward Chateau-Salins. As CCB pushed north, the Germans cropped up in small pockets of resistance, and always seemed eager to make a fight of it. German mortar and artillery fire chased the columns, and a series of defended roadblocks and minefields had to be cleared en route. The fighting intensified as the two task forces drew closer to the objective. CCB was still short of the city by nightfall, and stopped its advance rather than attempt a night attack over unfamiliar ground.

On September 18, a decision was made to outflank the German defenders in the city by capturing the town of Fresnes, located about 3.5 miles west of Chateau-Salins. TF Conley made plans to assemble in a bivouac area east of the objective, from whence it would prepare an assault. As the advance elements of the task force closed in on the assembly area, they spotted three enemy vehicles moving along a distant ridge. The Hellcats that were part of the advance guard fired on the moving targets, which were almost at maximum range for their guns. In an expert display of gunnery skill, the TD gunners blew the three targets to smithereens. The bivouac was established without further incident.

TF Withers was charged with advancing directly toward Chateau-Salins, and they did so while TF Conley was moving into position near Fresnes. The Germans held Withers' force in check, however, and so a decision was made to keep TF Conley disengaged, in case Withers needed assistance. TF Withers sat tight for the balance of the day.

General Eddy's original plan called for the XII Corps' general offensive to resume on September 18, but the torrential rain on the 17th had thrown the timetable off by a day. With CCB now in position outside Chateau-Salins and Fresnes, they felt confident they could begin their operation on September 19.

5. A Legend Is Born

Hitler Responds

With the invasion of German soil a near certainty, Hitler was increasingly desperate to find a formula that would alter the flow of the war. He would look in every nook and cranny in search of positive news that might be used to his advantage. And lo and behold, there were some slender traces of silver lining to be found, if one stared hard enough at the dark clouds descending upon the Third Reich.

For starters, every mile the Soviets advanced toward Germany extended the Russian Army's logistical tether that much further. To a corresponding degree, the Germans benefited from the contraction of their own supply lines as they retreated toward their own border. (Had Hitler acted on this reality and initiated an organized withdrawal in late 1942, when it had become clear that his invasion of Russia had faltered, his forces would probably have been in much better shape at that moment.)

Hitler was also buoyed by the promise of several "wonder weapons" that were finally making their way off the drawing board. If enough time could be bought, perhaps these new inventions could be brought to bear in enough numbers to stem the tide that was rising against the shores of Germany. The V2 rocket was just being pressed into service, and the first production jet fighter planes were not far behind. And looming on the tree was the possible fruit of nuclear research that German scientists had been pursuing since 1939.

These weapons held huge potential. But at the present moment, none of them could swing the balance of power in Hitler's favor. Outnumbered and outgunned at this stage of the war, Hitler would have to pin his immediate hopes on the fighting ability of his veteran soldiers, and the desire of green and experienced soldiers alike to fight with vigor and resolve in defense of their native soil.

It was not in Hitler's nature to rely on a defensive posture for his salvation. But as things stood in early September, there was no place on the map where he could hope to wrestle the initiative from his enemies; that would at least be the conclusion of any reasonable, realistic military mind. But Hitler was neither reasonable nor realistic in his thought process at this stage of the war. In the wake of the attempt on his life on

July 20, he was, by all accounts, a physical and mental wreck. Though he still had an iron clasp on his military machine and the German populace, he clearly did not have a firm grip on his own faculties.

Hitler was greatly concerned with the threat that Patton represented. The Third Army, spearheaded by the Fourth Armored Division, was closer to the German border at the start of September than any of the other Allied armies. If Patton continued on his current track, he would soon be in the heart of the Saar region, which was second only to the Ruhr as Germany's most productive industrial area.

On September 3, Hitler responded to the Allied threat by ordering the commander of his forces in the west, Generalfeldmarschall Ger von Rundstedt, to begin planning a counteroffensive designed to destroy Patton's spearhead on the right flank of the Third Army. Rundstedt's forces would assemble in the area of Nancy, thrust to the northwest, and capture Reims (a distance of approximately 100 miles). This would stop Patton dead in his tracks, and drive a wedge between the US Third and Seventh armies.

But where would Hitler gain the strength, after the debacle in Normandy, to launch such an ambitious attack? At the close of August, the West Front was a shambles. The remnants of the German Army were in full retreat toward their own border, and there were less than 200 tanks available across the entire front.

Hitler had at least one card to play. During the summer, his tank factories were churning out their strongest production quotas of the war, despite the attempts of the Allied Air Force to interfere with Germany's capacity for arms production. Rather than send his factory-fresh Panthers and Mark IVs to replenish the depleted panzer divisions that had limped back from Normandy (a course of action that many of his generals would have preferred), he ordered the creation of several special panzer brigades. The original intent was to send these tank-heavy formations to face the Russians. But with the rapid deterioration of the West Front, Hitler ordered their use as a means to blunt Patton's advance.

Generaloberst Johannes Blaskowitz, commanding Army Group G, was responsible for the southern portion of the German line on the West Front, including the sector facing Patton's Third Army. Unlike his counterparts in Normandy, Blaskowitz had managed to pull his forces back in fairly good shape from southern France and the Bay of Biscay region. He was attempting to stabilize his positions facing the Third and Seventh armies when he was assigned responsibility for the counterattack. To accomplish the task, he would be allocated the additional resource of the 5th Panzer Army.

The 5th Panzer Army

At the moment of Hitler's decision, the 5th Panzer Army was an army in name only. The battered formation was currently occupying positions in Belgium, and would have to move south to join Army Group G. Upon its arrival, it would be joined by the newly raised panzer brigades, which were to serve as the razor's edge for the offensive.

The commander of the 5th Panzer Army, General der Panzertruppe Hasso von Manteuffel, was a bold, brash officer who had cut his teeth as a cavalry officer during the First World War. Remaining in the military after the Great War, he assumed command of an infantry battalion in the 7th Panzer Division prior to the invasion of France in 1940 (his division commander was none other than Erwin Rommel). He went on to higher positions of command in Russia and North Africa, and after the collapse in Tunisia, returned to Russia as the commander of his old 7th Panzer Division. He would soon take over the command of the esteemed Gross Deutschland Panzer Grenadier Division. He so impressed Hitler with his prowess as a division commander, that he bypassed the corps level of command, and was appointed directly to the command of the 5th Panzer Army on September 1, 1944, just days before Hitler's offensive was to begin.

With the assignment of the panzer brigades to his army, the newly promoted general would have at his disposal the bulk of the armor then available on the West Front. But not all of the units were immediately available; some of the brigades were still in transit at the start of the offensive.

For the initial wave, Manteuffel would have three of the new panzer brigades (the 111th, 112th, and 113th) and three panzer grenadier divisions (the 3rd, 15th, and 17th SS). After the offensive was under way, three panzer divisions (the 11th, 21st, and Panzer Lehr) and three additional panzer brigades (the 106th, 107th, and 108th) were to be provided as reinforcements.

While Hitler had success at manufacturing tanks, he had less success in filling the turrets with experienced crews. The ranks of the panzer brigades were filled primarily with hastily called up recruits, who had no experience as tankers, and were given little time to train for their assigned duties (this was a problem that plagued the great majority of units being called to arms to defend the German border). The new recruits were buttressed, however, with veteran tankers and officers from units that had been battered in recent combat (primarily from formations that had been devastated on the Russian Font). The performance of the new panzer brigades would depend in large part on just how well the cadre could bring the new men up to speed.

All of the panzer brigades were not alike, in terms of their organizational structure. The 111th, 112th, and 113th Panzer Brigades each consisted of two tank battalions (one each of Mark IV's and Panthers, for a total of 90 tanks) and ten tank destroyers. In terms of panzer strength, each of these brigades was equivalent to a panzer division at this stage of the war. The 106th, 107th, and 108th Brigades, on the other hand, were composed of only 36 Panthers and eleven tank destroyers, making them the equivalent of a battalion in strength.

The structure of the panzer brigades was heavily influenced by the German experience against the Russians. In addition to the panzers, there were two battalions of panzer grenadiers, but very little in the way of specialized reconnaissance elements, and no integral artillery support. This type of tank-heavy organization had proven itself against the Soviets. But against the Americans, it would prove to be far less effective.

The standard panzer division, when at full strength, did not suffer from such an imbalance of force, and the original plan called for Manteuffel to have three of them. The preeminent division of the group was the 11th Panzer Division. It had withdrawn from the south of France with Army Group G, and though it lost an appreciable number of its tanks en route, its staff and enlisted ranks were in good shape. At the time it joined the 5th Panzer Army, it had 30 Panthers and 20 Mark IVs. The 21st Panzer

Division, which had been engaged ever since D-Day, was actually void of tanks. Not a single one remained (an experienced division, it would have been a great candidate to have received some of those factory-fresh Panthers). As for the Panzer Lehr Division, it was never brought to the front to participate in the attack (Hitler ended up having other plans for it).

The three panzer grenadier divisions would provide the bulk of the infantry to be used in the offensive. The 3rd and 15th Panzer Grenadier divisions were in good shape overall, having come from Italy via southern France. Each division had a battalion of tank destroyers for armor support. The 15th also had 36 Mark IV tanks, and the 3rd a battalion of StuG IIIs. The 17th SS Panzer Grenadier Division was another matter. It was in poor condition after having been virtually destroyed during Operation Cobra, and had been reformed using two SS panzer grenadier brigades that had been stationed in Denmark. It had very little integral armor, being equipped with only four Panzer IV/70 tank destroyers and a dozen StuG III assault guns.

It was with this force that Blaskowitz and Manteuffel were charged with reversing the course of the war in the West. Hitler had placed the vast majority of his reserves in their hands, and would keep close tabs on their progress.

German Setbacks

The original date for the German counter-offensive was September 12, but events along the Moselle River, as well as other sectors of the front, caused Hitler's timetable to fall apart. Patton's forces, though slowed by the gas crunch, still managed to push east far enough that they unknowingly infringed on the staging areas the 5th Panzer Army had planned on using for the attack. The situation was further aggravated on September 8, when the 106th Panzer Brigade was sucked into the fighting near Metz (about 32 miles north of Nancy, in the zone of General Walker's U.S. XX Corps). The brigade was virtually destroyed in a sharp action with the US 90th Infantry Division.

On September 11, Manteuffel's situation was compromised even further when the 107th and 108th Panzer Brigades were shipped north in response to the U.S. First Army's approach toward Aachen. This was the first major city on German soil to be threatened, and Hitler demanded that it be protected at all costs.

Thus, before he could begin his attack, Manteuffel was mugged and robbed of the resources he needed to carry out his offensive. A reluctant Hitler allowed Manteuffel to delay the 5th Panzer Army offensive until September 15, but not a day later.

As Manteuffel made plans for the new start date, more trouble broke out to the south. The US XV Corps threatened to encircle elements of the German 64th Corps, and the 21st Panzer Division and 112th Panzer Brigade were called upon to assist them. The two units arrived in the vicinity of Dompaire on September 12, and on the following day, the 112th took a thorough beating at the hands of the French 2nd Armored Division. The brigade limped away with only 4 Panthers and 17 Mark IVs intact (the remnants of the brigade were attached thereafter to the 21st Panzer Division). With these losses taken into account, the force immediately available to Manteuffel now con-

Another Panther meets its fate (courtesy K. Besedick).

sisted of only the 111th and 113th Panzer Brigades, the battered remnants of the 106th and 112th, and the 21st Panzer Division (which still had no tanks of its own).

It was clear that circumstances now prevented the Germans from pursuing their original goals. An advance toward Reims was out of the question. Rundstedt submitted an alternative plan to OKW, which was aimed at the destruction of the American divisions of XII Corps that had established themselves east of the Moselle River. Rather than driving to Reims, they would be content with restoring their line of defense at the banks of the Moselle. They could then ride out the autumn and winter months behind the natural barrier of the river. Inserting the 5th Panzer Army in this sector would also serve to close a dangerous gap that existed between the German First and Nineteenth armies.

The plan was approved, and the date for the offensive was moved back to September 18. The 11th Panzer Division, which was originally slated for the second wave of the offensive, was given to Manteuffel as an additional resource for the initial attack. Manteuffel continued to protest that his army was not sufficient for the task he had been assigned, but his warning fell on deaf ears. He would have to find a way to make do with what he had. Though the 5th Panzer Army was now a mere shadow of the force that had been originally envisioned for the offensive, the Fuehrer expected no less of it.

Genesis

Taking refuge at his field headquarters in East Prussia, Hitler studied his maps and the military situation laid out before him. His country was in an ever-tightening vise, with the Western Allies pressing from one direction, and the Russians from the other. He was desperate to find a way to reverse the course of events that had placed his country in such an untenable position.

It was clear that, after almost two full years of retreat in Russia and the failed offensive at Kursk, the East Front offered no opportunities for seizing the initiative; even *his* weakened mind could grasp that fact. But the West Front was another matter! Even as he awaited the commencement of his counterattack against Patton, he began to contemplate a grander scheme that would not only stop the American's spearhead, but indeed, reverse the course of the war.

Hitler began to reason that a surprise counterattack had the potential to drive a wedge not only through the Allied lines, but also between the members of the Western Alliance itself. He had long believed that the Americans and British lacked the resolve of the German people. If he could inflict a devastating blow, the Americans might actually say, "enough is enough," and settle for a separate peace. The British, weary after five years of continuous war, might also follow suit if they saw the Americans step aside. After all, the British could never muster the resources to carry on the war in the west by themselves.

But what sort of blow could have such an impact? Where and how could he attack in order to set the Americans and British on their heels?

On September 16, during his routine daily briefing, Hitler suddenly brought the proceedings to a dramatic halt. "Stop! I have come to a momentous decision. I shall go over to the counterattack!" Seizing the pointer from the grasp of the officer conducting the briefing, Hitler drove everyone's attention toward the situation map. "That is to say, *here*! Out of the Ardennes, with the objective: Antwerp!"

As Hitler saw it, it was time to seize the initiative and send the Americans and British packing. Then he would be free to turn the full fury of a rejuvenated Nazi war machine against the Soviets. With his infrastructure free of the harassing attacks of Allied long-range bombers, and the increased delivery of new weapons such as the marvelous jet fighter planes, he felt that he could turn the course of the war in his favor. But it all hinged on the Ardennes, and his ability to mount a decisive thrust. It would be a desperate gamble, for if he lost, his strategic reserves would be spent. But for Hitler, the perpetual aggressor, there was no hesitation in taking this course.

It is quite amazing that Hitler contemplated such a scheme when the situation in the west was so desperate. The German border was barely secured, and his local counterattack against Patton had been running into delays for days. If he could not successfully execute an attack on this scale, what made him think that he could assemble the type of force necessary to execute an attack as large as what he contemplated for the Ardennes? How could he have been so confident that the Allies would not have penetrated east of the Ardennes prior to his gathering of armies for the counterattack? In retrospect, it is really quite remarkable that Hitler was able to foresee where the front would stabilize, and where his opportunity would reside.

Thus was set in motion the great German counterattack in the Ardennes. Little did the men of the Fourth Armored know that three months after the genesis of Hitler's plan, they would play a key role in handing the Nazi leader one of his greatest defeats.

But before Hitler could launch such a massive blow, he had to deal with the task at hand. He had to stop Patton.

Luneville

Early on the morning of September 18, the 111th Panzer Brigade set out for the area of Arracourt, where it would assemble for an attack against the positions of CCA/4. Its axis of advance would take it through the town of Luneville, which was reportedly occupied by other German troops. Unfortunately for the men of the 111th, they had been given incorrect information regarding the status of Luneville. It was actually under the control of CCR of the Fourth Armored Division.

The Americans at Luneville had one important advantage on the morning of September 18: they had captured a German map that revealed the location of the opposing forces, their command posts, and their observation posts. When all of this information was reviewed, the 10th AIB determined that there were several hundred German infantrymen and 20 tanks poised to attack.

The Panther tanks led the way for the Germans as they advanced down the road toward Luneville. En route, they ran, quite unexpectedly, into an outpost of the 42nd Cavalry Squadron. A skirmish ensued, wherein the 42nd's M8 armored cars and assault guns tried to take on the Panthers, but the 37mm guns and 75mm howitzers were no match for the heavy German armor. Three of the assault guns were knocked out, and the balance of the American force pulled back.

Further down the road, the Germans ran into stiffer resistance when some of the cavalrymen dismounted from their vehicles and made a stand as infantrymen. While not able to stop the German tanks, they successfully delayed the grenadiers who were accompanying them. As a result of their effort, the balance of the Second Cavalry Group was able to withdraw through Luneville, and warned the Fourth Armored Division about the approaching enemy tanks.

The Germans pressed on toward Luneville. They zeroed in on the American positions with mortar and artillery fire, which caused some casualties within the medical support personnel of the 704th, as well as other men attached to CCR. The fight was not going well for the Americans, and was made worse when a mortar shell killed Lt. Colonel Bailey, the commanding officer of the 704th TD Battalion.

The Germans eventually punched into the south end of Luneville. Elements of CCR, along with the 2nd Cavalry Group, stood their ground in the north half of the village, and the battle was joined near the center of town. Elements of the 603rd Tank Destroyer Battalion were dispatched to the scene to help deal with the German tanks.

Realizing that a serious situation had developed at Luneville, a team consisting of A/37, B/53, and Battery C of the 94th AFAB was sent to lend a hand. The team, commanded by Major Hunter of the 37th Tank Battalion, raced to the scene, and upon its arrival, sent B/53 into the town while the Sherman tanks of A/37 formed a mobile reserve. Battery C staked out its firing positions and provided support, with Lt. Truitt spotting the fire for the armored infantry, and Lt. Kelly the tanks. Truitt used one of the houses in town for an observation post, and called down fire on at least one anti-tank gun and a number of German vehicles. An assembly area for several of the German tanks was spotted, and the artillery pounded away at their position.

While TF Hunter helped to maintain the Germans in check at Luneville, more reinforcements were being dispatched to the scene. Hunter was soon joined by elements of the 35th Tank Battalion, along with additional elements from the 10th AIB and 704th TD Battalion. The additional reinforcements helped tip the scales in favor of the Americans, and the Germans were forced out of the town.

When 2nd Lt. Richard Buss arrived with his platoon of Hellcats from C/704, he was led to the south portion of the town, where he reported to Captain Tanner from the 35th Tank Battalion. Together, they surveyed the scene. Facing down the main street, there was a row of buildings leading up to a railroad overpass, with several boxcars sitting on the tracks, all of which had the potential to provide the enemy with ample cover. On the right side of the road was an open field, the far end of which was lined by trees. Buss asked Tanner whether or not the Panthers had taken refuge in the area around the overpass; Tanner replied that he thought the tanks had moved out across the field to their right. There was no sign of them at the moment.

A while later, one of the officers in Buss's platoon, Lieutenant Walle, went on foot to the railroad embankment, and from that position spotted two Panthers hiding in the woods at the edge of the field, about 300 yards away. He headed back to Buss's position to advise him of his discovery, whereupon the two men ran back to the embankment so that Buss could have a look for himself.

Buss was beside himself when he saw that one of the Panthers was turned sideways toward his position. At this range, turned in this fashion, it represented a lucrative target for the Hellcats. Jumping on the opportunity, Buss used hand signals to call forward the TD of Sergeant Romek. Upon pulling forward, Romek left the TD and joined Buss and Walle on the embankment. Romek studied the location of the two Panthers, and then returned to his Hellcat.

The driver of the M18 nuzzled the tank destroyer up to the railroad embankment. The long, sleek cannon extended over the top of the rise; the underbelly of the gun could not have been very far above the railroad track. Romek briefed the gunner, Corporal Mazolla, on the location of the Panthers. Mazolla slowly traversed the gun into position, locked onto the target, and squeezed off a round on the command of Lt. Buss. The cannon let out a deafening roar, and Mazolla rose above the rim of the open turret and signaled that he had scored a hit.

To Buss's extreme disappointment, the round did not appear to damage the Panther; not even at the very close range of 300 yards. Buss quickly signaled for another round to be fired, and Mazolla struck the Panther with another armor-piercing shell. Yet again, it appeared that no damage had been done. What would it take to kill these beasts? But apparently the shells had indeed penetrated the enemy tank. As Buss told it:

> Suddenly, I saw billowing flames. It was not the dramatic kind of explosion that one
> would have expected. The flames were a transparent orange, rising with startling swift-

ness. They rose through the branches of the trees to a height of nearly sixty feet. When I looked for the second target, it was gone. It had backed into a culvert in the woods and was completely out of range of direct fire.

Buss ordered Romek's TD to back up into a hidden position behind the embankment, where he would wait to see if the enemy tried to reestablish their position at the edge of the field. It was not long after that when orders were received for Buss to pull back to his position further down the road. His TDs were thereupon relieved by some of the armored infantry, which had come forward to secure the southern approaches to Luneville.

It was a lucrative day for the 704th Tank Destroyer Battalion. During the engagement at Luneville, the Hellcats claimed eight Panther tanks without losing a single TD. Unfortunately, their success that day was marred by the loss of their commanding officer.

Having been kept at bay by the swelling American force in Luneville, Manteuffel ordered the 111th Panzer Brigade to disengage and proceed to the town of Parroy, where it would team up with the 113th Panzer Brigade for an attack scheduled for the following day. The unexpected presence of the Americans at Luneville had thrown off the tempo of the German offensive before it had even really started.

Prelude at Lezey

Luneville had been the key hot spot for the Fourth Armored Division on September 18. And once the German attack was thrown back, there would have been little reason to suspect that the Germans had anything else in the works, had it not been for an increasing number of reports that were coming in from civilians warning of large concentrations of enemy tanks heading in the direction of CCA.

On the night of September 18, the 37th Tank Battalion had only two of its four companies (C and D) available for outposting the approaches leading to Moncourt and Lezey. The primary outpost was held by the 1st Platoon of C/37, and was located at a spot about three quarters of a mile east of Lezey. The platoon leader, 1st Lt. Wilbur Berard, had placed his tanks in superb positions guarding the road. Lt. Berard's own tank was hiding behind some brush just a few yards from the pavement. Sgt. Earle Radlauer's Sherman was further to the east and to the north of the road, hidden in a gully about 200 yards from the road and concealed under a canopy of large trees. The only tank south of the road was that of Sgt. Timothy Dunn, who placed his Sherman on high, open ground about 150 yards south of the pavement. Dunn's crew had covered their tank with branches and foliage for concealment. The platoon's remaining two Shermans remained in reserve.

Late that night, there were signs that the civilian reports were well founded. At 11:30 P.M., Berard's outpost reported that a German column (probably from the 113th Panzer Brigade) had been heading toward its position, but then turned off the main road. The suspicion was that the enemy vehicles had moved into a bivouac area. Lt. Berard took a small patrol on foot down to the main road, and advanced to the point where the column had turned off. Groping in the dark with his hands, he felt the unmistakable impressions in the soil where tanks had left the pavement. Berard was able to judge from the width of the impressions that they were of German origin. If there was any doubt, the sound of German voices in the distance removed it.

The patrol returned and reported their observations to Major Bautz. Back at the battalion command post, arrangements were made with Captain Cook of the 94th to target the suspected enemy camp so that they could open fire immediately if called upon.

When Lt. Berard returned to his outpost, he stiffened his position by having Sgt. Dunn place a series of 12 mines on the road leading toward the outpost. In the meantime, Lt. Harris accompanied a squad from the Reconnaissance Platoon on an intelligence mission to gain more information about the enemy force.

At 1:30 A.M., the 94th was called upon to fire at the suspected enemy position. A short but intense barrage forced the Germans out of their camp. As they fled, they passed through a crossroad north of Ley. The Sherman assault guns from the 37th Tank Battalion had already registered their 105mm howitzers on this spot, and when the Germans appeared, the Americans hit them with more indirect fire.

The German offensive had stumbled coming out of the blocks. The chance meeting between CCR/4 and the 111th at Luneville had thrown the proverbial monkey wrench into Manteuffel's plan. And now, as the Germans tried to jockey for position under the cover of darkness, they found themselves being harassed by the ever-vigilant men of the Fourth Armored Division.

The Americans weren't the only ones gumming up the works for the 5th Panzer Army. Near the end of the day, Manteuffel was informed that his objective for the offensive had changed yet again. The immediate focus was shifted to the city of Nancy, in an effort to free the German troops that had been encircled by the pincers of CCA and CCB. The advance of the U.S. XV Corps, located south of CCR's positions, compounded Manteuffel's problems. In order to keep the XV Corps at bay, a sizeable portion of his force had to revert to a defensive posture (the units impacted being the 21st Panzer Division, 15th Panzer Grenadier Division, and 112th Panzer Brigade).

C/37 at Lezey

During the early morning hours of September 19, the 111th and 113th Panzer Brigades attempted to move into position to launch their hastily arranged attack against CCA. Unfortunately for the Germans, the column from the 111th got lost during the night while en route from Luneville, and would not make it to the assembly area in time for the attack. The 113th Panzer Brigade, which had already been harassed during the night by American artillery, would have to carry out the initial phase of the offensive on its own.

On the morning of September 19, the 113th Panzer Brigade's lead task force, built around some 40 Panthers and the 2113th Panzer Grenadier Regiment, moved out under the cover of dense fog and rain that limited visibility to less than 100 yards. From the perspective of the Germans, the poor weather was very fortuitous, since it robbed the Americans of their air support.

The Americans were on a high state of alert. The fireworks during the night near the outposts of C/37 had certainly gotten their attention. In addition, a German POW revealed that there were 21 Panther and Tiger tanks on the road from Ley to Lezey. There were plenty of reasons for the Americans to suspect that trouble was brewing.

The first contact with the 113th Panzer Brigade took place at Moncourt, where a platoon of light tanks, commanded by Sergeant Mallon, maintained an outpost overlooking the road leading into the town. The Germans were running some lighter vehicles at the front of their column, and Mallon's tanks quickly destroyed a German halftrack and truck. The platoon of M5s began to receive small arms fire in return, but it was nothing they couldn't handle. The complexion of the engagement changed radically, however, when five Panther tanks appeared out of the mist. The light tanks fell back in a delaying action toward Lezey, which is where the 37th Tank Battalion had established its command post.

The enemy tanks advanced through the dense fog toward the 37th's command post. Unfortunately for the Panthers, their path carried them directly toward the outpost commanded by 2nd Lt. Howard Smith, 1st Platoon of C Company. Fortunately for the Americans, a section of tanks from Smith's platoon had been sent to this position that very morning; Captain Lamison, the commanding officer of C Company, had dispatched them after being warned of the approaching enemy armor.

Lt. Smith was kept abreast of the Panthers' location via telephone. His Shermans stood ready, with one tank on each side of the road in well-concealed positions (one of the Shermans was hidden underneath a straw pile inside an open barn overlooking the road). At about 7 A.M., when three of the enemy beasts appeared out of the fog, Smith's gunners knocked out two of them at a distance of about 75 yards. The third Panther fled south, where it passed before the waiting Sherman tank of Sgt. Timothy Dunn.

As you will recall, Dunn's foliage-covered Sherman was part of the 2nd Platoon outpost guarding the main road leading into Lezey. When word came in that the Germans were advancing up the valley from the direction of Ley, his platoon leader shifted his tanks so that all of their guns faced to the southeast. This placed Dunn's tank in a perfect position to hit the retreating Panther in the flank. Dunn's gunner slammed three AP rounds into the Panther, setting it ablaze. As the German crew bailed out of their burning tank, Dunn fired a round of HE in their direction for good measure.

At this point, the Germans appeared to pull back to the south (due to the fog, the Germans were not observed; the determination was made based on the sounds generated by the enemy column). It was a good thing that C Company had gained the upper hand; with the balance of the 37th Tank Battalion still away on other missions, Captain Lamison's lone company of Sherman tanks and Mallon's platoon of M5s were all that stood in the way of the German attack. Had the Germans kept pressing with the full weight of the 113th Panzer Brigade, the outcome might have been different.

After the initial exchange, Captain Lamison brought Lt. Smith's 1st Platoon outpost to full strength, while the 2nd Platoon maintained its outpost east of Lezey. Lamison, anticipating that the Germans were headed south for Bezange, took a section of three tanks from the 3rd Platoon, in addition to his own, and raced south toward the high ground west of the town. It was here that a north-south ridge ran parallel with the road connecting Bezange and Lezey, and it was here that Lamison planned on heading off the enemy attack.

The tank and crew of Sgt. Timothy Dunn. September 26, 1944 (National Archives Photograph SC194707).

Lamison reached the crest of the ridge about three minutes before the German Panthers appeared. The enemy tanks were still moving south, and were following the axis of the road connecting Bezange with Lezey. The fog was now burning off, and visibility was greatly improved. As Lamison spied the first Panthers, they were at a distance of about 900 yards.

The Panthers were oblivious to the Shermans atop the ridge, and eight of the Mark Vs paraded directly past the barrels of Lamison's tanks. The thinner right flank of the Panthers presented welcome targets for the crack American gunners. Before the German tankers knew what had happened, the Shermans destroyed five of the eight Panthers. As the remaining Panthers slowly turned their cannons toward the ridge and began firing, Lamison pulled his tanks back behind the crest and moved to another position about 500 yards further south. With the Shermans fully hidden from view, the crews of the Panthers had not a clue as to where the American tanks would reappear. When the Shermans drove back up to the top of the ridge, they made quick work of the remaining three Panthers.

As the Panthers were being polished off, Lamison started receiving anti-tank fire from an unseen source, so he pulled his tanks back from the top of the ridge and advanced on foot to the crest. From his vantage point, he observed that the Germans had brought up a towed anti-tank gun and placed it near the knocked out tanks.

Returning to his tank, he provided directions to the other tank commanders, and all four tanks once again moved to the crest and quickly eliminated the 75mm AT weapon. Lamison now had a commanding view of Bezange from atop the ridge, and he kept the section of Shermans in position there to keep watch over the town and road.

While Lamison was dispensing with the two platoons of Mark Vs, another platoon of four Panthers proceeded up the main road from Ley to Lezey, headed straight for Lt. Berard's outpost. When the Panthers closed within a few hundred yards, all of Berard's tanks opened fire and quickly destroyed three of the four Panthers. At least one of the Panthers managed to return fire, but only succeeded in hitting the bogey wheel area of Lt. Berard's tank; the shot knocked off a couple of the wheels, but this wasn't enough to disable the tank. The fourth Panther ran for cover behind the wreckage of a downed American bomber resting in a nearby field. The plane was set afire by a round of high explosive from one of the Shermans. Whether the enemy tank was caught by one of the AP shells that followed was not known, but it was not seen fleeing, nor did it cause any more problems for Berard's outpost.

After the initial wave of Panthers was squashed, Berard's outpost had a series of fleeting encounters with the enemy throughout the balance of the day and night. In every case, the Germans approached down the main road from Ley. The first encounter involved a lone Panther tank that made its way down the road directly toward Berard's position. This Panther suffered the same fate as the others. All remained quiet around the outpost for the balance of the daylight hours. Before nightfall, the outpost was beefed up with some bazooka-wielding armored infantrymen, a heavy machine gun, and a 57mm anti-tank gun. All of these men came from A Company of the 10th Armored Infantry Battalion.

Around midnight, another panzer attempted to make the dangerous trip down the road from Ley. It hit one of the mines that had been strewn by Sgt. Dunn, and came to a sudden stop. A flurry of fire erupted from the Americans manning the outpost. The bazooka men, 57mm anti-tank gun, and tanks all opened fire (the 57mm gun crew was given credit for the kill).

Later that night, a German command car and motorcycle wandered down the road, probably by accident, and were taken out by the heavy machine gun. This was the last of the encounters for Berard's outpost. They had not relinquished an inch of ground, and ensured that the route to Lezey, and the left flank of the 37th Tank Battalion, was buttoned up tight as a drum.

Hellcats to the Rescue

There was yet another hot spot during the morning of September 19. It would become one of the definitive engagements of the battle.

Early that foggy and misty morning, Captain Dwight, the liaison officer of the 37th Tank Battalion, climbed in his jeep and departed from CCA headquarters after one of his routine sojourns. His destination was the headquarters of his own 37th Tank Battalion. He was approaching Bezange when he heard the sound of the battle between the Panthers and Lt. Smith's Shermans (he knew not who the antagonists were). After passing through the town, he was surprised by the sight of a company of Panthers. He used his radio to contact the command post of the 37th, and asked if it was "all right to come in." It was clearly not all right.

Anxious to do something to help his battalion, Dwight returned to CCA headquarters in search of reinforcements that he could lead back toward Bezange. He was given all that was available: the four Hellcats of the 3rd Platoon of C/704. After consulting with the platoon leader, Lt. Ed Leiper, Dwight jumped back in his jeep and escorted the platoon back toward the sound of the firing near Bezange. As the tank destroyers moved out through the dense fog, the crews had no idea where they were going, or what they would encounter.

Leiper's platoon advanced in column, with the Hellcat of Sgt. Stasi leading the way. Behind him followed the TDs of Sgt. Ferraro, Sgt. McGurk, and finally, Sgt. Krewsky. The fog was so dense that the men in the tank destroyer at the rear couldn't see the tank destroyers at the front of the column.

As the Hellcats began to ascend a hill, the unmistakable sound of cannon fire rang out. Several sharp "booms" cut through the misty veil clinging to the tanks, and the column came to a halt. Within a matter of minutes, Sgt. Stasi came back down the slope, bringing with him one of his men who had been killed (Pvt. Richard Graham), along with the news that his tank destroyer had been knocked out (Stasi and two other crewmen, Cpl. Stewart and Pfc. George Knoblach, were wounded; only the driver, Pfc. John Green, walked away unscathed). The three remaining tank destroyers continued their advance, and as they passed the point where Stasi's Hellcat had been knocked out, they saw two German tanks aflame. Sgt. Stasi's gunner, Cpl. Frederick Stewart, had gotten in the first shots of the battle, knocking out two Panthers at short range.

The Hellcats continued to climb the slope. It was only a matter of a few minutes before more shots were fired. Sgt. Ferraro's Hellcat accounted for three more Panthers, but now it too was hit, and came limping back to the rear. Two of his men had been wounded as well (Cpl. Valentine Folk and Pfc. Henry Godwin). The two remaining Hellcats continued to move, and passed by more burning Panthers on their way to the crest of the hill.

All was quiet as McGurk's and Kresky's TD crews sat perched on the fog-shrouded hilltop. After awhile, the fog began to thin, and the tankers realized they had a valuable vantage point when they spotted a long line of tanks in the distance. The tanks were on the move, with infantry clinging to their decks.

Though the fog had thinned, it was still thick enough to make the identity of the tanks less than certain. At first glance, they weren't sure if the vehicles were friend or foe. But when they made out the unmistakable feature of muzzle brakes on the end of the tank cannons, the ownership became clear; very few American tanks were so equipped, and McGurk and Kresky were confident that it was an enemy column parading beneath their gun barrels. Indeed, the tanks were from the 113th Panzer Brigade.

The Americans opened fire on the unsuspecting enemy. Paul Colangelo, the assistant driver in Kresky's Hellcat, described the action:

> After we realized they were German, we started to open fire with our two M18's. We would shoot and move, and with our speed and maneuverability, we were having a field day… like in a shooting gallery. The German's didn't know what was happening.

Sgt. Kresky's Hellcat was particularly productive at this stage. Its crew wiped out four more Panthers from its position overlooking the assembled German armor.

All was going the Americans' way until a Panther was spotted hiding behind a large pile of rocks. Either Capt. Dwight or Lt. Leiper directed the two remaining TDs to take out the tank. When the TD commanders looked at the location of the Panther, they were concerned that they wouldn't be able to maneuver for a shot without putting themselves at unnecessary risk, and tried to convince the officers that it was folly to try. Colangelo picks up the story:

Paul Colangelo, C Company, 704th Tank Destroyer Battalion (courtesy Paul Colangelo).

> We knew that he was going to get us before we could get him. While this discussion was going on, I had to make an important phone call that couldn't wait. I got out from my assistant driver seat to do my business. They went up the hill without me. As soon as they got up there — boom — an armored piercing shell (went) through the assistant driver's seat. Imagine if I was in there? God was with me that day. Fortunately for the rest of the crew the shell hit the bottom and they were able to bail out.

Sgt. McGurk's lone Hellcat continued the fight. Thanks to the skill of his gunner, Cpl. Dominick Sorrentino, McGurk's crew racked up another two Panthers during the balance of the engagement. When all of the 76mm ammunition was exhausted, the men of the platoon fought on against the German infantry using their .50 caliber machine guns and small arms.

At about 3 P.M., Lt. Smith of C/37 brought the first section of the 1st Platoon to assist Captain Dwight. When the Shermans rolled up on the other side of the hill, the men of Leiper's platoon breathed a collective sigh of relief. Smith's tanks now hammered away at the 200 to 300 German infantry that were down in the valley threatening the position held by the dismounted tank destroyer crews; there was no longer a threat from enemy tanks, as Leiper's platoon had knocked out eleven Panthers (virtually an entire company). The lone Panther that had survived the encounter near the rocks had apparently fled the scene. The Germans managed to knock out one of the Shermans with a round from a panzerfaust. But other than that, the affair was decidedly one sided.

While Leiper's platoon was playing "shoot and scoot" from behind the rise, the first platoon of C/704 had also raced into action. Unknown to Colangelo and the other men of Leiper's platoon, Captain Tom Evans, commanding officer of C/704, had been ordered to hustle his 1st Platoon into action soon after Leiper's 3rd Platoon had departed. The additional Hellcats joined the fray at a critical moment.

Rather than follow Leiper, Evans had his Hellcats take up other positions. He was supported by B Battery of the 489th AA Battalion and engineers from the 24th Armored Engineer Battalion, who dug in and quickly placed a minefield in front of their positions.

Captain Evans' outpost overlooked the same enemy column that Leiper was engaging. His own account does the best job of describing what happened next:

> We were in pretty good strategic position along a ridge over-looking a shallow valley. We could hear the Germans coming, but couldn't see them because of the fog. As the fog burned off, we saw at least thirty to forty German tanks with supporting infantry start up toward us in a frontal attack, coming directly at Leiper's platoon, only 200 yards from him. He knocked out three tanks. The Germans changed direction toward us. We waited and waited until they were within 1500 yards, then we fired. The two leading tanks were hit and stopped dead, aflame. The others, their crews apparently confused, turned sideways. I really don't know why. That's where they made a big mistake. It was a turkey shoot! From our position, with only turrets showing, we hit eleven more as fast as we could load and shoot. Then we moved from that position. "Fire and fall back," was our motto. Fall back to another good position with coverage and a good field of fire.

The tank destroyer crews from the 1st Platoon were as prolific as their peers in the 3rd Platoon. Pfc. Frank Amodio, the gunner in Sgt. Henry Hartman's Hellcat, knocked out five enemy tanks. The gunner for Sgt. Tom Donovan's TD, Corporal John Ewanitsko, accounted for three more panzers. In total, the first and third platoons put 19 enemy tanks out of action, at the expense of 1 man killed, five wounded (only two seriously), and three M18s knocked out.

Counterattack

Meanwhile, back near Luneville, the task force under the command of Major Hunter had been intercepting enemy radio messages emanating from the area around Lezy. Hunter urgently requested that his force be released to go to the aid of C/37, but given the situation at Luneville, he was held in place for the entire morning. Permission was finally granted, with Abrams urging him on over the radio: "Dust off the sights, wipe off the shot, and breeze right on through." It was 1 P.M. before A/37 was relieved and allowed to proceed back toward the headquarters of the 37th.

Once they were free to go, A/37 and a supporting battery of artillery raced toward Arracourt, arriving there at about 2 P.M. The artillery took up firing positions within the town while Captain Spencer's tanks continued on to link up with Captain Leach's B/37.

Jimmie Leach's tank company had also been very heavily engaged during the earlier part of the day. At the start of the day, B/37 had been assigned a supporting role with the 53rd AIB, which was holding positions back on the far left flank of CCA. As the fighting erupted during the early morning hours, Captain Leach was ordered to bring his company to the headquarters of CCA, near Arracourt.

Leach's platoons were spread out miles apart. As his platoon leaders went about bringing the tanks together for their road march to Arracourt, Captain Leach sped off in his jeep toward Clarke's HQ. When he received his orders, he had not been given any indication of what the situation was like, so getting there in advance of his tanks seemed to be more than prudent.

As Leach pulled up to the command post area, he found Clarke's position already under attack by enemy tanks. Colonels Clarke, Hyde, and Pattison were taking cover in a ditch as the M7s of the 66th AFAB were turning their 105mm guns against a group of advancing Panthers. As Leach approached, Clarke yelled out, "Where the hell is your company!" Leach replied, "Sir, they're on the way. They're rolling." Looking over toward the enemy tanks, Clarke quickly said, "You see those? I want you to take them out."

The M7s were only about 650 yards away from the Panthers. They lowered the barrels of their 105mm howitzers and took aim. At this short range, the howitzers were capable of packing a punch against the German tanks, and at the very least, could rattle their cage with some direct hits. The volume of fire they threw at the Panthers was enough to make the Germans think twice about continuing their advance during the critical time frame before the arrival of B/37.

The Shermans arrived at about 11 A.M., and Leach immediately moved them into positions on high ground about 400 to 600 yards from the command post of CCA. "Within a matter of minutes" after placing his tanks in position, Leach's company came face to face with a group of five Panthers. Leach's tanks fired first, and the Panthers retreated to the cover of some nearby woods. The Shermans continued to fire at the Panthers as they sat at the edge of the woods, but with little effect. The Panthers now had the advantage, as only their superior frontal armor was exposed, and they were at a range that was advantageous to their superior high-velocity 75mm cannon.

The Panthers soon found their range, and proceeded to hit all three of Lt. Marston's tanks. Marston's tank suffered the most damage. The German shell penetrated the turret, killing the gunner and loader. The Shermans began jockeying for better positions in anticipation of an advance by the Panthers, but the Germans did not come forward. Though they hadn't knocked out any of the enemy's tanks, B/37's response stopped them from overrunning the command post nevertheless.

There was one other key player involved in the action near CCA's command post at Arracourt: Major Charles Carpenter, the commander of the division's artillery liaison planes. Carpenter had taken to the skies in his Piper Cub earlier in the day, but the heavy fog had kept him from contributing to the battle. He stayed aloft, waiting for the conditions to improve, and by noon, his patience was rewarded. As he flew over the area of Rechicourt, he spotted a company of panzers moving toward Arracourt. As he watched, the enemy tanks advanced toward a half-dozen GIs that comprised CCA's water point crew. After reporting the enemy's position over his radio, Carpenter took matters into his own hands, and swooped down upon the enemy tanks. You see, Carpenter wasn't flying just any old Piper Cub. He had ingenuously mounted six bazookas on his aircraft, three under each wing. Using push buttons that he had rigged up in his cockpit, he could fire the rockets one at a time, or all six in unison. *Rosie the Rocketer* wasn't your typical Piper Cub, and "Bazooka Charlie" wasn't your typical pilot.

On his first pass, Carpenter launched two of his rockets, but failed to score a hit. Coming out of his dive, he ascended once again for another attack. On his second pass, he came in at a steeper angle, and once again launched two of his rockets. This time, one of the bazooka rounds found its mark, "damaging a tank and causing the crew to bail out and run." He climbed and descended yet again, unleashing his final two rockets. He scored another hit, and it was enough to halt the German's advance (by the end of the war, Carpenter would be credited with knocking out a total of five enemy tanks with direct fire from his Piper Cub). During the aerial assault by the lone plane, the men of the water point crew were able to scramble for cover in a nearby creek, where they remained in hiding until dark.

Once the situation around CCA's command post had settled down, Leach was ordered to bring his company to Arracourt, where he would link up with A/37 upon its return from Luneville.

At 2 P.M., B/37 and A/37 (minus one platoon of A/37, which was left at CCA's headquarters for security) joined C/37 and the tank destroyers near Rechicourt. At this point, German forces had assembled at a position on the low ground south of Hill 297, and the reunited members of the 37th Tank Battalion were ordered to eliminate the opposition in that area.

Prior to moving out, Captains Leach and Spencer, along with Major Bill Hunter (the 37th's Exec Officer), made a reconnaissance of the approaches to Rechicourt. They observed four enemy tanks in a draw southeast of town, and figured that was the sum total of their opposition. They planned on hitting them from the south and west, with A/37 on the left (attacking from the west with six tanks), and B/37 on the right (attacking from the south with fourteen tanks). The advance would be made under the cover of a smoke screen.

As A/37 drew into position for the attack, they saw that there were actually a dozen Panthers, not four. This didn't impact the plan, however. The smoke screen was laid down in front of the Panthers, and A Company began its advance to the east. Captain Spencer led the charge with his command tank, which was one of two in his company armed with the new 76mm gun. The three-tank platoon of Lt. Turner went in on his left, and a platoon of two tanks stayed to his right (Lt. DeCraene, who commanded the platoon on the right, had the other 76mm Sherman as his command tank).

Lt. Turner's three tanks swung around still further to the left, so that they could get into position to hit the Panthers' right flank. His Shermans closed to within 250 yards before the American gunners opened fire. Turner's platoon then took to the brow of a hill on the German's right flank, and continued to fire at the enemy.

As Turner was jockeying for position on the German's right flank, Captain Spencer and the platoon led by Lt. DeCraene continued their advance directly toward the Panthers. Unfortunately, Spencer's tank was knocked out during the first few minutes. Lt. DeCraene continued to advance, but then his tank was hit as well. When the shell struck, DeCraene was knocked unconscious for a brief moment. When he regained his senses, he ordered the tank to continue advancing toward the Panthers. Another round destroyed the tank, killing all but one of the crewmembers.

In the meantime, Captain Leach's tanks had advanced behind the smoke screen, and then moved unseen through a defilade position running along the Panthers' left flank. Leach's tanks then wheeled to their left and lunged downhill toward the assembled Panthers. The Shermans plowed forward with all guns blazing, and were soon driving straight through the German's position. The Panthers were still facing toward the initial threat from A Company, and were not anticipating Leach's surprise assault on their left.

With armor piercing shells coming at them from three directions, the Panthers didn't stand a chance. Nine German tanks were knocked out, against the loss of three Shermans (one of Lt. Turner's tanks was eventually knocked out atop the hill). Though considered a success overall, the sharp engagement was costly for A/37, as they had six men killed and four wounded. Captain Leach's B Company was unscathed.

The tanks of B/37 followed up on their success by pushing on toward Moncourt. Perched on the high ground to the west, Leach's tank crews spotted some Germans digging in along the edge of the woods near the town. Darkness was descending, but there was still enough light for Leach's men to shoot up the German positions. Once daylight was exhausted, B Company turned back in the direction from whence they came. There was no confusing the route, as the burning Panthers stood as a tanker's lighthouse guiding them home to Lezey.

During the evening of the 19th, General Patton paid a visit to Colonel Clarke's headquarters. He used the occasion to lavish some well deserved praise upon Captain Evans, whose C Company was responsible for so much of the damage inflicted on the 113th Panzer Brigade. Patton told the young company commander, "This is the kind of thing that's going to end the war quicker than anybody had hoped!" Patton had good reason to be excited, as the tally for the day stood at 43 enemy tanks destroyed (mostly Panthers), with the loss of only five Sherman tanks and three Hellcats (the Germans estimated their own losses to be an even higher total of 50 tanks). It was a remarkable display of skill by the men of the Fourth Armored Division.

Patton also met with General Wood that evening. They discussed the events of the day, and the course they should adopt for September 20. The feeling was that the German effort on the 19th amounted to nothing more than a local counterattack, and that the threat had been extinguished. Patton urged that the advance of the Fourth Armored should continue on the 20th as planned, despite the fact that he felt "Wood's division was spread pretty thin."

While Wood and Patton had underestimated the nature of the counterattack, their intuition regarding the success that might be gained by continuing to press the attack the following day was on the money. For at the headquarters of the 5th Panzer Army, the outlook had turned grim. Throughout the night, the progress reports being sent to General Blaskowitz were increasingly pessimistic. By 4 P.M., he was informed, "the attack of the 113th Panzer Brigade at Bezange is stuck." Less than five hours later, words of caution were sent expressing the fact that "the Army has no more units to block the [American] breakthroughs."

At 9:20 P.M., it was reported to 5th Panzer Army HQ that the Fourth Armored Division had "succeeded in breaking through the attack of the 113th Panzer Brigade between Lezey and Bezange and onto Moncourt with approximately 60 tanks." The Germans had nothing but "work units left at Dieuze by Mulcey and Blanche-Eglise," and that, due to the heavy casualties incurred, "there is no way possible for the 111th and 113th Panzer Brigades to attack further." As the night wore on, Manteuffel and Blaskowitz discussed their options for salvaging the operation.

The Battle for Chateau-Salins

As CCA and CCR dealt with the German threat, General Dager's CCB continued its offensive efforts to the left of CCA. Chateau-Salins still posed a major obstacle for Task Force Withers, and on September 19, CCB took another stab at entering the city. But to tell the story of Chateau-Salins, we must back up one day to September 18, when the battle for the city first began.

The 51st Armored Infantry Battalion was largely responsible for capturing the objective. As they approached the city on the 18th, they came upon a number of roadblocks, which the Germans defended with vigor. The Krauts hit them with a little bit of everything: AT weapons, artillery, mortars, and machine guns all chimed in against the advancing Americans. The armored infantry of B/51, which was in the lead, dismounted from their halftracks and called in artillery support to help deal with the enemy positions. As darkness descended, the entire column moved off the road into assembly areas, and plans were drawn up for an attack on Chateau-Salins.

The attack kicked off at 7:30 that same evening, with Company B of the 51st leading the way. The armored infantrymen were met with heavy return fire, which caused 12 casualties. But the company continued to advance, and soon occupied some of the buildings on the edge of town, where it remained until after midnight.

At 2:00 A.M., a change in the plan was announced. B/51 was ordered to withdraw, thus giving up its hard fought gains. It had been decided that a heavy artillery barrage would be laid on the town in the morning; B Company, being too close to the target area, would have to pull back for safety's sake.

Within two hours, B/51 had completed their withdrawal under the cover of darkness, and returned to the vehicle park. The Germans followed up behind them as though being sucked into a vacuum. They reoccupied the buildings that had been lost to the Americans, and moved further onto the high ground south of the town.

The 51st then received an incredible change in orders. The town-flattening barrage would not take place after all! Instead, A/51 and C/51, supported by Company B of the 35th Tank Battalion, were ordered to attack the town, commencing at 7:30 A.M. They would now have to fight to retake the ground that B/51 had already won and then abdicated to the enemy.

Before another attack could be launched directly against the city, the Germans would have to be kicked off the high ground to the south. The second platoon of B/51, commanded by Lt. Cassidy, led the attack and recaptured the heights. A/51 and C/51 then jumped off, each with their own platoon of Shermans in support.

The Germans brought down heavy fire on the advancing units. C/51, which was moving over fairly open terrain, was repeatedly pinned down. Artillery support from the 253rd Artillery Battalion was added to the mix, and after a hard day of fighting, A/51 managed to enter the town; they cleared a good chunk of it by about 3 P.M. At 7:45 P.M., C/51 finally reached the south edge of Chateau-Salins after bitter fighting. The Germans were hanging on tenaciously, and decided to make a final stand at an agricultural college located on the east edge of town.

The Germans pulled out all the stops in an effort to maintain their hold on Chateau-Salins. During the early morning hours of September 20, the Krauts brought

Captain James H. Leach, CO of B/37, near Vic Montcourt, France. October 1944 (courtesy J. Leach).

down heavy artillery fire on the men of A/51 and C/51. They also tried to interfere with the reinforcement of the Americans positions by shelling the main road leading into the town. The 51st AIB, in turn, brought down heavy artillery concentrations on the Germans holding out in the college; it was all to no avail. As stated in the 51st AIB's combat journal, "They still remained in the school and could not be dislodged." Elements of B/51 were moved into the town, and the balance of the day was spent mopping up other scattered German positions.

The attack on Chateau-Salins was made no easier by the fact that the population of the town had a strong German heritage, and their sympathies generally fell in the direction of the enemy. It was a far cry from the reception of flowers, wine, song, and embraces that they had received in so many towns during their race across France. Late in the day on September 20, the 51st AIB received orders once again to depart from Chateau-Salins.

The Battle at Ley

On September 20, CCA issued orders creating two extremely strong task forces: TF Abrams-West and TF Oden-Jaques. TF Abrams-West was built primarily around the 37th Tank Battalion, the 10th AIB (minus one company), and the 94th AFAB. TF Oden-Jaques consisted of the 35th Tank Battalion (minus two medium tank companies), the 53rdAIB, and the 66th AFAB. Urged on by Patton himself, the two task forces were to drive in tandem to the northeast — Oden-Jacques on the left, Abrams-West on the right — with the immediate objective of securing crossings over the Saar River, and the further objective of driving northeast toward the city of Sarreguemines.

At 9 A.M. that morning, reports filtered in to CCA that 150 to 180 enemy tanks were spotted in an area south of the Marne-Rhine Canal, and that 20 of them had already made it across the waterway. Despite this report, CCA's plans for resuming the attack to the northeast remained intact, and the column moved out as scheduled.

CCA began its advance before noon. The 37th Tank Battalion crossed its start line at 11:35 A.M., and brushed aside the enemy at Blanche Eglise. At 12:25 P.M., a report came in to the 37th that 16 enemy tanks had been reported south of Arracourt, and were advancing toward the Fourth Armored's rear area. The 37th continued its advance despite this development, and by 12:35 P.M., had passed through the town of Dieuze. It was then that they received word that the rear elements of the division were under attack.

In response to this threat, CCA issued new orders, and within minutes, Lt. Colonel Abrams turned his task force back toward its original assembly area near Lezey. The new mission for TF Abrams-West would be to counterattack to the south and west, with the goal of clearing out the German forces that had penetrated between Lezey and the Marne-Rhine Canal.

The panzers that were on the move were from the 111th Panzer Brigade, which had finally regained its bearings and was now prepared to enter the battle. The lead panzers first emerged near the positions of the 191st Field Artillery Battalion, just as its men were preparing to limber their weapons for a move to new firing positions. Eight panzers appeared through a misty veil about 1,000 yards from the 191st's 155mm howitzers. The artillery pieces were swung about and fired directly at the approaching tanks. Some nearby tanks and tank destroyers from the 35th Tank Battalion and 602nd TD Battalion arrived to lend support, and the Germans were beaten back.

TF Abrams-West was now reformed for its new mission, with TF Abrams being created specifically for dealing with the enemy threat. Abrams' force consisted of the 37th Tank Battalion, C/704, the 94th AFAB, and the 10th Armored Infantry Battalion (minus B Company, which was attached to CCB). They moved urgently back toward Lezey, and by 1:00 P.M., B/37 (the first unit on the scene) took up an outpost position, where it engaged the enemy, holding them at bay until the balance of Abrams' force arrived. Once reassembled, TF Abrams first objective would be to attack the German forces that had been reported in the vicinity of Ley, located about two miles southeast of their assembly area at Lezey.

As the commanders were meeting to discuss their plan of attack, two Mark IV tanks probed at the outposts of the 37th. The German panzers fired on the southernmost outpost of B Company, and the Shermans returned fire. Sgt. Litherland's Sherman destroyed one of the Mark IV tanks, while Sgt. Grady's tank engaged the second Mark IV, but missed. One of the German tanks scored a hit on the suspension of Litherland's tank, but failed to disable it. The return fire from Leach's company was enough to run off the pesky Mark IV.

The commanders emerged from their meeting, and immediately went to work assembling their force for the attack on Ley. Abrams' plan called for all three medium tank companies of the 37th and two companies from the 10th AIB to assemble north and east of Lezey prior to the attack. The entire force would then advance using a defilade route all the way to a position north of Ley, whence it would launch the attack.

For the actual assault, A/37 and B/37 would advance directly toward the town, with one company on each side of the road. A/37, which now had 9 Shermans available (two of which were armed with the newer 76mm gun), would advance to the right of the road, and B/37, with 13 Shermans, to the left. C/37 would seize and hold the high ground (Mannecourt Hill) east of Ley, and protect the left flank of the main force driving into Ley. The supporting artillery would shell the town prior to the tanks making their direct advance toward Ley.

As soon as the preparatory barrage lifted, A/37 and B/37 moved toward the town, with the supporting armored infantry from A/10 and C/10 following in their halftracks. The lead tanks pushed toward Ley without receiving any fire from the Germans. As the American tanks reached the outskirts of the town, a panzer was spotted backing out of a barn. The Sherman tank of Sgt. Noe (A/37) quickly knocked out the enemy tank. As they continued their advance toward the main buildings, A/37 came across some German infantry firing from a trench; the tanks of Sergeants Ellison and Griggs neutralized the enemy position. A/37 continued into Ley with the armored infantry following, and proceeded to clear out the town without too much trouble.

Meanwhile, C Company had begun its advance with little difficulty. As it proceeded toward its objective, the tankers spotted several panzers (probably Mark IVs), and engaged two of them. The two panzers were huddled near a cluster of trees, and C Company knocked them out before they could do any damage. The Shermans swung south, and soon encountered more resistance close to the road, this time in the form of an anti-tank gun and a pair of 20mm anti-aircraft guns. The Shermans had no problem knocking out the enemy guns positions, and resumed the advance. So far, so good.

More tanks were observed on the slope of Mannecourt Hill, and C Company engaged them. Captain Lamison's tanks destroyed three of the enemy tanks, without taking any losses among his own vehicles (Sgt. Dunn claimed two of the tanks, and Lt. Smith the other). The Shermans then turned east, and advanced through the throat of a small valley toward the hill. They drew some fire from German infantry, and lost one Sherman to a panzerfaust, but this barely slowed them down, and they proceeded down the length of the valley toward their objective, with the company's 3rd Platoon leading the way.

The Shermans left the valley to climb the slope of the hill. What they didn't know as they approached the crest was that the Mark IVs of Captain Junghannis' panzer company, supported by some towed anti-tank guns, were set up across a valley in an ambush position on another slope facing Mannecourt Hill.

As the leading Shermans of the 3rd Platoon emerged over the top of the slope, Junghannis' tanks opened fire, knocking out one of the Shermans as soon as it came into view. The other two platoons gained the top of the hill, and joined the 3rd Platoon in engaging the enemy tanks and towed guns. Four more Shermans were disabled early in the engagement (Lamison thought they were hit by the German anti-tank guns), but the balance of Lamison's Shermans knocked out seven Mark IVs — all that they could see — before pulling back down the slope from whence they came. C Company suffered 21 casualties on Mannecourt Hill, one of which was killed, and five of which were missing.

Realizing that they had come up against a strong enemy position, Lamison radioed for assistance. In response, Abrams pulled B/37 from the action in Ley, and sent it to the aid of C/37. Abrams also headed to the scene in his own tank.

Before Captain Leach brought his full company up to the positions of C/37, he dismounted from his tank to do a reconnaissance on foot. While he was out of his tank, "Blockbuster" took a hit from an enemy anti-tank gun. The shell penetrated the hull of the tank in the right-forward section, killing the bow gunner, Pfc. Popovitch, and the driver, T4 Boggs. Colonel Abrams then brought his own tank into action, advancing several hundred yards into a hull defilade position to fire on the enemy guns.

At this point, it appeared to Abrams that the enemy had pulled back after the engagement with C Company. With darkness approaching, he opted to forego a pursuit of the remaining Mark IV tanks. With the blazing hulks of shattered tanks offsetting the encroaching darkness, B/37 and C/37 pulled back from the hill via the same valley that Lamison had used on his approach, and joined the other elements of TF Abrams near Ley.

Lt. Colonel Abrams now went about reorganizing his force in preparation for an assault on Moncourt. The only interference from the enemy came when Lt. Donnelly (A/37) spotted a German tank about 1500 yards west of the 37th Battalion's assembly area. He fired one round from his tank, which missed. He then told Sgt. Walling to fire on the tank at a range of 1500 yards. Walling's first round fell short, so he adjusted the range to approximately 1600 yards, and then fired three more rounds, at least one of which found its mark and destroyed the panzer. With the display of Walling's gunnery skills in the books, Abrams' task force completed its preparation for the assault on Moncourt.

The Night Assault on Moncourt

The attack on Moncourt was a new venture for the 37th Tank Battalion. Up to this point, they had never engaged in a tank assault at night. "The book" said that tanks could not be successfully employed in the dark. The 37th was about to throw the book out the window.

A heavy artillery barrage signaled the start of the attack on Moncourt. It was here that the 94th employed, for the first time, the "on call" barrage. As described in the 94th AFAB's unit history, "All details were worked out in advance on several numbered concentrations in the target area. Fire was brought down by the task force commander through the artillery liaison officer and lifted by the forward observer with the leading element." This was a highly effective tactic that would be used many times in the future.

The barrage would be lifted at the very moment that the assaulting ground troops were ready to enter the target area. If the artillery barrage didn't kill or wound the enemy, it would certainly drive them to cover. By maintaining the barrage right up until the final approach of the assaulting tanks and infantry, it allowed them to charge in before the Germans could catch their breath and recover their wits from the shelling. Before they knew it, the Americans would be in their midst (usually with devastating consequences for the Germans). It worked in exactly that fashion at Moncourt.

All three medium tank companies and two companies of infantry from the 10th AIB moved toward Moncourt in a tight, cross country formation. All of the units opened fire in unison as they approached, which created an unbelievable spectacle in the night sky. Moncourt began to burn, its buildings set ablaze by the pounding of HE shells and incendiary bullets. The scene was unlike anything the members of the battalion had yet experienced.

The advancing juggernaut overran the enemy's forward positions, and when Moncourt itself was reached, A/37 and A/10 were sent into the town to clean it out. The Germans were completely shell-shocked by the cascade of fire that had rained down upon them, and the men of the 10th AIB raced in and slaughtered them as they cowered in their foxholes. After the enemy was routed, the two A Companies outposted the town, and the balance of the force returned to the battalion assembly area near Ley.

The 37th had more than earned its combat pay for the day, with 16 panzers destroyed and 257 enemy killed. That only 18 POWs were taken is a testimony to the ferocity of the attack (not to mention the nature of fighting at night, when the taking of prisoners becomes a bit more problematic and dangerous). One of the prisoners was a tank crewmember, and he revealed to his captors that of the 32 tanks the Germans had committed to battle, 28 had been destroyed (this total was probably a reflection of the enemy units' total action over several days, and not just this particular day's action versus the 37th).

The Hellcats of the 704th continued to play a pivotal role as well. In the area between Arracourt and Luneville, the M-18 of Sergeant Hicklin zeroed in on an enemy column consisting of an assault gun, a Mark IV, and two Panthers. All of the armored vehicles were moving left to right across his line of sight. Carefully estimating the range to the target at 2000 yards, the gunner then determined that, with a velocity of 2,700 feet per second, a round from his gun would take about two seconds to reach the target. Estimating the speed of the lead vehicle at 15 feet per second, he knew he would have to lead it by 30 feet. To hit the middle of the vehicle, which he knew to be 20 feet in length from his study of enemy armor profiles, the lead would have to be reduced to 20 feet. Conveniently, this equaled one vehicle length, thus making it easier to gauge.

Sure enough, the first round he fired slammed into the flank of the lead panzer. He then hit the panzer at the rear of the column, setting it on fire. The TD crew then slammed rounds into the two panzers in the center. All four vehicles were stopped, and the enemy crews abandoned at least three of them.

The Americans spent the following day consolidating their positions in the area. The 10th AIB and 37th Tank Battalion were ordered to seize the villages of Bezange, Coincourt and Parroy. Bezange was found to be under the control of friendly units, and fortunately, the task force had not called in a preparatory barrage on the town. Coincourt and Parroy, however, were indeed held by the enemy.

At Coincourt, American artillery and air support hammered the town, and when the tanks and infantry entered, they routed the stunned defenders. A similar plan of attack was used at Parroy, commencing at 4:15 P.M. The Germans had fled in advance of the attack, however, and had destroyed all of the bridges in the area that crossed the Marne-Rhine Canal.

A task force led by Major Kimsey was sent to mop up along the north bank of the canal, and destroyed five Panther tanks during the operation. But when Kimsey's Shermans tried to enter the town of Bures, they were driven off by several Panthers firing at long range.

The Germans Resume the Offensive

Reports on the offensive filtered back to OKW, and Hitler was furious when he learned of the losses that his coveted panzer brigades had suffered at the hands of the Fourth Armored Division. It was clear that his plan was unraveling, but that didn't stop him from pressing on in his usual fashion. On September 21, he relieved General Blaskowitz of the command of Army Group G and assigned General Hermann Balck in his place.

Despite the serious losses they had suffered, Balck continued to press the attack (no doubt at the Fuehrer's insistence), and decided to shift the axis of his offensive. On the same day that he assumed command, he pulled back most of his force out of harms' way in order to regroup (elements of the Fourth that pressed forward that day only found weak, isolated pockets of resistance). He also felt a need to stiffen the resolve of his troops, but the method certainly could not be placed in the category of inspired leadership: An order was issued that night that any crews deserting their combat vehicles "will stand before a court-martial and be sentenced to death for cowardice."

On September 22, the Germans launched an attack from Blanch-Eglise to Juvelize. This time, a battalion of panzer grenadiers from the 11th Panzer Division found a weak spot. Once again using dense fog as cover, the German tanks supporting the attack hit the assembly area of the lightly armored 25th Cav Recon Squadron. Seven light tanks were lost as the armored cavalry made a valiant but unsuccessful effort to hold back the

Panthers. The German armor succeeded in gaining the high ground west of Juvelize, overlooking Lezey.

As the battle progressed and the fog dissipated, air support was called in to help the hard-pressed cavalry. P-47s swooped in to attack the advancing enemy column. The appearance of the planes slowed the attackers, but did not stop them. The Germans continued to press, and were getting dangerously close to the 37th's bivouac area. Flames from one of the burning Panthers were visible just 600 yards away from the service company.

Just when things were looking desperate for the Americans, the omnipresent Hellcats of Captain Tom Evans' C/704 arrived to help stem the tide. As his tank destroyers engaged the enemy, Evans directed the fight from his armored car. The German infantry began to advance toward the TD's positions; they moved relentlessly forward, until Evans "fearlessly manned the machine gun of his armored car and drove off the hostile infantry." The battle was now left to the Panthers.

As Evans was having his personal successes against the enemy foot soldiers, his tank destroyers weren't sharing in his good fortune. Enemy rounds struck two of the Hellcats; one was burning, and the other had a track shot off and was immobilized. The crews had bailed out of both vehicles, and it appeared that the Panthers would continue to surge through their position. In a display of courage that earned him the Distinguished Service Cross, Evans mounted the disabled Hellcat, and then single hand-edly loaded and fired the main gun, destroying two of the Panthers. Sensing he had used up his luck, he abandoned the crippled tank destroyer and crawled away under enemy fire. His intuition was working overtime, as the Hellcat was soon hit and set ablaze. He then went on foot to direct the actions of another of his platoons. Evans later offered a glimpse into the horrors of the battlefield that day:

> There were burned vehicles all over the place. I'll never forget this. A German got out of the top of a tank. It was burning and he was on fire. He had his hands ups up and started walking toward us. We were 500 or 600 yards away, looking down into this valley. You could see his jacket smoking, burning on his back. He got within 100 yards of us and finally fell over. Nobody could go after him because of the gunfire. His jacket finally really started to burn and the poor sonofabitch burned-up, right in front of our eyes. But there was nothing we could do.

The Germans paused to regroup. And at that moment, an unexpected fortune of war fell into the laps of the Americans. As the Germans sat perched above Lezey, the officer in charge of their assault force sent a radio message to his commanding officer, informing him that he had achieved his initial objective, and would continue the attack upon further orders. He was informed in return that additional panzers would be sent forward to reinforce his advance, and that supporting artillery fire would be provided from an area near Bourdonnay. The good fortune for the Americans was that they had intercepted the radio message, and were now well aware of the German plan.

The tanks of the 37th launched a counterattack that would break the back of the German effort. B/37 and A/10 attacked the town of Juvelize, which was now a strong-point for enemy tanks and infantry. They knocked the Germans out of their positions in the town, and then advanced on toward the high ground to the southwest. Mean-while, A/37 and C/37 secured the other high ground in the surrounding area, and engaged the enemy tanks at distances ranging from 400 to 2,000 yards.

A/37 established excellent positions from which they could hit the flank of the enemy, and Captain Spencer's seven Shermans proceeded to destroy seventeen enemy tanks out of twenty-two that they faced (the remaining five retreated to safety). The commanding officer of the 111th Panzer Brigade, Colonel Heinrich von Bronsart-Schellendorf, was killed during the battle, and his unit was left in disarray. By the end of the day, the 111th was reduced to only seven tanks and 80 men; the LVIII Panzer Corps reported that a continuation of the attack "is absolutely impossible"; and Captain Spencer had earned the Distinguished Service Cross.

To this point, the primary tank unit engaged in the battle was Lt. Colonel Creighton W. Abrams' 37th Tank Battalion. The 37th's performance in September cemented its reputation as one of the premier tank battalions of the US Army. Abrams, who already had a solid reputation, saw his stock skyrocket, especially in the eyes of General Patton. As the war progressed, Patton lavished great praise on Abrams, saying, "I'm supposed to be the best tank commander in the Army, but I have one peer — Abe Abrams." Patton also once told a group of reporters that if they wanted to interview Abrams, they had better do it quickly, implying that with his bold, up front style of command, he wouldn't be on the list of battalion commanders likely to survive the war.

As we have already seen, Abrams made a point of inserting himself and his own personal command tank ("Thunderbolt") into the action on numerous occasions. His effort on September 20 involved one of those occasions, and he was awarded the Distinguished Service Cross in recognition of the great achievements of that day. During the course of the war, the crew of "Thunderbolt" racked up what is generally acknowledged as the highest kill count of any tank in the 37th Tank Battalion (though an official tally was not kept). The crewmembers of this great tank certainly deserve mention: gunner John Gatusky, loader Len Katz, driver Bob Stillwell, and bow gunner Emil Hanus. Abrams' determination under fire, and his willingness to aggressively engage the enemy, ensured that the 37th remained a hard-charging, high-performance battalion, right up until the end of the war.

The Attack Against CCB

Despite being out-maneuvered and out-fought by the American armor, the Germans didn't give up after their setback on September 22. On the morning of September 24, the 559th Volksgrenadier Division, supported by the remaining tanks of the 106th Panzer Brigade, struck from the direction of Chateau-Salins. After what had been predominately a CCA affair, CCB and the 8th Tank Battalion now found itself in the thick of the September tank battles.

The day began with an unusually heavy artillery bombardment that struck across the entire front held by CCB. It was a sign that something was brewing, and sure enough, the Germans attacked at about 5:45 A.M. The enemy tanks and infantry struck in three separate locations along CCB's defensive perimeter.

By 8:15 A.M., it appeared that one of the thrusts by the 106th Panzer Brigade was gaining ground against CCB's right flank. Over on the left flank, German infantry and

"Thunderbolt," the command tank of the 37th Tank Battalion. September, 1944 (courtesy J. Leach).

tanks emerged from the fog shrouded Foret de Chateau-Salins, and advanced over open ground toward the American positions.

CCB had selected good defensive positions. All of the medium and light tanks, tanks destroyers, and self propelled artillery pieces were arranged near the crest of a ridge that looked down upon the open terrain that the Germans were negotiating. As the enemy exposed themselves, all of the available guns opened up from the ridge. The German advance ground to a halt. The enemy infantry, caught out in the open, pulled back to the cover of the forest. The panzers halted momentarily, but soon resumed their advance without their infantry support.

The panzers were primarily a force of Panthers, with a few Tigers reportedly thrown in the mix. Normally, it would be imperative for the Shermans to jockey for position so that they could get a flank or rear shot on both of these tanks. The frontal armor was simply too thick, and in the case of the Panther, sloped to such a degree that shells would simply ricochet off the armor plate. When taking on a Panther from the front, an extremely precise — or lucky — shot was required in order to cause some sort of damage that would render the tank ineffective (such as a strike on the gun barrel, or perhaps knocking off a tread that might immobilize the tank).

In this instance, however, the nature of the terrain prevented CCB's tanks and tank destroyers from gaining favorable firing positions against the side or rear of the enemy tanks. To get to a good shot, the American armor would have had to descend from their ridge positions, and in the process, expose themselves to the powerful 75mm high velocity guns of the Panthers (not to mention the even deadlier 88mm cannons mounted on the Tigers). Even with the superior hydraulic turret traverse and gyro stabilizers of the Shermans and Hellcats, which allowed them to move and fire more effectively than their German counterparts, the open ground they would have had to cover in order to close within effective range would have simply become a graveyard for American tanks.

Instead, the American tankers and TD crews used the ridgeline to their advantage. Using a technique known as "turret defilade," they would pull their vehicles behind the crest of the ridge far enough so that the enemy could not see the tank. The tank commander, standing in the opening of his turret, would be able to instruct the driver to pull forward or back so that he could see over the ridge. He would then spot his targets, and give the gunner the bearings while the tank was still out of view. Then on command, the tank would pull forward in order to have the gun clear the top of the ridge. The gunner would engage the target, and typically try to squeeze off a few shots before the commander pulled the tank back from view. This tactic gave the enemy a very small target to shoot at (only the turret of the tank being exposed), and if the commander timed his departure from the ridge correctly, the enemy would not have time to draw a bead on the turret before it disappeared. If the terrain permitted, the tank or TD could then scoot to a different position along the ridge, and repeat the procedure (if the tank continued to reappear in the same position, it certainly would increase the risk that a German gunner would have the location targeted the next time he popped into view).

The problem that CCB was encountering, no matter how excellent the turret defilade position, was that the German armor was at a range that was unfavorable for the Shermans' 75mm guns. When the Panthers placed a Fourth Armored tank turret in its sights, it had a decided advantage. The men of the 8th Tank Battalion and 704th TD Battalion were scoring some hits, but not fast enough to deter the advance of German steel. It began to appear that the enemy tanks might manage a breakthrough.

But the Americans had an unexpected ace up their sleeve. Though the weather was absolutely miserable, two squadrons of P-47s from the 405th Fighter Group (the 509th and 510th) were dispatched toward the scene of the battle. After their attempts to climb above the cloud cover met with failure, the pilots had to rely on their instruments for navigation. One of the squadrons failed to find the battlefield, but while searching, attacked an enemy convoy they spotted from the air.

The other squadron reached the general area, and came down underneath the cloud cover, less than 800 feet above the ground. A ground controller then guided them during the final approach to the targets.

The Thunderbolts flew across the battlefield only 15 feet above the ground, skip-bombing and strafing the enemy tanks as they streaked by. The air attack threw the balance of power in favor of the Americans. The remaining panzers followed their support-ing infantry back to the woods, and the threat subsided. Smoking tanks littered both sides of the battlefield, but the German advance in this sector had been turned back. The Germans left behind 11 tanks and approximately 300 dead. The positions of CCB were secure, and they owed a large debt to the flyboys who come in to help them out.

The appearance of air support was not anticipated by the tankers of CCB, and certainly caught the Germans off guard, as they had attacked believing that the weather was on their side. Patton would later describe the effort of the 405th Fighter Group as "a very fine feat of air co-operation." For their effort that day, the 405th was awarded a Distinguished Unit Citation.

A Final Strike Against CCA

Manteuffel was running out of options. Hitler, who was now distracted by the events that had unfolded farther north in the wake of Operation Market-Garden and the assault on Aachen, refused to send additional resources to restock the depleted ranks of the 5th Panzer Army. Despite his losses and the decision not to replenish his com-mand, Manteuffel was still expected to continue the attack. He would have to forge ahead with the remnants of his battered army, and hope for the best.

The 11th Panzer Division, commanded by General Wietersheim, had now arrived on the scene, bringing with it a paltry 16 tanks. The panzer brigades were no longer effective fighting units, so Manteuffel merged the remnants of the brigades with the 11th Panzer, 21st Panzer, and 15th Panzer Grenadier divisions. All told, he mustered about 50 tanks. His last hope would be pinned to this hodge-podge of units.

Manteuffel was beginning to learn that, against his American foe, he could not employ the same tactics that had served him so well on the Russian front. He now took advance reconnaissance more seriously, and took greater care to scout the enemy's posi-tions prior to committing his main force. As a result of that reconnaissance, he was informed that the crossroads town of Moyenvic was vacant of Americans troops. He swept into the town on the morning of September 25; this helped secure his own right flank, and he planned on following up on his unopposed success by hitting the left flank of CCA.

Shortly after 10 A.M., up to three hundred enemy infantry were reported advanc-ing toward Juvelize from the north. Meanwhile, 30 enemy tanks were reported near Marsal, about two miles west of the enemy infantry formation. The enemy advanced at a steady rate, driving back the forward elements of the 25th Cav Recon Squadron, which had been screening the American positions. The Germans then hit the forward outposts of the 10th and 53rd Armored Infantry Battalions, driving the Americans out of their positions. B/37 was sent to support the armored infantry, and by shortly after noon, the line was restored and the Germans in the area driven off, save at the town of Moncourt, which the Germans captured and held (Art West had a narrow miss near the tail end of this engagement. He and his crew had just exited his light tank — a tank which had been given to him by Lt. Colonel Abrams — when an artillery shell landed directly on top of the M5, completely destroying it.)

Just as this situation was being cleared up, C/37 came under attack, and Abrams radioed back to CCA, "my position being attacked by unknown number of infantry and five tanks." A/37 was dispatched to counterattack the German force. The Shermans became heavily engaged, but they could not force the Germans to break off the attack. In the meantime, the German infantry continued to apply pressure on B/37 and C/37. The TDs that had been supporting the area had to withdraw when the enemy infantry closed in (their opened topped turrets being much too vulnerable to artillery and grenades). Battery B of the 94th AFAB, which had taken up firing positions at Juvrecourt, provided fire support to help hold back the German attack near the salt works at Lezey (the rest of the 94th was relocating toward Arracourt at the time).

All of the resources that Abrams had available were now committed, and the pressure on his position was mounting. He was without adequate flank protection, and was outnumbered in terms of infantry support. Aware that there was only one bridge leading out of the area through Lezey, Colonel Clarke realized that the situation was becoming perilous, so the decision was made to pull back and consolidate the line further to the west, before the Americans were trapped on the wrong side of the bridge. With the assistance of strong artillery support from B Battery, the 37th and 10th Battalions pulled back and took up positions straddling the Rechicourt-Bezange road. Fortunately, the Germans did not follow up on their limited success.

The Fourth Armored now worked to consolidate its positions, remaining ever alert for more enemy counterattacks. On September 26, the 35th Infantry Division took over the positions of CCB. Dager's command then headed south to occupy defensive positions on the right flank of CCA. This helped the situation significantly, as it shortened Wood's front and enhanced the Fourth Armored's logistical situation.

The 10th Armored Infantry Battalion was now assigned to CCB. Major West's men spent much of the day on the 26th moving south to their new positions along the line extending from Rechicourt to Bezange. The morning hours passed without incident, but at about noon, the enemy started pouring artillery fire into their area. The Americans answered with their own artillery, and the two sides continued to shell one another throughout the day.

At about 4 P.M., Company B finally rejoined the 10th AIB (they had been detached and assigned to CCB since September 10), and was placed on the battalion's left flank. A/10 continued to hold the battalion's right flank, and C/10, the center. The HQ Company's heavy weapons platoon was placed in support of A/10, with its machine guns positioned to cover a large draw and wooded area in front of A Company. To the left of the 10th AIB was the 53rd AIB, and to their right, the 35th Infantry Division, elements of which held the town of Rechicourt.

Near the position of A/10 was a dominating piece of real estate called Hill 265. In order to better the battalion's overall defensive position, A/10 was ordered to seize the hill. Little did the men of A Company know that Hill 265 was about to become a

Pvt. Kenneth Boyer, 37th Tank Battalion. September 26, 1944 (National Archives Photograph SC194706).

magnet, drawing both American and German forces into a pitched battle for control of the heights.

Before nightfall on September 26, two platoons of armored infantry, supported by the heavy weapons platoon and the howitzers of the 94th AFAB, ascended Hill 265. When they reached the top, they were engaged by a platoon of German infantry, who were supported by three Panther tanks and a complement of artillery. The Americans wiped out the enemy platoon, but suffered heavy casualties themselves; 55 men had climbed the hill, and only 13 returned from the mission.

With both sides spent, the hill was left vacant, resulting in a void in the 10th Armored Infantry Battalion's line. To fill the gap, the first platoon of A/10, under the leadership of 1st Lt. James H. Fields, was sent under cover of darkness to occupy the crest. Before dawn, the platoon dug in and established a firm defensive position on top of Hill 265. For the time being, the 10th AIB's front appeared to be in solid shape.

The withdrawal of CCA from Juvelize, the realignment of CCB on the right flank, and the insertion of all three armored infantry battalions on the front line marked the temporary end of the Fourth Armored Division's aspirations for offensive action in the area. The 37th was placed in reserve, while the 8th and 35th Tank Battalions remained forward to support the armored infantry. Back on September 23, Bradley had informed Patton that, due to the supply situation, the Third Army would have to revert to a defensive posture, and the Fourth now complied with that request. But the battle was far from over.

The Battle for Hill 265

Manteuffel claimed a victory when CCA withdrew from Juvelize. In the wake of Clarke's move to the west, the Germans swept back into the towns of Juvelize, Lezey, Moncourt, and Coincourt. Not being content to rest on their thin laurels, the Germans made plans to resume their attack on September 27. Combat losses and maintenance issues had significantly reduced the amount of armor available to Manteuffel, and he now went forward with only six Mark IVs, 24 Panthers, and a few assault guns.

Manteuffel's immediate objective was the capture of two key hills (318 and 293) on the right flank of the Fourth Armored, which was now held by CCB. Kampfgruppe Hammon, consisting of the remnants of the 113th Panzer Brigade and the 11th Panzer Division's reconnaissance battalion (about 25 tanks, in total), was charged with capturing the heights, and if successful, continuing the drive in the direction of Arracourt.

But before the assault on Hill 318 could take place, Manteuffel wanted to secure the right flank of his attacking force, which was now threatened by the 10th Armored Infantry Battalion's occupation of Hill 265. From their positions atop Hill 265, the Americans could observe the movement of the German forces and could potentially disrupt Manteuffel's attempt to capture Hill 318. The 111th Panzer Grenadier Regiment was assigned the task of recapturing Hill 265.

During the very early morning hours of September 27, the grenadiers advanced unopposed into the village of Bezange-la-Petite, and then moved into position just south of Hill 265 in preparation for the assault. At 6:00 A.M., the Germans began their attack. Lt. Fields' 1st platoon, which had occupied the hilltop during the dead of night, was still the only American unit defending the heights. The fighting was intense and at close range; Fields' platoon suffered numerous casualties.

Soon after repelling the first wave of the attack, Fields heard one of his men calling for medical aid. Knowing that there were no medics available on the hill, he left the protection of his own trench and went to assist the soldier. He had no sooner reached the man's foxhole than the fighting intensified again. Almost immediately, one of his squad leaders was shot through the head. Fields turned in that direction and saw the German who had pulled the trigger. But before Fields could fire and avenge the squad leader's death, an enemy round ripped through his left cheek, wreaked havoc on his teeth and tongue, and then exited through his right cheek. With his mouth filled with blood and the shattered remnants of his teeth and jaw, he was unable to speak.

Rather than leave the hilltop to seek medical aid for what was obviously a severe injury, Fields held his position. With no medic available atop the hill, he tended to his own wounds. He shoved a compress into his mouth, and then pressed another compress over his right cheek in hopes of slowing down the bleeding. Despite his wound, he maintained the composure and presence of mind needed to lead his platoon. Without the use of his voice, he relied on hand signals and written notes to direct the flow of the battle

The fight for Hill 265 intensified when three Panther tanks joined the attack. The German tank commanders rode into battle with hatches open and their heads exposed in order to better observe and guide the attack. Lieutenant Fields, shooting left handed as he held the compress against his shattered face, drew a bead on the tank commander of the lead Panther. He scored a hit. His platoon responded by pouring an intense volume of small arms fire against the other two Panthers. Now leaderless, the three tanks pulled back from the hill.

The fight was far from over. The German infantry continued to press the attack, and at one point, two German machine guns hit part of Fields' platoon with a deadly crossfire. Fields grabbed a light machine gun from one of his own positions that had been knocked out and, firing from the hip, silenced both of the enemy machine guns. Unable to wrestle the hill away from Fields' men, the Germans pulled back at about noon. They had tried in vain for almost six hours to kick Fields' platoon off the hill. He and his men wouldn't budge.

With the hill secured, Fields finally left his position and made his way back to the battalion aid station, located a half-mile from Hill 265. Though in need of treatment at a field hospital with better medical resources, Fields refused to be evacuated until he had time to draw a detailed sketch showing the enemy positions around the hill. Lieutenant Fields later offered the following assessment of the battle:

> I'll never know why they didn't overrun us. We didn't have a thing in the world to stop them, other than a bunch of fighting mad doughs who just wouldn't give up. My platoon was wonderful that day. No one ever thought of withdrawing. At one time those tanks were so damned close they were firing direct fire at the tops of our foxholes with their 75's.

The fight for Hill 265 took on special meaning for the Fourth Armored Division, as Lieutenant James H. Fields joined Sgt. Joe Sadowski as one of three men who would earn the Congressional Medal of Honor.

The Germans made one more assault that night at 9:50 P.M., and this time, the platoon of A/10 responsible for holding the hill was forced to withdraw, leaving the way open to the 10th AIB's command post. A platoon each of American engineers and tank destroyers were sent forward to retake the hill, which they accomplished before sunrise.

Hill 265 was not the only hot spot for the 10th AIB that day. Earlier, a heated battle had also taken place about two miles north of Hill 265, near the boundary between the 10th AIB and the 53rd AIB. The 110th Panzer Grenadier Regiment captured the town of Xanrey, and at about 4 P.M., while pausing to regroup, the Germans were dealt a devastating blow by the 35th Tank Battalion. The Germans suffered 135 casualties in the attack. The grenadiers were forced to retreat, and the left flank of the 10th AIB remained secure for the duration.

On September 28, the Germans continued their efforts around Hill 265. Shortly before 10 A.M., the enemy placed a smoke screen in front of A/10's positions, and behind it the Germans assembled six tanks and up to a battalion of infantry.

When the enemy tanks pinned down the armored infantry atop the hill, Pfc. R.M. Murray volunteered to drive a jeep through the enemy's line of sight in order to secure some supporting tanks. As he raced off, his jeep was peppered with shrapnel from the shells that chased him, but he continued on until he carried out his mission. American tank destroyers and a company of tanks, supported by fighter planes, then came forward to throw back the enemy attack, knocking out several of the enemy tanks in the process.

The Germans launched yet another attack at 7 P.M. This time, German tanks reached the crest of the hill, and fired point-blank into the forward foxholes of A Company's 3rd platoon, inflicting heavy losses. As the platoon pulled back, Pvt. Albert Knapp left the protection of his foxhole and took over an abandoned machine gun, with which he continued to fire at the enemy infantry at a range of only 30 yards. He remained in his position until he was killed (he was posthumously awarded the Sliver Star).

The 1st Platoon, now led by 2nd Lt. Adrian Tessier, took over the 3rd Platoon's positions. Tessier manned one of the platoon's two machine guns, and in addition to killing several Germans, forced the enemy tankers to button up. But despite his efforts, his platoon was also pushed back off the hill. He and his men fell back to positions on the reverse slope. Once the Americans had pulled back, American artillery support was called in to hammer the top of Hill 265. It was the best the 10th AIB could muster at the moment in the face of the relentless enemy assault.

During the following two days, the Germans continued to exert pressure across the front of the 10th AIB. With the aid of artillery and tank fire directed from their positions atop Hill 265, German tanks and infantry made a successful penetration into Bezange on September 30. The panzers were able to fire directly into the 10th AIB's command post and bivouac area, destroying three half tracks and damaging two more (Art West later commented to Captain Leach that he had lost nineteen halftracks during the entire engagement). Heavy return fire from the tanks and TDs supporting the 10th AIB helped push the German tanks away from the crest of the hill.

During the days that followed, the pressure in front of the 10th AIB began to decrease, as the Germans shifted their attention to other areas along the front of the Fourth Armored. The heavy losses incurred by the Germans also served to slow down the intensity of their efforts. The 10th AIB would basically hold in place until October 7, when the 104th Infantry Regiment relieved it.

The Germans' Last Gasp at Hill 318

Despite the failure to fully secure their right flank, the Germans opted to proceed the following day with their assault on Hill 318. But before we explore the details of the battle, we must back up a few days and examine how the defenders of the hill came into their positions prior to the German attack.

On the afternoon of September 25, the 51st Armored Infantry Battalion received word that it would be handing over its positions to elements of the 35th Infantry Division. The battalion would then move into a rear area position so that the troops could "secure as much rest, maintenance and rehabilitation as possible pending establishment of a greater flow of supplies from the rear." The spirits of the battalion were lifted as the news spread regarding their departure from the front line.

The battalion staff was instructed that "no undue haste be employed" during the transition of the troops to the rear. They were to take a methodical approach to the transfer of their positions.

Later that evening, the battalion liaison officer returned with an update to their orders. Manton Eddy had ordered CCB to move back at once, without waiting for relief from the 35th Infantry Division. The battalion would now have to hastily assemble in the dark, and make a night march to their assigned assembly area on the right flank of CCA. So much for rest.

The company commanders were highly concerned about the withdrawal orders. In order to reach their assigned assembly area, they would have to march their men through the Forest of Gremency, where the enemy was still reported to be operating. As they prepared to move, the prospect of an ambush was on everyone's minds.

For security purposes, the platoons were sent out in ten-minute intervals. Fortunately, the move to the assembly area took place without any mishaps. The only action that took place occurred when some panzers appeared near the positions of B/51. Captain Rockafeller called for support from the 8th Tank Battalion, which obliged by knocking out three Tiger tanks.

Upon the battalion's arrival at the assembly area, the platoons were crammed into trucks and jeeps, and at 1:15 A.M., began moving toward their next assignment. It was a chilly night, made more uncomfortable by a heavy rain that fell as the convoy started making its way south. Several vehicles got stuck in the mud, which slowed down the pace of the column. The rain continued all night, and it was still pouring when the convoy pulled into their assembly area between Hoeville and Serres. When they arrived, the sun was just beginning to rise, and with it, the hope that the temperature would rise as well.

Upon their arrival and assembly, the battalion was immediately ordered to move forward to relieve two battalions of the 320th Regiment, which had been holding a line south of Arracourt centered on Hill 318. It took some time for the battalion staff to work out the relief arrangements with the 320th, which in turn gave the men some time to recoup a little bit from the arduous nighttime drive.

The battalion moved out shortly after 11 A.M., and passed through Arracourt two hours later. It was here that guides from the Recon Platoon greeted them and escorted the companies to their new positions. Companies A and C took over the positions of two battalions of the 320th (a frontage of some 5000 yards), while B Company moved into the town of Rouville and the farms between Arracourt and Rechicourt. By nightfall on September 26, the relief was complete. Company A of the 10th Armored Infantry Battalion was positioned on the left (near Hill 265) of the 51st AIB, and Troop B of the 25th Cavalry Recon Squadron on the right.

As they traded places in the line, the men from the 320th made a point of telling the men of the 51st what a quiet sector this had been. The words of comfort were perhaps a curse, as heavy artillery fire soon began to fall on the battalion's positions and in the town of Rechicourt. Reports came in that enemy tanks were operating in the area, and it was feared that a German counterattack might be in the works. The concern was reinforced when two prisoners revealed that they had been ordered to attack twice that day (they were members of the 11th Panzer Division's reconnaissance battalion).

With an enemy attack appearing to be a real possibility, extra effort was made to ensure the front line was buttoned up. A platoon from A/51 was sent to establish contact on the flanks of the battalion. The report sent back by its commander, Lt. Lahey, was ominous: "I have made contact with the 10th Armored Infantry Battalion on my left and Tiger tanks on my right." With concerns over the German's intentions on the rise, a company of tank destroyers (A Company) from the 691st TD Battalion arrived to reinforce the 51st AIB's position.

The weather improved as the night wore on. The rain had stopped earlier in the day, and the night sky was clear, with the Moon making an appearance for the first time in a long while. From their hilltop positions, the horizon was aglow from the burning hulks of three tanks off in the distance; a silent, fiery testimony to the fierce battles that had been taking place in this sector for almost a week now.

As the men watched the eerie scene, they were disgusted with the situation they now found themselves in. Not much more than 24 hours before, they had been looking forward to a rest period where they could regroup and get some much needed rest. Instead, they had to suffer through a miserable truck ride only to be thrown into a hot section of the front. As some of the men tried to get some sleep amidst the sporadic artillery shells, others watched cautiously for signs of the enemy. The morning couldn't come soon enough.

When daylight arrived, an unusually clear sky and fair temperature greeted the 51st Armored Infantry Battalion. It was a welcome change from the weather that had become customary during recent days and weeks. As the day progressed, however, clouds rolled in and the temperature dropped. Then the rain returned, making this day just as miserable as the ones that had preceded it.

On September 27, the 51st AIB got busy improving its positions and lines of communication. Telephone lines were laid between the armored infantry companies, and communication with the supporting artillery from the 253rd Armored Field Artillery Battalion was buttoned up. All of this took place as both sides kept trying to disrupt the other with artillery fire.

The activity reached a fever pitch at about 10 A.M., when a large force of German tanks and infantry began advancing toward Hill 318. Six American artillery battalions responded, as did the tank destroyers from the 691st TD Battalion. The German advance was halted before it ever got close to the hill, and the enemy withdrew. The pressure against A/51 was greatest at their positions located near Rechicourt, and twice during the day they received assistance from B/51.

Despite the bad weather, planes from both sides flew over the battlefield during the day. Shortly after 1:00 P.M., a flight of three enemy fighters soared overhead, and a host of American machine guns swung to the heavens to throw up an ineffective curtain of lead. The German planes flew off unscathed. The pilot of an American P-51 wasn't as fortunate; late in the day, his plane was downed within sight of the 51st AIB's positions. Thankfully, the pilot was seen drifting slowly to earth beneath his parachute, and came down a few miles away from the battalion command post.

During the night that followed, a great deal of activity could be heard taking place out in front of the positions of the 51st AIB. Enemy tanks and vehicles could be heard moving nearby, and men could be heard digging in at positions not far from the armored infantry's forward positions. Artillery fire was unleashed in the direction of the sounds, but there was no telling what the effect was. The only damage that had been inflicted with certainty was the destruction of one enemy tank, a 88mm gun, and two halftracks that were knocked out during the night by the American tank destroyers.

At 2:30 A.M. on the morning of September 28, a German patrol stumbled into the command post of the cannon company. T/Sgt. Breece saw them approaching, and brought down machine gun fire and grenades that chased off the small band of enemy soldiers. The rest of the night was quiet, and at sunrise, the armored infantry were greeted by another day of unusually nice weather, relative to the usual rain, mud, and damp chill. The front line remained quiet throughout the morning.

All of that changed in the afternoon, when the Germans began shelling the positions of A/51 and C/51, inflicting some casualties in the process. Within a span of eleven minutes, some 70 shells fell into the positions of A Company; the Germans were firing the heavy stuff, as no shell that struck was less than 105mm. The Americans reciprocated by shelling suspected enemy positions at Bures and Parroy. After the shelling, things settled down once again until dusk.

As part of the defensive scheme for Hill 318, an American engineer unit was ordered to occupy prepared defenses (primarily slit trenches) that had been dug in the heavily wooded south face of the hill. These positions were to the right of C/51, which occupied the top of the hill. For some reason, however, the engineers had not appeared, and as night began to fall, the right flank of C Company was wide open.

The Germans hit C/51 with a heavy artillery barrage just as the sun was setting. Driven to their foxholes and trenches, the Americans atop the hill could not observe their right flank in the woods, and the German infantry used this to their full advantage. A battalion of panzer grenadiers advanced up the south face of the hill, worming their way through the empty slit trenches that had been reserved for the missing engineers. They were able to move extremely close to the forward positions of C Company, and began lobbing grenades into the American foxholes. The men stationed at the forward artillery observation post were injured, and had to retreat from their position when it came under pressure from the enemy.

After fierce fighting, C/51 was forced to abandon Hill 318. They remained on the rear slopes however, and called in the support of the division's artillery in order to knock the Germans off. German tanks came into play in the area around the hill, but tank destroyers from the 602nd TD Battalion forced them to break off the attack.

Fighting on the hill continued throughout the night at close range. But as sunlight struggled to cut through the thick early morning fog on September 29, the Germans still held Hill 318. Flush with the success of having occupied the hill, the Germans beefed up their units in the area. The 11th Panzer Division was now reinforced with a battalion from the 110th Panzer Grenadier Regiment, an armored engineer company, and the remaining panzers from the 111th and 113th Panzer Brigades. They were able to bring their tank strength up to 18 Mark IVs and 20 Panthers; eleven Flakpanzer IVs provided additional support.

With the approach of sunrise, CCB was faced with an urgent situation. Once daylight and good visibility arrived, the bowels of CCB would be exposed, and the Germans could easily direct artillery fire at their positions. In an attempt to head off a potential disaster, CCB planned a fresh assault on the hill that would take place at first light. The 51st AIB would be reinforced with elements of the 8th Tank Battalion, and the two units would attempt to take back the heights.

Fortunately for CCB, visibility at dawn was terrible, as a thick layer of fog and mist enveloped the battlefield. This severely limited the German's view from atop the hill. But it also limited the distance the advancing tankers could see to no more than 30 feet beyond the tip of their guns. But as the 37th had found during the tank battles a week earlier, the poor visibility gave the American tankers one important advantage: it negated the superior range of the panzer's high velocity guns.

The tanks of A/8 and C/8 led the charge toward Hill 318. At first, they did not encounter any enemy tanks. The German response was initially limited to small arms fire coming from the grenadiers dug in along the base and slopes of the hill. While the bullets and shrapnel couldn't tear through steel, it was not without effect. As usual, the tank commanders were riding with their heads out of the turret, so as to guide the tanks with maximum effectiveness. Platoon Sergeant George Carge (C/8) was killed when struck in the head with a single bullet.

With the tanks of the 8th now supporting them, C/51 renewed its attack toward the crest of the hill. The assault force surged its way to the top, and Hill 318 was once again in the hands of the Fourth Armored Division.

But the battle was far from over. As visibility gradually improved, German Panthers opened up on the forces from CCB that were now atop the hill. Enemy artillery opened up as well, and after a hefty barrage, German tanks and infantry moved once again toward Hill 318. Firing from their reacquired hilltop position, the Americans held back the Germans. The tanks of C Company scored eight confirmed kills of enemy tanks, without losing a single Sherman in the process.

While the German advance may have stalled, it had not yet turned into a retreat. As the battle continued, the fog and mist lifted, and sunlight bathed the battlefield. As if on cue, Thunderbolts from the XIX TAC descended upon the scene and broke the back of the German assault. The 25th Armored Cavalry and some TDs from the 704th also joined in the fight, circling around the woods and cutting off the enemy's route of retreat. The fighter-bombers then poured it on.

By 2:00 P.M., the Germans had been beaten back, and within another two hours, the 51st AIB reported the situation as being "well in hand." The nearest enemy concentration remained in the woods on the 51st's right flank, where the Germans continued to snipe at the Americans. Some additional casualties were suffered in that area; among them, Pfc. Heffernan, who was killed by machine gun fire while laying down telephone wire for C Company. But all in all, the Germans were spent. By the time the dust had settled on Hill 318, 400 Germans lay dead or wounded, and 24 of the 25 panzers they sent into the final battle were destroyed or disabled.

The impressive performance of the 8th Tank Battalion was a parting gift of sorts

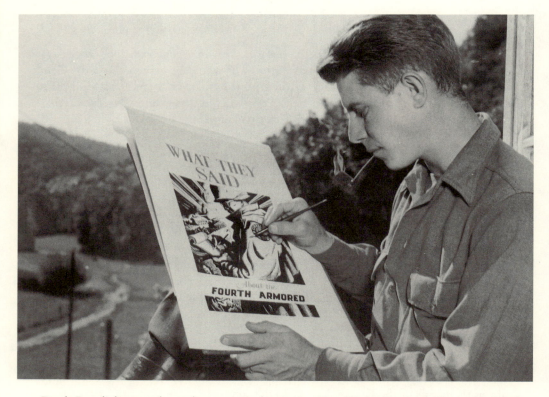

Frank Besedick at work on the cover art for the booklet *What They Said About the Fourth Armored* (courtesy K. Besedick).

for its commander, Colonel Conley, who was moving on to a position as G4 (Corps Logistical Staff Officer) for Maj. General Walton Walker's XX Corps (Conley was Walker's son-in-law). Lt. Colonel Henry (Pat) Heid was awarded the reins of the battalion. Heid had been the S-3 for Colonel Bruce Clarke's CCA for most of the campaign across France, and had commanded the 704th TD Battalion for a scant 11 days before taking Conley's place. The 704th was, in turn, handed over to Major Dan Alanis, who had been the S-3 for the 51st AIB.

The Germans tried to counter during the next several days in order to reverse the situation and make good on their losses, but the Fourth Armored Division dominated at every turn. The front was stabilized, and the artillery battalions were moved closer to the front, in order to extend their firing range deeper into the German rear areas. Each day that followed featured artillery and mortar barrages conducted by both sides. It was a far cry from the slashing, mobile warfare that had dominated the early combat experience of the division.

By the end of September, Wood's division had decimated one of the few panzer forces available to meet the advancing Americans. They had demonstrated that they could control the battlefield, even when the odds were stacked against them. The "Great Tank Battle at Arracourt," as it would become popularized, had given birth to a fighting legend.

6. Rest

Patton's Best

On October 1, General Patton paid a visit to his good friend "P," and together they toured some of the units of the Fourth Armored Division. The Third Army commander noted, "as usual with that division, the dispositions were excellent." He also commented to Wood, "I consider the 4th Armored Division the finest armored division in the United States Army." Wood in turn instructed his combat commanders to disseminate Patton's statement to all of the troops in the division.

The men of the Fourth were indeed worthy of Patton's high praise. They had captured Avranches, the gateway to Brittany and central France. They launched a bold encirclement of Rennes, setting it up for easy capture by trailing forces. They sliced across the Brittany Peninsula, and after turning east, made one of the fastest, boldest drives in the history of armored warfare. The division liberated countless villages, towns, and cities as it raced east across France. Nantes, Orleans, Troyes; these were just some of the more renowned objectives they captured on the way toward their crowning achievement: the encirclement of Nancy, and the great tank battles at Arracourt. They took on the heaviest armored counterattack the Germans could muster, and beat them back with heavy losses. After little more than two months in action, they had indeed established themselves as "Patton's Best."

Patton wasn't the only one who considered the Fourth Armored to be "the best." If you asked just about any infantry unit that fought alongside Wood's division, they would tell you that the Fourth Armored stood head and shoulders above the other tank units. By the time the war was over, men from the 80th Infantry Division had said it. So too did the men of the 35th. And the 26th. And the 87th. And the 101st Airborne. The accolades were seemingly endless.

One of the key reasons the tankers of the Fourth Armored were held in such high regard is that they didn't have a tendency, unlike many other tank outfits, to "button up" when going into action. As had been so amply demonstrated by the death of Sergeant Carge at Hill 318, the tankers of the Fourth Armored Division were a breed apart when it came to their protocol for working with infantry.

Other armored units did indeed tend to button up when in combat. Closing the hatches protected the crew from enemy fire, but limited the effectiveness of the tank. The veterans of the Fourth, in contrast, would maneuver and fight with their hatches open, keeping their heads exposed for better visibility and communication with their supporting infantry. As Lt. Colonel Abrams used to say, "the only thing the infantry has between them and the enemy is a wool shirt." He didn't expect his men to be bashful about keeping their heads out of the turret, given the sacrifices being made by the men with their boots on the ground. As a result, the infantry loved working with the tanks of the Fourth Armored Division. Whether or not this practice led to higher casualties among the tankers is debatable; after all, a more effective tank resulted in quicker identification and destruction of the enemy. In the end, more lives were probably saved than lost by the practice. Still, it was clearly selfless behavior on the part of the tankers. And it was one of the things that made the Fourth Armored the best.

A Welcome Rest Period

As the calendar flipped to the month of October, the autumn weather of the Lorraine region began to cast a pall over the battlefield. The rain, mud, and bone-chilling cold made for a miserable life. During those first days of October, the only consolation was that the front had grown relatively quiet. The Germans had clearly spent themselves during the past two weeks. Unfortunately, Patton's army was not in a position to exploit the opportunity this presented.

With much of the Allied line pausing to consolidate their positions (an undesired pause, as the lion's share of supplies continued to be funneled to Montgomery), Wood felt it was time for his men to get a breather. On October 2, on the heels of Patton's visit, he sent Patton a written communication, in which he expressed the hope that "we can get a little time out for maintenance and regrouping soon." While it took a few days to arrange, his plea was answered on October 7, when elements of the 26th Infantry Division began moving in to relieve the Fourth Armored. By October 12, the vast majority of the division was off the front line completely.

For the next 27 days, most of the Fourth Armored would be able to rest and refit (the artillery battalions remained in firing positions to support the 26th Infantry Division and Second Cavalry Group). It was a well-deserved pause. And it was well timed, since the road ahead would be, if not literally a rough one, a muddy and torturous one.

The rest period afforded Wood's men the opportunity to perform critical maintenance on their equipment, and to absorb replacements under more reasonable and manageable circumstances than the heat of battle allowed. And there were plenty of replacement officers and enlisted men coming in. On October 6, the 37th Tank Battalion welcomed six new lieutenants. Among them were two men who would figure very prominently in Fourth Armored's future: 1st Lt. Charles P. Boggess, who was assigned to C/37, and 2nd Lt. John A. Whitehill, who was assigned to A/37. During the course of the rest period, the 10th Armored Infantry Battalion welcomed 275 replacements and returnees; the 51st AIB greeted 206.

Lt. Colonel Abrams awards battlefield promotions to the rank of second lieutenant. Facing camera, from left, recipients S/Sgt. Mallon, S/Sgt. Walters, S/Sgt. Farese, T/Sgt. Smith, and S/Sgt. Grubbs. Sgt. Major Hogancamp stands behind Abrams with back to camera (courtesy J. Leach).

In addition to caring for vehicles and weapons, the rest period would be used for additional training, for the benefit of veterans and rookies alike. The fast paced action of the summer and early fall was likely going to give way to a more static form of warfare, and appropriate tactics were reinforced and practiced. In some cases, units experimented with new methods and equipment. As an example, the 51st AIB tried mounting their 57mm AT guns in the beds of their halftracks, rather than towing them (this improvised tank destroyer didn't work very well). C Company of the 10th AIB put in time on the firing range using the new grenade launchers that attached to their M-1 rifles. In preparation for the tough fighting that was anticipated near the German border, full-scale replicas of the Siegfried Line defenses were constructed in order for units to practice their assault tactics.

New weapons and devices were a curiosity, and often the top brass would attend demonstrations of the equipment. In one such instance, General Patton arrived to witness the firing of a halftrack-mounted flame-thrower. Before the commencement of the exercise, the Chemical Corps officer in charge instructed his audience, "Now, if everybody would just step back." Everyone started to move back, except for one: Patton. "What do you mean, 'Step back?' Don't you have any confidence in this weapon working?" was the general's retort. To which the captain replied, "Well, yes, Sir, I do." And then in his own inimitable way, Patton said, "Well, you damn well better have. You're going to stand right next to that thing and I'm going to stand right over here, too." The byproduct of Patton's exhortation was that the crowd reversed direction and now stood where Patton stood, close to the halftrack.

There was also time for rest and relaxation. Many men had been staring death in the face for weeks on end. Good friends had fallen, and men had died in the arms of those who would move on to the next battlefield, wondering when it might be their turn to be cradled by another man wearing the patch of the Fourth Armored Division on his shoulder. A trip to Nancy, or for the luckiest among them, a sojourn to Paris, would offer a brief interlude of sanity in an olive drab world of death and destruction.

Not everyone could travel to the rear on leave, so entertainment was brought forward. In some cases, the festivities were entirely self-made, such as the bash thrown by the 704th TD Battalion on November 1 at the town of Dombasle. Movies such as "Swingtime Johnny," "Jam Session," "Minstrel Men," and "Casanova Brown" graced the impromptu movie theatres set up at the battalion command posts. Ensuring that liquor was available helped with morale in some quarters, and on November 3, CCB issued cognac at the rate of one bottle for every ten men.

Not everyone was inclined to fill their free time with such distractions. Attendance at religious services rose, as men gave thanks for having been given the strength to endure the hardships of the past three months. Heartfelt prayers went out to the men that were not as fortunate to have survived the division's first three months in action. "There but for the grace of God go I" was probably on the lips and mind of every man inclined to worship. If a church were left standing in a liberated town, services would take place in a tranquil, deceptively normal setting. On some occasions, a farmer's barn would suffice as a place to worship away from the harsh elements of the autumn weather. When all else was lacking, open fields would serve as a cathedral for the men of the cloth who offered both prayers for peace, and for victory over their enemies.

The October rest period also afforded higher commanders the opportunity to visit and address the lower echelons. Major General Wood's presence was always an uplifting occasion for the units of the Fourth, and great energy would go into preparing for his visits.

On October 9, Wood visited with the 10th Armored Infantry Battalion. With the full battalion assembled before him, he surprised everyone in attendance by awarding Lt. Colonel West the Distinguished Service Cross for his actions during the battle of Troyes. West, in turn, presented Bronze Stars to two of his men, Tech Sergeant John Consalvi and Pfc. William Bonner. Consalvi's award was earned on August 1, when he grabbed a fire extinguisher in the middle of an enemy artillery barrage to douse the flames of a vehicle loaded with 57mm and .50 caliber ammunition. Bonner's award was given for his actions on July 31 during the attack at Avranches, when he discarded his M-1 in favor of a machine gun, which he promptly fired from the hip in order to increase the firepower of his unit.

The importance of Wood's sojourns can be felt when one reads the combat diaries of the battalions that hosted him. His visits were indelibly recorded, and the highlights of his comments often written down for posterity. His informal speeches were memorable and motivating. As an example, on October 11, he visited and addressed the men of the 51st Armored Infantry Battalion, and remarked that the Fourth Armored Division could not be stopped by the Germans. Any delay the division experienced was, in his words, the fault of those "who could not keep up with us."

Wood's itinerary also took him outside of the boundaries of his division. On Octo-

Men of the 4th AD attend a Protestant service being held in a barn near Arracourt. October 7, 1944 (National Archives Photograph SC195350).

ber 15, he and his immediate boss, General Manton Eddy, traveled with Patton to visit the 26th Infantry Division, where they witnessed "Old Blood and Guts" deliver one of his famous pep talks to the men of that unit. Patton was with Wood yet again on October 20, this time with General Spaatz in tow, to witness a demonstration of the "duck's feet" which had been invented to increase the flotation of the tanks.

During this visit, Spaatz took particular note of Wood's living conditions. Unlike most division commanders, Wood insisted on working under the same conditions that his men endured. Spaatz was distressed when he found that Wood's accommodations consisted of a wet, muddy tent. He was so concerned, in fact, he arranged for the delivery of his own personal trailer as a gift to Wood. The trailer was, as Patton described it, "a huge affair and most luxurious." Wood graciously accepted the gift when it was presented to him, but Patton was quick to point out that "I have never seen a man more pleased than Wood, and yet more determined not to use the trailer." In fact, Wood never did use it. One week later, he returned it to Spaatz.

During the latter part of the month, it appeared that some elements of the division might find themselves back in action. On October 21, the 37th Tank Battalion and A/704 (commanded by 1st Lt. John Preneta) were attached to the 26th Infantry

Division, which was preparing to launch an attack the following day. The 26th ID's objectives were Bezange and Moncourt (two very familiar towns from the days of the Arracourt Tank Battles). Thankfully, Abrams' tanks were not needed during the action. The 704th, however, was called upon to lend a direct assist in the attack.

During an infantry attack near Bezange-la-Petite, the Hellcat platoon commanded by 2nd Lt. Charles Kollin found itself in a minefield under heavy artillery fire. Kollin rallied his platoon, and then "went back and forth through the mine field directing the evacuation of the wounded, then led the attack forward." Meanwhile, his company commander, Lt. Preneta, scouted the area on foot in order to get the attack moving. While on his recon mission, he came across two enemy snipers, and killed them both with only his pistol. He then came upon two other Germans manning a pillbox, and forced them into surrendering. Both Preneta and Kollin were subsequently awarded the Distinguished Service Cross.

The 37th Tank Battalion was back in very fine form at this point. By October 24, it was just five Shermans shy of its full complement of 53, while D Company was at full strength with 17 M5 light tanks. October 25 was a somber day for the battalion, however, when they came upon the three Sherman tanks that A/37 lost to enemy fire back on September 19. "The enemy had despoiled the tanks and neglected to care for the dead." The bodies of six brave tankers, including Lt. DeCraene, were removed from the tanks and taken back for a proper burial.

On November 6, generals Patton, Eddy, and Wood met with all of the battalion commanders and some of the company commanders from Wood's tank and infantry units. The meetings were a preamble to the upcoming winter offensive that would kick off in just a few days. The men who attended came back elated by what the Third Army commander had to say about the Fourth Armored Division:

> The accomplishments of this division have never been equaled. And by that statement I do not mean in this war, I mean in the entire history of warfare. There has never been such a superb fighting organization as the Fourth Armored Division.

Patton also joked about the inability of Hodges' First Army to deliver as planned, and remarked "the First shall be last and the 4th shall be first." There was no doubting Patton's ability to inspire and motivate the men under his command.

An interesting sidebar to the November 6 session was that Patton had not planned on visiting with either the Fourth or Sixth Armored divisions prior to the start of the next offensive. He had scheduled a tour of several divisions for November 5, but left these two veterans units off the list. When word got around to the men of the Fourth Armored that they were not on Patton's itinerary, they requested that he come speak to them. In his words, "I did not include them … as there is nothing about war I can tell them…. I felt that they were such veteran and experienced divisions that it was painting the lily to talk to them; but they seemed quite hurt, so I talked to them."

Changes in Command

This particular rest period brought about a number of changes in the command structure of the Fourth Armored Division. The biggest move involved the helm of

CCA. Colonel Bruce Clarke, who had been the only commander CCA had known in combat, was promoted to brigadier general, and subsequently transferred to the 7th Armored Division, where he would take command of Combat Command B. Each armored division was allocated one brigadier general, and since Holmes Dager already held that position within the Fourth Armored, Clarke's promotion made the transfer a necessity.

Clarke had been a member of the Fourth for a very long time, and among other roles, he had served as the division chief of staff before taking command of CCA/4. He had a very close relationship with Wood, who leaned on him heavily for many affairs within the division. Clarke had made an extremely favorable impression on Patton, who personally argued for his promotion during a tour with General Marshall on October 10.

In the wake of Clarke's departure, Lt. Colonel Abrams was given temporary command of CCA; he would turn it over to Colonel Bill Withers on November 17. Abrams then returned to the 37th Tank Battalion (to the delight of the staff of the 37th, who thought his departure to be permanent).

As tough as conditions were out in the field, many men of the Fourth welcomed and savored the opportunity to serve, despite the inherent risks. One such example was that of Pat Heid, the newly appointed commanding officer of the 8th Tank Battalion. For some time, he had been hiding the fact that he had diabetes; he had been self-administering his insulin in secrecy. Dr. Scotti, the battalion surgeon of the 37th Tank Battalion, became suspicious and reported Heid's condition. This signaled the end of Heid's command, and the 8th Tank Battalion was passed into the hands of Major Tom Churchill.

The first phase of the Fourth Armored Division's campaign in Europe had come to a close. Rested and refitted, with its battalions brought back nearly to full strength after the losses suffered during its first three months in combat, the division would now embark upon the most challenging period in its history.

7. Back on the Offensive

Rain, Mud, and Misery

During the early morning hours of November 8, the rain that poured down upon the sleeping quarters of George Patton created a great anxiety within the general. Fearful that the torrential sheets of rain would hinder the start of his winter offensive, he found himself unable to sleep. To put himself at ease, he pulled down a copy of Rommel's book, *Infantry Attacks*, and by chance turned to a chapter dealing with a battle waged under similar conditions. The fact that the Germans were able to garner success while attacking during inclement weather gave him renewed confidence. He thought, "if the Germans could do it I could." Comforted by the thought, he fell asleep within the hour.

His sleep lasted barely an hour and a half. At 5:15 A.M., he was awakened by the booming guns of the Third Army. The massive display of artillery had seemingly chased the clouds away, and a star-filled sky now graced the battlefield. The day turned out to be "the brightest and best we had had for two months." The Third Army offensive was underway, and with any luck, clear weather would be Patton's ally.

During the first day of the offensive, Patton visited the headquarters of the 80th, 35th, and 26th Infantry divisions, and he also visited with General Wood. By nightfall, two of the three infantry divisions had achieved their assigned objectives. Despite the 35th being slightly behind schedule, the first day's action filled Patton with confidence. But his mood dampened when the rain began to fall once again that evening. After a promising day of clear skies, there would be no respite from the weather that had plagued the Third Army during the weeks preceding the attack.

The weather in November was no better than it had been in October. In fact it was worse, as colder temperatures turned the precipitation to sleet and snow, and higher winds made the cold air seem colder still. Conditions at night were especially miserable for the men that had to remain outside in the elements. It was almost impossible to keep clothing dry, and as the daily temperature readings began to sink lower and lower, trench foot became an increasing threat. A sheltered place to sleep was a luxury of the highest proportions, and some of the incentive for moving forward was the hope that one could take over a town that might offer refuge from the elements. The fields and roads were an absolute muddy mess. The earth, acting like some primordial ooze, sucked in everything that came in contact with it. Even pitching a tent was difficult, as pegs would simply slip out of the ground. All of this made for miserable living and fighting conditions for the men.

Needless to say, the conditions were highly unfavorable for the employment of armor. Most of the time, the tanks were confined to the limited roads in the region. This made their position all too predictable, and the German gunners took advantage of it. When the Shermans came under fire, they typically were unable to deploy off-road, for fear of bogging down in the muddy fields. The special tread extensions that had been demonstrated for Patton during the rest period had been added to the tanks to help improve their "flotation" (in other words, the extensions increased the surface area of the tank tracks, which helped keep the tank from sinking deeper into the mud). The extensions helped a little, but didn't solve the problem entirely.

When the conditions were such that the tanks not dare leave the roadway, the battlefield became a "one-tank front." Nothing to the left. Nothing to the right. No airplanes overhead. Just a single tank at the front of the column, moving forward with all other elements stretched behind it on the road. The front was literally the width of the lead tank. If there were any one way to describe the days that lay ahead, a "one tank front" was it. It was under these conditions that the Fourth Armored Division would be committed to battle on the second day of Patton's offensive.

CCB and Task Force Maybach

General Dager's CCB now consisted primarily of the 8th Tank Battalion, 51st Armored Infantry Battalion, and 22nd Armored Field Artillery Battalion. Some extra armor support was provided by the attachment of C/37 to the 51st AIB. Extra artillery support was provided by the 253rd AFAB. Units from the 24th Armored Engineer Battalion, 489th AAA Battalion, and 704th Tank Destroyer Battalion rounded out the command.

Brigadier General Dager formed two task forces: TF Churchill and TF Maybach. TF Maybach consisted of the 51st AIB, C/37, the 253rd AFAB, C/24 Armored Engineers, a section of C Battery of the 489th, and the 1st Platoon of A/704. TF Churchill contained the majority of the command's armor, as it was built around the 8th Tank Battalion. After leaving their respective assembly areas, the two task forces converged near the town of Manhoue. From that point, they advanced along different routes, with Task Force Churchill on the left, and Task Force Maybach on the right. It was envisioned that they would advance at the same pace, and remain roughly parallel to one another as they attacked through the forward positions of the 35th Infantry Division.

The advance guard of TF Maybach set out 30 minutes ahead of the main body of the task force. The vanguard consisted of A/51, supported by a platoon of Shermans from C/37, the 51st AIB's assault gun platoon, C Battery of the 253rd, the 1st Platoon of C/24, a platoon of Hellcats from A/704, and the AAA section from the 489th. The engineers carried 76 feet of bridge sections with them, in anticipation that swollen

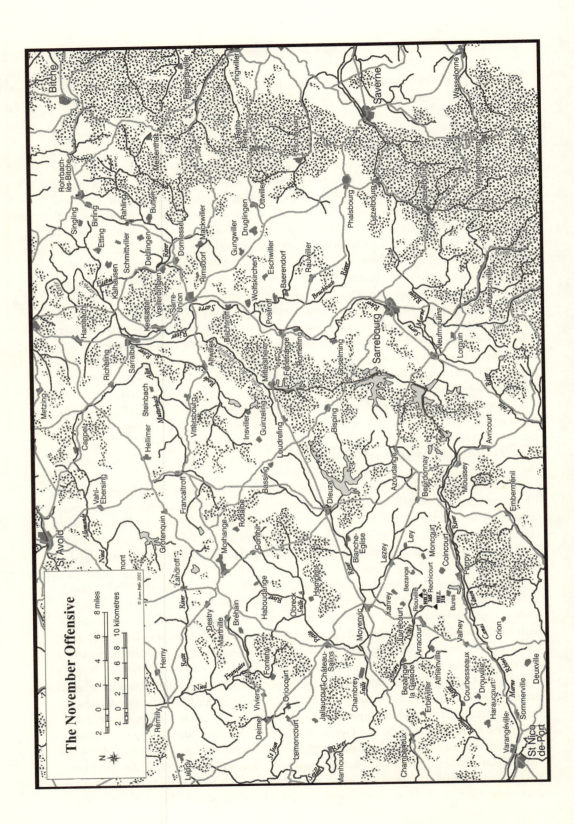

The November Offensive

N

2 0 2 4 6 8 miles

2 0 2 4 6 8 10 kilometres

© Jean-Paul, 2002

Bitche
Rohrbach-lès-Bitche
Singling
Birling
Eting
Schmittviller
Kalhausen
Hanlbach
Richeling
Sarralbe
Metzing
Cappel
Vahl-Ebersing
St Avold
Allmandé
Nied
Gromont
Grostenquin
Landroff
Remilly
Herny
Destry
Marthille
Brehain
Viviers
Oriocourt
Lemoncourt
Luppy
Deime
Manhoué
St Jean
Rejperswiller
Meisenthal
Butten
Rahling
Deflingen
Voellerdingen
Sárre-Union
Keskastel
Harskirchen
Altwiller
Hellimer
Steinbach
Mutterbach
Vittersbourg
Francaltroff
Morhange
Rodalbe
Conthil
Haboudange
Obreck
Fonteny
Jallaucourt-Château-Salins
Chambrey
Champenoux
Ingwiller
La Petite Pierre
Ottwiller
Drulingen
Gungwiller
Rimsdorf
Domfessel
Mackwiller
Wolfskirchen
Eschwiller
Baerendorf
Postroff
Bischtroff
Mittersheim
Guinzeling
Insviller
Loudrefing
Bassing
Harprich
Lezey
Bezange-la-Grande
Erbéviller
Saverne
Haselbourg
Phalsbourg
Lützelbourg
Rauwiller
Bruchbach
Fénétrange
Romelfing
Goselming
Bisping
Dieuze
Blanche-Église
Moyenvic
Xanrey
Bezange
Vaxy
Arracourt
Athienville
Courbesseaux
Drouville
Haraucourt
Varangéville
Wasselonne
Vanden
Rhine
Abreschviller
Sarre
Sarrebourg
Neufmoulins
Loquin
Azoudange
Bourdonnay
Ley
Monongourt
Rechicourt
Riouville
HILL 265
HILL 318
Bures
Coincourt
Pagny
Valhey
Crion
Moussey
Embermenil
Avricourt
Sommerville
Deuxville
St Nico de-Port

streams and blown bridges would be among the obstacles encountered. Due to the slow pace imposed by the terrible road conditions, the 30-minute gap evaporated, and the main body soon closed with the vanguard. From that point on, the entire force basically moved as a single column.

After moving through the forward positions of the 35th Infantry Division near Jallaucourt, TF Maybach headed for the enemy held town of Oriocourt. When the vanguard reached a point about midway between Jallaucourt and Oriocourt, it was greeted by anti-tank gun, machine gun, and mortar fire originating from a wooded area north of Jallaucourt. The Germans employed a tactic they would use repeatedly during the road-bound battles in the Lorraine region: They allowed the column to advance past their positions, and then opened fire on the vehicles at the center of the chain. On this day, 60 Germans, equipped with two anti-tanks guns, allowed the first five American halftracks to pass by "unmolested." They opened up on the sixth halftrack in the column and an assault gun that was next in line, destroying them both.

Captain Rockafeller dispatched three infantry squads and a section of tanks (half a platoon) from C/37 on a mission to suppress the enemy fire coming from the woods. The Sherman gunners knocked out the anti-tank gun, which seemed to bring an end to all of the German's harassing fire. But as the column resumed its advance down the road, the Germans opened fire again using their lighter weapons. Under covering fire provided by the tanks, TF Maybach continued its advance.

The task force was forced to halt when it encountered a strong roadblock at the town of Oriocourt. While patrols went out to look for an alternative route, the Germans began to hit the main body of the task force with heavy artillery fire. When the patrols came back, they reported that they had found another way into Oriocourt, and the task force was soon moving along that route.

The German artillery shells continued to follow TF Maybach right into the town. The Americans moved through Oriocourt with all guns blazing. German resistance was light, and many of the Krauts "came out into the streets with their hands up." The 1st Battalion of the 137th RCT, which was trailing Maybach's force, marched 150 prisoners out of the town. As the task force moved past Oriocourt, they ran into more towed anti-tank guns. Another assault gun and halftrack were lost before the enemy guns were silenced.

The next town in front of Task Force Maybach was Laneuveville-en-Saulnois, located about one mile beyond Oriocourt. German artillery and mortars continued to pursue the task force as it moved into the town. The vanguard came across two German field guns about 400 yards past the town, and overran the position before the Krauts had a chance to turn them against the task force. Three enemy anti-tank guns were also destroyed in this area.

Fonteny was the next town on the task force's list. It was now early afternoon, and despite the conditions and degree of enemy opposition, Task Force Maybach had been making good progress. They hoped to continue on that same pace by moving quickly into Fonteny. Unfortunately, the Germans were well prepared for just such an attack, having reinforced the town's defenses with guns from the 9th Flak Division.

When the head of the column reached the ridge overlooking Fonteny, it barely paused before starting down the steep slope toward the town. The 51st AIB combat diary described the mad, downhill dash toward their objective:

The enemy opened up on the column with a multitude of 20mm anti-aircraft guns, anti-tank guns and mortars. The (enemy) anti-aircraft had been depressed to ground level and laid down a withering fire of air bursts. The third platoon of Co "A," now in the lead, reached the edge of town and was able to take cover, while the first platoon was pinned down along the road. Meanwhile, 4 or 5 enemy tanks appeared on the left flank and opened fire on the advance guard artillery battery (from the 253rd). The battery was ordered behind the last mask and the remainder of Co "A" was emplaced along the ridge in front of Fonteny. Meanwhile, a total of 8 halftracks were knocked out and 7 of these could not be salvaged at all. The last assault gun was also destroyed.

The attack had come completely unglued. The Sherman tanks of Lt. Grubbs' 2nd Platoon were part of the vanguard, and they now found themselves in a tough predicament. Enemy anti-tank guns and tanks were firing at them from several different directions. Seeing that Grubbs was in trouble, the commander of C/37, Captain Lamison, ordered the lieutenant to pull back up over the hill. As Grubbs' tanks tried to withdraw, one of the Shermans was hit by anti-tank fire, killing the bow gunner, Private Hamann. A second Sherman stopped dead in its tracks, victim of a bad clutch. The crew had to bail out, and the Germans subsequently destroyed the tank. The remaining tanks of Grubbs' platoon made it back over the ridge, where they were out of the enemy's line of sight.

Maybach pulled back the rest of the bloodied vanguard as well, and subsequently reorganized for a stronger attack utilizing the main body of his task force. Maybach's plan called for a heavy artillery strike against all of the known or suspected German positions. The tanks of C/37 would then line up abreast and pull up to the top of the ridge overlooking Fonteny. From that vantage point, the Shermans would hit the town with direct fire, while the armored infantry advanced toward the town on foot.

As the Americans organized their attack, 2nd Lt. Edward Marshall had his 2nd Platoon of B/51 "in a holding position on the south side of the road leading into the town." Marshall went on foot to the crest of the ridge to observe an enemy strong point that was marked on his defense map, and spotted two panzers in the edge of the forest to the southeast. "The tanks appeared to be moving around the right flank of the task force."

Lt. Marshall took matters into is own hands. He called in on his radio to the commander of B/51, 1st Lt. Joseph Cassidy, and said, "I think I can get at them with a bazooka," and asked for permission to make the attempt. Cassidy gave him the green light, but quickly followed it with a caution, "but for God's sake be careful."

Marshall assembled two teams of bazooka men to hunt the enemy tanks. Marshall personally led the GIs toward the enemy position, and crawled to within effective firing range. A direct hit was scored on each of the panzers, and the teams retreated back to their position behind the ridge. En route, however, they came under fire from enemy machine guns. Three of the Americans were killed: S/Sgt. Sol Tennenbaum, Pvt William Bodner, and Lt. Marshall.

Maybach's primary attack was plagued with problems from the outset. When the supporting artillery failed to fire on cue, Captain Lamison called to find out what the problem was. He was told that the barrage would be delivered shortly. Twenty minutes passed, and there was no artillery to be seen or heard. Lamison called again, but this time was told that the howitzers had fired. Lamison informed them that he had been watching, and that no shells had fallen.

Lamison was no doubt frustrated by the situation with the artillery. But rather than sit idle, he ordered his tanks up to the crest of the hill, and from that position, they began firing on the town in order to soften it up prior to the planned advance by the infantry. The infantry failed to move up with his tanks, however, so after a few salvos, he pulled the tanks back behind the ridge. Maybach now planned another attack, this one scheduled to commence at 3:30 P.M.

The plan for the 3:30 attack was a bit different than the prior proposal. This time, the artillery would supplement their barrage with a smoke screen designed to shield Lamison's tanks from the German anti-tank fire originating from some nearby woods. The full company of tanks, supported by the infantry, would then descend the slope and advance into the town.

Once again, major elements of the plan failed to fall into place. The artillery hit the town this time, but only four rounds were delivered. The smoke screen didn't materialize, and the tanks were left with the prospect of advancing over the crest within full view of the enemy.

Lamison was not deterred by the initial glitches. He sent his three platoons over the crest, despite the fact that, without the smokescreen, the tanks of the 37th would be vulnerable. The Shermans churned down the steep muddy slope, and began drawing an almost immediate response from the enemy gunners. Captain Lamison's tank was hit and disabled just as soon as it came over the crest of the ridge (the entire crew bailed out safely). Now unable to advance with the main body of C/37, Lamison radioed Lt. Wrolson and turned the company over to him for the balance of the advance toward Fonteny. But one other element of the attack had gone awry in addition to the blunders by the supporting artillery: the armored infantry did not follow behind the tanks. The tankers soon discovered that they were descending the hill on their own.

As the tanks plunged down the slope toward Fonteny, they were unable to provide their own covering fire, for the hill was so steep that their 75mm guns could not be elevated enough to fire at the enemy positions. Wrolson directed the tanks down into the valley that formed at the base of the hill — a move that helped shield his force from some of the German guns. But the enemy tanks and guns firing from positions northeast of Fonteny had a good vantage point over the valley, and they began a duel with the Shermans. The American tankers knocked out two or three of the panzers, but they were not able to suppress all of the fire coming their way.

C/37 hung on in the valley throughout the afternoon. As the sunlight began to fade, so to did the Sherman's ammunition. It was becoming increasingly clear that the tankers would need to withdraw. But getting the Shermans out of the valley and back up the steep hill was going to be tricky. And dangerous.

Under the cover of a smoke screen provided by the Shermans themselves, the tankers began pulling back up the slope. The Germans hit two more tanks of C/37 as they struggled out of the valley. But it suddenly became clear that the enemy guns weren't the biggest threat facing Wrolson's tanks. For as the treads of the tanks strained against the steep, mud-covered slope, they dug deeper and deeper into the surface. One by one, they failed to gain the crest, and came to rest short of the safety of the infantry's positions.

The tankers worked under the cover of darkness in an attempt to extract the Shermans. The Germans made their task more difficult by hitting the slope with intermittent fire, but it was the mud and the grade of the hill that really foiled their effort. At 9 P.M., they gave up on their endeavor and abandoned the tanks, without having recovered a single one (the tanks would eventually be pulled out of the muck on November 11).

Lt. Colonel Maybach's tally sheet looked dismal at the end of the day. An entire company of tanks had been put out of action. A total of ten halftracks and three assault guns had been destroyed. The casualty list totaled 98 men, with 14 killed, 50 wounded, 22 exhaustion cases, 4 sick, and 8 injured.

On November 10, TF Maybach maintained its position behind the ridge fronting Fonteny. The Germans knew the task force was there, however, and continued to shell the Americans position. Another 57 casualties were incurred that day as a result.

The assessment of the situation at Fonteny was that the advance could not continue until the enemy positions in the Forest of Chateau-Salins were dealt with. To that end, elements of the 35th Infantry Division came up on the flank of TF Maybach. The 35th ID tried to carry the attack toward the woods, but the Germans kept them at bay with a high volume of fire.

Lt. Colonel Maybach was ordered to take another shot at Fonteny on November 11. The light tank company from the 25th Cav Recon Squadron was assigned to his task force as a replacement for C/37, which returned to its parent outfit in the wake of losing its tanks. The 3rd Platoon of A/704, commanded by 2nd Lt. Robert Lane, also provided support.

When the attacking force came up to the crest of the ridge, they encountered the same level of response from the enemy that plagued them on November 9. This time, however, the fortitude of the armored infantry had risen, and they accompanied the light tanks down the hill and into the buildings on the forward edge of the town. They also had some help: two battalions of infantry from the 35th Infantry Division participated in the attack. Together, they successfully cleared the southern half of the town by nightfall. Casualties had begun to mount, however, and once again, it was proven that rank did not provide immunity from personal harm.

While observing C/51's attack on Fonteny, Lt. Colonel Maybach was mortally wounded by a mortar round (Lt. Col. William Shade of the 253rd AFAB was also mortally wounded). Captain Hope and Captain Rockafeller, the S-2 and S-3, respectively, were both slightly wounded by the same blast. Maybach was transported back along the route that his men were using to advance to the front, and a "strange silence" fell over the men of the 51st AIB as they witnessed their commanding officer being hurried back to the rear. After receiving treatment at the forward aid station, he was sent back to a rear area hospital for more extensive care. When he left the aid station, there was hope for his survival, which was buoyed when word came back that he had survived the trip to the hospital and made it onto the operating table. Unfortunately, he didn't recover after the operation, and passed away the following day. Major Van Arnam, the 51st's executive officer, assumed command of the battalion following Lt. Colonel Maybach's evacuation.

The effort to clear the enemy from Fonteny resumed at first light on November 12. C/51 and two companies from the 35th Infantry Division completed the task, while other elements of the 35th finally cleared the Forest of Chateau-Salins. Before the end of the day, the tanks from the 25th Cav were released from their assignment with the task force, and were replaced by two platoons of light tanks from D/35.

With Fonteny and the forest finally secured, the battered task force resumed its advance. Despite their losses, they were now actually a little bit stronger, due to the addition of the 2nd Battalion, 137th Infantry Regiment. The task force moved through the villages of Faxe and Oron without meeting any opposition (more than 600 Germans surrendered as CCB pushed forward). The next objective was Chateau-Brehain, but the column had to stop when it encountered a blown bridge. The engineers spent the night making repairs, and the column resumed the advance at 7:15 A.M. the next morning. The movement of the task force that day (November 13) was frustrated by a combination of blown bridges, minefields, and muddy, impassable roads. The column even had to double back on one occasion in search of a passable route. The frustrations continued on November 14. The following day, the 51st AIB arrived in the area of Morhange.

CCB and Task Force Churchill

TF Churchill's axis of advance was to the left of TF Maybach. Major Irzyk commanded the vanguard, and he saw to it that good progress was made on the first day of the attack (November 9). Despite the mud, mines, and proliferation of enemy anti-tank guns, the tanks of D/8 and C/8 continued to rack up mileage on their odometers. Lemoncourt was one of the objectives on the list early in the day, and its capture was aided by the unexpected appearance of American fighter-bombers.

After leaving Lemoncourt, Irzyk had only traveled a short distance before experiencing delays from mines and a "formidable concrete roadblock which took time to reduce." The task force slugged its way forward, however, and by nightfall, had captured the towns of Viviers and Hannocourt. After an advance of slightly more than six miles, the task force set up a bivouac for the night. In August, six miles would have been considered a walk to the curb. In November, it was a marathon.

The following day brought bad news for the men of TF Churchill. For starters, they were ordered to halt in place due to the delays experienced by TF Maybach at Fonteny. With TF Maybach stalled, a continued advance by TF Churchill would leave both its flanks exposed and highly vulnerable. But the truly bad news was that the 35th Infantry Division had failed to follow behind TF Churchill as planned. The Germans took advantage of the resulting gap between the two American forces, and slipped a strong force of infantry, tanks, armored cars, and artillery, back into the town of Viviers. As the Germans moved into the town, they hit part of the 22nd AFAB, which was supporting TF Churchill from further back in the column. The net result of all this was that TF Churchill was, in effect, cut off behind enemy lines.

TF Churchill responded by sending a platoon of tanks back down the road toward Viviers to help out the 22nd AFAB, and to take a stab at reopening their supply route and line of communication. Fortunately, elements of the 35th Infantry Division were finally closing on Viviers at about the same time. The Germans found themselves being attacked from two sides, and they were pressured to withdraw from the town.

As the squeeze was being placed on the Germans at Viviers, the main body of Task Force Churchill, which was still located near Hannocourt, became the target of German artillery. Rather than sweat out the barrage in the relatively open terrain surrounding the town, the task force moved into the Bois De Serres, less than a half-mile to the southeast.

With Fonteny still in German hands on September 11, TF Churchill was ordered to remain in place for yet another day. By now, the Germans had figured out where Churchill had placed his force, and a cascade of artillery shells began falling in the forest. The "tree bursts" that resulted were far more dangerous than the prospect of being shelled out in the open, so Churchill moved the task force back closer to Hannocourt.

Soon after TF Churchill relocated, the Germans launched a counterattack from the direction of Oron. With the assistance of supporting artillery from the division and corps level, the Americans beat back the enemy attack. This wasn't the last that TF Churchill would see of the Germans that day, however. Later on, German tanks approached and managed to knock out five Sherman tanks (four from B/8 and one from C/8). Casualties among the tankers began to rise. In a short period of time, six platoon leaders from the 8th Tank Battalion were killed or wounded.

Task Force Churchill was forced to stand in place yet again on November 12. But on November 13, Churchill finally received his orders to move. The advance guard, once again led by Major Irzyk, was to advance toward the town of Marthille, and then continue on to Destry.

TF Irzyk got off to a tremendous start, unleashing all the pent-up energy and frustration of the past few days. After an early morning meeting with his advance guard commanders, Irzyk had his task force on the road by 8 A.M. The column moved quickly through the familiar Bois de Serres, with no interference from the enemy. They emerged from the forest and plunged into the village of Oron. The prisoners they captured there were sent back to the 35th Infantry Division, so that the advance could continue unencumbered. Resistance stiffened over the course of the next two and a half miles, and the pace of the advance slowed a bit. But Villers sur Nied fell to the vanguard, and there was still plenty of daylight left to continue the advance.

Marthille

The next stop was the town of Marthille. As Irzyk scoped out the approach, he thought better of making an advance straight down the road. His sixth sense — a "special battle sense" — was awakened by the nature of the surrounding terrain. To the right of the road was water, which left no room for maneuver to the east. To the left of the road, the ground rose sharply, culminating in a forested ridge that ran parallel to the road. If the enemy had established positions along the top of that ridge, they would be able to hit the left flank of his column as it moved down the road toward Marthille.

The road and ridge combination extended for almost a mile and half, and if an unseen enemy held its fire until the column got close to the town, virtually his entire task force would be in their sights, strung out along the road. It would be a perfect ambush, as the column could not back up, nor find safe haven off to the right of the road. And if the town itself were occupied, the column would not be able to race forward in hopes of escape. Just a couple of crippled vehicles on the road could block the movement of the entire task force. The only choice for the Americans would be to turn directly toward the enemy facing them on the high ground. And if the enemy *were* on top of the ridge, engaging them from the bottom of the slope would hardly be favorable.

Having weighed all the factors, Irzyk decided that he couldn't take the risk of parading his task force down the road. But what other choice did he have?

Irzyk reasoned that the high ground off to the left side of the road might be dry and firm enough to support his vehicles, so he decided to let his tanks take a shot at navigating the muddy slope to gain the top of the ridge. His armor would then advance down the length of the ridge, reconnoitering by fire as they went (in other words, firing at all potential enemy positions as they advanced, regardless of whether or not they identified a specific target). Once the ridge was deemed clear of enemy forces, the entire task force could continue its advance. If Irzyk desired, he could even bypass Marthiile altogether by staying on the high ground, which continued in the direction of Destry.

The light tanks of D Company led the way. The tankers found the slope firm enough to support their weight, and quickly ascended to the top of the hill, with the Sherman tanks following close behind. As the lead tank of Staff Sergeant Ellsworth Ranson reached the top of the ridge, it opened up with its .30 caliber machine gun, firing at the first suspected enemy position about 1000 yards further down the ridge at the edge of the woods.

The machine gun tracers appeared to bounce off something, so Ranson had his gunner fire a shot from his 37mm main gun straight at that location. The shell blew away some of the foliage, revealing two antitank guns laying in wait! The guns were manned, and the startled crews fired off wild rounds that had already been loaded in the chambers. The guns had been pointing toward the road, and they had no time to reposition them to face the American tanks now careening toward them along the line of the ridge. Irzyk's battle sense had indeed been working overtime.

The Sherman tanks trailing the M5s now opened up with their more powerful 75mm guns, and immediately destroyed the two antitank weapons. The tanks then fanned out, and began to fire at every suspected location atop the ridge. And then, quite unexpectedly, some 200 Germans spilled out of Marthille and raced as fast as the mud would permit toward the other anti-tank guns. As they struggled to climb the slope, the tankers mowed them down in droves. The German gunners that did manage to make it to their weapons found them either destroyed or pointed in the wrong direction. They died by their guns without hitting a single American tank. In fact, the only tank to be damaged during the assault was a Sherman that struck a mine.

The Americans ripped the Germans to shreds. In addition to the destruction of 21 anti-tanks guns (ten of which were powerful 88s), Irzyk's men killed 100 of the enemy and took 50 prisoners. Some of the surviving Germans fled, accompanied by two Panthers that fired wild shots while retreating toward the Sarre River.

The 8th Tank Battalion S3 tank and crew (courtesy Al Irzyk).

Had Task Force Irzyk advanced down the road as originally planned, it would have been dealt a devastating blow. And while Irzyk credited an increasingly keen battle sense for alerting him to the possibility of an ambush, he would also give a nod to Devine intervention for keeping him and his men out of harm's way that fateful day.

Buoyed by the success at Marthille, TF Churchill continued on the following day toward Destry, just over a mile north of Marthille. It had snowed during the night, which didn't help the ground conditions. The white stuff only served to add more moisture to the already soupy soil.

From Destry, Churchill was ordered to swing to the southeast in order to help shake loose the German defenders standing in the way of CCB's other task force. Major Irzyk took a task force on an excruciatingly slow trek toward Baronville. Mines and roadblocks slowed them down, while the mud conspired with the enemy to hold Irzyk in check. Normally, these obstacles might have been bypassed by moving cross-country, but doing so under these conditions was an invitation to lose your tank. In fact, some of the tankers tried, and as feared, the mud emerged as the victor. So most of the advance toward Baronville took pace only at the pace allowed by the work of the engineers, who in turn were slowed down by the harassment of German artillery. Irzyk was persistent, however, and by late in the day on November 14, his task force tied in with elements of the 35th Infantry Division, which were holding a position west of Baronville. They remained in place for another snowy night.

On November 15, Irzyk received orders to "follow behind the 51st Infantry Task Force as it moved on Morhange." But the 51st AIB was running behind schedule, so there was no movement by TF Churchill toward Morhange that day. The men of TF Churchill satisfied themselves by hitting the German positions with shells delivered by the 22nd AFAB and 8th Tank Battalion.

By the morning of November 16, the combined movements of CCB and CCA had outflanked Morhange. It was left to the 35th Infantry Division to attack and capture the town, which they accomplished that same day, after a heated, costly engagement versus the German 1127th Regiment.

CCA and Task Force Hunter

CCA, which was under the temporary command of Lt. Colonel Abrams, was heavily loaded with resources at the start of the offensive. It consisted primarily of the 35th

The command group of Task Force Hunter, on the road near Conthil. November 14, 1944. The Sherman tank is Hunter's tank, "Tornado" (National Archives Photograph SC196527).

and 37th(-C) Tank Battalions, 53rd and 10th Armored Infantry Battalions, and the 66th and 94th Armored Field Artillery Battalions. CCA was to attack through the forward positions of the 26th Infantry Division, which was located to the right of the 35th Infantry Division. CCA's axis of advance paralleled that of CCB, and ultimately, the two commands would converge on the town of Morhange. CCA formed two task forces for the mission: Task Force Hunter and Task Force Oden-West. The task forces would advance on parallel routes, with Hunter on the right, and Oden-West on the left.

Task Force Hunter consisted of the 37th Tank Battalion (minus C Company, which was attached to the 51st AIB operating with CCB), A/53, C/10, the 66th AFAB, and a platoon each from C/704 and C/24. Major Hunter's group got underway on November 10, with the immediate objective of "seizing the ground around the rail center of Benestroff."

The road over which TF Hunter advanced was heavily cratered in spots, and the battalion bulldozer was kept busy repairing the German demolitions. In one case, the Germans had thrown obstacles on both sides of a gaping crater, making it impossible for the task force to bypass it. Frustrated by the delays, the light tanks of D/37 were sent on a reconnaissance to look for an alternative route, but they came up empty. They did, however, destroy two anti-tank guns during the course of their mission.

The first point of enemy resistance was encountered at Morville, and the task force punched through it without too much difficulty. But the Germans made a tougher stand at the next village along Hunter's axis of advance. Near Hampont, Captain Spencer, the commanding officer of A/37, was seriously wounded by small arms fire while conducting a reconnaissance mission on foot. Spencer was evacuated, and Lt. Martin White took over command of A/37, using Spencer's command tank from that point forward.

Unfortunately, Lt. White wasn't in command for long. Once inside Hampont, a blast from a German panzerfaust struck White's tank, killing the loader, Pvt. Walter Hammerschmidt, and the gunner, Cpl. Jess Dingledine. White was seriously wounded by the blast, and so the command of A/37 passed into the hands of 2nd Lt. Charley Walters, who had been "a platoon sergeant only a month ago." Despite his rapid rise, he proved to be capable of handling the company.

Task Force Hunter finished the day by capturing the village of Obreck. The tankers and infantry halted soon thereafter, and remained in position for the night. They were now tied in with elements of the 104th Infantry Regiment.

The Germans were not content to let Hunter's men rest. They zeroed in on the American's bivouac area, and pounded them with artillery throughout the night and into the next morning. Casualties were heavy during the shelling; more than half a dozen men of the 37th were killed, and several light vehicles were destroyed or damaged. Among the wounded were Major Hunter and captains Stroup and Dwight (Major Hunter stayed with the task force after receiving his wound, but had to be evacuated several days later).

The lead elements of TF Hunter moved out again on the morning of November 11. The enemy continued to shell the column as it advanced. The German gunners also stayed zeroed in on the American units back in the assembly area (when viewing the situations encountered by both CCA and CCB, it appears that the Germans had no shortage of artillery and mortar ammunition). TF Hunter ran into heated resistance near La Moutelotte Farme. The Germans were no match, however, as Hunter's men proceeded to dispose of four 20mm AA guns, two halftracks (one of which mounted a cannon in the bed), a self-propelled assault gun, and a variety of anti-tank guns.

The German artillery continued to focus on the Americans still waiting to move out from the assembly area. The Krauts hit paydirt when their shells struck two ammunition trucks, resulting in a massive explosion when the trucks' cargo ignited. A platoon of Hellcats from C/704 was nearby, and several of the men were wounded by the blasts. Their platoon leader, Lt. Bunpass, was killed.

After clearing out the enemy at La Moutelotte Farme, the column continued its advance toward Haboudange. En route, the lead tanks found themselves moving along a treacherous strip of real estate. To the right was a steep railroad embankment. To the left, a "creek surrounded by low, swampy ground." If they ran into a problem while moving down this stretch of road, their only choice would be to continue forward or backwards. And moving backward in a column isn't much of a choice.

As the head of the column drew close to Haboudange, the vehicles were still confined by the nature of the road. The Germans were ready and waiting, and unleashed both AP and HE fire from a variety of weapons, including guns belonging to the 111th Flak Battalion, which depressed their barrels and employed them in a direct fire role against the American ground troops. Three of the light tanks near the front of the column were hit and destroyed, as was the Sherman tank of Captain Hays. A jeep carrying Lt. Lynn Dennison, the motor pool officer for D/37, was also hit, killing the officer.

The column was brought to a halt, not by choice, but by the circumstances. Unable to move forward or backward, the men and vehicles were sitting ducks. The Germans then unleashed an artillery barrage on the tail of the column that had a devastating effect. The tanks of B/37 returned fire, but they couldn't even see what they were firing at. The Germans continued to pound the column, and they added direct fire to the deadly chorus.

The mortar platoon commanded by Lt. Max Poore was receiving more than its fair share of enemy fire. He called Captain Leach, and asked that the forward artillery observer supporting B/37 adjust the fire of the 66th AFAB on suspected enemy positions to the northwest. The observer, Lt. Rejrat, pulled his observer's tank toward Leach's position. At that moment, an enemy AP round ricocheted off Rejrat's tank. A second round followed quickly behind, and struck Rejrat in the head, killing him instantly.

Several of the officers moved away from the column in an attempt to observe where the enemy fire was coming from, so that they could call in artillery support to suppress the German guns. Three officers were killed making the attempt (Lt. Poore of the mortar platoon, Lt. Frederick Lockwood of B/37, and one of the artillery observers for the 66th AFAB, Lt. Mitchell).

The tanks of D Company managed to worm their way through the wreckage at the head of the column, and proceeded to find some cover southwest of Conthil. En route, they captured a 30-man strong AA unit, along with the German commanding officer. Meanwhile, the balance of the column, which was unable to move forward, finally managed to turn the vehicles around on the narrow road, and made its way to D/37's location via an alternative route. Conthil was not yet in Americans hands, so an artillery barrage was called in on the town prior to the column moving through. After the shelling stopped, the Americans sped through uneventfully.

The next town down the road was Rodalbe. Captain Leach's B/37 was ordered to move on the town, and en route, he found two companies of riflemen from the 104th Infantry Regiment moving in the same direction. He hooked up with the doughs and carried them into Rodalbe on his tanks.

As night began to fall, Major Hunter ordered his tanks to move into an assembly area east of Conthil and south of Rodalbe. For Captain Leach, this meant leaving the two companies from the 104th to their own devices. He was aware that they had few anti-tank weapons — only a small number of bazookas — and no mines. Leach proposed leaving behind one of his platoons of Shermans in support of the infantrymen, but Major Hunter insisted that he bring his entire company back to the assembly area. Leach protested, but it did no good. The infantrymen would be on their own.

On the morning of November 12, the Germans launched a strong counterattack against the forward positions of the 26th Infantry Division in the Rodalbe-Conthil sector. The two infantry companies in Rodalbe came under heavy attack, as did another two companies holding Conthil. The men in Rodalbe held their positions (despite being fired on by tanks that had entered the town and were firing at point-blank range), but the two companies in Conthil had to evacuate the town after nearly being surrounded.

With Rodalbe under pressure, TF Hunter was called upon to restore the situation. The plan for the attack to relieve the German pressure on Rodalbe called for a simultaneous advance on the town from two sides. C/10 and B/37 were to deploy east of the town via a trail. Meanwhile, A/37 was to deploy just outside of the Bois de Conthil, while B/53 would attack through the woods and on toward the town.

The wheels came off the plan when the halftracks and tanks moving to the east side of Rodalbe bogged down en route along the muddy trail. The armored infantry from B/53 also ran into problems when they encountered strong enemy resistance in the woods (they never made it close enough to Rodalbe to launch their attack).

The German tanks north of the town became aware of the move by C/10 and B/37 on their flank, and moved into position to hit Jimmie Leach's Shermans with direct fire. B/37 lost three of its tanks to enemy rounds; the mine-roller tank that accompanied the column was also hit and knocked out of action. C/10 and B/37 maintained their presence in the area, however, and even tried to continue the attack toward Rodalbe. But the muddy terrain forced the Americans to suspend the effort, and at nightfall, they prepared to withdraw. Two tanks and a jeep were stuck in the mud, and the GIs could not free them when it came time to pull out. The Americans intentionally destroyed the vehicles before their departure, in order to ensure that the enemy would not put them to use under the Nazi banner.

The withdrawal of TF Hunter meant that the American infantry in Rodalbe were on their own. Strong artillery support helped the riflemen hold the Germans in check during the balance of November 12, but as they settled in for the night, they still had no anti-tank capability to speak of.

On November 13, the Germans continued their attack against the two infantry companies in Rodalbe. The initial attack was conducted predominately by grenadiers, and the Americans continued to hold. But as daylight was fading, the Germans managed to apply very effective counterbattery fire against the artillery supporting the American forces, which significantly reduced the support available to the men of the 104th. Without artillery support, the Americans were unable to hold back the onslaught that followed after dark. By morning, only two officers and 30 men had escaped the town. Approximately 200 men were lost, either killed or captured.

As the saga in Rodalbe was unfolding on the 13th, TF Hunter stood its ground in anticipation of Task Force Oden launching an attack on Rodalbe from the south (back on November 11, TF Oden-West, which had been on Hunter's left, passed behind TF Hunter and shifted to Hunter's right). The attack by TF Oden did not come off successfully, and TF Hunter remained idle.

November 14 was a relatively calm day. Major Bautz led A/37 on a mission supporting TF West in the area east of Lidrezing (the company would return at the end of the following day with two enemy tanks notched on its belt). At this point, the 26th Infantry Division was working hand in hand with CCA, and they "coordinated their activities and took up positions accordingly."

November 15 and 16 were spent in static positions alongside the 26th ID. On

November 17, the 37th Tank Battalion was pulled from the line and spent the following day heavily engaged in repair and maintenance activity.

On November 18, after having enjoyed several days of relative calm, orders were received for an advance toward Sarre-Union. A task force would be assembled under the command of Lt. Colonel Abrams, who had returned to his position as the CO of the 37th Tank Battalion. The planned axis of advance was Conthil-Rodalbe-Bermering-Virming-Francaltroff-Lening, and then the ultimate goal, which was Sarre-Union. The task force would jump off the following morning.

Guebling

Task Force Oden-West was the last of the Fourth Armored teams to join the offensive. On November 12, the powerful task force advanced through the positions on the left flank of the 104th Infantry Regiment. The tanks of the 35th Tank Battalion advanced cleanly through the front line, and seized their initial objective, which was the high ground three miles beyond Chateau Vous.

Though the front of the column did not meet any resistance, all did not go exactly as planned. The leading tank and infantry companies had advanced too far ahead of the balance of the column, creating a large gap between the forward and rear elements. The void was filled by three German tanks, which proceeded to block the route for the rest of the column. The lead elements did not backtrack to take care of the problem; instead, the trailing portion of the task force spent the balance of the day seeking an alternate route toward their objective. Six hours later, the rear elements rejoined the rest of the task force.

In response to the German capture of Conthil, Oden was instructed to detach a task force that would head due north to counterattack and take back the town (by capturing Conthil, the Germans had cut the main supply line leading to TF Hunter and the forward elements of the 104th Infantry Regiment). This was done successfully by the end of the day. That evening, TF Oden-West took up positions about a mile east of Kutzeling Farm, with the supporting artillery of the 94th perched atop Hill 330.

The task force remained in place on November 13 (according to after-action interviews conducted on November 23 with the staff of the 37th Tank Battalion, there seemed to be an expectation that TF Oden would attack Rodalbe that day. Apparently, the attack never materialized). Patton, accompanied by Omar Bradley and Major General Charles Bonesteel, visited with the Fourth Armored Division that same day, and observed first hand what the division was struggling against. They made special note of the terrible conditions when they witnessed tanks that had "bellied down" upon leaving the road.

On November 14, TF Oden-West advanced toward Guebling. The weather had a significant impact on the pace of movement, and a mixture of rain, snow, and bitter cold added to the men's misery. The mud was even worse than usual that morning. As testimony, most of the vehicles of the 10th AIB had to be towed out of the field where they had bivouacked for the night.

Plans were made for a coordinated attack to capture Guebling. Colonel Delk

Oden's 35th Tank Battalion and Major West's 10th Armored Infantry Battalion, supported by the 94th AFAB, would bear the brunt of the attack. They were soon to find themselves pitted in a tough battle against a familiar opponent: the 11th Panzer Division, which had been strengthened after the September tank battles and now stood ready with some nineteen Mark IV tanks and fifty factory-fresh Panthers.

Guebling was a small town that sat upon a ridge overlooking a fairly wide valley, through which ran a strong and swift stream that fed the farms in the area. CCA occupied positions on the opposing ridge to the west. The lone road leading into the town from the west descended from the ridge on the American side, crossed the open valley, and then crossed over the aforementioned stream and a railroad embankment. The road then made an uphill climb into the town. The surrounding terrain was fairly wide open, and American units advancing along the road would be in clear sight of the enemy sitting on the opposing ridge. The Germans added to the complexity of the approach by placing a generous amount of mines near the bridge and rail embankment. They also placed a number of Panther tanks into excellent hull-defilade positions that covered the approaches.

The tanks of A/35 drew the assignment of making the initial advance toward the town. With other Sherman tanks from the 35th providing supporting fire from up on the ridge, A/35 began its advance at 9:40 A.M., and it wasn't long before the lead Shermans came under fire from several of the Panthers. The commanding officer of A/35 was wounded early in the fight, and 1st Lieutenant Arthur Sell took the reins of the company.

Caught in an ambush by three of the enemy tanks, Lt. Sell deployed the other tanks from his platoon to cover the flanks, and then drove his own tank to within 50 yards of the Panthers. He managed to destroy two of the Mark Vs before his Sherman was knocked out of action by several enemy rounds. The other tanks in his company then opened fire and destroyed the remaining Panther (Lt. Sell later received the DSC for his actions at Guebling).

With the immediate threat of the Panthers eliminated, the main column resumed its advance, and had traveled another mile toward Guebling when it encountered yet more Panthers. The subsequent battle between Panthers and Shermans raged for nearly three hours. During the engagement, the pilot of one of the artillery spotter planes swooped down and destroyed an enemy halftrack using the bazookas mounted under the wings of his plane (three Fourth Armored pilots utilized this practice: Major Carpenter, 2nd Lt. Roy Carson, and 2nd Lt. Harley Merrick). One more Sherman was lost during the melee, but the Panthers finally withdrew, and the advance continued (apparently, some of the Panthers were abandoned, and the armored infantrymen of B/10 destroyed them as they advanced).

Before the column resumed its advance, disaster was avoided when the spotter plane picked up five more Panthers at the edge of the town, apparently laying in wait to ambush the approaching American column. In what the 10th AIB journal described as "one of the most brilliantly maneuvered tank battles ever witnessed," the five Panthers were destroyed. Only a single Sherman was lost.

A heavy artillery barrage was then brought down on the town as the men of the 10th AIB stood off and watched. With dusk approaching, the artillery fire was lifted, and the armored infantry, led by B Company, attempted to enter the town. The going was slow, as the creek and minefield posed barriers that demanded caution (three tanks supporting B/10 were disabled by the mines). T/Sgt. Clifford Turner raced to the area of the minefield in a jeep, and removed the mines and demolition charges.

A heavy smoke screen provided by the 94th aided the approach of the column (the artillery battalion exhausted all of their smoke shells in the effort). Engineers were brought forward, and a bridge put in place over the stream. At 4:30 P.M., the column started across the stream and headed straight for Guebling.

Despite heavy resistance, the American infantry managed to enter the town by nightfall. Their original objective had been to push through and take the high ground on the far side of town, but rather than continue their advance beyond Guebling in the dark, they opted to stake out positions inside the town. The 10th AIB moved its headquarters into the town as well.

It soon became apparent that West's force was in a vulnerable position. The Germans faced the Americans on three sides, and looked down on them from dominating positions above the town. The decision not to press on beyond Guebling was about to be exposed as a critical mistake.

At 11 P.M., the enemy brought down intense artillery and tank fire on the town. Buildings and vehicles were blown apart in front of the armored infantry, and fires raged throughout the town. The brilliant flames served to illuminate potential targets for the German observers, and the artillery fire became increasingly effective. The building housing the 10th Armored Infantry Battalion's command post was almost destroyed during the night, and the staff had to relocate to another building while the barrage continued. Three gasoline trucks that had been brought in during the night were caught in the barrage and destroyed. American GIs were mutilated and dismembered by the explosions; it was a horrific scene for the men lucky enough to survive the blasts.

The flames leaping into the night served as a poignant counterpoint to the cold rain that blanketed the men as they tried to find cover. As the temperature dropped, it turned to snow. The elements added to the misery being imposed by the Germans.

Casualties among the armored infantrymen were heavy, and there were incredible acts of bravery as soldiers raced through the rubble of the town to rescue comrades who lay

Major Abe Baum, 10th AIB (courtesy Abraham Baum).

injured. Men such as S/Sgt. Charles Bye, Pfc. Richard Eckert, Pfc. Anthony Di Girolme, and Pvt. James Moscato risked their lives by going to the aid of others in the face of enemy fire (all four of these men were awarded Bronze Stars for their selfless acts).

Not all of the men who braved the rubble-strewn streets of Guebling to assist others survived the attempt. Earlier in the day, 1st Lt. Robert Gutschmidt attempted to reach a man from his platoon who had been wounded. Gutschmidt was cut down by enemy machine gun fire, and died before he could reach his man. Just prior to this, the brave Lieutenant had led his platoon in an assault that broke up a strong counterattack by the Germans (he was posthumously awarded the Silver Star for his actions at Guebling).

During the night, German infantry attempted to infiltrate the American positions. They moved in close enough to use a panzerfaust to destroy the forward observer tank of the 94th AFAB. Lieutenant John Kelly, who had served with great distinction with the 94th, was killed in the attack. The other four crewmembers of Kelly's tank were badly wounded (Sgt. William Skyrmes, Cpl. James Tiehl, T4 Rufus Babb, and Pvt. Harold Smith). Lt. Guild of the 94th borrowed a tank from the 35th Tank Battalion and took Lt Kelly's place as the forward observer (Lt. Guild had lost his own tank in action the day before, near the town of Rodalbe, while supporting other elements of the 35th Tank Battalion. After having his tank knocked out, Lt. Guild and his gunner, Corporal Charles Easter, earned the Silver Star for rescuing the "wounded members of another tank crew while under fire").

The situation was bad, but the German attacks failed to push the Americans out of the town. After a night of terror inside Guebling, the rising sun revealed a horrid amount of destruction. Lt. Colonel West realized that his position was untenable, and began drawing up plans for pulling out of Guebling. In the meantime, the task force stayed in its positions, and weathered the continuing rain of artillery and tank shells that fell on the town.

The plan was slow in coming together. West and his staff had been rattled by the ferocity of the German attack. As the day progressed, the staff gathered themselves and worked out the details for getting out of Guebling.

The Germans had a line of sight to the only road leading out of Guebling, and it would be too dangerous to conduct the withdrawal under the direct fire of the enemy tanks. If just a few vehicles were disabled, the entire force might find their escape route blocked. To help cover the withdrawal, the task force wanted to bring artillery fire down on top of the Panthers. But the enemy tanks were too close to the forward American positions, and the fire mission could not be conducted without great risk. The panzers would have to be dealt with via other means.

In an act of great courage, the 94th's forward infantry observer, Lt. Elesworth Chamberlin, traded in his normal role to become a spotter for the tanks of the 35th Tank Battalion. Moving forward toward the enemy, he pointed out the location of the Panthers so that the Shermans could engage them.

At 4:00 P.M., the order was given to vacate the town. With the Panthers occupied, the infantry began withdrawing, and the 94th laid down a smoke screen to conceal their movement. It was effective, as the 10th AIB was able to withdraw without losing a single vehicle as they moved down the dangerous road. Lt. Colonel West and Lt. Lyons (who was now the CO of the HQ Company) were the last men out of the town. As they withdrew, the two men tossed grenades through the open doorways of the buildings still left intact, in an attempt to set fire to the remaining structures. Lt. Col. West jumped into a waiting tank at the edge of town, while Lyons "made a flying leap" into the back of a jeep, which "took off like a bat out of Hell."

A squad of American engineers remained at the bridge leading away from town. Their orders were to blow the bridge behind them after the last of the American forces withdrew. The engineers carried out their assignment as Lt. Donald Guild's Sherman stood nearby, blasting away at German infantry that were within sight at a nearby strand of houses. After destroying the bridge, the engineers mounted Lt. Guild's tank, and beat a hasty retreat.

Guebling was a place and a time that would be long remembered by the men who fought there. The 10th AIB alone suffered 181 casualties during the two days spent in the battered town. Coming off of this engagement, the 35th Tank Battalion had only 15 medium tanks fit for battle, and they lost one of their most experienced commanders, Captain Brady, when he had to be evacuated after losing his arm during the battle. The decision to occupy the town without having pushed to the high ground beyond had turned out to be a disastrous choice.

Recriminations

Patton seemed happy with the overall pace of the offensive during the first week. He noted: "As of November 15, the operation was quite satisfactory, except that the 4th Armored had been set back a little bit and the Seventh Army had not done as much as we had hoped." Patton's comment was probably a reflection of CCA's inability to hold Guebling; the performance of the combat command was perhaps a symptom of Bruce Clarke's departure.

Still smarting from the sting at Guebling, most of the Fourth Armored was either pulled out of the front line or sat idle on November 16. Their rest period would last for three days, as the XII Corps regrouped after a week of hard fighting under very tough conditions. XII Corps was not alone in having a rough go of it. Patton's above comment not withstanding, the XX Corps was having a heck of a time with the German defenders at Metz, some 40 miles to the northwest, and casualties were running high in virtually every unit engaged on the front line.

The unanticipated rest period was a blessing. During the respite, Colonel Withers, who had been in temporary command of the 2nd Cavalry Group, arrived to take over the reins of CCA. Upon his arrival, Lt. Colonel Abrams returned to his command of the 37th Tank Battalion (his men were overjoyed when they discovered he was returning). On November 18, CCB was placed in XII Corps reserve, and all was quiet for the division. Quiet for everyone, that is, except General Wood.

On what would turn out to be the final day of their rest period, Eddy and Wood had a strong disagreement regarding the performance of the Fourth Armored in recent days. Eddy's opinion was that the division was not driving hard. Wood couldn't disagree more, and the facts would seem to support him on that count. The division was certainly attacking forcefully, but the conditions were simply not suitable for the effective use of tanks. There was also the fact that he was facing a determined, experienced opponent in the form of the 11th Panzer Division.

On the morning of November 19, an ominous phone call took place. At 8:45 A.M., Manton Eddy rang Patton, and asked if he could come see him regarding his situation with Wood. When they met, he told Patton that Wood had been almost insubordinate. In response, Patton composed a letter, which he had his Chief of Staff, Hugh Gaffey, deliver to Wood. In his diary, Patton lamented having to do this, "as he is one of my best friends, but war is war...." The contents of the letter show signs of his reservations as a friend. But the letter was no less direct in its purpose:

> My Dear P:
>
> You know that no one has a greater affection for you, nor a greater opinion of your military ability than I; however, it is apparent to me that you are not complying with either the letter or spirit of instructions received by you from your Corps Commander. Furthermore, I believe that your actions toward him verge on insubordination.
>
> This letter will be handed to you by Gen Gaffey. I desire that you explain fully and frankly to him any possible arguments which you may have for the apparently dilatory manner in which you carried out the orders of your Corps Commander on November 18.
>
> If, when he leaves, you cannot assure him that you will carry out your instructions, both in letter and in spirit, I will be forced to relieve you.
>
> Very sincerely yours,
> G.S. Patton, Jr.
> Lieut. Gen., U.S. Army
> Commanding.

Later that day, Patton wrote in his diary, "Wood apologized to Eddy and everything seems all right." But the very next day, he made an ominous entry that seemed to reveal his continued unease with the situation between Eddy and Wood: "I am trying to find some nice way of easing him out."

Wood's division resumed the offensive on November 19. The two combat commands were separated by approximately eight to nine miles, with the 26th Infantry Division sandwich in between them. The plan called for CCA, led by Task Force Abrams, to advance on the left through positions held by recon elements of the 26th Infantry Division. The axis of advance for CCA would take it northeast toward Francaltroff, and then on to Sarre-Union. CCB, which had now been shifted over to the right flank of the 26th ID, would drive to the northeast on an axis of advance that would carry it through Dieuze, Mittersheim, and finally, Sarre-Union, where they would close the noose with CCA. The 26th Infantry was aligned with the 104th Regiment on the left and the 101st Regiment on the right (the 101st was centered on Guebling, having taken over CCA's positions in the area after the failed attack on November 14/15). The 328th Regiment was held in reserve north of Dieuze.

This was an extremely difficult assignment for an armored division, since there were no major roads running parallel with the assigned axis of advance. The tanks would have to advance over nothing much better than muddy logging trails. The area was heavily forested, and laced with swamps and bogs. It was not an inviting situation.

CCA's Drive to Francaltroff

At 7 A.M. on November 19, CCA, composed primarily of the 37th, 10th, and 94th Battalions, began moving through the 26th Infantry Division's positions. The specific axis of advance was Conthil, Rodalbe, Bermering, Virming, Francaltroff, Lening, and finally, Sarre-Union, where they would converge with CCB.

As the task force moved out, D Troop of the 25th Cavalry screened the left flank of the column, and a vanguard consisting of D/37 and the 37th's assault gun and mortar platoons, led by Captain Dwight, took the lead down the main road toward Francaltroff. The order of march behind the vanguard was the 37th Tank Battalion's recon unit, the 37th's Battalion HQ and HQ Company, A/37, B/10, A/24, B/704 (minus one platoon), the 94th AFAB, and finally, the headquarters of CCA.

Conthil was already in American hands. The first town the task force entered beyond the positions of the 26th Infantry Division was Rodalbe, which had posed so many problems for TF Hunter during the early days of the offensive. The 26th Infantry had since reoccupied the town, however, and the men of the 37th breathed a sigh of relief when they were able to pass through without a fight. There was a delay, however, due to a heavily mined roadblock that the Germans had created before their departure. After the engineers cleared the way — 911 mines were removed — the advance continued, and TF Abrams briefly passed through the zone of the 35th Infantry Division at the village of Bermering. The going was extremely slow, with several tanks becoming bogged down in the mud along the way.

As the vanguard drew close to the village of Virming, it was met by enemy tank and anti-tank fire. At 4 P.M., TF Abrams launched an assault on the village, destroying four German tanks and several anti-tank guns as they cleared the town. Two Sherman tanks were lost during the attack, one of them the lead tank of B/37 as it entered the town. Twelve Germans were taken prisoner, and ten bodies of the enemy tallied as dead. A battalion of the 320th Infantry Regiment (35th Infantry Division) moved in behind CCA to outpost the town, and TF Abrams moved into bivouac positions for the night.

The following morning, Abrams asked for C/37 to join the lead task force (it had been held in reserve prior to that point). D/37 took C/37's place in reserve, and at 7:30 A.M., the task force, with A/37 in the lead, advanced through the 35th Infantry Division's outpost at Virming. Francaltroff was now less than five miles away from the vanguard of TF Abrams.

Soon after moving into the open terrain northeast of Virming, the column came under fire from enemy mortars and artillery. This did not deter the advance, and Abrams' tanks closed on Francaltroff. The advance came to a halt, however, when a blown bridge and anti-tank ditch were encountered. It took some time to clear these obstacles, and it would be late afternoon before TF Abrams was in position for an attack on the town.

A company of armored infantry (B/10) and a company of medium tanks (B/37) assaulted Francaltroff. When the lead elements of B/10 entered the town, they found they could not continue further due to another blown bridge. At that moment, the enemy hit the tail of the column with heavy mortar fire, which set several vehicles ablaze. The barrage was followed by a strong counterattack by the enemy, and the part of the column that was already in the town had to pull back.

The units attempting to withdraw ran into an immediate problem. The burning vehicles at the rear of the column blocked the road, and there was no means necessary for moving them. With their path blocked, they had to look for an alternative route. The only other road was clogged with abandoned farm machinery and other heavy debris. The men of B/10, with enemy fire still cascading upon them, cleared away the obstacles and proceeded to evacuate the town. During the course of the withdrawal, ten Sherman tanks and three halftracks became bogged down in the mud west of the village, and the crews had to leave the tanks where they sat. The task force finally withdrew, and took up positions in the area of Obrick, where they remained for the night.

On November 21, much of the day was spent trying to recover the tanks and halftracks that were stranded near the forward positions at Francaltroff. The tanks had to be pulled from the mud by T-5 recovery vehicles operating under the nose of the enemy. The Germans complicated the effort by firing some 300 artillery rounds at the Americans as they struggled to unglue the tanks. Despite some problems with a broken winch, the tanks were finally pulled from the muck. The crews of the T-5s, led by Warrant Officer Charles Wathen, were singled out by Lt. Colonel Abrams for recognition (they later received the Bronze Star for their bravery).

CCA made virtually no progress after the rebuff at Francaltroff. The staff of CCA, which had been so well honed by Bruce Clarke, was not accustomed to failure on any level. Many eyes started to turn toward Colonel Withers, the new commander of CCA. It was already becoming clear to many of the men around him that Withers was having a tough time following in the footsteps of the dynamic Clarke.

CCB's Drive Toward Mittersheim

CCB started its attack on November 19, concurrent with CCA. The 51st Armored Infantry Battalion, working in conjunction with the 3rd Battalion of the 328th Infantry Regiment, paved the way for Brigadier General Dager's command. The objective for the 51st and 3rd Battalions was the large town of Dieuze. After Dieuze was secured, CCB would drive through the town to the northeast, with the 328th Regiment advancing on their left.

The 51st AIB set out at 1:00 P.M., and by 4:30 that afternoon, established a bivouac position two miles north of Dieuze. During the evening, they drew up their plans for a mid-morning attack on the town. The strength of the enemy in Dieuze was not known, but during the night, a great deal of vehicular movement was heard coming from the direction of the town. Based on that evidence, it was feared that the enemy was holding Dieuze in strength. In anticipation that the Germans would make a determined stand, plans were made for a heavy artillery barrage in advance of the attack by the infantry.

The attack on Dieuze jumped off at 10:00 A.M., with B/51 leading the way as soon as the 15-minute long artillery barrage had lifted. B Company was followed in column by A/51, while C/51 was held back in reserve. Fortunately, the enemy had withdrawn, and the town was quickly cleared and occupied by noon (they learned from a prisoner taken in the area that the enemy had pulled out during the night, which explained the sound of vehicles near the town). With their mission complete, the 51st was assigned to CCR, and placed in reserve.

The main body of CCB was now getting underway. Two task forces were formed: TF Jaques, built around the 53rd AIB and B/8, and commanded by Lt. Colonel "Jigger" Jaques of the 53rd AIB. The other was TF Churchill, commanded by Major Tom Churchill of the 8th Tank Battalion. His force consisted primarily of the 8th Tank Battalion (–B Company) plus one company of infantry from the 53rd AIB. TF Jaques would advance on the left, and TF Churchill on the right. TF Churchill's route was the primary axis of advance, and it would carry the tanks of the 8th through Dieuze and on toward Mittersheim.

Task Force Churchill entered Dieuze on November 21. The advance through the town went at a snail's pace, due to the streets being choked with rubble from the heavy barrage that had hit the town in support of the 51st's attack the day prior. Bulldozers were brought in to clear the debris, and after a long wait, the task force finally passed through the town. To their chagrin, Churchill's men were slowed yet again by the fact that the Germans had blown every bridge between Dieuze and Mittersheim. The familiar obstacles of mud, mines, and craters in the road also complicated the advance.

The division's 24th Armored Engineer Battalion worked hard, often under direct enemy fire, to make the way passable for the armored cavalry and tanks. They certainly earned their pay that day. By nightfall, TF Churchill had captured Loudrefing, a small town about three and a quarter miles from Mittersheim. They set up outposts in the area and rested for the night.

Shifting Gears

General Wood was concerned with his division's axis of advance before the attack toward Sarre-Union had even gotten underway. The amount of progress during the first three days only served to reinforce his skepticism about the orders he had received from General Eddy. Seeking an alternative that might speed his advance, at less cost to his division, Wood came up with a new idea.

There was only one high quality road in his current zone, and it led east toward the town of Fenetrange, which sits on the west bank of the Sarre River. Wood's orders were to drive to the northeast, so this road, while of much better quality than the muddy trails he was being forced to labor over, simply didn't take him in the right direction, which was toward Sarre-Union.

Upon close inspection of his map, Wood noted that once the road crossed over the Sarre River, it turned to the northeast, and followed the line of the river all the way to Sarre-Union. Another good road ran parallel to this one, just a bit further to the east. If he could seize a crossing at Fenetrange, and put the division across the Sarre, he might be able to forge a quick strike toward his objective.

There was one small problem. Everything on the east bank of the Sarre River, as well as Fenetrange itself, was in the zone of control of the neighboring 44th Infantry Division, which belonged to another corps (General Haislip's XV); which belonged to another army (the U.S. 7th); which belonged to another army group (Devers' 6th). Moving into the zone of another army group, army, corps, and division was not something that one did without permission. Even Wood wasn't that brazen.

Before taking the idea to his superiors, Wood paved the way by approaching General Haislip beforehand. Fortunately, they were old friends, with a relationship extending all the way back to their days together as cadets at West Point. Wood, who was not bashful by nature, felt no hesitation about making his case to Haislip, even though he was outside of his chain of command.

The proposal that Wood presented to Haislip called for the Fourth Armored to secure the crossing at Fenetrange, and then advance north via the two aforementioned roads, passing through Wolfskirchen and Eywiller. With the 44th Infantry Division advancing on his right, he would then cut back into the Third Army zone at Rimsdorf and Domfessel.

Haislip agreed with Wood's proposal, and with his confidential concurrence in hand, Wood took the proposal to Generals Eddy and Patton. The arrangements and approvals were then formally made between the two armies, all the while not knowing that Wood and Haislip had cemented the details in advance.

So with a new plan in place, Wood changed his axis of advance on November 22. The primary thrust would be launched by CCB, which was positioned on the right, closest to Fenetrange and the road leading to the east. CCB would have the critical objective of securing the bridgehead over the Sarre River at Fenetrange, and then would continue the advance toward Wolfskirchen. CCA would leave its positions to the left of the 26th Infantry Division, and would follow up behind CCB on the Dieuze-Mittersheim road, cross the Sarre, and then resume its advance alongside CCB.

CCB's Drive to the Sarre

On November 22, CCB set out along its new axis of advance. Mittersheim would have to fall en route to Fenetrange, and it was here that Dager placed his focus on the day before Thanksgiving. Major Churchill formed a small task force, led by Captain Bert Ezell, to spearhead the advance (Ezell had recently been given the role of S-3 for the 8th Tank Battalion, when Major Irzyk was shifted to the position of battalion executive officer).

The advance of TF Ezell was delayed when it came upon the remains of a destroyed railroad overpass that blocked the road. Once the engineers cleared the obstacle, the column resumed its advance toward Mittersheim. As the task force approached the town, it came under fire from machine guns, 20mm antitank guns, and panzers. A heavy volume of return fire from the tanks of the 8th forced the enemy to pull back from their forward positions, and the advance resumed.

The vanguard had not traveled far before another obstacle was encountered. A wide canal ran in front of Mittersheim (Canal des Houilleres de la Sarre), and the Germans had destroyed the bridge. It would require the construction of a 36-foot treadway bridge before TF Churchill could complete the final leg of its journey to Mittersheim. The engineers from B/24 got the job done in only 75 minutes.

Before entering the town, there was one other critical objective on the agenda. Less than a quarter mile south of Mittersheim was the Grand Etang de Mittersheim, a large body of water some three miles long and half a mile wide. The lake was held in check by a large dam located near the town; if the Germans blew the dam, the entire Sarre Valley would be flooded, and the advance brought to a screeching halt. Fortunately, the dam was captured by CCB without

Pfc. McGray of the 24th Armored Engineer Battalion. The engineers ensured the 4th AD could keep rolling when blown bridges and obstacles stood in the way (National Archives Photograph SC254744).

incident. The Germans had missed a key opportunity to disrupt the American offensive. Mittersheim was secured by 3:00 P.M., and the task force continued toward Fenetrange, which was now a critical objective for XII Corps.

Fenetrange was a fairly large town nestled on the west bank of the Sarre River. The layout of the town dictated that it would have to be completely swept clear of the enemy before it cold be used as a crossing site. With darkness approaching, the task force bivouacked for the night at a location short of the town, and made plans for resuming the advance in the morning.

Task Force Churchill got underway at 8:30 A.M. on November 23, and came under heavy artillery fire as it moved down the road toward Fenetrange. The Germans were also hitting them with direct fire from positions in the woods north of the road. The advance was slow and steady, but came to an abrupt halt when the lead elements came upon a very large crater in the road. The engineers from the 24th Armored Engineer Battalion were called forward to lay down a treadway bridge over the obstacle.

The Germans had no intention of letting the engineers do their work in peace. A wide range of German ordnance started hitting the muddy fields beside where the engineers labored. Mortar rounds, 75mm and 88mm shells rained down on the area. The incoming fire got so hot that the engineers dove underneath some nearby tanks from the 8th Tank Battalion. As the engineers hugged the ground, the tanks that shielded them fired on a German position they had spotted atop a hill to the north of the road. The engineer platoon, led by 1st Lt. John Anderson, was in a tough position.

At that moment, Staff Sergeant Vincent Morana suggested that they assemble the two bridge sections back behind the partial protection of a small house they had passed en route. They could then use their bridge truck to transport the sections one at a time down to the crater. The crane could then quickly drop it into place over the obstacle. Anderson gave the green light to give it a try.

The engineers retreated to the cover of the house, and proceeded to piece together the first 24-foot section of the bridge. As they started back toward the crater with the bridge section mounted to the truck, the German gunners adjusted their fire in the direction of the advancing engineers. The first round landed 100 yards over their position. The next round landed 100 yards short. At least one of the engineers quickly realized that the enemy gunners had bracketed their position with great precision; there was little doubt where the next round would fall. One man spoke what everyone was probably thinking—"Oh-oh, here it comes!"—and sure enough, a concentration of rounds started to rain down in the immediate area.

The truck continued forward in the face of the enemy artillery fire. As the engineers neared the crater, they encountered another obstacle: several mines had been strewn across the road just before the crater. Sergeant Lonnie Offut braved the artillery fire and pulled the mines from the road.

Given everything that was being thrown at them, Lt. Anderson had second thoughts about proceeding. Once his men started to work at the site of the crater, they would be sitting ducks. So he ordered Sgt. Morana to "get all hands under cover in that house and don't come out until I tell you to, or until you are absolutely sure it is okay." Anderson then ran back to find a radio from which he could call in counterbattery fire to help silence the enemy guns.

The need for a radio was eliminated when he came across the forward artillery observer's tank. He explained to him what he needed, and the observer quickly called in the mission. Anderson grabbed a spot on top of the tank to watch the response from the American artillery. What happened next is best described by Lt. Anderson:

> ...there was just one miscalculation—the order I gave Sergeant Moran had a loophole through which he now proceeded to leap. Since nothing had dropped in his vicinity in the past three minutes, and since he had found a bottle of bracing cognac in the cellar of the house to which he had been ordered, he decided it was now okay. The first I knew of it, he had the crew back at work assembling another (section of the) bridge with enemy shells banging all over the place. There were a lot of things to do. Sandbags had to be brought up for the approaches. Somebody found a wheelbarrow to cart dirt in. The picture of the anxious engineer madly shoveling dirt over and around it, but definitely not in it made most of them laugh at their own clumsiness.

When the engineers stumbled upon some mines further down the road, a mine detector crew was dispatched to work the other side of the crater and to sweep the road in the direction of Fenetrange. This job was no less perilous, as the minesweepers drew occasional sniper fire while completing the task.

When the second section of the bridge was assembled, the engineers began transporting it in the same fashion as the first. The Germans gave them the same vigorous response with their artillery and mortars. In the face of continued enemy fire, the engineers used their crane to move the two bridge sections into place. They even received a helping hand from a medic, who figured there would be less work for him to do in his normal trade if he helped get the engineers' job done that much sooner.

It was just about an hour after they started the job that the first tank rolled over the newly installed bridge and started its way down the last stretch of road toward Fenetrange. It wasn't long before TF Churchill rolled into the west side of town in force, having sliced through the positions of the 953rd Regiment of the 361st Volksgrenadier Division.

Crossing the Sarre

The bridges over the Sarre were located on the far side of Fenetrange, and could not be observed from the west. So a reconnaissance mission was ordered to see if the bridges had been blown or not. It was no great surprise when it was discovered that the bridges had in fact been destroyed.

The swollen Sarre River was a much more formidable obstacle than the streams and smaller rivers that the engineers had bridged during the balance of the advance, and they did not have the resources immediately available to tackle this imposing, swift flowing body of water. Nevertheless, the town itself had to be cleared, and elements of CCB spent the rest of November 23 securing Fenetrange up to the west bank of the river.

Meanwhile, the battalions assigned to CCA were taking up positions in the rear, as they waited for CCB to make their crossing. This gave the men of CCA some valued time to rest on Thanksgiving Day. Morale rose as the men got a chance to read their mail, grab some hot chow, and put on some dry clothes and shoes. The men of CCB, on the other hand, were as far as you could get from those luxuries.

While Fenetrange was being cleared, other elements of CCB pushed further south in pursuit of a more favorable crossing point. To everyone's surprise, a bridge was found at the town of Gosselming, about three and a half miles south of Fenetrange. If it could be captured intact, it would be a real coupe for CCB.

The German engineers responsible for blowing the bridge were apparently unaware that the Americans had moved into the area. Rather than outposting the bridge, they were enjoying themselves in a nearby beer parlor. The leading American elements (C Troop, 25th Armored Cavalry Squadron, under the command of 1st Lt. John Keenan) seized the opportunity to rush in and capture the demolition crew before they could trigger the explosive charges already laden on the bridge. By 1 P.M. on November 23, the Fourth Armored had its first bridge across the Sarre River.

CCB's plans changed immediately with the capture of the bridge. Task Force Jaques was now sent to this crossing site, and they proceeded to secure a firm bridgehead on the east bank. Meanwhile, the men from C Troop pushed on a little over a mile to the town of Bettborn, where they made contact with the 44th Infantry Division; the US Third and Seventh armies were now operating shoulder to shoulder.

The crossing site at Gosselming would not be CCB's lone bridgehead. That same day (November 23), the engineers went to work installing a treadway bridge over the Sarre at the small town of Romelfing, which was located midday between Fenetrange and Gosselming. The 8th Tank Battalion would cross at this site, rather than traveling as far south as Gosselming. By 8:30 A.M. on the November 24, the tanks of the 8th Battalion began crossing the Sarre River. The first stage of General Wood's plan was a success. Now, it was on to Sarre-Union.

Strike of the Lehr

Patton's winter offensive was creating growing pressure on the German defenses. But an even bigger challenge faced the Germans further south. The U.S. Seventh Army (of which the 44th Infantry Division constituted the far left flank) and the French First Army were attacking in force, and with great success.

Back on November 11, the U.S. Seventh Army's XV Corps launched an attack in the Baccarat sector south of the Marne-Rhine Canal. The XV Corps' main thrust came through the "Saverne Gap," a historic gateway through the Vosges Mountains. At the east end of the gap was the prized city of Strasbourg. Meanwhile, the French First Army, operating south of the U.S. Seventh, was attacking along an axis that in effect created a huge pincer movement. The Germans began to realize that the Allies were moving into position to trap the Nineteenth Army west of the Rhine River.

To avoid this disaster, the Panzer Lehr Division was sent south to participate in a counterattack designed to take back the city of Sarrebourg. At the time, the Panzer Lehr was being refitted for participation in Hitler's upcoming counteroffensive in the Ardennes; the refitting of the division was not complete, however, and the Panzer Lehr departed with only 65 tanks (30 Mark IV's and 35 Panthers) and two under-strength panzer grenadier regiments.

Before the commencement of the German counterattack, the French Second Armored Division made a bold drive through the Saverne gap and captured Strasbourg. This forced a change in the German plans, and the Panzer Lehr Division was ordered to attack through Phalsbourg and into the Saverne gap, rather than toward Sarrebourg. If successful, the Germans would cut off the French Second Armored Division.

There was one other key element to the German plan. Back on November 11, one factor that contributed to the success of the XV Corps attack was that it had struck at the boundary between the German First and Nineteenth armies. The Germans were painfully aware of the vulnerability inherent in organizational boundaries, and with that thought fresh in their minds, they planned their counterattack to hit the seam between the U.S. Third and Seventh armies; in other words, directly in the gap between the Fourth Armored and the 44th Infantry Division. What the Germans didn't know, however, was that the Fourth Armored Division would be across the Sarre River before the Panzer Lehr started its attack. The Germans thought they would only be hitting the weak left flank of the 44th ID.

On the morning of November 24, at the very moment the 8th Tank Battalion was rolling across the Sarre River, Fritz Bayerlein's Panzer Lehr Division struck the far left flank of the U.S. Seventh Army. The 44th ID and 106th Cavalry Group bore the brunt of the German attack, and by nightfall, Bayerlein's division had swept through the towns of Weyer and Hirschland. The Germans resumed their attack on the morning of November 25, dealing heavy blows to the American positions at Rauwiller and Ischermuhl. The strike against the seam between the Third and Seventh armies appeared to be shaping up as a success, and the Germans were moving forward with a full head of steam.

Bayerlein's momentum did not last long. As he attacked south, he was counting on the 361st Volksgrenadier Division to protect his right flank along the line of the

A mired Sherman tank shares the battlefield with three Panther tanks knocked out during recent fighting. November 25, 1944 (National Archives Photograph SC197268).

Sarre River. German engineers were prepared to destroy all of the bridges leading across the river from the west, which would make the 361st's job much easier. But as we know, on November 23 and 24, the Fourth Armored Division swept the volksgrenadiers aside, and stole across the river at Gosselming. Wood's division was now in a superb position to hit the right flank of the Panzer Lehr Division at the very moment that Bayerlein had the 44th Infantry Division on the ropes.

The Fourth was in an unusual position, however. It was now operating in the zone of the Seventh Army, but was still under the control of XII Corps and Third Army. As events would prove, however, Wood was not constrained by such artificial barriers. In his words, "such lines meant little to me and I went where the going was good." During the days that followed, the Fourth would demonstrate the kind of flexibility, innovation, and coordination that the Germans cold not muster when attacked on their own Army boundary line back on November 11.

CCB to the Rescue

Combat Command B struck out along two lines of advance from its bridgeheads on the Sarre River. The tank-heavy Task Force Churchill advanced toward the town

A convoy of 4th AD vehicles on the move, November 25, 1944. There was no escape from the mud (National Archives Photograph SC197159).

of Postroff, which rested on a dominating area of high ground overlooking the main road from Fenetrange. Postroff was also a critical waypoint on the route leading toward Wolfskirchen, which in turn was a waypoint en route to Sarre-Union.

TF Jaques was responsible for the important crossroad town of Baerendorf, approximately one mile to the south of Postroff. Baerendorf rested on the low ground below

Postroff, nestled at the opening of a valley that ran east toward Hirschland. The nature of the road net, so critical under the muddy conditions, made Baerendorf a choke point for the offensive operations of both John Wood's Fourth Armored Division and Fritz Bayerlein's Panzer Lehr.

Before TF Churchill attacked Postroff, it had to seize the high ground southwest of the town. This was accomplished with little difficulty, and Churchill now had a commanding view of the valley nestled below Postroff. The next move would involve an advance across the valley itself. And this would be no easy task, since the enemy positions on the opposite side of the divide afforded the Germans a clear view of any move the Americans would make toward Postroff.

As the task force moved down into the valley, it came under heavy fire from small arms, artillery, and panzers. The Germans had the approaches to the town zeroed in, and were taking full advantage of the excellent observation points on the high ground in and around Postroff. The American tankers' task was made all but impossible when they came up to the west bank of the river (a tributary of the Sarre) that ran down the spine of the valley, and found that the Germans had blown the only bridge leading across in that area. Casualties mounted as the Germans continued to pound on the Americans down in the valley. One of the tank platoon leaders, Lieutenant Rice, was among those killed during the advance.

Meanwhile, Task Force Jaques, moving along an axis about one mile south of TF Churchill, advanced toward the village of Baerendorf. The approaches to the town were heavily mined, and the hidden explosives disabled two Sherman tanks from B/8. As the men of the 53rd AIB approached the town, they had to form a human chain to cross over a swift flowing stream west of the town (this was a branch of the river that was causing the delay for TF Churchill).

Because Baerendorf represented such a critical spot on the right flank of the Panzer Lehr's attack against the 44th Infantry Division, the grenadiers from the 902nd Panzer Grenadier Regiment's 1st Battalion were prepared to defend it with great tenacity (the battalion also had the support of German pioneers and reconnaissance troops). Despite the German's best effort, however, the men of B/8 and the 53rd AIB proved to be the better warriors, and kicked the grenadiers out of the village by nightfall. But the battle for Baerendorf had only just begun.

The second stage of the battle began during the early morning hours of November 25. Bayerlein was now aware that his right flank was in serious jeopardy, so he turned his panzers, which now amounted to 33 Mark IVs and 20 Panthers, away from their attack against the 44th Infantry Division and cast them toward the Fourth Armored Division.

A German task force of tanks and infantry, attacking from the east, tried to drive its way back into Baerendorf. The Americans had consolidated their positions during the night, however, and were well prepared for the German assault. The severe mud made cross-country movement as difficult for the Germans as it was for the Americans, and the men of TF Jaques took advantage of the predictable route followed by the lead tanks. Two of the Panthers leading the charge were knocked out upon their approach, and the attack disintegrated.

As the battle for Baerendorf continued, elements of the 8th Tank Battalion from

Men of the 53rd AIB on the move near Baerendorf. November 25, 1944 (National Archives Photograph SC197206).

TF Churchill renewed their push toward Postroff. With the capture of Baerendorf, Churchill was able to change the axis of his advance, and now attacked from the south. This time, they managed to push their way in and secured the town.

With Postroff and Baerendorf firmly in the hands of CCB, General Dager began planning the next phase of the attack. During the fighting on November 25, he made what was considered to be a rare appearance at the front. (It seems that as the war dragged on, Dager spent less time at the front. Some under his command felt this was due to the increased confidence he had in their abilities, while some felt that he was less inclined to take the personal risk involved in coming up close to the action. Regardless of the reason behind the decline in his appearances, the fact that he visited with the front line units on this occasion was notable.)

Dager personally brought forward instructions to his battalion commanders regarding how they were to proceed. Major Churchill was to advance toward the town of Wolfskirchen (Churchill's task force was beefed up considerably for the task with the addition of the 51st AIB, which had moved up through Fenetrange on November 24 and was subsequently assigned to Dager's CCB). Lt. Colonel Jaques was instructed to take his task force abreast and to the right of Churchill. He was given the assignment of capturing Eywiller, about 2½ miles east of Wolfskirchen. For the time being, the forested high ground separating the two task forces would be left alone.

Fritz Bayerlein also had a visitor at the front on November 25. Major General F.W. Von Mellenthin came up from OKW to assess the situation, and after his visit, made a specific note that CCB/4 was "fighting stoutly at the village of Baerendorf." Bayerlein asked that he be allowed to break off his attack, but despite the fact that Von Mellenthin supported his request, OKW ordered Bayerlein to continue on the offensive.

CCB — November 25 and 26

Upon its attachment to CCB, the 51st Armored Infantry Battalion was ordered to hook up with TF Churchill for the drive toward Wolfskirchen. While en route, however, the 51st's orders were changed not once, but twice. Finally, the entire battalion was ordered back to the west, with the mission of clearing the large woods northeast of Fenetrange. Any German forces harbored within the Bois de-L'lisch would pose a threat to the left flank of Churchill's advance toward Wolfskirchen, so it became imperative that the 51st AIB secure the woods.

The 51st's plan of attack called for A/51 and B/51 to press into the woods, clearing them of enemy resistance. Meanwhile, C/51 would stay clear of the woods, and attack on an axis running parallel with the west edge of the forest, with the ultimate objective of capturing the village of Niederstinzel. If all three companies were successful, any enemy units remaining within the woods would be caught between the two advancing forces.

C/51 jumped off at 9:00 A.M., and the armored infantry reached the southern edge of Niederstinzel at 1:00 P.M. As they began their advance into the village, they drew heavy concentrations of artillery fire. After three hours of bitter fighting in Niederstinzel, the company was ordered to withdraw to high ground to the southwest. During the engagement, C Company had wiped out 5 machine gun nests, killed 15 of the enemy, and captured nine of them. But they were forced to withdraw nevertheless.

The attack into the woods by A/51 and B/51 would not get started until much later in the afternoon. At 3:20 P.M., the 22nd Armored Field Artillery Battalion laid down a ten-minute barrage to soften up the German positions. The two companies then began their advance. The armored infantrymen had to cross over open ground between their line of departure and the edge of the woods, and as they moved forward, they came under heavy artillery fire. They pressed on in the face of the shelling, and gained positions at the edge of the forest. The tempo of the enemy bombardment picked up when the Americans entered the woods. The casualty rate increased rapidly as the artillery shells crashed into the treetops, sending deadly splinters and shrapnel cascading downwards.

"Tree bursts" were the dreaded byproduct of being shelled while in a forest. Normally, when caught out in the open in an artillery barrage, a soldier would be inclined to lie down, thus reducing his profile and reducing the risk of being hit by shrapnel, which would typically be coming at him more or less horizontally. But in the forest, the tree bursts changed the trajectory of shrapnel from horizontal to vertical. A man lying on his stomach now had his torso exposed to fragments raining down from above. The men eventually learned that, while in the forest, their best protection was to remain standing and get in close behind the cover of a tree trunk (the infantry divisions of the U.S. First Army that fought in the dreaded Huertgen Forest campaign learned these lessons all too well, in what was probably the most horrific woods fighting of the war).

Despite the heavy shelling, the infantry of the 51st continued to press deeper into the forest. By nightfall, Companies A and B had dug foxholes in the muddy ground, and settled in for a cold, miserable night.

The two primary task forces operating to the east of the 51st AIB began their attack late in the afternoon that same day (November 25). They didn't get far, as intense artillery fire stopped them in their tracks. There seemed to be no shortage of German guns and ammunition, as almost every advancing unit that day was brought under heavy concentrations of indirect fire. By nightfall, both TF Churchill and TF Jaques were confined to their starting points at the towns of Prostroff and Baerendorf, respectively.

November 26 brought renewed fighting at Baerendorf. A strong task force from the Panzer Lehr Division struck once again against TF Jacques. There were heavy losses on both sides, but the German attack was beaten back. One of the most popular men in B/8, 30 year-old 1st Sgt. Melvyn Bailey, was killed during the attack (Bailey received five Bronze Stars and one Silver Star during the course of the campaign). After the repulse of Bayerlein's final effort to recapture Baerendorf, elements of TF Jaques pushed east into the village of Eschwiller. After securing the town, the task force attempted to move still further to the east, but they were hit yet again by heavy artillery fire as they emerged into the open terrain outside of the town.

The pressure placed on the Panzer Lehr Division by CCB finally came to a boiling point. By the end of the day, Bayerlein felt he had no choice but to assume defensive positions, despite the order from OKW to remain on the offensive. The Germans also had to bring in extra forces to deal with the threat of a breakthrough by the Fourth Armored, and to that end, a battle group from the 25th Panzer Grenadier Division arrived that same day to help shore up Bayerlein's left flank.

As the Germans abandoned their offensive operations, the 51st Armored Infantry Battalion continued its attack on the left flank of TF Churchill. It finished clearing out the woods, and then A and B Companies took up positions along the north edge of the forest. Of the two men killed in the battalion that day, it was unfortunate that one of them (a member of the reconnaissance platoon) was hit by gunfire from an outpost of the 53rd AIB, which now had elements screening the east edge of the forest.

CCA Arrives

As CCB was fighting hard east of the Sarre River, CCA had been enjoying some relative peace and quiet in its bivouac areas. On November 25, Colonel Withers' command, which now consisted primarily of the 35th Tank Battalion, 10th Armored Infantry Battalion, and the 94th AFAB, began moving east across the rear area of the 26th Infantry Division, toward Fenetrange. Task Force Oden led the way, and began crossing the Sarre River that same day. It moved into an assembly area near Romelfing.

Task Force West crossed the Sarre the following day, and moved immediately to an assembly area outside of Kirrberg (about a mile and a half south of Baerendorf). By 3:30 P.M., both task forces of CCA were on their way due east toward the town of Schalbach, which was held by the 44th Infantry Division. At that point, the two task forces split up, with TF West heading north toward Drulingen, and TF Oden continuing east and then north toward Ottwiller. These moves placed CCA to the right of CCB.

Task Force West passed through the town of Drulingen without meeting any opposition. By 9:30 that evening, it had taken up positions on and around Hill 311. The vanguard of the task force consisted of A/10, a platoon of B/704, a small detachment from the 24th Engineer Battalion, and the headquarters and HQ Company of the 10th AIB (C/10 was attached to TF Oden, and B/10 was placed in CCA reserve near Romelfing). The tanks of C/35 were attached to TF West, but did not advance with the vanguard. Meanwhile, TF Oden pulled up just shy of Ottwiller, about two miles due east of TF West.

As the two task forces of CCA moved into position alongside CCB, Colonel Withers issued a decree that limited the speed and scope of their pending attack. According to his executive officer, Hal Pattison, Withers stated "there would be no formal attack by either battalion task force." Instead, Oden and West were ordered to "reconnoiter extensively." Later, when Wood's staff made inquiries regarding the slow progress of CCA, Withers responded with the claim that CCA was confronted with heavy opposition, and that despite the level of resistance, his men "were probing vigorously." As we shall see, this was nothing short of a fabrication.

Withers did not have willing accomplices. The slow advance on November 26 gnawed at West and Oden. They felt they could do more on that day, and felt unduly constrained by Withers' orders to limit their activity. They knew they had a fresh, rested, and battle-ready force at their disposal, and that Withers was taking too conservative a course.

Though under the restraint of applying nothing stronger than extensive reconnaissance, Delk Oden made a liberal interpretation of his orders, and on November 27, began to push his task force north from Ottwiller. On that day, he advanced two miles, stopping just south of the village of Durstal. Opposition was light, but the shackle of Withers' orders kept Oden from exploiting the situation.

On that same day, Art West pushed the envelope of Withers' orders even further than had Oden. Advancing on Oden's left, West advanced his task force aggressively toward the key objective of Gungwiller. At 1:20 P.M., he attacked the town with the Shermans of C/35 and armored infantry of A/10. The infantry mounted the decks of the Shermans and rode on toward the objective. Artillery support was provided by the 94th AFAB and the Hellcats of B/704.

After hundreds of rounds had been unloaded on the town, the American tanks and infantry swept into Gungwiller. Resistance in the town was later described as being "half-hearted," but some of the Germans refused to give up. Fragmentation grenades, smoke grenades, and flamethrowers were used to rout the Germans from the cellars. By the time the town was cleared at 4 P.M., the Americans had captured 37 and killed 35. After the mopping-up was completed, A/10 pushed forward to the high ground outside of the town. Not long after the armored infantry had moved on, the

Germans hit Gungwiller with a heavy artillery barrage. The Americans had left just in time.

Though Colonel Withers had only been in command since November 17, his handling of CCA had already caused consternation among some of his staff, as well as the battalion commanders assigned to his command. Withers was increasingly unapproachable and unyielding in his dealings with them, and in the estimation of several of the officers, it was having a negative impact on the performance of CCA.

Colonel Withers was not aided by the reputation he carried into his new assignment. His qualities were known by the veteran officers of the Fourth Armored, by virtue of his holding prior positions within the division, dating all the way back to its training in the United States. As one of his staff members later wrote:

> He was mal-assigned as a commander; his bent was mechanical engineering, his talent was research and development. He was a grand gentleman and a perfect host. He was not a troop leader and, especially, he was not a tank unit commander. It seemed that everyone in the Division except General Wood knew Withers' failings. Wood's great weakness was his almost blind loyalty to, "my people." We could do no wrong in his eyes.

During his short tenure at CCA, Withers had established a peculiar habit. At dawn, he would depart alone from the command post, embarking upon a self-described "reconnaissance." He would not return until sunset. What he did, and where he went, was anyone's guess. He had already developed a reputation for undue caution, and in the words of one of his staff members, "he did not let us advance until there was very little in front of us." He had yet to gain the respect of his men, from top to bottom. His relationship with the commander of the 10th AIB, Lt. Col. West, was particularly strained. Hal Pattison later described that relationship:

> There was exceedingly bad blood between West of the 10th and Withers who, many believed, was waiting for a chance to "throw the book" at West. Withers considered West to be a wild man devoid of judgment and moral character. West, in fact, was a controlled fury in a fight and possessed sufficient moral character to achieve retirement as a Major General.

Withers' stature within CCA was pretty well summed up by the following reflection offered by one of the staff: "Colonel Withers lacked the moral courage to command and he was not a leader." He possessed other positive qualities, and those that knew him would be quick to recognize them, but the temperament and fortitude to lead a combat command was apparently not among them.

On November 27, the officers gathered together at the headquarters of CCA to meet with Colonel Pattison. They protested the methods and pace of the advance, and Pattison, being sympathetic to their cause, worked with them in his capacity as CCA's executive officer to develop an operation for the following day. Colonel Withers was unavailable for the meeting, as he was out on his daily "reconnaissance."

When Withers returned that evening, Pattison informed him of the plan that had been developed for November 28. Withers would have none of it. He cancelled the operation, and ordered that no one was to initiate any action without his explicit approval. Pattison's reward for attempting to kick-start CCA was a charge of insubordination and the threat of a court martial. Withers also erupted when he was informed of TF West's strong attack on Gungwiller. He viewed the attack as deliberate act of insubordination by Art West. Withers' response, and the events that followed, are best described by Pattison:

> When Withers learned of West's attack he went to the 10th AIB Command Post to place West under arrest for failure to obey orders but was foiled of his intent by the arrival of General Wood who congratulated both Withers and West on a fine and successful attack. West later told me there was nothing to it — as he had expected there was very little resistance to his front. Thus West was saved from Court Martial but battalion commanders and the CCA staff were jointly censured for irresponsibility.

On November 28, CCA barely budged from the positions it had reached the day prior. It wasn't for lack of objectives, for CCB, after many days in the fight, certainly would have benefited from immediate support on its right flank. A strong move by CCA would have protected the right flank of CCB, and perhaps even drawn off some of the resistance in front of them. But after the first day of engagement on November 26, Colonel Withers virtually sat his men down.

Given the rebuke they had received from Withers, the battalion commanders felt helpless to contribute. In reading the combat diary of West's 10th Armored Infantry Battalion, one readily senses the level of frustration that existed. The entry for November 28 reflects that no enemy activity, other than some light artillery shelling, took place on that day. The diary states: "All during the day the battalion was in readiness to push on, awaiting orders to push out and to the next objective, Rexingen and Battwiller." They were practically begging to continue the advance.

November 29 was a repeat of the day before. TF West remained in place on the high ground outside of Gungwiller. There was no enemy activity in the area, save for a few artillery shells that hit Drulingen, further to the rear, at about 5 P.M. Colonel Withers had CCA sitting on its hands. An opportunity had existed for them to outflank Sarre-Union, perhaps even pocketing the German forces facing CCB. But it was not to be, as Withers took counsel of his fears, and did not press the advance at a satisfactory pace.

The Advance on Wolfskirchen

On November 27, elements of the 8th Tank and 51st Armored Infantry Battalions struck toward Wolfskirchen. Their objective was not the town itself, but the high ground to the northeast. The plan called for bypassing Wolfskirchen to the south; they would only head there if they drew fire from the direction of the town. If the enemy were found to be holding strong positions in Wolfskirchen, they would change course and secure the town before proceeding to the northeast.

The advance got underway at 10:10 A.M. The 51st AIB moved out in a column of three companies (in order, B, C, and A). The column crossed over the bridge at the L'Isch River and then headed toward Wolfskirchen. As the infantry advanced, the light tanks of D/8 remained in position near the edge of the woods, where they would provide covering fire as needed.

As the men of TF Churchill would soon discover, Wolfskirchen was indeed occupied by the Germans. The Panzer Lehr Division had inserted the 7th Company of the 902nd PG Regiment into the town, with the mission of acting as a rear guard to cover the retreat of the 25th Panzer Grenadier Division from the area. The commander of the 7th Company, Oberleutnant Graf, received orders to defend his position and hold Wolfskirchen until 5 P.M. that evening, which would allow enough time for the 25th PG Division to make its escape. At approximately 11 A.M., their position was stiffened a bit when the 8th Company, led by Oberleutnant Ebner, took up positions on Hill 317 due north of the town in order to lend the support of its four 120mm mortars.

The American armored infantry made an uneventful approach to the town, and by 11:20 A.M., they had reached a position approximately 300 yards from the edge of Wolfskirchen. It was at this position that they came under fire from the small arms and machine guns of Graf's men located within Wolfskirchen. In reaction to the fire, the two lead companies of the 51st AIB deployed abreast (C on the left, B on the right), and with a company of Shermans from the 8th lending support, turned their attack directly toward the town.

Stiff resistance was encountered, and the entire balance of the day was spent clearing the town of the enemy. At about 3 P.M., two Mark IV tanks came up in support of the defenders, but they fled the area before sunset, having been driven away by the more plentiful armor of TF Churchill.

As the Americans drove deeper into the town, the Germans once again brought down heavy artillery and mortar fire, and the American infantry took refuge in the buildings they had already secured. As Graf's 5 P.M. deadline for holding the town approached, he prepared to pull his company out of the town. By nightfall, the Americans had pushed through the balance of the town, and all three companies of the 51st AIB set up a defensive perimeter. It was now suspected that the primary enemy stronghold was located on the high ground to the northeast.

CCB's Advance Toward Sarre-Union

On November 28, the burden of moving against Sarre-Union continued to fall on the back of Dager's CCB, as CCA sat idle on his right flank. TF Jacques, working with elements of the 71st Infantry Regiment, cleared out the woods east of Wolfskirchen (the Bois de Wolsthof). This helped secure the right flank of TF Churchill, and allowed the 8th and 51st to renew their advance to the northeast, with the objective of capturing the town of Burbach.

At 12:15 P.M., a single platoon of C/51 advanced to the high ground northeast of Wolfskirchen. There was no resistance encountered, and it appeared that the Germans had fled the scene (in fact, the Panzer Lehr Division had withdrawn in order to prepare for the Ardennes offensive; the 25th Panzer Grenadier Division had assumed responsibility for the sector).

With the heights overlooking their route secured, the three companies of the 51st AIB set out once again in a single column. They pushed on and captured Burbach without resistance, but once there, the Germans brought down more artillery fire on their

A light tank of the 8th Tank Battalion being put to use for the evacuation of a wounded soldier. This became a common use for the light tanks, when ground conditions did not allow wheeled vehicles to get to the wounded. December 1, 1944 (National Archives Photograph SC325974).

positions. By nightfall, the task force had moved on and occupied the high ground above the highway leading southeast from Sarre-Union to Drulingen.

On the morning of November 29, TF Irzyk (consisting of A/8 and B/51) struck out along a circuitous route from Burbach toward the town of Rimsdorf. The balance of the 51st would remain in position near Burbach, and would advance up the main road toward Sarre-Union if TF Irzyk were successful in capturing Rimsdorf (the capture of Rimsdorf would ensure protection on the right flank of the 51st as it advanced on the city).

The infantry of B/51 left their halftracks behind and mounted up on the Shermans of A/8. As soon as they advanced beyond Burbach, they came under fire from a combination of enemy tanks, artillery, and infantry. The Germans were firing from positions on the edge of the Le Bannholtz woods and the high ground northwest of Thalpres-Drulingen. The two forces battled all day, and TF Irzyk had to halt on the high ground short of Rimsdorf, where they secured their positions for the night.

At this point, the morale of the 51st was on the wane. The days of continuous

The men and tanks of the 10th AIB and 35th Tank Battalion advance on December 1, 1944 (National Archives Photograph SC197248).

action had reduced the ranks of the armored infantry companies to effective strengths of 70 to 80 men each. In some cases, men were pulled out of the towed 57mm anti-tank platoons and used as replacements for the under-strength infantry platoons.

During the same day (November 29), other elements of CCB had drawn up closer to TF Churchill. TF Jaques captured Berg, which placed them echeloned behind TF Churchill's right flank. CCA, which was not keeping pace, was echeloned still further back to the southeast of TF Jaques. Meanwhile, the 25th Cavalry had advanced to the west of Sarre-Union, and turned its assault guns against the city (the howitzers of the 22nd AFAB also joined in).

November 30th was spent consolidating their positions for the next big attack. The objective would be Sarre-Union itself, located to the northwest of Rimsdorf. The 101st Regiment of the 26th Infantry Division was brought in to assist with the attack. TF West finally inched forward that day, having been given orders to capture the high ground in the vicinity of Mackwiller. "The objective was taken without a single shot being fired." During the entire time that CCA had sat idle, it would appear that the Germans had already gone into retreat.

The attack toward Sarre-Union began at 8:00 A.M. on December 1. CCB, which now consisted primarily of the 8th and 51st Battalions, pushed off toward the intermediate objective of Rimsdorf, which had been denied to TF Irzyk two days earlier. The 101st Regiment, advancing in unison with CCB, supported the left flank.

C/8, with the infantry of B/51 mounted on its tanks, led the column toward Rimsdorf on the heels of a 10 minute artillery barrage that the Americans threw at the woods on both sides of the town. Following behind C/8 on foot were A/51 and C/51. Once again, they came under the heavy fire that was so typical of the Lorraine battles. But they pressed on, and found Rimsdorf vacant of opposition. C/8 and B/51 advanced into the town and secured it without suffering a single casualty. But A/51, following on foot, was caught by the German guns, and suffered heavily. Once the entire task force moved into the town, a perimeter defense was established around the outskirts.

Shortly after noon, the scene at Rimsdorf changed abruptly when the Germans launched a counterattack from the east with a force consisting of infantry and panzers. The Americans had been wise to prepare their perimeter defenses so soon after clearing the town, and thus were well prepared for the attack. The Shermans of C Company knocked out four panzers without the loss of a single American tank.

Changes in Command

December 1 turned out to be a day of major changes within the Fourth Armored Division. Among the wounded that day was the commander of the 51st Armored Infantry Battalion, Major Van Arnam. Captain Rockafeller took temporary command, and within 24 hours Major Dan Alanis, who had been the CO for the 704th TD Battalion, was assigned as the commanding officer of the 51st. Major Charlie Kimsey would, in turn, take over the reins of the esteemed 704th.

The 10th Armored Infantry Battalion also suffered a significant loss that first day of December when Lt. Colonel West was wounded and subsequently evacuated. He had been conducting a forward reconnaissance on the high ground west of Mackwiller prior to an attack by his battalion against the town. As he and the other officers accompanying him were lying along the crest of the ridge studying the scene, a lone German fired upon them with a submachine gun, striking West in the chest and arm (an officer from the 704th TD Battalion was also seriously wounded). As for the German, he was immediately dispatched for all eternity with a round from the main gun of Lt. Puff's tank.

Lt. Colonel West would not return; Major Harold Cohen was assigned command of the battalion. West had been one of the more vociferous battalion commanders, especially on the topic of Withers' performance, and his presence, after a very distinguished campaign across France, would be missed.

Two of the three armored infantry battalions had lost their CO's on the same day, and now had new officers at the helm. And as already mentioned, a byproduct of the moves to replace them was the assignment of a new commander for the 704th. It was not an auspicious start for the month of December.

The armored infantry battalions were not the only units impacted by a change in leadership. The following day, December 2, Major Irzyk, who was then the executive officer of the 8th Tank Battalion, was summoned to the command post of Brigadier General Dager. Without hesitation, Dager informed Irzyk, "Tom Churchill has not been able to move the battalion the way I would like him to, so I have had him reassigned to Reserve Command [Churchill became the S-3 of CCR]. General Wood and I would like you to take over the battalion right now. Continue the day's operations."

The Advance East of Sarre-Union

The advance of the Fourth Armored continued on December 2 along a broad front. A battalion from the 101st Regiment, along with the 51st and the 53rd Battalions from the Fourth, were positioned to advance in unison toward the high ground north of Rimsdorf, thus flanking Sarre-Union to the east.

A ten-minute preparatory barrage was provided by the 22nd AFAB, and the three battalions marched forward at 9:00 A.M. Soon after the advance commenced, the lead units came under small arms fire from nearby woods, and a platoon of M5 light tanks was sent forward to quiet the disturbance. The advance continued at a quick pace, despite constant harassment from the German artillery.

As the infantry approached the woods south of their objective, nine panzers were spotted to the north. Air support was called in, and the tanks were driven off by the flyboys of the XIX TAC. With the panzers no longer an immediate threat, the infantry consolidated their positions in the woods south of the Sarre Union-Domfessel road (Domfessel was a large town located about 2½ miles east-north-east of Sarre-Union). The medium tanks of A/8 then drove toward the objective, with the infantry following on foot. Despite continued shelling by enemy artillery, the tanks and infantry gained the high ground around Schlosshof Farm by 2:40 P.M., and the men of the 51st consolidated their positions and dug in for the night.

The advance toward Sarre-Union had been a slow, arduous, laborious affair. According to the division's After Action Report for the month of November, the Fourth Armored had lost "36 medium tanks, 10 light tanks, 7 artillery pieces, and 140 miscellaneous vehicles" since the start of the offensive on November 9. Casualties of the division were 220 killed, 805 wounded, and 38 missing in action." They estimated that they had inflicted losses upon the enemy that tallied "1575 killed, 939 wounded, and 1095 prisoners of war," along with the destruction or capture of "61 tanks, 104 large caliber artillery pieces, 11 anti-aircraft guns, and 63 miscellaneous vehicles." CCB had shouldered almost the entire burden for the division ever since crossing the Sarre River back on November 23. The battalions of CCB had been in the fight for more than 10 consecutive days without relief, while the balance of the division had a comparatively easy time of it (much to the consternation of the battalion commanders involved).

It was against this backdrop that General Eddy visited CCA's headquarters near the railroad station at Mackwiller on the late-morning of December 2. He was in search of General Wood, who was expected but had not yet arrived. Soon after Eddy's arrival, Colonel Withers left the CP, leaving Hal Pattison alone with Eddy to wait for Wood. "P" arrived at about 11 A.M., and he had no sooner entered the room when a sharp exchange occurred between the two generals. The tone was angry, and in retrospect, Pattison thought it was a continuation of an earlier argument. As Pattison tells it:

General Eddy said the division was not fighting hard, was not living up to its capabilities and would have to move faster. General Wood angrily disputed these charges and Eddy retorted that he, Wood, had promised to be out of the SEVENTH Army zone in a couple of days and it was still blocking the 44th Division's roads after more than a week and General Haislip was calling him every day to find out when Wood was going to get moving. To which General Wood, who rarely swore, replied, "God Damn it Matt, my boys have bought every foot of this ground with their blood, they have done everything humanely possible and I will not ask any more of them. We will get out as fast as we can but no faster" (that is a pretty accurate quote — I was awed by the intensity of their manner). General Wood then turned on his heel and stalked out leaving a very angry General Eddy behind him.

When Wood stood up for his men in the face of Eddy's accusations, he did so with the belief that his men were fighting as hard as they could, against a tough opponent, over tough terrain and in miserable weather conditions. Little did he know that the commander of CCA had been painting a false picture of the situation facing his command. Some of Eddy's criticisms were justified, but Wood was loyal to his men to a fault, and it was his blind trust in Withers that led him astray. The ramifications of Withers' betrayal, at worst, or incompetence, at best, would soon be felt across the entire division.

A Letter Home

When Staff Sergeant Frank Besedick first joined the Fourth Armored Division, he was assigned to the 22nd Armored Field Artillery Battalion. But when his gift for art was discovered, he was transferred to the division's operations staff to serve as a draftsman. His primary responsibility was the creation of map overlays and combat orders, but he soon found opportunities to indulge his artistic talents by contributing a large volume of work that served as illustrations for publications issued by the division (he would long be remembered by every member of the Fourth Armored for his Christmas Card designs and, most notably, the illustrations he provided for their official history, *From the Beach to Bavaria*).

Frank also had the opportunity now and again to create works that he would send home to his wife, Kay. December 2 provided an opportunity to do just that, and he spent some time that day creating an image of Fenetrange, where the Division HQ was located. Normally an uplifting spirit within the Division Headquarters (the citation for his Bronze Star made special note of his "cheer and efficiency"), it appears that Frank was in an uncharacteristically somber mood as the day drew to a close. Something was tearing at him, and he expressed his feelings to his wife in a note that he penciled beneath his rendering of the church overlooking the main street of Fenetrange:

Hello Darling,

It has been a terrible day — I feel much too low to even write a decent letter so have doodled this scene — it's the Church I shall attend tomorrow. Missing you terribly — and loving you always.

Always your loving husband,
Frank

Art. for Christmas Card for 4th Armored Div.

The 4th AD Christmas card for 1944, created by Staff Sergeant Frank Besedick (courtesy K. Besedick).

Hello Darling –
    It has been a terrible day – I feel
much too low to even write a decent letter
so have __doodled__ this scene – its the Church I
shall attend Tomorrow – Missing you
terribly – and loving you always –
                    always your loving
                    husband
                    Frank

Fenetrange on December 2, 1944 (courtesy K. Besedick).

Frank never wrote to Kay again about what may have been troubling him on December 2. Nor did he ever speak to her about it after the war. There were too many other things that would overshadow that day during the years that lay ahead. Returning to Kay, the love of his life. Raising a wonderful family. Launching a career as a commercial and creative artist. Indeed, the tidal wave of life washed over the events of December 2, 1944.

But December 2 had indeed been a terrible day, not only for Frank Besedick, but also for every member of the Fourth Armored Division. Most of the men of the Fourth turned in for the night unaware of what had transpired that day. But the news would be carried forth the following morning, and the date of December 3, 1944, would be emblazoned forever upon the collective memory of the division.

8. The Relief

Shockwaves

With CCB poised to outflank Sarre-Union from the east, and with CCA finally drawn up closer to Dager's right flank, there might have been reason for optimism, were it not for the startling news that rippled through the Fourth Armored Division on December 3. On that fateful day, it was announced that General Wood had been relieved of his command, and was ordered home to the United States. Many veterans of the division will always remember exactly where they were and what they were doing when they heard the news. Such was the case for Al Irzyk, the newly assigned commanding officer of the 8th Tank Battalion.

Brigadier General Holmes Dager ordered his two primary battalion commanders, Major Irzyk and Major Alanis, to report to his command post early on December 3. Upon their arrival, the two officers were ushered in to meet with their commanding officer. Dager, who had been in command of CCB since early 1942 and had a long relationship with Wood, immediately blurted out the bad news: "You won't believe it. You just won't believe it. General Wood has just been relieved of command of the division." The announcement swept over the two young majors like a tidal wave. Irzyk and Alanis sunk into the two nearest chairs, and a moment of silence passed as Dager, who was noticeably choked-up, allowed them to absorb the news.

Dager then explained the situation as it had been explained to him. He had been told that Wood was tired, sick, and in need of rest. But he immediately made it obvious to the two stunned men that he didn't accept that as the real reason. There had to be something else behind what had happened. After another pause ... perhaps reflecting on just how far he should carry the discussion with his subordinates ... Dager punctuated the finality of it all by saying "At any rate, 'P' is gone, sent home." He then announced to the men that General Hugh Gaffey would be taking over the reins of the division.

By the time Alanis and Irzyk returned to their respective battalions, the news had already started to spread. The men of the Fourth Armored were shocked. Disbelief and a sense of personal loss permeated the ranks of the division. Some men bowed their heads and cried at the news that "P" Wood was no longer their commanding officer. Groups of soldiers could be seen huddled together, lamenting Wood's departure. A platoon leader from the 53rd AIB, Lt. DeWitt Smith Jr., later described in writing how he felt when he heard the news:

> I cried. I was not alone. [Wood was a] great, gutsy, outgoing man ... with a tremendous sensitivity to human beings, a great love for his men, and a great faith in his division. He was brave; had great moral courage; was outspoken; was warm and compassionate; could fight armor better than any man in Europe; had the ability to infuse high morale and esprit through convincing, personal leadership; and was beloved by us all for this. He was the finest soldier I have ever known, and I shall never forget him.

The men of the Fourth could only agonize and commiserate over Wood's departure for so long. The necessities of battle dictated that they keep their head in the game, and by the end of the day, their focus came back to the job at hand. Their beloved leader was gone, but the enemy was not.

The Relief

The final decision to relieve Major General John Wood of his command was reached sometime on December 2. It is not certain when Wood was actually notified of the decision, but it was probably late in the afternoon or evening of that same day. The balance of the day and the early hours of December 3 were spent making the appointments that flowed from the decision to replace him.

At the time of his dismissal, Wood was told that he was suffering from fatigue — a claim that he strongly denied — and that it had been arranged for him to return to the United States for a 60-day period of detached service. He was reluctant to accept the relief, but finally did so with the understanding that he would return to the division after a prescribed period of rest. When he departed from the Fourth Armored, he assumed that he would be back. He left without ceremony; something that must have been difficult for him to do, but which was probably made a little bit easier by the prospect of his return.

On his way back to the United States, he paid a visit to Eisenhower's headquarters in Paris. There, he met with General Beedle Smith, Eisenhower's chief of staff. Smith assured Wood that Eisenhower had agreed to allow him to return to the Fourth Armored after four to six weeks of rest. Wood took the occasion to plead his case yet again, and continued to deny that he was sick or fatigued. But this had no effect on the decision, and Smith simply responded by informing Wood that he was being rested at the request of General Patton.

Upon Wood's return to the United States, he was allowed a brief rest, and was then placed in command of the Armored Replacement Center at Fort Knox. Based on his outstanding success with the Fourth Armored Division, and his superior qualities as a teacher, trainer, and coach, he was well suited for the assignment. But he longed to return to his beloved division.

After his first month back in the States, he went to see General Marshall about returning to Europe (a return that had been promised to him). To Wood's dismay, Marshall told him that his role at Fort Knox held greater value than the contribution he could make as a division commander. Wood felt betrayed, and he later expressed the view, in no uncertain terms, that he had been lied to by both Eisenhower and Marshall.

Subterfuge

The official reason for Wood's relief was a concern for his health. But ever since the relief took place, the "official" reason has been viewed as highly suspect. The kindling for the fire of suspicion is provided by Wood himself:

> They [Patton and Eisenhower] said they wanted me to get a rest from combat and wanted me back as soon as I had got it. I told them they were wrong, that all I wanted was to remain with my division, but that as a soldier I would carry out their orders. I think they were sincere in their expressions of concern ... but I think they knew they were only sugar-coating a very bitter pill.

John Wood went to his grave denying that he was sick or fatigued at the time he was relieved of his command. He protested the diagnosis from the moment he was presented with it, and he never wavered from his position. The veterans who served with him during those trying days of November 1944 concur. They did not sense a change in the way the division was being handled from the top. To his men, Wood seemed as driven and as engaged as ever. Was he concerned and troubled by the casualties suffered by his division during the slugfest in the Lorraine region? Certainly. It caused him great pain and anguish. Was he tired? Many would agree that he was, but they would also be quick to point out that he was no more tired than the division itself.

In the eyes of the men who served under him, Wood was fully capable of leading the division, and his skills had not diminished when faced with the grueling task of slugging his way toward the German border. A claim that Wood was rendered incapable of commanding the division due to fatigue simply did not ring true in the ears of the men of the Fourth Armored.

Despite Wood's denials and reassurances about his condition, Patton was intent on labeling Wood as fatigued and in need of rest. No one knew Wood better than Patton; perhaps he noticed changes in Wood that were missed by others. But suffering from exhaustion, in and of itself, is hardly reason enough to relieve an effective officer of his command. If Wood's supposed fatigue was of such grave concern, then it must have manifested itself in some sort of *behavior* that was of concern to Patton. If there were no changes in his behavior, there would have been no need for action on Patton's part.

So what was it about Wood's actual *behavior* that led to his relief? To find the answer to that question, we will start with the person who presumably determined Wood's fate. Patton wrote in his memoirs:

> On the second, it became evident that General Wood had to be sent home for a rest. This was arranged through General Eisenhower, and I sent General Gaffey, then Army Chief

of Staff, to take over the division, It was quite a favor to ask of the man, but there was no one else available, and the necessities of war demanded that the 4th Armored have a good commander. The subsequent exploits of this division showed that my choice was correct.

Given Patton's warm and lengthy relationship with Wood, it is perhaps surprising that the above paragraph is the entire sum of his commentary on Wood's relief. It lays out only the most basic facts, and does not provide any insight into the behavior that Wood may have exhibited that raised Patton's level of concern. When Patton wrote this passage, less than a year after the end of the war, perhaps the wound of relieving Wood was too fresh, and he felt it best not to elaborate further, out of respect for the man who he considered to be his best friend. Unfortunately, with Patton's untimely death in 1945, we are left to scrounge through other shards of evidence to paint a more detailed picture of Patton's opinions on the matter.

Fortunately, Patton left behind other correspondence relating to Wood's relief, and these documents provide some additional insight. In a letter to Lt. General Thomas Handy, Deputy Chief of Staff of the Army, written just three days after Patton made the decision to relieve Wood, he wrote:

> P. Wood got so nervously exhausted that General Eisenhower sent him home on a 60 day DS. I know that you are one of P's greatest friends, and he is my best friend. It is my considered opinion that due to P's inability to sleep, he should, if possible, be retained in the U.S. in his present rank. Unquestionably, in a rapid moving advance, he is the greatest division commander I have ever seen, but when things get sticky he is inclined to worry too much, which keeps him from sleeping and runs him down, and makes it difficult to control his operations. However, if it is a question of having him reduced, I will take him back even if I have to personally command him.

Several aspects of this letter are worth scrutinizing. First, exhaustion is clearly stated as the foundation upon which the relief was built. Second, he alludes to behavioral changes that resulted from his lack of sleep (though it is done in very general terms). Third, Patton offers the opinion that Wood should be retained in the United States (as we know, Wood was led to believe otherwise). Fourth, Patton's desire to protect his good friend's stature (i.e., rank) within the military is clear. And finally, there is the intriguing suggestion that it was Eisenhower who was actually responsible for the decision to relieve Wood (though that passage is certainly open to a different interpretation; it might only reflect Eisenhower's decision regarding what to do with Wood after Patton had made the decision to relieve him).

Patton also wrote to his wife about the decision to relieve "P." Bea Patton knew Wood very well by virtue of the close relationship maintained between Wood and her husband during the years since West Point, and it is not a surprise that Patton provided her with an update on his old friend. Patton confided:

> I got P sent home on a 60 day detached service. He is nearly nuts due to nerves and inability to sleep. I hope I can get him a job in the States. He is too hard to handle.

Three key points can be made after examining the three pieces of correspondence penned by Patton. First, it can be said that Patton remained consistent in regard to fatigue being the underlying reason for Wood's relief. Second, that he speaks of Wood's behavior in only very general terms. And finally, that there is a possible discrepancy regarding who was responsible for the decision.

Is there any outside corroboration of Patton's account of the relief? Unfortunately, neither Bradley nor Eisenhower mentions the affair in their memoirs. But in 1967, 'Hap' Gay, who replaced Hugh Gaffey as the Third Army Chief of Staff, shared his thoughts with Hal Pattison:

> Wood was not relieved of command ... for so-called cause. He was relieved because of health. He was a sick man and was so pronounced by all medical officers concerned; viz., corps, army, and army group. It was Patton's definite understanding and he so informed "P," that he was being sent home for a long deserved rest and to fit him physically for a higher command.

Gay's comments provoke more thought. His letter supports Patton's statements regarding Wood's fatigue. And it is the first that time that we find any mention that Wood may have been seen by not just one, but several physicians prior to his relief.

There is one significant problem with the fatigue argument, and that is the absence, on the record, of any behavior exhibited by Wood that would lead Patton, or anyone else, to conclude that he was severally fatigued. In the face of Wood's strong personal denials, and the supporting observations of the men under his command, it is arguable that more compelling evidence is needed in order to support such a claim.

Gay's insinuation many years later that Wood was seen by several medical officers would seem, on the surface, to provide such evidence. But it is hard to imagine that "P" would have denied Patton's diagnosis for all those years, had there been several doctors floating about that could have stepped forward at any time to support the "official" reason for his relief. Anyone who knew him would say that John Wood was not the type of man that could be that intellectually dishonest. Gay's claim that four different medical officers evaluated Wood is suspect.

The Real Motive

If a claim of physical and mental fatigue was indeed used as a sugar coating for relieving Wood, what might have really been at the root of Patton's decision? There are only two potential catalysts for Wood's relief. Either he was insubordinate, or he was failing to produce what was expected of him on the battlefield. Let us first examine the possibility of a performance issue.

On November 6, less than a month before his relief, Patton stated in the presence of Wood: "There has never been such a superb fighting organization as the Fourth Armored Division." While Wood's superiors had taken exception to his style from time to time, one can assume that, up to that point, there were no problems associated with the performance of the division itself. There is nothing in the record pointing to any serious disenchantment with Wood's results. His handling of the division near Rennes was the only matter of contention that had arisen up to that point, and by all accounts, that particular stream of water had passed under the bridge long ago. The first hint of any dissatisfaction came on November 15, when Patton noted that the "4th Armored had been set back a little bit." This was hardly a strong knock against Wood or the division, but it does stand in contrast to the usual superlatives that Patton extended toward the Fourth Armored.

The first sign of any sort of performance issue came on November 18, when Manton Eddy made a direct assertion to Wood that he was not driving hard enough during the opening stages of Patton's winter offensive. After what must have been a heated exchange between the two generals, Eddy took his case to Patton, who responded by sending Hugh Gaffey as a messenger to deliver the infamous letter of November 19.

What is most odd about that letter is the charge that Wood had carried out Eddy's orders of November 18 in an "apparently dilatory manner." The orders for the day in question supposedly involved Eddy's desire to have Wood assist the 26th Infantry Division in an assault against the town of Dieuze on that date. As we know, the Fourth Armored Division sat out the 18th without being committed, and it wasn't until the 19th that Wood resumed the attack. On that day, he did indeed commit one of his armored infantry battalions to support the 26th Infantry Division's attack on Dieuze. It would appear that Eddy's expectation was that the attack should have taken place on the 18th, not the 19th. The fact that the attack did not materialize when Eddy expected it to obviously was a cause for rancor between the two generals.

While Eddy might have been disappointed with Wood for not bringing his division to bear at Dieuze on the 18th, it is hard to find fault with the manner in which "P" drove the division during the days that immediately followed. His improvised move across the Sarre River was brilliant, and it carried with it the good fortune of spoiling the counterattack launched by the Panzer Lehr Division. But on the other hand, if there was ever a time in the Fourth's history when a charge of lackluster performance might stick, it was during late November, when CCA was suffering from the poor leadership provided by Colonel Withers.

But the performance of CCA was not indicative of the entire division. The fact is that CCB, under Brigadier General Dager, was charging hard across the Sarre River in line with Wood's improvised plan to advance through the zone of the 44th Infantry Division. CCB broke up the counterattack launched by the Panzer Lehr Division, and took immense pressure off the left flank of the Seventh Army. For every ounce of CCA's performance that was lackluster, CCB's performance was equal parts determined. So all things considered, one is hard pressed to build a case against Wood for poor performance. Certainly, his performance was not so poor during that time frame that a change in command would be required or prudent.

This leaves us with the specter of insubordination.

A well-known aspect of Wood's personality was his outspoken nature. His demeanor sometimes resulted in straightforward outbursts of contempt for the decisions rendered by his superiors. It was frequently said of Wood that he "did not suffer fools gladly." He had a low level of tolerance for the incompetent (though this sometimes was offset by an almost blind loyalty that he maintained for his own staff; something that came to haunt him in the case of Colonel Withers). Wood also had a tendency to bend his orders to suit his own idea of how an engagement should be fought. History has validated his choices, as the results of his liberal interpretations were always to the positive. Nevertheless, his methods irked his superiors on occasion.

Wood made a practice of pushing the envelope in his relationships with his superiors. This came home to roost with Manton Eddy back on November 18, and Patton had to intercede. Fortunately for Wood, Patton gave him adequate wiggle room to avoid losing his command at that time.

But then came the encounter between Wood and Eddy on December 2. Clearly, this confrontation played a pivotal role in Wood's fate. By defending his men to the hilt, without concern for Eddy's rank, Wood had pushed his luck too far. Under even the most liberal interpretations, it appears that Wood may have been insubordinate during their encounter on December 2.

Of all the possibilities, the most likely reason for Wood's dismissal was that the relationship between Eddy and Wood had become untenable. Eddy, having had to deal with two stinging episodes in barely two weeks time, would surely have been quick to protest Wood's behavior, and it is presumed that he contacted Patton to report the latest confrontation. With Eddy coming to him for the second time in two weeks, Patton was probably forced to choose between the two men.

On the one hand, he had Eddy, who had been the proficient and respected commander of the 9th Infantry Division, and who had proven himself to be at least an average corps commander since assuming command of the XII Corps from the disabled General Cook. On the other hand, he had the brilliant, unequalled Wood, who was, perhaps to a fault, equal parts brazen. Given the severity of the warning that Wood received just two weeks prior to the December 2 episode, his latest vociferous retort to Eddy's face would simply be too difficult for Patton to defend or deflect.

Given the events of December 2, one is left to wonder why Wood's relief was handled in the manner it was. Why was Wood not charged with insubordination, and relieved on those grounds, as opposed to the claim that he was suffering from fatigue?

The answer no doubt rests in the friendship between Patton and Wood. Had Wood been charged with insubordination, his military career would have been irreparably harmed. He would have been robbed not only of his command, but of his reputation as well. The prospect of seeing his best friend suffer the indignities of such charges probably led Patton to prescribe the "sugar coated pill" of fatigue.

An assertion that Wood's conduct toward Eddy was the result of fatigue could perhaps pass the test of a white lie; Wood was certainly tired, and his condition and state of mind in light of the attrition the division had suffered during the month of November might have contributed to a lapse in judgment when dealing with Eddy. But in the end, Wood's outspoken nature, more than anything else, is the most likely reason for his relief. Perhaps confident in his own performance, and confident in his relationship with Patton, he felt he could push back against Eddy with all his might in order to do what he thought was best for his beloved division.

In any event, when Patton played the "fatigue" card, he paved the way for his best friend to return home in good standing, with his career intact, as opposed to the embarrassment and stigma that would be associated with a relief based on cause. Anyone that had Patton's full confidence — such as Hap Gay — would likely have stuck to the claim that fatigue was the basis for the decision, even if he knew better.

But if this is indeed the case, then one lingering mystery remains. Did Wood know that the "fatigue" rationale was, in truth, Patton's way of avoiding a more serious charge?

The answer is most certainly no. Following the altercation with Eddy on December 2, it appears that Patton did not approach Wood with Eddy's charge of insubordination. For had he confronted Wood with Eddy's charge, Wood's position on the matter for all the years that followed would have been nothing more than a grand charade, as he would have known the real underlying cause for his relief, but chose to ignore it. So what happened when Patton *did* approach Wood?

The logical conclusion, based on all of the evidence (be it of submission or omission), is that Patton loved "P" Wood like a brother, and as a result, he made what was probably one of the toughest decisions of his life. Patton knew that Wood was not aware that Eddy had cried foul after their confrontation on December 2. Patton also knew that, if Eddy's charges were made public, "P" would not weather the storm; the events of November 18 made that a certainty. So Patton, without Wood's complicity, insisted on Wood's relief based on the "fatigue" factor.

Patton knew, under the circumstances, that Wood's return was impossible. He could not share that fact with his best friend, however, for it would force him to shed the cloak he had placed around the charge of insubordination. So despite promises to the contrary, Wood never stood a chance of returning to the Fourth Armored. Indeed, it wasn't Eisenhower or Marshall who had lied to Wood. It was Patton. And it was a lie that was made with the best of intentions, out of the sincerest affection for his best friend.

Patton's decision to deal with the situation in this manner is a reflection on the true depth of the friendship that existed between the two men. But it also offers insight into the great difference in priorities held by the two generals. Though great friends, they were not alike; especially in regard to how they saw themselves fitting into the overall scheme of things.

Patton was the consummate warrior. He lived for war, and he loved the experience. In fact, as the war was drawing to a close, he lamented over what he would do when the fighting ended. For him, if there was no war, there was no reason for being. His military career and ascent up the chain of command meant everything to him. He was the consummate showman, with a desire to be, for effect, larger than life in the eyes of the men he commanded (not to mention anyone else who was watching). Wood knew, perhaps better than anyone, the complex personality that resided beneath the character that Patton played in public:

> More than anyone I have ever known, George Patton was motivated by the desire for military glory. His patriotism and religion were real and not assumed, but to him they served best as a background for the glory of Patton the warrior. He strove to create and maintain the myth of "Old Blood and Guts," by concealing under a hard-boiled exterior and roughness of expression his natural fineness of spirit and tenderness of heart that I knew well from my personal experience. His mannerisms, his pistols, and his panoply of stars were all part of the act. I loved him like a brother.

The same did not apply to John Wood. In many respects, he was the antithesis of Patton in regard to his personal motivation for doing the job. Wood lived a life on the battlefield that was built on the foundation of suffering the same deprivations imposed upon his men. Patton put himself at risk at times, but he came nowhere close to the level that John Wood maintained for willingly suffering the day-to-day hardships of the common soldier. His desire to share and understand the experiences of his men was a fundamental aspect of his philosophy for leadership. Here is how he described the characteristics he believed necessary for the effective leadership of men in combat:

> First, there is the disregard of fear which passes for bravery; second, there is an unceasing endeavor to spare the men one has the honor to lead unnecessary hardships and useless losses; third, there is a willingness and desire to share their needed hardships and face their same dangers; fourth, there is the quality of sympathy and human understanding that inspires confidence and trust and willing effort and initiative among one's troops.

While Patton was depressed by the prospect of not having a war to fight, John Wood's choices after the war stand in stark contrast. He retired from the military in 1946, and chose a course that was diametrically opposed to the infliction of death and destruction. He joined the Intergovernmental Committee for Refugees as the director of field operations serving Germany and Austria. When this organization merged with the International Refugees Organization, he became chief of the mission in Austria, where he served until 1951. He then moved on to a similar role for another two years with the United Nations Korean Reconstruction Agency. The post-war proclivities of the two men could not have been more opposite. One was bent on finding an opportunity to wage war for war's sake. The other saw the opportunity to rebuild what had been, out of necessity, torn apart.

As Patton considered his options with Wood, there is no doubt that his primary concerns were those that *he himself* would have had if he were in Wood's shoes; i.e., the preservation of his military career. His statement to the effect that he would take Wood back under his personal command in order to avoid a reduction in Wood's rank speaks volumes. He would go the extra mile to ensure Wood did not take an extraordinary hit against his career, but would not go to the same lengths to stand behind Wood on the merits of his debate with Eddy. What is so ironic, in retrospect, is that "P" would have probably shrugged of such concerns for his rank and privileges, and would have much rather seen Patton stand by his side versus Eddy.

Given Patton's own priorities, he was in no position to take sides with his best friend in the debate with Eddy. Despite all of Patton's fame and renown with the general public, he was still on the hot seat with Ike and Bradley.

Patton was fortunate to have been given command of the Third Army after the huge trouble that befell him over the soldier-slapping incident in Sicily. And he had almost done himself in again when he made some serious missteps during a public appearance prior to the campaign in France. His commanding officers tolerated his personality quirks and pompous behavior for one reason, and one reason only: as the commander of an army, he was without equal. But his record of accomplishment on the battlefield was not enough to thicken the ice that supported him above troubled waters. Patton knew that he was always on thin ice with his superiors, and thus the prioritization of his personal career above and beyond all other concerns caused him to stop short of supporting Wood to the hilt. Surely, if Eddy had not been satisfied with the manner in which Patton addressed the second insubordination complaint, he would have taken his concern further up the chain of command. It is doubtful that Bradley, or Ike, would have taken sides against Eddy, all things considered.

Another intangible that may have prevented Patton from suppressing Eddy's complaint was that Eddy would not have been a lone wolf crying for Wood's dismissal. General Walton Walker, the commander of XX Corps, had urged Patton to relieve Wood in the past, and might have well come forward to support Eddy's side of the argument. Wood and Walker's relationship dated back to their days in West Point, where they were both graduated in 1912; Wood near the top of his class, Walker near the cellar. Wood served under Walker's corps on two occasions during their training period, and the rapport between the two men was very poor. Some of their personal clashes were played out in public, and it was fairly common knowledge that they did not enjoy each other's respect.

In later years, "Tiger Jack" (the nickname by which the Germans knew Wood best) said, "I will never know the entire story." If this was his honest sentiment, it is perhaps the best evidence indicating that Patton had indeed sheltered him from the truth. Patton and Gaffey were probably the two men who could have filled in the blanks for Wood after the war, but the tragic and premature deaths of both men, Patton in December of 1945 as a result of an automobile accident, and Gaffey in 1946 in an airplane crash, left Wood with a lifetime of speculation. Despite the lingering doubts, however, he never appeared to harbor any resentment toward Patton for what had happened. Such was the strength of their friendship.

Wood's Replacement

General Hugh Gaffey, who had most recently been General Patton's Chief of Staff, now took on the task of filling Wood's shoes.

Gaffey's relationship with Patton extended back quite some time. He served with Patton at the Desert Training Center in the United States, and then became the Deputy Commander of the 2nd Armored Division (Patton's old unit) in North Africa. He was later awarded the position of Commanding General of the 2nd Armored, and led that division as part of Patton's Seventh Army during the campaign in Sicily. Patton made him Chief of Staff of the Third Army in April 1944, when General Eisenhower placed pressure on Patton to replace Brigadier General Hobart "Hap" Gay, who had served in the position since January of that same year, and as chief of staff for Patton's Seventh Army prior to that. Gaffey was reluctant to give up command of the Second Armored Division, but accepted the position out of loyalty to Patton (General Gay would take over the Chief of Staff position for the second time in his career when Gaffey departed for the Fourth).

If General Wood was a tiger whose tail Patton and Eddy could not grasp, Hugh Gaffey was anything but. There is little doubt that, unlike Wood, Patton could count on Gaffey to follow instructions without debate (this would become glaringly obvious within a very short time). Given recent events, a streak of independence was not at the top of Patton's list of attributes that he looked for in a division commander. In fact, during the very week that Wood was relieved, Patton commented to General Bradley, "Hell, a division commander doesn't have to know anything. He can be as dumb as a sonovabitch just as long as he's a fighter." Gaffey would fit the bill.

The appointment of Gaffey produced one more major change within the command structure of the division. Brigadier General Herbert L. Earnest, who had worked with Gaffey at Third Army HQ, was appointed to CCA. Colonel Withers, whose performance had been so suspect during his first month in command, stayed on as his second in command. Apparently, Withers' lackluster performance had not gone unnoticed.

The assignment of Earnest was a most unusual arrangement, since armored divisions were only authorized to have one brigadier general, but now the Fourth was sporting two (Dager being the other). The position of second in command of a combat command was also a non-authorized position (Withers would hold that unique position until March of 1945). This type of flexibility was not at all common. After all, the limit of one brigadier general per division was the very reason that Bruce Clarke had to be transferred in order to gain his own promotion to that very rank.

The appointment of Earnest was preceded by some interesting moments. At midnight on the night of December 2/3, a message was sent to the 37th Tank Battalion HQ for Lt. Colonel Abrams, instructing him to take command of CCA at first light on the morning of December 3. Command of the 37th was passed to Major Bautz, and Abrams departed for CCA's headquarters. Later in the day, Bautz was summoned to CCA, and when he returned to the HQ of the 37th, he arrived with word that Abrams would be returning to the command of the 37th Tank Battalion. Somewhere along the line, Withers was relieved, Abrams covered, and finally, Earnest was appointed. The entire chain of events gives the impression that what was transpiring within the command of the Fourth was impromptu (more circumstantial evidence that the decision regarding Wood was reached on very short order, after the affair with Eddy).

As the new leadership came into place, a rumor circulated among the division staff that Gaffey was being "purified in a combat division" prior to his assignment to a new corps that was due to be activated. Further, there was hope that "P" would return and resume command of the Fourth once Gaffey moved on (the promise that Wood had been given regarding his return surely provided plenty of fuel for that portion of the rumor). There was probably some foundation behind the belief that Gaffey would be moving on after only a short tenure, for when Brigadier General Earnest took over CCA, it was with the expectation "that if he did well with CCA he would get a division of his own." (Earnest had been told this directly; presumably by Patton.) Earnest's hope was that his reward would be none other than the Fourth; he did not expect Gaffey to be with the division for long, and he did not expect Wood to return.

But as it turned out, Gaffey would remain in command until March 1945; the promise made to Earnest was fulfilled in January, when he was given command of the 90th Infantry Division. If there had been some sort of plan for passing on the command of the Fourth in more rapid fashion, it was probably torn asunder by the events that were about to unfold in the Ardennes.

A new era in the history of the Fourth Armored Division was about to begin. After almost two and a half years under the command of General Wood, a new leadership team was now at the helm. They would soon be put to the test in a way that no one could have ever imagined.

The Legacy of John S. Wood

"Tiger Jack" was the most proficient, dynamic commander of armor in Europe. He was loved and respected by his men to an extent that any division commander would envy, and this emotional attachment strengthened the performance of the unit.

During the four and a half months since the Fourth had arrived on French soil, it had established a record of performance that was nothing short of excellent. The men of the Fourth had proven themselves as masters of exploitation during their heady drive across France. During the encirclement of Nancy, and the armored battles that followed in the vicinity of Arracourt, they proved themselves to be superior in tank versus tank warfare. Even during the tough, slogging fight across the Lorraine region, they managed to press forward, gaining ground in quantities well in excess of what was being registered by the vast majority of Allied divisions all across the front in western Europe. In their most recent battle, they had turned the tide against the powerful Panzer Lehr Division, shutting down yet another of Hitler's personal campaigns, just as they had done at Arracourt.

Among the men of the Fourth Armored Division, you will find no shortage of accolades for their beloved commanding general. But lest one think that the words of those who served under him are in some way biased, consider the high words of praise submitted by the esteemed British historian B.H. Liddell Hart. Writing in his classic work, *History of the Second World War*, he said of John Wood:

> The break-out at Avranches was made by the U.S. 4th Armored Division under John S. Wood. I had spent two days with him shortly before the invasion and he had impressed me as being more conscious of the possibilities of a deep exploitation and the importance of speed than anyone else. Even Patton had then, in discussion with me, echoed the prevailing view at the top that the Allied forces must "go back to 1918 methods" and could not repeat the kind of deep and swift armoured drives that the Germans, especially Guderian and Rommel, had carried out in 1940.

In one of his other works, Hart said Wood was "The Rommel of the American armored forces ... one of the most dynamic commanders of armor in World War II and the first in the Allied Armies to demonstrate in Europe the essence of the art and tempo of handling a mobile force."

Indeed, there was not a single armored division commander better than Major General John S. Wood. He was in a league all his own.

9. Pressing Toward Germany

Sideshow at Sarre-Union

On the night of December 2, General Eddy made a request of Patton that was quite ironic, considering the rebuke he had given General Wood: he wanted permission to pull the Fourth Armored Division from the line for a rest. Wood's division — it was and always *would* be his division, no matter who followed him as its commander — would indeed come off the line soon, but not before making one last offensive push toward the German border.

December 3 was a day of relatively light activity for most of the division. CCA and CCB stood their ground, as the new commanders took stock of their situation and prepared for the next leg of their journey toward the German border. The exception occurred near Sarre-Union, when a company of German infantry, supported by four to six panzers, engaged the 104th Infantry Regiment. To help the 104th counter the German attack, the Sherman tanks of A/37, along with a platoon of tank destroyers from the 704th, were ordered to the vicinity of Sarr Warden. The M18s arrived late, however, and A/37 set off without them. That evening, Lt. Walters, the CO of A/37, consulted with the commanding officer of the 104th, and plans were drawn up for an attack that would commence early the next morning. After almost four weeks of battle, XII Corps was finally prepared to attack Sarre-Union.

At 8:00 A.M. on December 4, A/37 and elements of the 104th attacked the Germans defending city. The action was a resounding success, and Sarre-Union was declared clear of the enemy only 45 minutes after the start of the assault. The object of General Wood's bold move across the Sarre River had finally fallen into American hands. Due to advances made both west and east of Sarre-Union, the fall of the city was a somewhat anti-climactic affair. The main show had already moved to other segments of the front.

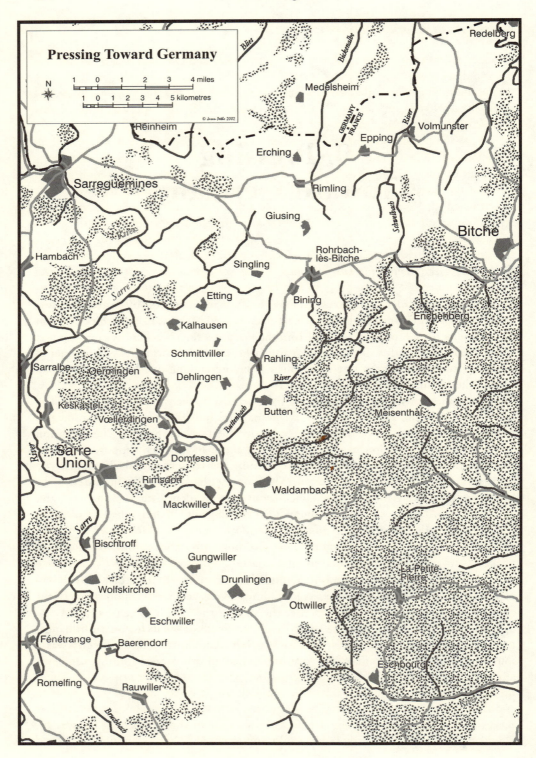

Pressing Toward Germany

CCB's Assault on Voellerdingen

On the morning of December 4, the Fourth Armored Division began the next leg of its journey toward the German border. CCB was still operating on the left, and CCA on the right. The two combat commands were to continue driving to the north-northeast, in the general direction of Bining. Once again, the division was cast in the familiar role of Patton's spearhead.

A 30-minute artillery barrage kicked off the renewed effort of CCB. The 8th Tank Battalion and 10th Armored Infantry Battalion moved quickly on the heels of the barrage, and encountered only light resistance as they advanced toward the high ground north of the road running from Sarre-Union to Domfessel. As soon as the two battalions reached the elevated terrain, they received a heavy volume of enemy fire from antiaircraft guns and small arms positioned in some woods located to the north.

Dager's next objective was the town of Voellerdingen, located to the northeast, and any move in that direction would expose his left flank to the troublesome woods, so bypassing the enemy position was out of the question. A task force of tanks and infantry was assembled and sent in to clear the enemy from that area. This was accomplished with little difficulty, and by 11:30 A.M., CCB was moving on toward its objective. After advancing only a short distance, it was discovered that yet another heavily wooded area (le Grand Bois) had to be cleared en route to Voellerdingen. This was accomplished by 1:00 A.M., and the task force that cleared the forest also took hold of Hill 280, located about one mile west of the town. Several tanks from the 8th took up covered positions atop the hill and stood by for their next set of orders.

Voellerdingen was a moderate size town nestled in the middle of a deep valley. The Eichel River formed the spine of the valley, and split the town into two unequal halves. A railroad line and embankment followed the line of the river on the west bank. While Hill 280 afforded a good view of the western approach to the town, the village itself was almost completely hidden from view by the crest of the valley on the west side of the town. The church steeple and a couple of taller rooftops that rose above the rim offered the only visual evidence that there was even a town there at all.

As Major Irzyk studied his map and contemplated the best way to assault Voellerdingen, his attention was suddenly diverted by the appearance of ten enemy tanks. The panzers had emerged from concealed positions in the woods and were now charging from the north over open ground. The enemy tanks were greeted with a hail of fire from the Shermans sitting atop Hill 280. The result was the quick destruction of two of the enemy tanks, and the retreat of the other eight, which sped back to the cover of the woods.

With the threat of the panzers turned aside, CCB redirected its focus on Voellerdingen. Irzyk called on his assigned artillery support (the 22nd Armored Field Artillery Battalion, commanded by Pete Peterson), and requested that the M7s hit the town with a barrage as soon as possible. Peterson responded with an alternative proposal: a "time-on-target" barrage executed by 12 artillery battalions. It would take up to an hour to coordinate the effort, but the simultaneous arrival of shells from almost 200 artillery pieces would be sure to send the defenders into a state of shock, opening the way for a bold charge into the town by Irzyk's tanks and armored infantry. Though concerned that the afternoon was waning and the early winter sunset would soon be upon him, Irzyk agreed to the plan. He would take the chance that there would be just enough daylight left to execute the attack.

The attacking elements of CCB moved closer to the town in anticipation of the barrage. As soon as the friendly artillery fire lifted, they were to charge in as aggressively as possible, before the defenders could recover from what was sure to be a shattering bombardment.

The barrage hit as scheduled, and it was everything that Peterson had promised. A dense cloud of smoke and dust rose above the crest of the valley, and vibrations raced through the ground, reverberating below the feet of the attackers poised to deliver the coup de grace. As the final salvo echoed through the valley, the tanks of the "Rolling Eight Ball" descended upon Voellerdingen. Charging from the high ground at full tilt down the steep slopes of the valley, they quickly entered the town's narrow streets, and for the moment, were unopposed. It appeared that the barrage had been completely effective.

The tanks barreled down the streets in a rapid descent toward the river, but they were forced to stop when they came to a high, extended embankment that supported the railroad. Now bottled up at what was basically a dead end near the bottom of town, it appeared that they could not continue the advance. An alert tank crew, however, found an underpass through which the tanks could gain access to the other side of the embankment.

As the tanks moved toward the opening of the underpass, they were greeted by direct fire at close range from some enemy self-propelled guns positioned on the opposite side of the railroad embankment. The enemy had set up their guns to hit anything coming underneath the overpass. It was a natural choke point that threatened to bring the advance to a complete halt.

The American tanks responded with a strong dose of return fire directed back through the underpass. After firing heavy salvos in that direction, the lead tanks charged through the opening. It appeared that the enemy had fled to fight another day, as the tanks swarmed through the narrow artery and beyond without receiving any further hostile fire. The area of the overpass could have been a major bottleneck, but the tenacity of the American tankers carried them through and beyond the obstacle.

The Eichel River was now just ahead of the advancing Shermans. To the delight of the tankers, the bridge leading to the east bank was intact! They quickly moved forward and darted across to the other side. With little daylight left to work with, more tanks and armored infantry poured into the town behind them, and pushed across the river. A bridgehead was fully secured before nightfall.

The enemy probed at the bridgehead that night in an attempt to find a weak spot, but the 8th TB and 10th AIB had closed ranks around the perimeter, forming an impenetrable defense that would sustain them until morning.

There is an interesting footnote to the capture of Voellerdingen. A contemporary article published in the *New York Times* credited Lt. Colonel Abrams, whose exploits to date had received a good deal of press coverage, with the capture of Voellerdingen. This was, of course, an error, as it was Major Irzyk who commanded the task force that had seized the town and bridge.

CCA Captures Domfessel

As the advance resumed on December 4, CCA, now under the command of Brig. General Earnest, was still aligned to the right of CCB. The plan for December 4 called for CCA to attack on a parallel course with CCB. This would take it over the Eichel River further down stream from Dager's command. CCA's crossing point would be just north of the town of Domfessel, located south-southeast of Voellerdingen.

The 35th Tank Battalion and 53rd Armored Infantry Battalion, which were now the primary components of CCA, encountered a series of obstacles as they advanced toward Domfessel. The roads leading into the town were well defended, and Earnest's men had to work their way through a combination of mines, heavy anti-tank fire, and artillery. The 35th Tank Battalion lost two tanks to the mines, and another five were disabled by enemy artillery. The fighting was fierce and at close quarters. Sgt. Paul Porter of B/53 was a key figure in the action. He was relentless in his advance, and even took on the enemy in hand-to-hand combat (he was awarded the DSC for his heroism that day).

The Shermans of C/35, commanded by 1st Lt. Eugene Berky, tried another route in an attempt to avoid the withering fire the Germans were bringing down on the main approach to Domfessel. Berky took his tank company off the road, and made his way cross-country instead (a risky proposition, given the ground conditions).

The Sherman tanks advanced through an orchard, and then maneuvered close to the tightly packed stone houses on the edge of town. Once there, they realized that the houses were so close together that they could not squeeze a tank in between them. It seemed that they were left with no way in, and would have to double back across the field.

Having come this far, the lead tank, a 105mm assault gun Sherman commanded by Sergeant Earl Eckard, honed in on a narrow 5-foot-wide path between two of the homes. Concrete posts blocked the center of the path, but it didn't stop Eckard from charging through. Half of the assault gun smashed into the house on one side of the path and plowed forward through the crumbling structure. The concrete posts snapped underneath the weight of the Sherman, and Eckard's tank emerged onto the street at the center of town. The other tanks of C Company raced in behind him, and the defenses of the town soon crumbled in the wake of the unexpected Shermans. The German officer (a major) in charge of the defense of the town was taken prisoner, along with 140 of his troops.

Domfessel had fallen, but not before the Germans destroyed the bridge that CCA needed in order to cross over the Eichel River. When darkness fell, the tanks of CCA were still on the wrong side of the river, while CCB had made their crossing at Voellerdingen.

A Confused Advance Towards Rohrbach

On the morning of December 5, CCB began to expand its bridgehead at Voellerdingen. General Dager's immediate objective was the high ground southwest of the town

The village of Rohrbach, as seen by S/Sgt. Frank Besedick (courtesy K. Besedick).

of Schmittville. Dager ordered Major Irzyk to advance no further than Schmittville, since CCA was slow in keeping up on their right; an advance beyond Schmittville would leave their right flank exposed to a possible enemy counterattack. Given the tank-led counterattack the 8th Tank Battalion had beaten off the day prior from their perch atop Hill 280, they were very aware that the Germans had panzers in the area, and thus had good reason to be wary.

At first light, B Company of the 8th Tank Battalion, with the men of the 10th Armored Infantry Battalion riding on the decks of the Shermans, began to push out of their bridgehead on the Eichel River. They received some light fire from the woods to their right, so the infantry dismounted and, with the support of the Shermans, chased off the enemy. The advance continued, and by noon, they had progressed over two miles from the bridgehead and secured their objective, which was the high ground southwest of Schmittville (this area was also known as "Langenwald Farms"). The lead elements of CCB came to a halt at that point, as Dager had instructed, and waited for further orders.

Irzyk returned to his command post at Voellerdingen, and while en route, he heard the movement of vehicles and firing of weapons off to the east. He assumed that the origin of this activity was CCA, and that Brigadier General Earnest must now be making progress, and would be coming abreast of his right flank. This would surely trigger the movement of CCB, so Irzyk, anticipating the green light from Dager at any moment, began preparing his men to resume the advance.

No word came from CCB to that effect, however, and Irzyk's command sat tight in their positions. Late that afternoon, he was summoned by Dager, and given his instructions for December 6. The plan called for CCB to attack toward the northeast and capture the town of Rimling. The general axis of advance toward their objective would take CCB through the area of Schmittville and Singling. At the same time, CCA would be attacking on the right of CCB, with the objectives of Bining and Rohrbach les Bitche.

Irzyk returned to his own command post and met with his battalion staff, as well as Major Hal Cohen, the commanding officer of the 10th AIB. They developed a plan for the following day, and tried to grab a decent night's sleep before setting out early the next morning.

As Irzyk and Cohen settled down on the night of December 5, they were not aware that other elements of the Fourth Armored would soon be infringing on CCB's zone of advance. The sounds Irzyk heard off to the east were *not* a sign that CCA was finally pushing up in force on his right flank. The sounds were originating from Lt. Colonel Creighton Abrams' 37th Tank Battalion.

Abrams had been called into the Fourth Armored Division HQ on the morning of December 5, after CCA and CCB had already resumed their advance for the day. This was unusual in and of itself, since a battalion commander normally would have been receiving his orders from the combat command HQ his battalion was assigned to. The orders Abrams received from Division were to wait for CCA and CCB to "secure the high ground across the river south of Dehlingen. After this was accomplished the 37th Tk Bn would push through and continue northward with Rohrbach-lès-Bitche as its objective."

What was also unusual about these orders, apart from their point of origin, is that the 37th would be moving ahead without any infantry support. This would make it difficult to take and hold any prepared enemy positions they might encounter, and depending on the nature of the fight, might leave the tanks of the 37th very vulnerable to German infantry armed with panzerfausts. Sending a tank battalion out on its own in this fashion was far from normal protocol for the division.

The 37th Runs into Trouble

As the morning of December 5 faded, the 37th was informed that CCA and CCB had secured their objectives. At 11:15 A.M., Abrams began his advance through the positions of CCA. C Company, which with 14 tanks was nearly at full strength, took the lead on the drive to the northeast. Batteries B and C of the 94th followed to provide artillery support (Battery A stayed behind to provide fire support during the opening stages of the advance).

The road leading toward the 37th Tank Battalion's objective passed through the town of Bining. Expecting strong enemy resistance in the town, Abrams sent C/37 off-road in order to circle around the left side of Bining. Some caution had to be exercised, however, since the town of Singling was still further to the left (west), and any Germans in that town would be able to observe C/37's move around the west flank of Bining. If the enemy had tanks or anti-tank guns in the vicinity of Singling, they would be able to strike against the left flank of C/37 as it moved across the open ground.

To help counter any threat that might exist at Singling, Battery A of the 94th laid down a smoke screen to the left of the route to be taken by C/37. But the screen proved to be inadequate; as the Shermans moved across the open field, heavy anti-tank and artillery fire rained down on the tanks from locations in the immediate vicinity of Singling, as well as from the high ground northeast of there.

Several of the tanks were hit and destroyed, while the others became bogged down in deep mud as they tried to maneuver. The combination of enemy fire and the natural elements put all 14 tanks of C Company out of action (including the forward observer tank for the 94th). The tankers fled the scene on foot to join the rest of the battalion. In the blink of an eye, Abrams had lost a third of his medium tanks.

As December 5 drew to a close, Abrams assembled his remaining two medium tank companies in a position out of sight of the enemy guns, and cast plans for continuing the assault the next day. The M7s of the 94th AFAB were assembled in Schmittville, and were readied to lend support when the advance resumed.

The men of the 94th were anxious about their position in Schmittville, as they knew it was an objective of CCB, and at the moment, they were not sure that CCB was aware that they had occupied it! This created the possibility that they might come under friendly fire from Dager's units. Fortunately, they were finally able to get word to CCB that they were there. As the 94th's battalion history states, "It took several radio messages to convince them we were correctly located."

Even before the 37th had run into problems, efforts were under way to provide Abrams with belated infantry support. At noon on the December 5, just a short time after the 37th had advanced through CCA's positions, the 51st Armored Infantry Battalion was given orders to move out in support of Abrams' tanks. Due to heavy vehicle traffic generated by other units of CCA trying to use the same route, it would take two hours for the battalion to assemble for the march, and another four hours to complete the trip to their assembly area at Schmittville (where they joined the 94th). This was yet another sign that things were not working with full precision at CCA (it is difficult to imagine that Bruce Clarke would have encountered such problems).

On the night of December 5, Abrams received his orders for the following day. He was to attack Bining, and then press on toward Rohrbach. He would now have the 51st AIB to work with, as well as two platoons of Hellcats from B/704. The 94th Armored Field Artillery Battalion would continue to support him.

As Abrams attacked, CCB would also attack on his left, in a continuation of its advance toward Rimling, and CCA's Task Force Oden would push out of its bridgehead over the Eichel River near Domfessel in pursuit of the objectives of Dehlingen and Rahling. These towns were off to Abrams' right, and well south of his current position near Singling (CCA still continued to trail the rest of the division).

After the disaster with C/37, Abrams realized that he would not be able to advance on Bining as long as the enemy occupied Singling and the high ground beyond. If he advanced toward Bining, he would be exposing the left flank of his units to the same intense firepower that had crippled C/37 the day before. He had three options: wait for CCB to secure Singling (he assumed incorrectly that CCB had specific orders to capture Singling; they did not), secure Singling himself before moving toward Bining, or risk the move toward Bining with the Germans still in control of Singling.

After due consideration, he worked up a plan to have at least six battalions of artillery pound the area in and around Singling. A barrage of this intensity would certainly suppress the enemy, and he would be able to move toward Bining with the threat to his flank significantly reduced (or so he hoped). Abrams sent a liaison officer to CCA with the revised plan of attack (the important element being the request for the six battalions of artillery support). General Earnest did not send back a communication to Abrams, however, and Abrams interpreted this to mean that the attack was to be conducted according to the original plan.

The attack that took place the following day is, on the surface, not one of the more important actions in the history of the Fourth Armored Division. But for some reason that is not fully understood, this particular battle — the battle of Singling — became scrutinized unlike any other of its kind. Extensive after action interviews were conducted with many of the participants, and a blow-by-blow account was prepared that is virtually unparalleled in its detail. Perhaps this happened because the division went into an extended rest period immediately after the battle, and this afforded the Army the time to conduct such extensive interviews (the interviews were conducted on December 10 and 18, while the participants were in a rest area near Mittersheim).

The following chapter is devoted to the battle for Singling. It offers a glimpse into small unit tactics of the period that many readers may find of interest. This is made possible due to the depth and quality of the information available from Army records. I also had the opportunity to personally interview three of the principles involved, Captain Leach, Lt. Guild, and Major Irzyk. Their recollections of the activities in and around Singling were still sharp and fresh.

There were also acts of bravery and courage at Singling that certainly deserve to be put on the record. When men are engaged in battle, they are generally not thinking about how important the moment is in the greater scheme of things. They are primarily fighting for their lives, and for the lives of the men who surround them, and to whom they owe their devotion. And in this respect, the battle of Singling becomes just as important or noteworthy, to the men who fought it, as any other battle.

10. The Battle for Singling

The Approach to Bining

On the morning of December 6, Task Force Abrams set out on its mission. The two remaining medium tank companies and all three of the armored infantry companies would be involved in the advance on Bining. The tank destroyers of the 704th would remain back in order to provide direct fire support. The mortars, artillery, and assault guns would supplement the indirect fire of the 94th AFAB's howitzers. This level of support was tremendously shy of the 6 battalions of artillery that Abrams had desired, but it would have to do.

Company B of the 37th (commanded by Captain Leach) and Company B of the 51st (commanded by 1st Lt. Daniel Belden) were paired up to lead the assault on Bining. Their team totaled 14 Shermans (one of which was a 105mm Assault Gun) and 57 infantrymen (B/51 was not even at half strength after the recent weeks of heavy fighting). B/37 packed a bit more punch than most of the Fourth Armored's tank companies, since it was equipped with five Sherman tanks mounting the new 76mm high velocity gun.

The plan called for the "B Team" to set out at 8:00 A.M., with the armored infantry riding in halftracks interspersed with Captain Leach's tanks. When they reached the outskirts of Bining, the infantry would dismount from the halftracks and support the tanks in the assault of the town. As they advanced, the aforementioned artillery, mortars, and assault guns would cover their left flank with smoke and high explosives.

The tanks and armored infantry assembled as planned early that morning. But it was quickly discovered that the muddy terrain was not going to allow the halftracks to advance with the Shermans. So the decision was made for the infantry to leave the halftracks and mount up on the tanks. This delayed their start, and it was 8:35 before they were ready to go.

As the B Team assembled, the tanks of A/37 advanced to a position approximately one mile ahead of the rest of the task force. The Shermans drew very heavy fire from

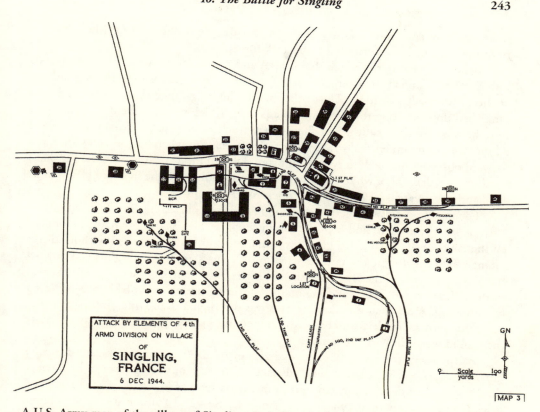

A U.S. Army map of the village of Singling, including the axis of movement for the elements of the "B Team," CCA (courtesy U.S. Army).

the same direction that C/37 had been hit the day before. But unlike C Company, A Company avoided taking losses.

At 8:30 A.M., the M-7 self-propelled 105mm howitzers of batteries B and C of the 94th AFAB began firing smoke in the face of the Germans. Despite accurate placement, it seemed to do little to effect the volume of incoming fire. For the next hour, the tanks of both A/37 and B/37 tried without success to neutralize the enemy guns. German tanks and assault guns were visible in the distance, and their high velocity, long-range guns gave them a distinct advantage over the Shermans. Under the circumstances, Abrams' team of tanks and infantry could not advance down the road toward Bining. It would have been disastrous.

The Move into Singling

Faced with a stalemate, Abrams took matters into his own hands and decided to make a somewhat impromptu attack on Singling in order to remove the threat on his left flank. His plan called for B/37 and B/51 to divert from their advance on Bining, and lead the assault on Singling instead. With Singling secured, the way would be clear for D/37, elements of the 25th Armored Cavalry, and the 1st Battalion of the 328th

Infantry Regiment (26th Infantry Division) to advance toward Bining (the battalion from the 26th had been attached to his task force).

Before the start of the attack, Batteries A and B of the 94th AFAB fired 107 rounds into Singling. Among their targets was a Panther tank parked between two buildings at the forward edge of town. Up to this point, the long-range shots from the 37th's tanks had done nothing to chase away the panzer, which guarded the direct approach into the town from the south. Ricochets off the thick, steeply angled frontal armor were all the American tankers had to show for their efforts. But when Lt. Donald Guild, the forward observer for the 94th AFAB, adjusted the fire of the artillery onto the Panther's position, and deadly hot white phosphorous was substituted for the standard HE rounds, the Panther retreated, leaving the way open for the assault.

For the move toward the town, Captain Leach deployed his 2nd Platoon on the left, the 1st on the right, and kept the 3rd in support. The infantry remained mounted on the tanks of the 1st and 3rd Platoons, while the 2nd Platoon went in without direct infantry support. Before the tanks started to roll, the 105mm assault guns laid down a smoke screen between the Shermans and the high ground north of Singling. A/37 stayed to the right of the B Team, and maintained covering fire on the road between Bining and Singling. A platoon of tank destroyers was positioned to provide direct support as well, but German artillery fire chased the vulnerable, open-topped Hellcats away before they could weigh in with any effect.

As the shells from the 105mm howitzers of the M7s continued to rain down on Singling, B/37 and B/51 began their advance, with the tanks firing toward the town as they moved. But the B Team ran into problems as soon as it came out of the starting gate. One of the Shermans in 2nd Lt. James Farese's 2nd Platoon developed engine trouble, and fell behind the rest of the tanks. One of the tanks in 1st Lt. Robert Cook's 3rd platoon dropped out when it was discovered that its radio was broken (a tank rendered deaf and mute was a potential liability). The other tanks of the 3rd platoon ran into some problems during their deployment and got bunched up; three of the tanks had to stop firing, lest they hit the two tanks in the front of the formation.

The lead tanks reported that they were not receiving enemy fire of any consequence. As they got closer to Singling, 1st Lt. William Goble's 1st Platoon swung to the right, Farese's 2nd Platoon swung to the left, and Cook's 3rd Platoon (which included Lt. Guild's forward observer tank and Leach's command tank) moved up through the center. The three platoons now formed a line that stretched from one end of Singling to the other (a distance of about 700 yards). As the B Team drew closer to the town, Lt. Guild shifted the artillery fire deeper into the town, and then lifted it completely as the tanks reached the edge of Singling.

On the left, Lt. Farese's tank moved out about 50 yards ahead of the rest of his platoon, and set out for a slight rise in the ground from where he would be able to observe the road leading into the west end of Singling. The rise was covered with an orchard that would provide some concealment as he jockeyed for position.

Unfortunately for the 2nd Platoon, the Germans had the western approaches well covered in anticipation of just such a move. A towed 75mm anti-tank gun, several Panther tanks, two self-propelled guns, and a machine gun emplacement were in position less than 100 yards from the north edge of the orchard, on the opposite side of the rise and hidden from the view of the American units advancing from the south. In addition to hitting anything that would come over the crest of the hill, they had a line of fire that extended straight down the main street that ran from west to east through Singling. It was a superb defensive position.

As soon as Farese's command tank reached the crest within the orchard (about 200 yards from the German positions), three armor piercing rounds slammed into the tank and set it ablaze. Farese and his loader, Pfc. William Bradley, where both killed. The other three crewmembers fled the tank and sought cover back down the orchard-covered slope.

S/Sgt. Sowers and Sgt. Parks, the commanders of the platoon's two remaining Shermans — Sgt. Joseph Hauptman's tank, which had experienced the engine problem, had yet to catch up to them — remained behind the crest, and told Hauptman over the radio not to come forward. All Sowers and Parks had to do to draw enemy fire was to show their radio antennae above the crest of the hill. They didn't know exactly what the enemy was shooting with, but they knew that it was more than they could handle. Advancing all the way to the crest would certainly result in the same fate that befell Farese and Bradley, so they remained on their side of the hill.

Before Farese's 2nd Platoon had ground to a halt, the 3rd and 1st Platoons had already started toward the edge of town. When they reached a line of hedges running along the south edge of the village, the armored infantry dismounted and followed their company commander, Lt. Belden. They ducked behind the shrubbery and organized their platoons. Belden doled out their orders: one platoon, under the command of Lt. William Cowgill, would bypass the three buildings closest to them and move forward to secure the left (west) side of the town. The platoon of 2nd Lt. Theodore Price would take the right side of town. The final platoon, under the command of 1st Lt. Norman Padgett, was to follow behind Cowgill's platoon and secure the three buildings that Cowgill's men were going to bypass.

As Lt. Belden sent his men off on their hastily arranged missions, he did so with the fog of war swirling about him. He didn't have any idea what type of resistance he would meet in and around Singling. All he knew with certainty is that the 94th had hit the town with a fairly heavy barrage, and that his unit had drawn limited, ineffective fire as it approached the town. His best hope would be to move swiftly, and count on the experienced men of his company to carry the load.

Unknown to Belden, the Germans had built up a considerable defensive position in Singling. In addition to the forces that had already faced off against the 2nd Platoon of B/37, the Germans were holding the town with the better part of a battalion of grenadiers from the 11th Panzer Division (1st Battalion, 111th Panzer Grenadier Regiment, to be precise). They also had the benefit of heavy weapons support, which included a towed 75mm AT gun, a number of 81mm mortars and machine guns, three 20 mm anti-aircraft guns, and a weapon known as a Wurfgeraet, which was a rocket launcher capable of firing two 200-pound rounds, each 36 inches in length. They also had direct support within the town in the form of two self-propelled guns. Topping all this off was a considerable array of artillery support: five 105mm howitzer batteries of the 199th Artillery Battalion (part of the 11th Panzer) and portions of at least five battalions from the 207th Volks Artillery Corps, whose guns ranged in caliber from 75 to 210 mm.

The grenadiers of the 111th PG Regiment were no strangers to the Fourth Armored. In fact, this was the same unit that held Voellerdingen prior to the assault by CCB's TF Irzyk. When the panzer grenadiers fled Voellerdingen, they headed northeast toward Singling, which had been the location of their battalion HQ. After regrouping, they received orders to attack Oermingen, a key town located back to the southwest, midway between Voellerdingen and Hebitzheim. But before they became engaged in that effort, their orders were changed to a defensive mission at Singling. They were aided in that assignment by the fact that Singling sat atop the Maginot line, the string of French-built fortifications facing the German border. This provided them with a number of strong, prepared emplacements that would serve as anchors for their defense. The battalion was under-strength after arduous fighting during the past several weeks, but they still outnumbered B/51 by a margin of over 3 to 1. Capturing Singling would be no easy task.

The men of B/51 moved in against this formidable defensive position, ignorant of its composition and strength. In an effort to establish the nature of the enemy force, Lt. Cowgill and Pfc. John Stanton (normally Cowgill's radio operator, but on this day he would serve as his runner) worked their way forward of the rest of the armored infantry platoon. Visibility was very poor, as some sections of the town were blanketed with thick smoke from the buildings set ablaze by the artillery bombardment that had preceded the attack. They were nearly to the main square of the town when they observed a self-propelled gun guarding the approach from the west. The commander of the SP gun did not appear to see them; he kept his head out of the hatch, seemingly without fear that an enemy soldier could draw a bead on him at any moment.

Lt. Cowgill, fearing that the advancing Shermans would stumble into the line of fire of the enemy SP gun, shouted back a warning not to approach. The warning made its way back to Captain Leach, whose tank had been among those following behind the armored infantry as they moved toward the center of town. Leach dismounted and went forward on foot to Cowgill's position in order to take stock of the situation for himself.

The two officers decided to chase off the German SP gun by firing at the exposed commander with their small arms. At the very least, they wanted him to button up his assault gun, which would limit his visibility. The shots failed to hit the commander, but the swarm of bullets forced him back inside the assault gun, and he closed the hatch behind him. The gun then backed out of its position, and started moving in reverse toward the west. As it fled, the SP gun sent a hail of machine gun bullets flying toward some of the other men of B/51, who had congregated in a tight cluster near the street. The spray of bullets quickly scattered the men, and they raced for cover in the nearby houses.

The SP gun then tried to turn around, during which time Leach continued to fire at the vehicle with his submachine gun. His command tank, 'Blockbuster 2d', had entered the street behind him, and the gunner, Cpl. John Yaremchuk, now had a bead on the SP gun. But Leach was standing directly in between the SP gun and his own tank, and Yaremchuk held his fire, lest he take off his commander's head. The SP gun escaped down the road to the west (in a hand-written footnote entered into his copy of the U.S. War Department's "Small Unit Actions" report on the battle of Singling,

Leach would later write: "The words: 'Thank You Corporal Yaremchuk' are long over-due.")

As Leach dealt with the enemy SP gun, Lt. Guild was busy trying to establish an observation point from which he could direct artillery fire against the enemy. After parking his tank in a concealed position south of the main square, he and his bow gunner traveled on foot for about 250 yards, skirting the buildings along the south edge of town. Unable to find a suitable vantage point, the two men were about to double back, when suddenly, they came upon an enemy machine gun position from the rear. The lone German occupying the nest was taken by surprise, and did not offer any resistance. Guild disarmed the German, destroyed the machine gun, and escorted the prisoner only as far as it took to turn him over to the crew of the closest Sherman tank. Now unencumbered, Guild returned to his search for an observation post.

The highest point overlooking the town was the steeple of the church located back near the town square. Guild and his bow gunner headed that way. He climbed a ladder leading to the steeple, and was greeted by the sight of the German SP gun elevating its gun directly toward him. Sensing that the gun would fire at any second, Guild "jumped for the ladder and slid down with (his) hands on the side rails." An armor-piercing round slammed into the steeple, leaving Guild unharmed, but serving as notice that the church would be useless as a vantage point.

Lt. Belden appeared on the scene right after the self-propelled gun had withdrawn. When he asked someone for information regarding what his men were up against, he was told it was a machine gun, to which he replied, "If it is a machine gun nest, we'll bring up a tank." No one bothered to clarify that the machine gun fire was from the self-propelled gun. Based on that misunderstanding, a tank from the 1st Platoon was ordered forward to destroy a non-existent machine gun emplacement.

The tank of Sgt. Kenneth Sandrock drew the assignment. His tank had been in place well to the east of town, behind the cover of an orchard. As he approached the town square, he took aim at the steeple of the church—the same steeple from which Lt. Guild had been chased—and blasted it in the event that it housed enemy observers or snipers. Of course, Sandrock never found a machine gun nest, but he did find Captain Leach, who sent Sandrock's tank into a position guarding the left side of the force that had assembled in the area of the town square.

Leach decided that it would not be prudent to have his tank follow after the enemy assault gun. By now, word had reached him about the fate of Lt. Farese's tank, and he realized that some caution was due. Instead of pursuing directly after the German armor, he would send the tanks of Lt. Cook's 3rd Platoon on a flanking movement. They would cut behind the buildings lining the south side of the main street, and then enter into the town further to the west. Hopefully, they would take the enemy gun by surprise, and if good fortune prevailed, catch it from the rear or side. After issuing the order, Leach pulled his own tank into a secure position overlooking the town square, from whence he could command the battle.

Two Sherman tanks and a Sherman 105mm assault gun of Lt. Cook's 3rd platoon drew the assignment. They advanced though an orchard south of town, and then cut in between some buildings that lined the main east-west road that sliced through the center of Singling. The smoke from the burning buildings was very thick in this area, and Cook's tank, which was leading the way, plowed into a stone retaining wall with one of its treads. This almost forced the tank to overturn, but the wall crumbled and the embankment it was built upon caved in beneath the weight of the tank, which allowed the tank to right itself. With the embankment leveled, the other two tanks followed without difficulty.

The tankers of the 3rd Platoon now found themselves within a garden area that was enclosed by a wall of stone varying in height from 4 to 6 feet. The wall didn't offer all that much protection, as the ground to the north rose to a higher elevation, and enemy guns firing from that direction would easily have a line of sight into the garden, and could shoot over the top of the wall.

The tankers paused to take stock of their situation. They had hoped to catch the German assault gun in this area, but there was no sign of it. Not knowing what might lurk around the corners, and with no supporting infantry to scout ahead for them, they stayed put for the moment in the garden.

As Cook's tanks plowed into the garden, Lt. Cowgill and a few of his infantrymen were working their way west down the main route through town, moving from house to house on the south side of the street They eventually worked their way into a building adjacent to the garden where Cook's tanks had stopped. From his vantage point, Cowgill could now see not one, but *two* German assault guns located about 200 yards further to the west. Seeing Cook's three tanks perched behind the garden wall, they warned the tankers of the location of the SP guns. This warning came just in time, as Cook had been contemplating leaving the cover of the garden in search of the enemy SP gun, despite not having infantry in direct support of his tanks. Had he pulled out into the street, he probably would have met an ugly fate.

Lt. Cook couldn't see the assault guns from his position in the garden. But based on the position reported to him by the infantry, he figured that he could knock off the corner of the building that concealed one of the guns. Cook had his tanks fire at the masonry, but as it turned out, he had misunderstood what the infantrymen had told him, and was chipping away at the wrong structure. The fire of his tanks revealed his own position to the enemy, who delivered a response in the form of a 75mm round that slammed into the building behind Cook's tanks.

As the enemy assault guns and Cook's Shermans engaged in a game of cat and mouse around the corners of the buildings, Cowgill's infantry continued to clear out the houses further to the east on both sides of the main street. It was not an easy task, as the machine guns mounted on the SP guns continued to dominate the thoroughfare, making it very dangerous for the infantry to venture out of the buildings. Anyone attempting to cross from one side of the street to the other was running straight across the line of sight of the enemy gunners.

If any further progress were going to be made, the enemy SP guns would have to be dislodged. Cook's tank platoon was clearly not in a position to take on the guns from its current position in the garden. In an effort to break the logjam, Captain Leach ordered the 2nd Platoon, now commanded by S/Sgt. Sowers in the wake of Lt. Farese's death, to leave its position in the orchard on the west side of town. They were instructed to pull back and then advance into the town at a point west of Cook's position, with the hope of taking the SP guns in the flank or rear.

Sowers led his two Shermans on the mission. But as soon as he stuck the nose of his tank around the wall of a burning barn, the Germans launched a volley of anti-tank fire in his direction. Sowers saw no opportunity for further advance, and returned his tanks to the orchard from whence they had started.

As the day progressed, some of the infantrymen wormed their way into advantageous positions in some of the buildings farther to the west of Lt. Cook's tanks, which were still behind the stone walls of the garden. Lt. Cowgill managed to lead a patrol into an attic that afforded a very close view of the enemy assault guns. Not being able to see beyond the guns, the patrol bravely made their way even further to the west, getting within spitting distance of the enemy armor. It was then that they made a most important observation: There were three additional panzers within 200 yards of the assault guns. He reported back to Lt. Cook, who now realized just how serious the situation was.

Lieutenant Cook saw a potential remedy in the form of his supporting artillery. He sought out the forward observer (Lt. Guild), who was back at the infantry command post, along with Lieutenant Belden and Captain Leach. After Cook joined them, the four officers discussed the best way of dislodging the enemy from their positions on the west side of town.

Cook stated his preference for bringing down a heavy artillery barrage on the enemy positions. Lt. Guild advised him that the men of B/51 were too close to the enemy, and that a barrage could not be delivered safely unless he had a good vantage point from which to guide and correct the fire (Earlier, Guild had made his way to the same house that Lt. Cowgill had used to observe the enemy tanks, and felt that he could use this position as his artillery observation post. The infantry had insisted on maintaining it as a position from which they would eventually fire upon the enemy, which would no doubt draw return fire, and render it useless as an OP for Guild.) Someone suggested that he adjust the artillery fire by "sound," but that was clearly not an option, given the narrow margin for error. They discussed using mortars, but as it turned out, none had been brought along due to manpower shortages in the company (the mortar squad, which was down to three men, were armed with a bazooka instead).

The men then tossed around some other options. Lt. Cook suggested that a smoke screen should be placed down in front of the enemy SP guns, which would allow his Shermans in the garden to cross the street and gain favorable firing positions from the northeast. Captain Leach preferred to send the bazooka-wielding infantry in to flush out the guns. In the end, it was Leach's plan that was put into action.

Lt. Cowgill put together two bazooka teams that would carry out the mission. His plan was to have the men take aim from the attic of his forward command post, which afforded a clear line of sight to the enemy gun. He assembled some infantry to protect them, and they prepared to go into position for the attack. But in the meantime, things were heating up in the other sections of Singling.

Action at the Center of Singling

While Cook and Leach struggled to find a way to budge the German assault guns on the west side of town, the armored infantry were occupied with other threats. Once they had cleared the buildings on the north side of the street, they were able to look out over the valley that was nestled to the north of the town. In that area, clustered near a pillbox, were some fifteen to eighteen German soldiers. The American infantry launched a fusillade of small arms fire, hitting some of them, and sending the rest running into the pillbox. Lt. Cook's tanks could also see this area from their garden perch, and they joined in the shooting as well.

The Germans reflected on their situation, and decided to give up the fight. They hung out white clothes from the pillbox to indicate their desire to surrender. The Americans ceased firing, but the Germans failed to come out. Lt. Guild, who was nearby, stepped out and waved the Germans in. A dozen Germans left the cover of the pillbox, marched up from the valley, and surrendered to Lt. Price of the 1st Platoon. One of the Germans spoke English, and reported that five others from his unit were anxious to surrender, but were afraid to leave the safety of the pillbox. In an effort to coax them out without any risk to his own men, Price sent one of the German prisoners back to the pillbox. Hopefully, the German could convince his comrades that it was safe to venture out toward the American positions.

It was then that a volley of mortar and artillery fire rained down on the square where the Americans were assembled. The GIs raced for the cover of nearby houses. The German POWs, who had a golden opportunity to escape if they wanted to make a run for it, stayed put, apparently deciding that they were better off in the hands of the Americans than they would be if they tried to return to their own lines. Once the shelling ended, the prisoners, who had been joined by a couple of other stragglers that had wandered in and surrendered, were marched south out of the immediate battle area (the men of the 51st AIB would bag over 60 prisoners during the battle).

After the enemy artillery subsided, four men from the 1st Squad of Price's platoon wandered down to the pillbox to flush out the remaining Germans. When they arrived, they discovered that the fortification was empty. Their only reward was a hail of machine gun bullets that came from about 500 yards to the north (from the direction of the Welschoff Farm). One of the men received a serious leg wound, and the squad was pinned down for the next several hours.

The situation in the center of town would remain relatively stable for the balance of the day. The same could not be said of the west and east sides of town.

The East Side of Singling

Over on the east end of Singling, Lt. Padgett's 2nd Armored Infantry Platoon also had a vantage point overlooking the valley. But he was able to see a couple of things that evaded Lt. Price's attention from the position at the center of town: a German rocket launcher, firing from a position about 800 yards west of Welschoff Farm, and seven panzers sitting atop a dominating ridge to the northeast.

Lt. Padgett's position provided an excellent view of the surrounding terrain. His perch was located in the next to last building on the east edge of town, and was at a higher elevation than any of the other buildings to the west. It was a veritable fortress, as its walls were made of steel reinforced concrete some three feet in thickness. The citizens of the town must have been well aware of the quality of its construction, as several of them had taken refuge there during the battle.

The soundness of the building gave Padgett great confidence about weathering the fire from the rockets and enemy artillery. But the panzers were another matter, as their high velocity cannons could perhaps penetrate the walls of the house. For defense against the enemy tanks, he would have to rely on the presence of Lieutenant Goble's 1st Platoon from B/37 (minus the one tank that had been sent back toward the town square). Lt. Goble brought his four Sherman tanks into position behind the building at about the same time that Padgett's men had originally occupied the house; this was also about the same time that Lt. Farese's tanks were advancing on the left, and Lt. Cook's tanks were advancing in the center.

Lt. Padgett wanted to get word to his company commander, Lt. Belden, regarding his observations from the east end of town. He sent his runner on two missions: go to Belden's command post to report on the situation, and then look for the 2nd Squad (led by Pfc. Phillip Scharz), which had become separated from the rest of the platoon. When the runner did not return in what Padgett thought was a reasonable amount of time, he dispatched Private Lonnie Blevins with the same orders: report to Belden, and return with the 2nd Squad.

Private Blevins struck out for the company command post, which he believed to be at a building south of the main square, near the point where the Americans had first entered the town (we can presume this is where the first runner headed as well). What neither man knew when they departed on their respective mission was that, after the battle started, Lt. Belden moved his command post closer to the town square. Fortunately, after checking with other troops in the area, Blevins discovered the correct location of the CP.

In order to reach the command post, Blevins had to cross the main west-east road that was under fire by the German self-propelled gun. The enemy gun fired a heavy blast of machine gun bullets as he darted across, but he made it without getting hit. He hunted down Lt. Belden, and made his report regarding Lt. Padgett's situation and observations over on the east side of town. With the first half of his mission accomplished, Blevins set out in search of Pfc. Scharz's 2nd squad.

Scharz's men had a good reason for falling behind the rest of the platoon. As you will recall, Lt. Belden's entire company entered Singling by coming in cross-country, moving due north toward the main body of buildings on the southeast edge of town. At the point where they entered the village, there were two isolated houses located to their right; the closest at a distance of about 50 yards, and the second another 75 yards beyond that. As the main body of Lt. Belden's company advanced north up the main road toward the town square, Scharz's squad was given the assignment of clearing out the two houses on the right. As Scharz investigated the houses, Lt. Belden set up his initial command post in the third house from the edge of town, adjacent to one of the homes that Scharz was about to clear.

Scharz's men selected the house furthest to their right as the first one they would enter. They then planned on working their way back north up the street to the second house. At the first house, they came upon a Frenchman, and questioned him about the presence of German troops in the area. The civilian shook his head no, in effect telling them that there were no Germans nearby. But just as he was making his denial, one of the GIs noticed a radio antenna sticking out from one of the cellar windows.

Four men from the squad quickly surrounded the house, while Scharz and one of his men, Pfc. Lewis Dennis, entered the building. They came out with quite a bag: two German officers and 28 enlisted men! Fortunately, the Germans offered no resistance. In addition to the prisoners, a further search of the home turned up a large cache of small arms and ammunition. Having discovered so many of the enemy in the first house, the squad carefully checked out all of the other houses that had been bypassed by the main body of troops. This is what had led to their separation from the rest of their platoon.

As Private Blevins started back from Lt. Belden's CP, he stumbled into Scharz's squad by accident. Scharz's unit had just reached the area close to the town square following their successful roundup of the enemy (the homes they searched after the first one ended up being vacant). Blevins informed Scharz of the location of the rest of the platoon on the east side of town, and the 2nd Squad then set out to join them.

Panzers on the Move

The B Team was in a tough spot. By now, it was clear that they had walked into a bit of a hornet's nest in Singling. In addition to the strong enemy forces that opposed them inside the town, the Germans had additional forces firing at them from the north and northeast. It wasn't a pretty picture.

The most immediate goal at this point was to try and clear the enemy from the town. By now, the Americans had reasonable control of the east and central portions of the village, and all that remained to be done was to push the enemy out of their positions on the west side of Singling. To that end, Lt. Cowgill's bazooka teams were preparing to strike against the German self-propelled guns that ruled over the main avenue.

Right about the time that the bazooka teams were moving into position, the Germans began to take matters into their own hands. An intense, 5-minute barrage of artillery, mortar, and rocket fire fell on the American positions. While the Americans ducked for cover, the Germans began to press forward on every sector of the town occupied by the Americans. Given all of the simultaneous activity that subsequently took place, the story of this phase of the battle is not easy to tell; for the purposes of our narrative, we will start on the west side of Singling, and work our way east.

To the west (the American "left"), the 2nd Platoon of B/37 still occupied their position in the orchard. Sgt. Hauptman had finally brought up his lagging Sherman, which brought the platoon's strength up to three tanks. All three of the Shermans were tucked down behind the slope, presumably out of the line of sight of the powerful Panthers, SP guns, and towed AT guns that had destroyed their platoon leader's tank at the start of the battle.

When the artillery barrage hit in their area, it came dangerously close to the tanks, so they backed the Shermans up a few yards to avoid the most intense fire. The accuracy of the enemy artillery on their hidden position immediately explained the presence of a German soldier who had appeared at the top of the ridge just before the start of the barrage (a sighting that, at the moment it occurred, didn't mean much to the tankers). It was now obvious that the man had helped his artillery set the range to the American tanks on the rear slope of the hill.

No sooner had the tanks shifted position when, in a stroke of either incredibly bad luck or unbelievable gunnery, a German armor piercing shell ricocheted off the crest of the hill at a point about 100 yards in front of the tanks, and hit Sergeant Hauptman's Sherman. The shell penetrated the right side of the turret, killing his loader, Pfc. William McVicker. A passage from the "Small Unit Actions" report on the Battle of Singling best describes the nature of the shot:

> If the German tanks west of town aimed that shell to carom into the tanks parked where they had been observed by the lone (German) infantryman, the accuracy of this shot was most remarkable.

Not being aware at the time that the shot had been delivered from a location on the other side of the hill, the tankers of the 2nd Platoon now feared that they were under direct fire from some other location. After receiving permission, they pulled back to a position behind the 3rd Platoon, where they were sheltered by some of the buildings of Singling.

As the 2nd Platoon was scrambling for cover, the 3rd Platoon of B/37, located in the center, also came under fire from German guns. From positions on the high ground to the north, a lone Panther launched an AT round toward Grimm's and Hayward's tanks, which were still near the garden west of the town square. Grimm realized that his 105mm assault gun Sherman was in an extremely vulnerable position, and that he could not respond effectively against the one German Panther that he could see (the range was approximately 1200 yards). He decided to back the tank out of the garden in order to find cover. At that moment, another AT round slammed into the sprocket of Hayward's tank, immobilizing it. In just a matter of seconds, four more enemy rounds slammed into Hayward's tank, setting it ablaze. Two of the crewmembers were killed (the gunner, Cpl. Angelo Ginoli, and the bow gunner, Pvt. John Furlow), and two wounded (the loader, Pfc. Vern Thomas, and Hayward). Grimm's tank made good its immediate escape, but got bogged down in some heavy mud in the field behind the buildings (S/Sgt. Sowers would later tow him out with his tank).

With the American tanks now forced out of their forward positions, they were of little help to the infantry manning the buildings nearby. All of the tanks of the 2nd and 3rd Platoons, the artillery observer tank, Leach's command tank, and one tank of the 1st Platoon (Sgt. Sandrock's) were all clustered in an area southwest of town, surrounded on three sides by buildings. The best they could do at the moment was brace for a continuation of the enemy attack, and to try to hold their current positions. The infantry of Lt. Price's platoon were ordered to stay put in the relative safety of the buildings they had captured, while Lt. Padgett's men took to the cellar of the house they occupied on the east edge of town. Given the strength and composition of the enemy force, they now knew that their best bet was to wait for the arrival of CCB, which they understood to be on the way.

Though they had pushed the American tanks back on both the west and center

"Backbreaker," the B/37 105mm Assault Gun Sherman commanded by Sgt. "Pappy" Grimm. Standing in front of the tank is Cpl. Raymond Darke (courtesy J. Leach).

sections of town, the Germans did not choose to follow up their success in these areas. Instead, they made their next move from the east. During the artillery barrage, the Germans had begun to reposition their armor for an attack on Singling. Several panzers that had occupied the high ground to the north began to shift east. And from the east-northeast, several more panzers began to advance toward the positions of Lt. Padgett's infantry and Lt. Goble's tanks on the east side of town.

Fortunately, Lt. Guild (the forward artillery observer) had spotted the German tanks in the distance, and reported his sighting to Captain Leach, who in turn, reported the news to the commander of the 1st Tank Platoon, Lt. Goble. Anticipating that the Germans might try to approach via the road entering the town from the east, or perhaps cross-country from the northeast, Goble sent the Sherman tank of Sgt. Robert Fitzgerald down the hill to a position further east where he could better observe an enemy threat coming from either of those two directions. A house on the north side of the street provided concealment for Fitzgerald's tank, and he lay there in wait as the enemy tanks moved closer. Fitzgerald's tank was the right one for the job, in that it was armed with one of the new 76mm high velocity guns.

Fitzgerald's gunner set his gun sight at a distance of 1,400 yards, which was the last reported position of the Panthers (the 75mm gun on a standard Sherman wouldn't have stood much of a chance engaging a Panther at that range). To Fitzgerald's surprise, the first German Panther to appear cropped up at a range of only 150 yards! Fitzgerald saw the Panther as it passed through his line of sight between two of the buildings on the north side of the street. Apparently, the commander of the Panther saw Fitzgerald's tank at the same time. Both tanks started to swing their guns toward one another, but the power traverse of the Sherman won the race, allowing Fitzgerald's gunner to draw a bead first. He slammed a 76mm AP round into the Panther, setting it ablaze. Only one man was seen bailing out of the tank, after which Fitzgerald slammed two more rounds into the Panther, ensuring that it was no longer a threat.

As the German tank burned, there did not appear to be any more enemy tanks advancing. But shortly thereafter, some of Lt. Padgett's infantry holed up in the last house on the edge of town spotted more panzers driving cross-country from the northeast. They raced into the street to warn the tankers, and Fitzgerald moved his tank further east to gain an even better firing position over the route that the Germans appeared to be using.

From his new vantage point, Fitzgerald saw another Panther coming across the field. Before he could lay a shot on the enemy tank, however, his opponent must have spotted his Sherman, and rather than engage, the Panther commander used his smoke screen device to cover his retreat.

The retreat of the Panther was followed by a barrage of rockets that fell on Fitzgerald's position. He backed his tank out of harm's way, and then dismounted to go meet with his platoon leader, Lt. Goble. The two men then went to visit with Lt. Padgett at his command post in the house on the east edge of town. From a vantage point in the house, Fitzgerald and Goble spotted another Panther that appeared to be parked with its gun covering the road leading east out of Singling.

Fitzgerald decided to take a crack at the Panther. He returned to his tank, and then moved the Sherman still further to the east. He framed the Panther between two trees, and his gunner took careful aim. The first round missed, but the second one found its mark. A third shot followed, this one setting the Panther ablaze.

As the Panther began to burn, Fitzgerald spotted yet another Panther facing directly at him at a distance of about 800 yards. Sgt. Del Vecchio's Sherman (armed with a 75 mm gun) was already engaging this Panther from a position further back up the hill behind Fitzgerald's tank. Fitzgerald's gunner took aim with the 76mm gun, and fired off one round, and then another. The frontal armor of the Panther proved to be too much for even the 76mm gun; the shells bounced harmlessly off the Kraut steel. Fitzgerald backed his tank away, and once again dismounted to take a look at the scene from the vantage point of Lt. Padgett's command post.

Fitzgerald spotted yet another German target on the move. A self-propelled assault gun was headed east, coming from the direction of the Welschoff Farm. Fitzgerald returned to his tank, expecting the enemy assault gun to cross his line of fire. The SP gun never emerged, however, and as Fitzgerald waited in his ambush position, the Germans managed to place Lieutenant Goble's command tank in their sights. Two armor-piercing shells spiraled towards Goble's tank in quick succession. The first round wounded Goble and his gunner, Cpl. Therman Hale, and started a fire inside the tank. The second round penetrated through the steel turret. The aftermath of that shot is best described by the driver of "Bottle Baby," Cpl. John "Swede" Nelsen:

> I had the motor off so we could hear the Kraut shells come in. I had just finished cleaning my periscope and had stuck it back in place when — wham! It sounded and felt like our own gun firing, but it wasn't. A shell had it our turret. I looked back and saw smoke behind me. I was thinking of getting out when — blam — again. And I'll be damned if I didn't have a German armor–piercing shell in my lap. It came through in front of me and must have had just enough force to get through the armor plate and drop. I looked at the slug in my hands. I remember thinking that it felt heavy. It was so hot, it burned my gloves. I didn't look at it long, though, I can tell you. In exactly two seconds I was out of that driver's seat. As I slid out of the hatch another shell clipped the tank inches from my legs. I dropped into the mud and did some fast crawling until I got to a building and took time out to find out that I wasn't hurt. Of course, my gloves aren't much good.

With Lt. Goble wounded, Staff Sergeant Fitzpatrick took command of the 1st Platoon. He ordered the remaining tanks to back up into a defilade position that would protect them from enemy fire coming in from the north. The American positions were now constricting, and it was becoming clear that they would not be able to clear the enemy from Singling.

But what of Cowgill's bazooka teams over on the west side of town? It was about this time that the infantrymen had moved into position, and were ready to strike. The two bazooka teams climbed into an excellent firing position in the attic of one of the buildings. In the basement, Sergeants Patrick Dennis and Harold Hollands maintained firing positions from where they could cover the bazooka teams. Right before the bazooka teams went into action, they were joined by Company 1st Sgt. Cannon and Corporal Ralph Harrington, who had come forward to do some reconnaissance.

The bazooka teams prepared to fire at the SP gun through holes in the attic. One of the bazookas malfunctioned, and never launched a round. But the other team got off five rounds, of which the first four missed the target. The fifth round struck the right side of the upper portion of the assault gun, but did not appear to cause much damage, as only a fragment of steel splintered off the beast. It was an effective shot, however, since it resulted in the crew of the assault gun abandoning the vehicle. The GIs gunned down two of the Germans as they fled. The success of the bazooka team was short lived, however. A Panther tank rolled up right next to the abandoned assault gun and fired a shell directly into the house being used by the bazooka teams. Another shell hit the building from the north. Fortunately, none of the men in the attic or basement were hurt, and they made their way to safety.

CCB Arrives

As the battle for Singling raged, a task force from CCB, commanded by the new CO of the 8th Tank Battalion, advanced toward the town. Major Irzyk was not aware that Abrams' task force had already occupied part of Singling, let alone moved into CCB's axis of advance. The fact that no one had informed Irzyk of either Abrams' presence or the enemy's positions in and around Singling, which by now were all too familiar to Abrams' B Team, stands as testimony to the confused state of affairs at the top of the division following General Wood's departure.

Expecting to find nothing but the enemy in front of him, Irzyk was shocked as he closed in on Singling. There before him, deployed over the open ground south of Singling, were the elements of Abrams' task force that were supporting the men and tanks fighting it out with the Germans in town. Irzyk, who was rightfully puzzled by the situation, thought to himself, "What the hell; what gives here? Where in the hell did they come from, and how did they get here?"

Irzyk was even more amazed when he got close enough to study the markings on the vehicles, and realized that they were from the 37thTank Battalion. To his knowledge, the 37th was still in reserve. He was totally unaware that they had been committed. If he were to have guessed, he would have bet that it was the 35th and 53rd; perhaps they had moved west out of their assigned area. But the 37th?

Major Irzyk immediately sought out Creighton Abrams. Irzyk's driver jockeyed his command tank up to Abrams' Sherman. Irzyk dismounted and jogged over to "Thunderbolt." As he approached, he quickly greeted Major Dan Alanis, the CO of the 51st AIB, who was already near Abrams' command tank. Abrams was perched in his usual position in the turret of "Thunderbolt," barking into his radio mike. The 27-year-old Irzyk climbed atop the deck of Abrams' tank, and Alanis followed him up.

The two majors now found themselves struck by a "thunderbolt" of a different sort. Abrams jerked the mike away from his face, and before Irzyk could say a word, the senior officer unloaded on his junior peer. "Where have you been? What took you so long?," Abrams shouted. Then, displaying a lack of insight into what had been happening within the division that day, he said:

> You're too slow. I'm occupying your axis of advance. I've attacked your town. I can't stay here any longer. I've got to get right out. I've got to get back on my own route, on my own mission. It's about time you took over the town! I've got a tank/infantry team in it. I want your tanks and infantry to relieve them in place. Do it right now! I can't spend any more time here.

Then, amazingly, he added:

> The town is clear, so you can move right in — you won't have to fight.

Caught totally off guard by the verbal lashing he had just received from the most esteemed battalion commander in the division, and perhaps even in the entire Third Army, Irzyk could only reply, "Yes, sir." Devastated and shaken, he quickly left Abrams' tank and dashed back to his own battalion, where he began making plans with his staff for the relief of the American forces in the town.

The Sherman tanks of C/8 (commanded by 1st Lt. Bill Marshall) and the armored infantry of B/10 (1st Lt. Robert Lange) were assigned the task of taking over TF Abrams' positions in Singling. They were also instructed to send out patrols to the north (all of this on the assumption that the town was totally secure). The men of B/10 mounted Marshall's tanks, and proceeded toward Singling along the same routes that Captain Leach's company had followed that morning. They literally followed in the tracks of B/37's tanks.

The 1st Platoon of Marshall's company led the way. Once they reached the south edge of town, the platoon commander, 2nd Lt. George Gray, ordered his tanks to veer off to the northwest. This was the exact same route taken by the ill-fated tank platoon of Lt. Farese.

As Lt. Gray approached the west side of the town, he noticed two Shermans up ahead in the orchard area. He assumed that they were operative and occupied as he continued his advance. He moved slightly to the right, toward the building closest to the orchard. As he approached the corner of the building, he saw a tank further ahead near the road. He assumed the tank was from the 37th (after all, he had been informed that the town was clear of the enemy). At that moment, Lt. Marshall radioed to Lt. Gray, and asked him how his advance was proceeding. Gray replied, "OK, as soon as I get around this corner." The words had barely left his lips when his tank was hit by two rounds (probably from the Panther that had moved up to shoot at the building housing Cowgill's bazooka teams). Gray received a serious wound, and his gunner, Corporal Tauno Aro, was killed. The armored infantry mounted on his tank jumped off and scrambled for cover near one of the buildings.

Marshall now realized that something was terribly wrong. Unaware of the jockeying that had been going on all day to clear the west side of the town, he ordered his 2nd Platoon, led by Staff Sgt. Edwin DeRosia, to move east and attempt to circle behind the tank that had fired on Gray's Sherman. As DeRosia moved out, however, he came under fire from the German guns located to the north and east (though he was unsure at the time of the direction of the fire). For a town that had supposedly been cleared of the enemy, Marshall realized that his tanks were taking a hell of a lot of heat. He ordered his entire company to pull back south of the town, behind the protection of the ridge. The infantry of the 10th AIB had remained on the decks of the tanks, and pulled back with him.

At this point, everyone went in search of better information. Lt. Marshall left the scene in his command tank in search of Major Irzyk, while 1st Lt. Lange went in search of his counterpart with the 51st, Lt. Belden.

Before finding Lt. Belden, Lange stumbled upon Captain Leach, and together they went to consult with Belden. The three men worked out a relief plan for the armored infantry, and as Lt. Lange passed the plan on to his platoon leaders, Captain Leach went in search of 1st Lt. Marshall in order to work out the relief of his tanks.

At about this time, Abrams radioed Captain Leach to find out how the relief of his force was progressing. Since Leach was off hunting down Marshall, Lt. Cook took the call. He informed Abrams of the presence of up to five enemy tanks on the west edge of town, and that from three to five more had been observed moving toward them from the ridge overlooking Singling. He went on to tell him that the relief of the infantry was in process, but that he was not in contact at the moment with Captain Leach (Leach later recalled that he himself had placed a radio call to Abrams earlier in the battle, and had reported that the west side of the town was not clear. Additionally, he advised Abrams that any forces moving forward to relieve the B Team should stay to the right of the church steeple. Had this information been passed on, Lt. Gray's tank and crewmember would have surely been spared).

An impatient Abrams called back a little later. Once again, he got Cook on the line instead of Leach. Abrams told him to organize his tanks, pick up the infantry of B/51, and move out of the town, regardless of whether or not Leach had returned. Cook quickly got the tanks ready to move, but the 10th AIB was still in the process of relieving B/51, so Cook had to sit tight for another half hour.

Captain Leach arrived at the assembly area for Marshall's company. Marshall was absent, as he had gone to meet personally with Major Irzyk. Leach got a hold of Marshall on Sgt. DeRosia's radio, however, and briefed him on the enemy positions as best he knew them at the moment. He then asked Marshall how soon he could get his tanks back into town to relieve B/37. Marshall's reply was not what Leach had expected to hear: he was not coming into the town until he was ordered to do so by Major Irzyk, who had, at least for the moment, ordered Marshall's tanks to stay put on the back side of the slope south of town.

The infantry commanders were unaware of the confusion between the two tank companies, so the relief of the infantry continued unabated. Positions were transferred, and the wounded were taken away from the scene. Darkness was descending, and with the relief of the infantry nearly complete, Cook started to pull out the tanks of B/37. With the men of B/51 mounted on their decks, the Shermans pulled back to the south.

About 400 yards south of Singling, Cook came across both Captain Leach and Lt. Marshall, who were now finally face to face with one another. (As Marshall had approached in his tank, Leach noted that his peer was almost cowering within the turret. In Leach's estimation, Marshall was suffering from combat fatigue.) At that moment, another barrage of enemy artillery struck in that immediate area. Luckily, only one man was wounded.

To help cover the rest of the withdrawal, the tanks of B/37 turned their guns back toward Singling and hit suspected enemy positions with direct fire (all the while being mindful of where the men of the 10th Battalion were now positioned). The German tanks returned fire, and Lt. Marshall's tanks now added their weight to the battle. A heavy volume of fire was exchanged, but no losses were incurred on either side. The B Team was finally out of Singling.

The men of the 10th AIB, however, were now alone in Singling, waiting for their supporting tanks from the 8th Tank Battalion. They held their positions for over three hours in the dark without seeing a single Sherman. Fortunately, the German armor never struck against their positions.

Singling was not void of activity, however. After dark, the Germans sent some men out to the two knocked out tanks of Farese's platoon with the apparent intent of driving them off. They got the engines started, and when the men of B/10 heard the familiar sound of the Shermans, they thought that the supporting tanks of Marshall's company had finally arrived. They sent out a small patrol to greet them, and when the two GIs got within about 25 feet, they noticed that the darkened silhouettes of the three men on the tanks looked a heck of a lot like Germans! Armed only with a carbine at the moment, they returned to pick up another man and heavier weapons. As they approached a second time, they were spotted by the Germans, who opened up on them with a burp gun. The Americans returned fire with rifles and hand grenades. They chased the Germans off, but later that night, the Krauts returned. Unable to steal the tanks, they settled for setting them ablaze.

Lt. Lange was greatly concerned about the position of his armored infantry inside the town. His company was very under strength (he was operating with only about 40 men; B/10 was in effect not much stronger than a platoon). With enemy tanks close at hand, but no armor of his own immediately available, he knew he was extremely vulnerable.

Lange went in search of Bill Marshall to try to persuade him to bring the tanks in. Arriving at the assembly area for Marshall's company, he found not Marshall, but Major Irzyk, who was conferring with Sgt. DeRosia, the new temporary commander of C/8. Lt. Marshall had become distraught over what had happened to his company as it initially moved into Singling, and Irzyk felt compelled to send him back to the 8th Tank Battalion HQ (apparently, Leach's take on Marshall's condition had been on the mark).

Lt. Lange, Major Irzyk, and Captain Abe Baum (S-3 of the 10th) now discussed the merits of holding the town for the remainder of the night. Irzyk had been planning to send a platoon of tanks in to support the infantry, but after further discussion with Lange, he opted for a withdrawal from the town. A key factor influencing his decision was the fact that at about 7 P.M. that evening, a German kitchen truck had been captured near the town square, and in it was found enough hot soup to feed at least a full strength company. Irzyk figured that Lange's depleted company was outnumbered in and around the town by a margin of at least three to one. He concluded that there was little they could accomplish in Singling, and that the presence of friendly infantry in the town only served to preclude the use of artillery against the Germans.

The men of B/10 soon pulled out to positions about 400 yards south of the town, where they dug in and provided security for the tanks. Very shortly after the infantry had reported their departure from the town, a heavy "time on target" barrage was delivered by corps artillery. Enemy casualties were unknown, but there was some satisfaction in handing the Germans a powerful parting gift.

That evening, Irzyk received orders that he was to hold his position the following day. There would be no further attempt to capture Singling. This came as good news to Irzyk, and he managed to have an unusually restful night's sleep knowing that there would be no call to action in the morning.

The final toll at Singling for December 6: Twenty-two American casualties, including six men killed in action. Five medium tanks were knocked out. Add to this the loss of C/37's 14 tanks on December 5, and the sum total represented a costly engagement for Abrams' 37th Tank Battalion. The number of German casualties was unknown, but the prisoner count totaled over 60. Two Panther tanks were confirmed destroyed, courtesy of Sgt. Fitzgerald's tank.

While the Fourth failed to secure Singling, it is important to note that the action created a diversion that enabled D/37, the 25th Cav, and the 1st Battalion of the 328th Infantry Regiment to capture Bining. The enemy they faced at Bining was less substantial than the force the Germans had positioned at Singling; at Bining, the German defense consisted of one company from the 61st Anti-tank Battalion (11th Panzer Division). This amounted to about 50 men and eight 75mm AT guns.

The Advance Comes to a Halt

For the Fourth Armored Division as a whole, December 7 represented the high water mark of its drive toward the West Wall. Singling and Bining would be as close as the Fourth Armored would get to the German border during this particular offensive. The only unit to remain heavily engaged on December 7 was D/37, which along with the battalion of infantry from the 26th Infantry Division, continued to hold Bining in the face of several enemy counterattacks.

For the rest of the division, December 7 was a day of relative calm. The medium tank companies of the 37th Tank Battalion licked their wounds at Schmittville. The men of the 51st AIB, who had pulled back from the action as well, found good reason to rejoice when they received word that 60 enlisted men and five officers had been selected from the Fourth Armored to go on "rotation." Seven enlisted men from the 51st would be among the chosen few to be granted 90 days away from the front, 30 of which could be spent at their home back in the United States. After all of the hard days that were behind them, and the prospect of still more trying days ahead, the news generated a lot of excitement.

Back near Singling, where the tanks and infantry of TF Irzyk were holding positions 400 yards south of the town, Major Irzyk received great news as well. The 8th Tank Battalion would soon be relieved by elements of the 12th Armored Division. That evening, the lead elements of the 12th Armored arrived, and Irzyk's staff started planning the transition of positions between the two units. At 6:00 A.M. on December 8, the 12th Armored began to relieve the Fourth, and Irzyk's men assembled south of Schmittville. From there, they departed for their final destination: the town of Domnom les Dieuze (the 12th Armored would capture Singling once and for all on December 10).

A similar scene was repeated across the entire front of the Fourth Armored Division. The 37th moved to the rear shortly after midnight, and in the morning, relocated to Mittersheim for reorganization and rest. The 94th FAB moved to Langiumberg. The 51st to Bidestroff. The 10th to Bassing. Every battalion was pulled back and given a chance to rest, perform direly needed maintenance, and sadly, to absorb a significant number of replacements.

The fighting during the past month had been some of the most bitter the Fourth

Pfc. Allen Kohlwaies, 24th Armored Engineer Battalion, strikes a holiday pose on December 16, 1944. An M1 Carbine stands on the window ledge, along with a 4th AD Christmas card and a German helmet (National Archives Photograph SC326569).

Armored had experienced since landing on the continent of Europe. On December 6, the strength of the 51st AIB stood at only 160 men, and the 53rd AIB at 126; these numbers serve as testimony to the heavy load that the infantry had to bear during the November offensive. Shortly before he was relieved of his command, General Wood had argued vociferously for a rest for the division. His wish had been belatedly granted, and the men of the Fourth now relished the opportunity to pull themselves back into top fighting shape.

11. Recuperation

A Well Deserved Rest

During a time of the war when advances were often measured not in miles, but in yards, the Fourth Armored stood out as one of the few divisions that continued to make consistent progress. Their effort during November and early December had been a costly one, however, and it was now imperative that they take advantage of the rest period being afforded them. Allied plans called for a resumption of the Third Army offensive in mid–December, with the 19th being set as the anticipated launch date. This gave the division a window of ten days to prepare itself before potentially being returned to combat.

When they were pulled from the front line, the men of the Fourth Armored were sent to the unglamorous, manure-filled towns and villages that characterized the Lorraine region of France. Most of these towns offered few luxuries. A roof over their heads and some occasional indoor plumbing were about the best that many of the men could hope for. No matter how primitive, however, it was a wonderfully welcome change from the battlefield. On second thought, when compared to the rigors of the front, their new surroundings might have actually qualified as luxurious after all.

As with earlier rest periods, the men filled much of their time with maintenance duties. But after more than four months of action in France, it was increasingly important for the human body and spirit to receive as much attention as weapons and vehicles. The medical staff kept busy with dental exams and the dispensing of medication, such as booster shots to fend off typhus. Hot showers were a welcome luxury after weeks of slugging through mud, rain, and snow. Religious services were well attended, as were the hastily arranged movies brought over from the States. The Red Cross Clubmobile made its rounds, bringing hot coffee, doughnuts, and the opportunity to catch the eye of a real American girl. Passes to Paris were offered to some of the men, while others were sent off to large regional cities. All of these things helped uplift the physical and psychological condition of the men.

There was also a need to absorb a slew of replacement soldiers. There was a dire need for riflemen, and as soon as the armored infantry battalions made it to the rear,

Clockwise from left, Pfc. Thomas Gardner, Pvt. William Frazier, and Pfc. J. Martinez, all from the 24th Armored Engineer Battalion, have a seemingly light-hearted moment during the 4th AD's rest period. December 16, 1944 (National Archives Photograph SC326568).

they began to see their ranks swell once again with rookies, who typically arrived via the "repple depples." (The replacement system, which, according to General Bradley, "developed an infamous reputation for callousness and inefficiency in their operations," was run by none other than Lt. General Ben Lear; the same General Lear that "P" Wood had so many problems with during the Tennessee maneuvers.)

In some cases, the new riflemen had been culled from other units, such as the towed anti-tank gun platoons. The light 57mm anti-tank guns were not of great value within the organization of an armored division, given their lack of mobility and, by comparison, the superior anti-tank capability of the tank destroyers and Shermans (though as we have already seen in, they were used with good effect on several occasions). Thus the men trained to operate the 57mm guns were viewed as being much more valuable in the role of a rifleman, and were reassigned accordingly when manpower shortages got to a critical stage. The ranks were also replenished by the return of men who had been wounded and hospitalized during past battles (though, much to their disappointment, not all of the returning troops were able to rejoin their original units).

Men were also culled from the Corps and Army Headquarters. At the end of

November, Patton took 5 percent of the troops assigned to the headquarters units, and had them reassigned as replacements for the front line divisions (he would eventually reduce the HQ units by up to 10 percent). On December 9, the 51st AIB received 98 replacements in one shot. This stands as testimony to just how understrength they had become.

The tank battalions were also short crewmembers for their tanks. Most of the replacements arriving at this stage of the war had no armor-specific training, so a great deal of time had to be spent teaching them the specialized skills that would be required in order to be a productive member of a tank crew. Fortunately,

Officers of the 8th Tank Battalion. *Kneeling:* Maj. Sam Diuguid (S-3). *Left to right:* Maj. Bert Ezell (Executive Officer), Major Al Irzyk (CO), Capt. Chuck Stauber (S-2), and Capt. Mac McGlamery (CO of B Company).

the replacements arrived en masse when the tank battalions pulled out of the line, and they would have the luxury of the entire rest period to provide orientation and training. Replacement officers were also in the mix, and the battalion commanders were thankful for the opportunity to bring them into their positions under the calm of the rear area, as opposed to injecting them during combat.

Indoctrinating the new men would be a key task during the rest period. Firing ranges were set up, and rookies and veterans alike sharpened their skills.

A firing exercise carried out by the 8th Tank Battalion provided one of the lighter moments of the war for that unit. Early on the morning of December 15, some of the battalion's tanks were in position at the range, ready to squeeze in some more practice. The session was made a little out of the ordinary when, without prior notice, General Dager and his staff appeared on the scene to observe. After a good display of gunnery by the tankers, Dager expressed his approval and moved on. Irzyk, satisfied with the session, also prepared to depart. Just as Irzyk began to leave, a large deer bolted across the far end of the firing range. The platoon of five tanks stationed at that end of the range acted as one, and opened up on the deer simultaneously with their .30 caliber machine guns. With bullets kicking up all around it, the deer ran for its life, and managed to flee the scene without so much as a scratch. Laughter blanketed the range, followed by an awful ribbing directed at the rookie gunners, who sunk into their seats in embarrassment. This experience got a lot of mileage as a long-standing battalion joke.

During this window, some of the units took the opportunity presented by the rest period to realign some of their command and staff positions. The changes that had taken place in early December had descended upon some of the units while they were heavily engaged in combat, and now with the luxury of time and relative tranquility to contemplate the strengths and weaknesses of their staff, they shuffled their resources.

The situation within the 8th Tank Battalion serves as a good example of the ripple effect that can result when a few key slots are changed. Bert Ezell, the S-3 (operations officer) of the 8th, would move into the role of S-1 (battalion executive officer). The commander of A Company, Chuck Stauber, would move into the S-2 position. Sam Diuguid moved to S-3 to replace Ezell. The CO of D Company, Jerry Tuszynski, became the assistant S3.

These changes meant that new commanders would be needed for D Company and A Company (Lt. Roy Erdmann and Lt. Len Kieley, respectively, were appointed to the positions). A new commander was also needed for B Company, when Irzyk learned that Mac McGlamery was one of the 5 officers of the Fourth selected to go home on rotation; 1st Lt. Ben Fischler would take over command of B/8. C Company was left with only one officer after the action at Singling, Lt. Steve Stephenson, who up until that point had been the maintenance officer for the company. He now became the CO of C/8. By the time all of the moves were completed, every position of command at the company level had changed hands.

Depending on the personalities, ability, and tenure of the men involved, changes of this sort could range from seamless to tumultuous. Fortunately, despite the losses incurred by the division since Normandy, the Fourth still had sufficient depth to fill many of the command positions with officers who were more than capable and qualified to handle the job.

As the units got deeper into the rest period, the disciplines of military life found their way back into the soldiers' routine. Weapon inspections were conducted, reveille formations greeted the day, and calisthenics sessions were held. Officers contemplated the performance of their men during recent weeks, and took the time to write up recommendations for decorations. There was also a stream of visits from the upper echelons, including an announced visit from General Patton.

Patton had a tremendous, uplifting effect on the men. During his visit to the 8th Tank Battalion, he managed, over the course of about 30 minutes, to interact informally with almost every man in the battalion. His rapport rested on a foundation of good old backslapping encouragement. Words of appreciation flowed freely, along with the occasional wisecrack or good-natured dig. With his visit complete, he concluded with a slap on the shoulder of the young battalion commander, accompanied by the words "Keep up the great work!"

Major Irzyk saw immense value in Patton's visit, since the end result was a jolt of enthusiasm and energy that helped raise the battalion's performance yet another notch. Irzyk would later write:

> There is almost nothing in the world like recognition and pride, and they (the men of the 8th) were handed a big dose of both this day.

The recognition continued in other forms. Award ceremonies were scheduled, wherein General Gaffey, the commanding officers of the combat commands, and some staff members would come down to the battalion level and present the awards that had been granted, based on the recommendations submitted by the officers of the unit. The awards were treasured, and congratulations flowed freely among the men.

Back into the Breach

Some of the units were called upon for action sooner than originally planned. On December 13, Lt. Col. Abrams was informed that his 37th Tank Battalion would be attached to the 87th Infantry Division, which had just recently arrived in the combat zone from England. Without its own attached battalion of tanks or self propelled tank destroyers, the green division would have the benefit of not only Abrams' 37th, but also the 704th TD Battalion.

The 37th had yet to fully replace the tanks it lost during the recent weeks of heavy fighting. On December 14, its strength consisted of 25 Shermans and 13 M5 tanks. In fact, none of the three medium tank battalions received sufficient replacement tanks during the rest period to make good the losses incurred in the recent offensive.

The commanders at the top often had a mistaken impression of the actual fighting strength of the tank battalions. While visiting the maintenance area of the 37th, Patton asked the battalion's executive officer, Major Ed Bautz, "Now, how many tanks are you short?" Bautz was well aware of the total, since it was part of his responsibilities as the exec to keep track of such things. In fact, he kept a log in a small notebook, with the tanks tracked by serial number (the battalion was supposed to receive back the same tanks they sent in for repair. It didn't always work out that way, however). Bautz's reply to Patton was, "Well, right now, we're short thirteen medium tanks." Patton shot back, "We're not short thirteen medium tanks in the whole Unites States Army." General Gaffey, perhaps embarrassed at the suggestion that his division was not in the shape Patton expected it to be, interjected. "Well, I think he (Bautz) includes those that are in ordnance and so on." Bautz, knowing the reality of the situation, and not of a mind to sugarcoat the situation, added, "yes, Sir, and a lot of others." The reality is that, after Normandy, the division's tank battalions were rarely at full strength, and the type of shortage reported by Major Bautz was routine. In fact, it was often worse.

On December 13, Abrams received his new orders from the commanding general of the 87th Infantry Division. The battalion prepared to depart from its bivouac at Mittersheim, and would begin its first assignment two days later.

On December 15, Company A of the 37th Tank Battalion was attached to the 346th Regiment for an attack on Hill 378, located northwest of the village of Erchins. Lt. Waters of A Company was seriously wounded during this action, and 2nd Lt. John Whitehill assumed command of the company. At dusk, the 346th was relieved by the 345th Regiment. A/37 was the only company from the battalion committed that day. The balance of the 37th was brought forward that afternoon.

On December 16, the 345th moved into position to launch an attack against a plot of woods north of Hill 378. A/37 was positioned one kilometer north of the hill in a position where it could provide supporting fire. Their firing positions were actually across the German border, and in moving there, A/37 became the first company of the Fourth Armored to touch German soil. During the day, the balance of the 37th moved to a position about a mile and a half east of Rimling. That afternoon, C/37 relieved A/37 north of Hill 378.

On December 17, Captain Leach returned from the hospital after receiving treatment for an old leg wound, as well as a bout of severe diarrhea. He took back command of B/37 from Lt. Cook, who had held the reins in his absence. On the day of his return, Leach's company was ordered to support an attack by the 87th against the town of Walsheim. The route to their assigned positions carried them through the village of Gersheim, where they discovered that the only bridge crossing a stream had been destroyed. The stream in the immediate vicinity of the bridge could not be forded, so Leach had to search for another place to cross.

When Leach finally found a location that he thought was suitable, he had the engineers check the crossing site for mines. The report came back that the site was clear, but as Leach's unit began moving across the stream, one of the Shermans hit a mine, which destroyed the tank's suspension system. The engineers returned, and upon further inspection, found a field of Reigal and Tellermines. The engineers installed a treadway bridge that crossed over the mined stream, and the advance toward Walsheim continued.

The delay imposed by the mines and subsequent bridge installation prevented B/37 from supporting the attack on Walsheim as planned. The 87th went forward anyway, and moved into the town. When Leach's tanks arrived, they outposted Walsheim in support of the infantry. All was not quiet, however. After assuming their positions, Leach's own command tank was knocked out by an unobserved enemy tank. The blast wounded his driver, T4 Hobart Drew, who had to be evacuated.

C/37 was also busy that day, having been assigned a mission in support of the 345th Regiment. The Shermans were employed in an attack into the woods, which was described in the battalion journal as "an unsatisfactory mission for tanks." The tanks were primarily used for providing direct fire against machine gun positions, and for evacuating wounded infantrymen to the rear. By this time, word had filtered down about the German attack in the Ardennes, accompanied by an unusual order from the 87th Infantry Division: "No one will give up a foot of ground without pain of a court-martial." The men of the 37th needed no such admonishment; obviously this was for the benefit of the green, untested troops of the 87th.

December 18 saw the 37th stay in the positions they held the day prior. The following day, they were released from the 87th Division and moved back to Mittersheim. The battalion command staff assembled there first, and began to discuss the situation, as they understood it. Facts were few and far between, so Colonel Abrams decided to depart ahead of the battalion in the hope of gathering better information before his battalion departed for the Ardennes. Before he left, he intuitively capsulated the situation by telling his men, "This is an opportunity to get 'em."

After Abrams' departure, it was up to Major Bautz to assemble the scattered tank companies and move them back to Mittersheim. Not long after issuing the orders to move to the designated assembly area, Bautz received a call from Captain Leach, who reported that the infantry battalion commander he was working with was only going to allow him to depart on one condition: "over his dead body." Unable to convince the officer from the 87th that Leach's orders were legitimate, Bautz headed over to the command post of the regiment to which Leach's company was attached. Once there, the regimental commander confessed to forgetting to tell his staff that the 37th was being released. With the situation resolved, the remaining Shermans of B/37 joined the others as they rolled toward Mittersheim.

The Final Party

The 37th was the exception to the norm, as the majority of the division continued to get some much-appreciated rest away from the dangers of the front. On the evening of December 16, there was a battalion officers' party held at the Town Hall in Dieuze. All of the commanding officers and staff of the division's battalions were invited, and General Gaffey attended as well. Invitations were also extended to all of the nurses and Red Cross Clubmobile girls that could be found. The companies, in turn, were given beer and held their own parties that night.

Sgt. Hobart Drew, the driver of "Blockbuster 2nd" (command tank of B/37) (National Archives Photograph SC277320).

As the men of the Fourth Armored tipped their glasses and longed for the arms of American girls that were all too few, they were unaware of the events taking place along what had been, up until that morning, a quiet portion of the front in the scenic Ardennes sector. As the men of the Fourth basked in a night of peace in the middle of a world drenched in war, the men of the U.S. First Army's VIII and V Corps were engaged in the fight of their lives. As they settled down after a long night of revelry, they had no way of knowing that they would soon be embarking upon what would become the most historic mission of their division's illustrious career. The Battle of the Bulge was on, and the Fourth Armored Division would soon be called upon to drive a stake into the heart of the German attack.

12. The Stage Is Set

German Preparations

As revealed in Chapter 5, September 16 marked the day when Hitler announced his intention to launch a counteroffensive through the Ardennes. Given the eventual impact on the Fourth Armored Division, it is worth examining the German's preparation for the offensive.

As the month of September progressed, Hitler could take some solace from the fact that the pace of the Allied advance on the West Front had slowed significantly. Though his counterattack against Patton's Third Army had been crushed, the Nazi leader could draw some satisfaction from events on the northern section of the front, where Montgomery's Operation Market-Garden had gone incredibly sour for the Allies. Aided by the logistical situation faced by the Allied Armies and an overall Allied strategy that had become suspect, Hitler's generals had indeed performed a miracle in the West. The front had been stabilized.

During the days following his dramatic pronouncement, Hitler added more depth to his scheme. On September 25, he unveiled the details to select members of OKW (Oberkommando der Wehrmacht). Following the meeting, operational planning for the Ardennes Offensive would take place with great vigor.

Due to legitimate concerns for intelligence security, combined with Hitler's growing paranoia after the July 20 attempt on his life, the number of staff involved in the next level of planning would be limited to a tight circle of men that had retained Hitler's trust and confidence. The chief of operations at OKW, General Alfred Jodl, left the September 25 meeting charged with developing the operational plan, while Field Marshal Keitel was responsible for developing estimates for the quantity of fuel and ammunition that would have to be stockpiled to support the effort. These two men carried the burden of finding a way to make Hitler's dream a reality.

On November 2, after several weeks of operational planning, the commanders of the field armies assigned to the offensive were brought into the loop. Great pains had been taken to conceal the blossoming plan, and so far, those efforts had been very successful. In light of prior victories the Americans and British had scored on the intelligence front, it was truly a win for the Germans that they were able to hold the plans for the offensive so close to the vest.

The German Resources

The original German plan to seize Antwerp called for a force of 30 divisions, organized into three armies: the Sixth SS Panzer, the Fifth Panzer, and the Seventh. They would be provided with as much artillery and air support as could be mustered at this point in the war. The Germans would also employ a special force designed to infiltrate the American front line in unique fashion. Led by Major Otto Skorzeny of the Waffen-SS, the 3,300 men strong 150th Panzer Brigade would disguise themselves as an American unit. They would dress in American uniforms, and would be equipped with U.S. vehicles and weapons (when it turned out that a sufficient quantity of captured vehicles were not available, the difference was made up with German vehicles mocked up to look like American vehicles). At the start of the offensive, they would follow behind the panzer spearheads, and then advance behind the American lines in order to secure critical objectives in the rear. Skorzeny also assembled nine small teams of men, all fluent in English, who were to roam the American rear areas and engage in acts of sabotage and disinformation.

The Germans would employ the latest weaponry available to them, in the greatest numbers that could be spared. Among the 800 aircraft eventually gathered to support the attack would be 60 of the new jet fighters, which promised to outperform anything that the Americans could send aloft to face them. The 70-ton Tiger VIB heavy tank was a monstrous, imposing weapon; two battalions of the beasts were available for use by the 6th SS Panzer Army. Some of the Panther tanks were now equipped with infrared night vision equipment (a state of the art advance not possessed by the Allies). And Hitler would make it a point of personal focus to bring the latest heavy tank destroyer, the massive JagdTiger, off the assembly line in time to participate in the attack.

The technical superiority of the German army was not limited to the "big ticket" items. The volksgrenadier divisions were equipped in large numbers with the latest assault rifle, the MP-44, which could be fired in either semi-automatic or automatic mode. The Luftwaffe paratroop divisions were armed with a successful variant of this weapon, the Fallschirmjager Gewehr 42 assault rifle. The common perception of German infantry is that they were armed with bolt-action rifles. The truth of the matter is that, by 1944, the ratio of submachine guns to rifles in the volksgrenadier divisions stood at 1.3 to 1.

The Germans had an excellent machine gun, the MG-42, which was extremely well designed and portable. At only 26 pounds, it could be handled relatively easily by a single gunner (the lightest American machine gun, by comparison, weighed in at over 42 pounds). When equipped with a heavy-duty tripod and telescopic sight, the effective range of the MG-42 was 2000 meters. The MG-42's rate of fire of 1,200 rounds per minute was more than double that of American machine guns.

The Germans also had an edge in anti-tank weapons. A large supply of panzerfausts (single-use bazookas) greatly increased the tank killing capability of the German infantry formations. Their primary towed anti-tanks guns were the 75mm Pak 40 and the dreaded 88. Their various assault guns and tanks were equipped with high velocity cannons that could penetrate virtually every American armored vehicle at long range (the one exception to this being the M4A3E2 Sherman, which had substantial armor above and beyond that of the normal Sherman tank).

Despite their technological edge in many areas, the Germans had one glaring area of weakness when it came to equipment, and that was in regard to transportation. Despite all the glory and notoriety achieved by Hitler's vaunted panzer divisions, the German army was still over-reliant on horses for moving supplies, artillery, and heavy weapons. The volksgrenadier divisions had very little motor transport, and the pace of their advance was limited to the speed at which an infantryman could set one foot in front of the other. Even the panzer and panzer grenadier divisions, which were built on the premise of being fully motorized, did not always have adequate vehicles to mobilize their infantry component. Halftracks were in short supply, and trucks were used as a substitute. But in many cases, there were not enough trucks to be had, and not all of the division's infantry could be motorized.

If German industry delivered as expected during the weeks leading up to the offensive, Hitler could count on having a generally well-equipped, powerful force at his disposal (hampered as it might be by the lack of transport). But there was one more lingering, irresolvable issue that stared the Germans in the face as they planned their offensive. They did not have enough petrol.

The simple fact of the matter was that gasoline was in short supply. Though their factories had withstood the pounding of the Allied air forces, and were even producing some items in record numbers (such as tanks), gasoline and oil production was another matter altogether. Allied efforts to cut into the German petrol supply had been quite effective. In fact, this was the most successful aspect of the Allied strategic bombing campaign. Though the Germans managed to stockpile some 500 million gallons for the offensive, about half of that supply remained east of the Rhine River.

At the start of the offensive, the German command knew that they did not have enough gasoline to get their forces to Antwerp. Even getting to the Meuse was in doubt. Their success was dependent upon capturing allied stockpiles of gasoline. The decision to proceed under this circumstance is perhaps the greatest testimony to the degree of desperation that laced Hitler's plan.

The German Plan

Hitler never wavered on the ultimate objective for this formidable force: the vital port city of Antwerp. The route of attack would take the Germans through the Ardennes region, across the Meuse River, and on to Antwerp. If successful, Montgomery's 21st Army Group (which consisted of the Canadian First and British Second armies), plus the American Ninth and First armies (save for whatever elements of the First that found themselves south of the penetration), would be trapped north of the advancing German forces and would be cut off from their primary source of supply at Antwerp. The

Germans would then go about rolling up the Allied forces trapped north of the penetration. In Hitler's own words: "If all goes well, the offensive will set the stage for the annihilation of the bulk of twenty to thirty divisions. It will be another Dunkirk."

Each of the three German armies participating in the offensive had a specific mission. The Sixth SS Panzer Army, attacking on the German right, would carry the main weight of the attack, and held the responsibility for capturing Antwerp, which was slightly more than 100 miles (as the crow flies) from its starting positions. As the Sixth SS Panzer Army advanced, its infantry divisions would peel off and face north to protect the base of the salient and right flank of the advance. The panzer divisions would continue the thrust toward Antwerp.

The Fifth Panzer Army, occupying the center position of the three armies, would advance in tandem with the Sixth SS Panzer. Their primary role was the protection of the left flank of the Sixth SS beyond the Meuse River. Their main axis of advance would carry them toward the city of Brussels.

The Seventh Army, located furthest to the south, would attack in tandem with the Fifth Panzer Army, but would advance only as far west as the Meuse River. As they advanced, the divisions of the Seventh Army would peel off and face south with the intent of creating a defensive barrier against any counterattack that might come courtesy of Patton's Third Army, which was located south of the Ardennes.

As the German attack progressed, the plan called for secondary strikes to take place against portions of the Allied line both north and south of the Ardennes. These supporting attacks would be on a limited scale, and would presumably serve to tie down Allied forces that might otherwise be dispatched toward the Ardennes in response to the main German attack. Should the Allies thin their lines out north and south of the Ardennes in order to send units toward the main German threat, these attacks might also exploit whatever opportunity became available by virtue of a diminished enemy force in their sector.

The timetable for the whole affair was aggressive. The plan called for the lead units to cross the Meuse on the very first day of the offensive, and for Antwerp to be in German hands well within the first week. Oddly enough, the plan for what was to be done after the capture of Antwerp was very nebulous. This was no doubt a reflection of the German generals' lack of hope for reaching Antwerp in the first place.

Obstacles, Delays, and Alternatives Considered

The original timing for Hitler's attack was mid to late November (later refined to November 25). The date was influenced by two key factors: 1) the initial estimates for putting the requested 30 divisions into position, and 2) the anticipated onset of poor flying weather typical of late autumn/early winter in northwest Europe.

Given the challenges faced by the Germans, this timetable was simply too aggressive. During September and October, the few German reserves that were available were either attacking Patton in the Lorraine region, or were being thrown into the breach to halt the vanguard of the Allied armies as they approached the German border. In fact, the very day after Hitler's original announcement of his counterattack scheme, the

Allies launched Operation Market-Garden, to which the Germans had to respond by committing reserve forces.

The dilemma of holding the Allied advance in check while keeping the units assigned to the Ardennes offensive out of the line continued during the month of November. The Americans resumed the offensive early that month, forcing the commitment of German reserves in several areas. The most negative repercussion occurred south of the Ardennes, when the Panzer Lehr Division was drawn from the reserve in an attempt to blunt the advance of the U.S. Third and Seventh armies. The Panzer Lehr was one of seven panzer divisions slated to participate in the opening of the Ardennes offensive, and it was dealt a heavy blow by the Fourth Armored — a blow from which it would not fully recover prior to the start of the offensive in the Ardennes.

Given these circumstances, not even the will and iron fist of Adolph Hitler could make a mid-November start date a reality. And even with the grace of three extra weeks beyond the initial date set for the offensive, the Germans failed to muster the 30 divisions originally envisioned for the attack.

On December 15, as Hitler's three armies sat poised to attack the following day, only 20 divisions were available for the initial wave. The Sixth SS Panzer came to the party with four SS panzer divisions, a parachute division, and four volksgrenadier divisions (this roll call is a bit of an overstatement, since two of the panzer divisions, the 2nd and 9th SS, arrived so close in time to the start of the attack that they were not available to participate in the initial assault). The neighboring Fifth Panzer Army consisted of three panzer divisions and four volksgrenadier divisions. The Seventh Army consisted of only four divisions (one parachute and three volksgrenadier). More panzer, panzer grenadier, and volksgrenadier divisions would be made available after the start of the offensive, bringing the total number of divisions engaged during the full course of the battle to twenty-eight. But some of these arrived far too late in the battle to have a decisive influence on the outcome.

Even though the initial force was limited to 20 divisions, this was enough to guarantee overwhelming force for the Germans during the initial assault. At some specific points of concentration, the Germans would be attacking in numbers in excess of 8 to 1. Given that a ratio of 3 to 1 is considered the desired minimum for success when on the offensive, the German commanders felt very confident of their chances coming out of the starting blocks. Their enthusiasm flowed right down to the combat soldiers on the front line, and German morale reached a point that had not been seen in months, if not years.

But the German commanders also knew that the force at hand was not large enough to achieve the objective of capturing Antwerp. With this realization in mind, some of the German staff lobbied hard for what became known as "the small solution." This was an attack designed to encircle the American First and Ninth armies, and to capture the Allied stocks and airfields in the vicinity of Liege. But Hitler, after allowing for an airing of differences, dismissed all alternative suggestions. He insisted in the end that his original plan not be compromised. Attempts to persuade him to adopt the "small solution" continued until just days before the start of the offensive, and he grew increasingly irritated by the efforts to change his mind.

In the end, perhaps the most prescient observation was made by Field Marshal Walter Model. On November 27, he warned:

Should the attack be stopped at the Meuse due to lack of reserves, the only result will be a bulge in the line and not the destruction of sizeable military forces... The widely stretched flanks, *especially in the south* [emphasis added], will only invite enemy counteraction.

The German Armies

The three attacking armies were organized under Army Group B, which was commanded by Field Marshal Model. The 15th Army, located to the north of the 6th SS Panzer Army, also fell under the command of Army Group B, but would not participate directly in the offensive. Model's forces were arrayed from north to south along a 60-mile stretch of front that ran roughly concurrent with the border between Germany and the countries of Belgium and Luxembourg. In a few areas, the Americans had penetrated the West Wall, and held positions slightly inside the German border.

The 6th SS Panzer Army, commanded by Sepp Dietrich, was the best equipped of the three armies. The nucleus of the 6th Panzer consisted of four SS panzer divisions (1st, 2nd, 9th, and 12th), all of which were fairly well rested prior to the start of the battle. Only the 1st and 12th were near full strength in manpower, however, and the 1st SS was the only one of the four close to its full complement of 100 Panzers (the 9th SS being the most under-strength, with only 66 tanks available). Some of the tank shortages were offset by the attachment of heavy Panzer battalions (equipped with the huge Tiger VIB tanks) or tank destroyer battalions (equipped with a variety of TD designs, the best of which was the JagdPanther, but perhaps the most awe-inspiring of which was the JagdTiger, with its mammoth 128mm cannon). Perhaps the panzer divisions' biggest weakness, aside from the fuel shortage, was that training was not up to par in all of the units, especially in regard to offensive tactics. The divisions had been reconstructed with new, inexperienced soldiers after the debacle in France, and there had not been time enough to complete their training.

With the 2nd and 9th SS Panzer divisions unavailable at the start of the offensive, the burden of spearheading the 6th SS Panzer Army's attack fell on the 1st and 12th SS Panzer divisions. Dietrich's panzer divisions would not be used in the initial attack against the forward American defenses, however. This was the result of a direct order from Hitler, who insisted that the opening attack would consist of a massive artillery bombardment, followed with an assault by the volksgrenadier divisions. After the infantry had torn holes in the forward American defenses, the panzer divisions would be inserted for the drive to the Meuse River.

The two panzer divisions would advance in tandem, with the 12th on the right, and the 1st on the left. The infantry divisions (arranged from north to south, the 272nd VG, 326th VG, 277th VG, 12thVG, and 3rd Parachute), having completed their initial mission of opening the way for the panzer divisions, would then peel off and face north to protect the right flank of the penetration from counterattacks. At the start of the offensive, only two American infantry divisions and portions of two cavalry groups opposed this impressive force.

The 5th Panzer Army was commanded by General der Panzertruppen Hasso von

Manteuffel, who had held the position since mid September. His force consisted of regular Wehrmacht units, as opposed to the Waffen SS troops that gave the 6th SS Panzer Army its name. Manteuffel's three panzer divisions (the 2nd, 116th, and Panzer Lehr) were commanded by experienced generals, and there were a number of seasoned veterans within their ranks. But they were handicapped by equipment shortages to a greater degree than the SS units, who benefited from special consideration when it came to filling their equipment quotas. As with the 6th SS Panzer Army, the training time available for the units of the 5th Panzer was well below what Manteuffel desired.

The 2nd Panzer Division was the best equipped of the three panzer divisions. The other two divisions were barely at 50 percent strength in tanks. As with the divisions of the 6th SS Panzer Army, the shortfalls were made up for in part by attaching separate tank destroyer or assault gun units. These weapons could function in a tank-like role, and would have to suffice. The 559th and 653rd Anti-Tank Battalions and the 243rd Assault Gun Brigade were all attached to the Panzer Lehr Division (the 653rd would not arrive in time for the start of the offensive, but a small portion of the battalion would play a key role later in the battle). Infantry support for the Fifth Panzer Army consisted of the 18th, 62nd, 560th, and 26th Volksgrenadier divisions (listed as they were positioned from north to south at the start of the offensive).

While lighter in firepower than Hitler's pet 6th SS Panzer Army, Manteuffel's force would have the advantage of taking on the Americans at the thinnest portion of their line. In all, his seven divisions would be engaging slightly less than two American infantry divisions and a portion of one cavalry group on the first day, and they were spread out along a much broader front than the two infantry divisions facing the 6th SS Panzer Army.

In addition to the advantage of attacking at the weakest points in the U.S. VIII Corps' line, Manteuffel would enjoy a better road system than was available to Dietrich. Making full use of that road system depended, however, on the capture of two very critical road junctions: St. Vith, which was located just south of the boundary separating the 5th and 6th armies, and Bastogne, which lay squarely in Manteuffel's zone. Short of the Meuse River crossings, these were the most critical objectives on the agenda for Manteuffel during the first day or two of the offensive. Given the relative proximity of both of these towns to the German start line, it was considered a given that they would fall in rapid fashion. In fact, the German command was so confident of the capture of the towns, they ordered a significant portion of the lead panzer forces to bypass them and head for the Meuse. Capturing the towns would be the responsibility of the volksgrenadier divisions (this would turn out to be a devastating error).

The German 7th Army, commanded by General Erich Brandenberger, had the unenviable role of providing protection for the southern flank of the advance. Of the three armies, the 7th was the least equipped for the task at hand. Consisting of the 352nd, 212th, and 276th Volksgrenadier divisions, plus the 5th Parachute Division, it would be charged with securing the southern shoulder and flank of the offensive. Its task would be made more difficult by the fact that it would have to keep pace with the motorized elements of the 5th Panzer Army. The divisions of the 7th Army had little integral motorized capability, and if the 5th Panzer Army advanced according to the original timetable, the volksgrenadiers and paratroopers (Fallschirmjagers, in the German vernacular) would be very hard pressed to keep up with the advance.

If the attack went according to plan, the 7th Army would have to defend a line that was some 65 miles in length. This would be an extremely tough task for only four divisions. This was recognized as a weakness in the plan, however, so additional resources were to be added to the 7th Army after the start of the battle.

Making matters even tougher for Brandenberger was the paucity of armor he was allotted. There were approximately 30 self-propelled assault guns available to support his entire army. The 352nd Volksgrenadier Division was equipped with perhaps a half dozen Hetzer tank destroyers, the 212th VG Division had perhaps five StuG IIIs, and the 5th Parachute Division had 18 to 20 StuG IIIs, courtesy of the attached 11th Assault Gun Brigade (some accounts claim the 11th had as many as 30 StuG IIIs available, but if this were true, the count for the Seventh Army would have to be raised by up to 10 assault guns). The 276th VG Division had no armor support at all.

As the 7th Army moved west, its divisions would eventually turn and face south, where they would assume defensive positions in anticipation of an American counterattack. From east to west, the defensive alignment would be the 212th, 276th, 352nd, and 5th. The 5th Parachute Division (in German, the term for Parachute Division is "Fallschirmjägerdivision"; the abbreviation FJ is commonly used), being the westernmost of the four units, would have the greatest distance to travel before assuming its blocking positions, and thus would be under the greatest pressure to keep up with the advance of the 5th Panzer Army to its right. Led by Colonel Ludwig Heilmann, the 5th FJ Division was over 16,000 men strong (with attachments) at the start of the battle, making it the most powerful of the 7th Army's divisions.

Heilmann's division could trace its roots back to the early days of the German elite paratroops. The division was formed during April 1944, when it was built around a nucleus of battalions from the 3rd and 4th FJ regiments, supplemented by volunteers from various Luftwaffe ground units. The 3rd FJ Regiment's history extended as far back as 1940, and it had been involved in the airborne attack on the island of Crete. But by the spring of 1944, the title of "parachute division" was deceiving, since incoming members of the division were not trained to conduct drops.

When the Allies invaded Normandy, the units of the 5th FJ Division were scattered across the Brittany region of France. The division's elements were eventually drawn into the American portion of the front in Normandy. They arrived piecemeal from their various stations, and were thrown into the line upon their arrival. The division suffered heavy losses during the fighting in Normandy, and was eventually decimated during Operation Cobra and the subsequent breakout through Avranches. The remnants of the division limped back toward the German border.

Colonel Heilmann, who would be promoted to the rank of Generalmajor while the Battle of the Bulge was in progress, was a highly experienced officer. He had been involved with the Fallschirmjäger during the days when they actually jumped from planes. He was recognized as a hero during the airborne operation at Crete, and went on to command the paratroopers who conducted the famous defense of Monte Cassino in Italy. The commander of the German Tenth Army, to which Heilmann belonged while serving in Italy, said that "No troops but [Heilmann's] could have held at Cassino."

Hitler himself insisted that Heilmann should take command of the 5th FJ Division when it was being reformed during the autumn of 1944.

In all likelihood, if Patton struck from the south, it would be the 5th FJ Division that would bear the brunt of his attack. More than anything else, it was the nature of the terrain that made the positions of the 5th FJ Division the most likely magnet for the Third Army. While beautiful in peacetime, the dense woods, deep ravines, and swollen streams and rivers that characterize the country of Luxembourg pose a nightmare for would-be attackers. Additionally, the Sure River, which flows on a zigzag course through the country, provides a superb natural defensive barrier against attacks advancing along a north-south axis. Quite simply, the nature of the terrain in Luxembourg would not allow for the deployment of armor in force. Any attack by Patton through this area would have to be primarily an infantry affair, and it would be relatively easy to defend against it. The three volksgrenadier divisions would take up their positions within this region. If Patton were to strike an armored blow against the German salient, it would likely come elsewhere.

The only decent terrain for an armored advance was to the west of Luxembourg. The Sure River extends from Luxembourg into the neighboring country of Belgium; the river continues to provide an excellent defensive barrier, but the countryside in this region, especially north of the river, is less heavily wooded and less severe in terms of elevation changes (increasingly so as one moves further west). More importantly, there were several key highways that led from France across the border into Belgium, and they were well suited for mechanized forces. In the original German plan, it was the 5th Parachute Division's responsibility to cover the terrain from the town of Martelange all the way to the Meuse River, which meant that the Fallschirmjägers would be solely responsible for defending those quality roads.

Of the Seventh Army's four divisions, the 5th FJ was the best equipped for this demanding task. In addition to the anti-tank capability provided by the 11th Assault Gun Brigade, the division was bolstered by a high complement of towed anti-tank guns of both the 75m and 88mm variety. They would begin the battle with 51 towed AT guns (this number did not include any of the additional guns held by the 7th Army, which could be made available to the 5th FJ). In fact, the 5th FJ Division had more AT guns at its disposal than any of the divisions participating in the entire offensive.

In addition to their beefed up anti-tank capability, the 5th Parachute Division also benefited from an organizational structure that gave it much greater strength than the typical volksgrenadier division of 1944. The parachute divisions were composed of three regiments, with each regiment consisting of three battalions of infantry. The volksgrenadier divisions, in contrast, were composed of only two battalions per regiment. As a result, the 5th FJ Division was nearly 50 percent larger than its volksgrenadier counterparts. Due to the nature of its mission, it would need all the strength it could muster … and then some.

The Allied Situation

When the Allied forces approached the German border during the autumn of 1944, it was anticipated that the next great effort on the West Front would involve the securing of bridgeheads across the Rhine. But the enemy defenses coalesced once the Allies drew close to German soil, and it started to become clear that the road ahead would be a tough one. The German defense of places like Arnhem, Aachen, Huertgen, and Metz had been tenacious, and the cost for the Allies in these battles had been quite high. In fact, more American lives had been lost during the first two months of the autumn campaign than had been lost in the first three months following D-Day. Despite these losses, the gain in territory during the months of October and November was but a small fraction of what had been gained in the period prior to that. A high price had been paid, and arguably too little accomplished in return.

Much to the consternation of some of the generals involved, Eisenhower had elected to execute the advance to the Rhine River along a broad front, as opposed to a concentrated thrust on a narrow sector. But despite the advantages in men and material accumulated by the Allies, the advantage was not so tremendous that offensive concentrations could be achieved in every zone. In fact, some areas would have to be thinly manned in order to allow for reasonable offensive concentrations to be achieved in the desired sectors. The Ardennes region was the most notable area where units were overextended.

When American forces first arrived in the Ardennes in mid–September, they were greeted by a strong enemy response at the German border. Bradley quickly assumed defensive positions there, and the Ardennes sector soon settled into a state of relative calm, with both sides seemingly content to not disrupt the status quo. For the Americans, the Ardennes become an area used for the rest and refitting of exhausted divisions, and a training ground for green divisions entering the theatre of operations. The American divisions positioned here would have to be content remaining relatively idle as the offensive resumed along other parts of the front.

The Positions of the U.S. VIII Corps in the Ardennes

The U.S. VIII Corps was responsible for the lion's share of the front in the Ardennes. By mid December, the VIII Corps, commanded by Maj. General Troy H. Middleton, consisted of the 4th, 28th, and 106th Infantry divisions, two thirds of the 9th Armored Division (CCB/9 was on loan to V Corps to the north), and the 14th Cavalry Group. There were other supporting elements as well, such as artillery and engineer units.

VIII Corps was responsible for some 88 miles of winding front, stretching from well below Echternach in the south, to the small village of Lanzerath in the north (Lanzerath being located on the northern edge of a sector called the "Loshiem Gap," which was a historic gateway into the Ardennes).

The 4th Infantry Division, commanded by Maj. General Raymond O. Barton, had moved into the southern part of the region, taking up positions along a 35 mile stretch of front tucked along the west bank of the Sauer and Moselle Rivers. In this position, it held the right flank of VIII Corps, all the way down to the boundary between the U.S. First and Third armies. Barton's division had been dealt a severe blow during the battle of the Huertgen Forest, and was in the process of absorbing replacements.

**The Ardennes
December 1944**

Inserted on the left of the 4th Infantry Division was approximately one third of the green 9th Armored Division, in the form of CCA/9, commanded by Colonel Thomas Harrold. The 9th Armored, commanded by Major General John W. Leonard, had arrived in the Ardennes in November, and was untested in combat. It was well equipped and at full strength, however, and its tank battalions had the benefit of some of the latest 76mm Sherman tanks, as well as the M24 "Chaffee" light tank, which was a superb upgrade over the M5 light tank. On the morning of December 16, only one element of CCA would be in a defensive position near the front, this being the 60th Armored Infantry Battalion, which held positions close to the line of the river, near the towns of Dillingen and Bigelbach. CCA's 19th Tank Battalion would be in reserve positions at the start of the battle.

Continuing north along the west bank of the Our River were the positions of the veteran 28th Infantry Division. The Keystone Division — so named due to its roots in Pennsylvania — had received a terrible beating in the Huertgen Forest during the first half of November. In fact, it suffered such heavy losses both there and in Normandy, that the unofficial nickname of the division became "the Bloody Bucket" (a sad interpretation of the red keystone patch worn on their shoulder).

While in the Huertgen, the 28th had struggled in vain for two weeks to capture the town of Schmidt. The effort exhausted and depleted the division, and it was transferred to the Ardennes for rest and refitting on November 19. Commanded by Maj. General Norman D. "Dutch" Cota, it occupied a line that was some 23 miles long. If there was any good news for the division, it was that their units had been brought up to full strength by the time the German offensive began, and they had had almost a full month to dig in and prepare their defensive positions.

Another element of the 9th Armored Division was held in VIII Corps reserve further back behind the lines of the 28th Infantry Division. Combat Command Reserve, commanded by Col. Joseph H. Gilbreth, was about the same strength as CCA/9, with a tank battalion, armored infantry battalion, and artillery battalion providing the bulk of its firepower. It was based near the town of Trois Vierges.

To the north of Cota's division was the newly arrived 106th Infantry Division, commanded by Major General Alan Jones. The division arrived on the continent on December 2, and had just recently moved into its positions in the Ardennes. Its first assignment was to relieve the veteran 2nd Infantry Division, which was being pulled out of its positions in the Schnee Eifel to participate in an offensive by V Corps to the north. Two regiments of the 106th (the 422nd and 423rd) were holding positions along the Schnee Eifel ridge (a location that would prove to be extremely vulnerable to encirclement). The third regiment (the 424th) was located further south, and just east of the Our River. Attached to the 106th was the 14th Cavalry Group, which occupied positions north of the 422nd and 423rd regiments in what was known as the "Loshiem Gap." Including the positions of the 14th Cavalry, Jones' green division had to hold a front that was 22 miles in length.

The zone of control of Middleton's VIII Corps ended with the left flank of the 14th Cavalry Group. It was a huge expanse of territory, and under normal conditions, would be viewed as untenable from a defensive standpoint. But conventional wisdom within the Allied command structure held firm that the Germans did not have the capacity for a major counteroffensive. And even if they did, the Ardennes would surely be the last place they would strike, since there were no objectives of significance in the area behind the American lines.

The U.S. V Corps

Just north of Middleton's VIII Corps was the U.S. V Corps, commanded by Maj. General Leonard T. Gerow. Unlike the quiet defensive posture of VIII Corps, Gerow's force had resumed the offensive in its sector just three days prior to the German counteroffensive. Gerow's attack was part of a general offensive north of the Ardennes that also involved the U.S. VII Corps. The timing and nature of this attack would have a direct impact on the course of the German attack in the Ardennes.

On December 9, VII Corps (located north of V Corps) had kicked off the U.S. First Army offensive designed to push the Germans back to the line of the Roer River, and in the process, capture the vital dams that controlled the depth and flow of the Roer. The mission of capturing the dams belonged specifically to V Corps, and on December 13, it began its role in the offensive. Two of Gerow's divisions, the 8th and 78th Infantry, were operating north of the Ardennes, and were attacking east toward the river. To the south, in an area concentrated between the Loshiem Gap and the scenic village of Monschau, were the 99th and 2nd Infantry divisions.

The 2nd Infantry Division was beefed up considerably for its role in the offensive. There was extra artillery support provided by V Corps, and CCB of the 9th Armored Division (on loan from VIII Corps) was available to exploit any success achieved by Robertson's division. The 2nd ID was also allocated an extra tank destroyer battalion above and beyond its normal attachment of one tank battalion and one tank destroyer battalion. Most of the 99th Infantry Division, commanded by Major General Walter E. Lauer, was serving in a relatively passive role; the 2nd Infantry would attack through its positions in a northeasterly direction, ultimately driving north toward the dams.

The Final Days Before the Storm

During the fading days of autumn, Field Marshal Model's Army Group B began assembling its forces ever closer to the line of engagement with the U.S. First Army. Assisted by several days of thick, leaden clouds that blanketed the German's assembly area, they were able to avoid the prying eyes of Allied aircraft, and managed to position 18 divisions within striking distance. The Germans maintained their routine activities close to the American's forward outposts, and General Hodges' divisions showed no sign that they suspected anything was brewing.

On December 12, Hitler assembled his staff at his underground HQ bunker near Frankfurt. He was a physical wreck, as his condition had continued to worsen since the July 20 assassination attempt (some accounts have laid blame on his physician, who was prescribing dubious medications for the Fuehrer's ailments). On this occasion, he summoned up a great deal of energy and emotion that fueled a diatribe about the political and military ramifications of the pending attack. While he probably convinced not a single person that the offensive could succeed, he did manage to instill the will to give it their best shot.

December 12 marked another meeting, this one on the Allied side, which would ultimately influence the course of events. On that day, Patton expressed concern over the possibility of a German attack, either against the First Army's VIII Corps or his own XX Corps. He was aware of a build-up of enemy forces around Trier, and as a precautionary move, he positioned the III Corps (then consisting of the 6th Armored and 26th Infantry divisions) near Saarbrucken. With his resources so positioned, he felt he could respond to a threat to either of the corps. He was already thinking about what would be required if he had to turn elements of the Third Army to the north; his foresight would pay great dividends.

During the final days leading up to the German attack, the VIII Corps went about its usual business. For the 28th and 4th Infantry divisions, routine patrolling and the business of absorbing and training replacements dominated the agenda. The green 106th Infantry Division started settling into their new positions. They had a lot of work to do, since the veteran 2nd Infantry had, upon their relief by the 106th, taken with them some of their valued communications equipment, leaving the 106th with the task of restructuring the communication network between the regiment and division head-quarters, as well as communications back to VIII Corps HQ. The "Golden Lions" were also still in the preliminary stages of developing operational plans for holding their sector.

On the front of V Corps, the 2nd Infantry Division had gone on the attack on December 13. Progress was slow during the first three days, but on the night of the 15th, they managed to tear a 1000-meter hole in the German line, and plans were made to commit some of their reserves the following morning in order to exploit their success. Prospects for the offensive were bright, and Robertson was looking forward to blowing the front wide open on the morning of the 16th.

There would indeed be a strong blow delivered in the Ardennes on the morning of December 16. Little did Robertson — or anyone else in the Allied command — know that it would be the Germans who would be the aggressor.

13. Out of the Mist

The Opening Salvos

Shortly after midnight on December 16, under a cold, dark, moonless sky, the Battle of the Bulge began, not with a bang, but with the stealth of rubber boats paddled cautiously across the Our River. Here, in front of the positions of the U.S. 28th Infantry Division, soldiers from the 26th Volksgrenadier Division stole across the ice cold waters of the river that separated them from their enemy. They infiltrated the positions of the 28th Infantry Division's 110th Regiment, and then waited in silence for the start of the barrage that would mark the start of the main show.

And what a show it was. At approximately 5:30 in the morning, the artillery, mortars, and rocket launchers of Model's Army Group B opened fire on the American positions in the Ardennes, delivering the largest barrage the Germans would ever mount in the west. Up and down the winding, 85-mile front, shells and rockets cascaded through the dark fog and mist, and rained down on the unsuspecting men of the U.S. VIII and V Corps.

Hitler's plan had come together about as well as anyone under his command could have expected. Against all odds, the Germans had assembled a potent offensive force of three armies, backed by a strong contingent of artillery and air support. While the size of the force fell short of Hitler's original aspirations, it still greatly outnumbered the American forces aligned against it on December 16. The question now was simply a matter of whether or not the objectives chosen for it were realistic and attainable.

There was another element of the Fuehrer's plan that had fallen into place on the morning of December 16. Hitler had been counting on weather that would favor his efforts, and as the calendar rolled past the midpoint of the month, nature delivered just what he had hoped for. Gray, sullen skies hung over the Ardennes throughout the night of December 15, and continued to blanket the Ardennes on the first day of the attack, providing the best possible defense against the American *jabos*. Heavy fog, characteristic of the region during this time of year, severely limited the visibility at ground level until the sun rose high and bright enough to burn it away. The temperature during the night of December 15 had dropped into the low 30s to high 20s, which was a mixed blessing. On the negative side, it made for an uncomfortable night for any soldier not fortunate enough to have accommodations in a building. On the positive side, it helped firm up the ground, thus making vehicular movement over the dirt roads and fields a bit easier.

There was one other natural condition that favored the Germans, and this one could be planned for with certainty. During this time of year in northwest Europe, the days grow increasingly short, with the longest night of the year falling at the winter solstice on December 21. Darkness was the friend of the Germans, as it reduced the amount of time the *jabos* could spend overhead hunting down their troop and supply columns. It meant less daylight for ground operations, but this was an acceptable trade-off.

The opening barrage did not last long in the 5th Panzer Army's zone, since Manteuffel wanted to get his attack underway as rapidly as possible. Within 30 minutes, firing had subsided in his sector, and the aforementioned volksgrenadiers got to work. In front of the 6th SS Panzer and 7th armies, however, the bombardment continued for up to an hour and a half, depending on the location. Whether for 30 minutes or 90 minutes, the barrage was an extraordinary and unusual event for this section of the American front.

The opening artillery fire certainly caught the Americans by surprise. But despite the unexpected timing and weight of the barrage, the damage done to American positions was relatively light. The fact that the Americans had been in prepared positions for so long prior to December 16 was a decided plus in their favor, as many of the trenches were reinforced with log roofs that helped protect them during the withering fire. Perhaps the biggest impact was on communications, as the rain of shells severed telephone wires along several sections of the front. It is fair to say that American senses were rattled a bit by the intensity of the strike, but for the most part, it did not create the wholesale panic or abandonment of positions that the Germans were hoping for.

The Sixth SS Panzer Army

The script for the 6th SS Panzer Army was a simple one: disrupt and numb the untested troops of the U.S. 99th Infantry Division with the opening barrage, and then smash their forward positions with the full weight of the volksgrenadier and parachute divisions. The 1st SS and 12th SS Panzer Division would then burst through into the American rear, and advance unimpeded along their assigned routes toward the bridges spanning the Meuse River. From there, the advance would continue toward Antwerp. The only problem was, someone forgot to give the Americans the script.

When the first day drew to a close, the Americans facing the 6th SS Panzer Army had given up little ground. From Monschau south to Lanzerath, V Corps held firm. To be sure, there had been heavy casualties among some of the units of the 99th Infantry Division. But the Germans had suffered more (the U.S. 2nd Infantry got through the day relatively unscathed, since their presence in the line had not been anticipated by the German planners). Instead of racing for the Meuse River, the vaunted SS panzer divisions were stuck behind the German infantry, waiting for the opportunity to move forward. There would be no breakthrough by the 6th SS Panzer Army on December 16.

During the next two days, the 2nd Infantry Division pulled off a masterful withdrawal from the salient they had carved out during their attack toward the Roer River dams. Together with the 99th Infantry Division, they executed a valiant delaying action, falling back through the villages of Rocherath and Krinkelt, and eventually settling into prepared positions along Elsenborn ridge. Together with reinforcements from the 9th Infantry Division and the 5th Armored Division, and supported by a massive array of artillery, they formed a solid wall that anchored the American line along the northern shoulder of the expanding German salient.

Other reinforcements had been sent with great haste to extend the defensive line further to the west. By midday on December 17, the 1st Infantry Division's 26th Regiment was in place near Butgenbach, with two of its battalions digging in near Dom Butgenbach, midway between Butgenbach and Bullingen. Later, the 16th Regiment would take up positions on the right flank of the 26th, thus extending the American line as far west as Waimes. On December 18, the American line was extended still further to the west, when the 30th Infantry Division arrived and placed its left flank near Malmedy, tying in with the right flank of the 16th Regiment.

When the 30th Infantry Division started out for the Ardennes, their original mission orders were to launch a counterattack toward the southeast (presumably to seal the gap that existed between Dom Butgenbach and St. Vith). But upon the 30th's arrival, the plan was changed in response to a lone armored penetration that had finally been achieved by the 6th SS Panzer Army. The 30th Infantry was now charged with containing the spearhead from the 1st SS Panzer Division and solidifying the American line west of Malmedy.

The German spearhead was that of Kampfgruppe Peiper, a powerful combined arms force that now posed a serious threat to the American rear area, including the First Army Headquarters at Spa. Given the role that the 1st SS Panzer Division would soon play in the history of the Fourth Armored Division, it is worth exploring the events surrounding KG Peiper in more detail.

The Breakthrough by Kampfgruppe Peiper

On the night of December 16, an impatient Jochen Peiper brought his panzers forward to the tiny village of Lanzerath, which had finally fallen that evening to the 3rd FJ Division. A lone I&R platoon from the 99th Infantry Division had held the 3rd FJ at bay for the entire day, and in the process, upset the timetable for getting KG Peiper on the road toward the Meuse River. Frustrated by the delay, Peiper decided to push through on his own during the hours after midnight.

Many of the same Americans who had resisted with such fortitude during the daylight hours of December 16 were now literally caught sleeping by Peiper's advancing tanks and infantry. Jolted from their beds, many of the U.S. soldiers at the village of Honsfeld were rounded up in the early morning darkness. Here the men of the SS committed what would be the first of several atrocities during the Ardennes offensive, as they gunned down some of their American prisoners in cold blood. Half-dressed GIs, barefoot and shivering in the streets, were mowed down with burp guns. Some of the Americans in the village tried to fight back, but Peiper's tanks and infantry had penetrated too far and too fast. Peiper's force quickly mopped up Honsfeld, and prepared to continue its advance to the west.

Peiper's assigned route leading west from Honsfeld was nothing more than a dirt trail. The temperature had climbed during the past day, and most of the snow was melting. He was greatly concerned that the "road" he was to follow would turn into a muddy quagmire under the weight of his heavy vehicles. So rather than stick to this route, he decided to veer north into the zone of the 12th SS Panzer Division. He would take the higher quality paved road that led to Bullingen, and from there, would swing back to the southwest, eventually picking up his assigned route.

As the eastern horizon began to brighten on December 17, Peiper closed in on Bullingen. Some American engineers offered resistance along the road leading into the town, but there wasn't much they could do in the face of Peiper's overwhelming strength. When Peiper's force entered Bullingen, they caught many of the Americans by surprise. Most of these men belonged to rear area elements supporting the 2nd and 99th divisions. Some tried to resist, while others tried to hide (those that initially found hiding spots were rounded up over the course of the next three days). Unfortunately, the Americans at Bullingen allowed some 50,000 gallons of gasoline to fall into Peiper's hands. Adding insult to injury, some of the captured Americans were forced to refuel Peiper's vehicles with the captured petrol.

Peiper's presence at Bullingen represented a critical turning point in the battle. At that moment, it was within Peiper's power to completely unhinge the U.S. V Corps. If he had advanced north, through Wirtzfeld, he would have been in the rear area of the 2nd Infantry Division, and the forces opposing the 6th SS Panzer Army's divisions to the north would have been hard pressed to hold their positions. If he had advanced to the west, he would have easily swept into the town of Butgenbach, which was where the 99th Infantry Division was headquartered (the 1st Infantry Division had yet to arrive to block the route). This would have enabled him to outflank virtually the entire front of V Corps. The 99th and 2nd Infantry divisions might easily have been surrounded and destroyed.

But Peiper's priority was not the destruction of these American divisions. His mission was to advance to the Meuse River, and to that end, he turned his task force to the southwest, in order to place it back on a route closer to his original assigned roads. The U.S. V Corps had dodged a bullet of immense proportions.

KG Peiper left Bullingen at about 9:30 A.M. on December 17. His route to the southwest carried him to the tiny crossroad village of Baugnez. It was here that Peiper's task force collided with Battery B, 285th Field Artillery Observation Battalion. This unit was near the tail end of one of the columns of the U.S. 7th Armored Division, which was racing south toward the crucial town of St. Vith.

The Americans traveling with B Battery were caught completely by surprise, and were in no position to put up an effective fight against the overwhelming might of Peiper's task force. Approximately 150 Americans were taken prisoner, and were subsequently rounded up in a field near the crossroad. Accounts of exactly what happened next vary, but what is known with certainty is that the Germans opened fire on the assembled prisoners, killing 84 of them. The slaughter of the Americans from B Battery became forever known as the "Malmedy Massacre." While it would become the most infamous, it was not the only act of brutality committed by the SS during the Battle of the Bulge. The savagery put on display at Honsfeld had been a prelude to what happened at Baugnez, and other acts would follow that were of equal ruthlessness (if not more so).

The bodies of the men massacred at Baugnez were discovered by a group of American engineers that passed the site later that same day. Word of the atrocity spread like wildfire through the American Army. The latest act of brutality by the SS simply confirmed and deepened the resentment that most GIs held for this branch of the Nazi war machine.

[handwritten: resentment? hatred would be a better wor]

The vanguard of Peiper's task force never stopped moving, even as the incident at Baugnez was unfolding. By dusk, the lead elements of the kampfgruppe had arrived at the heights overlooking the bridge over the Ambleve River at the town of Stavelot. After a tussle with a small contingent of Americans defending the town, Peiper stopped for the night, and consolidated his position for a coordinated attack on the town first thing in the morning. Up to that point, Peiper's advance from Lanzerath to Stavelot was the highlight of the entire German offensive.

On December 18, KG Peiper stormed into Stavelot, captured the town, and immediately pushed west toward Trois Ponts. He had planned on crossing back over to the south bank of the Ambleve River at Trois Ponts, but the Americans foiled his plan when they blew the bridges over both the Ambleve and the Salm Rivers before he could force his way across. With his route barred, he turned his column north, in the direction of La Gleize.

As the day progressed, Peiper found that the Americans were casting a net around his task force. More bridge demolitions forced him to change direction once again, and he settled on the road to Stoumont as his best available route of advance. The route was not well suited for armor, but if he could navigate it successfully as far as Remouchamps and Aywaille, his reward would be access to more favorable roads from that point forward.

The Americans were indeed tightening the noose around Peiper's force. The combination of air reconnaissance and the repeated brushes with American ground forces had provided the Americans with adequate knowledge of the location and strength of the German column. Elements of the 30th Infantry Division and the 82nd Airborne Division were now moving into position to halt and contain the rogue column of panzers. On December 18, a battalion from the 30th Infantry Division recaptured Stavelot just hours after Peiper had passed through the town. With Stavelot back in American hands, Peiper's route for supplies and reinforcements had been cut.

After the first three days of the offensive, the vaunted 6th SS Panzer Army had little to show for its effort and casualties. While KG Peiper had some early successes, all of Dietrich's other divisions were locked in intense combat with the American units manning the northern shoulder of the "Bulge." Attempts to wrestle Stavelot away from the 30th Infantry failed repeatedly on December 18, and Peiper was at risk of remaining cut off behind enemy lines. The Americans had suffered high casualties as well, but that didn't change the fact that the U.S. V Corps held its ground in almost every vital sector along the northern shoulder.

The Fifth Panzer Army

Manteuffel's 5th Panzer Army was a clear second fiddle to the 6th SS Panzer. But despite being cast in a supporting role, the 5th Panzer would soon find itself taking the lead in Hitler's offensive.

Positioned on the right flank of the 5th Panzer Army, the 18th Volksgrenadier Division was assigned the task of enveloping the two regiments of the 106th Infantry Division that were dug in along the Schnee Eifel. A combination of good execution on the Germans' part, and lack of communication and planning by the Americans, resulted in the 422nd and 423rd Infantry gegiments being quickly cut off on the snowy heights of the Eifel. The division commander hoped to launch a counterattack to stabilize his position, but the desperate situation in the balance of the sector would soon dash all prospects of a mission to save the two regiments. By the evening of the 18th, it was clear that if the regiments were going to be saved, they would have to fight their way out, with little support from other American forces in the area.

The nature of the German attack in this sector posed a clear and present danger to the vital crossroad town of St. Vith. Reinforcements were sent to the area on an urgent basis in order to counter the near collapse of the 106th Infantry Division and its attached 14th Cavalry Group. Brigadier General William Hoge's CCA/9, which was standing by in reserve to support the 2nd Infantry Division's attack toward the Roer River, was transferred from V Corps to VIII Corps. Also, the U.S. 7th Armored Division, which was in Ninth Army reserve, was ordered south by Eisenhower late on December 16.

The commander of the 106th had originally planned on using CCA/9 to relieve his threatened regiments in the Schnee Eifel. But when word came that the entire 7th Armored was en route, he decided to wait for its arrival, figuring that he would use the 7th for the relief mission instead. But the lead combat command, led by Brigadier General Bruce Clarke (of Fourth Armored fame), would not arrive soon enough to launch a counterattack to rescue the 422nd and 423rd regiments. The roads in the American rear area leading toward St. Vith were clogged with traffic, and Clarke's column had to push against the tide of American troops and vehicles fleeing from the front. Clarke's forward elements arrived in St. Vith late on the 17th, but by that point in time, St. Vith itself was under the threat of attack. Clarke would have to devote his full attention to holding the town, at the expense of rescuing the 106th's troops in the Schnee Eifel.

During the course of the night, Clarke hustled his units into defensive positions around St. Vith. By dawn on December 18, a defensive scheme had been implemented. Though he was not the senior commander on the scene, Clarke became the defacto commander overseeing the defense of St. Vith.

Despite the importance of St Vith, Manteuffel's strongest elements were further south, aligned against the very thin positions of the 28th Infantry Division. Their primary axis of advance would take them through the town of Clervaux, and on to the all-important crossroad town of Bastogne. A single volksgrenadier division (the 26th) was assigned the task of capturing Bastogne, while Manteuffel's three panzer divisions raced ahead toward the bridges over the Ourthe River, and then on to the Meuse.

The northern and southern regiments of the 28th Infantry Division were more or less able to roll with the punches they received during the first three days of the offensive. The 112th Regiment, located to the north, eventually tied in with the defensive perimeter around St. Vith. The 109th Regiment, located furthest south, fought a smart battle in its zone, and tied in with the units to their right in order to form a cohesive line of defense along the southern shoulder of the German salient.

The fate of the 110th Regiment was a different matter. It soon found itself engaged in a sharp battle for the village of Marnach, which was a key waypoint for the Germans en route to Clervaux. The Americans threw back the first German attack, but soon realized that the enemy was sweeping around both flanks. In response, the Americans committed some of the armor from the 707th Tank Battalion. But that night, the defenders of Marnach folded. They had bought valuable time, however, along the road to Clervaux and Bastogne.

By the morning of December 17, the Germans had pushed their lead tanks down the road toward Clervaux. After a sharp engagement east of the town between Shermans from the 707th and Mark IVs from the 2nd Panzer, the battle was carried into the streets of Clervaux itself. The commitment of more American armor, including a company of Shermans from CCR/9, failed to deter the Germans.

By nightfall, the panzers were moving freely through the town and on to the west. But the trailing German infantry and light vehicles were delayed by a group of Americans holed up in a chateau overlooking the main road (these brave men of the 110th would finally be forced to surrender the following day). Almost an entire day was spent clearing the town, and the 2nd Panzer Division was now seriously behind schedule. By the evening of December 17, General Middleton knew that the center of the 28th Infantry Division's front was on the verge of collapse. If the 110th Regiment folded, the road to Bastogne would be wide open.

Middleton was desperate to repair the tear in his line. His only immediate resources were CCR/9 and four battalions of engineers. There were more resources on the way, however, in the form of the 10th Armored Division, which was being transferred from Patton's Third Army (late on December 16, Eisenhower had suggested that Bradley have Patton dispatch this uncommitted division to assist Middleton). CCB/10 was sent to Bastogne, while CCA and CCR were sent further east, to shore up the positions along the southern shoulder facing the German 7th Army.

On December 17, Eisenhower made another critical and timely decision regarding the commitment of his reserves. The 101st and 82nd Airborne divisions, which had been recuperating from their role in Operation Market-Garden, were released from SHAEF reserve on his command. The 82nd was dispatched toward the north side of the Bulge. There was significant confusion, however, about where the 101st was to be committed, and the situation was still fuzzy even as the troops were en route to the Ardennes. They eventually were routed to Bastogne, where they took on primary responsibility for the defense of the town.

To delay the German advance toward Bastogne, Middleton decided to use CCR/9 to form a series of roadblock positions along the main roads leading toward the town. CCR/9 was split up into three task forces: Rose, Harper, and Booth. On December 18, TF Rose was dealt a heavy blow, and was flushed to the northwest, toward Houffalize. It ran into more trouble during its retreat, and the task force was virtually wiped out. TF Harper met an even quicker demise when it was struck by grenadiers, Mark IVs, and Panthers. The shattered remnants of TF Harper fell back to Longvilly, where the command post of CCR/9 was located. TF Booth was not engaged during the day on December 18, but that evening, after realizing it was cut off, the task force stumbled back through the darkness to try to hook back up with the American front line (wherever that might be). TF Booth ran into the enemy repeatedly, until finally, the Germans boxed the task force in and cut it to shreds.

As the 2nd Panzer Division was decimating the task forces of CCR/9, Fritz Bayerlein's Panzer Lehr Division was getting on track after a series of delays to the east. Having finally broken free of the traffic jams that were clogging the Our River crossing sites and the Clerve valley, he was ready to begin his advance toward Bastogne in earnest.

Faced with a decision over which of two routes to take toward Bastogne, Bayerlein chose a secondary dirt road that passed through the village of Mageret, as opposed to a quality paved road that he feared would be well defended by the Americans. Unfortunately for Bayerlein, the condition of the dirt road deteriorated the further west the column moved, and his progress was slowed considerably. Despite the delay, the Germans moved into Mageret during the early morning hours of December 19, and expelled a small detachment of American engineers who had been holding the town. But once in the town, Bayerlein refrained from continuing his advance toward Bastogne. Instead, he consolidated his position at Mageret, out of fear that American forces were operating to his rear (toward Longvilly).

The remnants of CCR/9 and the 110th RCT were indeed located to Bayerlein's rear at Longvilly. In their shattered condition, however, they posed no serious threat to the Panzer Lehr Division. But as dawn approached on December 19, the aforementioned American forces were not alone. Late in the afternoon of December 18, CCB/10 had arrived at Bastogne, and had thereupon sent roughly one third of its strength toward Longvilly. En route to Longvilly, Task Force Cherry had passed through Mageret before Bayerlein's arrival.

This situation was more a problem for the Americans than it was for the Germans. The American force near Longvilly was now faced with the very real prospect of being cut off from Bastogne. They also had the additional problem of straightening out a huge snarl in traffic that had developed when Team Cherry, moving east, ran into elements of CCR/9 that were heading west in an attempt to flee Longvilly during the night of December 18. The situation along the Mageret-Longvilly road had all the makings of a disaster.

TF Cherry was but one of three task forces formed by CCB/10 to delay the German advance toward Bastogne. Team Desobry moved to the northeast and secured Noville, while Team O'Hara moved to the southeast, and picked up responsibility for guarding the road leading through Marvie. Hopefully, the men of CCB/10 would buy time for the 101st Airborne Division to deploy in and around Bastogne.

The Seventh Army

The four divisions comprising the 7th Army were collectively the weak sisters of the German offensive. The fact that their goals were not as far-reaching as the other two armies was offset by the fact that the resources they had to work with were so slim by comparison.

The two volksgrenadier divisions operating on the left of the 7th Army (the 276th, and 212th VG divisions) succeeded in crossing over the Our River, and were soon engaging the U.S. 12th Infantry Regiment and elements of CCA/9. The American positions were spread as thin here as anywhere in the Ardennes, and during the first two days, the GIs were hard pressed to keep from being outflanked by the German infantry. But the lack of armored support for the 7th Army came home to roost, and the American tanks and tank destroyers, along with strong artillery support, were able to hold the Germans in check within four to five miles of the Our River.

With only one regiment of the 4th Infantry Division under assault, the commander of the division, Major General Raymon O. Barton, had the luxury of pulling in some reserves from the balance of his division. The timely arrival of two thirds of the 10th Armored Division, as well as the 159th Combat Engineer Battalion, went even further in helping the Americans shore up their line on the southern shoulder. They even began local counterattacks to take some pressure off of more critical areas. While there were some touchy moments during the first 48 hours, the Americans on the southern shoulder had the situation fairly well in hand by the evening of December 18.

The attack by the 7th Army's 5th FJ Division and 352nd VG Division met with greater success. All that stood before the Germans in this sector was the 109th Infantry Regiment of the 28th Infantry Division.

The 352nd VG Division was the southernmost of the two German formations that comprised the LXXXV Corps. After crossing the Our River, it advanced about three and three-quarter miles, and spent the following day constructing a bridge for its vehicles to cross the river. While the division waited for the bridge to be put in place, the infantry that had already crossed via other means continued to expand their bridgehead. The 352nd's fortunes were relatively good until December 18, when a sharp counterattack by two companies of the 1st Battalion, 109th Regiment, supported by some Sherman tanks, threw the Germans back toward Bastenndorf.

The 5th FJ Division had drawn the toughest assignment of the 7th Army's four divisions. From the outset, they would be under pressure to keep pace with the 5th Panzer Army on their right, lest a gap open up between the two armies (a gap that the enemy could perhaps exploit). And as it turned out, the paratroopers would be short some of their resources at the start of the offensive, since the division's heavy mortars and towed anti-tank battalion were both late in arriving at their assembly areas.

Before dawn on December 16, the 5th FJ's Pioneer (engineer) Battalion ferried the assault units from the 14th and 15th FJ regiments across the Our River. They quickly penetrated the forward outposts of the 28th Infantry Division, and began their advance toward the first towns on their list. The 15th FJ Regiment, advancing on the division's left, captured Vianden, and the 14th FJ Regiment, operating on the right, captured Putscheid. During the first day, the German paratroopers advanced just shy of four and a half miles beyond the Our River. The advance might have been greater, had it not been for delays that were experienced during bridging operations at the village of Roth.

On the second day, American resistance in front of the 5th FJ Division began to stiffen. Nevertheless, the 15th FJ Regiment advanced to positions overlooking the Wiltz River and captured Bourscheid. During the evening, the regiment attacked the town of Hoscheid, and secured it by dawn. As the 15th FJ Regiment crossed the Sure River near Bourscheid, the 14th Regiment advanced toward Wiltz.

The division had not been able to get its own bridges in place yet over the Our River, but on December 18, it utilized a bridge in the 5th Panzer Army zone to bring its motor transport, artillery, and assault guns across. After the first three days, the 5th FJ Division was maintaining contact with the 5th Panzer Army, though the paratroopers were echeloned further to the southeast. During the days that followed, the 5th FJ would be under increasing pressure to keep up with the 5th Panzer, and to take up blocking positions facing to the south.

The Intelligence Game

The attack on December 16 had caught the Allied command by surprise. Hitler's efforts to maintain secrecy had borne fruit, and his generals and staff deserve the credit for pulling off the assembly of the three armies without the Allies having any firm evidence of what was about to happen. But later examination revealed that, while the Germans deserved credit, there was also a portion of blame to be doled out on the Allied side. There had been a breakdown in Allied intelligence second in consequence only to the failure at Pearl Harbor.

In hindsight, the clues regarding the German's intentions were there to be seen, but the Allies simply ignored or overlooked them as they plotted their own course into Germany. Perhaps the key reason for the evidence being cast aside is that no rational military mind believed that the Germans had enough strength to take on an offensive that stood any chance of achieving a meaningful objective at the strategic level. Those who believed that were actually correct. But what they overlooked was the fact that Hitler was not looking at the same facts with a rational mind. Allied intelligence did not take into account what might be possible when a man as desperate and wounded as Adolph Hitler commanded the available German resources.

By the end of the third day of the offensive, ULTRA, the interception and code breaking operation that had served the Allies so well throughout the war, was returning critical information about the German's plans and dispositions. The Germans preattack precautions had protected their communications from interception by ULTRA. But once the offensive was underway, the Germans went back to routine communication procedures, and an increasing amount of intelligence began flowing into the SHAEF headquarters. Perhaps the most significant indication of the nature of the German attack was found in a message sent by von Rundstedt for dissemination to all of the troops participating in the offensive:

> The hour of destiny has struck. Mighty offensive armies face the Allies. WE GAMBLE EVERYTHING!

When ULTRA intercepted a German request for a photoreconnaissance mission covering the Meuse bridges near Liege, they had their first really solid clue regarding the ultimate direction of the German attack. Another valuable interception revealed the order of battle for the 6th SS Panzer Army, and the general positions of its divisions. Combined with the intelligence coming from the battlefield, the Americans were now getting a handle on exactly what they were up against.

It was time to solidify the plan for dealing with Hitler's desperate gamble. As a start to that process, Eisenhower expressed his view to the American commanders of the 12th and 6th Army Groups: "My intention is to take immediate action to check the enemy advance; to launch a counter-offensive without delay with all forces north of the Moselle." Even the day before, less than 48 hours after the German attack had begun, Ike was considering ways that he might be able to profit from Hitler's move. He reasoned that, by leaving the protection afforded them by the Siegfried Line, the German forces were far more vulnerable than if they had remained in their fortified nests. Though painful at the outset, the Allies were being afforded the opportunity to crush the last substantial reserves of the Wehrmacht.

14. Patton to the Rescue

Patton's Prognostication

When the Allied armies drew close to the German border in September, Eisenhower had to make some difficult decisions regarding how and where he would concentrate his strength. When he opted to leave the Ardennes so thinly manned, he did so with the knowledge that there were inherent risks involved. After almost three months of relative quiet there, it appeared that his decision had been a wise one.

Patton was not to be counted among those who thought the minimal allocation of force in the Ardennes was prudent. He stood alone as the only high-level commander who gave credence to the notion that a substantive danger was lurking behind the German side of the thinly held front in the Ardennes. On November 25, Patton made a portentous, nay, almost prescient entry in his diary:

> …the First Army is making a terrible mistake in leaving the VIII Corps static, as it is highly probable that the Germans are building up east of them.

Patton had good reason to be concerned about the Ardennes. The VIII Corps formed the right wing of the U.S. First Army, and was thus adjacent to the left wing of his own Third Army. The Germans could easily exploit the weakness of the American positions in the Ardennes in order to disrupt Patton's own offensive efforts. A German right hook across the Our River, for example, would pose a serious hazard to the rear of General Walker's XX Corps (whose own left flank was thinly held as well).

Toward the middle of December, Patton had been gathering his forces for the next leg of his offensive. Many of his divisions were in dire need of rest and refitting after the hard fighting in November and early December. The date for his next push was set for December 19 and, with the intent of creating a Cobra-like breakthrough, substantial air support was allocated to soften up the German defenses prior to the attack.

As he moved closer to December 19, Patton's concerns regarding his left flank grew more extreme. When Colonel Koch, the Third Army G-2 officer, issued a warning about German reserves that were known to be accumulating in the area of Trier, Patton's prognostication of November 25 appeared to be coming true.

It was time to turn his intuition into action. On December 12, he instructed his staff to make a study of how the Third Army should respond in the event of a German attack against Middleton's corps. His intent was purely that of safeguarding the start of his own operation on December 19. As an immediate contingency on the 12th, he decided to assign the 6th Armored and 26th Infantry divisions to III Corps near Saarbrucken. From this location, III Corps could be employed to either the north, in the event of trouble in the Ardennes, or to the east, in support of the December 19 offensive.

Patton's Early Response to the German Offensive

News of the German attack on the morning of December 16 was slow to arrive at Patton's doorstep. The first substantive information was delivered that evening, when General Allen, the chief of staff for the 12th Army Group, telephoned Patton with details of the day's events (as best as they were understood at the time). But Allen had a specific purpose for the call beyond a general sharing of information: the Third Army was to send the 10th Armored Division, which had been in reserve with XX Corps in preparation for the December 19 offensive, to the aid of General Middleton's VIII Corps.

Patton was incensed. He launched a strong protest, saying that, "the loss of this division would seriously affect the chances of my breaking through at Saarlautern." He went on to tell Allen that he had "paid a high price for that sector so far, and that to move the 10th Armored to the north would be playing into the hands of the Germans." Having received an earful from Patton, Allen apparently turned the conversation over to Bradley.

That his boss was now on the other end of the telephone made no difference. Patton continued with his protest; his words came easily, since the situation now reflected the concerns he had been harboring since November 25. "But that's no major threat up there. Hell, it's probably nothing more than a spoiling attack to throw us off balance down here and make us stop this offensive," he said. Bradley tried to sooth Patton a bit by telling him his reasoning was logical. But throwing Patton that bone did not change the fact that Bradley was determined to make the order stick.

Bradley could have nipped Patton's retort in the bud by informing him that it was actually Ike who had ordered the move of the 10th Armored (Bradley was actually at Ike's headquarters while talking to Patton). But rather than lay the "blame" directly on Eisenhower, Bradley kept the matter at his level, saying to Patton "I hate like hell to do it, George, but I've got to have that division. Even if it's only a spoiling attack as you say, Middleton must have help." Patton acquiesced (not that he had any choice), and lamented to himself that Bradley had taken counsel of his fears in ordering the move of the 10th Armored, adding further that "I wish he (Bradley) were less timid." But upon reflection, he offered the caveat that "He probably knows more of the situation than he can say over the phone."

Though he slept on that conciliatory note, Patton's actions the following morning remained that of a general who did not yet have an appreciation for the danger that faced the U.S. First Army. He was not alone, as Ike was perhaps the only person in a position of high command who sensed the true danger from the outset of Hitler's offensive. Early on the morning of December 17, fearing that he would be stripped of more resources, Patton ordered General Eddy to get the Fourth Armored Division committed to action (Patton would later acknowledge just how mistaken he had been about the gravity of the situation after the first day of the German offensive, and cited his employment of the Fourth Armored as evidence of it).

At the same time that Patton was trying to ensure that his own offensive was launched on schedule, the figurative light bulb above his head was beginning to brighten in regard to the opportunities the German offensive might present. During a briefing with his staff that same day (December 17), Patton entertained their thoughts regarding what the Third Army should do in response to the attack in the Ardennes. His G-3, Colonel Maddox, suggested that the best response would be to push east, cutting deep behind the attacking German armies, in order to trap them west of the Rhine River. Patton concurred with Maddox's view, but chimed in that "My guess is that our offensive will be called off and we will have to go up there and save their hides." In anticipation of just such a mission, Patton had a substantive conversation with General Millikin regarding the "possible use of the III Corps in an attack to the north in case the Germans continued the attack on the VIII Corps of the First Army." This was the very role that he had foreseen for Millikin's corps back on December 12.

Patton and Bradley Confer

On December 18, Bradley called Patton and his staff to meet with him at the 12th Army Group HQ in Luxembourg City. The German penetration had split Bradley's command in two: the First and Ninth armies to the north of the Bulge, and Patton's Third Army to the south. Thus Patton was the only one of Bradley's three direct reports with which he could meet face to face with convenience (a trip to visit with Hodges or Simpson required either a trip by air, or a circuitous drive to the north).

At the meeting, Patton was briefed on the size and scope of the German attack, and of the serious, and in some instances, dire situation the First Army faced in the Ardennes. With Bradley spurred on by Ike's comment regarding the need to launch a counterattack in order to regain the initiative, the commander of the 12th Army Group asked his subordinate what he could do to help. Patton immediately offered that he could "halt the attack of the 4th Armored, and concentrate it near Longwy, starting that midnight." He also stated that the 80th Infantry Division could be pulled from the line and be on its way to Luxembourg in the morning. Further, the 26th Infantry Division could be alerted to move within 24 hours. He then told Bradley that he could have all three divisions attacking the German's left flank by December 21, which was not much more than 48 hours from the point of their discussion. If Patton could pull that off, it would be a monumental feat.

Patton was beginning to see the opportunity that was before him, and he no longer needed Eisenhower's prodding to get his units moving north. The farther the Hun advanced, the more vulnerable his southern flank would become. The German's left flank was seen as the "ripe underbelly" that was begging to be struck in force. In Patton's words, "the krauts have stuck their head into a meatgrinder, and I have hold of the handle." Though he inwardly still wanted to continue with his own offensive on December 19, he had resigned himself to the belief that he would be asked to do otherwise. Somewhat to Bradley's surprise, and certainly to his relief, Patton did not take a combative position against having to cancel his attack. Instead, he acquiesced, saying "But what the hell, we'll still be killing Krauts."

Their discussion complete, Bradley escorted Patton to his jeep. As the Third Army commander prepared to drive back to his headquarters at Nancy, Bradley tried to console him in the wake of canceling his offensive in the Saar, and for having pulled away the 10th Armored. "We won't commit any more of your stuff than we have to. I want to save it for a whale of a blow when we hit back — and we are going to hit this bastard hard."

The Wheels Go in Motion

Not wanting to waste a moment, Patton telephoned his chief of staff soon after the end of the meeting with Bradley on December 18. After canceling the ground attack and air strikes planned for the following day, he told him:

> Stop Hugh and McBride (CG's of the 4th Armored and 80th Infantry Divisions) from whatever they are doing. Alert them for movement. They should make no retrograde movement at this time, but this is the real thing and they will undoubtedly move tomorrow. They will go under General M. (Millikin) Arrange to have sufficient transportation on hand to move McBride. Hugh can move on his own power. I am going to leave here and stop to see Johnnie (Walker, CG of XX Corps). It will probably be late when I come home.

It was Patton's intent to get the three divisions moving north as soon as possible, as he had promised Bradley. Patton also instructed Major General Millikin to move his headquarters from Metz to Arlon. His only other instruction for Millikin was that he prepare for an attack "somewhere north of Luxembourg City."

With the wheels set in motion, Patton went to visit General Walker of XX Corps, and then returned to his headquarters at Nancy on the evening of December 18. While he was en route, Bradley placed a telephone call to Patton's chief of staff, General Gay, and inquired if one of the combat commands of the Fourth Armored could be ready to move that night. Apparently, with Middleton's situation deteriorating, he wanted to get additional forces into the Bastogne area as soon as possible. Gay confirmed that CCB/4 was indeed ready to move that night, and that the 80th Infantry Division and the balance of the Fourth Armored would be ready to depart the following day. Bradley closed the conversation by asking that Patton call him at 8 P.M.

The Fourth Armored and 80th Infantry responded in lightning fashion. Amazingly, Brigadier General Dager's CCB was assembled for the move by 11 P.M. that evening, and would get underway just after midnight. Meanwhile, the 80th Infantry Division spent the night preparing for the move, and managed to depart at dawn on the 19th. Most of the balance of the Fourth Armored would start its road march during the late afternoon of December 19.

Having finally returned to Nancy, Patton made the 8 P.M. phone call to his boss. Bradley told him that the situation up north was now much worse than it had been when they spoke earlier in the day. He emphasized to Patton the speed with which he needed to get his units moving north. It was Bradley's intention to put Patton's forces to work as soon as possible to assist Middleton's VIII Corps (an intention that Bradley failed to express adequately to Patton, and as we shall see, his intention had direct consequences for the Fourth Armored Division).

Bradley then informed Patton that Eisenhower had called for their attendance at a top level meeting the following day at Verdun. After three days of scrambling to react to the German offensive, this meeting would be the Allies' first opportunity to plan an overall strategy for countering Hitler's offensive.

Before Patton retired for the evening, he had at least one other piece of important business to tend to. After his final conversation with Bradley, he called in his staff to discuss the options for employing III Corps and VIII Corps (Bradley had suggested to him that VIII Corps would fall under the command of Third Army once Patton arrived on the scene). He left it to his staff to develop a set of proposals overnight, which they would present at a meeting he scheduled for the following morning, prior to his departure for Verdun.

At 7:00 A.M. the next morning, Patton assembled his principal staff members, the two corps commanders who would be moving north (Millikin and Eddy), and the VIII Corps Artillery Officer. After listening to the options that his staff had prepared, Patton's team agreed upon three possible axis of advance for III Corps. He instructed his staff to draw up specific plans for each route. At 8:00 A.M., with the rough outline of the plan agreed upon, the meeting was expanded to include General Weyland and the staff of the XIX TAC, as well as the entire Third Army general staff. On what was supposed to have been the first day of the Third Army offensive to push through the Seigfried line, he instead delivered the following pep talk before departing for Verdun:

> What has occurred up north is no occasion for excitement. As you know, alarm spreads very quickly in a military command. You must be extremely careful in a critical situation such as this not to give rise to any undue concern among the troops. Our plans have been changed. We're going to fight, but in a different place. Also, we are going to have to move very fast. We pride ourselves on our ability to move quickly. But, we're going to have to do it faster now than we've ever done before. I have no doubt that we will meet all demands made on us. You always have and I know you will do so again this time. And whatever happens, we will keep on doing as we have always done, killing Germans wherever we find the sons-of-bitches.

Of the proposals that had been submitted by his staff, Patton's preferred plan called for a thrust at the base of the German salient, along an axis of advance extending from Diekirch through St. Vith. As Patton considered this scenario, the 7th Armored Division was still in possession of St. Vith. If Bruce Clarke held on long enough, Patton could forge a link with the First Army there, and the entire Fifth Panzer Army would be isolated west of the Our River.

His two back-up plans called for strikes further to the west. Of the two remaining axis, the Arlon-Bastogne route was preferred. It was not as aggressive as the Diekirch-St. Vith axis, since it struck at the center of the Bulge and thus offered less opportunity for cutting off the German spearheads. But it did ensure the security of Bastogne, the road net of which would be required to continue the attack further to the north (Houffalize) or northeast (St. Vith). The third scenario called for a drive from Neufchâteau toward St. Hubert. This would hit the Germans closer to the tip of the salient and would constitute pushing the German back, rather than cutting him off. This was Patton's least favorite of the three options.

Patton did not want to waste a moment after the Verdun conference. Figuring that he would emerge from the meeting with specific directions from Ike and Bradley regarding how to proceed, and that one of his three plans would ultimately be the foundation for his counterattack, he assigned a simple codeword to each plan. When he exited the meeting, he planned on telephoning his chief of staff, "Hap" Gay, to deliver the codeword for the axis of attack that had been accepted. Gay was then to put the selected plan into immediate effect.

Having discussed the situation so thoroughly with his staff, Patton left for the meeting in Verdun well equipped with the knowledge of what he could and would commit to on the southern flank. In fact, since Patton had gone the extra step of actually putting the divisions on the road before he ever reached Verdun, he would enter the meeting with the knowledge that the majority of III Corps was already closing in on the south flank of the Bulge.

Patton departed for Verdun at 9:15 that morning, and arrived at 10:45, fifteen minutes before the scheduled start time. With the wheels and treads of the Third Army already churning toward the Ardennes, and the major contingencies planned for, he was surely a confident man as he headed into the meeting room.

The Meeting at Verdun

By 11 A.M., the Allied commanders had assembled at the 12th Army Group's main headquarters at Verdun. Surrounded by the gray, cold, and damp skies that blanketed most of northwest Europe, Generals Eisenhower, Bradley, Patton, and Devers, and Air Marshal Tedder, all accompanied by a large number of staff members, convened in the second floor squad room of an old, dank French army barracks. A single pot-bellied stove struggled to warm the chilled air in the hall. The only key player not in attendance was General Hodges of the First Army; his headquarters was in the process of being relocated from Spa to Liege (KG Peiper having come too close for comfort).

The meeting began with a briefing of the current situation, delivered by General Strong, the SHAEF G-2. In Patton's words, it "was far from happy." Here is the situation as understood by the Americans on the morning of December 19:

The north shoulder of the "Bulge," as it had already become known, was holding firm from Monschau south to Dom Butgenbach, and thence westward to Malmedy. The 30th Infantry Division had recaptured Stavelot, thus cutting off the elements of the 1st SS Panzer Division that had penetrated as far as Stoumont (the deepest penetration of any German unit at that point). The German spearhead appeared to have been contained, and plans were being made to eliminate the cancer it represented in the American rear. Elements of the 30th Infantry Division, 82nd Airborne Division, and 3rd Armored Division would be made available to assist in the task.

Meanwhile, the 7th Armored Division had made its way into St. Vith, and along with CCB/9 and the shattered remnants of the 106th Infantry Division, had formed a defensive perimeter around the vital cross road town (the 112th Infantry Regiment would soon be brought into the fold as well, as it fell back to the north and joined the right flank of the St. Vith defensive line). The grimmest news on this section of the front was that the two forward regiments of the 106th had been encircled on the Schnee Eifel, and attempts to relieve them had to be abandoned before they even started, in favor of the defense of St. Vith.

The VIII Corps front between the 112th Infantry Regiment and the forces assembled at Bastogne was practically void of American soldiers. The roads leading to Houffalize, which sits astride the key highway leading from Bastogne to Liege, were wide open for use by the Germans; the gap in the VIII Corps line in this sector was nearly 20 miles wide. If there was any one area of the front that was ripe for exploitation by the Germans, this was it.

Nearly as grim as the fate of the 106th Infantry Division was that of the 110th Infantry Regiment, which had been all but wiped out along the roads leading to Bastogne. CCR/9, the only armored reserve in the area, had already been engaged, and had sustained heavy losses. But the good news was that CCB/10 had arrived just in time to place additional armored roadblocks in front of Bastogne, and as a result, the 101st Airborne was able to enter Bastogne before the Germans had a chance to capture it. The leading regiment of the "Screaming Eagles" had arrived at about midnight, and was now in the process of moving into positions east of Bastogne. A following regiment was dispatched to positions north and northeast of the town. Reinforced with a battalion of Hellcat tank destroyers (the 705th) and supported by nearly 130 artillery pieces, the 101st had been ordered to hold the town at all costs.

The situation southeast of Bastogne was a bit fuzzy. The only organized resistance to be found between the defenders of Bastogne and the positions of the 109th Regiment, which anchored the left flank of the southern shoulder, was at the town of Wiltz. This is where the headquarters of the 28th Division was located, and it became a rallying point for some of the shocked remnants of the Keystone Division's forward positions. The defenders at Wiltz were reinforced with a battalion of combat engineers, and hoped to hold their position on December 19.

The 109th Regiment, CCA/9, and the Fourth Infantry Division had done a fine job of holding their line on the southern shoulder after only modest gains by the Germans. Now reinforced by CCA/10 and CCR/10, the Americans were confident that the Germans would not be able to move any further south in this sector.

Across most of the Ardennes, American engineers were put to work. Orders were sent out to create roadblocks and prepare bridges for demolition in order to slow down the German drive. This was done not only along the routes leading to the Meuse River, but also along the line of the Sure River, where it was feared the Germans might turn south and drive for Luxembourg City.

In addition to the conventional attacks launched by the Germans, some details had become available regarding the special operations the Germans had employed. A nighttime parachute drop had taken place in the American rear behind the defenses of the northern shoulder. The Americans were forced to commit a disproportionate amount of force to the task of hunting down the enemy paratroopers. By now, the Allies had also become aware of Otto Skorzeny's commandos dressed in American garb. A brilliant ruse by the Germans had led them to believe, however, that the commando's destination was SHAEF's HQ, and that their mission was the assassination of Eisenhower (out of fear that he was being hunted, Ike traveled to Verdun in a special armor plated automobile). Of course, the commandos were actually at work in the Ardennes (some of the commandos had actually reached one of the bridges over the Meuse River). The commando's impact was disproportionate to their small numbers; as word of their presence and mission spread, GIs became increasingly subject to questioning in order to confirm their identity. Bradley himself had been detained three times on his way to Verdun, and was quizzed about American sports figures, movie stars, and state capitols.

The final noteworthy item was the weather. Conditions on three of the first four days had limited the response of Allied airpower (a temporary clearing on December 17 allowed for a large number of sorties to be flown that day). Unfortunately, there was no immediate prospect for an improvement in the weather. The Americans would be unable to play one of their most powerful cards.

The American generals could be proud of the manner in which their front line divisions in the Ardennes had reacted to the weight of the German attack. They also could take great satisfaction in the rapid fashion that reserves were dispatched from the 9th, 1st, and 3rd armies to assist the V and VIII Corps. Had the Americans not acted with such speed, the situation could have been much, much worse. But time after time, the prompt response by units ordered to the Ardennes ensured that they arrived in the nick of time at crucial areas of the battlefield.

But signs of satisfaction were not reflected in the faces of the generals assembled at Verdun. Their mood seemed to echo the weather that enveloped the Ardennes. Ike admonished those in attendance: "The present situation is to be regarded as one of opportunity for us and not disaster. There will be only cheerful faces at this conference table." Patton responded in his characteristic manner: "Hell, let's have the guts to let the sons of bitches go all the way to Paris. Then we'll really cut them off and chew 'em up!"

Patton's spontaneous comment caused some smiles to break out around the room. But Ike wasn't laughing; he chose the opportunity presented by Patton's comment to establish just how far the Germans were to be permitted to advance. "George, that's fine. But the enemy must never be allowed to cross the Meuse." Ike told Montgomery later that day via radio that the weakest spot in the American line was in the direction of Namur. He informed Monty: "The general plan is to plug the holes in the north and launch co-coordinated attack from the south."

So it was indeed clear to Ike that the primary opportunity for the Americans to seize the initiative was to the south. And so, when the discussion turned to the plans for the southern portion of the Bulge, General Patton became the obvious focus of attention. Ike asked Patton when he could get to Luxembourg to take charge of the battle, and Patton responded that he could take the reins that afternoon.

The decision to attack already announced, Ike then asked the flamboyant commander of the Third Army, "When can you start?" Unknown to Ike, Patton had already been preparing for just such an eventuality, and his response was short and to the point: "As soon as you are through with me." Not necessarily impressed with Patton's bravado, Eisenhower pressed for a more specific answer. Patton refined his response, stating that that he could launch his attack "The morning of December 21st, with three divisions, the 4th Armored, the 26th, and the 80th."

His response startled the assembled generals. Patton's aide, Colonel Charles Codman, described the reaction:

> There was a stir, a shuffling of feet, as those present straightened up in their chairs. In some faces, skepticism. But through the room the current of excitement leaped like a flame. To disengage three divisions actually in combat and launch them over more than 100 miles of icy roads straight into the heart of a major attack of unprecedented violence presented problems which few commanders would have undertaken to resolve in that length of time.

Of course, Patton could make the statement with confidence, since he already had two of the divisions on the road at that very moment.

Eisenhower, who was among those unaware of Patton's proactive planning, perhaps did not take the response seriously at first; this might be some of Patton's characteristic hyperbole on display (Patton himself sensed that some in the room thought his proclamation was a boast). But after realizing he was serious, Ike cautioned him. "Don't be fatuous, George. If you try to go that early, you won't have all three divisions ready and you'll go piecemeal. You will start on the 22nd and I want your initial blow to be a strong one! I'd even settle for the 23rd if it takes that long to get three full divisions."

It was agreed upon in the meeting that Patton would assemble the III Corps in the vicinity of Arlon, and then attack toward Bastogne. Other alternatives were discussed, such as Patton's desire to cut into the German salient further to the east, but Ike dismissed all other ideas. He appeared determined from the outset that Bastogne was to be the centerpiece of the attack, and so it was. Though filled with the desire to take the more aggressive route, Patton did not belabor the point. He quickly placed his focus on the mission that he had been given. He responded to the assignment with an air of total confidence, perhaps bordering on cockiness. Patton felt, and let it be known, that he could accomplish the drive to Bastogne in short order; hopefully within 48 hours of the start of the attack, and certainly before Christmas, at the very latest.

Ike felt that Patton was underestimating the Germans in this instance, and that he was taking the task too lightly. Ike later wrote, "I felt it necessary to impress upon him the need of strength and cohesion in his own advance." He went on to express some concern that three divisions might not be enough to get the job done in total. He also told Patton that he wanted the advance to be "methodical and sure," and he cautioned him not to engage in piecemeal attacks. Patton assured Ike that he would bring another three divisions into the battle, for a total commitment of six.

Six divisions represented almost two thirds of the Third Army. In order to pull this much strength to the north, Patton would need relief for some of his divisions currently holding positions in the line. To facilitate this move, it was agreed that Devers' 6th Army Group would extend its line northward and assume some of the Third Army's line in the Saar region. The 6th Armored Division, which had also been in reserve in preparation for the December 19 offensive, was ordered to stay in the area of Saarbrucken until relieved by elements of the Seventh Army. To help Devers cover his extremely long front, Patton had to relinquish the 42nd and 87th Infantry divisions to the Seventh Army. Even with the addition of the two divisions, Devers armies were over-extended by the move. But that was a risk the Allies would have to take if they were to make a concentrated strike into the south flank of the Bulge.

At the close of the meeting, Eisenhower took a moment to joke with the man he was now counting on to regain the initiative in the Ardennes. Pointing to the fifth star that he had recently been awarded, he said, "You know, George, every time I get promoted I get attacked." Patton countered with a good-natured dig that had its foundation in Patton's role in North Africa after the American defeat at Kasserine Pass, which came soon after one of Ike's other promotions: "Yeah. And every time you get attacked I have to bail you out."

The 90 Degree Turn

Patton was now at a place where he was most comfortable and satisfied: center stage. He was the only Allied general in position to strike back at the German "Bulge." Fate had placed him in the right place, at the right time. And there was not a single commanding general better equipped for the task at hand.

The challenge before the Third Army was indeed one of great proportions. It would impose upon Patton the greatest test of his career. In essence, he had to pull more than two thirds of his army out of their positions facing the West Wall, and wheel them 90 degrees to the north. In some instances, units would have to travel distances in excess of 160 miles. The move would have to be made at great speed, under very poor weather conditions. The necessity for rapid movement would leave no choice but to move large columns of vehicles at night (a practice that carried with it inherent difficulties). If he pulled it off, it would represent the largest mass-movement of troops, in the shortest amount of time, in the history of the United States military.

Once the Verdun meeting adjourned, Patton immediately telephoned Hap Gay. Using the prearranged password, Patton signaled that the Arlon-Bastogne axis was the way they were headed. And with that order, the specific direction of the three divisions was determined. In addition to the Fourth Armored and 80th Infantry divisions, which were already en route, the 26th Infantry Division was ordered to move on the morning of December 20 to the vicinity of Arlon, from whence it would be placed in the front line. The XII Corps was ordered out of the line on the Third Army's right flank, and was to proceed to Luxembourg on December 21. The Third Army forward HQ was to move to Luxembourg City on December 20, as was the HQ of Eddy's XII Corps.

Later that day, Patton took inventory of his new command. He would now have control of four corps: the VIII, III, XII, and XX. As the III Corps moved into position for the primary attack, he would have Eddy's XII Corps take over responsibility for the southern shoulder. In addition to the 4th Infantry Division and elements of the 10th Armored, 9th Armored, and 28th Infantry Divisions, which were already holding this part of the front, Eddy would bring forward the 35th and 5th Infantry divisions for additional support. The 35th, which was presently in the line for its 160th consecutive day, would first report to Metz for some rest and rehabilitation before moving north; the 5th Infantry was coming to Eddy via reassignment from the XX Corps bridgehead at Saarlautern. Walker's XX Corps, which, after the release of the 5th Infantry Division, consisted of the 90th and 95th Infantry divisions, and Task Force Polk (the 6th Armored would join Walker's corps after it was relieved by the Seventh Army), would hold its positions near Thionville, on the new right flank of the Third Army.

III Corps

Major General John Millikin, a West Point graduate from the class of 1910, had not been under Patton's command for very long. His background was in cavalry, having commanded the 2d Cavalry Division (Horse) for a little over a year, up until it was disbanded in July of 1942. He moved on from there to command the 83rd Infantry Division for a period of only four months, and then moved on to command the 33rd Infantry Division during its jungle warfare training in Hawaii. He had no combat experience, and his appointment to the prominent position of a corps commander within the Third Army must have been a mystery to some. Patton did not have high expectations of him, and Millikin's appointment surely was forced upon him (in fact, he had earlier lobbied for Wood to be given this appointment instead).

Up until this point, Millikin's role had been limited to overseeing the rest and refitting of worn and tired divisions. At present, the 6th Armored and 26th Infantry divisions were the only units assigned to him. He would retain the 26th for his move to the Ardennes, but the 6th Armored would be reassigned to XX Corps while it waited to be relieved by elements of the Seventh Army. With the assignment of the 80th Infantry and Fourth Armored divisions to his command, Millikin had as seasoned a group of divisions as any commander could have hoped for at this stage of the war. Given that Millikin and his staff were a new and untried team, he was fortunate to have such a solid trio of divisions at his disposal.

While all of Millikin's divisions were experienced, they were not in their best fighting condition. All three had suffered heavy losses during the campaign in the Lorraine and the Saar regions. The 26th and 80th had been brought back up to full strength, but this was done largely through the assignment of headquarters troops to the divisions' rifle platoons. The 26th Infantry Division had just received 2,585 of these men on December 18, and thus had little time to get them indoctrinated. It was a plus, however, that they were able to bring them into the fold while away from the front. The 80th Infantry Division had been afforded a little more time to assimilate its new members. They also had the advantage of being fairly well rested, having been pulled from the line for that purpose well in advance of Patton's now defunct December 19 offensive.

Of the three divisions, the Fourth Armored was certainly the most accomplished. But this had come at a price, especially during the hard fighting during November and the first week of December. While they had received some replacements during their rest period, they had not yet been brought up to full strength. The division records show they were short 713 men and 19 officers; the majority of the shortage was in the armored infantry, tank, and armored cavalry units. In addition, new tanks had not come through in sufficient quantities to make up the heavy losses incurred during the Lorraine battles. Though the division's assistant G-4 would later report that the division was short only 21 Shermans before their departure for the Ardennes, the situation was definitely far worse than that. In terms of battle ready medium tanks, the Fourth Armored was short more than a third of its full complement, triple what was on record from the assistant G-4. They would head to the Ardennes with no more than 100 combat ready Shermans (the number was almost certainly closer to 90, not counting the 105mm Assault Gun Shermans).

Though short on resources, the Fourth was not short on experience. Despite their recent losses, they were still flush with seasoned veterans, and had the immeasurable benefit of receiving almost 10 days of rest, since most of its units were withdrawn to rear areas on December 8.

In addition to the three primary divisions, the III Corps was provided with a number of independent units for additional support. Patton culled the Third Army for as many artillery, engineer, tank destroyer, and AAA units as he could muster, in an effort to ensure that as much weight could be brought to bear on the advance as possible. Eleven artillery batteries had been pulled out of their positions to the south, where they had been emplaced to support the December 19 offensive. They were now all attached to III Corps in support of Millikin's offensive. He would have no shortage of resources with which to accomplish his mission.

The Mission

Though Patton had more ambitious desires, the primary mission for III Corps became the drive to relieve the American forces defending Bastogne. At the time that Patton's counterattack was first conceived, Bastogne had yet to be surrounded. But it was not long thereafter that word came back that the last road into Bastogne had been severed by the Germans. As the bulk of III Corps stood at the starting gate, Bastogne was the prize they were after.

As evidenced by his caution to Patton during the meeting at Verdun, the Supreme Commander was concerned that Patton would commit his forces piecemeal. Ike was also worried that Patton would broaden the offensive beyond the immediate objective of securing Bastogne. As relayed in the U.S. Official History of the Battle of the Bulge, authored by Hugh Cole, Eisenhower told Bradley "the American counterattack via Bastogne should be held in check and not allowed to spread, that it was, after all, only a steppingstone for the main offensive."

Given this directive, it is a bit surprising that Patton elected to execute the attack in the manner he did. Instead of organizing a heavily concentrated thrust along an axis of advance that would carry III Corps to Bastogne, Patton carried out his attack along virtually the entire length of the German southern flank.

The front of III Corps was almost 30 miles long at the start of the attack, stretching roughly from Neufchâteau in the west, to Ettelbruck in the east. An average front of 10 miles per division is quite large for offensive operations; but no effort was made to provide for a greater concentration of strength along the axis of advance toward the primary objective (Bastogne). In fact, of the three divisions, the Fourth Armored was operating over the *widest* front. Its original zone was defined as extending from Neufchâteau to Bigonville, a distance of over 15 miles (fully half of the III Corps' front). To the credit of the Fourth Armored, it planned its attack in such a way that it maintained concentration of force at the combat command level at the start of the offensive, but this was soon eroded due to the inherent weakness of advancing over such a wide zone, and against an enemy who, if not greater in firepower, was greater in number, with the added advantage of very favorable terrain for defensive operations. All of these factors would not make for any easy mission, and they serve to underscore the fact that Patton was underestimating the challenge that lay in front of III Corps.

In addition to the attack by III Corps, Eddy's XII Corps, which would soon be reinforced with the arrival of the 5th Infantry Division, began an escalating series of attacks in its zone east of III Corps. Eddy was doing exactly what Eisenhower had feared, which is that he was committing his troops in piecemeal fashion (a situation that the CG of the 5th Infantry was none too happy with, as he watched his regiments, which were arriving in staggered fashion, go on the attack immediately upon their arrival).

Patton had even considered reinforcing the attack of XII Corps with two more divisions (the 35th Infantry and 6th Armored), but events in the area around Bastogne in the days ahead finally convinced him to mass greater strength along the roads leading to Bastogne. If he had provided greater concentration along that part of the front to begin with, the history books would no doubt be due for a drastic revision. For example, had all or a substantial part of either the 26th or 80th Infantry divisions been employed directly with the Fourth Armored Division, and only one of the infantry divisions been employed in the rugged area east of Bigonville, it is arguable that the drive to Bastogne might have succeeded within a matter of 48 hours, as Patton had envisioned. There are other implications that arise from this "what-if" scenario, some of which we will explore later.

In any event, the attack toward Bastogne was to be executed by a single division, on a rather broad front. And it was the Fourth Armored that drew the assignment. The decision to employ the Fourth on the cutting edge of the drive came as no surprise to anyone. If there was any division that Patton felt he could count on, the Fourth was it.

There was another reason for assigning the mission to the Fourth Armored, and it was a purely practical one. The terrain south and southwest of Bastogne was the only tank-friendly terrain in this part of the Ardennes. The terrain east of the Arlon-Bastogne highway became increasingly rugged. It was liberally covered with dense forests, and lacked quality roads that could support a mechanized advance. A great many streams could be traced through the area, many of which ran through deep gorges. All of this made the area east of the Arlon-Bastogne highway ill suited for armored operations. Unfortunately, this also made the Arlon-Bastogne highway, and all points west, the obvious rallying point for the German defense.

Thus, as the III Corps' attack got underway, all eyes would be focused on the progress of the Fourth Armored Division. None were more interested than the men who were now manning the perimeter defenses around Bastogne. Though ideally suited for a mission that called for holding out behind enemy lines for an extended period of time, the 101st Airborne could not hold out indefinitely. Poor flying weather had hampered efforts to supply the 101st by air, and so they were increasingly at risk of running out of ammunition and medical supplies. The need to evacuate the wounded also became a critical concern.

Once Bastogne was secured, the view of the high command, as developed shortly after the Verdun meeting, was that the Third Army would drive toward St. Vith. This would take place in conjunction with a complementary attack launched along the north flank of the Bulge. As Patton issued his order for the attack, he added the rather ambitious goal of driving on to the northeast, in order to secure crossings over the Rhine River. If there was ever an example of putting the cart before the horse, this was it.

As noted previously, the Fourth Armored was not the only division striking back at the German flank, and the contribution of those divisions should not be overlooked. The 26th Infantry Division would attack alongside the Fourth Armored, maintaining contact with Gaffey's right flank. The 80th Infantry Division would attack to the right of the 26th Division. Thus Millikin's divisions were lined up three abreast across that very long, 30-mile line of departure.

The downside to this arrangement, as noted previously, was the absence of concentration of force. There was virtually no depth to the attack. The other major negative was the nature of the terrain over which the two infantry divisions would have to attack. As discussed above, it was ill suited for armor. But it was no friend to the foot soldier, either. The respected military historian Charles B. McDonald summed it up best when he wrote, "whoever picked the terrain over which the 26th and 80th Divisions advanced had a taste for shit."

Patton's expectation was that the Fourth Armored would be in position to attack starting on December 22. Despite the lack of depth in the attack, he was confident that Gaffey would ram his way through to Bastogne within 48 hours. Their plan called for the Fourth to follow the axis of the Arlon-Bastogne highway; CCA would come directly up the highway, while CCB followed a parallel path along a secondary road to the west of CCA. (Middleton wanted the main thrust of the Fourth to come up the Neufchâteau-Bastogne highway, but his suggestion was cast aside). As was the usual protocol for the Fourth Armored, CCR would remain uncommitted at the start of the offensive.

Meanwhile, the two infantry divisions would in essence by providing protection for Gaffey's right flank. The Fourth's left flank would be screened by Task Force Lyons, which had at its core the 178th Engineer Combat Battalion. The remains of the 110th Infantry Regiment (few in number as it was) also contributed to some blocking positions along the roads leading to the southwest.

It should be added that the situation facing the III Corps was incredibly uncertain. While the Americans had identified the four divisions comprising the German 7th Army, their exact dispositions and intentions were unknown, especially in the area extending west from Ettelbruck. It was assumed that the enemy had cut through the Arlon-Bastogne highway, but there was no reliable conformation to that effect. And in the event the road had been cut, there was no substantive information regarding the forces that might be defending it. The fragmented remnants of the 110th infantry division, along with small units of engineers and other stragglers, had been filtering back through the dense terrain to points south and southwest, but they brought with them little in the way of intelligence. With the situation on the ground being what it was, and with the weather conspiring to keep American air reconnaissance out of the sky, there was a tremendous lack of knowledge about enemy movements through this region. The degree of opposition in front of the Fourth Armored would be a matter of guesswork, and it was apparently Patton's guess that the opposition would be light. He guessed wrong.

Patton's Fingerprints

It is worth noting that Millikin's lack of experience would, in the end, be of little consequence to the outcome of the coming battle. From the outset, Patton held a tight rein on the execution of the attack, and was practically running III Corps himself. In fact, he violated many of his own principles by exercising direct control all the way down to the division level, and even lower in some cases. He even went so far as to prescribe the specific tactics that were to be employed by the Fourth Armored during their advance, dictating the favored attack formation (tanks, artillery, tank destroyers, and armored engineers out in front, with the armored infantry bringing up the rear to clean up what the armor bypassed). If strong enemy resistance was met, it was not to be tackled head-on. The enemy positions were to be enveloped, with the pincers starting anywhere from a mile to a mile-and-a-half back from the point of contact. He even dictated the use of specific weapons, calling for the available M4A3E2 "Jumbo" Shermans to be employed at the point of advance (there were very few of these available, but as we shall see, his idea was very prescient).

This level of over-control was very uncharacteristic of Patton. In the past, he had chastised commanders who commanded "too far down." In his memoir, Patton wrote:

> This habit of commanding too far down, I believe, is inculcated at schools and maneuvers. Actually, a General should command one echelon down, and know the position of units two echelons down. For example, and Army Commander should command corps, and show on his battle map the locations of corps and divisions, but he should not command the division. A Corps Commander should command divisions and show on his map the location of combat teams. A Division Commander should command combat teams and show on his map the location of battalions. The Regimental Commander should command battalions and show on his map the location of companies; similarly, with the Battalion and Company Commanders.

He continued:

> It has been my observation that any general officer who violates this rule and at, let us say, the Army level, shows the location of battalions, starts commanding them and loses his efficiency.

Patton's dabbling with the Fourth Armored division might well have been a prod-uct of the forced absence of John Wood. The division was now embarking on the most important mission of its combat history, and it was doing so without the man who had trained and nurtured them, and who had been at the helm during all of their exploits in combat, save for a handful of days in early December before the division was pulled from the line. Certainly, "P" would have never stood for Patton's meddling. But with the loyal Hugh Gaffey running the Fourth, Patton was able to run roughshod over the division staff. If Gaffey had any concerns over Patton's heavy hand in the affairs of the division, it would seem that he kept it to himself.

On December 20, General Patton made an inspection tour of the three divisions of III Corps. He was content with their preparation, and on December 21, issued the order for the attack, which was to officially commence on December 22. As he sent his commanders off, he demanded the attack be carried out in columns of regiments, "or in any case, lots of depth." This order was almost impossible to follow, due to the width of the III Corps front. But the situation did not at all dampen Patton's optimism that his troops would soon be in Bastogne. He left them with one final dose of classic Pat-ton inspiration, telling them to "Drive like hell."

The days that lay ahead would be unlike any that the Fourth Armored had yet experienced, as its men and machines were about to be pushed to the limit of endurance. The greatest chapter in the history of the Fourth Armored Division was about to be written.

15. Task Force Ezell

Preparing to Move

General Dager's CCB was awarded the distinction of being the first element of the Fourth Armored Division to begin the journey north toward the Bulge. Less than 36 hours after its embarkation, it would also earn the less heralded achievement of being the first of the Fourth Armored Division's combat commands to reach Bastogne. The story of CCB's march to the Ardennes is a unique one indeed.

During the 17th of December, the men of CCB listened with interest to the rumors about a German attack against the U.S. First Army. The Fourth Armored, being positioned on the far right flank of XII Corps and the Third Army, was farther from the Ardennes than any of Patton's other divisions. Many of the men of the Fourth probably figured the attack would be of little consequence to them.

Toward the end of the day on December 17, the 8th Tank Battalion was told to prepare to move on short notice. With their usual vigor, the tankers prepared to head back into action, not knowing that their latest orders were the result of Patton's desire to safeguard the Fourth Armored from being pulled away from his grasp.

Not long after midnight, the events to the north began to impact the men of CCB, but in a totally unexpected fashion. Reports were coming in that enemy paratroopers had landed in the vicinity of Nancy. The battalion commanders were raised from their sleep and were ordered to send out patrols as a security measure. As it turned out, the German paratroopers were just a rumor grown out of control. The one real drop conducted behind the front of V Corps had, in all likelihood, been its inspiration. By mid-morning, the patrols were cancelled.

Shortly before noon on December 18, orders were passed down to the units of CCB placing them on a one hour alert. They soon discovered that they would be moving into the area occupied by the 35th Infantry Division (a direct result of Patton's maneuver to hoard the division). Advance teams were sent out to prepare for the move, and much work was done to ensure a smooth road march. They were soon ready to go, with all of the units loaded with full supplies and ready for combat. But at about 5 P.M., CCB was ordered to remain in place; it was an unusual situation, to be sure. Wary that something out of the ordinary might happen yet again, the men were ordered to remain in a state of readiness.

It wasn't long before new orders came in. CCB was ordered to move at 11 P.M. toward a new line of departure, from whence they would leave at midnight. The specific destination was unknown, but the direction was not. They were heading north.

"The units of CCB fell into their proper place after midnight on December 19," and headed in the direction of Longwy. At precisely 12:50 A.M., amidst the nervous chatter of men who were unsure about exactly what lay before them, the lead tank of the "Rolling Eight Ball," with Major Irzyk in the turret, crossed the I.P.

The composition of CCB at that point was fairly typical. On this occasion, it consisted of:

8th Tank Battalion

10th Armored Infantry Battalion

22nd Armored Field Artillery Battalion

A Battery, 489th AAA SP Battalion

B Company, 24th Armored Engineer Battalion

Platoon of Engineers from the 995th Engineer Battalion

B Troop, 25th Cavalry Reconnaissance Squadron

Elements of the 704th Tank Destroyer Battalion were conspicuous by their absence. The tank destroyers were still attached to the 87th Infantry Division, and due to their late arrival back with the Fourth, they would be assigned to CCR at the start of its move to the Ardennes. In the event that CCB encountered German armor, Dager would be relying completely on the 8th Tank Battalion.

When Irzyk's battalion departed for the Ardennes, D Company was at, or very close to, its full compliment of 17 light tanks. The three medium tank companies were well short of full strength, however, as there were only 32 Shermans available between them (including Irzyk's command tank). The 8th Tank Battalion was entirely equipped with the older 75mm Sherman variants (to date, the 37th Tank Battalion had been the primary recipient of the few 76mm models that had been made available to the division).

Supplementing the Shermans were the battalion's six 105mm assault guns. Three of the assault guns were from the platoon that was part of the headquarters company. The other three assault guns were pulled from the three medium tank companies (each company had a compliment of one assault gun). In essence, Irzyk had created his own highly mobile artillery battery. He used the assault guns primarily in an indirect fire role, and they packed the same punch as a battery of 105's from one of the division's armored field artillery battalions. The difference was that they were at his immediate beck and call.

The Road to Bastogne

It was a long, arduous trip — the likes of which the men under the umbrella of CCB had never experienced before. The road ahead would test them both mentally and physically, and it would become a time in their lives that they would never forget. It became forever known as "The Firecall."

To ensure that the column didn't become too spread out, and that the entire force moved at an even tempo, the Shermans were at the head of the column (if faster vehicles took the lead, it would be more difficult to maintain even spacing within the column). The initial leg of their journey was made a bit easier when the drivers were allowed to turn on their headlights. The necessity for speed overruled the normal blackout procedures.

CCB drove northwest from its assembly area toward the town of Morhange. The column, with its long stream of evenly spaced headlights stretching as far as the eye could see, crossed back over the Moselle at Pont-a-Mousson. The column then turned north toward Longwy. The 8th's recon platoon raced out ahead of the tanks, securing the crossroads that lay ahead and ensuring that all pedestrian traffic was kept out of the way. The recon platoon continuously leapfrogged from town to town, intersection to intersection.

The column stopped periodically to allow the men a momentary respite from the rigors of the road. The stops gave the men a chance to relieve themselves and get their blood circulating (it was bitter cold). But despite the occasional stops, many of the men urinated over the tailgates of the trucks and sides of halftracks as the column moved over the icy roads.

The decision to send the Fourth Armored toward the Ardennes had been done in such haste that there were was but one map available that covered the areas they were moving through. General Dager took ownership of the priceless piece of cartography, and would frequently pull his jeep up to Irzyk's tank at the head of the column to keep him informed of the route to be followed.

The column rolled into Longwy, and despite the narrower street, the drivers never let up on their speed. Dager stood at the center of town, waving the column through and urging them to keep up the pace. About two miles north of Longwy, Irzyk's tank crossed the Belgian border. The column pulled away from the city, with Dager holding the answer to the question that everyone was asking: where are we headed?

At 8:30 A.M., a 45-minute stop was taken so that the appetites of hungry men and the thirst of drained machines could be quenched simultaneously. The tanks pulled off to the side of the road, which cleared the way for the fuel trucks to move up alongside the column. Five-gallon cans were quickly passed from truck crew to tankers, and in bucket brigade fashion, the precious gasoline flowed into the thirsty tanks and halftracks. Empty cans were loaded back into the trucks as efficiently as they had been offloaded, and the trucks did a smart turnabout and headed back toward the rear of the column.

Refueled and refreshed, the column continued on a straight shot to the north out of Longwy, and some 12 miles later entered Arlon, the next large city located only two miles from the southwest border of Luxembourg. General Dager was once again in prime form as he stood smack in the middle of the road facing the oncoming column. It was here that he signaled Irzyk to branch off to the left, down a road that would carry them to the northwest. The change in direction sent a buzz through the column. Where could they be headed?

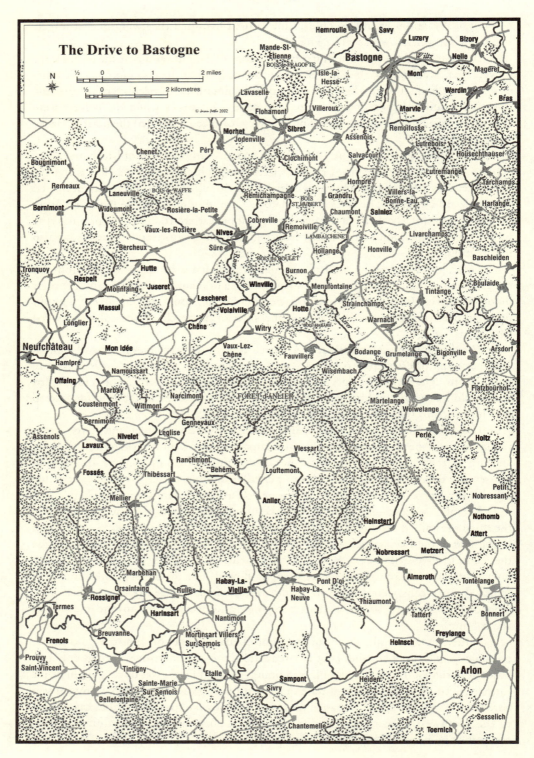

The Drive to Bastogne

The III Corps headquarters was not yet in operation at Arlon, and Dager soon discovered that VIII Corps was responsible for the zone into which he was now advancing. Middleton's corps had yet to be placed under Patton's command, so technically, CCB/4 was now in the zone of General Hodges' First Army.

Dager reported in to Middleton by radio, and discovered that he was now under the command of VIII Corps. This development took place without the immediate knowledge of the Third Army chain of command above Dager. Gaffey, Millikin, Patton ... none were aware of what had just happened. In no position to chart his own course within VIII Corps' zone, Dager had no choice but to abide by whatever Middleton wanted to do with his command. Colonel Clay Olbon was sent ahead to the headquarters of VIII Corps to receive instructions from Middleton regarding where he wanted CCB to move.

In the meantime, CCB kept churning down the road. The next significant waypoint was Neufchâteau, some two-dozen miles from Arlon. The exhausted men of CCB had been driving almost non-stop for 18 hours, and had covered some 140 miles during that time. It was now dark again, and the final leg of the trip was made more difficult by the fact that the vehicles now had to operate under blackout conditions; they were too close to the front to risk being spotted by the enemy. The drivers' nerves were scratched raw, as they had to stay intensely focused on the small sliver of light shining through the "cat's eyes" of the vehicle ahead of them. Irzyk's tank driver, by virtue of being at the head of the column, failed to have even that luxury. With no vehicles ahead of him, he pushed his Sherman through the pitch-black darkness.

As the lead tanks pulled into Neufchâteau, Dager radioed Irzyk and instructed him to bring the column to a stop. The brigadier general raced forward in his jeep to see Irzyk face to face, in order to issue the most critical order of the march: up ahead, at the next main intersection, the column would make a right hand turn. Their heading would now be to the northeast, traveling along the Neufchâteau-Bastogne highway.

Bastogne. To Irzyk, and all the men that trailed behind him, Bastogne was just another landmark that lay along their route. Little did they know the magnitude of the role this Belgian crossroad town was about to play in their lives. CCB would not head into Bastogne this evening, however. Dager instructed Irzyk and Cohen to set up a bivouac about a mile or so northeast of the highway, while CCB established its command post in the town of Vaux-lez-Rosieres

Irzyk and Cohen selected an area close to the small towns of Nives and Sure. Their men were dog-tired from the trip, but they realized the importance of securing their position for the night. So before anyone was allowed to bunk down, the area had to be thoroughly outposted. Teams of armored infantrymen and light tanks were sent out to patrol between the bivouac area and Bastogne. The situation was highly charged, since they didn't know where the enemy was located.

At about 11 P.M., the men settled into the cold interior of their tanks and half-tracks to grab whatever rest they could. The long, 161-mile trip had carried them from the dead of night, through the weak rays of the winter sun, and into the cold depths of a second night. They surely needed the rest.

Nervousness over what lay ahead offset the fatigue that every man was feeling.

Sleep did not come easy. It became even more difficult at 1:30 A.M., when it was reported that enemy tanks and infantry were moving toward the positions of A/10. Nothing came of the alert, however, and patrols sent out to identify the threat "failed to find traces of the enemy in the vicinity."

The arrival of CCB/4 just 8 miles southwest of Bastogne represented the delivery of a promise that Bradley had made to Middleton on the night of December 18. When Bradley became aware that at least one combat command of the Fourth would be on the way north on the 19th, he promised Middleton that more reinforcements were on the way. At noon on the 19th, as CCB/4 was traveling north, Middleton telephoned his immediate boss, the commander of the First Army (General Hodges), and asked him if he could employ CCB/4 upon its arrival. Unsure of what the total picture was on the south flank of the Bulge, Hodges sent Middleton's request to Bradley, who in turn informed Middleton that CCB was available for his use, but only for the purpose of holding his position, and only if necessary. Thus, when Dager reported in to VIII Corps later on the 19th, Middleton took him under his command without hesitation.

On the morning of December 20, Middleton plotted how to use his newly arrived resource. The commander of VIII Corps wanted to split up and dish out the elements of CCB/4 into yet more task forces and teams that could be scattered about the area in front of Bastogne, just as he had done with CCR/9 and CCB/10.

Dager argued vociferously against his command being split up in this fashion, and managed to satisfy Middleton by agreeing to send just a single task force into Bastogne; the majority of his command would remain in place southwest of town. Dager then turned to Major Irzyk to form the task force.

By now, Patton had been made aware of CCB's predicament. His response to the situation, however, was almost that of indifference. In his diary on December 20, he wrote:

> In the morning I drove to Luxembourg arriving at 0900. Bradley had halted the 80th Division at Luxembourg and had also engaged one combat command of the 4th Armored Division in the vicinity east of Bastogne without letting me know, but I said nothing.

The 33 Tanks

Before continuing the story of CCB, there must be a discussion of one long-standing error in the historical record. As mentioned in the Preface of this book, the Official Army History of the Ardennes Offensive, authored by Hugh Cole, states on page 513: "the 8th Tank Battalion alone had thirty-three tanks drop out because of mechanical failure in the 160-mile rush to the Ardennes." Unfortunately, Cole's statement is repeated ad nauseam by countless authors who have followed in his wake. What makes it so unfortunate is that the claim is not even remotely true. It is a complete falsehood, and does a great disservice to the men of the 8th Tank Battalion.

The root source for Cole's statement is a sloppily typed, page-and-a-half set of notes from an undated interview conducted with Major Abrams, the assistant G-4 of the 4th Armored Division. This document can be found within a large collection of after-action interviews conducted with a wide range of officers from the division. Unlike literally every other interview, this document does not contain the date or location where the interview took place, nor does it indicate the staff member who conducted the interview with Abrams (no relation to Lt. Col. Creighton Abrams).

Within this document, it is written: "On the move northward the 8th lost 33 because of mechanical failures. A reason for this: th (sic) 8th had most of the original tanks that were issued on arrival in England." After the page was typed, the hand-written word "medium" was inserted after the 33 (in the pre-computer era, it is extremely common to find that these sorts of documents were edited by hand, probably by higher-ups who were reviewing the work of their staff). This is also the source document for various authors' claims that the entire Fourth Armored Division was only short 21 medium tanks when it set out for the Ardennes (a review of the individual tank battalion records expose this as a gross misrepresentation of the combat-ready tank strength of the division).

The assertion regarding the 33 tanks is repeated in summaries of the battle scribed by the members of the Army's historical division, who compiled and bundled the after action reports. For example, the 33-tank claim is mentioned in a document titled: "*Narrative summary of Operation of the 4th Armd Div in the relief of Bastogne, 22-29 Dec*," authored by one L.B. Clark, Captain, AUS. (Captain Clark figures prominently in many of the interviews conducted with the 4th AD during this period). Clark also repeats the claim in "*Narrative summary of CCB's part in the relief of Bastogne, 20 through 29 Dec 44.*" It is unknown whether Hugh Cole drew his "fact" from the original, sloppy interview with Major Abrams, or from the narrative summaries prepared by Clark.

The truth of the matter is that the 8th Tank Battalion set out for the Ardennes with approximately 32 medium tanks. And every one of them arrived. Not a single tank failed to reach its destination. This is the recollection of (ret) Brig. General Irzyk, as stated during my correspondence and discussions with him. It is also the figure that matches up well with my own extrapolations, based on data culled from contemporary after-action interviews and the account Irzyk penned several years before we first met.

It is indeed a shame that no one, including the highly respected Hugh Cole, took greater care to examine the records or interview the participants who were closest to the story. An after-action interview was conducted on 7 January 1945 with Brigadier General Dager (CCB), and a joint interview on 9 January 1945 with Captain Bert Ezell (the 8th TB's Executive Officer) and Captain C.J. Stauber (the 8th's S-2). Neither of these interviews includes even one word about the loss of 33 tanks en route to the Ardennes. Not a single word. This would have been big news, and it is conspicuous by virtue of its absence in these interviews.

In Al Irzyk's words, the loss of 33 tanks in the fashion suggested by Cole would have been "an unprecedented mechanical and vehicular disaster." He later offered the following:

> If 33 tanks dropped out because of mechanical problems, they would be strewn out along the whole route of march. I had a very talented maintenance platoon in my service company. They marched closely behind the combat vehicles. They would pull off the road the minute they spotted a tank with mechanical problems. They had the proper tools and spare parts. Often they would get a tank rolling after a very short pause. But this did not happen on our approach march to Bastogne. ALL our tanks made it. We had no chance

to do maintenance for six weeks — from the time we kicked off in early November until our rest stop at Domnom les Dieuze. It was the great work our tankers did during that brief rest period that got us successfully to Bastogne.

After continued discussion and speculation regarding how the assistant G-4 and/or the interviewer, and subsequently, Hugh Cole, could have made such a glaring error, Al Irzyk wrote, a bit tongue-in-cheek,

> 33 was about my battalion's worth of tanks. If they all dropped out how in the hell did we get to Nives — walk? If what I have out lined is not fact, then I must have had amnesia or combat fatigue. I do remember that my tank and I got to Nives, that I was surrounded by tanks in the bivouac area, and there were enough tanks the next morning to go into Bastogne with Ezell. There must have been some phantom maintenance organization that in an instant repaired 33 tanks. The historians make the assertion about the 33 tanks, but they never correlate the drop out with the fact that the tanks somehow were immediately involved in operations.

It is also interesting that, in his narrative summary, Captain Clark dismissed the suggestion that the Fourth Armored was only short 21 medium tanks leading into the Battle of the Bulge. He participated in most of the interviews conducted with the staff of the combat commands and tank battalions, and heard first hand about the number of tanks each battalion drove into action at the start of the counterattack. So it is no surprise that he wrote off the suggestion that the division was only short 21 Sherman tanks.

It is a shame that Clark did not perform at least equal due diligence regarding the outrageous claim that 33 tanks of the 8th Tank Battalion had dropped out due to mechanical failure. Given that the interview with the assistant G-4 does not carry a date, we do not know if the information was garnered before or after Captain Clark had the opportunity to speak with the officers at the combat command and battalion levels. If he gained this information prior to his interviews with Brig. General Dager and the staff of the 8th Tank Battalion, you can only scratch your head and wonder why he would not have thought this worthy of corroboration with the men who rode with the column. If the information from the assistant G-4 was garnered *after* the other interviews, one has to wonder why he didn't backtrack for confirmation. Such post-interview follow-ups were not unheard of. In fact, none other than Captain Clark conducted a supplemental interview with (then) Lt. Colonel Cohen on April 29, 1945, in order to clarify some of the details regarding the fight at Chaumont that took place on December 23. This was almost four months after his original interview with Cohen.

Had Captain Clark been thorough on this point, he clearly would have uncovered a gross mistake on the part of either assistant G-4 Abrams or the unidentified interviewer (one must consider the possibility that the interviewer misinterpreted or recorded incorrectly a comment made by Abrams). But the bottom line is that, had Captain Clark been more thorough in his work, the mistake would have been revealed at its point of origin. Instead, we have a fallacious account of the 8th Tank Battalion's movement to the Ardennes that has lingered all these many years, unchallenged, uninvestigated, and uncorrected — until now.

The record has now been set straight. It is a shame, however, that the mistake will linger on in so many other published works. The men of the 8th Tank Battalion, who worked so diligently on their vehicles, and who took such pride in their performance, deserve much better than that.

Task Force Ezell

When General Dager informed Al Irzyk that he had to send a task force into Bastogne, the young major's response mirrored Dager's reaction to Middleton. He "protested vehemently," arguing that, with the situation ahead being so unclear, this was no time for "a piecemeal commitment of his forces." Somewhat to Irzyk's surprise, Dager, without hesitation, agreed with him, and told him about his own disagreement with Middleton just a short time ago. In the face of Dager's honesty and forthrightness, Irzyk saw little purpose in further debate, and went about pulling together the task force.

Irzyk chose Captain Bert Ezell, the executive officer of the 8th Tank Battalion, to lead the task force into Bastogne. Task Force Ezell consisted of the Sherman tanks of A Company, C Company from the 10th Armored Infantry Battalion, and the M-7s of C Battery from the 22nd AFAB. Accompanying Ezell was the S-3 of the 10th AIB, Captain Abe Baum.

At 10:30 A.M., Ezell set out with his force, which represented roughly one third of the core fighting strength of CCB. Not knowing what they would find at Bastogne, Irzyk's orders to Ezell were to report to General McAuliffe, from whom he would then receive further instructions, and to report back to Irzyk on the situation in Bastogne.

As the men of TF Ezell advanced up the highway toward Bastogne, they had no knowledge of what was ahead. Rumor had it that the Germans had cut the road. If so, would they have to fight their way in?

The ride into Bastogne was nerve-wracking. En route, TF Ezell passed some GIs moving on foot away from Bastogne, in the direction of Sibret. The Americans appeared disorganized and beaten, but neither Ezell, churning ahead in his tank, or Baum, bouncing along in his jeep, stopped to get their story. Nor should they have. Their mission was in Bastogne.

The cracking sound of distant, sporadic small arms fire punctuated the cold winter air as TF Ezell continued up the road. Closer to Bastogne, they were surprised to find several batteries of 155mm towed howitzers sitting idle along the side of the road. A lone lieutenant colonel stood amongst the guns and transports with tears in his eyes. The task force moved on without inquiring as to the fate of the lieutenant colonel's command.

The unidentified officer would have had quite a story to tell, had he been asked. The artillery pieces belonged to the battalions of the 333rd Artillery Group; specifically, the 969th (Colored), 333rd (Colored), and 771st Field Artillery battalions. The day before, the 333rd Group had been attached to the 101st Airborne Division, and had established firing positions north and west of Bastogne. After receiving small arms fire, the group commander ordered all three of the battalions "to displace toward St. Hubert, west of Bastogne." There was "considerable confusion" as the artillery battalions pulled up stakes and headed away from Bastogne. The route they followed was to the southwest, along the Bastogne-Neufchâteau highway.

The following morning, there was even greater confusion in store when the 101st Division Artillery could not make contact with the 333rd Group. Early that afternoon, the 101st learned that the 333rd Group had moved, having been so informed by the group's executive officer. As it turns out, the group commander had not asked for permission to displace his battalions (he was relieved of his command later that day). The 101st sent a party down the Bastogne-Neufchâteau highway to intercept the fleeing artillery battalions, and ordered them to return. During the period of time that followed, the crews had apparently left their guns and the distraught Lt. Colonel at the roadside.

The men that were seen walking down the highway southwest of the abandoned guns may have very well belonged to the artillery battalions of the 333rd Group. They may have also been, or included, members of the 28th Infantry Division. Earlier that day, the CG of the 28th, Norman Cota, had requested and received permission from Middleton to extract the battered remnants of his division from Bastogne. Cota had just established his division command post at Sibret (having fled Wiltz the day before) and was now trying to rally his remaining troops at that location. Traffic was so snarled in and around Bastogne that day that, at one point, an order was given to at least some of the men from the 28th Infantry Division to abandon their vehicles and march toward Sibret.

The remainder of the advance into Bastogne was uneventful. Upon contacting the 101st, Ezell radioed Irzyk to update him on his status. If it was the Fourth Armored's mission to drive to Bastogne, they had succeeded!

Once in Bastogne, Captain Ezell and Captain Baum hunted down the 101st Airborne Division's chief of staff, who passed the two captains over to the G-3 of the 101st, who in turn brought them to General McAuliffe, the acting commander of the 101st. McAuliffe was still in the process of working out the mechanics of the relationship between his division and the supporting elements from CCR/9 and CCB/10. So perhaps with enough on his plate already, he turned Ezell over to Colonel Roberts, the commanding officer of CCB/10.

To Abe Baum, Roberts appeared to be fatigued by the hard fighting his combat command had experienced during the past two days. In Baum's words, "he had no idea of why we were there or what to do with us." Of course, how could he; seeing someone from the Fourth Armored suddenly appear in Bastogne was probably something that no one would have laid odds for on the morning of December 20. Baum asked, "Where would you like to deploy us?" Apparently not having an immediate need to plug TF Ezell into a position directly in the face of the Germans, Roberts instructed Ezell to assemble his force at the village of Villeroux, about two and a half miles southwest of Bastogne. As Roberts talked with the two captains, his glazed eyes stayed glued to a map of the Bastogne defenses. Abe Baum sensed that the situation at Bastogne was not good.

As all of this was unfolding on December 20, III Corps' headquarters finally got up and running at Arlon, and the Fourth was now officially attached to Millikin's corps. Also during that time, Dager managed to reach General Gaffey, and raised hell about how his command had been commandeered and was now being scattered about the Belgian landscape. Gaffey, faced with executing the most important part of III Corps' mission, was equally disturbed by the fact that one third of his division had been stripped from his command. He immediately ordered Dager to pull back TF Ezell, consolidate it with CCB, and move the entire command back in the direction of Arlon.

The new orders were immediately passed on to Major Irzyk, who in turn tried to raise Ezell on the radio. But Ezell was not immediately available, as he and Baum were meeting with Colonel Roberts at the very moment Irzyk was calling. Irzyk shouted into the radio "Get him!," and the operator ran to summon Ezell, who came immediately to the radio, while Baum remained with Roberts.

Captain Ezell was relieved when he was told he would be rejoining the main body of CCB, but was nonetheless mystified by the way events were unfolding. Ezell returned to see Roberts, and informed him of his new orders. Ezell "had a difficult time convincing a confused Colonel Roberts that after just arriving, he was turning around and returning with his force." Ezell departed, but Baum remained behind for about 15 minutes with Roberts, with the hope that he could offer some comforting words in light of the situation.

TF Ezell's trip back down the road toward Vaux-lez-Rosieres, which started during mid-afternoon, would prove to be much more eventful than the trip into Bastogne earlier in the day. Once outside of Bastogne, the task force came across a truck that had come to rest in a ditch along the side of the road. Stopping to investigate, they found the driver still in the seat behind the wheel, but the top of his head had been completely blown off above the eyes. A short distance ahead, they found further evidence that the enemy might be lurking nearby: the telltale tracks left by German tanks. Judging from the width, they were believed to be Panthers or Tigers.

A short distance further down the highway, they once again came upon the artillery pieces that had been left at the side of the road. Some of the trucks and prime movers were still idling, and now a lone captain was on the scene, laboring by himself to hitch up the guns and move them to the road. The company commander of A/8, Lt. Len Kieley, left some of his men behind to help the unidentified captain recover the howitzers. Meanwhile, Kieley hitched three of the guns to the rear of his Shermans and brought them back to CCB. Some of the pieces were returned directly to their owners (the howitzers and crews would be reunited by that evening, and would go on to make a better account of themselves during the defense of Bastogne).

Obviously, the Germans had cut across the Neufchâteau-Bastogne highway sometime during the day on December 20, and had made contact with some of the men from the 28th Infantry and/or the artillery battalions assembling near Sibret and Villeroux, respectively. This contact came during the period when TF Ezell was actually in Bastogne. But where were the Germans now?

The task force was wary as it headed back to the southwest, but other than three artillery rounds that fell within earshot, they didn't hear or see any other sign of the enemy. As they moved, they came across signalmen laying telephone wire parallel to the highway, and they seemed to be unnerved. Apparently, they had been able to do their work uninterrupted by the Germans.

Given TF Ezell's free passage back down the road to the southwest, it would appear that the highway between Neufchâteau and Bastogne was still open during the mid to late afternoon of the 20th. General McAuliffe himself used the road to go to Neufchâteau late in the day on the 20th for a meeting with Middleton at VIII Corps HQ; he was able to make it back into Bastogne before sundown without running into the enemy.

But the Germans were indeed nearby. Late that afternoon or early evening, Sibret came under attack by a small force from the 5th FJ Division, which managed to enter the town and occupy the police station. Sibret is located approximately one kilometer north of the Neufchâteau highway; the Germans had to have crossed the highway en route to Sibret.

Later that evening, elements of the 26th VG Division and Panzer Lehr Division followed behind the 5th FJ. The 26th VG recon battalion added significant weight to the attack by the small band of paratroopers from the 5th FJ Division, and forced the remnants of Cota's division to abandon Sibret (he relocated his command post to Vaux-lez-Rosieres, further down the Neufchâteau highway). Apparently, both TF Ezell and Brigadier General McAuliffe managed to squeeze in their travel in between the elements of the 5th FJ and 26th VG divisions.

Before the fighting at Sibret erupted, Dager's command was released from VIII Corps and assigned to III Corps. Thankfully, Dager was now back under the command of his parent division. Later that afternoon, CCB saddled up and headed back toward Neufchâteau. CCB then turned to the southeast, and after traveling about five miles, the 8th Tank Battalion stopped at Leglise. Major Cohen's 10th AIB, supported by a platoon of AAA guns from the 489th, continued on for another three miles until it reached the crossroads at Beheme. It then turned left, and traveled another mile to the town of Louftemont, arriving there at 6 P.M. Company C/10 was sent south to outpost the crossroads at the village of Anlier. The 22nd AFAB and 126th Armored Ordnance Battalion were sent east as far as Habay-la-Neuve. CCB's HQ spent the night of the 20th at Mellier, and then on the 21st, moved to Habay-la-Vielle (slightly southwest of Habay-la-Neuve).

After all of the movement of the past three days, the morning of December 21 brought the promise of being able to stay put in one place. While the balance of the Fourth Armored was assembling further east, CCB was able to spend the day tending to the maintenance of their vehicles. Rather than relax, Major Irzyk saw to it that the tankers of the "Rolling Eight Ball" were "squeezing in as much maintenance as they possibly could during the obviously brief time available to them."

What If?

For decades to follow, those familiar with the story of Task Force Ezell's foray into Bastogne would speculate about what would have happened had CCB been ordered to hold open the Neufchâteau-Bastogne highway. Some suggest that the German encirclement of Bastogne would never have been completed. Others are of the opinion that CCB did not have the strength to stand in the way of what was coming toward them, and would have been either forced into the Bastogne perimeter with the rest of the defenders, overrun, or pushed away from Bastogne.

The outcome of such a battle would have been largely determined by the subsequent role played by CCA and CCR. Had CCB remained committed along the Neufchâteau highway, a critical decision would have been forthcoming regarding the best use of the rest of the Fourth Armored Division. Should they have continued with the attack up the Arlon-Bastogne highway? Should CCA and CCR been shifted to the Neufchâteau highway as well? If they *were* shifted west, what unit(s) would have covered their right flank? What would the German reaction have been? Would they have held more of their panzer forces in the vicinity of Bastogne to deal with the Fourth Armored Division, which they respected and feared? Once one starts down the road of hypotheticals related to CCB and TF Ezell, a quagmire awaits, as the number of variables that arise outpace one's ability to project an outcome with any certainty.

To say that the withdrawal of CCB to a position further to the southeast was a mistake is to deny the fact that the Fourth Armored Division's attack was, in the end, successful. Had the Fourth Armored failed to relieve Bastogne, then the decision to attack along the chosen routes would be ripe for criticism. But that was not the case.

All that can be said with certainty is what actually happened. And what happened is that General Gaffey was alarmed when he discovered that one third of his division had been, without his prior knowledge, wrestled from his control. He had a specific mission to fulfill, and it was not his place to change the axis of the attack. To do so would have involved significant shifts in the dispositions of the entire III Corps. This might have been possible, had Patton had the desire to make them. It is not known whether, upon learning of CCB's close proximity to Bastogne, Patton gave the idea any consideration.

All we *do* know is that he was in full support of Gaffey's need and desire to get CCB back under the control of the Fourth Armored. Despite his initial acquiescence upon hearing of CCB's attachment to VIII Corps, he was later quoted as saying "I want that son of a bitch back here. I want him back as fast as shit goes through a sick duck." And so it was done.

The Move to New Positions

During the day on December 21, Irzyk and Cohen were called back to the headquarters of CCB. There, the staff briefed the team that Bastogne had indeed been encircled during the prior night. TF Ezell had avoided the trap by the thinnest of margins. Dager then informed the men of their mission, which was to drive north toward Bastogne. They would be operating on the left flank of the division, and their axis of advance would run parallel to that of CCA. Dager laid out the route to be taken to the I.P., and the axis of the attack thereafter. CCB's mission orders were simple: relieve Bastogne, and provide a secure route of supply into the town.

At 4 P.M., they received specific orders for taking their first intermediate objective: Chaumont. The general axis of advance would be from Fauvillers due north over a secondary road to Menufontaine, then across the Sure River at a bridge just south of Burnon. From the banks of the Sure River, they would be approximately 7 miles from the 101st Airborne Division's defensive perimeter south of Bastogne. From Burnon, the advance would continue to Chaumont, slightly over three miles north of the Sure River crossing site. At that point, only four miles would separate CCB from the 101st. The terrain over the remaining miles was more favorable for offensive operations, and the exact route they would take, after passing through Grandru, would be opportunistic. One contingency for their advance was that they be prepared to swing east to the Arlon-Bastogne highway, should CCA have a difficult time gaining a crossing of the Sure River at Martelange.

By the early evening, the orders had been passed down to the individual units. The 8th Tank Battalion's A Company, reinforced with armored infantry, would take the lead. Extra artillery support was brought in for CCB, in the form of the 253rd Armored Field Artillery Battalion (M7s), and the 776th Field Artillery Battalion (tractor-drawn 155mm Howitzers).

The mood within the 8th Tank Battalion had become "progressively more tense and grim" as their time for commitment drew near. There had been no contact with the enemy up to this point, but that evening, at about 10 P.M., Company A of the 10th AIB captured two Germans near Louftemont. It was the first sign that the enemy might have indeed pushed that far south.

Though CCB had already been in the Ardennes sector since the late evening of December 19, and had even sent elements into Bastogne on the 20th, December 22 would mark its first day of full engagement at the Battle of the Bulge. As we shall see, getting into Bastogne the second time around wouldn't be so easy.

16. Nuts!

Critical Decisions

As the sun rose behind the thick morning fog and mist on December 19, the Germans found themselves well behind schedule in their drive to Antwerp. Thoughts of reaching the port city faded from the forefront of the Germans' minds, and they now focused almost exclusively on reaching the line of the Meuse River. But even that goal was at risk, due to the valiant and, at times, desperate defense that the Americans had offered at key locations throughout the Ardennes.

If life were to be breathed into the German drive to the Meuse, there was no question that Bastogne had to fall to Manteuffel's Fifth Panzer Army. If the vital road junction remained in American hands, the Germans would have a difficult time supplying and reinforcing the spearheads that might manage to move further west. Given the necessity of capturing Bastogne, Hitler's insistence that only the 26th Volkgrenadier Division be used for the task ranks at the top of the list of blunders committed by the Germans during the offensive. Those close to the battlefield understood the necessity of capturing the town, and were desperate to use more force than what the 26th VG Division alone could provide. But Hitler would have none of it, and insisted that the panzer divisions bypass Bastogne in favor of driving west for the Meuse River. Hitler's penchant for meddling in the business of his generals was about to wipe out any slim chance of success that the offensive had to begin with.

During the initial stages of the German advance toward Bastogne, both the Panzer Lehr Division, driving from the east, and the 2nd Panzer Division, driving from the north, had a grand opportunity to push into Bastogne. The 101st would have certainly made a fight of it, but the odds of them holding back the full weight of two panzer divisions, plus the 26th VG Division, are highly improbable. Instead, the 2nd Panzer, after getting its nose bloodied by Team Desobry at Noville, moved on to the west-northwest, completely bypassing Bastogne. They would never play a direct role in the battle for Bastogne, other than the tangential repercussions of the battle at Noville.

The Panzer Lehr Division was a different story. Though the majority of the division would eventually bypass the town to the south, elements of the division made repeated attempts to break through the American defenses. The full weight of the division was never thrown into the effort, however, and Bayerlein's own focus seemed to be cast with his spearheads moving west, as opposed to the more critical job of capturing Bastogne.

Tightening the Noose

General Kokott had the burden of figuring out how he was going to take the town. An axiom of war is that the attacker should afford itself at least a 3 to 1 advantage when planning an attack. Kokott had no such superiority. In fact, the opposing forces were closer to equal in infantry strength, and the Americans actually had an advantage in both armor and artillery. The Americans also had the distinct advantage of defending along interior lines. As a result, the American's linear front was shorter than their opponents. Firing from within the perimeter, their artillery could strike any area threatened by the Germans. They were also able to use the excellent road network stemming from Bastogne for the quick dispatch of mobile reserves that could react to potential German breakthroughs.

Having witnessed the rebuff of the Panzer Lehr Division's initial attack from the east, the Germans began to test the waters in other areas. On the morning of December 20, the lead elements of the 901st Panzer Grenadier Regiment moved into the town of Marvie, located only about a mile and a half southeast of Bastogne. The German force consisted of only a company of grenadiers supported by four tanks. The Americans had just bolstered their defenses west of Marvie with the addition of the 327th Glider Regiment's 2nd Battalion, with several medium tanks from Team O'Hara located nearby for support. Rather than allowing the German vanguard to steal the town, the Americans counterattacked, and within an hour, destroyed all four of the German tanks and drove the grenadiers back from whence they came. It was the last the Americans saw of the Germans at Marvie for the balance of the day.

That evening, the 902nd Panzer Grenadier Regiment attempted to attack the positions of the 501st Regiment west of Neffe. The German infantry, some two battalions in strength, were observed moving toward the 501st's positions, and heavy American artillery fire, along with the firepower of the 501st and Team O'Hara, broke up the attack before it ever had a chance. This would be the final attempt by the Germans to attack the perimeter from the east.

Once the 26th Volksgrenadier Division caught up with the Panzer Lehr Division, the 902nd Panzer Grenadier Regiment was pulled from the line. The grenadiers were sent along the same road taken by Bayerlein's reconnaissance battalion, which had skirted Bastogne to the south. In a move that was critically important to Kokott, the 901st Panzer Grenadier Regiment was detached from Bayerlein's command and attached to the 26th Volksgrenadier Division (someone had finally recognized and acted upon the necessity to provide more muscle for capturing Bastogne). Some Mark IVs and Panthers also remained behind to support the 901st. This provided Kokott with some much needed armor.

Kokott began moving his two lead volksgrenadier regiments, the 77th and 78th, across the north side of the American perimeter. The 77th advanced furthest to the west, cutting across the Houffalize-Bastogne highway, while the 78th remained east of that road. The 26th VG Division's Pioneer Battalion would later slide in and occupy the axis of the highway itself. Once established in these positions, Kokott used his volksgrenadiers to strike from the north and northeast. In the dense woods that dominated the sector, the Germans went head to head against the experienced 506th and 501st regiments, in what boiled down to a pure infantry battle. The attacks failed, and Kokott added these avenues to the list of approaches he would no longer consider.

As Kokott's two volksgrenadier regiments were moving into position north of Bastogne, the 39th Fusilier Regiment, which had been serving as the 26th VG Division's reserve, was put in motion around the south flank of Bastogne. They would screen the perimeter to the south and southwest, and position some of their units to partake in the offensive activities being planned for the west side of the perimeter.

Kokott's headquarters followed in the wake of the 39th Regiment, and settled in at the village of Hompre, which was located about three quarters of a mile west of the Arlon-Bastogne highway, four miles south of Bastogne, and about a mile and a half north of Chaumont. In the area south of Bastogne, there were very few roads leading from east to west, and the most prominent one passed through Hompre. This made the small village an important nexus not only for Kokott's units that were sweeping around Bastogne, but also for Bayerlein's Panzer Lehr Division, which advanced over the same route before continuing west toward the Ourthe River.

Kokott would not make an immediate push toward Bastogne from the south. His plan called for an attack from the west side of the perimeter, in the area of Senonchamps. His only integral mechanized unit was his reconnaissance battalion, command by Major Rolf Kunkel. He used this unit as the core of a mobile kampfgruppe, which he sent south of Bastogne. Kampfgruppe Kunkel passed through the lines of the 39th Regiment, and across the Neufchâteau highway. Some of Kunkel's men reached the area of Sibret late on the night of December 20, where they ran into remnants of the 110th Infantry Regiment and the division HQ of the 28th Infantry Division, who were engaged, much to Kokott's surprise, with advance elements of the 5th FJ Division.

KG Kunkel joined with the company of paratroopers from the 14th FJ Regiment, and by 9 A.M. on December 21, the Americans had been flushed from Sibret. KG Kunkel then moved on toward positions in the woods west of Senonchamps, from whence he prepared to launch an attack down the Senonchamps-Bastogne road on the following day.

On December 22, the Germans had a fairly contiguous ring of units surrounding the Americans at Bastogne. But Kokott did not have the strength to launch an all out attack across the entire perimeter. He would only be able to concentrate sufficient force for offensive operations at one or perhaps two select points at any given time. Cognizant of his limitations at Bastogne, General Heinrich von Luttwitz, the commander of the XLVII Panzer Corps (the corps to which Kokott's division belonged), tried to steal Bastogne by making what might be considered one of the worst bluffs in military history.

The Ultimatum

At 11:30 A.M. on December 22, in the midst of a swirling snowfall, four Germans bearing a white flag approached the front line of Company F, 327th Glider Regiment, which was guarding the southern perimeter near the Arlon-Bastogne highway. The German party consisted of two officers and two enlisted men. Some Americans went out to meet them, whereupon the junior officer among the Germans, who spoke English, asked to speak with the commanding general.

All four of the Germans were brought to the nearby farmhouse of Jean Kessler, which was serving as a command post for one of the platoons of F Company. The two officers were blindfolded, and led back to F Company's command post, further to the rear. Upon their arrival, the American company commander was presented with a note from "The German Commander," which contained an ultimatum: surrender within two hours, or see your forces annihilated by the guns of a full German Artillery Corps and six heavy A.A. battalions massed beyond the American perimeter.

While the Germans were detained, the note was brought to the headquarters of the 101st Airborne Division. Upon reading the demand, McAuliffe reacted by simply saying, "Nuts," and then turned away from the matter. He departed his headquarters, and headed to the front to go congratulate some men who had recently repelled a strong enemy attack in their sector.

When he returned, his staff reminded him that he should send a formal reply to the German demand. Stumped for an appropriate response, he asked them for advice. His G-3, Lt. Colonel Kinnard (obviously a man with a sense of humor) said, "That first remark of yours would be hard to beat." McAuliffe couldn't recall what his one syllable response had been, and when reminded, agreed with his G-3 that it was appropriate. A formal reply was typed up, which simply said:

> To the German Commander:
>
> Nuts!
>
> The American Commander

Colonel Harper, the commanding officer of the 327th, carried the note by hand back to the command post of F Company, where the two German officers were still being detained (the two enlisted men had been kept back at the front line). When he presented the note to the German major, the enemy officer was uncertain as to the meaning of the word "Nuts," but seemed to think it was an indication that the Americans would indeed surrender. Harper informed the Germans that the reply was "decidedly not affirmative," and left it at that.

The party soon reached the forward line of F Company, where the two German officers were reunited with the two enlisted men. Harper gave the Germans a parting point of clarification about the response of the American Commander:

> If you don't understand what "Nuts" means, in plain English it is the same as "Go to hell." I will tell you something else — if you continue to attack, we will kill every goddamn German that tries to break into this city.

As it turned out, the Germans were in no position to attempt the massive bombardment promised in Luttwitz's ultimatum. Lacking adequate transport, much of their artillery still sat east of the Our River, and the artillery that *had* been moved to the west was short of ammunition. General Luttwitz had failed miserably at bluffing the Americans into surrendering. If anything, his note, and more precisely, McAuliffe's response of "Nuts," served as a rallying cry for the men of the 101st.

When Manteuffel discovered what Luttwitz had done, he was furious, for the failure to make good on the threat would send a signal to the Americans that the Germans had not amassed the kind of artillery that was suggested in Luttwitz's ultimatum. Desperate to inflict some sort of wound on the Americans in response to the rebuff, Manteuffel requested the Luftwaffe's support in bombing the town during the days that followed. The Luftwaffe delivered on Manteuffel's request, and they put together a series of night bombing raids that spilled much American and civilian blood into the streets of Bastogne, but came nowhere close to pounding the "Screaming Eagles" into submission.

Enter the 5th Parachute Division

As Kokott tried to discover the formula for taking Bastogne, he kept a wary eye on the progress of the German 7th Army, and in particular, the 5th FJ Division. Heilmann's paratroopers had the responsibility of keeping pace with Kokott's division, and once south and southwest of Bastogne, they were to turn south and take up defensive positions as a precaution against American counterattacks from that direction. Kokott was depending on Heilmann to watch his back as he dealt with Bastogne

Kokott was not very enamored with Heilmann's division. The 5th FJ's performance during the opening days of the offensive was a bit tainted in his eyes, first by the slow progress of the paratroopers after crossing the Our River, and then by an incident that occurred at the town of Wiltz.

Wiltz was in the 26th Volksgrenadier Division's zone. Kokott's plan was to bypass the town, since alternative routes would allow them to sweep north of the town against limited opposition. To his surprise, elements of the 5th FJ wandered north out of their own zone and decided to attack Wiltz on the evening of December 19. Heilmann had not ordered the attack, for he, too, wanted his troops to continue heading west. Wiltz was of no value to him.

Apparently his paratroopers felt otherwise. Some of his men decided to find refuge from the cold winter night, and the houses of Wiltz looked inviting. So without orders, they manufactured their own axis of advance, and plunged into the town. Wiltz was still held by elements of the 28th Infantry Division, and until earlier that day, had housed General Cota's headquarters.

The attack netted the capture of 520 Americans and six Sherman tanks in town (the tanks were later adorned with swastikas and pressed into German service). American troops that tried to flee under the cover of darkness were dealt harsh blows by the enemy paratroopers as their columns were caught on the roads leading out of Wiltz. Some of the American drivers raced out with headlights blazing, they were so desperate to break out of the net that the 5th FJ had thrown around them.

By morning, Wiltz and the surrounding road net was firmly in the hands of the German paratroopers. Most of the retreating Americans had been killed or captured. An uncounted number of survivors spent the coming days struggling alone or in small groups to make their way back toward the American lines.

Despite the success of capturing the town and routing the American defenders, to Kokott, this represented a serious breach of discipline and order within the 5th FJ, and significantly influenced his opinion of its ability during the balance of the offensive. While Heilmann shared Kokott's dissatisfaction with his paras taking it upon themselves to attack Wiltz, it must not be overlooked that his men had handed the Americans a stunning defeat, impromptu or not.

As later events would prove, Kokott had perhaps placed too much emphasis on this one aspect of the 5th FJ Division's performance. For as the seventh day of the battle dawned, Heilmann's paratroopers had kept up with the 26th Division just fine. A company of paras from the 14th FJ Regiment had even managed to get as far as Sibret on December 20, arriving there ahead of Kokott's own forces. In fact, Heilmann had good reason to be proud of his young division. In their first action since being reconstructed after the disaster at Normandy, they had earned the distinction of being the only division in the entire offensive to have achieved its objectives.

After kicking Norm Cota's division out of Sibret on the 21st, elements of the 14th FJ Regiment pushed down the Neufchâteau-Bastogne highway as far as Vaux-les-Rosieres, where, on December 22, they once again encountered the HQ of the perpetually retreating 28th Infantry Division. General Cota did not have many resources with which to defend the town or his headquarters. Perhaps 200 to 300 exhausted men from the 110th Infantry Regiment had filtered back to his headquarters, and they now formed the centerpiece of his force. All that he had available to support them was an engineer light pontoon company (which he pressed into service as infantrymen), a platoon of tank destroyers from the 602nd TD Battalion, and a few howitzers. The scratch force repulsed the paratroopers' early morning probe, and the Americans managed to retain their positions around the town.

Vaux-les-Rosieres was important to Heilmann, as it was the designated anchor point for the defensive line that defined his mission. So at dusk, he ordered the 14th Regiment to launch a coordinated assault on the town. In support of this attack, the Germans employed "a platoon of long-barreled 88-mm assault guns mounted on an old model Tiger body with exceptionally heavy armor." (This is the description offered on page 328 of Cole's Official History of the Battle of the Bulge; no unit identification was provided) The shells from the 76mm guns of the American tank destroyers simply glanced off the armor of their German counterparts, leaving the infantrymen and engineers little recourse but to give way. Cota's headquarter was once again in flight, this time all the way back to Neufchâteau, where they settled in near the headquarters of Middleton's VIII Corps.

The 14th FJ Regiment, with its objectives now achieved, began digging in along the routes heading north to Bastogne. They established their headquarters at the small village of Chaumont, astride the road leading from Burnon to Grandru.

The 15th FJ Regiment had established itself along the main axis of the Bastogne-Arlon highway, having advanced through Kaundorf, Boulaide, and Tintange. As early as the afternoon of December 19, paratroopers from the 15th FJ had pushed as far south as Martelange, where they came in contact with the men of the 299th Engineer Battalion north of the town. At about 2 A.M. on December 20, the American engineers reported that 6 enemy "tanks" were located near Martelange (these were actually assault guns from the 11th Assault Gun Brigade). Heavy fighting broke out the following day between the two forces, and by 3:40 P.M., it had been decided that the main bridge carrying the Arlon-Bastogne highway (N4) would have to be blown.

As daylight began to fade, the American engineers, who had already prepped the two bridges in town for demolition, fell back to the south bank of the Sure River. The engineers continued to hold their position on the south bank in the face of the advancing Germans. When the Krauts drew too close for comfort to the N4 bridge, Sgt. Cook lit a short five-second fuse and jumped aboard the truck that carried him and the other engineers west toward the secondary bridge on N45-46.

Another squad of engineers had been guarding the secondary bridge, and now the entire group climbed aboard the truck, save for Sgt. Caufield, who set the fuse on the bridge before boarding. By 5:20 P.M., Company B of the 299th had destroyed the only two bridges crossing the Sure at Martelange (later that evening, a team of engineers from the 299th would blow the bridge at Bodange located 2.5 miles to the northwest). The engineers then withdrew some 6 miles to the west, to the town of Witry.

What Sgt. Caufield didn't know as he sped away from the second bridge was that the span was still sufficiently intact to support men crossing on foot. Though they could not move their pursuing assault guns across the river, German paratroopers crossed over the bridge, and a small group set out on foot toward the west. The Germans then took hold of the town of Fauvillers, which barred the secondary route leading from Habay La Nueve to Bastogne.

It was a good thing for the Americans that the Sure River bridges had been destroyed, for they did not have much available to stop the 15th FJ Regiment from driving south. On the evening of the 20th, all that stood in the Germans' way along the road to Arlon were elements of three American engineer battalions (the 511th, 299th, and 1278th).

At 5:45 P.M. on the evening of December 20, a team of engineers was assembled from elements of the 299th and 1278th Engineer battalions, and the 342nd Engineer General Service Regiment. The task set before them was to occupy and defend Martelange. A two-pronged attack was planned; one group of engineers, assembled in Wiltry, would attack Martelange from the west; another group would attack from the south, via the Arlon highway. Major Kohlar, the executive officer of the 299th Engineer Battalion, was to coordinate the two attacks.

The engineers attacking from the west were dubbed "Company B Force," while the engineers moving up from the south received the title "Buick Force." Both teams took up positions around the outskirts of Martelange, and sent out patrols to determine the enemy's strength inside the town. The attack was planned for the following day.

That evening, a report came in that the Germans were in Fauvillers, which straddled the road leading from Wiltry to Martelange. It now appeared that Company B Force was cut off in between Fauvillers and Martelange, so Company C of the 299th was rushed to Fauvillers to reopen the road. At 10:05 A.M. on December 21, C/299 attacked and quickly cleared the enemy from Fauvillers. Apparently, the 5th FJ had only sent a small patrol into the town, and was not holding it in force. The engineers killed two paratroopers and took four prisoners.

As C/299 was attempting to establish contact with Company B Force, the engineers of B/299 continued on their mission toward Martelange. The vanguard of the force, led by Captain Steen, weaved its way into the town from the west, and met their first opposition at the site of the bridge on road N45-46. The Germans greeted them with machine gun and mortar fire. The Americans were pinned down until they managed to get a .50 caliber machine gun into position to counter the enemy positions. But the presence of the American heavy machine gun was trumped when the Germans brought up some assault guns, which proceeded to advance and fire on the engineers at "point blank" range.

C/299 continued to advance east toward Martelange and the suspected positions of Company B Force. A mile and a half east of Fauvillers (about two thirds of the distance to Martelange), they came under heavy enemy machine gun and mortar fire. The men on point were cut off from the rest of the company, which fell back a short distance to a crossroad along N45-46. They established a roadblock, and the rest of the company returned to Wiltry. By 11 A.M., the engineers were ordered to fall back "as best they could." For S/Sgt. Stanley Green of the 1st Platoon, this meant swimming down a nearby creek with a floating log tucked against his head for protection and concealment.

Attempts to relieve Company B Force from the west were abandoned. Eventually, the survivors of B Force broke out to the south, in the area where Buick Force had assembled. The combined force, which had taken heavy casualties, pulled back further south of Martelange. Two enemy armored vehicles were spotted south of the river, which fueled concerns that the Germans might be preparing to advance toward Arlon. The engineers blew a large, deep crater in the Arlon-Bastogne road, which served as a very effective roadblock against vehicles. By 3:00 P.M., the engineers pulled back and rejoined their battalion at their CP.

Further to the east, the 15th Regiment had made a deeper penetration across the Sure River, capturing the town of Bigonville on December 21. The paratroopers that occupied the town had traveled on foot all the way from the Our River. As they climbed and descended the steep grades that characterized this part of Luxembourg, their shoes were literally falling apart (the paras looted a store along the way to pick up some new footwear).

By noon, the 12th Company of the 15th Regiment's 3rd Battalion had entered Bigonville, and began setting up their mortars to support the defensive positions the Germans were setting up facing south. Rumors were already circulating among the men that Patton's Third Army was being turned north against them. The sound of heavy vehicle traffic in the distance that night began to serve as confirmation that the Americans might be drawing near.

By the evening of December 21, Oberstleutnant Kurt Groschke, commanding officer of the 15th FJ Regiment, had established his forward command post at the town of Warnach, just a tad over two miles north of Martelange. Despite the loss of the bridges at Martelange, Heilmann decided to push some of his reconnaissance forces south of the Sure River (the German force that had moved into Fauvillers was one element of this mission). These were primarily small units, moving on foot. At best, they would act as his forward eyes and ears, and would stay on the lookout for the expected American move against the German 7th Army. On the evening of the 21st, Groschke received a visit from Heilmann, who was pleased with the progress of the 15th FJ Regiment (though in a later account Heilmann would state that "quite a few things had gone wrong" at Martelange).

Meanwhile, the 13th Regiment, which had been in Seventh Army reserve, was now turned back over to Heilmann. The relatively fresh paratroopers were being hastily deployed on the division's left flank; one of their three battalions moved into Bigonville, following on the heels of the elements of the 15th FJ Regiment that had already established defensive positions there. Another of the 13th's battalions moved into Boulaide.

Heilmann's integral artillery support was the only portion of the division that had not made it to the Bastogne area. There was insufficient motorized transport available to move the guns out of their original firing positions of December 16, and so the batteries remained to the east, where they lent support to other elements of the 7th Army. To make up for the shortage, the commander of LXXXV Corps, General Baptist Kniess, assigned to the 5th FJ Division three battalions of self-propelled artillery (36 guns) from the 406th Volksartillerie Corps. For added measure, he attached a battalion of rocket launchers from the 18th Volkswerfer Brigade (a total of 18 launchers).

The 11th Assault Gun Brigade had managed to cross over the Our River in force by this point in time, and was now well positioned to support the paratroopers. It appears that two thirds of the brigade's StuG IIIs were at the disposal of the 14th FJ Regiment, while the balance were sent to assist the 15th FJ. Some of the Sherman tanks captured at Wiltz also supplemented the firepower of Heilmann's force.

Bracing for the Attack

Heilmann had done well to get his three regiments into their respective positions by the morning of December 22. He had done so not a moment too soon, as the Fourth Armored Division was about to challenge his paratroopers at their forward outposts.

Heilmann had no way of knowing where the main weight of an American counterattack would fall. But one thing was for certain: unless the Americans struck from the southwest, they would have to cross the Sure River en route to Bastogne. The Sure was a formidable water obstacle that could not be forded by vehicles. If the Americans were going to attack from the south, they would have to either capture an existing bridge, or build one. In either event, the river provided Heilmann with a natural place to build his primary line of defense. Geographically, there was no better place between the Americans and Bastogne to make a stand.

The most prominent crossing site over the Sure River was at Martelange. As Heilmann's troops shifted from offense to defense, the bridges that had been blown by the retreating Americans engineers now turned from a liability into an asset. If an American attack followed the axis of the Arlon-Bastogne highway, the blown bridges would surely pose a significant delay for the Americans. Knowing that the Americans would have to install a bridge, Heilmann could easily craft a defense of the river that would disrupt the efforts of the American engineers. The layout of the town lent itself to just such an effort, since the river split the town in two, and many of the buildings on the north bank sat on elevations overlooking the river. There would be ample places for the 15th FJ Regiment to bring down fire on the potential bridge sites. From the sanctuary of nearby buildings, forward observers could call in artillery and mortar fire that would seriously hamper the American effort to cross the river.

The Germans did make one significant oversight at Martelange, however. As mentioned previously, while the American engineers had destroyed one of the bridges completely, the second span on the west side of town was only partially destroyed. It could not support vehicles, but it could support infantry moving across on foot. It does not appear that the 15th FJ Regiment made any provisions to finish the work that the American engineers had started. Perhaps they wanted to keep the bridge open for their own men that had taken up positions on the south bank of the river. If that were the case, they would have been better served if they had pulled everyone back to the north bank, and blown the bridge completely.

Heilmann could be fairly criticized for the modest attempt he eventually made to hold the line of the river at Martelange. A lone company of paratroopers from the 15th FJ Regiment was the only force employed in the town on December 22. It was not for lack of resources, for just two miles up the road, at the village of Warnach, the headquarters and main body of the 15th FJ had set up shop.

If Warnach was intended to be the spot where the 15th FJ Regiment would make its primary stand, the choice is somewhat befuddling. The highway did not even pass through Warnach. Rather, it bypassed the town to the west. For sure, the ground between the highway and the village was wide open, and traffic passing along the highway was clearly visible from the buildings on the south and southwest edges of the town, and could be fired upon from the village. In that sense, it provided a good position to delay an enemy advance up the highway. But if the goal was to stop an American advance, and not simply delay it, it certainly would have been much wiser to build the regiment's primary defensive positions along the line of the Sure River at Martelange.

Martelange was not the only potential crossing site for the Americans. The Sure River runs west out of Martelange, and then takes a sharp bend to the north, before finally cutting back to the west at a point south of Hollange. The nature of the road net, the river, and the surrounding terrain virtually ruled out a crossing in this area (besides, the 299th Engineers had destroyed the two bridges that could have carried the American tanks across the river; one at Bodange, and the other near Strainchamps). But the river narrows as it turns back to the west, and the surrounding terrain is less severe. Another bridge is then found south of the village of Burnon. The road it carries is a relatively poor one, being nothing more than a dirt road or logging trail running north into Burnon.

A short distance north of Burnon, the road comes to a fork; the right prong running to Hollange, the left to Chaumont. While not viewed as a primary route for an

American attack, it still received almost an equal amount of attention in the German's defensive scheme. The 14th FJ Regiment was assigned responsibility for this area.

Unlike Martelange, the area around the bridge south of Burnon consisted of very open terrain. Burnon was well north of the bridge, and provided little value to a defender trying to maintain positions at the line of the river. There were some hills on the north side of the river, however, that would provide good defilade positions for the defenders. For the attacker, there was little cover to be found as he approached the bridge from the south. Here too, the bridge had been blown.

The 14th FJ Regiment moved an unknown number of men into an area close to the crossing site. But it does not appear that it was a substantial force (perhaps a company in strength). The main defensive positions for the 14th FJ Regiment were to be found much further north, with some forces at Burnon, and the main body at Chaumont. The 14th Regiment was a bit more extended than the 15th Regiment to its left. In addition to the Burnon-Chaumont road, the 14th FJ Regiment had to cover the line as far west as the Neufchâteau highway. Its primary defensive positions, however, appeared to be clustered around Chaumont.

So, as the sun rose on the seventh day after they had set out from their positions east of the Our River, Heilmann's paratroopers had successfully advanced to their assigned positions on the left flank of the German salient. Of all the German division's committed to the Ardennes Offensive, the 5th FJ was the only one that would ever be able to claim that they had done what was asked of them.

But their mission had only just begun. Reaching their assigned blocking positions was simply a means to an end. They were there for a purpose; and that purpose was to prevent a successful American counterattack against the south flank of the "Bulge." Little did they know that the toughest portion of their mission was about to begin, and that their opponent would be none other than "Roosevelt's Butchers."

17. The Arlon-Bastogne Highway

The Departure of CCA

Brigadier General Herbert L. Earnest had only been in command of CCA for slightly more then two weeks when the call came to head for the Ardennes. He had inherited a bad situation from Colonel Withers, and as evidenced by the continued lagging of CCA during the final leg of the drive toward Bining and Singling, the change of command did not bring about an immediate improvement in the situation. The fact that Colonel Withers was still present at CCA in his improvised role as assistant combat commander certainly did not help matters. The officers that had been victimized by Withers' intolerance must have felt there was no escape from the man.

Though Earnest came to the Fourth Armored Division from a staff position at Third Army, it wasn't one of the pure paper-pushing assignments held by many of the rear echelon types. He was in charge of the Tank Destroyer Group, a role in which he oversaw the independent tank destroyer battalions assigned to the Third Army. One of his virtues was that he was not a complete stranger to leading men in combat. After the breakout at Avranches, he commanded a collection of armored cavalry and tank destroyer units dubbed "Task Force A," which had the mission of charging into Brittany to secure some 17 miles of trestle on the railway leading east from Brest (if the railway bridging had been destroyed, the value of the port of Brest would have been diminished). Along the way, his task force sealed off some 12,000 Germans at the port of St. Malo (the 3,500 men of Task Force A were ill-equipped to take on the German garrison, so the task of capturing the city was turned over to the 83rd Infantry Division). It was with these credentials that General Earnest stepped into the shoes of Bruce Clarke.

Earnest would soon be afforded the opportunity to step out of Clarke's lengthy shadow and into his own spotlight. At 3 A.M. on the morning of December 19, he issued assembly orders to his command. He had no shortage of resources to work with, as CCA consisted of:

35th Tank Battalion

51st Armored Infantry Battalion

53rd Armored Infantry Battalion

66th Armored Field Artillery Battalion

94th Armored Field Artillery Battalion

B Battery, 489th AAA Sp Battalion

A Company, 24th Armored Engineer Battalion

A Troop, 25th Cavalry Reconnaissance Squadron

274th Armored Field Artillery Battalion (M7's)

177th Field Artillery Battalion (minus one battery) 155mm Howitzers

In addition to having greater resources than CCB, Earnest also had the healthiest of the division's three tank battalions. Delk Oden's 35th Tank Battalion had 35 Shermans ready for combat (37, if the two battalion HQ tanks were included in the count): A/35 had 13, B/35 had 14, and C/35 had 8. Like the 8th Tank Battalion, the 35th relied primarily on the older 75mm Shermans.

The units of CCA began moving toward their assembly area south of Longwy on the morning of December 19, with the first units departing at about 8:30 A.M. The column reached the village of Trieux at 4:25 P.M., and halted there with plans to spend the night. Unlike CCB, the staff of CCA had time to round up the appropriate maps covering the area to the north, and they were distributed during this stop.

CCA had barely begun to settle down for the night when orders were received to resume the march to the north. By 7:30 P.M., Earnest's command was back on the road. Its new destination was an assembly area located a short distance across the Belgian border, near the Luxembourg town of Clemency.

The column now moved under cover of darkness, and the pace slowed accordingly. CCA pulled into Longwy at 10:40 P.M. and continued north without pause. The column pulled off the main highway about five miles north of Longwy, and traveled over secondary roads toward Clemency, located about two and a half miles east of the Arlon-Bastogne highway.

At 1:25 A.M., the lead units began pulling into their assembly areas in and around the towns of Clemency, Houdelange, and Selange. CCA was now at a point roughly midway between Longwy and Arlon. Though this area was well south of the fighting in the Ardennes, the situation was uncertain enough that defensive positions were taken inside the town. Many of the men were fortunate that they were able to stay inside the buildings during the balance of the night, which afforded them some welcome protection against the cold weather.

Compared to the events swirling about CCB on December 20, General Earnest's Combat Command A awoke that morning to a more certain situation. Unlike CCB, CCA was still under the direct command of the Fourth Armored Division, which was in turn assigned to III Corps. As such, it was immune from the confusion that General Dager was wrestling with at CCB. This didn't mean that the situation wasn't fluid, however. CCA had its own fog of war to cut through, though it wasn't as thick as CCB's.

One of the first units to move on December 20 was the 51st AIB. It received orders to move to the town of Hondelange, less than three miles to the north. But before the column could start, its destination was changed to Toernich, located about three miles southwest of Arlon. When the armored infantry arrived, they were to outpost the town and guard against enemy attacks from any direction.

The column departed at 1:30 P.M. and arrived at Toernich at 3:35 P.M. Less than an hour later, a task force under the command of Captain Rockafeller was ordered to guard the roads north and northeast of Arlon (TF Rockafeller was composed of C/51, D/35, one platoon of A/24, a section from the 51st I&R platoon, and the Assault Gun Platoon from the 35th Tank Battalion).

Meanwhile, all of the remaining units of CCA were ordered to move west of the Arlon-Bastogne highway in order to make room for the 26th Infantry Division, which was advancing north to take up positions to the east of the Fourth Armored Division's zone. The balance of the day was spent with the entire combat command in place near Arlon.

The Mission Is Defined

Brigadier General Earnest received his mission orders on December 21. They were simple and concise: Commencing on December 22, CCA would drive up the Arlon highway and relieve Bastogne. The men of CCA would soon discover that the brevity and conciseness of their mission order did not equate to an easy task.

Of all the roads leading north in the zone of the Fourth Armored Division, the Arlon-Bastogne highway was of the highest quality. The paved, wide surface would sustain any weight or type of vehicles placed upon it, under virtually any weather conditions. It was also the most direct route to Bastogne. Clearing this route would be vitally important not only for the purpose of bringing in supplies and reinforcements to the defenders of Bastogne, but for sustaining meaningful offensive operations after the relief had taken place.

Bastogne would be the springboard for Patton's continuation of the attack against the German salient, and if the Arlon-Bastogne highway were not under the complete control of the Americans, the Third Army would have a difficult time expanding its offensive.

Given the above, it was to be expected that if the Germans chose any one place to stand their ground, it would be along the axis of the Arlon-Bastogne highway. But even if by some chance the highway was lightly defended, CCA was not in a position to ram its tanks past the opposition in a freewheeling charge into Bastogne. Getting into the town wasn't the critical piece, especially when it was confirmed that the Germans had completely encircled Bastogne. Rather, the most important thing was to ensure that enemy resistance had been cleared and pushed back along the entire length of the road, so that vehicles could make it in and out of the town without being caught in the crosshairs of German guns.

The Advance to Martelange

The most significant waypoint between Arlon and Bastogne was the large town of Martelange. This picturesque Belgian community straddled the Sure River, with its many houses and shops carved into the slopes that descended toward the waterway. The Arlon-Bastogne highway passed directly through the east side of town and across the river, whereupon it continued for 12 miles to Bastogne. By car, the trip from Martelange to Bastogne was less than a 15-minute ride. In a tank, 30 minutes would do. That assumes, of course, that no one is shooting at you, and that no roadblocks have been thrown in the way. The men of CCA knew they wouldn't be that fortunate, but to what extent the enemy would greet them was anyone's guess.

The American engineers outposting the roads south of Martelange were the sole source of information regarding the disposition of German forces in the area. They had reported that the enemy was operating both in Martelange and the town of Perle, which was located just shy of two miles south-southeast of Martelange and only one mile east of the Arlon-Bastogne highway. But they had few specifics, if any, regarding the nature of the forces occupying these towns.

The distance between Arlon and Martelange was 10 miles, and the first 7 miles or so of that trip was thought to be free of the enemy. There was little concern for security on CCA's left flank. Starting about 4 miles south of Martelange, the highway was bordered very close on the west side by the Foret d'Anlier. There were no significant roads leading through the east portion of the forest, thus the prospects of a threat from that direction were minimal. Some additional security would be gained by the fact that CCB was advancing on a parallel route through the center of the forest, about 4 miles west of CCA's axis of advance.

The area to the east of the Arlon-Bastogne highway was a bit more problematic. If the enemy had advanced in strength south of the Sure River, they could be in position to strike at CCA's right flank as it drove up the main highway. As a precaution, General Earnest decided to advance with two task forces moving abreast in columns. One column would advance directly along the Arlon-Bastogne highway, while the second column would advance on a parallel route approximately 2½ miles to the east. A secondary road through the towns of Petit Nobressart, Holtz, and Flatzbourhof would serve as the axis of advance for the east column.

The task forces were formed on December 21. On the left was TF Alanis, led by Major Dan Alanis, CO of the 51st AIB. The advance guard of TF Alanis was composed of the recon elements of the 51st and 704th battalions, a platoon from B/35, a platoon from A/704, and a squad from A/24. The main body of the column was composed of A/51, two platoons from B35, A/24, the HQ Company of the 51st, B/51, and another platoon from A/704. The 274th AFAB was attached in direct support of the advance guard. On the right was TF Oden, led by the CO of the 35th Tank Battalion, Lt. Colonel Delk Oden. The task force consisted of D/35, A/35, C/35, C/51, the 66th AFAB, a platoon of A/25, and a platoon of Hellcats from A/704.

TF Alanis moved out from its positions near Toernich at 6:20 P.M. on December 21. Traveling at night didn't help matters; some of the vehicles went off the road into a ditch just outside of Toernich, slowing the progress of the column. At 8:40 P.M., TF

Alanis entered its assembly areas near Attert, about five miles north of Arlon. Once at Attert, the men moved into buildings for the night. For many of the men, this would be their last night tucked away from the harsh winter elements for many days to come. As TF Alanis settled in for the night, TF Oden also moved into positions in the vicinity of Attert.

Early the next morning (December 22), TF Alanis was ready to begin moving north into enemy territory. The task force set out at 5:15 A.M., employing the same order of march used the day before. The column began its advance over a secondary road to the west of the main highway, and at 7:55 A.M., it entered Heinstert. At about 8 A.M., elements of the 25th Cav, which had been at the rear of the column, moved up to the front and advanced cautiously on foot toward a major crossroad where the secondary road they were traveling on merged with the Arlon-Bastogne highway. Soon after the column closed up on the crossroad, it was ordered to halt. The reason for the delay was that TF Oden had run into some problems along their axis of advance east of the Arlon-Bastogne highway.

TF Oden had departed at 6:00 A.M., and was advancing along the secondary road east of TF Alanis. The order of march for TF Oden was one medium tank company from the 35th, followed by C/51, the 66th AFAB, HQ/35, the second medium tank company, the 174th Field Artillery Battalion, and finally, the supply trains. Departing from Attert, TF Oden moved through the small town of Nothomb, and then headed northeast via a dirt trail to the village of Petit Nobressart, where Oden intended to pick up the secondary road that led north to Holtz. At 8:00 A.M., after traveling only three tenths of a mile north of Petit Nobressart, the column was literally stopped in its tracks by a blown bridge. This was just about the same time that TF Alanis had turned on to the Arlon-Bastogne highway at a point due west of Oden's furthest point of advance. The two task forces were thus abreast of each other at that moment, and if Alanis continued, he would be doing so without the flank protection that TF Oden was supposed to provide.

The engineers went to work on installing a bridge, but it became clear that the delay would be substantial. So rather than delay the advance any further, a decision was made to merge the two task forces on the single highway leading into Martelange. TF Alanis took the lead, while TF Oden doubled back from Petit Nobressart, and fell in line behind TF Alanis.

The advance continued without incident until 9:30 A.M., when the column came to a halt about one and a half miles south of Martelange, where a secondary road branched off to the east in the direction of the town of Perle. It was here that the armored cavalry came upon the huge crater that had been created by the American engineers during their retreat from Martelange. This fine bit of demolition work drew no distinction between friend or foe, and it now effectively blocked the advance of TF Alanis. The engineers from the 24th Engineer Battalion, operating under the watchful eyes of a detachment from A/51, put a bridge in place over the gaping cavity. The work was completed by noon.

Help from Above

The weather on December 22 was not helping CCA's cause. Visibility was greatly reduced by the falling, swirling snow. Cold temperatures, hovering right around the freezing mark, made for an uncomfortable ride for men standing in open hatches and huddled in the open-air halftracks and tank destroyers. Patches of ice posed a hazard for wheeled vehicles, but the tracked vehicles handled the conditions without too much difficulty.

For several weeks, bad weather had been nothing short of a curse for the Third Army. Their efforts in the Lorraine region had been seriously hampered by the caustic conditions. In preparation for the renewal of the Third Army offensive in the Saar, which had been slated for December 19, Patton had even gone so far as to have his Chaplain, Colonel James O'Neill, compose a prayer asking for good weather. Though the occasion for the prayer had changed, he was no less inclined to have it printed and distributed to his troops. It read:

> Almighty and most merciful Father, we humbly beseech Thee, of Thy great goodness, to restrain these immoderate rains with which we have had to contend. Grant us fair weather for Battle. Graciously hearken to us as soldiers who call upon Thee that, armed with Thy power, we may advance from victory to victory, and crush the oppression and wickedness of our enemies, and establish Thy justice among men and nations. Amen.

As of December 22, it appeared that his prayer was falling on deaf ears.

Preparing for the Assault on Martelange

Up to this point, the combined task force had advanced along the Arlon-Bastogne highway without any threats appearing on its right flank. But now that the column had advanced to a point due west of Perle, Oden needed to be increasingly wary of a potential attack from that direction. Having received reports from the American engineers regarding an enemy presence in Perle, a decision was made to push some of the 25th Armored Cavalry to the east, in order to provide the main column with some protection as it continued to the north. The possibility of German forces in Perle had to be explored, for if the column bypassed the town, TF Alanis would be an easy target for an enemy attack against their exposed right flank.

The eastbound patrol found the town occupied by a very small German force, which it easily swept aside. The armored cavalry advanced another mile beyond Perle, to the village of Holtz, which they also found occupied by a handful of Germans. These were in effect small, isolated groups of paratroopers who posed no threat of any consequence.

The cavalry then pushed on boldly toward the small village of Flatzbourhof, located two miles north of Holtz. Near Flatzbourhof, the armored cavalry discovered 80 Americans from the 28th Infantry Division and 44th Engineer Battalion, who had taken refuge in some nearby woods. These men had fallen back from Wiltz after the devastating attack by the 5th FJ Division on that town, and had trekked through the snow, mud, and rugged terrain for more than a dozen miles before settling into their hiding place near Flatzbourhof. Once found by the men of the 25th Armored Cavalry, the battered men were escorted back to safety. As the cavalry drew closer to Flatzbourhof, they encountered stiff resistance, which brought their advance to a halt.

As the eastbound patrols scouted the column's right flank, the northbound cavalry closed on Martelange, and quickly discovered that, unlike Perle and Holtz, Martelange was held in strength. Oden would have to advance on the town with more firepower than his leading armored cavalry could bring to the party.

Martelange posed a specific challenge for General Earnest, and that was the fact that American engineers, while retreating south, had blown the bridges spanning the Sure River in order to stop or delay the Germans from advancing south toward Arlon. The Sure, while not terribly wide at this point in its course, featured banks that were steep and rugged, making it unfordable by vehicles. A bridge would have to be put in place by the engineers, and this was certainly the most important consideration facing CCB on December 22.

In order for the engineers to do their work, Oden would have to first secure the portion of the town south of the Sure River. He would then have to push his armored infantry across the river to secure and expand a bridgehead that would afford the engineers ample room to operate with a reasonable degree of safety.

Before Oden pushed some of his men into the town, he saw to it that his immediate flanks were secured, and that the heights overlooking the portion of the town south of the Sure River were in American hands. To that end, he sent his original tank-heavy task force to occupy the high ground north of Perle. The task force met little opposition, but the enemy paratroopers did manage to take out one tank from A/35, which reduced it to an even dozen Shermans. He also moved a company of medium tanks and the armored infantry of C/51 to a ridge southeast of the town of Wolwelange, which overlooked the southeast and east portion of Martelange (Wolwelange was located less than a half mile southeast of Martelange). There were no enemy forces present in that area, and Wolwelange was taken without opposition. With his right flank secured, he could now support an attack on Martelange with direct fire from the heights overlooking the town.

At 1:30 P.M., the armored infantry of A/51, accompanied by a platoon of Sherman tanks, began moving on foot toward the wooded heights overlooking the southwest portion of Martelange. There was no immediate resistance, and within 30 minutes, they occupied the Haut-Martelange. By 2:00 P.M., Oden was ready to send his force into Martelange.

The Attack on Martelange

The drive into town was spearheaded by a tank/infantry team consisting of C/51 and two platoons of Shermans from B/35. The 2nd Platoon of B/35 pressed into Martelange from the southeast, and then the 1st Platoon of B/35 passed through the 2nd Platoon's positions toward the center of town. As the tanks moved onto the main street that ran along the south bank of the Sure River, they came under heavy panzerfaust, small arms, and machine gun fire, all of which originated from the west side of town. The 1st Platoon tanks were unable to advance in the face of this fire, so some of the 2nd Platoon's Shermans came forward and took up firing positions near the church at the center of town, to the left of the 1st Platoon. The Shermans managed to knock out the panzerfaust positions, as well as several American trucks and jeeps that had been captured by the Germans and painted with swastikas.

The battle within the city streets soon evolved into a bitter fight between the armored infantry and enemy paratroopers. Eventually, most of the 51st Armored Infantry Battalion was engaged inside the southern half of the town. The Germans held several commanding positions in buildings at higher elevations, and using automatic weapons, managed to pin down a platoon of B/51 on an embankment west of the main highway. Artillery support was called in to silence the enemy positions, but the shells could not effectively be laid upon their targets through the densely packed buildings.

A coordinated attack, supported by two tanks, commenced in the dark at 6:00 P.M. It was a clear, cold night in Martelange, with a bright moon reflecting off the snow. The illumination probably hurt more than it helped, as the advancing armored infantry became easier targets for the Germans as they moved against the moonlit white back-drop.

Martelange had turned into a significant obstacle, courtesy of a stubborn company of paratroopers from the 15th FJ Regiment. As CCA pressed its attack into the town, the enemy pulled back to the north side of the river, where they continued to harass and frustrate the Americans' attempt to secure a crossing. The Germans maintained their positions near the north bank of the river until about 3:00 A.M., when, inexplicably, they fell back, save for a single squad of men that stayed behind with a radio to observe and report on the activity of the Americans. The German withdrawal allowed A/51 and B/51 to close up on the south bank of the river, and to clear the entire west side of the town.

The armored infantry confirmed that the main bridge carrying the Arlon-Bastogne highway had indeed been destroyed. But on the west side of town, the task force discovered that the second bridge over the Sure had been only partially damaged. It could not support vehicles, but would support the armored infantry on foot. This was indeed a welcome break for the men of the 51st AIB, since it meant they would not have to wade the icy, dark waters of the Sure River.

C/51 took advantage of the German retreat, and crossed the damaged span unopposed. The German withdrawal was indeed a major blunder on the part of the 15th FJ Regiment. There is no telling how long a determined stand on the north bank would have held back the advance of CCA, but such are the fortunes of war, and by 5:00 A.M., the armored infantry had secured the high ground to the northwest of the bridge without any interference from the enemy. With the north bank around the bridge site secure, engineers from the 188th (3rd Platoon of A Company) and 24th Engineer battalions came forward, and at 7 A.M., started construction on the new bridge. A 90-foot span was required in order to cross the gorge through which the Sure River traversed, and the better part of the day on December 23 was spent putting it in place. As the engineers toiled, the Germans lobbed in some mortar rounds that fell wide of the target, causing no casualties. It would be 2:30 P.M. before the first vehicles crossed the river. Later that evening, the engineers constructed a second Bailey bridge, which enabled traffic to flow both ways across the river simultaneously.

Though the engineers' work on the Sure River was complete, the installation of the bridges did not spell the end of their support for CCA. The engineers would be kept busy enough during the days ahead. An entry from the unit history of the 188th Engineer Combat Battalion speaks for itself:

> It was plain from the start that being attached in direct support of the Fourth Armored Division meant immediate action and varied tasks, with an emphasis on speed and resourcefulness. The constant chatter of small arms, and the proximity of artillery of all calibers put everyone on the alert, and kept him there.

Answered Prayers

The unexplained withdrawal of the paratroopers wasn't the only bright spot that greeted the men of CCA on December 23. The snow of December 22 was followed by the arrival of a cold front sweeping in behind the line of storms. After starting off with the seemingly ubiquitous morning fog, the weather had improved steadily throughout the day. Though the passage of the front dropped temperatures to an increasingly uncomfortable level, it also brought with it blue skies that gradually embraced the entire Ardennes region. Visibility had improved dramatically, and virtually all the clouds had been swept from the sky. The wispy contrails of fighter planes began taking the place of the gray blanket that had hung low over the battlefield for so many days.

That very morning, having had to struggle with the limitations imposed by the weather during the first day of III Corps' offensive, Patton wrote a lengthy prayer in which he spoke to the Almighty as through he were giving Him a lesson in battlefield tactics. Just in case He wasn't aware, Patton included the passage: "I've sent Hugh Gaffey, one of my ablest generals, with his 4th Armored Division, north toward that all-important road center to relieve the encircled garrison and he's finding Your weather more difficult than he is the Krauts." And in one of his prophetic moments, Patton wrote:

> Sir, I have never been an unreasonable man, I am not going to ask You for the impossible. I do not even insist upon a miracle, for all I request is four days of clear weather. Give me four days so that my planes can fly, so that my fighter bombers can bomb and strafe, so that my reconnaissance may pick out targets for my magnificent artillery. Give me four days of sunshine to dry this blasted mud, so that my tanks roll, so that ammunition and rations may be taken to my hungry, ill-equipped infantry. I need these four days to send Von Rundstedt and his godless army to their Valhalla. I am sick of this unnecessary butchery of American youth, and in exchange for four days of fighting weather, I will deliver You enough Krauts to keep your bookkeepers months behind in their work. Amen.

Patton got exactly what he asked for, as the 24th through the 27th were the clearest days of the battle. Air support and reconnaissance were now back in the American arsenal, and as a secondary benefit, the cold temperatures firmed up the soft ground, making cross country movement more practical.

The freezing weather wasn't necessarily an answer to every infantryman's prayers, however. The high temperature for each day would linger briefly in the mid 20's, and then drop into the teens during the long winter nights. The shivering, bone-chilling days and nights to come would live in many a soldier's memory for decades to come.

The snow that had fallen on December 22 would remain on the ground in most areas throughout the balance of the battle, adding to the discomfort of the infantrymen who had to slog through the wet stuff. The snow and underlying frozen ground made digging-in a more difficult task. More snow would come on December 28 and 31, in amounts that greatly exceeded what had fallen on December 22.

The Advance Continues Beyond Martelange

Delk Oden was still in command of the consolidated task force as CCA prepared to advance beyond Martelange. It was Brigadier General Earnest's vision that the advance to Bastogne would be predominately an armor affair, and he thus felt it best to empower the commanding officer of the 35th Tank Battalion as the leader of the charge. Having started across the Sure River, it was now Oden's intent to drive north up the main highway, while Major Alanis' task force would peel off to the northeast to secure the towns of Warnach and Tintange, which presented potential threats to the right flank of their advance.

Alanis was not happy with the assignment of taking Tintange, and submitted a protest to Earnest to that effect. He was "fearful" that it would be "almost impossible" to control his battalion in an attack toward Tintange (his concern was probably the very hazardous terrain that separated the two towns). The commander of CCA "dressed down" Alanis, and told him "he would do as he was instructed." Given CCA's difficulties during recent weeks, this was not a particularly good sign.

As the long American column snaked across the river, Lt. Colonel Oden took the forward elements of his task force up the main highway. Oden's Sherman tanks led the way, with the infantry of C/51 riding on their decks. A company of Hellcats from the 704th also drove near the front to provide support. At this point, CCA was just slightly more than 11 miles south of the 101st Airborne Division's defensive perimeter around Bastogne.

The advance out of Martelange was fraught with danger. A large wooded hill to the left of the highway overlooked the entire town, its peak rising some 80 meters above the level of the highway. In the immediate vicinity of Martelange, the Sure River hugged the right side of the road. After the road departed from the line of the river, it traced its way around the north side of the hill, and then started to climb up a steep, wooded grade that rose about 50 meters. It then leveled off on a 200-yard plateau. There were numerous places along the route where the Germans could delay the advance, if they so desired. Fortunately, up to this point, the Germans had not shown themselves. When the company of paratroopers pulled away from the line of the river, it would appear that they pulled well away from the town, as well (save for the small radio team).

Oden's good fortune ran out at about 4 P.M. When the vanguard reached the open plateau, it met its first resistance outside of Martelange. As the leading armored cavalry units hit a bend in the road on top of the plateau, the Germans opened fire with 20mm AA guns, small arms, and machine guns. The infantry riding on the decks of the tanks were extremely vulnerable, and two of them were killed by bursts from automatic weapons. The commander of A/35's 3rd Platoon dismounted from his command tank to see what was holding up the column, and soon became another casualty when he was wounded by machine gun fire. At that point, the Shermans of A Company left the road and deployed in a protected defilade position west of the highway. They remained there for about 30 minutes while the forward artillery observer called for an artillery strike against the enemy positions. A/35 then continued its advance to the north, remaining in defilade to the west of the road. A scene that would be repeated a number of times during the days to come occurred when a German paratrooper, brandishing a panzerfaust, knocked out the Sherman advancing closest to the highway.

For the tank crews of the 35th, the panzerfaust would be one of the most serious threats they faced during the days and nights that lay ahead. When the tankers had to move within the close confines of the woods and villages, they became more vulnerable to attacks by the German paratroopers who would sneak into position at close range with the dreaded anti-tank weapon. Along the road to Bastogne, the terrain provided the enemy with many such opportunities.

As CCA's artillery support continued to hit the enemy positions, elements of the 51st Armored Infantry Battalion started to make their way up the highway, sticking to the pavement as they advanced. The tank and artillery fire hit the suspected enemy positions for some 30 minutes. Their effort silenced the enemy guns, and 60 enemy paratroopers were taken prisoner.

The nature of the terrain beyond this point was friendlier to the Americans. At a spot just shy of 2 miles north of Martelange, the road reached yet another plateau, this one overlooking an expanse of open terrain to the north and northwest. The ground ahead was laced with more gentle, rolling elevation changes. The main feature on the map in this area was the town of Warnach, nestled about 500 yards to the east of the main highway. In the distance, further beyond to the north and east of Warnach, ran an extremely dense and rugged forest called the Schockbesch. Beyond the plateau, there were woods to the left of the highway as well. But in this direction, at a distance of about 1,000 yards from the highway, the terrain fell away rather sharply. The Sure River and its small tributaries were not very far beyond the edge of the woods, and their influence on the lay of the land effectively limited both sides to the 1,000 yards of open terrain between the trees and the road. For the next two and a half miles beyond Warnach, the Arlon-Bastogne highway ran roughly parallel with the forested area to the east. Near Warnach, the edge of the woods sat about two-thirds of a mile away from the road. But as the highway continued north, the woods grew progressively closer to the pavement, until in the area just east of the village of Strainchamps, the woods clamped down upon the roadway, and remained that way for some 1,000 yards leading to the north. The thick woods provided a natural choke point and potential defensive position for the Germans.

Just as CCB had been ordered to advance through the night of December 22/23 (see Chapter 19), Oden now found himself ordered to continue the attack during the night of December 23/34. With darkness drawing near, a decision was made to bypass

Warnach. The 14 light tanks of D Company, along with six 105mm Assault Guns, were brought forward to advance through the positions of A/35. Rather than head up the road in a single column in darkness, they spread out across the available open terrain on both sides of the road (one platoon of tanks east of the road, and the balance to the west).

As Oden prepared to continue the advance, what he did not know was that Warnach was heavily defended, and the Germans were keeping a watchful eye on the highway as it crossed over the plateau south of the town. Warnach would soon become a "hot spot" for CCA.

The Battle for Warnach

With the last remnants of daylight clinging to the battlefield, the leading vehicles started up Highway N4 west of Warnach. The tanks moved by without incident, but when the vulnerable halftracks of C/51 came into view, German anti-tank gunners within Warnach opened fire, and quickly knocked out two of the halftracks. With darkness descending, bypassing the town was now out of the question. There was no telling at the moment just how strong the enemy force was. If it was large, CCA could not risk leaving an enemy stronghold smack in its rear area as they continued moving to the north. So D Company was brought to a halt, and the light tanks and Sherman Assault Guns were turned to face Warnach.

At 8:15 P.M., orders were issued to capture Warnach. The 105mm assault guns deployed into positions where they could hit the village with direct fire. As they laid down a supporting barrage, Oden sent the five light tanks of D/35's 3rd Platoon and a 26-man armored infantry platoon from C/51 into the town. Due to the hazards of attacking at night, neither the tank platoon leader nor commanding officer of D/35 was very happy about the assignment. But the tankers' concern did not produce a change in the orders, and the team of infantry and light tanks set out across the open field toward Warnach. As they moved closer to the buildings at the edge of town, the commander of one of the M5s instructed his gunner, Private W. King Pound, to fire the tank's .30 caliber machine gun at the thatched roofs of the houses, with the hope of setting them on fire with their tracers. Hopefully, the light from the flames would reveal the enemy.

Private Pound poured lead from his machine gun into the buildings until the desired effect was achieved. But as the roofs began to burn, the enemy returned fire, and sent an anti-tank round slamming into Pound's tank. The private had been so engrossed in his mission that he hadn't even felt the impact. It was only the voice of his tank commander yelling, "Get the hell out, Pound! We've been hit!" that made him aware he had better separate himself from the tank, and in a hurry.

Pound erupted from the tank, and along with the other crewmembers, began to race toward a distant tree line that reflected the fires burning at the edge of Warnach. Small arms fire arced overhead as the men scrambled through the deep snow. Pound had gotten about 50 yards away from the tank when he was struck by the startling realization that he had left the turret of the tank positioned in such a way that the driver couldn't exit out of his hatch. "Squirrel" Hayden was still inside the disabled M5, trapped as a result of Pound's understandable oversight.

Private Pound turned about and ran back to the tank as fast as he could. He called to "Squirrel" from outside the tank, and the reply was not good: "I can't get out. I think my foot's been shot off." Without hesitation, Pound climbed into the tank and moved the turret in order to free the driver's hatch. He then climbed up on the front of the tank, and helped pull Hayden out through the hatch. Unable to walk, Hayden held on to Pound's back, and the private carried him the length of the field to the tree line, where they joined the other two members of the crew. After a close brush with some Germans who came within 20 yards of their hiding place, the tankers later navigated the half mile or so back to the lines of CCA.

Though Pound's tank was stopped short of the town, the rest of the tanks and infantry made it into the forward section of Warnach. A short, vicious street fight erupted, and the Americans discovered that they were seriously outgunned when the Germans brought forward four StuG III Assault Guns. Only one of the light tanks made it back, but fortunately, the infantry managed to remain fairly healthy, and made it out under cover of darkness with light casualties.

As the light tanks and infantry were battling for their lives inside Warnach, the other two platoons of light tanks from D/35, along with some of the mediums from A/35, move up the road a bit further to the north, where they attacked and cleared some buildings outside of Warnach. Perhaps with Patton's admonishment ringing in their ears, CCA ordered A/35 to continue moving through the darkness. Their immediate objective was to secure the next ridge to the north. The lead tanks advanced too far beyond the ridge, however, and wandered into a marsh. Two of the tanks got stuck, and the advance stalled for lack of a firm route. During the balance of the night, A/35 found itself under fire much of the time, and spent the time until sunrise maneuvering over the open ground to avoid being hit hard by the enemy. This represented the farthest advance north for CCA during the early morning hours of December 24.

After the rebuff of the first assault on Warnach, it was absolutely clear that the town had to be taken, since there would be no safe passage for the column heading to Bastogne as long as the Germans remained entrenched there. B/35 had finally advanced up the main road from Martelange, and shortly after midnight, its Sherman tanks were available to support another assault on the town.

B/35 sent two of its platoons toward the town, while the third stayed to the rear in support. One platoon of Shermans approached Warnach from the south, while the other came at the town from the west. The armored infantry of B/51 advanced alongside the tanks in the dark. After the two platoons of Shermans entered the town, the 1st Platoon moved out of its support position and circled around the north side of Warnach. The Americans now had the town surrounded on three sides, and started to press forward down the narrow streets. To this point, they had not run into any resistance. So far, so good. In fact, things were going so good, that at 1:00 A.M., a report came back to the 35th Tank Battalion HQ to the effect that Warnach had been cleared. As we shall soon see, this report was premature.

Once the Americans moved deeper into the town, there was an abrupt change in the situation. Heavy enemy anti-tank fire erupted, some of it reportedly coming from two Panther tanks. The advance of the Shermans and armored infantry stalled under the weight of the German response. It was now abundantly clear that the Germans were intent on making a stand at Warnach. The 15th FJ Regiment, which had its regimental command post at Warnach, had committed at least a battalion of paratroopers for the task, supported by the StuG IIIs of the 11th Assault Gun Brigade and the two aforementioned Panthers. During the fight, the command tank of the 2nd Platoon destroyed one of the Panthers, but was then immediately knocked out by three successive blasts from panzerfausts. The battle continued through the dark early morning hours.

Daylight brought a renewed intensity to the fight, and a street brawl between the opposing infantry forces ensued. Meanwhile, the Shermans from B/35 engaged some of the StuG IIIs at close range within the confines of the town. Three more Shermans were lost in the process, but the balance of B Company knocked out the remaining Panther tank and two of the StuG IIIs. The paratroopers of the 5th FJ Division, who had been so maligned by the German command during the early days of the German offensive, were now fighting like seasoned warriors. And unlike many Germans at this stage of the war who would surrender all too willingly, these men fought fanatically, with no sign that surrender was an option they were willing to consider. CCA had a real dogfight on its hands.

Throughout the morning hours, the Germans launched local counterattacks within the town, as they attempted to retake buildings that the Americans had wrestled from them. They seemed particularly anxious to get within panzerfaust range of the Shermans, but the men of B/51 did an able job of keeping the German raiding parties at bay (ultimately, the one aforementioned command tank was the only Sherman the FJs were able to notch on their belts by the time the fighting in Warnach was over).

The American attack stalled. Unable to rout the Germans from the east side of Warnach, the Americans shifted gears and tried a different approach. The infantry and tanks pulled back to the west side of town, which they now had under control. They then allowed two battalions of supporting artillery, plus some 4.2-inch mortars, to hammer away at the areas occupied by the Germans. The attack then resumed, with no letup in the intensity.

After the artillery barrage, the armored infantry received an unexpected assist. When the hot tracer bullets from one of the Sherman tanks set a barn aflame, the wind carried the heavy smoke from the burning building straight through the center of town. The dense smoke served as a screen behind which the Americans could operate. This was apparently the difference that allowed them to close in on the German positions. By late in the afternoon, the town was once again reported as being cleared, and the Germans had apparently fled to the neighboring woods.

But just when the American command thought the battle had subsided, the Germans launched yet another counterattack. The enemy paratroopers emerged from the woods and stormed across the open field separating Warnach from the forest. Another artillery barrage was called in, and the German assault broke under the weight of the howitzers. The enemy paratroopers lay crumpled on the snow-covered ground between the woods and the edge of town. Those that were not killed pulled back to the safety of the woods from whence they came. The Germans had finally exhausted themselves, and by 5:15 P.M. on December 24, the Americans were able to claim a victory at Warnach. Groschke ordered his remaining paratroopers to pull back into the woods lying between Warnach and Tintange. Fortunately for the Americans, this took them away from CCA's primary axis of advance.

While the battle raged inside Warnach on December 24, other elements of CCA had continued moving north. A/51 and C/35 moved out at noon to clear the woods north of Warnach, and by 4:45, they reached the edge of the woods about a mile and a quarter north of the town. They secured a position just north of the Tintange/Strainchamps road, where they stayed for the night.

Meanwhile, C/51, D/35, and A/35 had advanced west of the highway, captured Herrenburg, and advanced on to clear the woods to the north and the Bois de Morieval. "Very little resistance" was met by this part of the task force. C/51 then took up positions on the left flank of A/51, while B/51 remained at Warnach. After the difficult time they had experienced at Warnach, B/51 was in need of some rest. They still had to be alert, however, due to the continued threat of German attacks from their positions deep in the woods between Warnach and Tintange.

The contest in and around Warnach was a costly affair for CCA. Over the course of three days, the 51st Armored Infantry Battalion had suffered 69 casualties (fortunately, 67 timely replacements arrived on December 24). German casualties during the battle for Warnach had been far heavier, however. On the 24th alone, enemy losses were estimated at 160 killed and 140 wounded, with 135 paratroopers taken prisoner. Three self-propelled assault guns, two Panthers, and an armored car had been destroyed. In the process of clearing the town, several men from C/51 that had been taken prisoner early in the battle were rescued, along with some men from the engineer detachments who had been fighting in the Martelange area prior to the Fourth Armored's arrival.

By Christmas Eve, General Earnest had come to the conclusion that the advance to Bastogne was going to be best accomplished not by his tanks, but by his infantry. The change in operational philosophy manifested itself in the appointment of Major Alanis as the commander of the main task force attacking north. The 51st AIB would now carry the main burden, with Delk Oden's tanks in support.

Tintange

With Warnach secure, CCA could now turn its full attention to the north. But there turned out to be one more potential threat on the right flank that had to be dealt with, and that was the town of Tintange, located 1.5 miles northeast of Warnach.

Tintange was not in the immediate path of the forces advancing toward Bastogne, but it did provide an excellent assembly area for any troops the Germans might be harboring for a counterattack against CCA's right flank. The Americans decided that Tintange would be cleared out at the same time that the main body of CCA was advancing up the Arlon-Bastogne highway.

Warnach and Tintange were separated by a tributary of the Sure River called the Grausse Mauischt. The creek ran deep within a gorge that extended from northwest to southeast through the dense forest of Schockbesch. Warnach was west of the gorge, and Tintange to the east, atop an open plateau. The ground sloped away from both villages toward the Grausse Mauischt, bottoming out in the gorge at an elevation of about 380 meters. The eastern face of the gorge was particularly steep and rugged, rising some 75 yards above the creek. It is no wonder that Alanis had reservations when he was presented with the prospect of attacking through this area back on December 23.

As Earnest considered his options for dealing with Tintange, his biggest problem was one of resources. Though his combat command was the strongest of the three, he could not afford to fragment his force by sending a large contingent to secure Tintange. The problem was solved when he received word that the 1st Battalion of the 318th Infantry Regiment would be attached to CCA.

When Major Connaughton's battalion reported to CCA, its fighting strength had already been reduced to approximately 450 men (see Chapter 19 for details regarding the battalion's action in the Ardennes prior to December 24). The officer ranks had been particularly hard-hit, and all of the company commanders were brand new. Major Connaughton was new in his role as well, having been awarded command of the battalion just prior to its attachment to the Fourth Armored (he was previously the battalion's executive officer).

The 1st Battalion's truck ride from the 80th Division zone to Martelange was long, cold, and miserable. The battalion arrived just after sunset on December 24, and upon his arrival, Major Connaughton met immediately with Brigadier General Earnest. He was briefed on the situation, and given his orders for Christmas Day.

The 1st Battalion would line up on the right side of CCA. Its axis of advance would initially extend to the northeast, in order to eliminate any enemy resistance that might reside in Tintange. Once Tintange was secured, the battalion would continue driving north alongside the primary elements of CCA. The start time for their attack toward Tintange was set for 8:00 A.M.

Major Connaughton was assigned a bivouac area for Christmas Eve. The designated area was 800 yards southeast of Warnach, and amounted to nothing more than an open, snow covered field. By midnight, the battalion was ready to settle down, and the 450 infantrymen spent the night huddled under whatever cover they could construct.

At 2:30 in the morning, Connaughton brought together his green company commanders and provided them with their instructions. They were to assemble the troops early and depart from the bivouac area at 7 A.M. The line of departure was the Grausse Mauischt, and it would be crossed at 8 A.M., with A Company on the left and C Company on the right. The road connecting Warnach and Tintange would form the left boundary for A Company, while the Belgium-Luxembourg border would serve as the boundary for the battalion's right flank (in this area, the Surbach River defined the border between the two countries). After crossing the line of departure, A Company would seize the high ground southwest of Tintange, and then assault the northwest part of the town. C Company would be responsible for capturing the balance of the town, while B Company would circle Tintange to the east and sweep around the north side, linking up with A Company north of the village. Major Connaughton's battalion was given the support of all eight Sherman tanks of C/35, and two tank destroyers. Air and artillery support would also be provided for the assault on Tintange.

On the morning of December 25, the 1st Battalion assembled as scheduled, and began to move toward their line of departure. The march to the Grausse Mauischt carried them through the woods, where they encountered enemy resistance west of the creek. This resulted in a delay of about 30 minutes before reaching the LD. When they arrived, they found that the Grausse Mauischt was quite different than the impression they had formed from their map; they were not expecting to see the imposing gorge that contained the creek. They also found that the Germans were there, ready and waiting, to defend the road leading to Tintange

Though cold, tired, and under strength, Major Connaughton's men rushed down the heavily wooded slope leading down to the stream. They were hit by small arms fire as they descended into the gorge, but this did not deter them from advancing and wading across the creek at the bottom. Though the Germans atop the opposite side of the gorge threw down hand grenades and pelted the Americans with small arms fire, the men of the 1st Battalion scaled the opposite side of the gorge, and carried their assault over the top.

The American advance was slowed a bit by the appearance of Germans in American uniforms. In all likelihood, this was an example of the poorly clothed paratroopers donning American uniform components in order to gain some extra measure of protection against the elements, as opposed to creating some sort of intentional deception. Regardless, it had the net effect of creating caution among the American infantrymen, as they feared they might be firing upon some of their own men in the dense woods.

The GIs emerged at the edge of the woods facing Tintange. About 500 yards of open ground lay between the forest and the buildings on the south side of town. As the infantry began advancing, the Germans opened up once again with heavy small arms fire. But this time, the Germans also had the benefit of a large-caliber assault gun, which started firing high-explosive shells at the American infantry.

Company B, commanded by Captain Reid McAllister, was in a fixed position supporting the assault formations, and was to remain there until it was time to make their move around the east side of Tintange. McAllister's men seemed to be on the receiving end of a disproportionate volume of fire from the assault gun, however, and soon grew frustrated by the casualties they were taking while in their static position. Having finally had enough, B Company volunteered to take over the assault.

McAllister's request was granted, and he immediately sent two platoons of infantry racing through the two forward companies, while his third platoon circled the town from the east, as had originally been planned. The advance of the third platoon was aided by a defilade formed by a small hill southwest of the town.

The sight of the two oncoming platoons was enticing for the German infantry, and they began firing at the scampering GIs. But when they did, they revealed their positions to the third platoon, which was now on the German's left flank. The third platoon proceeded to lay down an effective volume of return fire, which, at least for the moment, silenced the German infantry. Then, with magnificent timing, eight fighter-bombers from the 377th Squadron swooped in on Tintange, further discouraging and pinning down the enemy force inside the town.

The two forward platoons of B Company rushed the village on the heels of the air strike and took on the enemy assault gun. Seeing the American infantry swarming toward them like ants, the assault gun crew decided to abandon the gun before they were over-run by the fanatical Americans. B Company, enraged by their losses, went on a rampage through the streets of Tintange and overwhelmed the defenders, taking 161 of them prisoner. This was "the biggest haul the Bn (had) ever taken in a single day."

The 1st Battalion, despite all the hardship it had faced during the past three days, and now led by a brand new set of battalion and company commanders, had pulled of a marvelous assault on Tintange, and had cleared away any immediate threat to the right flank of CCA's advance. Their effort was not without cost, however. At the end of the day, the three rifle companies were reduced to a total of 124 men (the company strength is based on the recollections of Major Connaughton, which were collected in a combat interview on January 29, 1945). With the road leading through the woods and into Tintange now secured, C/35 was brought up to support the 1st Battalion. The Sherman tanks moved into the village at about 4 P.M. on Christmas Day.

Even though Tintange was now firmly in American hands, there was still some concern that a German attack could come from the direction of the large town of Surre. There was only one road leading from Surre to Tintange, however, and that road had to cross a bridge over the Surbach Ruisseau. The Shermans of C/8 were sent toward the bridge to guard it until American engineers could come forward to destroy it. As they pulled up within sight of the bridge, which was about 1500 yards north of Tintange, they spotted an enemy column headed back toward Surre, and blasted it with deadly fire. The engineers then came forward, and blew the bridge later that evening.

A few of the tanks were also sent to the southeast, to help clear the area around Tintange where the Germans might have fled, while the remaining tanks and two tank destroyers stood guard over the crossroads north of Tintange. The infantry battalion moved north before nightfall to establish a defensive line that extended from the destroyed bridge on the right, in a northwesterly direction toward the Grausse Mauischt on the left. Patrols were sent out during the night in order to maintain contact with the enemy, while the balance of the battalion settled down for another cold, shivering night in the snow.

The Christmas Day Advance of CCA

While the 1st Battalion spent Christmas Day capturing Tintange and providing protection on CCA's right flank, General Earnest's main force resumed its advance along the Arlon-Bastogne highway. The 51st AIB pushed off at 8 A.M., with C/51 on the left and A/51 on the right. B/51 remained back at Warnach in reserve, but late that night, found itself attached to the 1st Battalion (more on that later).

Due to the gap that existed between CCA and CCB, the vanguard of CCA still had to worry about the possibility of an enemy presence on its left flank as well as its right. The most likely harbor for German troops to the immediate left of CCA was the village of Strainchamps. So as C/51 and A/51 started their march to the north, a small team was dispatched to capture the town.

Strainchamps was located about three quarters of a mile west of the main highway. A platoon from C/51 peeled away from the rest of the company, and headed down into the small valley where Strainchamps was nestled. Before they descended upon the town, tanks from A/35, D/35, and some Hellcats from A/704 moved onto the high ground overlooking the town from the north, east, and south. If the armored infantry met any resistance, the American armor was in position to deal a heavy blow.

Once the armored infantry moved into the village, two platoons of Shermans from A/35 moved in to support them. Fortunately, the Germans had abandoned Strainchamps, and the town was taken without a fight. The balance of A/35 moved into the town, and remained there for the better part of the day (A/35's only loss on Christmas Day was one Sherman, and that was due to mechanical failure).

Visibility on December 25 was excellent, and the men at Strainchamps could look to the west and see elements of CCB about two miles away as they moved along the road between Burnon and Chaumont. They could also see an "extensive enemy pocket" of resistance dug-in southwest of Hollange. This enemy force was scissored in between the axis of advance of CCB and CCA, and had been left alone by the Americans up to this point (had Dager chosen to advance further to the east, toward Hollange instead of Chaumont, CCB would have run head-on into this enemy position). Though this German force was not in line to be attacked by either CCA or CCB, it made too inviting a target to be ignored. The mortar and assault guns platoons of the 51st AIB, along with supporting artillery, hammered the enemy position.

With Strainchamps in Americans hands, the left flank of CCA was relatively secure, and C/51 and A/51 continued to advance abreast to the north. Both companies met resistance as they approached the wooded areas less than a mile north of Strainchamps. Company C met light resistance. Company A, which was closer to the main highway, came under heavy small arms fire from the north edge of the Bois de Melch. At this point, the light tanks from the 35th were brought forward to help clear the edge of the woods.

The Germans decided to stand their ground in the face of the machine gun and 37mm high explosive rounds being dispensed by the light tanks. A round from a panzerfaust hit one of the tanks, stopping it dead in its tracks. The other M5 light tanks nearby opened up with a blaze of machine gun fire, and cut down several of the paratroopers who had ambushed the now smoking tank. The wounded Germans made gestures for surrender as the armored infantry swept in to clean up the paratroopers that the M5s had missed. In the distance, a lone, pathetic German crawled away on his hands and knees. The Americans let him continue on across the open field. After several minutes, he disappeared over a hillock some 300 yards away.

Beside the smoldering M5, a tearful tank commander mourned the loss of his bow gunner and driver. They had been together as a crew ever since the early days at Pine Camp. The Kraut who ruined the tankers' collective dream of all returning home in one piece stood a short distance away, his panzerfaust thrown aside, his hands now high over his head. The look of fear in the German's eyes was magnified through the tears of the American tank commander. One can only imagine the thoughts that raced through the tanker's mind. You cowardly Kraut bastard! If you were going to give up so easily, why did you have to squeeze off that damn shot from your panzerfaust? Why?

What did you accomplish? In a flat voice that belied the depth of his pain, his only words were "Take the bastard away."

D Company exacted a heavy toll on the 15th FJ Regiment that day. Colonel Hal Pattison, the executive officer of CCA, would later report, "The light tanks ... had a field day shooting up enemy personnel and vehicles." By the end of the day, D Company had rounded up 40 to 50 prisoners, and had killed many more.

The skies on that Christmas Day were picture perfect, and American P-47s now arrived to help clear the way for the next leg of the advance. Unfortunately, some of the American pilots attacked the lead elements of CCA by mistake. This event didn't dampen the Fourth's enthusiasm when American fighters appeared overhead, however. Sam Ridley later recalled that, when he and his men saw American planes in action, "We all cheered like we (were) at a football game." Nevertheless, the confusion generated by this particular incident caused a considerable delay.

When the advance resumed late that afternoon, C/51 and A/35 pushed across difficult, elevated terrain. Tanks and infantrymen alike were sent skidding and slipping on the icy slopes. By 4:30 P.M., with daylight fading, they reached a position on high ground about 500 yards south of Hollange. At 5 P.M., C/51 sent a patrol toward the town. The armored infantrymen returned with a report that they had drawn small arms fire from the buildings. An air recon mission also brought back word that the Germans were holding Hollange with a force of considerable size. With the prospects of a tough battle in front of them, and with a bitter taste in their mouths from the nighttime assault on Warnach, the 51st AIB sat down for the night and planned to make its assault on Hollange the following morning. Throughout the night, the Americans were content to register heavy artillery concentrations on the town in order to soften the Krauts up for the following day.

The waning hours of Christmas Day offered no peace, even for those that had been taken prisoner. That night, a twin-engine German plane flew in low over a band of 220 German POW's that were being searched and processed by the military police. The unarmed Germans took advantage of the distraction to break for the cover of some nearby buildings. The MPs quickly rounded up the Germans, and told them they would be shot if they tried to escape again.

The POWs would soon test the MP's resolve. The German fighter came back on a return pass, and this time, its cannons were blazing. The German officers in the group shouted to their men, who then broke and ran once again. A German officer charged directly at one of the MPs, who was manning a .30 caliber machine gun. The MP, Pfc. Paul Carrafiello, trained the barrel of his machine gun on the racing figure, and peppered him with a burst when he was only a couple of feet away. The MPs went after the prisoners, but this time, showed little mercy in the wake of the Germans' lack of compliance. Ten of the Germans were killed, and 22 wounded (the German fighter plane probably accounted for some of those casualties).

German planes put at least one other target in their sights that day, and if they had had better aim, they would have changed the course of history. General Patton decided to come forward that day to visit with the Fourth Armored. While driving along a road in the zone of CCA, two enemy airplanes descended on his vehicle, dropping bombs and strafing the road. While coming close, they did no damage. Patton later noted that this was the only occasion during the war in northwest Europe when he came under direct attack by German fighter planes.

Amidst the intense fighting that continued along CCA's front on Christmas Day, an attempt was made by some of the men to make something special of the day. Sam Ridley of D/35 managed to scrape up a hot meal along with some of his fellow officers. They took to a local house, which was stocked with wine, and even had the luxury of using glasses with which to enjoy their drink. Ridley later recalled:

> We were very happy that day and very thankful. After we had (finished) eating we broke all the dishes and glasses, just like we were Greeks. Hell all broke the next A.M.

The mood throughout most of the frontline units of CCA was not particularly merry, however. The 51st Armored Infantry Battalion reported, "the morale of the men was not very high on Xmas day." They were finishing up their fourth consecutive day of heavy fighting without a break, and the cold weather only weakened their condition. The recent snowfall wasn't welcome either. According to the battalion's diary, "It was a 'white' Xmas but that added to the general discomfort." The number of casualties they had incurred so far also served to diminish their spirit. On this one day alone, the 51st suffered 62 battle and non-battle casualties combined. Still, they were chipping away at the 5th FJ Division at a more rapid rate. On that same day, the 51st claimed 40 FJ's killed, 50 wounded, and 73 prisoners. And within 24 hours, the 51st AIB was right back where it had started from, after having picked up their replacement troops.

Replacement troops were indeed a valued commodity at this stage of the fight. All of the armored infantry battalions were suffering high casualties, and Patton had ordered that the rear area units and headquarters were to be used as a source for rifleman. Of course, not too many men were crazy about the prospect of being ripped away from their existing unit and job responsibilities for the purpose of becoming a rifleman.

Near Martelange, two men of the 704th TD Battalion came face to face with that prospect. Having just completed the refueling of the Hellcats of A Company and the battalion's recon platoon, the two soldiers "were told to park their truck and stand by for possible reassignment as infantry replacements." The two men followed the instructions they had been given, and then found protection from the cold in "a shot up house along the road that still had two good rooms." They soon found they were not the only ones with the same idea. Another half dozen GIs already occupied one of the rooms. An elderly couple that occupied the house were doing their best to make the American soldiers at home by serving up hot coffee. A 2nd lieutenant suddenly appeared on the scene, and "raised hell and threatened to court-martial anyone not on the road in five minutes, and a couple of GIs who knew him offered their unsolicited opinion of his behavior, the weather, and the war in general."

There would be no peace this Christmas along the cold, dark stretch of highway leading from Arlon to Bastogne. For the men of the 51st and 35th battalions engaged on the front line, the dangers were the same that day as they had been the day before, and as they would be on the day after. Nevertheless, it would be a Christmas they would never forget for the rest of their lives, as each and every one of them carried forth a mixture of sentiments that would rise to the surface every Christmas thereafter, sometimes to be shared with those gathered around them for the holidays, but more often than not, simply to be reflected upon in silent meditation. Christmas would never be the same.

18. Bigonville

CCR Moves North

Colonel Wendell Blanchard's CCR was the last of the three combat commands to head north to the Ardennes. At the time of its departure, CCR consisted primarily of the 37th Tank Battalion and the 704th TD Battalion, both of which had been attached to the 87th Infantry Division when the Germans struck against Hodge's First Army. Thus, they had to be disengaged and reassembled for the trip north, as opposed to the rest of the division, which had already been off the front line, preparing for Patton's winter offensive scheduled for December 19.

Of the division's three tank battalions, Abe Abrams' 37th was currently the most under strength, with only 27 medium tanks ready for combat at the time of the move. This tally did not include Abrams' own Sherman, however, nor did it include any of the other four Shermans Abrams retained at his Battalion HQ. By the book, a tank battalion headquarters was allocated only two medium tanks (one for the battalion commander, and the other for his executive officer). But from the very start of the Fourth Armored's campaign in Europe, Abrams had pulled one Sherman from each of his three medium tank companies, and assigned them to his S-2, S-3, and liaison officer. These men were among his most experienced and trusted officers, and he wanted to have them in a position where they could directly influence the course of events (something they could do much more readily in a tank, as opposed to a jeep).

Abrams had to shuffle some of his company commanders just prior to moving to the Ardennes. The commanding officer of A Company was wounded and evacuated during the operation supporting the 87th, and Lt. John Whitehill became the new CO of the company. C Company also sported a relatively new commanding officer, and he came with lofty credentials: Captain Trover, who had commanded D Troop of the 25th Cavalry so capably in the past (Trover had briefly left D Troop for an assignment as the S-3 of the 704th Tank Destroyer Battalion, but finding that job too boring for his taste, and wanting to make a stronger contribution in a fighting role, he volunteered to take command of C/37 when it became available). The return of Captain Jimmie Leach, who had just recently come back from a brief hospital stay, added immeasurably to the battalion's effectiveness. Lt. Donahue now commanded D Company, as Captain John McMahon had moved to the S-2 staff position.

In contrast to the 37th's depleted inventory of tanks, the 704th Tank Destroyer Battalion was only one vehicle shy of its full compliment of 36 Hellcats. While assigned to CCR for the moment, its tank destroyers would soon be doled out as deemed necessary among the combat commands.

The 37th Tank Battalion moved out at 8:30 A.M. on December 20. It traveled 120 miles along a route that began at Mittersheim and passed through Morhange, Pont-a-Mousson, Conflans, and Longwy. The tanks held up well during the road march, and no dropouts were reported. The balance of CCR moved on December 21. "The military police and traffic controllers did a magnificent job" of keeping the columns moving on schedule. During the trip to their assembly area near Arlon, the column only stopped once, and that was for refueling. While the rest of the combat command was moving to join the 37th, Abrams' unit spent the day performing equipment maintenance. It was at this time that the 53rd AIB was reassigned from CCA to CCR. Of the three armored infantry battalions, the 53rd was the most under strength, with each company being short approximately 50 men.

As CCR headed north, there was no immediate plan to involve it in combat operations. As was almost always the case in the Fourth Armored, CCR was being used as a true reserve. Its units would be doled out to either CCA or CCB as needed. So as dawn broke on December 22, the men of the 37th Tank Battalion sat on the sidelines, as their peers assigned to CCA and CCB began the drive to Bastogne.

All of that began to change, however, on the night of December 22, when it was reported that German armor had appeared near the seam between the 26th Infantry Division and the Fourth Armored. Elements of CCA had already pushed to the northeast as far as Flatzbourhof, and while no enemy armor had been encountered, it was discovered that the Germans had moved their infantry into position to threaten CCA's right flank. There indeed seemed to be cause for concern, though the degree of the threat was still uncertain.

In order to gain an effective concentration of force, Gaffey had left both the left and right flanks of the division virtually unguarded. If the intelligence regarding German armor to the east were true, there was the potential for a serious problem on the Fourth Armored's right flank; for if the Germans drove down through the town of Bigonville, and subsequently gained control of the main road that ran west toward Martelange, CCA would be open for a strike at its rear as it advanced north along the Arlon-Bastogne highway. If the Germans recaptured Martelange, CCA would be cut off north of the Sure River.

Gaffey decided that he had to secure Bigonville. It would be a limited offensive, since there were no objectives of any great value beyond the town (a single road continued to wind north from Bigonville, passing through increasingly rough terrain, until it reached the steep bank of the Sure River; there was only one bridge in the area, and even if it was intact, there was little benefit to be gained by crossing it, as the Americans would be heading away from Bastogne at that point). But what force would he use? CCA and CCB were fully engaged on their respective missions and could certainly not spare any of their strength for this particular assignment.

The decision was made on the night of the 22nd to utilize CCR as a fighting command, with the specific mission of securing the division's right flank at Bigonville. The 94th AFAB was reassigned to CCR, along with a battery of 155mm howitzers from the 177th Field Artillery Battalion.

The units of CCR moved that same evening from Arlon to Quatre Vents. Blanchard now had a balanced force at his disposal, and he would put it into play on the morning of December 23. The full composition of CCR at that point was:

53rd Armored Infantry Battalion

37th Tank Battalion

704th TD Battalion (minus A Company)

94th Armored Field Artillery Battalion

C Company, 24th Armored Engineers

D Battery, 489th AAA SP Battalion

C, D, and E Troops of the 25th Cavalry Squadron

C Battery, 177th FAB

995th Engineer Battalion (minus two platoons; one each having been assigned to CCA and CCB)

The Advance Toward Bigonville

At 6 A.M. on the morning of December 23, CCR departed from Quatre-Vents and set out along the main road toward Martelange. The column was led by Lt. Marion Harris, the CO of the 37th Tank Battalion's recon platoon. Behind the recon platoon came B/37 and B/53, followed by the HQ Company of the 37th Tank Battalion. A/37 and C/37 were next, followed by the balance of the 53rd AIB and the self-propelled howitzers of the 94th AFAB.

Approximately two miles south of Martelange, the column turned off the main Arlon-Bastogne highway and headed for the town of Perle, which had been cleared the day before by CCA. The advance toward the town was now a much more hazardous affair, as the hard freeze the previous night had cast a thick coat of ice on the road. Some of the tanks and halftracks slid from one side of the road to the other as they ascended to the higher ground east of the Arlon highway. The column labored at a slow pace, with the engineers having to come forward at times to cut down logs to be laid across the road for traction.

The column continued though Perle and on to the northeast, toward the small village of Flatzbourhof. The guns of the 94th AFAB remained near Perle, where they set up their firing positions to support the attack toward Bigonville. The 155mm howitzers of the 177th Field Artillery Battalion's C Battery also displaced to Perle.

Lt. Harris brought the column through the positions of the 25th Armored Cavalry, which had established outposts south of Flatzbourhof. Having delivered the column to the front, he pulled his vehicle off to the side of the road and saluted Captain Leach as his tank rumbled past, followed by the other six Shermans of B Company.

With Captain Leach's command tank "Blockbuster 3d" in the lead (it was a brand

"Blockbuster 3d," the command tank of B/37. This photograph was taken shortly after the Bulge, while the division was in Luxembourg (courtesy J. Leach).

new M4A3E8 delivered to him after the recent loss of Blockbuster 2d), the column continued on toward Flatzbourhof. Almost a foot of fresh snow covered the road, but the route could still be distinguished. As they advanced, they came upon evidence that the enemy might be near: the wide, unmistakable tank tracks of German armor carved in the virgin snow. Studying the tracks, Leach could tell that the enemy tanks had moved south toward the positions of the 25th Cav, but had then turned about and headed back in the direction of Flatzbourhof. The chance of imminent contact was confirmed when Captain Dwight relayed word that an Army recon plane had spotted the enemy up ahead. Radio silence had been in effect for the column, but it was now lifted as Leach's company prepared to meet the enemy.

At about noon, the Americans approached the crossroads, which, along with the nearby rail line and train station, defined Flatzbourhof. They were now just one mile south of Bigonville, and were making good progress. Anticipating that the enemy might be present near the rail station, Leach deployed the tanks and infantry of the "B Team" in order to lay down the highest volume of fire possible on the area. Sure enough, as Leach approached the station, Germans clad in white capes and helmets opened fire from the edge of the nearby woods. A combination of rifle, machine gun, and mortar fire came in at a steady rate, punctuated by some incoming rounds from two 75mm anti-tank guns, one of which claimed one of B/53's halftracks.

Leach called the artillery battalion for support, and at 12:40 P.M., the 94th AFAB proceeded to hit the woods with a sustained barrage that lasted for about an hour (they also began firing on Bigonville). Unfortunately, some of the shells fell short, wounding some of the men from B/53 who had dismounted in preparation for clearing the enemy from the woods. The artillery seemed to have done its job, however, as the German guns fell silent. Some of the armored infantrymen from B Company proceeded into the woods, where they found little resistance. With the threat apparently removed, the men of B/53 returned to the road to remount their halftracks

Unknown to the Americans, the Germans had apparently stolen away during the artillery barrage, and had returned after the shelling had stopped. As the armored infantry began to mount up, the Germans opened up with an even heavier volume of fire, catching the Americans by surprise.

The Germans were using their small arms with deadly accuracy. The armored infantry, who were exposed on the open ground near the road, were taking casualties. And the tankers, who, per their custom, were riding with their hatches open, also fell victim to bullets; Sgt. John Fitzpatrick received an extremely serious wound when he was shot in the mouth. The Germans also started hitting back with anti-tank fire once again. Sgt. John Parks and one of his crew, Edward Clark, were both killed when their Sherman tank was hit and destroyed west of Flatzbourhof.

The battle at the Flatzbourhof crossroad had been raging since noon, with the only lull being the time it took for the Germans to evade the American artillery fire. Lt. Colonel Abrams now came to the fore to see what was delaying the attack. Just as he arrived, the Germans launched a counterattack with at least two StuG III Assault Guns and a captured Sherman tank (Horst Lange, who was at his mortar position inside Bigonville, had a clear view of the German armor as it emerged from the woods onto the high ground outside the town; he counted five tanks or assault guns).

Leach's Sherman was in a hull defilade position behind the railroad embankment. His gunner drew a bead on the advancing Sherman adorned with the telltale cross of the Wehrmacht. The gunner's first shot with the 76mm was low and hit the embankment. After making an adjustment, Cpl. Yaremchuk squeezed off a second round, but this one caught the rail itself. One more adjustment, and a third armor piercing round was on the way. This one found its mark, destroying the pilfered Sherman. Meanwhile, Lt. Cook's platoon took on the two assault guns, and destroyed both of them with multiple rounds.

Leach's company had been under-strength from the very start of the engagement, having headed north to the Ardennes with only seven tanks. Now with one destroyed, and the commander of another seriously wounded, Abrams decided to bring up Lt. Whitehill's A Company to continue the advance.

Whitehill's eleven Shermans moved up quickly through the positions of the "B Team." As the tanks churned through the deep snow, they unwittingly entered a minefield near the railroad crossing. Lt. Whitehill's tank struck one of the hidden mines, which blew off a three to four foot long section of one of the tracks as well as one of the bogey wheels, and caved in the floor of the tank, injuring the driver. At the time, Whitehill wasn't sure if the damage came from a mine or an incoming round of high explosive, but S/Sgt. Herman Walling, who was observing from the following tank, confirmed that it was indeed a mine.

A mine also blew off the bogey wheel of the 94th AFAB's forward observer tank, but fortunately, neither the observer (Lt. Guild) nor any of his crew were injured. With the tank immobilized, Guild ordered his crew to stay put in the tank, as he expected the Germans were going to hit the area with artillery fire. Eventually, he and his bow gunner, Pfc. Susceta, left the Sherman and headed for the woods. This was the same patch of forest that the M7s of the 94th AFAB had pounded earlier in the day, and Guild found a horrific sight lying within. As he walked deeper into the woods, he found "absolute carnage," with dismembered and mutilated bodies scattered about the forest floor. The artillery had done its job after all.

Due to the depth of the snow covering the field, Whitehill had no idea just what sort of a mess his company had driven into. It could be a dense minefield, or they could have had the bad luck of striking an isolated mine. Whitehill turned his damaged tank and its crew over to S/Sgt. Walling. He then took over Walling's Sherman as his new command tank.

Whitehill pulled back his newly acquired Sherman, skirting what he now suspected to be a larger minefield. He shifted his advance to the east side of the road and approached the rail station from that direction. Meanwhile, his company of Shermans deployed in a line formation on the north side of the railroad tracks, facing north toward Bigonville.

Up to this point in time, all of the enemy fire, except for the assault guns, had been emanating from the woods to the east and northeast. Suddenly, anti-tank fire erupted from the northwest, where the enemy apparently held a position along a ridge overlooking the approaches to Bigonville. Lt. Whitehill's tank was struck in quick succession by three armor-piercing shells, all of which found their mark on the turret of the Sherman. Fortunately, none of the shells penetrated, but two of the crewmen were injured (the driver's hatch was blown open, cutting the arm of the driver, and the loader sustained some rib injuries, apparently from the shock and concussion of the shell impact). After absorbing the three rounds, the crew realized they were sitting ducks, and bailed out of the tank. Lt. Whitehill was not as quick to do so, and realizing that the tank could still move under its own power, he drove it back to the rear, where he turned it back to the original crew so they could use it to take the two wounded men in for medical attention. Meanwhile, another Sherman of A/37 was hit by armor piercing rounds emanating from the ridge. This one belonged to Lt. Robert Gilson, the only other officer available in A Company. Gilson was wounded and evacuated, leaving Whitehill as the only able-bodied officer in A/37.

Having lost two tanks from underneath him in less than 20 minutes, Whitehill decided to lead the attack on foot. Using hand and arm signals, he led his company forward toward the enemy positions. When radio contact was necessary, he jumped to the rear deck of S/Sgt. Rowland's tank to use his equipment. Whitehill positioned his tanks to cover the south and southwest sections of Bigonville, and held those positions for the time being.

With A Company experiencing difficulty, and daylight becoming a scarce commodity, Abrams brought up Captain Trover's C Company in an effort to move around the German's right flank at Flatzbourhof. The plan called for Trover to bring his Shermans in between A/37 and B/37, and then swing east to cut the road leading from Flatzbourhof to Bigonville.

Captain Trover's tanks moved easily around B/37, which had been on the right side of the formation. But after moving behind Flatzbourhof, heavy enemy sniper fire wreaked havoc on the tankers, who were, in the tradition of the 37th, riding with their heads out of the turrets. Captain Trover was killed by a sniper's bullet, and several of the other tank commanders were hit as well. With C Company rocked by the loss of their leader, and several of the tanks now dealing with wounded officers in their turrets, Abrams decided to halt his move toward Bigonville rather than continue in darkness. He would resume his push in the morning.

Both Sides Reorganize

Abrams now had his men improve their positions for the night. B/53, which had suffered 30 casualties during the fighting near the woods, was sent back to the rear and placed in reserve, while A/53 and C/53 dug in near the front. The Sherman tanks of C/37 were dispatched to the right flank, where they guarded the only road leading into the area from the east (twenty to thirty enemy tanks had been reported operating in the area east of Bigonville, and there was some concern that they might swing to the west via this road).

Eight engineers from the 188th Combat Engineer Battalion, led by Sergeant Bruce Burdett, were sent further east to set up a roadblock along the same approach being guarded by C/37. About midway between Flatzbourhof and Koetschette, they placed demolition charges on trees close to the road, so that if the need arose, they could create an instant roadblock by downing the timbers. They also laid a number of anti-tank mines on the paved road. Should the enemy approach, their orders were to "fire briskly for an honest five minutes, and then fall back to the Flatzbourhof position."

Fortunately, the Germans never made an appearance from the east during the Bigonville operation, despite the fact that they weren't all that far away (the Germans held the nearby town of Arsdorf in force, and would give the 26th Infantry Division and 249th Combat Engineer Battalion a difficult time there on Christmas Day).

There was plenty of activity during the night of December 23/24. Abrams put his engineers to work in the darkness clearing the minefield outside of Flatzbourhof, and the tank recovery crew from the 94th AFAB tried to rescue the artillery observer's disabled tank. Efforts to move the tank failed at first due to the slippery roads, and then failed again when the tow cable snapped. The recovery crew gave up on it for the night (the tank was recovered and repaired the following day). The front line troops of CCR didn't encounter any trouble with the enemy that night, but the 94th AFAB continued to shell suspected enemy positions just to keep them honest.

Meanwhile, on the German side of the front, the forward paratroopers used the cover of darkness as an opportunity to slip out of the woods. They moved north, and joined the battalion of infantry from the 13th FJ Regiment currently holding Bigonville.

The company commanders of the 37th had a lot of work to do to rally and reorganize their force. 1st Lt. Charles Boggess, the executive officer of C Company (he was also pulling duty as the company motor officer), was placed in command of that unit by Abrams following the death of Captain Trover. Some replacement crewmembers were brought forward, and Captain Leach, with the help of 1st Sergeant Louis Guffey and Lt. Cook (Cook was Leach's executive officer and leader of the 3rd platoon), got them assimilated into the company. Leach later described a memorable event that took place as his staff was discussing the reorganization of the company following the day's turbulent action:

> As we were discussing replacement of platoon Sergeant Fitzpatrick, our tank trained company supply sergeant, Staff Sergeant Walter P. Kaplin, asked me if he could take command of a tank. Since he had been out of tanks for awhile, I was skeptical until he volunteered some professional fire commands and superb radio procedure. He was ready.

CCR outposted their positions, and settled down as best they could under the clear, cold winter sky. The nights prior to this had been cold, but the night of December 23/24 was now colder still. For the men that had to remain outside in the elements, the bone chilling air seemed unbearable at times. If the men weren't lucky enough to get to the shelter and warmth of a building, they tried to improve their situation however they could. Getting close to the heated exhaust of a tank engine was one way to gather a little bit of warmth. As Sgt. Harry Feinberg of the 37th's assault gun platoon later recalled:

> A few of the boys got too close to the exhaust, soaked up some carbon monoxide and keeled over. They didn't realize they were inhaling fumes that could have killed them. But luckily, we were outdoors and there was enough fresh air to sort of dilute the exhaust fumes. We helped them up and walked them around until they got their senses back.

The rising sun brought with it the promise of a little bit more warmth. It also signaled the start of another day of combat. And if a soldier's prayers were answered, he would have the good fortune of suffering through another frigid night.

The Attack on Bigonville

The area in and around Bigonville represented the left flank of the 5th FJ Division, and as the sun rose on December 24, CCR/4 would find itself squaring off against a battalion from the 13th FJ Regiment, as well as small contingent from the 15th FJ Regiment. The 13th was a relatively fresh unit, as it had been held in the German 7th Army's reserve for most of the battle. They had been following in the footsteps of the 15th FJ Regiment, and their march had terminated at Bigonville.

For the Germans, the coming battle would be an infantry-only affair. The rumor that a strong force of German tanks had moved into the area immediately east of the Fourth Armored had not been true; there were some strong tank and panzer grenadier elements of the Fuehrer Grenadier Brigade moving into position further to the east, square in the zone of the 26th Infantry Division, but they would not become involved in the battle at Bigonville.

On December 24, Abrams kicked off the attack at 8 A.M. with a short but sharp artillery barrage fired against the suspected enemy positions in and around Bigonville.

Most of the artillery fire was confined to the approaches north and east of the town. As an extra precaution, the 94th delivered some shells into Bilsdorf and Arsdorf, well to the east of Bigonville, just in case the Germans had any plans of concentrating at these points for a move against Abrams' right flank (the artillery fire on these towns was adjusted by spotters flying overhead).

Captain Leach's B/37 and two companies of armored infantry (A/53 and C/53) pressed directly up the road toward Bigonville. As they advanced over open ground, the Germans hit them with heavy doses of mortar, artillery, and small arms fire. The armored infantrymen dropped to their stomachs in the face of the enemy fire, and crawled forward in the snow along the ridges overlooking the town.

Once in position, B/53 was brought forward to join B/37 in the attack on the town. Lt. Cook led the Shermans of the 3rd Platoon into the village streets, while the armored infantry moved in on foot alongside them.

The pace of the tankers' advance depended upon the armored infantrymen's ability to clear the houses lining the streets along the route. Leach was none too happy with the level of enthusiasm the infantry seemed to have for the task. Twice he descended from his turret to place some pressure on B/53 to pick up the pace.

As Leach was urging on his supporting infantry, he received a call over the radio from Lt. Cook, who informed him that he had been seriously wounded. A German bullet had struck him in the chest, exited, and then lodged in his arm. Leach had Cook turn command of the 3rd Platoon over to Sergeant Max Morphew. Leach then asked Cook if he could make it under his own power back to the medical jeep parked at the edge of town. Cook replied that he would head back.

Lt. Cook dismounted from his tank and started making his way back toward the edge of town. Apparently, the armored infantry supporting his tanks had failed to clear all of the buildings they had already passed, for as he walked by the doorway of a house, a squad of German paratroopers reached out and grabbed him off the street. The wounded lieutenant now found himself a prisoner of the German paratroopers. Fortunately, as the battle started going the wrong way for the Germans, they abandoned the lieutenant without doing him further harm. In fact, they helped tend to his wounds and made him as comfortable as possible before leaving. Despite a heavy loss of blood, he finally managed to make it back to the rear for medical aid and evacuation.

As Lt. Cook was having his brush with the enemy, Captain Leach was still trying to prod the supporting infantry to hasten the clearing of the houses lining the town's main streets. While standing up in the turret of his tank, Leach unknowingly found himself in the gun sight of an unseen sniper. A bullet penetrated the side of his helmet at an oblique angle, creasing the side of his head with enough impact to render him unconscious. Two of his tank crewmembers, Corporal Yaremchuck and Specialist 4 Jefferis, bandaged his wound and helped bring him back to consciousness.

At the time he was struck by the sniper's bullet, Leach's company had advanced about halfway into the town from the south. Faced with the temporary loss of his most experienced company commander, Abrams had the tanks of B/37 withdraw from Bigonville, while the infantrymen of B/53 continued to work their way forward through the town. After pulling back, the remaining Shermans of B/37 circled the town to the west. The platoon of Shermans commanded by Sgt. Morphew took up positions north of the town to cut off the only route of retreat available to the enemy. After Leach regained consciousness, he was right back in the fight — and subsequently found himself in the gunsight of yet another German sniper. This time, a bullet caught him in the right arm. But it was not enough to take him out of the contest, and he continued to lead his company throughout the action.

As B/37 completed the encirclement of Bigonville, A/37, which now consisted of nine tanks, was brought up from the south to resume the push that B/37 had started. Whitehill's company now had the additional goal of linking up with B/37 on the north edge of town. Some additional muscle was added to the attack by bringing A/53 forward with the tanks.

S/Sgt. MAX MORPHEW
ACTing Platoon ldr
B-37th TankBn

Sgt. Max Morphew of B/37 (courtesy J. Leach).

Lt. Whitehill's company advanced up the main highway leading toward Bigonville from the southeast. S/Sgt. F. Woods led the first platoon of four tanks up the highway, while the platoon of S/Sgt. Rowland covered Wood's left flank by advancing in a wedge formation. A/37 and B/37 now formed a contiguous line facing Bigonville from three directions. As Wood's platoon approached the town, it ran into some of the same stiff resistance that Leach had encountered. The Germans poured mortar rounds and machine gun fire on the tanks, while paratroopers bearing panzerfausts tried to close in for the kill. The advance stalled, and Whitehill brought his command tank to the front in order to inspire his men to keep moving forward. Whitehill's tank entered the village, and Wood's platoon soon followed behind.

The battle that ensued in the streets of Bigonville was intense. The men from one of the companies of the 53rd AIB were still struggling a bit in clearing the buildings. Their efficiency was further reduced when they lost their commanding officer during the fight. Lt. Whitehill took charge of directing the infantry inside the town at that point, in addition to managing his own company of Shermans.

The tanks and infantry continued to push through Bigonville. Whitehill's Sherman kept moving up the main street, and eventually came to a stop alongside a barn. From this position, Whitehill could make out the shadows of German paratroopers hiding around the corner, panzerfausts at the ready, trying to close in for a shot at his tanks. The progress of the entire attack had stalled at that point, and as Whitehill was contemplating his next move, the voice of Colonel Abrams suddenly came over the radio. "Why was the attack not moving forward as planned?" he asked. Whitehill explained the tactical situation, and Abrams "immediately countered with a verbal lesson in tactics which covered direct fire versus high trajectory fire." Abrams also reinforced that moving tanks could usually advance against soldiers on foot without too many problems. Captain John McMahon, the battalion S-2, was listening in on the conversation, and perhaps feeling some sympathy for Whitehill's situation, broke in on the radio channel and interrupted Abrams without identifying himself: "If Whitehill could move, he would."

Captain McMahon's comments provided some motivation for Whitehill's next move. Thinking fast, he decided to toss a grenade into the barn in order to set it on fire. As the flames began to engulf the building, the panzerfaust-wielding paratroopers were forced to abandon their hiding place. Having cleared the immediate threat, the advance continued.

Small arms fire continued to patter off the tanks like hail. Sgt. Woods' Sherman took a larger round in the area of one of his bogey wheels, but fortunately, it didn't disable the tank, and no one was injured. Despite the volume of fire, Whitehill continued to stand in his turret in order to direct the action. At one point, an enemy sniper took aim at Whitehill's head, but missed with several shots that ricocheted of the turret. Whitehill thought he had the sniper's location pegged, but rather than direct his gunner to take out the position with a round from his 75mm gun, he decided to pull out his submachine gun for the task (ammunition for the main gun was running low, and he wanted to conserve it). As Whitehill began to rise out of the hatch opening in preparation for taking aim, the sniper finally found his mark, sending a bullet that caught Whitehill's right hand. At that point, he figured using a round of 75mm HE was worth it, and put his gunner to work. The sniper didn't bother him again.

As the battle raged, four P-47s descended on the battlefield, but they mistook the tanks of B Company on the north side of town for enemy tanks. Despite Leach's men displaying their identification panels on the rear decks of their tanks, as well as setting off red signal smoke, the planes from the XIX TAC made two bombing and strafing runs against the Shermans. The tank crews were furious. Fortunately, none of the Shermans were damaged.

With the escape routes sealed off, and Whitehill's force pushing through the center of town, the Germans had nowhere to go. They began to surrender in droves (conflicting records indicate that somewhere between 328 and 482 prisoners were taken). Among those taken prisoner were some women who had been pressed into service. Officially, approximately 350 Germans had been killed or wounded (Leach, however, calls this "a doubtful figure"). In addition to the Sherman tank that had been employed by the Germans, the victorious men of CCR also found a number of other American weapons that had been turned against them, including two 40mm anti-aircraft guns, four 81mm mortars, and a variety of small arms. The Fourth Armored also rescued 39 American officers and enlisted men from the 299th Engineer Battalion who the Germans were holding captive in the town.

Horst Lange was one of the Germans taken prisoner on December 24. After being marched out of the combat area, along with about 100 other prisoners, he later recalled that the Americans forced any German caught wearing American shoes to remove them, and carry on barefoot. Lange ripped his sweater into fragments, which he wrapped around his feet in an attempt to stave off frostbite. About two hours later, a sympathetic American officer rounded up shoes for the prisoners' naked feet. Obviously, the American GIs were not very fond of seeing the boots of their dead brothers-in-arms put to use by the enemy. Who could blame them?

B/37 wasn't fortunate enough to emerge unscathed from the battle on December 24. Among the American casualties that day was the intrepid Sergeant Kaplan, who had so gallantly volunteered to take over one of the tank commander vacancies. Captain Leach would later recall what a tragedy it was that this fine young man would be struck down less than 24 hours after passing his field test. Fifty-seven years later, I will never forget sitting in Jimmie Leach's living room as he told the story of Walter Kaplin. The sense of needless loss still reverberated after all those many years, along with the sense that Kaplan's premature death had robbed B Company of a special leader who would never see his full potential realized.

There were no plans to advance beyond Bigonville, and once the Germans in the town were rounded up, CCR settled in to outpost the town and await further orders. Those orders came in earlier than expected.

Now that the threat of a German attack toward Martelange had been alleviated, CCR served no substantive purpose on the Fourth Armored Division's right flank. The 26th Infantry Division was thus ordered to extend its left flank west to Bigonville, in order to release CCR for commitment elsewhere. Elements of the 6th Cavalry Group were committed in the area as well, in order to bridge the gap between the two divisions. All of this was done quickly, and starting at midnight, CCR mounted up and headed west. Its destination: the far left flank of the division. Though they had no hint of it at the time, their deployment there would develop into one of the key turning points in the Fourth Armored Division's drive to Bastogne.

19. Chaumont

CCB's Advance to the Sure River

As you will recall, General Dager's command had arrived in the Ardennes before any of the other elements of the Fourth Armored Division. After the fascinating foray into Bastogne by TF Ezell, CCB had moved south, taking up positions to the west of CCA, whence they would commence their attack on December 22.

Even though his men had the disadvantage of advancing over roads that were marginal at best, it was anticipated that General Dager's CCB would be the first of the two combat commands to reach Bastogne. Why that was the case is not entirely certain. It might have been because CCB had arrived in the Ardennes first, and was in position to get a jump on CCA. It could have also been that Dager, as the most experienced of the three combat commanders, carried the burden of high expectations due to his track record heading into the battle. Certainly, CCB had outperformed CCA during the final weeks leading up to the division's rest period. Perhaps this trend was expected to continue. Perhaps Gaffey and Patton felt that the secondary road assigned to CCB would be less heavily defended. Regardless of the reason, the expectation was clear that CCB would get to Bastogne first.

CCB got an early start on the morning of December 22. The 8th Tank Battalion left its bivouac area at 4:30 A.M. and headed for the forward positions of the 10th AIB at Louftémont. Advancing in the dark was reason enough for tempering the pace of the advance, but poor weather conspired with the veil of night to further restrict the speed at which the column moved. The temperature was well below freezing, and the roads were covered with ice. A fresh blanket of snow started falling before sunrise, which reduced visibility even further. The net effect was an understandably slow and deliberate advance during the pre-dawn hours.

After leaving their bivouac area, the column of tanks from the "Rolling Eight Ball" moved southeast for a distance of about four miles. At the village of Beheme, they made a left turn onto a narrow dirt road that led north to Louftémont and the outposts of the 10th AIB. As the tanks moved through Louftémont, the 10th AIB fell into place in the column. By this time, the sun had broken above the horizon, but it was shrouded by the falling snow and early morning fog. The sky was a leaden gray, and the clouds hung low over the column, serving as notice that there would be no air support this day.

The first major obstacle along CCB's route was the Foret d'Anlier. The road through the forest was intimidating. The stately, thick evergreens were tucked so close to the road that the tree branches formed a canopy, making the next three and a half miles akin to driving through a tunnel.

The lead tanks continued to move cautiously, yet deliberately. The tankers scanned the woods diligently for signs of the enemy. If there was even the slightest suspicion of danger ahead, the lead tanks opened up with their machine guns to flush out any potential adversaries. One advantage that the column had in its favor was that an enemy seeking to engage them would have to do so from the edge of the woods, directly at the side of the road. The forest was simply too thick to allow for a field of fire from deep within the timbers; this made reconnaissance by fire along the edge of the road a very effective means of preempting any attack or ambush the Germans might have in the works.

As the lead tanks emerged from the forest, they were less than a mile away from the large town of Fauvillers, which was their first objective along CCB's axis of advance. Fauvillers was an important place on the map, since the only good quality east-west road ran directly through the town (Fauvillers would later serve as the location for General Dager's headquarters).

The terrain both to the left and right of the road leading into Fauvillers was now void of trees, and the buildings on the edge of town were clearly visible up ahead. As the column drew close to the town, it drew scattered small arms fire. This was the first confrontation with the enemy that day, and the lead tanks quickly rendered them silent. The column picked up the pace a little bit, and reached Fauvillers at about 10:15 A.M. Major Irzyk's vanguard moved through the town without meeting any resistance (unknown to Irzyk, the engineers of C/299 had cleared Fauvillers of a small enemy force the day before).

Irzyk wasted no time before moving his task force beyond Fauvillers. He continued north using a secondary dirt road that led toward the towns of Hotte and Menufontaine, some two miles ahead. Once again, the column entered into a wooded area, but the Bois Habaru was nowhere near as dense and intimidating as the forest they had just negotiated. When the task force emerged back into open terrain, it was only about three tenths of a mile from the village of Hotte. Freed from the woods, the column picked up speed again, occupied Hotte without opposition, and arrived at Menufontaine at 1:00 P.M.

The lead cavalry and tanks had just started moving beyond Menufontaine when they encountered their first strong resistance in the form of small arms fire coming from the direction of Burnon, north of the Sure River. Confined on the right by a swollen stream, the Shermans of A/8 deployed to the left of the road and spit out a steady stream of suppressive fire. The terrain in the area was wide open, so the enemy was not able to draw close to the column without fully revealing themselves. Company A of the 10th AIB took up positions on the high ground west of Menufontaine. The enemy fire subsided without having done any notable damage, and the tanks from A Company, along with elements of the 25th Armored Cavalry, continued the advance toward the Sure River, which was only a couple of hundred yards up ahead.

Crossing the Sure

Upon reaching the Sure River crossing site north of Menufontaine, Major Irzyk found that his task force was in a situation similar to that which confronted CCA: the bridge upon which he depended had been blown. The architects of the demolition hailed from the same outfit that had taken out the Martelange bridges. Up until Noon on December 21, the bridge had been in the hands of B/299's 3rd Platoon, with Sgt. Leon Tobin in charge of the bridge site. Despite the fact that the engineers had reported "no activity in this vicinity," "Lt. Russell gave orders to blow the bridge." After the bridge demolition was complete, the engineers departed for other assignments (half of this group of engineers left for Cobreville, where they would destroy yet another bridge eventually needed by the Fourth Armored Division).

CCB's engineers would have to put a temporary bridge in place. Since the site of the bridge was under the watchful eyes of the enemy located on the high ground to the north and northeast, a bridgehead would have to be established before the engineers from the B/24 and C Company of the 188th Engineer Combat Battalion could get to work.

Major Irzyk's first step in establishing the bridgehead was to position some of his units to provide covering fire for the crossing site. A platoon of Shermans from A Company, supported by a platoon of armored infantry from A/10, were positioned on the forward slope of Hill 470, which overlooked the bridge site from a distance of about 500 yards. Another platoon of Sherman tanks from A/8 was positioned somewhat closer, due south of the bridge site. Meanwhile, Irzyk called for the support of the 22nd AFAB. The M7s quickly deployed in firing positions, and answered Irzyk's call for a brisk barrage in the area near the bridge site.

At 2:30 P.M., two platoons of armored infantry from C/10 were brought forward to the line of the river for the unenviable task of wading across. As the tanks of A/8 fired in support, Lt. Charles Ingersoll led the infantrymen across the chilled waters of the Sure, and then quickly pushed forward a few hundred yards to establish a perimeter around the bridgehead. The Germans made their presence known, and continued to throw small arms fire in the direction of C Company's positions on the north bank of the river.

As the armored infantry formed their defensive perimeter, the engineers came forward to begin their work. They arrived near the site at 3:45 P.M., and immediately commenced work on the bridge. The river was about 20 feet wide at this point in its course, but due to the softness of the ground along the banks, some extra bridging was needed. By 5:45 P.M., the engineers of B/24 and C/188 had completed the installation of a 36-foot span, with the final touches being performed under the cover darkness. The protection provided by the armored infantry north of the river, and the tanks to the south, was invaluable.

With the bridge complete, the balance of C/10 crossed the river, followed by the tanks of Lt. Kieley's A/8. The bridgehead was then expanded toward Burnon, as the balance of the 8th and 10th battalions prepared to slowly snake across the bridge.

Two platoons of armored infantry from C Company pushed north into Burnon. As they attacked, T/Sgt. Roscoe Albertson moved into position with his 60mm mortar to strike at a German machine gun emplacement. While braving heavy fire from the enemy machine gun, Albertson adjusted his fire and placed several rounds directly onto the enemy position. The gun was silenced, and Roscoe then single-handedly captured the 19 surviving Germans that had been manning the position (Roscoe received the Silver Star). Resistance in the town faded, and the armored infantry secured it in less than an hour.

Darkness did not deter CCB from pressing forward as soon as the bridge was ready to support traffic. Tanks and halftracks continued to pour across the Sure River, and the main body of CCB had soon pushed forward to link up with the two platoons of C/10 holding Burnon.

Major Irzyk was not content to rest on his laurels at Burnon. The next town beyond Burnon was the small village of Chaumont, which had been earmarked as the primary objective for December 22. Only two miles separated the two Belgian villages, and had it not been for the blown bridge (courtesy of the 299th Engineer Combat Battalion), CCB would have, in all likelihood, reached Chaumont before sunset. There was always the possibility that CCB could reach Chaumont during the evening of the 22nd, but traveling at night through hostile territory could turn two miles into a marathon. The terrain to the left of the road was favorable for a night advance, as it was open and sloped gently downward to the west for about 500 yards before reaching the wood line of the Bois du Boulet. But to the right, about 500 yards north of Burnon, the forest of Lambaichenet hugged the right side of the road, and offered a superb hiding place from which the Germans could snipe at the column.

A platoon each of armored cavalry, light tanks (D/8), and Shermans (A/8) formed the point of the advance. As the tanks and infantry advanced and fanned out, they received periodic harassing fire from within the woods. Under the cover of darkness, it was difficult to determine exactly where it was coming from.

Up to this point, CCB's progress had been significant. From its starting point, it had covered half the distance to Bastogne, and had advanced significantly further north than CCA. The downside of CCB's success was the fact that a 6-mile gap had developed between the two combat commands. With CCA stalled at the line of the Sure River at Martelange, any further advance by CCB served to widen the gap. As the evening progressed, concern over the gap grew to the point that CCB was brought to a halt for the balance of the night.

Major Irzyk went to work immediately on refueling and supplying his forward elements. The armored infantry and light tanks were sent out to guard both sides of the road, in order to protect the vulnerable supply vehicles that would have to come all the way forward past Burnon. Tank and infantry teams were set up for the night, with A/10 remaining back at Menufontaine, B/10 near Hotte, and C/10 at Burnon. Gassed up and resupplied, they would resume their advance with the rising sun, and hopefully drive the remaining seven miles to Bastogne on December 23.

Patton Intervenes

That evening, General Patton took stock of the progress III Corps had made during the daylight hours. By all accounts, an objective observer would surmise that things were shaping up nicely. The two infantry divisions of III Corps had moved into the line without meeting heavy resistance, and the only immediate problem facing the Fourth Armored Division was the need to construct a bridge at Martelange. But Patton had expectations beyond what had been achieved that day, and by evening, he was unsettled and only grudgingly satisfied. That night, he wrote to his wife:

> We jumped off at 0630 and have progressed on a twenty mile front to a depth of seven miles. I had hoped for more, but we are in the middle of a snow storm and there were a lot of demolitions. So I should be content which of course I am not… John Millikin is doing better than I feared. I told him he had to go up and hear them [the shells and bullets] whistle. I think he will.

In his diary, he confided:

> I am satisfied but not particularly happy over the results of today. It is always hard to get an attack rolling. I doubt the enemy can make a serious reaction for another 36 hours. I hope that by that time we will be moving. The men are in good spirits and full of confidence…

Patton's course of action that evening was not that of a man content with his accomplishments for the day. He instructed Millikin to have his divisions continue the attack through the night. With characteristic hyperbole, he told the impotent commander of III Corps that the very outcome of the entire offensive could be decided by his efforts. He really need not have wasted his time inspiring or selling Millikin, since he was only Patton's marionette. It was Patton who would dictate the pace and course of events for III Corps.

CCB had just established its bivouac positions when the order came to continue the advance through the night (it was clear enough to all concerned that Patton himself had sent the directive). At 9 P.M., Dager radioed the forward elements of CCB and ordered the advance to continue as instructed. The order was stated simply enough: "Move all night!" This was not an easy task for men that had been up since 3 A.M. that morning, and who had had little rest ever since setting out for the Ardennes after midnight on the 19th. Fatigue was a very real factor that Major Irzyk had to wrestle with.

After the radio message was sent to the forward battalions, the formal movement and attack orders were prepared at CCB's headquarters, which was now located at Fauvillers. The written orders included details such as the composition of the force, and the timetable for the following day's activities. Though the standard operating procedure between Irzyk and Dager was for such orders to be communicated orally, on this rare occasion, the 8th Tank Battalion's liaison officer, Bill Marshall, was to hand-deliver the orders in their written form.

Marshall, along with one other liaison officer, climbed into a jeep and started out for Major Irzyk's command post at Burnon. Fauvillers was only about 3 miles south of Burnon, but traveling at night, through territory that had only recently been purged of the enemy, made this anything but a short drive. There was no assurance that the enemy paratroopers had not infiltrated back though the woods into positions along the roads, and the two men would need to exercise caution as they traveled back to the front.

As it turned out, Marshall and his partner would never discover whether or not the road to Burnon held any danger for them. As they left the town, they made a wrong turn in the dark, and instead of heading north, toward Burnon, they turned east, toward Martelange. Approximately mid way between these two towns, nestled along the banks of the Sure River, was the town of Bodange. This town was still held by the enemy (in fact, 1st Lt. Jack Bartow of the 10th AIB had run into an ambush in Bodange earlier that same day. His jeep was hit with numerous machine gun bullets, but he managed to make his escape, and returned to Fauvillers). Now Marshall, the carrier of vital information regarding CCB's upcoming drive toward Bastogne, was heading straight for the town of Bodange in the dead of night. Marshall was captured, and the orders presumably fell into the enemy's hands. One can only speculate as to the impact this may or may not have had on events during the next 24 hours.*

Irzyk now went about the task of reassembling his force for the advance. By the time they were ready to go, it was just past midnight. Elements of the 25th Armored Cavalry took the lead, once again supported by the light tanks of D/8. A company of Shermans and a company of armored infantry mounted in halftracks followed close behind the cavalrymen. Groping their way through the dark amidst the cold winds and swirling snow, they advanced slowly up the road toward Chaumont, as the main body of the combat command formed up behind them (B/10 and a company of tanks from the 8th remained behind as a rear guard).

As the column advanced, there was significant concern for the security of CCB's flanks. Some elements of the task force operated off to the west side of the road, screening the left flank of the column. Fortunately, there appeared to be no Germans to the left, as no fire from that direction was ever reported. The situation to the right of the road was altogether different, however. Here, where the woods closed within just a matter of yards of the dirt road, the advancing Americans were most vulnerable. And the woods were flush with German paratroopers from the 14th FJ Regiment.

As the American column advanced, it drew small arms fire from the woods on the right. With the Germans protected by the cover of darkness, the Americans had to settle on raking the wood line with automatic fire, hoping that the sheer volume of lead would silence the enemy. Panzerfausts claimed a couple of the armored cavalry's jeeps, with the casualties one might expect from such an impact. The column continued to move at a slow, deliberate pace, and as the eastern horizon began to reflect the gray light of dawn, CCB had drawn close to the village of Chaumont.

As the sun rose, the vanguard of the task force, led by some of the light tanks, began climbing the gentle slope leading up to the crest of the heights overlooking Chau-

---

Marshall eventually ended up at Oflag XIIIB at Hammelburg, Germany. This was the same POW camp where Patton's son-in-law, Colonel John Waters, was being held toward the end of the war. Toward the end of March 1945, Patton ordered a dangerous rescue mission, which was led by Abe Baum of the 10th AIB. While the mission failed to rescue the POWs from Oflag XIIIB, it stands as one of the most daring and courageous missions ever carried out by the men of the Fourth Armored Division.

A Jeep of the 25th Cav destroyed on December 23, on the road south of Chaumont. Photograph taken on December 27. Some of the buildings of Chaumont are visible in the background, as is a portion of the wooded ridge situated behind the village (National Archives Photograph SC198405).

mont. The woods still hugged the right side of the road, but just up ahead, as the road took a slight jog to the right, the woods peeled away. There was no telling what was around the bend.

As the light tanks of D/8 and the jeeps of the 25th Armored Cavalry came around the corner of the forest, the Germans, who were laying in wait, launched a stiff counterattack. This was the toughest resistance yet encountered by CCB during their advance. Several German 75mm self propelled assault guns (StuG IIIs) hit the head of the column, destroying three vehicles from the 25th Armored Cavalry and one of the M5 light tanks from D/8 (three of the four crewman in the light tank were killed). The Germans brought down artillery fire in support of the attack, and panzerfaust-wielding paratroopers emerged to take pot shots at the American column. The Shermans weren't far behind, however, and they were quickly engaged in the fight. They destroyed one of the StuG IIIs before chasing off the rest, and sent the enemy paratroopers scampering back into woods.

The forward elements quickly regrouped in the wake of the attack, and Major Irzyk ordered them to press on. Visibility on the morning of December 23 was still poor;

early morning fog and haze still blanketed this portion of the battlefield (many popular accounts of the battle cast the impression that with the coming of dawn, the skies were sparkling blue with tremendous visibility; this was not the case in all areas, as the cold front descending on the Ardennes from the north was still in the process of sweeping through). By noon, CCB reached the top of the high ground overlooking Chaumont from the southwest. Resistance had been sporadic after the German's early morning counterattack; the woods to their right seemed to be harboring the primary enemy threat at the moment.

The distance covered since the time of Patton's order to advance all night was less than a mile. Casualties during the advance had not been heavy, but an intangible that Patton had overlooked was that the men were exhausted. In the light of day on December 23, they could have covered the mile between Burnon and the heights south of Chaumont in a fraction of the time it took them during the dark morning hours. Instead, they traded sleep and recovery time — which would have served them well the next day — for a mile of real estate that could have been taken with relative ease under the sun.

Setting the Stage at Chaumont

Rather than rush immediately down the slope into Chaumont, the forward elements of CCB pulled back behind the crest, so as not to be visible from the town. Major Irzyk then coiled his task force on his side of the hill while he considered his options.

Irzyk personally went to the high ground overlooking Chaumont to study the scene in advance of preparing his plan of attack. One thing was clear: due to the nature of the terrain and road net, the advance *had* to go through Chaumont. There was no bypassing it. The aborted counterattack by the StuG IIIs stood as evidence that the Germans might intend to make an issue of the town. Additionally, foot patrols sent toward Chaumont during the early daylight hours had drawn enemy fire from inside the town itself.

Chaumont was just like dozens of other towns that the Fourth Armored had captured in recent weeks. It wasn't a large town; perhaps no more than 50 dwellings, many of which were half-home and half-barn. The village was dotted with manure piles, each one piled high in front of the home of its owner. The whole town didn't stretch much more than a quarter of a mile. If you were searching for it on a map, it would be a challenge finding it, if you didn't know exactly where to look.

If there was anything unique about Chaumont, it was the nature of the terrain that surrounded it. Chaumont is often described as sitting at the bottom of a saucer, and rightly so, as it is ringed by elevated ground in all directions. Two roads led toward the town from the area occupied by CCB; one from the southwest, which was the road the Americans had traveled from Burnon, and another from the west-southwest, emanating from the village of Remoiville. The two roads merged just south of Chaumont, thereupon forming a single road that entered the south end of the village. Both of these roads descended gradually over completely open terrain for a distance of approximately 1000 yards before merging in front of Chaumont. Any American forces advancing toward the village over these routes would be extremely vulnerable, as they would be exposed to enemy guns that might be located within the town, or on the high ground overlooking it to the north, northeast, and east.

The area to the west and northwest of Chaumont was wide open as well, with about 900 yards of open space between the village and the Bois-St. Hubert. The woods were far enough back from the top of high ground, however, that an enemy force located within the forest could not hit Chaumont or the approach roads with direct fire.

To the north-northwest of the village, the lone road leading into Chaumont from that direction ran through a tight draw leading toward the town of Grandru. This approach was well concealed by virtue of the steep slopes on both sides of the road and the thick woods to the east of the draw.

To Major Irzyk's right, a long ridge looked down upon Chaumont from the south and east. The top of the ridge was open, while the forward slope was dotted with trees (the back side of the ridge was more heavily forested). If the enemy were present along this ridge, they would have an excellent view of any troops advancing north up the main road into Chaumont. Securing this ridge would be a major priority.

There was one other road leading out of Chaumont, and it ran along the base of a large, ominous, ridge that overlooked the village from the northeast. The road followed the banks of a stream running from behind Chaumont to the southeast, and could not be seen from Irzyk's position, since both the road and stream were nestled in the depression carved out by the waterway. The forested slopes leading to the crest of the ridge rose more than 50 meters above Chaumont, and the heights provided an excellent vantage point from which to observe every point of entry into the town.

Having gotten a good first-hand look at the situation, Irzyk put together a thorough plan for capturing Chaumont. He would send Lt. Steve Stephenson's C Company, which was eleven Shermans strong at that point, to sweep over the open ground west of the town. This would accomplish three things: First, it would prevent an enemy threat from coming out of the woods on the left flank. Second, it would cut off the road leading into the village from the direction of Grandru. And third, it would place the tanks of C Company in position to provide supporting fire for the elements assigned the task of pushing into Chaumont. Lt. Len Kieley's A Company, consisting of nine tanks, would sweep to the right and ride the ridge that overlooked the southeast portion of the village. Kieley's position would also afford the tankers a point of observation and fire toward the large, wooded ridge that stared down on Chaumont from the northeast. Since the ridgeline was in close proximity to the woods, the tanks would be supported by a company of infantry from Major Cohen's 10th AIB as a deterrent against German infantry that might decide to emerge and take some shots at the tanks with their panzerfausts. The infantry would ride in on the decks of the tanks and then jump off to secure the woods.

The primary attack would come down the main road straight into Chaumont. The eleven Shermans of 1st Lt. Ben Fischler's B Company, with the men of A/10 riding on some of the tanks, would plunge into the town on the heels of a preparatory artillery barrage. A platoon from B/10 would follow behind on foot. Once the town was secured, the three medium tank companies, along with the infantry and armored cavalry, would continue to advance toward Grandru. Irzyk was very confident in his plan, and indeed had no reason to feel otherwise. He was bringing virtually the full weight of CCB to bear against a critical objective, and he was doing it in a way that took into account just about every contingency he or anyone else could think of.

The Germans also recognized the importance of Chaumont. But it was not only the 5th FJ Division that was concerned. As it turned out, the commander of the 26th Volksgrenadier Division, Generalmajor Heinz Kokott, had turned a wary eye toward the south.

> I had my Command Post at Hompre on 23 December 44. Technically speaking, I was in the zone of 5 FJ Div, Seventh Army, which was blocking to the south; however, this was no time to be concerned about boundary lines. The action of 5 FJ Division was of vital concern to me. I was facing Bastogne. The American 4th Armored Division drive north threatened my rear. It is an uncomfortable feeling to have someone launching a drive to your rear; so boundary or not, 5 FJ Div was of constant concern to me. The situation was not aided by my knowledge that 5 FJ Div was a very poor division. I feared 4th Armored Division. I knew it was a 'crack' division. Furthermore, Generalmajor Heilmann, Commander of 5 FJ Div, was in Lutrebois. He had a very wide front and could not be everywhere. As it happened, I was nearer to this danger point than he; therefore I gave orders to build a resistance line near Chaumont.

As Irzyk was about to launch his attack, CCA was still stuck at Martelange, a victim of the time it was taking to get a Bailey bridge in place over the Sure River. Obviously irritated by what he perceived to be a lack of drive, Patton telephoned Millikin with a very specific directive: "There is too much piddling around. Bypass these towns and clear them up later. Tanks can operate on this ground now." Clearly, Patton thought the hard freeze of the previous night had given his tanks the opportunity for cross-country maneuver. He was about to be proven wrong.

CCB Attacks Chaumont

Right on cue, the 22nd AFAB delivered its salvos into the heart of Chaumont. Artillery fire was also delivered into the woods west of C/8's axis of advance (the Bois–St. Hubert) and into the wooded ridge northeast of town. Hopefully, this barrage would suppress any enemy anti-tank weapons that might be lurking, as yet undiscovered.

The attack began in earnest at about 1:30 P.M. As soon as the artillery barrage ended, all three companies of tanks moved out simultaneously. The artillery strikes seemed to work, as the enemy response from those areas during the initial move toward Chaumont was sporadic. But no matter the intensity, the Germans were shooting back, thus sending a signal that their intent was to hold their ground.

Everything was progressing as planned, with the two tank companies swinging around the flanks as B Company moved down the hill straight toward the town. Most of the tanks of B Company had 6 or 7 men clinging to the decks of each of the tanks. A small number of the Sherman tanks out in front, however, went in without any infantry on board.

"Big Deal 2," commanded by Jimmy Dandrellis and driven by Corporal Tony

Giallanza, was near the front of the pack. Giallanza, expecting return fire from Chaumont, was buttoned up, but pushed "Big Deal 2" as fast as it could go down the hill. After getting about three-quarters of the way down the slope, an armor piercing shell (Giallanza thought it was an 88mm) struck the tank. No one inside was injured, but the Sherman had to be abandoned. Dandrellis' crew bailed out not a moment too soon, as a second round struck the tank, causing an explosion that totally destroyed it. With shells and bullets flying back and forth over their heads from both sides of the battlefield, the tank crew ran up the snow covered slope as fast as they could, trying desperately to reach the protection of the woods atop the hill. Fortunately, all of the men made it. Giallanza would later credit the other American tanks for hitting the Germans with so much firepower on their descent into Chaumont that it kept the enemy pinned down, thus allowing the crew of "Big Deal 2" to reach the woods.

As the tanks rumbled into the streets of Chaumont, the armored infantry dismounted and started to clear the houses. The artillery barrage had apparently done its job, since the Germans didn't offer much in the way of resistance at first. Staff Sergeant Stanley Kosiek, who served as the 1st platoon sergeant of B/10, said:

> We went into town and didn't find too much against us. We got eight Germans out of buildings, other platoons got more prisoners. These Germans — some of them at least — were wearing American field jackets and leggings. They had American cigarettes and candy. They wore the jackets under their overcoats. Most were young squirts and mean.

As the tanks and armored infantry began working their way through Chaumont, Major Irzyk received an alarming message from Lt. Stephenson, the commanding officer of C Company, which was leading the sweep around the west side of Chaumont. He reported that his lead platoon of five tanks had become stuck in what was apparently soft ground underneath the new fallen snow. For fear of losing the balance of his company, he brought the remaining six tanks to a halt.

Popular accounts of this stage of the battle have long been in error, for it was not thawing ground that the tanks had succumbed too, as is so often stated. Unknown to Irzyk and Stephenson — their 1:100,000 map wasn't detailed enough to show the true nature of the terrain west of Chaumont — the stream leading toward Chaumont from the southeast did not terminate behind the town. In fact, it separated into two branches, one of which continued to the northwest of the village, the other due west. A snow-covered marsh surrounded both of these extensions. Stephenson's tanks had, quite unwittingly, driven into the marsh.

Fifty-seven years later, Al Irzyk and I would stand with magnifying glass in hand, studying a more detailed 1:50,000 map of the area, which clearly showed the branches of the stream, and the surrounding marsh. The map was placed side by side with a copy of Irzyk's original 1:100,000 map, upon which there was no evidence of either the branches of the stream or the marsh. Reflecting on how things might have gone differently, had he had a more detailed map, Irzyk said, "I had no way of knowing." Indeed, he did not.

C Company was unable to complete its assignment on the left flank. The balance of Stephenson's Shermans were in position to guard against an attack from the woods to the west — that part of their mission was achieved — but they did not have a line of sight to the road leading south from Grandru, nor into Chaumont itself. Stephenson's company was basically out of the battle.

As C/8 regrouped, the operation in Chaumont continued. As the Americans pushed further into the town, a company of German paratroopers decided to make a fight of it, providing the armored infantry with what they later called "some of the heaviest opposition this battalion has yet encountered." After the first hour of battle inside the town, reinforcements were called for, and another platoon of infantry from B/10 was sent into Chaumont. At 4:00 P.M., another call for assistance was sent back, and another platoon of infantry, this time from C/10, was sent into the fray. At one point, an enemy machine gun nest inside one of the houses held up the advance. S/Sgt. Lumpkin Glenn volunteered to launch a solo attack against the enemy position. He crawled up to the building and tossed in hand grenades that flushed out the machine gun crew. Glenn's actions were characteristic of the effort that was required in order to wrestle the town away from the paratroopers.

Casualties among the armored infantry began to mount, and some of the infantrymen found themselves taking on roles usually reserved for medics. When Pfc. James Carey was seriously wounded, he would not allow himself to be evacuated. Unable to stay in the fight in a direct combat role, "Carey seized an ambulance which the Germans had abandoned in Chaumont, assisted wounded comrades into the vehicle, and made repeated trips through artillery fire to the aid station until his strength was exhausted." He was later decorated with the Silver Star for his selfless act of courage.

After a hard fight, the weight of the tanks of B/8 and almost two companies of armored infantry finally carried the day, and the Americans rounded up most of the remaining paratroopers (over 100 members of the 14th FJ Regiment were taken prisoner). With the village cleansed of the enemy, the tanks and infantry pushed through to the road leading toward Grandru, and started setting up outposts at the edge of Chaumont. Major Irzyk had gone into the town in his command tank behind B/8, and now saw first hand that the town was in firm possession of his task force. Using his radio, he issued instructions for the other elements of CCB to start down the main road into Chaumont. There was still enough daylight to continue the advance, and Irzyk was determined to get his column organized and moving on toward Grandru.

General Kokott Responds

General Kokott was at his division headquarters at Hompre, just two miles north of Chaumont, when he became aware that the men of the 5th FJ Division were falling back from their defensive positions. Should the Americans break through, his own command post would soon be in the shadows of the rumbling Shermans. Already none-too-happy with the performance of the 5th FJ Division, Kokott took matters into his own hands. He gathered up the retreating paratroopers, and ordered them to return to Chaumont. He sent along some officers and men from his own 26th Volksgrenadier Division ("assault troops" from the Division Combat School and a small group of engineers) to help restore some backbone and resolve to the 14th FJ Regiment.

Kokott also had available some unexpected resources that would serve to strengthen the counterattack at Chaumont. That afternoon, seemingly out of nowhere, four JagdTigers from the 653rd Heavy Panzerjager Battalion had appeared in Hompre. Without inquiring into the identity of the orphaned tank destroyers, Kokott commandeered the JagdTigers and sent them south toward Chaumont. Kokott later described his stroke of good fortune:

> An unknown major in command of four Tiger tanks came into Hompre. I don't know where he came from, or where he was going, but I ordered him south to aid the 5th FJ Div at Remichampagne and Chaumont.

Kokott erred by describing the huge tank destroyers as "Tigers."* He cannot be judged too harshly for that mistake, since it is very unlikely that he would have been familiar with the identity of the brand new JagdTigers, which had yet to make a combat appearance on the West Front. The unforeseen and, from the German perspective, fortuitous presence of Hitler's prized JagdTigers would soon play a pivotal role in the fortunes of Brigadier General Dager's CCB.

The German Strike at Chaumont

It was a short trip south for the JagdTigers as they moved from Hompre to Chaumont. They were unobserved by the Americans as they lumbered forward, and were apparently moved into concealed positions along the heavily wooded ridge northeast of Chaumont. Facilitating their movement was a dirt road that entered the woods from the northeast, at a point completely hidden from the Americans' view. They used this road to gain access to their positions overlooking Chaumont and the open terrain south of the town.

The paratroopers, volksgrenadiers, engineers, and assault guns that Kokott dispatched toward Chaumont prepared to strike back at CCB/4. Having taken up positions along the wooded ridge, they would advance from the heights directly into the town. Artillery, mortars, and the huge JagdTigers would provide ample support for their advance. To help cover their movement from the ridge into the town, provisions were made for a smoke screen to be laid in front of the American positions.

Just as the remaining elements of CCB started forward, all hell broke loose in front of Chaumont. A cascade of armor piercing and high explosive shells rained down from the wooded ridge. Under the cover of the smoke screen, the StuG III assault guns, with German infantry riding on board, came rolling off the wooded ridge toward the village. The Luftwaffe even managed to contribute to the counterattack, but return fire from the Americans on the ground destroyed two of the planes.

---

*In his classic work A Time for Trumpets, the respected historian Charles B MacDonald also points out that Kokott incorrectly identified the "Tigers" that appeared at his doorstep. MacDonald, however, incorrectly identified the "Tigers" as Ferdinand Tank Destroyers. Not long before departing for the Ardennes, the 653rd had been reequipped with the JagdTiger. Shortly before the start of the Ardennes offensive, the battalion had been attached to the Panzer Lehr Division. None of the battalion's tank destroyers reached the Ardennes prior to December 16, and only a portion of one company (the 3rd) was unloaded at the rail station at Blankenheim on December 21. There was only one route available that would take the handful of JagdTigers toward their assignment with the Panzer Lehr Division, and that route passed south of Bastogne ... through Hompre.

The Germans jumped down from their assault guns and raced into Chaumont. The enemy armor took on the Shermans of B/8, while the massive 128mm guns of the JagdTigers lent support from up on the ridge. Staff Sergeant Stanley Kosiek described the sight of the advancing Germans:

> We began to outpost the place when we spotted three German tanks coming down a draw toward us. Infantrymen followed them. Seventeen more German vehicles, including three American peeps, were moving around us. They laid smoke on us.

There was an initial moment of panic, but the veteran tankers of the 8th immediately tried to do what they had been trained to do: move and fire. But the tanks of B Company were at the bottom of a fish bowl, the village at their back, and a stream running in front of them that kept them from charging forward. There was no place to run. The tank gunners fired, but at what? Much of the enemy fire seemed to be coming from concealed positions, and the volume of incoming was so incredibly heavy, the scene so confusing, that picking out a target became extremely difficult.

One by one, the tanks of B Company were picked off by enemy rounds, until all were silenced. The surviving crews scrambled to make their way back out of the town, but not all of them made it. Lt. Blackmer, a platoon leader for B Company, was among those killed during the melee. The forward artillery observer was killed in the early going as well, robbing Major Irzyk of a quick retort from the guns of the 22nd AFAB. It probably didn't matter much anyway, since the enemy was engaged at such close range that an artillery response might have caused as much damage to the Americans as it would the Germans (especially without the benefit of a forward observer to coordinate the fire).

The tankers weren't the only ones having a rough go of it inside the town. Company A of the 10th AIB was catching a hell. They were outgunned and outnumbered, and knew they had to get out. In a desperate effort to leave no one behind, many men risked their lives to pull out the wounded. In one instance, S/Sgt. Charles Bennett of the 10th AIB saw that one of the tanks of B Company had been crippled, and its crew wounded. He crawled over a hundred yards under enemy fire to get to the tank. Once there, he managed to crank it up, and drove it back toward his own lines (he was awarded the Silver Star for his actions).

T/Sgt. Samuel English also stepped up to save another member of his unit. When his lead scout was wounded, English carried the man for 25 yards over open ground that was "exposed to hostile shell fire." Pfc. Louis Worst was another man who was at his best. While under machine gun and artillery fire, Worst carried a wounded member of his patrol back to adequate cover where the man could be treated.

Bennett, English, and Worst weren't alone in trying to save others. But despite their best efforts, not everyone could be rescued. After his platoon leader became a casualty, Staff Sgt. Kosiek rallied his men and led them out of the trap that had become Chaumont.

> We were ordered to withdraw. My men started back 50 yards apart moving fast. We found a wounded tanker and Pvt. William McIlvaine, morterman from Charlestown, Massachusetts, had ahold of him and was pulling, helping him back. It slowed us down. We went by another of our tankers sitting in a ditch. His foot was shot off. He saw we

couldn't take him too. He just said, "Hi'ya fellas." We were the last out. Had to wade a creek with them shooting burp guns at us, but we got through.

Those that made it back to the south end of the ugly, manure strewn hell of a village were faced with the prospect of crossing over completely open, exposed ground, as they climbed back up the slope whence their attack had originated. Second Lieutenant William Patton crawled up a small, snow covered hill in search of an escape route for his platoon, only to be cut down by a burst from a German machine gun (he was posthumously awarded the Silver Star).

Acts of courage became epidemic as the Americans struggled to find a safe way out of the town. Staff Sergeant Wallace Marcinkiewicz set up his light .30-caliber machine gun in position that would cover A/10's withdrawal. His machine gun chattered away at the approaching Germans, until a round from a panzerfaust killed him at his position.

Lt. Charles Gniot knew that someone had to cover the south end of the village, so that the remainder of the men could make it back up over the crest of the hill about 700 yards south of the town. If the Germans weren't held in check, they would come nipping at the heels of his men as they tried to pull back. The losses they were taking were already bad enough, but it could become a complete massacre if the Krauts followed the armored infantry and dismounted tankers back up the hill.

Lt. Gniot was now the last officer left in A Company. Rather than setting up his remaining automatic weapons to cover the withdrawal of his men, he grabbed a BAR and stayed behind to cover their retreat single handedly, in what was later described in the 10th AIB journal as a "suicide mission." He stayed firmly planted, dispensing covering fire from his BAR, until the advancing Germans killed him. The heroic efforts of the last men remaining in Chaumont were not in vain, as it allowed some of their brothers to escape (Gniot was posthumously awarded the Distinguished Service Cross).

There was at least one other officer doing the best he could to salvage the situation. When the avalanche of enemy anti-tank rounds fell upon the men in the town, Major Irzyk was just behind the tanks of B Company, toward the center of the village. Irzyk immediately had two concerns: directing the battle, and directing his tank crew. He knew he had to somehow get control of the situation, but he was now in the worst possible position to do it. Being smack in the middle of an enemy armored assault was not the place he needed to be.

Irzyk immediately began barking orders over the radio to his three company commanders. C/8 was out of the picture on the left flank, but A/8 was still riding the ridge east of Chaumont, and had much better firing positions than did B Company down in the village. Company A responded with a high volume of fire, which probably kept the enemy assault guns from plunging right through the town. A/8 was taking some punishment as well though, since they were exposed to the JagdTigers and any other anti-tank guns positioned along the wooded ridge. But they were not deterred, and held their ground long enough to provide covering fire for the men withdrawing from Chaumont.

At the same time that Irzyk was attempting to retain control of his force, he knew that he had to get out of the town. His tank was a sitting duck, and if he didn't keep moving, it was just a matter of time before he would suffer the same fate as the tanks of B Company. There was not much room within the narrow streets of the village for Irzyk's driver to turn the tank about; in any event, turning the thin armor of the rear of his Sherman directly toward the enemy was an almost certain invitation for disaster. So Irzyk had his driver back the tank out through the village, a process that seemed to take an eternity. Irzyk's own gunner maintained a heavy rate of fire at suspected enemy positions as they pulled back. When the tank reached the outskirts of the village, with only open ground remaining behind it, the driver picked up the pace. But now Irzyk's tank was in the open; surely one of the German gunners up on the wooded slope would draw a bead on him. To try and hasten the pace, Irzyk decide to turn the tank turret to the rear, so that he could see exactly where they were going, and thus give the driver better directions over the intercom. With the benefit of Irzyk serving as his eyes, the driver could accelerate back up the hill as fast as possible.

Major Irzyk could now see the crest of the hill before him. Just a few more yards and they would make it to safety. Irzyk later described what happened next:

> there was a low, load, deafening, earsplitting sound, followed by a terrible, horrible, frightening blow. The tank was shoved violently forward. It was as though the tank had been hit in the back by a huge sledge hammer, and picked up and thrown forward by a superhuman hand.

An armor piercing round had slammed into the tank with a thunderous shock. The three men in the turret were thrown violently to the floor, amidst a cascade of gun shells that had broken loose from their mounting around the turret and were tossed around like matchsticks. Everything that was loose, and some things that were not, were thrown together on the floor. As Irzyk described it, "The inside of the tank looked as though a bunch of tables at a rummage sale had been picked up and upended." The tank stopped for what seemed like an eternity, but Irzyk quickly urged the driver to continue toward the crest of the hill. "Keep moving!," he shouted. Irzyk had two things to be thankful for at that very moment: that he was alive, and that the tank was still capable of moving. Thank God, they hadn't been disabled and left exposed on the open slope.

As the tank started backward again, Irzyk turned toward the rear of the turret, where his radio equipment was located. To his utter amazement, he saw that his turret had been cracked! He could actually see daylight penetrating through a seam that had been created behind his radio. Based on the power of the impact, he knew that the shell that had struck his tank traveled at an extremely high velocity. At the range involved, it was certainly something bigger than one of the StuG III's 75mm guns. If the shot had been fired from all the way back on the wooded ridge, it would have hit him from a distance of at least 1000 yards. And to crack the turret? The power of the shell must have been immense.

Later, when Irzyk examined his tank from the exterior, he realized just how lucky he had been. The shell had struck an appendage of solid steel mounted to the back of the turret. The slab was only about 4 inches high and five inches wide, but it was at least 6 inches thick, and cut at an oblique angle. This seemingly innocuous object was located in a position just to the right of the radio antenna well, squarely behind where

Irzyk was normally positioned in the turret. Irzyk had never even taken notice of this object before (to this day, he does not know what function it served). Though not by design, it had served one key purpose: it had saved his life, and probably the lives of his entire crew. The armor piercing round, which could very well have come from the 128mm cannon of one of the JagdTigers, simply could not penetrate the 6 inches of angled steel. The shell ricocheted off the slab, but the impact was still powerful enough to crack the turret. Yes, the likelihood was great indeed that one of the beasts from the 653rd Heavy Panzerjager Battalion had placed Irzyk's command tank in its crosshairs.

Fortunately, the men inside of Irzyk's tank were only shaken; none were seriously injured. Once over the crest of the hill and out of harm's way, Irzyk realized that he had received a wound to his hand. It was of little concern to him, as he now had the urgent task of rallying his force south of the ridgeline, in anticipation that the Germans would follow up their success by pushing south from Chaumont. The Sherman tanks of A Company were still out on the ridge, and he now pulled them back to shore up his defense.

Thankfully, and somewhat to Irzyk's surprise, the Germans did not pursue the last vestiges of his force as they withdrew. Once the Shermans were back at a safe distance, the howitzers of the 22nd AFAB pounded the area in and around Chaumont, just in case the enemy harbored any thoughts of coming forward. But the Germans seemed content to have wrestled control of the village, and did not move beyond it. This gave CCB some valuable time to collect itself.

Company A of the 10th AIB had been dealt a horrendous blow, with 65 casualties suffered in and around the village (its three platoons were at a strength of about 30 men each prior to the attack). With the loss of Lt. Gniot, there was not a single officer left in the company. The platoon from B Company that had waded in behind the tanks fared better, and was able to withdraw 26 of the 31 men who entered Chaumont.

The 8th Tank Battalion had also suffered heavily. All eleven tanks of B Company were destroyed or disabled. Most of the survivors of B Company would go to the rear, as was the normal procedure, and wait for replacement tanks to become available. Company C, which had advanced with eleven tanks, left five of them stuck in the marsh west of Chaumont; when they regrouped with Irzyk, they had six tanks available. Company A, which had taken nine tanks down the ridge east of the village, returned with seven. In a matter of not much more than an hour, the medium tank strength of the 8th Tank Battalion had been reduced by more than half.

As Irzyk organized his defense atop the hill overlooking Chaumont, the total assets of the 8th Tank Battalion were fourteen Shermans (including Irzyk's, which was quickly repaired with the aid of a welder's torch and pressed back into service), six 105mm assault guns, and the remaining light tanks of D Company. Major Harold Cohen's 10th Armored Infantry Battalion was in no better shape. A Company was, at least for the time being, a mere shell of a fighting force. Companies B and C were already under strength. CCB had been rocked. The mission of getting through to Bastogne had changed in the blink of an eye.

CCB Regroups

The mood at CCB's HQ was sober in light of the rebuff they had suffered at Chaumont. That evening, Major Irzyk went to the rear to report directly to Brigadier General Dager on the events of the day. Irzyk briefed Dager on CCB's attack on Chaumont and the German counterattack that followed. He advised him of the current state of the combat command, and of the dispositions of his units for the evening. Dager did more listening than talking, and in the end, endorsed the decisions that had been made that day.

The fact that CCB was still more than 5 miles ahead of CCA made it a clear magnet for the enemy's attention. Dager decided to have CCB stand firm during the following day (December 24). This would allow his men some time to gather their strength after the battle at Chaumont, and would hopefully provide CCA with enough time to draw abreast of his position. This would relieve CCB of the added pressure of having to protect its extended right flank.

As Irzyk and Dager wrapped up their meeting, the general concluded with a bit of bad news: Bill Marshall was missing in action. Al was despondent over the news, since he and Bill had developed a close relationship during their tenure together in the 8th Tank Battalion.

On the evening of December 23, almost two days after the start of the attack, the situation facing George Patton was not what he hoped it would be. His 48-hour time frame for reaching Bastogne was dashed, as all three combat commands were slowed or rebuffed during the second day of the offensive. CCB was in a holding pattern, licking its wounds. CCA was stalled at Warnach. CCR was stopped short of Bigonville.

At Bastogne, the 101st had spent much of the 22nd and 23rd holding back strong German attacks. By the morning of the 23rd, the logistical situation was looking grim, with artillery shells and medical supplies being in particularly short supply. But thankfully, the improved flying weather on December 23 brought with it the opportunity to airdrop supplies within the American perimeter, which eased the situation somewhat. Still, the 101st was feeling the pressure of being surrounded. They were especially desperate to get their wounded out for treatment. On the night of the 23rd, General McAuliffe sent a message of regret to the Fourth Armored: "Sorry I did not get to shake hands today. I was disappointed." This was followed by another message just past midnight: "There is only one more shopping day before Christmas" (a reference to Patton's promise that he would certainly be in Bastogne before the holiday). Unfortunately, Patton's boisterous promises had fostered false hope within the Bastogne perimeter.

When word of the German counterattack at Chaumont reached Patton's headquarters, it caused him to reflect on his order to continue the advance during the night (CCB was not the only unit to suffer as a result of the misguided order; CCA was also engaged needlessly, as were the infantry divisions to the east). On December 24, he wrote in his diary:

> This has been a very bad Christmas Eve. All along our line we have received violent counterattacks, one of which [Chaumont] forced ... the 4th Armored back some miles with the loss of ten tanks. This was probably my fault, because I had been insisting on day

and night attacks. This is all right on the first or second day of the battle and when we had the enemy surprised, but after that the men get too tired. Furthermore, in this bad weather, it is very difficult for armored outfits to operate at night...

In his memoirs, Patton paraphrased his diary entry, repeating some of it word for word (including the acceptance of blame for the decision and outcome). He added a final thought:

I remember being surprised at the time at how long it took for me to learn war. I should have known this before.

While Patton didn't have all the facts correct regarding the attack, he was indeed correct for taking the blame. His meddling in the method of advance for the combat commands was counter to all that he preached, and in this case, his breech had serious consequences. To his credit, he realized his mistake, and took responsibility for it.

CCB spent December 24 in position south of the charred, demolished remnants of Chaumont. General Dager's plan was to rest and refit his weary troops, but the Germans saw to it that the fighting would continue, though not with the same intensity as the day before. The Germans poked and prodded at Irzyk's positions. Heavy artillery and mortar fire rained down periodically, and bands of paratroopers armed with panzerfausts attempted to get at the Shermans and M5s. The men of the 10th AIB and 25th Armored Cavalry remained busy all day safeguarding the tanks.

Most of the enemy activity originated from the pesky woods off to the right of CCB's positions. This was getting to be really old; for three days running, the woods had been a source of aggravation. The 25th Cavalry and 10th AIB launched a foray into the woods in an attempt to flush out the enemy. When the Americans nailed down the locations of three German machine gun nests, B/10 sent out a combat patrol to deal with them. They succeeded in knocking out one of the nests.

The Germans turned it up a notch later in the day. Rather than harassing CCB with small patrols, they launched an infantry attack on a larger scale. The 25th Armored Cavalry troop attached to CCB shouldered the main burden of repulsing this attack, and while engaged, lost its commander, Captain Sklar. The able and highly respected officer became missing in action during the fight in the woods. His body was never found, and he was later presumed killed. After the 25th Cav repulsed the attack, Major Irzyk decided that he had had enough of the Germans using the forest as an enclave from which to repeatedly harass his force. Shortly after noon, he turned all of his available artillery against the forest. Eight P-47s happened to arrive at the same time, and strafed and bombed the area suspected of harboring the enemy. Elements of the 10th AIB then pushed into the woods, and by about 2:30 P.M., had cleared out some of the primary areas of concern.

As progress reports came in from CCA and CCB, Gaffey and Millikin realized that the Fourth needed more support if it were to press on. What they desperately lacked was infantry. The three armored infantry battalions had been short on riflemen to begin with, and losses during the opening stages of the advance had rendered some of the companies virtually ineffective for offensive operations. Millikin then did what should have been done from the very start: he attached two infantry battalions from the 80th Infantry Division's 318th Infantry Regiment to the Fourth Armored. The 1st Battalion was assigned to CCA, and the 2nd Battalion to CCB.

The Journey of the 318th RCT

Prior to its attachment to the Fourth Armored Division, the 318th Infantry Regiment had been deployed on the right flank of the 80th Division. They had a successful day on December 22, when they advanced toward the line of the Sure River near the town of Ettelbruck. But that evening, Patton insisted that they continue the attack under the cover of darkness. While the regiment did indeed gain the heights around Ettelbruck during the night, and even pushed one of the rifle companies into the town, it is debatable whether or not the toll taken in casualties and fatigue was worth it.

Patton's decision to push the infantry into a night attack through the woods was in direct conflict with his own battlefield philosophies:

> Night Attack in Woods: It is not necessary or advisable to attack through woods at night. In the first place, the woods themselves give the cover which the darkness does in the open. In the second place, it is almost impossible to move through the woods at night except in column on roads.

He would violate his own tenants on more than one occasion during the fight in the Ardennes, and never once showed a positive result for doing so.

The terrain around Ettelbruck placed severe limits on the use of the division's attached tanks and tank destroyers, and the subsequent battle became strictly an old-fashioned infantry affair. At first light on December 23, the 1st Battalion tried to reinforce its lone company that had infiltrated the town during the night. Their first three attempts to reach them failed, and the only thing they had to show for their effort was a high rate of casualties. Before making a fourth attempt, they finally managed to bring a few tanks up to the point of the advance. The additional firepower made the difference, and the 1st Battalion was able to move in and relieve its forward company.

The infantry and tanks attempted to advance further through the town. But the debris-choked streets proved impassable for the tanks, and the division commander, Major General H.L. McBride, decided to call off the attack. The 1st Battalion withdrew, and after they were at a safe distance, Ettelbruck was hammered by American artillery. The battle had been an expensive affair, with the 1st Battalion losing a third of its strength. The unit also experienced the loss of its battalion commander, Lt. Colonel Tosi, and all the company commanders who served under him. There must have been some bitter feelings as the infantrymen walked away from the prize they had shed so much blood over.

On December 24, both the 1st and 2nd battalions, along with some supporting engineers, received their orders to move west in support of the Fourth Armored Division. Disengaging from the front wasn't easy, and they regretfully left the 3rd Battalion to fend for itself. After assembling and loading up into trucks at separate locations, the two battalions and the 318th's Regimental HQ departed at 5:00 P.M. for a miserable ride to the zone of the Fourth Armored. They arrived late that evening, and the 1st Battalion was the first to detruck at the town of Ell, where it hooked up with CCA.

The 2nd Battalion, which had only 350 combat infantrymen at the time of their departure, was met at Ell by a guide from the Fourth Armored Division, who escorted the battalion to Fauvillers and the command post of CCB. After the losses CCB had taken on December 23, the arrival of the 2nd Battalion on the evening of December 24 was nothing short of the most marvelous early Christmas present Dager could have received. Lt. Colonel Glenn Gardner, the new commanding officer of the 2nd Battalion, arrived at CCB's headquarters and subsequently moved forward to meet with Major Irzyk. The 2nd Battalion, along with E Company of the 305th Engineer Battalion, was then moved toward the front.

At 11 P.M. that evening, Irzyk huddled with the other battalion officers, his own company commanders, and the commanders of the attached engineer and armored cavalry units. General Dager had delegated the operation to Irzyk, who now devised a plan of attack for Christmas Day in consultation with the other officers present. Though still short on tanks, the confidence level of Irzyk and his staff began to rise with the arrival of the 2nd Battalion. They were certain that Christmas Day would mark the renewal of their advance toward Bastogne.

As Major Irzyk celebrated the arrival of his reinforcements on Christmas Eve, General McAuliffe was in Bastogne with visions of a different sort of Christmas gift dancing in his head. Earlier that day, he had received a promising message from General Patton: "Xmas Eve present coming up. Hold on." After it appeared clear that the 24th of December was going to fade with Patton's promise unfulfilled, McAuliffe, while on the phone with Middleton, said, "The finest Christmas present the 101st could get would be a relief tomorrow."

On December 24, the Germans were busy shuffling their deck. After their success at Chaumont, the Germans pulled back the StuG IIIs that had supported the counterattack. And what of the JagdTigers? It would appear that, after having received orders to participate in Operation Nordwind in Alsace, they began their return march to the railroad yard at Blankenheim, where they would eventually load and depart after the start of the New Year. This left the defense of the Chaumont sector in the hands of the German paratroopers, supported by a plethora of towed anti-tank guns. The experienced Generalmajor Kokott lent a hand once again to the 5th FJ Division:

> I was to participate in an attack on Bastogne on 25 December, and in preparation, I moved my Command Post to Gives on 24 December. Just before I departed, I left a few guards and directed the placing of anti-aircraft guns on the heights around Hompre. There was only one good thing about 5 FJ Division: it was heavily equipped with weapons. I assisted by giving instructions as to how some of these weapons could be used to best advantage. That night I talked to General von Manteuffel on the telephone. I told him that I could not watch two fronts, and that the southern situation was most dangerous. I did not think that 5 FJ Division could hold, and I was in no position to prevent a breakthrough. He told me to forget about the American 4th Armored Division, that it was quiet for the moment.

Chaumont — Round Two

Christmas Day dawned with clear blue skies that once again paved the way for the air force to play an active role in both the resupply of Bastogne and the provision of tactical support for the Fourth Armored on the battlefield. In his diary that day, Patton made note of the wonderful weather:

> A clear cold Christmas, lovely weather for killing Germans, which seems a bit queer, seeing Whose birthday it is.

The immediate goal for CCB on Christmas Day was to recapture Chaumont. The Germans had spent the time since their successful counterattack improving their defensive positions. They were now well dug in along the ridge behind the town, and had once again infiltrated the Lambaichenet woods to the east of the Chaumont-Burnon road.

Before the direct attack on Chaumont could begin, the Lambaichenet had to be cleared of the enemy. The mission was assigned to the 2nd Battalion, with the eight Shermans of A/8 in a supporting role. Elements of the 10th AIB, supported by the tanks of C/8, advanced on the 2nd Battalion's left flank.

The attacked started at 8:50 A.M., with two infantry companies attacking side by side into the woods: Company F on the right, Company G on the left (E Company was maintained as a reserve). The Germans were dug in and appeared determined to stay put within the forest. The 2nd Battalion reported that, "It was difficult to oust the paratroopers out of their foxholes and many were bayoneted while still in them. The infantry advance was assisted by the tank fire which was placed indiscriminately within the woods." After heavy fighting, the woods were finally cleared, and Companies G and F prepared to move on.

The next objective for the 2nd Battalion was to clear the ridge and woods southeast of Chaumont (the area where A/8 had advanced on December 23). As the lead platoon of G Company advanced across the open ground between the two woods, two German machine guns opened up, sending the infantrymen diving for cover. The nests were firmly dug in along the edge of the second plot of woods, and enemy infantry provided ample protection for the machine guns. It appeared for the moment that the attack had stalled.

It was at that moment that Private Paul Wiedorfer took matters into his own hands. What he was about to do would earn him the Medal of Honor, and his actions are best described by the citation that accompanied his award:

> The platoon took cover behind a small ridge approximately 40 yards from the enemy position. There was no other available protection and the entire platoon was pinned down by German fire. It was about noon and the day was clear, but the terrain was extremely difficult due to a 3 inch snowfall the night before over ice covered ground. Pvt. Wiedorfer, realizing that the platoon advance could not continue until the 2 enemy machine gun nests were destroyed, voluntarily charged alone across the slippery open ground with no protecting cover of any kind. Running in a crouched position, under a hail of enemy fire, he slipped and fell in the snow, but quickly rose and continued forward with the enemy concentrating automatic and small-arms fire on him as he advanced. Miraculously escaping injury, Pvt. Wiedorfer reached a point some 10 yards from the first machine gun emplacement and hurled a grenade into it. With his rifle he killed the remaining Germans, and, without hesitation, wheeled to the right and attacked the second emplacement. One of the enemy was wounded by his fire and the other 6 immediately surrendered. This heroic action by 1 man enabled the platoon to advance from behind its protecting

ridge and continue successfully to reach its objective. A few minutes later, when both the platoon leader and the platoon sergeant were wounded, Pvt. Wiedorfer assumed command of his platoon, leading it forward with inspired energy until the mission was accomplished.

Fifty-seven years later, I would show Paul Wiedorfer's Medal of Honor citation to Al Irzyk, who for all those years was unaware that a rare Medal of Honor had been earned by a man serving in a unit attached to CCB, and who was, in effect, under his command as the task force leader. Irzyk seemed pleased by the revelation, and said proudly, "So! We had our own Hendrix!" (The exploits of Pvt James Hendrix are detailed in the next chapter.)

Wiedorfer had single-handedly created the break the 2nd Battalion needed in order to clear out the woods southeast of Chaumont. But the fight was far from over. It was time for the 2nd Battalion to tackle the dreaded ridge northeast of Chaumont, which had been the origin of so much deadly fire on December 23.

The Sherman tanks moved forward in support of the infantry and hit the German positions with effective high-explosive rounds (fortunately, the StuG III's and JagdTigers that had done so much damage on December 23 had since left the scene of the crime). The men of the 2nd Battalion continued up the wooded slopes, their goal being the capture of Hill 490. It was during the assault on Hill 490 that they had the misfortune of being hit by friendly fire from the 66th AFAB, which had been called in to help support the attack. The 2nd Battalion reported 30 casualties from the shells of the 105mm howitzers. Even with that setback, however, the brave men of the 80th Infantry Division continued on. Several light tanks from D/8 were brought up to assist them, and the added firepower helped the advance to resume. The 2nd Battalion wrestled the wooded heights from the enemy, taking some 100 Germans prisoner in the process.

While the 2nd Battalion had been setting up for the attack on Chaumont by seizing the area to the south, east, and northeast, the 10th Armored Infantry Battalion was hard at work to the west and northwest. At 11:05, the armored infantry, supported by the seven Sherman tanks of C/8, attacked toward the high ground northwest of Chaumont. As they advanced along the ridge fronting the Bois–St Hubert, they received enemy fire from the direction of Remoiville, which was to their rear. Not having the resources to attack in two directions simultaneously, the threat had to be left alone for the time being. The only course of action taken was the establishment of an outpost along the road between Remoiville and Chaumont, manned by elements of the 25th Armored Cavalry. A minefield was hastily laid in front of their positions to help deter an enemy counterattack from this direction.

Enemy resistance near the Bois–St. Hubert was light. With the additional support of the mortar and assault gun platoons of the 10th's HQ Company, the Americans established positions overlooking the road from Grandru, thus shutting the back door on Chaumont. To ensure that their left flank was fully secured, the armored infantrymen pushed into the woods and advanced to hill 510, which was located in the middle of the Bois–St. Hubert (they remained there for the night). The armored infantry also penetrated into some of the buildings on the far side of Chaumont. In one instance, Sgt. Julius Perger advanced on a German machine gun nest in one of the houses, getting close enough to toss in some grenades that neutralized the enemy position.

Meanwhile, A/8 and Company E of the 2nd Battalion advanced straight toward Chaumont from the south. The Germans responded with artillery and mortar fire as the infantrymen attempted to close on the town over the open ground. American artillery fire was sent back in support. The team from the 2nd Battalion pushed into the town, where they found heavy resistance. General Dager offered the commander of the 318th RCT the use of D/8's light tanks to assist the 2nd Battalion, but the offer was declined. The men from the 318th decided to tackle it with what they had available. The fighting was ultimately done at very close quarters, with the skilled use of bayonets and grenades sometimes being the deciding factors.

With the ridge overlooking Chaumont now penetrated by the 2nd Battalion, the Germans in town must have realized how vulnerable they were, and many of the defenders withdrew to the north. Capturing the village was now an easier matter. The light tanks of D Company supported the final infantry advance through the town (the 2nd Battalion finally taking up the offer of support), and by 7:15 P.M., it was deemed secure (100 prisoners were taken inside the town). The fight had lasted more than 10 hours non-stop, and CCB finally had the prize that had eluded it on December 23. The 2nd Battalion now outposted the town for the night, with Company G, reinforced by the heavy weapons company, taking up positions north of the town, and Company F remaining on the high ground northeast and east of Chaumont, where they provided protection for the tanks of A/8. Company E, which was now reduced significantly in strength, remained in Chaumont for the night.

Company E wasn't the only unit reduced in strength that day. The entire 2nd Battalion had suffered significantly during the day's continuous attack. F Company had been reduced to only 29 men and G Company to 49. To help beef up the greatly reduced ranks of the infantry platoons, the I&R Platoon was attached to E Company. It was hard to believe that as of that morning, the battalion had gone into battle with 350 infantrymen. This was all that remained. The courage of the men from the 2nd Battalion was beyond question.

Once inside Chaumont, the 8th Tank Battalion received an unexpected Christmas present. Of the eleven tanks from B Company that had been destroyed or disabled, two were found to be in recoverable condition. And amazingly, all five of the C Company tanks that had been stuck in the marsh were still intact. The Germans, who had had almost two full days to do so, had not torched the tanks. The Shermans were sent back for repair and maintenance, and B Company would soon find itself back in action. With the 8th Tank Battalion back up to 21 tanks in strength, CCB would be able to resume the drive to Bastogne with greater confidence.

Before the day was out, the 10th AIB launched one more important mission. Lt. Charles Ingersoll led his platoon of armored infantrymen toward Grandru. Sensing that it was too dangerous to move his entire platoon toward the town, Ingersoll set out with a single volunteer, Sgt. Joseph Noel, to perform a reconnaissance of the area around the village. Braving enemy sniper fire, the two men observed the Germans as they occupied the houses at the extreme south edge of Grandru. This information would be of "inestimable aid" to the 10th AIB and 2nd Battalion when the advance resumed in the morning (both men received the Bronze Star for their daring mission).

CCB Picks Up Steam

December 26 was another day of clear and cold weather. With Chaumont under control, CCB now planned on advancing through Grandru, after which it would be faced with one more large patchwork of woods before breaking out into open terrain in the area of Hompre. Two primary teams were formed: one built around the 2nd Battalion and a company of medium tanks, and the other consisting of the 10th AIB and two companies of Shermans (under strength as they were). Throughout the course of the next three days, the team built around the 10th AIB advanced on the left, and the 2nd Battalion on the right.

Some of the Shermans supporting the 10th AIB launched an attack against the woods east of Remichampagne, along the left flank of CCB's axis of advance. The tank of Staff Sergeant Frank Gill was on the move when suddenly an unseen 88 slammed two high velocity rounds into the Sherman. The crew bailed out of the tank, but rather than beat a hasty retreat to the rear to wait for a replacement tank, they decided that they weren't going to take the loss of their current Sherman that easily. The tank was immobilized, but the gun and turret still worked. So Gill, along with Corporal Michael Kotus, crawled in the direction they thought the rounds had emanated from. If the enemy gun could stop them in their tracks, then surely they could put the gun in their own sights, barring its removal by the Germans. They just had to find it.

And find it they did. The 88 had been well camouflaged, but just like a lost golf ball found in the woods, once sighted, they weren't going to lose it. Now under fire, the men crawled back to their wounded Sherman. Apparently the Germans thought the tank was completely out of action, for no other rounds were launched at it. Back inside the turret, Cpl. Kotus loaded the chamber with a high explosive round, and Sgt. Gill took aim and fired. It took more than one round, but the end result was the destruction of the enemy position. During the balance of the day, several more 88's were cleaned out of this area as well.

As the 10th Armored Infantry Battalion advanced that day, they suddenly realized that they had company on their left flank when ten Sherman tanks were spotted east of Remoiville (the area whence the 10th AIB had received harassing fire the day prior). The two American units came dangerously close to firing on each other before positive identification was made. The appearance of these tanks, which were soon identified as being from the 37th Tank Battalion, certainly came as a surprise to the commanding officer of the 10th AIB. Major Cohen had not been given any prior indication that CCR would be operating on the left flank of CCB. The identification of Abe Abrams' Shermans was the first indication that American units were attacking to the west.

While the fighting on December 26 wasn't as fierce as the buzz saw at Chaumont on the 23rd, the men of the 10th AIB still had their moments. This was proven by 1st Lt. Andrew Puff and T/Sgt. Stephen Bardohan. Coming upon an enemy stronghold manned by 19 German paratroopers, the two men advanced alone against the position, and killed or captured all 19 of the enemy (Puff was awarded the Silver Star, and Bardohan the Bronze). Puff wasn't the only officer of the 10th AIB making things happen that day. 1st Lt. Robert Lange, who commanded one of the armored infantry companies, saw his men pinned down by heavy sniper fire as they advanced west of Grandru.

Braving enemy fire, he exposed himself to rally his troops, who then continued the advance and neutralized the enemy. Lange was awarded the Silver Star for his actions.

As the 10th Armored Infantry Battalion continued to push forward on the left wing of CCB, the 2nd Battalion maneuvered into position to capture Grandru. Company F advanced first, moving directly north from its positions east of the line Chaumont-Grandru. As the supporting tanks fired into the Boise du Harje, the infantrymen moved north and cleaned out the southern edge of the woods, thus securing the right flank of the battalion. E Company then advanced to the immediate east of Grandru, about 500 yards away from the edge of the town. Once E and F Company had secured their positions, G Company moved due north out of Chaumont via the main road leading through the draw. The battalion's 57mm towed anti-tank guns were brought forward, and were used to plaster the forward houses in the village were the enemy was known to have holed up the night before. Company G then moved west of the town, as though they were going to bypass it. This was a ruse, however, for once they drew due west of Grandru, they made a quick right turn and descended into the village. The Sherman tanks supporting them knocked out several German halftracks during the fight, and also destroyed some captured American halftracks that had been pressed into service by the Germans. Forty Germans were taken prisoner, along with a wealth of captured American supplies, such as rations, clothing, M-1 rifles, and a 57mm AT gun.

As Grandru was falling to G Company, Companies E and F were coming under heavy fire from the woods further to the east. F Company, now down to only 25 men, was ordered to stand firm, while Companies E and G continued to attack. G Company advanced due north out of Grandru, and soon ran into heavy machine gun fire. The enemy emplacement was disposed of, and G Company resumed its advance. For some reason, the normally hardy German paratroopers began to surrender in large numbers, and G Company soon reported that they had more prisoners on hand than they could handle (during the advance out of Grandru, the 49 men of G company captured 150 Germans). At a subsequent crossroad, they captured two 88s, and in a nearby house, came upon a German command post, where they captured three officers.

E Company had no such luck. Their axis of advance took them through the woods east of Grandru, where they ran into stiff resistance. Command of E Company had been passed to the leader of the I&R Platoon, Lt. Willinghoff, who, in the words of the Battalion commander, "was really getting a work out." As the casualties began to mount within E Company, Colonel Gardner took a direct hand in the battle. He ordered E Company to cease-fire, and then directed it to head east out of the woods, and into the south edge of another small patch of woods located further north. The Germans took advantage of the resulting lull to fall back, and they chose as their place of refuge the northern half of that same small patch of woods.

After dark, Gardner ordered E Company to clear the northern half of the woods. Rather then duke it out in the forest, the Germans slipped out into some nearby houses that lined the road west of Hompre. The Americans followed quickly on their heels, and descended upon them before they could prepare an organized defense. The Americans took 40 prisoners and captured a loaded 88mm gun. The infantrymen also encountered a Mark IV tank, which they knocked out with a bazooka. Company E then proceeded to dig in along the road, while F Company remained to the rear guarding the tanks, which had not been able to advance through the woods.

By nightfall on December 26, the 2nd Battalion had pushed to within 4,000 yards of the 101st Airborne Division's positions south of Bastogne. The 10th AIB had remained on their left, and were approaching the woods near Assenois. Its advance was hampered by German forces in the village of Salvacourt, which lay nestled in a shallow valley running roughly between Hompre and Assenois. The tanks had to remain to the rear during this leg of the advance, since a swollen stream and railroad embankment prevented them from staying with the infantry. As the tanks provided covering fire from a distance, the 10th AIB closed on the forest, but with darkness approaching, a decision was made to halt for the night. Major Cohen's battalion would attack the woods in the morning.

Late that night, 1st Lt. Walter Carr took a patrol of four men from E Company on a foray through the German lines. His goal was to make contact with the 101st Airborne Division. Carr succeeded in his mission at 4:30 A.M. on the morning of December 27. After his arrival, Lt. Carr was escorted to General McAuliffe's command post, where he was given a map overlay marked with the positions of the 101st.

As Carr and his brave band of men headed back to their own lines with the valuable information, they probably thought that they had earned the honor of being the first unit to come in contact with the 101st. Little did they know that someone else had beaten them to the prize.

20. Breakthrough

The Shift to the Left Flank

After CCR's rout of the Germans at Bigonville on December 24, the only orders it received were to outpost the town. Colonel Blanchard's plans for December 25 consisted of cooking up a big Christmas dinner; little else was on CCR's plate that snowy Christmas Eve, as it appeared they had earned a brief respite by virtue of securing the division's right flank.

When Blanchard received his next set of orders later that evening, they were certainly unexpected: He was to move his command at once to Neufchâteau, which was all the way over on the division's far left flank. He hastily assembled his troops and vehicles, and had them on the road by 12:30 A.M. on Christmas Day. The dreams of a timely, hot Christmas meal would not be realized.

As CCR left Bigonville, it consisted of the 37th Tank Battalion, the 53rd AIB, the 94th AFAB, C Company of the 704th TD Battalion, and a battery of 155mm howitzers from the 177th Field Artillery Battalion. The thirty mile trek to the division's left flank was aided by the bright moonlight reflecting off the snow covered ground, but was hampered by the slippery, iced roads and bitter cold. The most direct path to the west was the Martelange-Fauvillers road, but there were reports of bridges being out along that route, so a longer, alternative route was taken. After leaving Bigonville, the column, guided by MPs along the way, passed through Perle, Heinstert, Habay-la-Neuve, Leglise, and Offaing. It then turned northeast along the Neufchâteau-Bastogne highway. D/37 entered the town of Bercheux shortly before dawn, where they encountered a company of American engineers who had been outposting the village. The rest of the 37th Tank Battalion went into an assembly area southwest of Bercheux. CCR spent the morning resting and refueling after their all-night trek.

The vast majority of vehicles made the journey without incident. An exception was one of the 105mm Assault Guns from the 37th Tank Battalion's HQ Company, which developed a mechanical problem and had to drop out of the column. When the tank commander, Sgt. Feinberg, radioed his platoon leader to inform him of his dilemma, he was told not to worry about catching up for the moment, but rather, to stay put and try to fix the problem where they were, and then to catch up in the morning.

Feinberg's assault gun was stranded near a frozen, snow-covered farm. During the night, the Belgian who owned the land approached and invited the tankers to use his barn and hayloft for the night. It was a welcome invitation, since the barn would provide much more warmth than could be found in their immobile tank. Feinberg, who spoke Yiddish, was able to converse with the farmer, who knew German (the two languages being similar enough for them to have at least a rudimentary understanding of what the other was saying). The farmer guided the Americans to the barn, and once the GIs had begun to settle in, he returned with a treat: some hard alcohol that helped warm them even further. Feeling very fortunate to have come upon such a generous host, the tankers drank up, and eventually feel asleep.

Early the next morning, the farmer approached the barn with three strapping American officers in tow: a Colonel, a Captain, and a Lieutenant. They weren't from the Fourth Armored, and were complete strangers to Feinberg and his crew. Suddenly and unexpectedly, Feinberg found himself under interrogation! After asking Feinberg and his crew what unit they were from, and how they ended up where they were, the officers started checking for dog tags. Upon looking at Feinberg's, they asked, "What in the hell is that 'H' for?" The Sergeant explained to them that he was Jewish, and that the 'H' stood for 'Hebrew'. The Lieutenant quickly inserted a totally unrelated question: "What do they call the Brooklyn Dodgers?" It then dawned on Feinberg that these fellows thought they were Germans! When Feinberg had conversed with the farmer in something passing for German, it must have aroused the farmer's suspicions. Well-founded rumors about Germans trying to pass as Americans had been running rampant around the Third Army as well as the civilian population, and this Belgian citizen was apparently not taking any chances.

Every man on the crew chimed in to help convince the officers of their true nationality. Finally convinced, the officers departed, leaving Feinberg and his men to conduct their repairs. They would soon rejoin the 37th Tank Battalion after what had certainly been an unexpected vignette.

As Blanchard's force neared its assembly area, he received a little more detail regarding his mission. He was to attack on the left flank of the division, in the direction of Bastogne. The primary purpose was not to force a breakthrough, but rather to protect the left flank of CCB, due to concerns that the Germans were building up strength in the area of Sibret. Other than the specter of German armor and infantry at Sibret, there was little, if any, information regarding what lay before them. They were not even sure of the exact positions of CCB, which was operating to their right.

At 6 A.M., Colonel Blanchard met with his commanders to review the plans for the coming day. The command would be given a few hours rest after the trying drive from Bigonville. At 11 A.M., they would get underway.

CCR's Christmas Drive

At the appointed time, Wendell's force started up the paved road toward Vaux-les-Rosieres. D/37 led the way, followed by the armored infantry of B/53, a platoon of

Hellcats from C/704, and a squad of engineers riding in a halftrack. Following the engineers were paired teams of tank and armored infantry companies.

If the town of Vaux-les-Rosieres sounds familiar, it should: CCB/4 had occupied it while bivouacked southwest of Bastogne on December 19/20. After CCB had departed, it became the very temporary site of the headquarters of the battered 28th Infantry Division. The Germans had driven Norm Cota's men out of the town on the night of December 22. It was now CCR's turn to take it back.

Intelligence had reported that the Germans were holding Vaux-les-Rosieres with only a light force, and that the next town along the route, Petite Rosieres, was held in greater strength. Concerned that a deliberate attack on Vaxu-les-Rosieres would sound the alarm for the German force at Petite Rosieres, Abrams decided to have the light tank company, tank destroyers, B/53, and engineers race through the first village without stopping. It would be up to the trailing medium tank companies and armored infantry to clear Vaux-les-Rosieres, while the vanguard, commanded by Captain McMahon (S-2 of the 37th) continued on to Petite Rosieres, which was less than a mile up the road.

As the vanguard approached Vaux-les-Rosieres, it came upon the outposts of the 46th Replacement Panzer Engineer Battalion. The Germans dove for cover at the sight of the oncoming M5 tanks. The tankers swept beyond the German outposts and on through Vaux-les-Rosieres, receiving nothing more than scattered rifle fire as they drove by. The Germans must have quickly realized that the tankers had sliced through their position and, in effect, cut them off from the 5th FJ Division. The engineers were quick to surrender to the main body of Abrams' column as it followed in behind McMahon's tanks.

The light tanks of D/37 moved swiftly up the road, and drove straight ahead through Petite Rosieres. The tankers fired their machine guns as they raced through the town, in order to pin down the enemy paratroopers. They continued on toward the high ground to the northeast, where the Hellcats of C/704 soon joined them. The armored infantrymen from B Company dismounted and swept through Petite Rosieres, taking 65 prisoners in the process. In total, it took two and a half hours to capture and secure the two towns of Vaux-les-Rosieres and Petite Rosieres.

With both towns in the bag, the column turned off the main paved highway, and headed northeast along a secondary road in the hope that it would be lightly defended. A/37 and A/53 now took the lead and headed for the village of Nives. At the same time, C/37 and C/53 moved forward to the village of Cobreville. After preparatory barrages provided by the 94th AFAB, both towns were quickly cleared of the enemy. Fifteen prisoners were taken at Nives, and another five at Cobreville.

At about 2:00 P.M., the advance came to a halt at a small creek outside of Cobreville, where Lt. Boggess reported that the bridge had been blown (once again, the handiwork of the U.S. 299th Engineer Battalion). Abrams ordered the battalion bulldozer to come forward. Under the watchful eyes of C/37 and A/37, the bulldozer demolished a stone wall, and then pushed the debris into the creek to form an improvised bridge. The work was completed by 3:15 P.M., and the C Team immediately raced due east toward Remoiville, where it occupied the high ground overlooking the town from the west.

At this point, there is an odd twist in the history of CCR's advance. The official history, authored by Dr. Hugh Cole, tells a story of how Abrams was wary of Remoiville, and that he called in *four battalions* of artillery to level the town. There is no record of this massive barrage in the unit histories of either the 37th Tank Battalion or the 94th AFAB. Various combat interviews and records are at odds regarding exactly what happened at Remoiville. The 37th Tank Battalion's daily combat diary makes a specific point of saying that artillery support was *not* used at Remoiville, due to the fact that CCB was known to be operating close to the east; CCR was not exactly sure of CCB's positions, and they were afraid of hitting them with friendly fire. Other post-battle interviews indicate that perhaps four *batteries* of artillery (the 94th AFAB and the single battery from the 177th FAB) were used for a 5 to 10 minute preparatory barrage against Remoiville (this was nothing out of the ordinary, since Abrams had worked out the artillery concentrations for each town along his route, and assigned them each a number so that he could quickly call them into action). It is also noted in the record of the Fourth Armored's divisional artillery how communication with CCR was very problematic after they moved to the left flank of the division; the only confirmed use of artillery other than the 94th AFAB and 177th during this stage of the battle is that which took place at Assenois on December 26.

Thus, it is virtually certain that the account of an artillery barrage by four *battalions* is an error. The difference between four battalions and four batteries is huge; in this case, at least 66 guns versus 22, so it is worth clearing the record on this matter. Like the erroneous report of the mechanical failure of 33 tanks of the 8th Tank Battalion, many authors have repeated the false account of the artillery barrage at Remoiville.

If the recollections of Major Parker are relied upon (the commanding officer of the 94th AFAB was interviewed on January 7, 1945, just two weeks after the engagement), the 94th hit Remoiville for 5 to 10 minutes with 20 volleys from each of its guns, while C Battery of the 177th FAB fired about a dozen volleys, before the town was entered by American troops.

The Shermans of C/37 lined up on the high ground overlooking the town from the west in order to support the advance into the town by A/37 and A/53. Meanwhile, Captain Leach's B Company moved to Hill 480, about one kilometer to the northwest. From this position, his tanks overlooked the main road connecting Remoiville with Remichampagne. B/37's presence ensured that the Germans would not make a surprise move from the north.

As A/37 and A/53 raced toward Remoiville, the guns of C/37 fired high explosive shells into the town. The weight of the American artillery and tank fire drove the 3rd Battalion of the 14th FJ Regiment into the buildings and cellars, and the A Team charged in so fast that the Americans were among them before the paratroopers could pull their heads out of the sand. As some of the Germans tried to take to the windows and doorways, they found the Americans already there with guns blazing.

The tanks quickly penetrated to the center of the village, while the armored infantry, who came into town riding in their halftracks, dismounted and began clearing the buildings, one after another. The Shermans blasted away point blank at the houses lining the streets of the village. As the attack progressed, the C Team charged down from the high ground, and sealed off the west side of the town.

Every cellar was cleaned out, typically by the use of grenades tossed in by the racing infantry. The Germans did manage to hit two tanks with panzerfausts. One of the tanks received some damage, but was still operable. By dusk, 327 prisoners had been taken, 35 to 50 of the enemy were counted as dead, and 42 Germans had been wounded.

While the main body of Abrams' force gathered itself, the light tanks of D Company advanced toward Remichampagne, which was slightly more than one mile to the north. The road connecting Remoiville and Remichampagne followed the course of a valley, with the Rau de Remichampagne laying immediately to the right of the road (this was the same road under observation by B/37). East of the stream, the wooded ground rose steadily away toward a series of three consecutive hills, from which the Germans, if present, could observe CCR's advance. To the west of the road, the ground rose more gradually, culminating in a large area of woods due west of Remichampagne. This area also offered an excellent position for observing the road heading north through the valley.

The light tanks had only advanced a couple of hundred yards when they were stopped cold by a huge crater that had been dug across the road. The obstacle couldn't be bypassed, since the stream blocked their movement to the right, and an embankment on the left was too steep for the vehicles to climb. With darkness approaching, Abrams decided to halt his task force for the night. At 6 P.M., A/37 exchanged positions with B/37 guarding the left flank atop Hill 480, and the balance of the command remained in position north of Remoiville, with C/37 outposted on the high ground due north of the town. Abrams would let the engineers work on the crater, and then continue the advance in the morning.

As night fell, CCR was roughly abreast of CCB. But Dager and Blanchard were not in communication with one another, and neither commander knew the exact location of his counterpart's forces. Though both commands were now roughly an equal distance from Bastogne, the expectation remained that it would be Dager's CCB that would lead the charge into Bastogne. In fact, the expectation was so high that General Maxwell Taylor, the commander of the 101st, was sticking close to Dager's command post, waiting for the opportunity to join his men inside the encircled town. (Taylor had been on a special assignment off the continent, and thus missed the opportunity to enter Bastogne with his division).

Lt. Colonel Abrams also came close to missing *his* anticipated entry into Bastogne. Earlier that same day, while traveling amongst his advancing units, his jeep struck an American mine close to his own command post. The jeep was destroyed, and the driver seriously injured. Abrams, however, escaped without a scratch. (In fact, he would serve out the entire war without receiving a single wound; his fortune was quite good, given his proclivity for being in the middle of the action)

Friction at the Top

That evening, Patton and Bradley met for a low-key Christmas dinner. Montgomery, who had been given command of the forces on the north side of the Bulge back on December 20 (much to Bradley's open disgust), had spoken with Patton earlier that day, leaving Patton fit to be tied. The British Field Marshal had informed Patton that the "First Army could not attack for three months." Montgomery's view was that Patton was the only one in a position to strike. Monty felt his own forces — American forces — were too weak to go on the offensive. Given the situation, Montgomery felt it best for Patton to fall back to the Saar-Vosges line, and perhaps even as far back as the Moselle River, in order to shorten the line, which would presumably allow more resources to be brought against the south flank of the Bulge.

Both Patton and Bradley were furious at the prospect of doing this, and began a lobbying effort that same night to have the 1st and 9th armies placed back under the 12th Army Group, so that the offensive could be executed with the zeal necessary to inflict maximum damage upon the Germans. Taking the sort of time that Montgomery envisioned would simply allow the Germans to strengthen their positions, or slip away at their convenience back to the safety of the West Wall. Unfortunately, their request to realign the 1st and 9th armies was denied by Ike, who while not ready to embrace the ambitious proposals of his two American generals, was even more reluctant to go along with a plan as conservative and cautious as Monty's.

The Opposing Plans

As Bradley and Patton stewed over the big picture on Christmas Night, Blanchard and his battalion commanders plotted their strategy for the following day on a much smaller scale. They had just received a new map showing the American positions along the Bastogne perimeter. Also marked were the known German positions facing in toward the 101st and out toward the Fourth Armored. Details regarding the former were more plentiful, since the 101st had been engaged and patrolling the perimeter for several days now. Regarding the latter, there were more questions than answers.

Abrams and Jaques met at the CCR command post at 8 P.M. on December 25, where they received their orders for the following day. The plan for December 26 called for an advance north over the newly repaired road leading out of Remoiville, with the immediate objective being Remichampagne. CCR would then seize the high ground north of the town, and advance to the Neufchâteau-Bastogne highway, via Clochimont. From there, they would drive toward Sibret.

Air reconnaissance flights had sent back reports of a strong concentration of Germans in Sibret. An enemy force in this area could pose a serious threat to the left flank of the Fourth Armored Division. If CCR secured the town, CCB could continue its final drive for Bastogne with its left flank reasonably secure. Thus the capture of Sibret became the most important objective for CCR on December 26.

Before the advance resumed, CCR's supporting artillery moved into new firing positions south of Cobreville. The artillery would play a critical role in CCR's advance on the 26th. The four batteries had to exercise caution in their targeting, however, due to the fact that the exact location of CCB was still in doubt. If their fire drifted too far east, they feared it might hit some of CCB's positions.

The Germans were also busy making plans for the 26th of December. With the appearance of American armor on the right flank of his division, the commander of the 5th FJ Division knew that he was being stretched to the limit. He warned his superiors "a breakthrough of the enemy is imminent." Certainly, General Kokott of the 26th VG Division, whose 39th Fusilier Regiment was fighting almost literally back to back with Heilmann's paratroopers, knew that this spelled trouble for his men south of Bastogne.

> The 39th Grenadier Regiment had its principle strength in Assenois, Salvacourt, and Sibret. I told Kaufmann to continue facing towards Bastogne, and not to form a front to the south. I warned him, of course, to watch his rear and, when it became worse, to prepare an all-around defense, using all his anti-tank guns.

Kokott was not the only one watching the situation around Bastogne. Finally admitting that the force surrounding the town was not suited for the task of capturing it, Hitler decided to reinforce the effort at Bastogne. Some additional units were already heading into the area, such as the 15th Panzer Grenadier Division. On December 26, Hitler bolstered his forces in the Bastogne area even further by ordering the 1st SS Panzer Division to head south. Though weakened by the losses inflicted upon KG Peiper, the 1st SS was still a formidable force to be reckoned with. Its armor strength still amounted to perhaps a battalion of tanks, made up of a combination of Panthers and Mark IVs. It also had in tow the remaining Mark VIBs of the attached 501st Heavy Panzer Battalion (13 of which were battle ready; another 14 were in need of repair). The 1st SS Panzer Division's two panzer grenadier regiments were still in very good fighting condition, and together with the remaining panzers, they would soon play an active role in the fighting around Bastogne. But for the moment, the battle remained in the hands of the 26th VG and 5th FJ divisions.

From Remichampagne to Assenois

At 9:25 on the morning of December 26, the artillery plastered the woods west of Remichampagne (the Bois De Cohet), as well as the road that led from that town to the northwest (toward Morhet). American spotter planes had identified German tanks along this road, and the artillery barrage was designed as a preemptive strike to discourage enemy movement against CCR's left flank.

Abrams' task force began moving north while the artillery banged away at the suspected enemy positions. The light tanks of D Company, along with seven Hellcat tank destroyers from C/704, moved out first in order to screen the left flank of the advance. As the main body of CCR began advancing on Remichampagne, they received a welcome surprise when sixteen P-47 Thunderbolts appeared overhead and joined the action. The 37th Tank Battalion diary described the advance in glowing terms:

> The coordination of tanks, infantry artillery and air was to perfection. Planes came over tanks at antenna altitude and strafed to the front. The combination of artillery and planes took care of the Bois de Cohet, which was the unknown quantity.

As it turned out, there were few Germans present in the woods on the American's left, and the tank threat on the road from Morhet didn't materialize at the moment. Remichampagne quickly became the main cause of concern.

Here again we find some conflicting information regarding the degree of artillery fire that was employed. The aforementioned interview with Major Parker cites a continued concern about the location of CCB as a reason for constraining the fire of the 94th AFAB; he reported that his howitzers did not fire on Remichampagne that day. This seems a bit odd, however, since Remichampagne was further from CCB's axis of advance than was Remoiville. It leaves one to wonder if some of the records and recollections about the two towns have not been reversed (there are some contradictory statements in other unit records indicating that artillery support *was* brought to bear against Remichampagne).

In any event, the B Team advanced due north along an axis parallel with the main road leading from Remoiville to Remichampagne. The ground was frozen solid, so the tanks and halftracks had no problem deploying off road for the attack. Meanwhile, the C Team took up positions on the high ground west of the town, whence they prepared to offer supporting fire for the B Team.

As Leach's Shermans approached, artillery fire (perhaps from the 177th, or indirect fire from the 37th Tank Battalion's own 105mm assault guns) continued to pour into Remichampagne. When the artillery fire lifted, the tanks of C Company started hitting the town with direct fire from the west. As it turned out, the enemy was not present in high numbers, and what was there simply wilted before the extraordinarily well coordinated attack (the Germans taken prisoner were from the 3rd and 6th companies of the 104th Panzer Grenadier Regiment, 15th PG Division, which was newly arrived on the scene). "The effect on the enemy was demoralizing. The enemy at Remichampagne was stunned, straggling out in small groups."

CCR continued on toward Clochimont. The B Team advanced to the hills overlooking Clochimont from the southwest, and Lt. Colonel Abrams came forward to B/37's positions to have a look for himself. Now that Abrams was drawing appreciably closer to the Bastogne perimeter — Clochimont was but a mere 2.5 miles away from the positions plotted for the 101st — he became increasingly sensitive to the fact that, sooner or later, he was bound to hit strong German resistance.

CCR had made very strong progress over the course of the past two days. The overall opposition it faced was lighter than what CCA and CCB had been tackling, but that does not diminish the magnitude of its success. Some of the towns had been only lightly defended, but when heavier opposition was faced, such as at Remoiville, Abrams and Jacques executed textbook combined arms attacks that rocked the enemy back on their heels.

Success had come with a price tag attached, however. CCR was starting to show signs of wear and tear after its battles on both flanks of the division. The 37th, which had begun the offensive with about 27 tanks, had lost a few during the four days of fighting, and now had about 20 combat ready Shermans and 13 M5 light tanks. Jacques' 53rd AIB was short 230 men. But CCR had one very important thing going for it. Unlike CCA and CCB, Blanchard's command had not been engaged in the same sort of non-stop attack since December 22. From the outset, they managed to avoid Patton's directive to attack at night, which reduced their casualties and ensured they were as well rested as possible under the circumstances.

It was now 3 P.M., and the next step, according to the plan that had been laid out the previous night, called for Abrams to turn his tanks toward Sibret. As "Abe" Abrams and "Jigger" Jaques were discussing their next move, a huge armada of cargo planes began to fill the sky. Their destination was Bastogne, and in a matter of minutes, the battalion commanders saw crates of supplies swaying beneath the billowing parachutes to which they were attached. Transport planes appeared with gliders in tow, which were then cut loose for their silent descent toward the landing sites within the perimeter. Not all of the aircraft made a safe return, as bursts of flak from the German AA guns peppered the flight path of the transports. The odd cargo plane could be seen falling out of formation, sometimes aflame, dropping toward an unseen fate over the horizon.

As Abrams and Jaques watched the precious supplies drift downward and out of sight, and witnessed the bravery of the unarmed pilots risking their lives to deliver the lifeblood of supplies to the surrounded paratroopers, a fresh sense of urgency stirred within them. Abrams suggested to Jaques that, instead of heading for Sibret and the possibility of an uncertain fight that would put them no closer to Bastogne, why not continue along the road from Clochimont to Assenois, and then on to Bastogne itself? Assenois was the only village that remained between CCR and the 101st Airborne. If they could make a dash through the town, there was a good chance they would make contact with the "Screaming Eagles." When Jacques agreed, the wheels were put in motion.

Abrams now ordered A/37 to pass through B/37's positions in order to secure the hill northwest of Clochimont, which also overlooked Sibret. The C team remained behind in a position northwest of Remichampagne, where they would guard the road leading in from Morhet, thus protecting the flank and rear of CCR. D/37 and the tank destroyers of C/704 also continued to screen the left flank of the command.

Just after Lt. Whitehill's tanks had passed through Captain Leach's position, A/37 began receiving dangerous anti-tank fire from its right rear. Abrams ordered Leach to destroy the camouflaged enemy gun position, and Leach in turn handed the assignment to Staff Sergeant Robert "Pappy" Grimm (so nicknamed because, at the age of 42, he was the oldest member of the battalion), who commanded one of the 105mm Sherman assault guns. Grimm was out of high explosive ammunition, however, and had to resort to his remaining solid shot rounds, which were not as well suited for taking out a "soft" target. With a masterful shot, Grimm's gunner plucked off a German truck sitting near the gun, and followed that score with a few less effective rounds directed at the 88mm anti-tank gun. Impatient, Abrams rolled up to the scene in his tank. "Thunderbolt" came to a stop just a couple of tank lengths from Leach's tank, with Abrams riding high in the opening of the turret, as was his custom. Abrams immediately barked out fire orders to his gunner, John Gatusky. "Gunner — anti-tank — HE (x-range) — (gunner ready) fire." And with one high explosive round delivered from his 76mm cannon, the enemy anti-tank gun was sent skyward.

When Whitehill gained his position overlooking Sibret, he reported over the radio that he did not observe any enemy activity there. So while B/37 and B/53 guarded the heights at Clochimont, Abrams had Captain Dwight bring the C Team (C/37 and C/53) forward from its positions guarding the road between Morhet and Remichampagne. These two companies, under the command of Captain Dwight, would form the vanguard for the attack through Assenois and on to the Bastogne perimeter. (It is interesting to note that the selection of C/37 was based on their supply of ammunition. B Company had used up all of their 75mm ammunition, and A Company was nearly out. Of the three companies of mediums, only C/37 had ample ammo.)

There was no hesitancy among Abrams' and Jaques' men. They too had been witness to the drama being played out in the skies above Bastogne, and it provided all the motivation they needed.

Before the commencement of the attack, some prudent coordination had to be conducted. The 101st was advised that American armor would be coming in toward their lines (the last thing that C Company needed was to be fired upon by American troops as it charged toward Bastogne). More importantly, a fire plan was put together and communicated to the supporting artillery batteries. In addition to the 94th AFAB, and the one battery from the 177th that was attached to CCR, three more artillery battalions joined in the shoot, courtesy of CCB (the 22nd, 253rd, and 776th). Even though Assenois was easily within range of the artillery batteries positioned within the defensive perimeter around Bastogne, communication with the guns supporting the 101st was not such that it would allow for them to throw their weight into the attack.

Assenois

At about 4:15 P.M., the C Team, commanded by Captain Dwight, pushed off down the road toward Assenois. The Shermans of 1st Lt. Boggess' C Company led the way, followed by the halftracks loaded with the armored infantry of C/53. Following the C Team would be A/37 and B/53, which would be responsible for cleaning out Assenois after the C team charged through. Captain Leach's B/37 would remain positioned on the high ground south of Clochimont; the armored infantrymen of A/53 were held in reserve.

Before Boggess departed, Abrams had a few words with him. Actually, it was more than that, as he studied the map with him and laid out where Boggess should head. Most of their discussion focused on the road between Assenois and Bastogne, and what Boggess might expect to encounter there (it was anyone's guess, really). No doubt Abrams intended the conversation to be equal parts educational and motivational, and he accomplished the latter with his final words: "Get to those men in Bastogne."

Lt. Boggess later revealed what he was thinking as the final leg on the drive to Bastogne got underway:

> We were going through fast, all guns firing, straight up that road to bust through before they had time to get set. I thought a lot of things as we took off. I thought of whether the road would be mined, whether the bridge in Assenois would be blown, whether they would be ready at their anti-tank guns. Then we charged, and I didn't have any time to wonder.

At 4:34 P.M., Lt. Boggess radioed Abrams to request the artillery concentration on Assenois. At that moment, Abrams radioed the 94th AFAB, saying "number nine, play it soft and sweet." With that prearranged code dispatched over the airwaves to the 94th, thirteen batteries of artillery placed a blanket of steel on top of Assenois. In all,

420 rounds plastered the area in and about the town. Batteries A and C of the 94th fired on the woods on both sides of the road, where it was suspected that the enemy had placed anti-tank guns. B Battery hit the south end of town, and would lift its fire when Boggess' lead tanks were ready to enter the area. Battery C of the 177th would begin by hitting the center of town, and would roll its fire to the north once the American troops had entered from the south. The balance of the supporting artillery would fire ten rounds each into the center of Assenois. Lt. Chamberlin, the infantry forward observer for the 94th AFAB, would be near the front of the attack, and would be responsible for making the call to lift the fire at the proper time. Additionally, the spotter plane of Lt. Billy Wood was overhead.

Unlike some of the villages that CCR had swept through in the past 48 hours, Assenois was heavily defended. Eight anti-tank gun emplacements were well situated around the approaches to the village. In addition to the paratroopers from the 5th FJ Division, men from Colonel Kokott's 26th Volksgrenadier Division were also in position inside the town. Indeed, Abrams had great foresight when he called for the punishing artillery support.

As Lt. Boggess' tankers moved closer to the town, they saw billowing smoke and dust rising above Assenois. Boggess himself was leading the way, his M4A3E2 command tank, nicknamed "Cobra King," charging down the road under the control of his driver, Private Hubert Smith. The M4A3E2's 6-inch thick turret provided extra security, making it the perfect tank to be on point (just as Patton had envisioned). The Germans met the charging tanks with a high volume of anti-tank rounds, but none of the enemy gunners hit their targets. The Shermans opened fire as they came plunging down the road, and their machine guns eliminated any threat that escaped the shells lobbed in by the artillery.

Before the signal could be given to lift the artillery fire, the jeep carrying the artillery observer received a direct hit. The driver (Pfc. Draper Charles) was killed, and Lt. Chamberlin was thrown into a ditch. As "Cobra King" came to a dip in the road at the edge of the village, Boggess asked for the barrage to be lifted. But rather than wait for the firing to stop, Boggess and his entire C team plunged into Assenois.

The Germans had sought refuge from the punishing artillery in the buildings and cellars of Assenois, and the Shermans and halftracks were now among them before they could reorganize their defense. The barrage in Assenois was of such intensity that an overlay of smoke and dust blanketed the streets, reducing visibility for both sides. As the halftracks drove into the town, the armored infantry fired over the sides, all guns blazing, to pin down the enemy soldiers that began to emerge through the billowing smoke. The Shermans never stopped firing as they raced through the streets of Assenois. The gunner of "Cobra King," Corporal Milton Dickerman, described the scene:

> I used the 75 like a machine gun. Murphy was plenty busy throwing in the shells. We shot twenty-one rounds in a few minutes and I don't know how much machinegun stuff. As we got to Assenois an anti-tank gun in a halftrack fired at us. The shell hit the road in front of the tank and threw dirt all over. I got the halftrack in my sights and hit it with high explosive. It blew up.

The smoke and dust kicked up by the shellfire made it none too easy for the lead tank. Private Smith struggled to see through his dirt-smeared periscope.

I made out okay, although I couldn't see very good. I sorta guessed at the road. Had a little trouble when my left brake locked and the tank turned up a road we didn't want to go. So I just stopped her, backed her up and went on again.

Smith wasn't the only driver having problems finding his way. The lack of visibility resulted in two of Boggess' other Shermans also taking a wrong turn inside the town, but unlike Smith, they didn't make their way immediately back to the main road, and became separated from the column. Shells continued to fall even as the column raced through the town, and unfortunately, a loaded halftrack from C/53 was knocked out by a shell burst from an American artillery piece, resulting in three casualties. Apparently, Boggess' radio call to lift the barrage had not gone through. In the confusion, a halftrack managed to insert itself into the middle of the tank portion of the column.

Further back in the column, a telephone pole fell on top of one of the halftracks, bringing that portion of the column to a halt. With 155mm howitzer shells still falling at the center of the town, the armored infantry, save for the squad that was riding in the halftrack in the column with the Shermans, dismounted from their vehicles in search of cover from their own artillery. As they scrambled to find a safe haven, the German paratroopers and volksgrenadiers began emerging from their own hiding places (these men were primarily from the 39th Regiment's 1st Battalion, whose HQ was located in the town). Vicious fighting ensued. Men found themselves face to face with the enemy, and hand-to-hand combat was often the result. As Boggess' tanks and the lone halftrack raced on, the men of C/53 fought for their lives in the streets and alleys of Assenois.

Finally, the artillery fire on the center of town ceased when Lt. Wood, flying overhead, called in for the fire to be lifted. Lt. Colonel Abrams' tank was in the column, not far behind where the felled pole had brought them to a dead stop. He and his crew dismounted from their tank, and raced toward the pinned halftrack. They muscled the pole from the vehicle, and the armored portion of the column continued to advance.

The resolve demonstrated by Abrams and his crew was not the only act of bravery to take place within the streets of Assenois that afternoon. During the melee inside the town, Private James Hendrix, a 19-year-old rifleman from C/53, decided to single-handedly take on two 88mm guns that had survived the artillery barrage. Armed only with his M-1 rifle, he killed one of the crewmembers and captured the rest. He later described his actions:

We ran up on 'em yelling "come out" but they wouldn't. One poked his head out of a foxhole and I hit him through the neck. I got closer and hit another on the head with the butt of my M1. He had American matches on him. Others came out with their hands up.

With at least these two 88s no longer a threat, some of the armored infantrymen, including Hendrix, mounted their halftracks again and continued their advance through the now rubble-strewn town. From his vehicle, Hendrix saw a halftrack that had been hit by a round of high explosive. The occupants were lying dead and wounded near the vehicle. German machine gun crews showed the downed men no mercy, as they continued to throw bursts of lead at them as they huddled for safety in a nearby ditch.

The halftracks, including the one that Hendrix was in, used their .50 caliber machine guns to try and silence the enemy machine gun positions, but to no avail. On his own initiative, Hendrix left the protection of his halftrack to go to the aid of his wounded comrades. As the enemy machine guns continued to direct their fire toward the wounded men, Hendrix raced into a position where he could take aim at the enemy guns, and proceeded to silence them both. He then held his position and protected the wounded men until they could be evacuated.

But that was not the last act of bravery that Hendrix would commit in the hell that was Assenois. Once again on the move, he witnessed a German grenade plunge into the rear of another American halftrack. Most of the crew and soldiers riding in the vehicle bailed out safely as their mount went up in flames. But one man, who had been badly injured by the grenade blast, remained in the open rear of the vehicle. Hearing the wounded soldier's plaintive screams for help, Hendrix braved enemy fire and raced to the man's aid. He later told what happened once he arrived at the burning halftrack:

> I pulled at him and got him out on the road, but he was burned bad. I tried to find water to put out the fire, but the water cans were full of bullet holes, so I beat out the flames as best I could. He died later.

Hendrix was later awarded one of the three Medals of Honor earned by members of the Fourth Armored Division during the Second World War.

As Hendrix and the men of C/53 battled to clear the streets of Assenois, Boggess' column continued to drive on toward Bastogne. With his own M4A3E2 still in the lead, the small column now consisted of three Shermans, followed by the rogue halftrack, and then two more Shermans (one of which was Captain Dwight's).

The road leading out of Assenois quickly ascends between two thick sections of forest. The trees are tucked in close to the road for a distance of about a thousand yards, making it a perfect place to conduct an ambush. This did not deter Boggess' crew. They simply sped down the road at full throttle, blasting away at any and all spots along the edge of the woods that might harbor the enemy. Their .30 caliber machine guns and 75mm gun were fired non-stop as they moved.

As the three Shermans at the head of the column raced ahead, the halftrack started falling behind, unable to keep up with its heavy load of infantrymen. In so doing, they delayed the two Shermans behind them that were anxious to gallop at the same speed as Boggess' tank. A gap of some 300 yards opened up in the column, and the Germans hiding in the woods took advantage of it to hastily throw a string of a dozen teller mines across the road. Unaware, the halftrack rolled over the first mine, causing an explosion that turned the vehicle into a flaming wreck. Captain Dwight had the two following Shermans pull to the shoulder of the road while he dismounted and rallied the infantrymen from the wrecked halftrack to help him pull the remaining mines off the road. As one of the Shermans provided covering fire with its .50 caliber, the men threw the mines into a ditch alongside the road.

Despite the problem on the road behind him, Boggess never looked back. The three lead Shermans continued to blast their way down the road, sending a cascade of machine gun rounds into the trees and brush that lined both sides of the road. Boggess, who was keeping a close eye out from his open turret, suddenly spied a concrete pill-box up ahead within a slight opening ringed by pines. Corporal Dickerman placed the green pillbox in the sights of his 75mm cannon and sent a round crashing into the con-crete emplacement. He quickly followed it with another two rounds, with the loader, Private James Murphy, feverishly replacing each spent casing with another shell.

As dust and smoke rose from the shattered pillbox, Boggess ordered the tank slowly forward. His bow gunner, Private Harold Hafner, kept his machine gun trained on the woods near the pillbox. As he got closer, Boggess spotted several uniformed figures in the forest. But they were not the uniforms of the fanatical German paratroopers. They were American.

The GIs, who were from the 326th Airborne Engineer Battalion, were in the process of launching an assault on the pillbox that Boggess' gunner had just snuffed out (a dozen dead Germans were counted). Boggess shouted out from his turret "Come here, come on out. This is the Fourth Armored." At first, there was no response. Boggess called out again, this time louder, his voice cutting through the cold, fading light of day. Then a lone figure emerged from the edge of the woods facing the pillbox. As he strode toward the tank, Boggess maintained a wary eye; there had been too many instances of Krauts donning G.I. uniforms, either for deception, or simply to add an extra layer of clothing for protection against the sub-freezing temperatures that had blanketed the battlefield for days on end.

When the approaching soldier was within speaking distance, he said "I'm Lieu-tenant Webster of the 326th Engineers, 101st Airborne Division. Glad to see you." At 4:50 P.M., after nearly five days of slugging, brutal combat, the Fourth Armored Divi-sion had broken through to Bastogne.

Contact had been made, but the mission was far from over. Three lone tanks in touch with the 101st represented only a thin umbilical cord between the Fourth Armored and the Screaming Eagles. The primary elements of CCR had yet to push through, and bringing them up the road from Assenois would be no simple task.

Once Dwight's men had cleared the mines from the road, the trailing tanks were quickly underway, followed by infantry-laden halftracks that were now coming out of Assenois. Small arms and panzerfaust fire continued to snap at the column. The tanks plunged ahead, but four more halftracks were set ablaze by the determined defenders lurking in the woods. The armored infantrymen took to the ground, and started to take on the enemy lurking by the roadside. They slowly began working their way in the direction of Boggess' tanks.

As the armored infantry advanced on foot, Captain Dwight's tanks continued on and soon caught up with Lt. Boggess. Within a matter of minutes, Dwight drove up to an observation post were General McAuliffe was waiting (after having been told of the approach of the Fourth Armored, McAuliffe had come forward to greet the reliev-ing force). After a formal salute, Dwight casually asked: "How are you, General?" McAuliffe's reply echoed that of Lt. Webster, and probably represented the feelings of every Screaming Eagle at Bastogne: "Gee, I am mighty glad to see you."

After having helped clear the streets of Assenois, Lt. Colonel Abrams continued in his command tank toward Bastogne. Joined by two trailing tanks of C/37, he began leading C/53 down the road from Assenois. His radio message to higher headquarters at 5:25 P.M. imparts the sense of urgency that was probably felt by every soldier fighting along that road: "Everyone should attack, get off their high horse. Have everyone attack, CCB."

As the advance toward Bastogne continued, the situation in Assenois was still not under control. Company B of the 53rd was now brought forward, along with the light tanks of D/37, to continue the fight. But as daylight gradually faded from the Ardennes, so did the Germans' resolve to hold the town. With the flames from the burning buildings serving as their work light, B/53 and D/37 finally wrestled control of the town. They had quite a bag of prisoners to show for their effort: 428 Germans were rounded up, including several officers from the battalion and regimental staffs of the 39th Fusilier Regiment (26th VG Division). Four more 88mm guns were captured or destroyed, along with two batteries of 105mm howitzers, several smaller caliber anti-tank guns (a total of 17 AT guns were found in the area), five halftracks, and two armored cars.

At 5:50 P.M., Lt. Colonel Abrams, who was later awarded the DSC for his leadership at Assenois, pushed "Thunderbolt" down the final stretch of road and joined up with Captain Dwight. Abrams soon found himself shaking hands with General McAuliffe. But the battle was still raging behind Abrams as the Germans tried furiously to keep the road closed. Volksgrenadiers continued to filter into the woods lining both sides of the road, and it became clear that a dedicated effort was going to have to be made to clear them out. General Kokott later described their attempt to close the narrow corridor.

> When the US 4th Armored Division broke into Assenois in the afternoon, Kaufmann called me. He said there were twelve enemy tanks in the village. The tanks were through Assenois and going to Bastogne. I knew it was all over. I told Kaufmann just to block the road. The corridor was still very small, the width of the road itself, and I hoped that with road-blocks and barriers, we could close the ring around Bastogne. It was a difficult task, however, because 39th Grenadier Regiment had been scattered on both sides of the road by 4th Armored Division tanks, which were firing in all directions. Now it was difficult for the 39th Grenadier Regiment to fight back without firing at each other. We tried to get reinforcements there, but the troops of the 26th VGD were so tired from their fighting that they couldn't make the effort. The Fuehrer Begleit Brigade was ordered by Corps to move to Sibret to close the circle, but it didn't get there in time. When it arrived, the US 4th Armored Division had already taken Sibret.

A/53, commanded by Captain Frank Kutak, was given the assignment of cleaning out the woods. Kutak, who had been wounded in both legs earlier in the battle, was confined to his jeep, but continued to lead his men from his vehicle. At midnight, the men of A/53 entered the woods to flush out the enemy. For the next three hours, they engaged in a heated battle. Given their proximity to the positions of the 101st, they couldn't risk bringing their supporting artillery into play, and had to rely entirely upon their integral heavy weapons for support. During the battle, Kutak's men only took four prisoners. But in the morning light, they discovered 30 to 35 dead Germans in their foxholes. The enemy had abandoned a dozen panzerfausts and two 75mm AT guns; weapons that would no longer harass the ambulances and supply trucks as they raced in and out of Bastogne (Kutak was awarded the DSC for his actions at Assenois).

A light tank of the 4th AD leads a column of trucks toward Bastogne, via the Assenois road. December 27, 1944 (National Archives Photograph SC198451).

The 53rd AIB had taken heavy losses. Since its initial commitment near Bigonville on December 23, it had suffered a total of 210 casualties (30 KIA, 180 wounded). And so at 8 P.M. that evening, Jaques was certainly glad to hear that 111 replacements were coming his way courtesy of the 87th Paratrooper Replacement Battalion (no source was being left untapped). Unfortunately, when the new GIs were marched to the front during the night, they were inadvertently led into a German bivouac area. There were no casualties, but all of their equipment was lost.

By approximately 1 A.M. on December 27, the enemy was finally pushed back a sufficient distance from the edge of the woods lining the road to allow vehicles to move toward Bastogne. With the light tanks of D/37 providing security, some 40 trucks and 70 ambulances were escorted into the battered town. After 6 days of encirclement, the siege of Bastogne had been lifted. But the battle was far from over.

A Postscript to Assenois

There has always been a bit of a mystery surrounding the identity of the architect who drew up the plan for shifting CCR over to the left flank of the Fourth Armored

Division, and for the subsequent decision to drive up the previously untested route from the southwest.

The decision to move CCR to the left had to rest with one of three people: Gaffey, Millikin, or Patton. It is not entirely certain, but for the reasons discussed below, I believe that it was General Gaffey who orchestrated the move.

The decision to move CCR away from the Bigonville area was not a difficult one to make. Due to the nature of the terrain and road network, there was nothing beyond Bigonville that would aid the Fourth Armored Division in its assigned mission of opening a relief corridor to Bastogne. CCR had played an important role on December 23 and 24 by protecting the right flank of the division, but that mission had been brought to a successful conclusion. Given the eroding resources of both CCA and CCB after the first three days of the offensive (December 22–24), leaving CCR in a defensive posture on the right flank of the division would have been a blunder. It was essential to add the weight of CCR to the primary attack toward Bastogne, which meant that Blanchard's command *had* to be shifted somewhere further to the west.

A case could have been made for inserting CCR directly into the zone of either CCB or CCA. With both of the primary combat commands significantly under strength on Christmas Day, a plan could have been formulated wherein the 37th Tank Battalion and 53rd Armored Infantry Battalion attacked alongside, or through, the units of CCA and/or CCB. The 8th Tank Battalion was fighting with only 14 medium tanks on December 25, and the additional 20 some-odd tanks of the 37th would have given CCB a real boost in firepower.

Someone wanted to send CCR further west, however, into its own zone over on the left flank of CCB. In his memoirs, Patton mentions the shift of CCR, writing:

> …it was necessary to move Combat Command "R" of the 4th Armored Division (Colonel Wendell Blanchard) from the right flank to the left flank of the III Corps in order to attempt a break-through to Bastogne.

Though it is conjecture on my part, I believe that if the move of CCR had been Patton's idea, he would have taken direct credit for it. It would have been out of character for him not to do so (especially since the breakthrough by CCR was viewed as the crowning achievement of the Third Army counterattack). Given Millikin's very low-key role during the offensive, it is difficult to imagine the rookie corps commander consummating the decision to employ CCR on the left. It seems fairly obvious that it was Gaffey's call, made in the due course of deciding how to employ his reserve once the mission at Bigonville had been completed.

The issue of CCR's mission once it arrived on the left flank is a much more interesting affair. Documents from within the Fourth Armored itself become a bit confusing on the matter. An after-action report prepared from an interview with the Assistant G-3 of the division, Captain Stedman Seay, was very specific on one point:

> The original plan of commitment was to use CCR on the left of CCB to guard against a possible enemy thrust from the northwest. It was anticipated that CCB would make first contact with the beleaguered troops in the BASTOGNE pocket.

A review of an after-action report based on a January 6, 1945 interview with Colonel Blanchard paints a different picture. Blanchard indicated that the oral order to move to the left flank came directly from the division command post. And then it is written, almost emphatically:

> Primary mission to make contact with the encircled elements, situation permitting. Secondary mission: cover the left flank.

A couple of things became clear once CCR became engaged on the division's left flank on Christmas day:

1. The axis of advance chosen for CCR certainly respected the left flank of CCB. Rather than launch the attack up the Neufchâteau-Bastogne highway, Blanchard set an axis of advance that kept CCR hugging General Dager's left flank (and it is a good thing he did, since there would have been substantial German forces left in the seam between CCB and CCR).
2. On December 26, the secondary part of the mission had taken precedence, as Blanchard gave Abrams and Jaques very specific instructions to protect the left flank of CCB by attacking Sibret in response to intelligence indicating a strong enemy presence there.

Patton made an interesting diary entry on December 26 that pertains to this matter:

> At 1400 Gaffey phoned to say that if I authorized the risk, he thought that ... Colonel Wendell Blanchard could break through to Bastogne by a rapid advance. I told him to try it. At 1845 they made contact and Bastogne was liberated. It was a daring thing and well done. Of course they may be cut off, but I doubt it... The speed of our movements is amazing, even to me, and must be a constant source of surprise to the Germans.

If Gaffey had indeed had this brainstorm at 2 P.M. on the afternoon of December 26, orders to execute such a mission had not filtered down to Abrams and Jaques. It is well documented that at 3 P.M., Abrams and Jaques decided on their own initiative to make the push through Assenois, rather than attack Sibret. An after-action report prepared by Captain L B Clark, based on a January 5, 1945, interview session with Lt. Colonel Abrams, Major Edward Bautz (the executive officer of the 37th), Captain William Dwight (S-3), and 2nd Lt. John Whitehill (CO A/37), states:

> Except for transmission of orders from division and the prescribing of the route to be followed in shifting from east to west flank of the division, CCR apparently had little to do with the direction of the action of 37th Tk Bn and 53rd AIB. Col Blanchard, CCR Commander, was ordering an attack after the 37th had made contact with 101 AB Div elements. Decisions were made by Lt. Cols Abrams and Jaques without consulting CCR [Maj Bautz and Capt Dwight both said this].

The most telling bit of evidence supporting the fact that Abrams and Jaques made the plunge on their own initiative is found in the radio transcript maintained by the 37th Tank Battalion. At 4:40 P.M. on the 26th, at the very moment that Lt. Boggess' tank was charging up the road from Assenois, just minutes away from the link-up with the 101st, Colonel Blanchard sent a radio message to Major Bautz: "We are going to do it tonight. Get everything together. I want Abe and Jaques at CP 74 in about 45 minutes." Bautz, knowing that Abrams was up front with the attacking forces, replied, "Can I meet you?" to which Blanchard answered, "yes." It appears that Blanchard was soon in the loop on what was transpiring, and at 4:55, ordered Bautz to find an assembly area for the entire command in the area of contact with the 101st. Clearly, he still did not understand the nature of the battle from his position in the rear, as both Bautz and Abrams cautioned that the town and road were ablaze. There was also the continued threat of an attack against Blanchard's left flank. In fact, at 5:55 P.M., just slightly over an hour after the first contact with the 101st, Lt. Donahue, the CO of D/37, reported that an estimated 15 to 20 enemy tanks were located north of Morhet, thus confirming the recon plane report from earlier in the day. Had all of CCR been pulled up through Assenois, the command would have been extremely vulnerable to attack from the left rear.

Thus, it appears most likely that General Gaffey ordered CCR to the left flank as a practical matter, and that as CCR's fight evolved, their mission had indeed taken on the flavor of protecting the left flank of CCB. This changed dramatically on the initiative of Abrams and Jaques, as they engineered the bold breakthrough at Assenois.

With Lt. Boggess' dramatic plunge through Assenois, and the subsequent link up with the 101st Airborne, CCR/4 earned its place on the pages of countless history books for decades to come. Lt. Colonel Abrams, who at the pinnacle of his career would become Army Chief of Staff, would forever be associated with the improvised sweep over to the left flank of the division, and the subsequent drive to Bastogne. Lt. Boggess' tank, "Cobra King," would become one of the most famous Sherman tanks of the Second World War (perhaps second only to Abrams' own "Thunderbolt"). Somewhat ironically, "Cobra King," with a different commander in the turret, would meet its fate three months later while participating in the famous raid on the POW camp at Hammelburg.

General Patton was greatly relieved that his promise to relieve Bastogne had finally been fulfilled. Reflecting on the achievement, he wrote to General Gaffey:

> The outstanding celerity of your movement and the unremitting, vicious, and skillful manner in which you pushed the attack terminating at the end of four days and four nights of incessant battle in the relief of Bastogne, constitute one of the finest chapters in the glorious history of the United States Army. You and the officers and men of your command are hereby commended for a superior performance.

Patton was obviously proud of the achievement of the Fourth Armored Division. To his wife, he wrote:

> The relief of Bastogne is the most brilliant operation we have thus far performed and is in my opinion the outstanding achievement of this war. Now the enemy must dance to our tune, not we to his.

As daring as CCR's attack was, and as brave as the men were who executed it (among those decorated for their actions between Bigonville and Bastogne were Lt. Whitehill and Captain Leach, who both earned the Distinguished Service Cross), it is a major oversight, even an injustice, if one provides CCR with all the laurels for breaking through to Bastogne. When Patton wrote to Gaffey and implied that the success was gained by the efforts of his entire division, he was absolutely correct. For the fact of the matter is that CCR could not have done it, were it not for the roles played by both CCA and CCB. Prior to CCR's breakthrough on the late afternoon of December 26, CCB and CCA had traded blows with the strongest part of the German defenses south of Bastogne. When CCB moved perilously close to Bastogne on December 23, they became a magnet for the available German armor, and secured the dubious distinction of being the first opponents in combat of Hitler's massive JagdTigers. Likewise, CCA had drawn its share of armor and towed anti-tank weapons, and had to fight over terrain that was more difficult than that faced by the other two combat commands.

This isn't to say that CCR had a cake walk on December 25 and 26; it was far from that, to be sure, and Abrams and his team carried out attacks by combined arms along the way that were unequalled by the other combat commands up to that point in the battle. But the perspective on the true team effort must not be forgotten. Success was achieved through the combined efforts of all three combat commands. General Wood certainly would not have wanted it recognized any other way.

21. Widening the Corridor

Hitler Responds

Adolph Hitler was enraged at the news that the Fourth Armored Division had broken through to Bastogne. The division that had foiled his counterattack back in September had now struck again, this time driving a stake through the heart of his last, great offensive. Having learned of the Fourth Armored's achievement, he shifted his attention from the fanciful goal of Antwerp, to the seemingly more realistic objective of Bastogne. Under the rallying decree that "Bastogne must be cleared," Hitler ordered that the SS panzer divisions were to be pulled from the line in the north and sent south to digest Bastogne. The Fuehrer Begleit Brigade and 3rd Panzer Grenadier Division would join them. Other reserve units, such as the 167th Volksgrenadier Division, would also be sent to the scene.

Hitler, in all his madness, continued to believe that somehow, someway, victory could be forged from the mountain of defeats that had been piled upon his doorstep. He beckoned his followers to fight on, to the last:

> We have had unexpected setbacks — because my plan was not followed to the letter, but all is not lost. The war cannot last as long again as it has already lasted. Nobody could stand it, neither we nor the others. The question is, which side will crack first? I say that the side that lasts longer will do so only if it stands to lose everything. We stand to lose everything. If the other side announces one day, 'We've had enough!' no harm will come to them. If America says, "Cut! Stop! No more American boys to Europe!" it won't hurt them. New York remains New York… Nothing changes. But if we say "We've had enough, we're packing up" — then Germany will cease to exist.

Hitler was not about to call off the fight. In fact, the "Battle of the Bulge" was about to enter its period of greatest intensity. And Bastogne, which had already played a pivotal role in the battle, would now become a magnet for the Germans, as they threw all of their available resources against the capture of the elusive town. If nothing else, Bastogne had become a symbolic trophy that Hitler was determined to win.

417

CCR Maintains the Corridor

As the sun rose over the battlefield on the morning of December 27, there were plenty of reasons for the Americans to celebrate. But there was also an incredible amount of work remaining to be done.

The most immediate imperative was that the corridor be widened so that safe passage in and out of Bastogne was more certain. To say that the corridor into Bastogne was narrow and dangerous would be an understatement.

On December 27, the light tanks of D/37 spent the entire day escorting vehicles in and out of the town via the dirt road connecting Assenois to Bastogne. The first column of ambulances and trucks reached Bastogne at 5 A.M., under the cover of early morning darkness. The ambulances returned with the most precious cargo of all: 652 wounded men who were in need of medical attention after six days of isolation. Another airlift of supplies took place that day, in some respects serving as testimony to the fragile nature of the corridor.

An even greater imperative for widening the corridor was that, in the long run, Patton needed more breathing room for inserting additional units into the Bastogne area for the continuation of his offensive. In the grand scheme, Bastogne was but a waypoint. The battle could not be called complete until the German salient had been severed or reduced (Patton's preference being the former). In order to accommodate these goals, the Neufchâteau-Bastogne highway had to be opened from the southwest, and most important of all, the Arlon-Bastogne highway had to be opened from the south.

To the surprise of the staff of the 37th Tank Battalion, Colonel Blanchard issued an order early on December 27 for all of CCR to "pick up everything and move it all into Bastogne." Major Bautz called Blanchard's order into question, saying, "Sir, I don't think we want to do that. You know we've been fighting along here. We've got a light tank company over here, on the flank, we've got B Company over here on this flank, and A Company over here, while C Company is in there with contact." Blanchard was apparently in no mood to debate Bautz. His reply was gruff: "I said move it in."

Following Blanchard's order would have resulted in the removal of all of the flank protection for the corridor. It could have been a disaster. Cognizant of the potential repercussions, Bautz raised Abrams on the radio in his tank, and explained to him what was going on. Abrams didn't hesitate in his response. "Hell, no," he said. "You do as you suggested. Just bring in the trains of the 101st and the other stuff in the headquarters." Blanchard, who had been conspicuously absent from the scene of any of the fighting during the advance into Bastogne, was apparently none the wiser.

While Major Bautz and Lt. Colonel Abrams had balked at Colonel Blanchard's order to move all of CCR into Bastogne, some of its elements did continue into the town. The 94th AFAB and the battery of 155mm howitzers from the 177th FAB moved forward and took up firing positions on the southeast edge of the town. The tanks of A/37 and B/37 continued to hold positions to the left of the main road leading into Assenois, in order to protect against a possible German counterattack from that direction; they would hold those positions until 8:15 A.M. on the morning of December 29. Later in the day on December 29, the 37th Tank Battalion was pulled back to a reserve

Men of the 10th AIB advance toward Bastogne. December 27, 1944 (National Archives Photograph SC198452).

position near Clochimont. All was quiet there, save for the night of December 29/30, when its positions were bombed six times by German planes.

Traveling the road from Assenois to Bastogne was not for the faint of heart. Even though the biggest news story of the war was in Bastogne, some very famous correspondents spent December 27 in the shattered ruins of Assenois, unwilling to take the risk of driving down the highway that the Fourth Armored had fought so hard to open. Walter Cronkite (then employed by United Press), John Driscoll (New York Herald Tribune), Norman Clark (London News Chronicle), and Cornelius Ryan (London Daily Telegraph) had taken a stab at getting into Bastogne, but the enemy still had portions of the road under fire, and when the whistling of bullets got too close for comfort, the newsmen retreated back toward Assenois.

The four men sought cover and warmth in a battered, abandoned house near Assenois (the daytime temperature had settled in the 20's for the fourth consecutive day). Though well ventilated from the prior day's battle, the structure still offered a windbreak that made it a better option than standing out in the open. They were not alone, as some officers from the Fourth Armored joined them for precisely the same reason. One of the men from the Fourth stood watch outside; this was no time to get

Armored infantrymen from the 10th AIB advance on December 27, 1944 (National Archives Photograph SC199295).

careless, since the enemy was not much more than half a mile away on either side of the corridor.

As the men huddled away from the cold, they heard the sound of a lone American jeep approaching from afar. As the jeep sped down the road, it seemed to draw the enemy's attention, and the Germans started throwing small arms fire toward the vehicle at an increasing rate. But the driver was not deterred, and continued speeding forward in the direction of the newsmen's enclave.

As he watched the lone jeep plow ahead with seeming ambivalence toward the enemy threat, John Driscoll remarked, "Look at that nut! When are they going to learn?" To the newsmen, the jeep driver was like other reckless men they had seen during their coverage of the war. And recklessness often had but one reward.

None too sure that the jeep would make it as far as their shelter, the newsmen placed bets on its fate. The odds were one in three that the jeep would make it. Had they known who was in the jeep, perhaps they would have bet the other way.

The vehicle screeched to a halt in front of the impulsive gamblers. Sgt. Charlie Kartus leapt from the driver's seat and darted for cover in the building. His passenger, in stark contrast, strolled leisurely toward the doorway where the newsmen and officers stood.

The passenger was General Maxwell Taylor, commander of the 101st Airborne Division. He was determined to rejoin his men at Bastogne, having missed the battle up to this point by virtue of having been in Washington, D.C., when the German offensive began. He returned to the battlefield as soon as he could, and up to this point, had been counting on entering Bastogne in the company of General Dager's CCB. But having heard the surprise news that CCR had broken through the evening before, he was now looking to exploit the only opening into the town, no matter how fragile and narrow its width.

Taylor explained to Cronkite and the other correspondents how anxious he was to link up with his proud division. An officer from the Fourth Armored cautioned him on the danger: "The corridor is so narrow you can spit across it. The Jerries have this road zeroed in for now." An offer was made to commandeer a tank or armored car to carry Taylor into Bastogne. When the men from the Fourth were unable to guarantee the timing of the trip, Taylor decided to take his chances with the jeep. With room for more passengers, he offered the correspondents a ride. Apparently, the general's courage had not rubbed off, as all four men declined the invitation.

With daylight fading, Sgt. Kartus revved up the jeep, and he and his lone passenger darted down the road toward Bastogne, where Taylor later enjoyed an evening cognac with General McAuliffe, who had so ably filled in for him in his absence. The correspondents, in stark contrast, spent the night shivering among the ruins of Assenois.

CCB Widens the Corridor

When Abrams decided to bypass Sibret in favor of his charge through Assenois, it was indeed a risky move. Had the Germans held Sibret in force, they might have struck a hard blow against CCR. But Abrams' gamble paid off, and there was no immediate German strike against his flank. The challenge now before the entire Fourth Armored Division was to widen the corridor into Bastogne.

On the morning of the 27th, CCB was echeloned just slightly behind and to the right of CCR. As mentioned previously, a patrol from the attached 2nd Battalion, 318th Infantry Regiment had made contact with the 101st during the small hours of the morning. CCB was now in a position to play a critical role in widening the corridor. If it advanced in force to the positions of the 101st, the existing corridor would stretch almost to the Arlon-Bastogne highway (it would remain the mission of CCA to clear the Arlon highway itself). The night before, Irzyk, Cohen, and Gardner had met over dinner and resolved to launch an "all-out effort" the following day to make firm contact with the 101st (the men were unaware at the moment that the patrol from Gardner's battalion was in the process of sneaking through to the perimeter).

Before CCB could close the final distance, the village of Hompre had to be secured. This turned out to be a quick, easy affair, despite Generalmajor Kokott's attempts to firm up the defenses of the town. The Germans had pulled out before the start of the attack, and Company E of Gardner's 2nd Battalion secured the town by 8:15 A.M.

As E Company moved into Hompre, G Company advanced on E's left, and F Company followed with the supporting Shermans of A/8. As they advanced, they drew fire from some 88s located in the woods east of Hompre. The tanks fired back, and called in air support to strike at the woods. The fighter-bombers soon arrived, and took out a dozen of the deadly guns.

With the threat to its flank relieved, the infantry battalion continued to advance north, until it drew close to the woods east of La Lune. Apparently, the 10th AIB was supposed to clean out this area, but they had either missed some Krauts, or the Germans had infiltrated back into the woods. In any event, they now fired on Gardner's weary troops. By nightfall, Gardner's battalion had drawn up to a line southeast of Assenois, where it settled in for the night. It was a nervous time, since reports had come in that 4,000 enemy troops, with 25 to 40 tanks, had been spotted in the woods east of his positions. Had the enemy attacked with a force of this magnitude, he was virtually powerless to do anything about it. His depleted infantry and handful of Shermans would have been overwhelmed. He warned his men to stay alert, and sweated out the night, no doubt hoping and praying for the best.

As the 2nd Battalion moved north, so too did the 10th AIB, supported by C/8 and B/8. The two infantry battalions advanced in tandem across more than a mile of open ground between Hompre and the woods. By 3 P.M., Major Cohen was ready to carry the attack into the forest. It was understood between Gardner and Cohen that the 10th AIB would carry the heavier burden of fighting in the woods, due to the depleted condition of the 2nd Battalion. The attack would primarily be an infantry affair, since the tanks were limited in their movement by a stream running south of the woods.

The attack commenced at 4:11 P.M. The armored infantrymen ran into brisk enemy fire as they advanced toward the forest. Though the tanks could not move all the way forward with the infantry, they came as close as possible in order to provide covering fire. To assist them, S/Sgt. Lewis Brazik "ran out into the open to direct a friendly tank against the enemy positions." The fight in the woods was extremely heavy, with the Germans determined to maintain their positions. But the American infantrymen were persistent in their cause, and by 7 P.M., the 10th AIB made contact with elements of the 101st Airborne Division. By a bit after 8 P.M., the armored infantrymen had punched completely though the woods, reaching the northern edge overlooking the Assenois road.

The Assenois corridor was now significantly more secure. And though CCR had opened the corridor some 26 hours earlier, the men of CCB were no less elated at their achievement on the evening of December 27. In the face of adversity unlike what either of the two other combat commands had faced, CCB had accomplished its mission. The infantry dug in for the night, no doubt relieved that, at least for the time being, they were no longer attacking. After six days of constant fighting, they were glad to have a moment of rest.

During the next two days, life for CCB would indeed take on a new tenor. Brigadier General Dager now had two primary concerns: guarding the long secondary road over which CCB had traveled, and defending the gap that still existed between CCB and CCA (the gap had narrowed considerably, however, and now stood at only 1.25 miles). All was relatively quiet on the front of CCB, but one notable exception to the calm occurred on the front of the 10th AIB, where 2nd Lt. James Swinderman led a patrol to attack an enemy machine gun nest that had been harassing his company. While Pfc. Frank Marieno braved small arms and artillery fire to set up his light machine gun in support of the Lieutenant, Swinderman "advanced in the face of enemy fire, silenced the enemy weapon, killed six Germans, and wounded three."

The 2nd Battalion, which had not yet drawn up to the line of the 101st, started the morning of December 28 with the objective of reaching the positions held by the airborne engineers. The attack was delayed when it was discovered that some of the mechanical components of the Sherman tanks were frozen from the harsh temperatures the night before, and had to be thawed before they could push off. When that was remedied, Companies G and E began their advance, with F trailing in reserve.

At 10 A.M., the infantry reached the 101st Airborne. The immediate reward for the infantrymen was that they continued on into the buildings on the southeast edge of Bastogne, and during the afternoon, earned a chance to clean up, change clothes, and get out of the cold. A belated Christmas Dinner was distributed to the men that evening. Turkey with all the trimmings was the featured item.

That evening, the 2nd Battalion was released back to its parent 80th Infantry Division. The unit's strength of only 126 men stood as stark testimony to the bitter fighting the battalion had endured during the four days it was attached to CCB. The toll had also been extremely high among its officers. When the battalion reached Bastogne, there were only four officers remaining between the three rifle companies. But even these numbers fail to paint the entire picture: the battalion received 79 replacements during its advance (only four of which were trained infantrymen; more evidence that the Americans were nearing the bottom of the barrel for replacements). Even with these replacements added to the total, they still only had 126 men standing.

Reinforcements and replacement vehicles were starting to come through for the other units as well, and on December 28, Major Irzyk was delighted when he received news that his battalion had just received seven brand-new M4A3E8 Sherman tanks. The improved 76mm gun would lend some weight to the 8th Tank Battalion's inventory.

That evening, at the HQ of the 8th, the commanders of the units that had participated in the relief of Bastogne assembled for a meeting that soon turned into a victory celebration. The mood of the group swung from "jovial" to "euphoric" when Irzyk informed them that there were no operations scheduled for the following day. With a great deal of emotion welling up within him, the 27-year-old major thanked everyone profusely for the effort they and their men had put forth during the trying days that were now behind them. He held out special thanks to Colonel Gardner and his 2nd Battalion, for they "were clearly instrumental in tipping the scales." He closed with the celebratory words: "We accomplished our mission," which grew a round of applause and cheers that punctuated their ordeal as nothing else could. The meeting collapsed into a casual celebration that lasted through the night and into the early hours of the morning.

As the officers celebrated, things were not completely quiet along the front of CCB. During the night, enemy planes bombed and strafed the positions of 1st Lt. Kenneth Hoffman's company from the 10th Armored Infantry Battalion. When a supply parachute containing 105mm howitzer shells caught fire, Lt. Hoffman, concerned not only that the ammunition would explode, but that the sight of the flames would draw back the enemy aircraft for another strafing run, threw himself on top of the fire in an attempt to smother it. Tec 5 Robert Hager (C/10) would perform a similar feat the very next night, when passing JU-88 bombers hit his company's position and set his half-track on fire. Wounded in the hands, he "disregarded the severe pain he was suffering and proceeded to fight the fire that was blazing in the engine and from several bedrolls." Even when the planes returned for another strafing run, he continued his fire-fighting effort until the flames were doused.

The night of December 29 saw one of the heaviest bombardments that the Germans threw against Bastogne during the entire battle. That night, enemy planes made several runs over the town. The positions of the 94th AFAB were hit by a string of five bombs that fell into the positions of A Battery. Sgt. Charles Kosiorowski was killed, and seven men of the 94th were wounded. Sensing that his support vehicles were too vulnerable, Lt. Colonel Parker ordered the ammunition and gasoline trucks out of Bastogne. They went to safer bivouac positions to the southwest, near Remoiville.

Parker had indeed been wise to send his vehicles out, for at 10:00 P.M., the heaviest bombardment of all struck Bastogne. Buildings crumpled underneath the power of the falling bombs, and men from the 101st Airborne and 53rd Armored Infantry Battalion were caught in the rubble. Some of the men from the 94th ran to the scene and, working by the light of the blazing ruins, began digging out the survivors.

West of the Corridor

While the situation looked bright on the east side of the corridor, the same could not exactly be said of the west side. CCR's long flank stretching down the Neufchâteau highway was indeed vulnerable. Some of the Hellcats from the 704th had already picked off a couple of German tanks that had attempted to close from that direction, and it was clear that more work was required to button up the this critical route leading into Bastogne. The most immediate need was to secure Sibret, which Abrams had bypassed in favor of taking the plunge through Assenois.

There were no more resources to be found from within the Fourth Armored Division, so Patton and Millikin would have to look elsewhere. With the situation on XII Corps' front now stable, Combat Command A of the 9th Armored Division was pulled from the line and reassigned to the Fourth Armored Division. It was a valuable addition, since the medium tank strength of the Fourth was down to less than 50 Shermans. CCA/9 was ordered to move to the left of CCR/4, and when it arrived on December 27, it would launch the attack against Sibret that Abrams had avoided the day before.

CCA/9 formed two task forces on the morning of December 27, and then began its drive up the Neufchâteau-Bastogne highway. TF Collins took the lead, but was held up by a minefield north of Vaux-les-Rosieres (the mines had been laid by the retreating Americans of VIII Corps). By nightfall, TF Karsteter had circled around toward Villeroux, but stopped outside of the village for the night. Meanwhile, TF Collins had finally navigated the minefield, and closed on Sibret. Collins sent in his lone company of Shermans to clear the town, but a small detachment from the 104th Panzer Grenadier Regiment managed to make a fight of it the entire night. The Germans pushed more men from the 39th Regiment into Vileroux, but American artillery, fighter-bombers, and the tanks of TF Karsteter chased them out.

On the morning of December 28, TF Collins tried to tighten its grip on Sibret by pushing north to the village of Chanogne. Upon reaching the crossroads there, the task force drew concealed small arms fire. The tanks quickly snuffed out the resistance, but with daylight fading, TF Collins stayed put at the crossroads for the night.

On the morning of December 29, TF Collins had quite a surprise served for breakfast. As the men chowed down their morning meal, a column of troops emerged from some nearby woods. An American captain shouted to the approaching soldiers, and in reply came a hearty "Good Morning" ... in German! What Generalmajor Kokott of the 26th Volksgrenadier Division had intended as a counterattack to retake Sibret quickly turned into a slaughter, as the Americans dropped their food and grabbed the nearest available weapons. Before the Germans could react, fifty of them were cut down, their bodies arranged neatly in the column formation they had held at the moment they stumbled into TF Collins.

The Germans were able to take some revenge on Collins' force, however. Late in the day, as TF Collins moved through Chenogne, the Shermans tanks leading the advance came under heavy anti-tank fire. Four Shermans were knocked out in rapid order, which led to the task force pulling out of Chenogne. That night, VIII Corps' artillery responded with a heavy barrage against whatever enemy forces had reoccupied the town.

TF Karsteter was not having much luck either at the end of the day on the 29th. While advancing on the town of Senonchamps, they ran into heavy German opposition, in the form of the 3rd Panzer Grenadier Division. Losses among the armored infantry were heavy, and when four American tanks managed to push into Senonchamps, they found themselves alone, as the armored infantry had failed to follow them in. The Shermans pulled back.

Unknowingly, on the afternoon of December 29, CCA/9 had stumbled into the positions of German units that were assembling for a large-scale counterattack against the Bastogne corridor. Set to take place on the morning of December 30, it would provide one final — and dramatic — test for the Fourth Armored Division during the Battle of the Bulge.

"We Must Have Bastogne!"

During the days following the relief of Bastogne, Adolph Hitler continued to lament the failure of his offensive. Despite the fact that he alone had chosen the time, place, and method for the attack, he wallowed in self-pity as he blamed everyone and everything other than himself for the course of events. "The horrendously bad roads" had thrown of the timetable; traffic congestion had plagued his SS panzer divisions as they tried in vain to negotiate the terrible routes that he himself had forced upon them; he blamed the petrol shortages on his tankers, accusing them of running their engines all night in order to stay warm in their panzers. And rather than giving due credit to the spirit and ability of the Americans who had held his last, great army in check, he pegged "remarkably bad luck" as one of the key ingredients of the recipe for failure.

Of all the American efforts in the Ardennes, none irked him like that of the 101st Airborne Division's stand at Bastogne, and of their subsequent relief by the Fourth Armored Division. Having pledged his remaining reserves to the capture of the town, he told his generals, "Above all, we must have Bastogne!"

22. Hitler's Last Gamble

Hollange

On the day that Lt. Boggess was destined to spur "Cobra King" toward a rendezvous with Lt. Webster of the 101st Airborne Division, Bastogne was just a faint glimmer in the distance for CCA. Some seven miles still separated Brigadier General Earnest from the culmination of his mission. As CCR and CCB stood on the eve of gratification, Earnest had only the prospect of stiff resistance from 5th FJ Division waiting for him.

On the morning of December 26, CCA took on the challenge of assaulting Hollange. This was another case of a town that did not rest directly along CCA's axis of advance, but Earnest could not afford to bypass it; his attack lacked depth, and there were no trailing units available to invest the enemy position. Making it a further necessity was the fact that the Germans had established a considerable force at Hollange. A sizeable portion of the artillery supporting the 5th FJ Division was located in this area, along with a battalion headquarters. And in the surrounding hills, estimates were that some 30 machine gun nests were in place to guard the approaches into the town.

At 8 A.M., a platoon of C/51, supported by a platoon of tanks from A/35, started off the attack by driving for Hill 490 northeast of Hollange. At 9:40 A.M., they were just south of the road running east from Hollange when the Germans brought down heavy fire on their positions. A Sherman was knocked out by anti-tank fire coming from their right. Artillery and rockets pounded them from the northeast, while direct fire came in from the north and northwest. Small arms fire snapped at them from within Hollange itself. The Americans called for an air strike on the town, and an air recon mission was requested for the area around Hill 490. Amidst all of this activity, C/51 was brought to a halt east of Hollange.

While C/51 struggled west of the Arlon highway, A/51 continued to advance north along an axis east of the highway. When the armored infantrymen reached a position north of the road that connected Strainchamps and Honville, they too were hit by heavy artillery fire, and like C/51, came to a halt. At 10:15, the Shermans of B/35 moved forward to assist the stalled armored infantrymen.

With the tanks now working in close support, A/51 resumed its advance. Its left flank was anchored on the highway, and its right flank extending out 1200 yards to the east. By 11 A.M., the Americans reached the reverse slope of Hill 460 (southeast of Hollange). A/51 had now drawn roughly abreast of C/51; A Company was still operating east of the highway, while C Company remained to the west.

Meanwhile, the requested air support had arrived. The pilots located several gun positions 600 yards north of Hollange, and attacked them at 12:10 P.M. A platoon of armored infantry from C/51, with two platoons of tanks in support, gained Hill 490 at 2:00 P.M. The Germans were not inclined to abandon Hollange, however, and continued to send small arms fire in their direction.

At 2:25 P.M., the Americans hit Hollange with a ten-minute artillery barrage. The tanks fired high explosive rounds over the heads of the American infantry as the supporting artillery pounded the town. The strength of the barrage allowed several elements of CCA to close on the town. Two platoons of C/51, supported by one platoon of Shermans from A/35, struck Hollange from the northeast. Some of the armored infantry, followed by three other Shermans from A/35, advanced toward the town from the south, moving along the railroad line running in from that direction (they were completely confined to the railroad embankment, due to marshes that were on both sides of the tracks). Meanwhile, the Shermans of B/35, which had just come up from the Warnach area, moved into position to the east of Hollange. As they advanced, they lost three tanks to enemy anti-tank fire coming from the woods off to their right. They neutralized the gun, but not before it had done significant damage to their already reduced numbers.

The American infantry and tanks attacking from the north carried the main weight of the attack against the Germans defending Hollange. They plunged into the town just as the artillery fire was lifted, and by 5:30 P.M., had secured the town for CCA. A/51 was then placed in position on the heights overlooking the town from the northeast.

In the process of capturing Hollange, CCA overran over half the artillery that had been supporting the 5th FJ Division. One of the self-propelled howitzer battalions from the 406th VAK, along with a battalion of Nebelwerfers from the 18th Volkswerfer Brigade, were taken out of action by the end of the day. All told, the Americans raked in some 300 Germans as prisoners at Hollange (174 of these were taken by the 51st AIB).

As for the Americans, the 51st AIB suffered 26 casualties during the fight. Lt. Carl Green, commander of C/51, was among the wounded, and was awarded the Silver Star for heroism during the battle for Hollange. A/35 lost one tank to enemy anti-tank fire during the assault.

Clearing the Highway   •

With CCA's left flank protected by the units attacking Hollange, the light tanks of D Company, supported by the 105mm assault guns, resumed the attack up the axis of the main highway. There was a significant crossroad located east of Hollange, and it fell on D Company's shoulders to take it.

There were several buildings near the crossroad, and the Germans were holding them in strength. The enemy paratroopers fired panzerfausts at the approaching M5s and Sherman assault guns, but the fire was ineffective. The assault guns moved in close, and began shooting up the houses. In fact, they moved up so close that the tankers were tossing grenades into the houses from the open turrets of their Shermans. Fifty enemy soldiers eventually surrendered, but not before 15 to 20 of their fellow paratroopers had been killed. The Americans began to see signs of wear, fatigue, and discouragement among the German prisoners. The relative lack of German artillery support, which was primarily due to ammunition constraints, was demoralizing for the German troops (especially when they were continuously on the receiving end of the American howitzers).

As the forward elements of CCA dug in for the night near Hollange, B/51 was moved forward to take up positions to the right of A/51. But this was not B/51's first movement of the day; for that, we must return to the early morning, and pick up the story of the 318th RCT's 1st Battalion.

The 1st Battalion Attacks

On the morning of December 26, the 1st Battalion continued its attack from the area of Tintange, advancing over incredibly tough, heavily wooded terrain. The battalion's primary mission remained the protection of CCA's right flank. To help give its depleted ranks some additional support, B/51 was taken out of its reserve position at Warnach and attached to the 1st Battalion.

The armored infantry had been sent to their positions the previous night, and they now occupied a stretch of woods along the Warnach-Tintange road. On the morning of the 26th, they would attack north through the woods to the west of the Grousse Mauischt, thus clearing the right flank of the 51st and the left flank of the 1st Battalion. Four tanks from C/35 would be attached for support. The 1st Battalion's left flank would rest on the east bank of the Grousse Mauischt, and they would advance alongside B/51, accompanied by the other four Shermans of C/35.

Both the 1st Battalion and B/51 were scheduled to attack at 8:00 A.M., but Major Connaughton was concerned that if he pushed his 1st Battalion ahead at 8:00 A.M., his men on the left flank (on the opposite bank of the creek from B/51) would be in danger of pushing into the line of fire of the armored infantry. The 1st Battalion was already echeloned farther north than B/51; ideally, he wanted the two elements to draw abreast of one another and then advance in tandem. He asked Brigadier General Earnest for a half hour delay in the advance of the 1st Battalion, which he figured would give B/51 time to draw even with his left flank. Earnest gave him permission to execute the attack in this fashion.

Major Connaughton began his morning with a visit to B/51, to help ensure that they got rolling on schedule. It was after 8:30 when Connaughton returned to his battalion, only to find that his men had not gotten off on schedule. The major approached his S-2, who he had charged with overseeing the start of the attack while he was visiting with B/51. He asked the 2nd lieutenant what the delay was, and the S-2 replied,

"There isn't much in the way of orders that a second lieutenant can give to captains and first lieutenants." He supplemented his excuse by saying that the requested artillery support had been delayed.

Shortly after this exchange between the two men, the artillery support began to fall, but the first rounds came dangerously close to the positions of the 1st Battalion. An additional delay was thus incurred as the artillery fire was adjusted. Unfortunately, the next salvos seemed to grossly overshoot the target area, as the rounds could not be seen or heard on impact. A third adjustment was called for, but the result appeared to be no better than the second concentration.

At this point, having lost valuable time, and knowing that B/51 was already working its way north on the opposite side of the stream, Connaughton called off the artillery concentration, and pushed his men forward without the benefit of the howitzers. It was now nearly 10 A.M., almost two hours after the time that Brigadier General Earnest had initially wanted the attack to take place.

B/51's advance through the woods west of the creek was largely uneventful. When the company reached the line defined by the road running generally east-west from Strainchamps to Tintange, it reverted back to the control of the 51st AIB. A vignette from one of the combat interviews with Major Alanis presents an interesting picture of the goings-on at CCA:

> Actually, the company was not supposed to revert to battalion control until grid 64 was reached. This grid line was about 800 yards north of the road. Capt. Daniel M. Belden, CO of Company (B/51), said when General Earnest gave him the grid line as a point of reversion he thought it quite peculiar since "grid lines are not distinctive on the terrain." So he said he was very happy when he was contacted by Major Rockafeller, the Bn Ex. O, at the road and began once again to work with his own Bn—this on December 26th.

Then in another sign that the new commander of CCA was still going through a learning curve:

> Lt. Col. Alanis said that he did not know until the time of the interview that his B Company was attached to the 1st Battalion, 318th. Capt Belden had received this verbal order direct from General Earnest.

This is confirmed when reading the daily battalion diary of the 51st AIB, wherein they report B Company as being in reserve at Warnach all the way through December 27!

The advance of the 1st Battalion was a more eventful affair. During the battalion's advance, the air force launched repeated strikes by P-47s against the Auf Berg Chateau, located on the north bluff of the Grande Molscht. German prisoners of war, captured the previous night, had stated that the Germans were holding the chateau in force, and the Americans were apparently not going to take any chances with it. The chateau afforded the Germans a commanding position overlooking the route the 1st Battalion would have to take toward Honville, their next major objective. It became imperative that the Americans capture the chateau.

After a thorough going over by the flyboys, one of the Sherman tanks from C/35 advanced toward the chateau "and took several unresisting prisoners." The infantry then continued to lead the advance, with the tanks trailing behind in support. They moved over the open ground east of the Bois de Melch, and then entered the woods via a trail leading toward Honville. Four of the Shermans continued to follow the riflemen of the 1st Battalion, while the other three Shermans were ordered to move further west to tie in with B/35.

Up to this point, Major Connaughton had reported that enemy resistance was lighter than it had been the day before at Tintange. Within two hours of his belated start, he had reached his next phase line (though he had lost contact with B/51 in the woods). It is interesting to note that as the 1st Battalion swept through this area, stragglers from the 28th Infantry Division made their way into the 1st Battalion's aid station, seeking treatment for exposure. In some cases, their combat boots were frozen to their feet and had to be cut off. These men had been isolated for at least a week, and were probably stealing their way back from the battle at Wiltz.

The next stage of the attack was the assault on Honville. As the 1st Battalion arrived at the edge of the woods south of the town, the four tanks from C/35 took up positions in support of the infantry. The doughboys closed on the town by pushing out across an open field and on toward the Nathelet River. The Air Corps was then called in once again, and proceeded to plaster Honville with great effectiveness (it was reported back to the 35th Tank Battalion that the town had been "flattened" by the air strikes).

As the infantry battalion prepared to advance over the remaining open ground to take Honville, the tank destroyers accompanying the task force spotted some Germans east of Sainlez (a key road running northwest to southeast connected Sainlez to Honville). The TD gunners opened fire, and immediately were fired upon themselves by Germans still hiding in the rubble of Honville. The telltale sound of 88mm shells creased the air, and the TDs and Shermans, which were sitting out in the open in plain view from Honville, pulled back to the south behind the crest of a hill. The tanks then circled south of the Le Chay woods in order to advance up the main road into Honville in support of the infantry. They were delayed en route, however, by a mined bridge and roadblock.

The 1st Battalion went ahead with the attack without the support of the tanks. B Company was sent around the east side of Honville, while C Company approached the town from the west. As they attacked, they disposed of the towed 88mm gun that had chased off the American armor. The 1st Battalion proceeded to clear Honville on its own.

The three Sherman tanks of C/35, which had made contact with B/35, now returned to Honville, where they joined the balance of C Company's four Shermans. All seven tanks of C/35 then took up mutually supporting positions with the infantry in and around Honville, where they remained for the night.

As the attack against Honville was in progress, a very regrettable incident took place involving Major Connaughton, who, in the eyes of any objective observer, had done a terrific job leading the battalion during the past two days. His commanding officer, Colonel McVickar, arrived on the scene with one burning question in mind: What time had the morning attack jumped off? The major replied, "About 0930 or 1000." MacVickar then relieved Connaughton of his command on the spot, and turned the battalion over to Captain Gaking. Connaughton tried to explain the events surrounding the morning attack, but "he did not have a receptive listener."

The Right Flank of CCA — December 27

On December 27, a new problem began to emerge for Earnest's command. As CCA made greater progress up the Arlon highway, a gap began to develop between the Fourth Armored and the neighboring 26th Infantry Division. Initially, the 6th Cavalry Squadron had been brought up to fill the zone in between the two divisions. But as CCA continued its trek to the north, the cavalry was hard pressed to cover the increasing distance between them.

There was also a growing concern that, with CCR's breakthrough to Bastogne on December 26, the Germans might make a concerted effort to cut the fragile umbilical cord that ran through Assenois. A German attack with that goal in mind would probably be launched from the east, since that was the area of the battlefield most easily reached by German reinforcements. CCA/4, even with 1/318 attached, didn't have enough strength to prevent such an attack and still continue its drive up the Arlon highway.

The solution was to bring up the 35th Infantry Division to take over the area held by the 6th Cavalry Group. The 35th would also go on the offensive, attacking to the north alongside CCA/4. If successful, the entire right flank of the Fourth Armored would be shielded, and CCA could drive hard as they sought to become the last of the three combat commands to achieve their mission.

The 35th Infantry Division began their attack on December 27, and attacking through the area around Tintange, pushed through to capture the large town of Surre. Progress by the 35th along other portions of the front provided a measure of relief for CCA/4.

On December 27, the task force built around the 1st Battalion was assigned the mission of capturing Liverchamps and securing the road leading north toward Losange. Due to the terrain in that area, the tanks of C/35 were restricted to the road. En route to the first objective, the Americans encountered a battery of six-barreled nebelwerfers. The task force got the drop on all four of the nebelwerfer crews, and before the Germans could fire a shot, the Americans destroyed the rocket launchers. Upon reaching the area of Liverchamps, the Shermans of C/35 took up positions on the high ground south of the village. From there, they shelled Liverchamps in preparation for the advance of the 1st Battalion. The infantry moved in against light resistance, and soon controlled the town. (Late in the day, paratroopers from the 15th FJ Regiment, who were retreating from Sainlez (see below), stumbled into the rear area of the 1st Battalion. A sharp fight ensued, and the fight didn't conclude until after dark. But the Americans held their ground).

The casualty rate for the 318th's 1st Battalion had continued to rise. After 6 days of virtually non-stop action, the infantrymen were getting absolutely worn down. The freezing temperatures and deep snow made frostbite and trench foot problems of a magnitude almost equal to that of combat casualties. The dire shortage of infantrymen was really being felt.

To help fill the void, thirty military policemen were pressed into service as infantry, and were assigned the mission of accompanying the tanks on the second leg of their mission. The MPs mounted up on the tanks, and started north to secure the road leading to Losange.

The mission came to an abrupt end about 1000 yards outside of Liverchamps. A dead end in the road had accomplished what the Germans could not, and the task force had to turn about. Unfortunately, even though the enemy was not encountered during the mission, the 35th lost two more tanks along the road; one got stuck, and another threw a track. The five remaining Shermans of C/35 now took an alternative route, and headed down the road leading out of Liverchamps to the east. They had advanced about 1500 yards northeast of Liverchamps, when they were greeted at a crossroads by fire from a panzerfaust. The lead tank was knocked out, and with darkness drawing near, this was enough to discourage any further advance. The four remaining Shermans returned to Liverchamps, where they spent the night. They would remain there the following day until relieved by the newly arrived 3rd Battalion of the 134th Infantry Regiment (35th Division). The arrival of the 134th RCT also allowed for the withdrawal of the battered 1st Battalion of the 318th RCT.

CCA's Main Axis of Advance — December 27

At 8:00 A.M., A/51 and C/51 resumed their march northward astride the Arlon highway. They were supported by the remaining tanks of A/35 and B/35, which advanced strictly along the area west of the road, which provided better defilade from the suspected enemy positions near Sainlez. The plan called for the tanks and infantry moving on the west side of the highway to advance to a point north of Sainlez, and then swing east to support the infantry that would be assaulting the town from the south.

The advance was conducted behind a rolling artillery barrage, and had gone about 800 yards when small arms fire erupted from some buildings about 400 yards west of Sainlez. C/51 was held up until Shermans from the 35th plastered these buildings with direct fire. The armored infantrymen then closed on the enemy positions and cleaned them out. During the fight, however, an enemy assault gun appeared at the mouth of a trail leading out of the woods north of Sainlez, and destroyed two or three Shermans before P-47s supporting the attack descended and silenced the enemy armor.

With the areas to the north and west of Sainlez cleared, the infantry prepared to attack the town. At 10 A.M., A/51 moved into position to attack Sainlez. B/51 moved up to support their right flank. A/35, which had by now been reduced in strength to only five Shermans (but only had enough crewmembers for four of them), provided direct support from north of the village, while the seven remaining Shermans of B/35 fired from the west.

An artillery barrage hit the town, and A/51 followed quickly behind it, applying marching fire as it advanced. As the armored infantry reached the edge of Sainlez, the Germans brought down mortar and artillery fire of their own. The supporting Shermans added the weight of their 75mm guns to the attack; one of the infantry platoon leaders mounted the deck of the tank platoon leader's Sherman and relayed the requests for direct fire support missions that were being called in by his men via a "walkie-talkie." The 15th FJ Regiment provided stubborn resistance at Sainlez. "After savage house-to-house fighting, the town was taken at 1350."

With Sainlez secured, B/51 advanced through the positions of A/51, and drew abreast of C/51. B/51 and C/51 then resumed the advance in tandem. Meanwhile, A/51 remained behind to consolidate their positions and outpost Sainlez.

B/51 had only been on the march for about an hour when, at 2:55 P.M., they were pinned down by machine gun and 20mm fire emanating from the northeast. American artillery support was brought into play once again and silenced the enemy guns. Both companies of armored infantry, supported by B/35, continued to advance north, and penetrated into the very thick woods north of Sainlez. Upon reaching a clearing, the tanks encountered hostile anti-tank fire that soared over their heads. The Shermans pulled back behind some cover on the south edge of the woods.

The two armored infantry companies drew to a halt when daylight was spent. C/51 remained on the left of the highway, while B/51 took up positions on the right. A/51 remained in its positions back at Sainlez.

It had been another tough day for the men of the 51st. The battalion had suffered 47 casualties, 15 of which were the result of frozen feet and exposure. New men were often the most vulnerable, due to their lack of experience. This applied to enlisted men and officers alike. Lt. Hoke, a new officer in place for less than 24 hours, was among the four men from the 51st killed that day by enemy machine gun fire.

The battle was also taking its toll on the men and machines of the 35th Tank Battalion. On December 28, the 35th reported that only nine medium tanks remained out of the 35 they had at the outset of the battle on December 22. But the German losses continued to exceed what the units of CCA were suffering (for example, on the 27th, 161 prisoners were taken from the 5th FJ Division). CCA had dealt the 15th FJ Regiment a series of deadly blows during the days since December 22. They had done likewise to the 14th FJ Regiment at Hollange. And they now found themselves squared off against elements of the 5th Engineer Battalion and the 13th FJ Regiment. They were getting a taste of everything that the 5th FJ Division had to offer.

CCA — December 28

The frigid weather continued on December 28. It was wearing on the men, who had been trudging through snow and up and down the steep hills and ridges that characterized the area along this section of the Arlon highway.

C/51 and B/51 moved out abreast at 8:00 A.M., but were slowed after only 400 yards by a minefield between Bois du Vicars and L'Ardoisiere. They continued their advance, however, and the engineers came forward to clear the obstacles.

At 11:15 A.M., B/51 prepared to attack Chateau Losange, which had earlier been the HQ for Heilmann's 5th FJ Division. Dense woods flanked the castle to the east and west, and the approach from the south was blocked in part by a pair of lakes and a stream. Tough resistance could be expected, as the chateau was now reported to be housing a regimental command post.

One platoon was sent through the woods to the west of the chateau, while another platoon moved through the woods on the right. Shermans from B/35 moved into position on open ground south of the chateau, from where they would provide direct fire support. The enemy responded with brisk small arms fire, but the flanking maneuver conducted by the infantry, combined with the firepower of the tanks, resulted in the capture of Chateau Losange by 3:50 P.M.

The two armored infantry companies continued their march to the north, with C/51 on the left and B/51 on the right. As C/51 began to emerge from the L'Ardoisiere Forest, it received heavy small arms fire from Hill 530. B/51 tried to advance further on the right, but it received heavy mortar and small arms fire from the east. The Sherman tanks supporting the advance of B/51 and C/51 encountered two enemy tanks near Lutrebois, and were successful in driving off the panzers. The American tanks then took up positions along the edge of the woods, where they watched over the approaches to the town. About four hours into their watch, the German infantry launched a local counterattack. At one point, the 2nd Platoon of B/35 was surrounded, but when they started to maneuver in order to comply with an order to withdraw, their movement seemed to scare off the Germans. The Shermans pulled back toward the relative safety of the clearing near Chateau Losange. The headquarters of the 51st AIB joined them later that afternoon.

In response to the stiffening German defense, A/51 was now brought forward for extra support, and was inserted on the right of B/51, since that was where most of the German resistance seemed to be focused. The enemy's resolve had indeed stiffened, especially in front of the 35th Infantry Division. Very little progress was made that day by the 35th, which left CCA concerned that yet another gap might open up on their right flank. Compounding Earnest's worry was the news that the 1st Battalion, worn as it was (only 96 riflemen remained), had been ordered to return that day to the 80th Infantry Division.

But the 35th hadn't played all of its cards, as it was still holding one of its three infantry regiments in reserve (the 134th, commanded by Colonel Butler Miltonberger). Earnest asked that the 134th be inserted on the right of CCA, and that the fresh infantry regiment be given the task of seizing Lutrebois, a village east of the Arlon highway. That night, the 134th moved up to positions near Hompre, and would, on the following day, launch an attack toward the east, cutting across the Arlon highway toward Lutrebois.

On December 28, D/35 was assigned the mission of linking up with either the 101st or CCB. They contacted CCB that day near the woods east of Assenois. For the first time in the battle, the gap between the two combat commands had been closed.

CCA — December 29

On December 29, D/35 completed the second half of its mission when it linked up with the 101st at a point west of the Arlon highway. Eight days of hard fighting had preceded the rather uneventful link-up. Coming almost three full days after CCR's celebrated breakthrough, the men were probably just thankful to have survived the ordeal.

On this eighth day of constant attacking, the 51st AIB found itself hung up by German forces at Remoifosse, which was located astride the Arlon/Bastogne highway. The enemy troops on Hill 530 prevented C/51 from mounting an attack on the town, and also managed to pin down B/51. Meanwhile, the Germans had reinforced their position in Lutrebois with some self-propelled guns, which continued to hit the right flank of the 51st AIB with direct fire. Things were not getting any easier.

It was essential that Hill 530 be taken. At 9:30 A.M., under the cover of a heavy artillery barrage designed to pin down the Germans at Lutrebois, B/51 and B/35 captured the hill. This allowed C/51 to continue the advance and capture Remoifosse. Engineers were brought forward to clear the minefields and obstacles the Germans had placed along the main highway. The enemy at Lutrebois continued to attempt to harass the American forces now at Remoifosse, but every time the Germans raised their heads, the 51st AIB brought down an artillery strike to pin them down. Meanwhile, two platoons from A/51 came up to guard the right flank east of the Arlon highway.

The tanks of B/35 and infantry of C/51 continued moving north with the hope of contacting the 101st, which they knew was just a short distance ahead. At 11:30 A.M. on December 29, they made contact with the airborne midway between Remoifosse and Bastogne. Word quickly spread around the 51st that their mission had been accomplished, which served to bolster their sagging moral. After eight days of constant fighting, they were exhausted and spent.

The link-up had an ugly punctuation to it, however. Despite having general knowledge of their positions, the tank commanders still mistook the white-caped "Screaming Eagles" for the enemy, and proceeded to fire on the house that the paratroopers were using for a strongpoint (47 holes were later counted in the building). After the identity of the paratroopers was ascertained, and the link-up forged, B/35 was relieved by the four tanks of C/35, and then pulled back to the south to positions near Remoifosse.

The pressure on the 51st AIB was relieved a bit that afternoon when the 3rd Battalion of the 134th Infantry Regiment began its attack on Lutrebois. The 51st also received 90 replacements that day, which they desperately needed.

The Arlon highway was now clear all the way into Bastogne. The 51st AIB now turned to the east to face whatever threat the Germans might throw at the corridor. C/51 took up positions on the left, while B/51 occupied the right. A/51 remained back on the west side of the Arlon highway in reserve. The 35th Tank Battalion, depleted as it was, and the Hellcats of A/704 provided much needed anti-tank support covering the open ground now occupied by the armored infantry.

Hitler's Last Gamble

On the morning of December 30, the Germans launched their first large scale attempt to sever the Bastogne corridor since CCR's initial contact with the 101st on December 26. Hitler had set the attack in motion several days prior, but it took time to get the assigned divisions into position. Fortunately, CCA had concluded its portion of the Fourth Armored's mission just in time, with literally just hours to spare, and was positioned to meet the threat.

Hitler's attack was designed to strike at the relief corridor from both sides. If successful, two powerful forces — one attacking from the west, the other from the east —

would burst through the American defenses and link up at Assenois and, in the process, once again encircle the American units operating in Bastogne. Additional forces en route to the Bastogne area would then take on the task of ripping the town away from its defenders.

The attack from the east was to be carried out by the 167th Volksgrenadier Division, the 1st SS Panzer Division, the 14th FJ Regiment, and the 901st PG Regiment. General Field Marshal von Rundstedt laid the groundwork with his order of December 25, which read, in part:

1. It is of decisive importance that the enemy attack wedge in the area of Bastogne is smashed very quickly and with sufficient and sweeping forces and means.

2. For this I am in agreement that the 1.SS Panzer Division is to be quickly led into the Bastogne area in order to add force to the concentrated attack of the 3. Panzer-Grenadier Division and the 167. Volks-Grenadier division against the deep flanks of the American units. The units of the 1. SS-Panzer Division are to apply their forces in local strongpoints where necessary.

The 1st SS Panzer Division received its orders to move to the Bastogne sector on December 26. Shifting the division south from the Stavelot/Trois Ponts area was not an easy task, as the presence of American fighter bombers limited much of the division's road movement to the dead of night, when they could avoid the strafing and bombing of the *jabos*. As units of the 1st SS were relieved from the front, they assembled in an area stretching between Vielsalm and St. Vith. Portions of the division left the assembly area during the late afternoon of December 28. The column continued to snake through St. Vith during the early morning hours of December 29, but due to a lack of fuel, some of the units had to remain behind until they could be resupplied; most of those units finally departed at midday on the 29th.

Even though 100 percent of the division did not arrive on time, and even though they were running short of tanks due to the losses sustained by Kampfgruppe Peiper, the 1st SS Panzer Division was still a force to be reckoned with. It had two powerful regiments of panzer grenadiers, commanded by Hansen and Sandig. These units had been relatively inactive since December 22, and had not taken the sort of beating that other units along the northern part of the Bulge had experienced. Their towed divisional artillery was still intact. The reconnaissance battalion, however, had been decimated, and now stood at only one hundred men and two armored cars (it had started the battle with over one thousand men). And as for the most vital ingredient, the panzers, the division was able to field approximately 50 for its latest role in Hitler's offensive.

Mohnke's panzer division was inserted into the line to the right of the 14th FJ Regiment. There was no love lost between these two units (probably a function of the rivalry between Himmler of the SS and Goering of the Luftwaffe). The 14th FJ Regiment had taken a terrible beating at the hands of the Fourth Armored during the course of the past week. It would operate on the left of the 1st SS, with some elements working in direct conjunction with the panzer division.

The 901st Panzer Grenadier Regiment had also suffered heavily during its attempts to break into Bastogne. Though listed as a participant on the attack on December 30, its role was negligible. It had simply fought itself out during the preceding two weeks.

The 167th was a veteran division brought in from the Russian front. It had just arrived in the Ardennes, and was at full strength and well rested. The division had no assault guns or other mechanized support weapons, however, and very little transport. It would march into position to the right (north) of the 1st SS Panzer Division.

The boundary between the 167th and the 1st SS Panzer ran directly through the village of Lutrebois. The plan called for the 167th to attack toward the village of Remoifosse, astride the Arlon highway. Its regiments were arriving at the front in column formation, and rather then take the time to assemble in a linear formation, they would be fed into the battle in the order they marched in.

Model arranged for considerable artillery support. The 401st and 766th Volks-Artillerie Korps yielded 321 guns (the limitations on supply would hinder their effectiveness, however). In addition, the 15th and 18th Volks-Werfer Brigade and the 306th Nebelwerfers were assigned to support the attack. The 1st SS Panzer Division also had 34 towed guns and five self-propelled artillery pieces available to throw into the mix.

The 1st SS Panzer Division would attack with two kampfgruppes. KG Poetschke would launch its attack from Lutrebois, while KG Hansen struck from Villers-la-Bonne-Eau. The 14th FJ Regiment would supply additional infantry support for their attack, while the 15th FJ Regiment, operating still further to the south, would maintain defensive positions on the left flank. The German plan was upended late in the evening of December 29, however, when the 35th Infantry Division captured Lutrebois and occupied a portion of Villers-la-Bonne-Eau. Unexpectedly, the 1st SS had lost its staging areas for the attack.

Kampfgruppe Hansen

The 1st SS moved into position on the night of December 29, and thus had virtually no time to prepare for the attack over unfamiliar terrain. At dawn, the southern task force (KG Hansen) struck at Villers-la-Bonne-Eau. KG Hansen was composed of Hansen's own 2nd SS PG Regiment (minus one battalion), a reconnaissance platoon, a company of engineers, and the 1st SS Anti-Tank Battalion. They also were to have the support of paratroopers from the 14th FJ Regiment, and several of the massive Tiger Bs from the 501st Battalion.

The weather had once again turned in favor of the Germans, as a thick, low layer of clouds hung over the Ardennes. The rays of the morning sun began to cut dimly through the dripping, misty air that reduced visibility at ground level. As the Germans began moving into position for the attack, they were confident that they would not have any interference from the dreaded American fighter planes.

The paratroopers of the 14th FJ Regiment, which had already been holding positions in the area, led the way. They quickly surrounded the town, cutting off two companies from the 137th Regiment of the 35th Infantry Division. Seven of the Tiger B tanks were bought forward to hammer the American infantrymen at close range. Even in the face of the Tigers, the two companies (K and L) of American infantrymen held on. About two hours into the attack, Hansen was compelled to reinforce the effort with additional tanks and flamethrowers (some bitter animosity developed between the 5th FJ and 1st SS commander over the performance of the paratroopers). Faced with certain defeat and death, the Americans surrendered (only one American soldier managed to escape). The Germans tried to push out beyond Villers, but the 35th Infantry was fairly well dug in, and the SS could not expel the Americans from the surrounding woods.

Kampfgruppe Poetschke

The other Kampfgruppe had the benefit of advancing over terrain more favorable for tanks. KG Poetschke was given all of the division's combat-ready Panthers and Mark IVs. Its infantry support consisted of Sandig's 1st SS PG Regiment, and a single battalion from the 2nd SS PG Regiment. The plan called for KG Poetschke to capture Lutrebois, and then drive down the main road to the northwest. The terrain opens up considerably there, and would allow them to drive cross-country toward the Arlon highway, in the vicinity of Remoifosse. If all went well, the 167th VG Division would be driving in tandem on their right, and would emerge from a draw leading through the woods toward the area of Marvie. After achieving their initial objective of cutting the Arlon highway, they would continue on toward Assenois, where they would link up with the German units attacking simultaneously on the west side of the corridor.

As noted previously, the 35th Infantry Division had captured Lutrebois the night prior to the German attack. On the morning of the 30th, the 3rd Battalion of the 134th Infantry Regiment, commanded by Lt. Colonel W.C. Wood, was responsible for holding the town. One of his companies (L Company) held positions inside the town, while Companies I and K had dug in east of the village. Their heavy machine guns were emplaced so as to cover the road west of the village.

At about 4:45 on the morning of December 30, German tanks and infantry began moving into position. As they headed toward Lutrebois, they crossed over the open ground in front of I and K companies. The Americans called in a heavy artillery barrage to disrupt the attack. Some of the American guns lobbed shells at Lutremange, which was a key point on the road net leading to both Lutrebois and Villers-la –Bonne-Eau.

Unable to advance straight down the road under the peering eyes of the American artillery spotters, the Germans decided instead to make a sweeping attack around the north side of Lutrebois. Company L fought hard, but was eventually overrun by the Germans. The German infantry continued to press toward the west, but were held in check by the heavy machine guns that were positioned to cover the road.

As the German infantry struck at Lutrebois, seven panzers swept north of the town and continued to the west, but all were taken out of the battle before they could do any more damage. A platoon of tank destroyers from the 654th TD Battalion knocked out four of the enemy tanks; another two were knocked out of action by high explosive rounds delivered by the supporting artillery; the final tank was immobilized by a mine.

Shortly after 6:30 A.M., General Earnest of CCA/4 received news of the German attack. The 35th Infantry did not have an attached tank battalion, so the veteran division relied on their good friends from the Fourth Armored to provide them with some help against the strong armored thrust that the Germans appeared to be mounting.

In response to the new threat, Earnest turned all of his assets to the east. In order to free up CCA to face this threat, General Dager's CCB, which had by now virtually completed their part in the drive to Bastogne, began shifting its units to pick up some of the positions formerly occupied by CCA.

CCA Comes to the Rescue

The 51st AIB was the first unit from CCA to come to the aid of the 35th Infantry. The men of A/51 loaded up their halftracks and moved into position to back up the thin lines of the 2nd Battalion south of Lutrebois. Here, grenadiers from the 1st SS Panzer Division's 2nd PG Regiment had managed to slip through the woods in several places, and had infiltrated into the rear area of the 2nd Battalion (commanded by Major C.F. McDannel). The 2nd Battalion held on to its front line positions in the woods, despite the SS troops prowling behind them.

The 51st AIB command post was still located at Chateau Losange. During the early morning hours, men from the 3rd Battalion started falling back, along with their heavy weapons, and found their way to the area of the chateau. The Germans had followed on their heels, and at 8:45, the German machine guns were set up along the edge of the woods north and east of the chateau. It wasn't long before they opened up, sending a hail of bullets that struck the outer walls of the castle. Tracers bounced of the sturdy exterior and struck the vehicles parked around the Battalion CP.

The 51st HQ had outposted the area around the chateau with dismounted machine guns, and it was these guns that kept the Germans at bay at the edge of the woods. The Germans then brought down mortar fire on the American troops in and around the chateau. Two Sherman tanks from A/35 came forward to provide direct fire support, and they drove the enemy back into the woods with blazing fire from their machine guns and 75mm cannons.

The 167th VG Division made a heady advance toward and across the Arlon-Bastogne highway. Of all the German units that day, the 167th came closest to achieving their objective when they reached the edge of the woods southeast of Assenois. Once again, elements of the 51st AIB arrived just in time to stifle the German advance. Without the benefit of any tanks or assault guns of their own, the volksgrenadiers had to push across open ground without protection. American machine guns and artillery hammered the volksgrenadiers every time they left the cover of the woods. Some American fighter planes also appeared to take part in the deadly repulse of General Hoecker's vanguard. In the German general's own words, his lead battalion was "cut to pieces."

At about 11:00 A.M., the main body of German armor, which consisted of approximately 25 tanks, began to push northwest up the Lutremange-Lutrebois road. American artillery liaison planes spotted the tanks at 10:20 A.M., and they reported 20 to 25 Tiger tanks moving northwest from Lutremange to Lutrebois (the number was correct, but the type of tank was not). American ground attack aircraft moved in on the column, and knocked out 7 of the tanks. The remaining 18 panzers turned tail.

As the Thunderbolts from the XIX TAC were hitting the German tanks, war correspondent Martha Gellhorn happened to be at a forward command post (presumably of CCA), and had a ringside seat for some of the radio chatter taking place between the pilots and their ground controller. She overheard the ground controller calling the lead pilot to check on their success against the enemy armor formation:

GROUND CONTROLLER:	"Argue Leader, Beagle here. Did you do any good on that one?"
PILOT 1:	"Can't say yet"
PILOT 2:	"Three Tigers down there with people around them"
PILOT 1:	"Go in and get them. Don't stand there talking about it"

After a period of time, the lead pilot's voice came back over the speaker in the command post: "Got those three. Going home now. Over." The ground controller voiced his approval. "Good boys. Best there is. My squadron."

As the fighter planes roared over the landscape, I and K Companies of the 134th Regiment were still in position south of Lutrebois with a clear view of the road. From this vantage point, they too saw the enemy tanks in motion. Having used up all of their bazooka rounds earlier in the fight, some of the inexperienced replacements shot at the tanks with their rifles. The enemy tanks turned toward the woods and flushed out the GIs. The Americans were ordered to fall back and join the defensive line forming near Chateau Losange.

Some thirteen panzers, which were probably part of the original group of 18 that had been chased off the road by the American fighter planes, now reached the woods southwest of Lutrebois. They remained unseen for the moment by American ground forces. But one of the Fourth Armored's artillery spotters, 1st Lt. Robert Pearson, was flying overhead in a small cub plane, and spotted the Mark IV tanks from the air. Not totally sure of their identity at first, he dropped his altitude to only 75 feet, and made a pass over the tanks. If there was any doubt about the nationality of the tanks at that point, it was removed by the flurry of small arms fire that sailed toward his plane.

The spotter planes were observed by the German tankers, as evidenced by the recollections of Rolf Ehrhardt, a member of the German 7th Panzerkompanie, whose 10 Mark IVs were part of a larger group of German tanks advancing toward the Arlon-Bastogne highway. Ehrhardt later recalled that the spotter planes were so close that they could have hit them with rocks, let alone bullets. The artillery fire chased Ehrhardt's unit as it moved across the snow-covered ground, and knowing that they were under constant observation, the German tankers grew increasingly nervous.

The Americans did indeed have a close eye on the movement of the German tanks. In a bit of improvised communication, Lt. Pearson jotted down on a map the position and direction of movement of the German tanks. He dropped the map from the air, and the invaluable information soon made its way into the hands of Lt. John Kingsley, the commander of B Company of Delk Oden's 35th Tank Battalion.

Kingsley only had six Shermans remaining in his company after the long, trying

Shermans of the 35th Tank Battalion deployed near Sainlez. December 31, 1944 (National Archives Photograph SC198523).

fight up the length of the highway from Martelange to Bastogne. But he also had as a resource a platoon of Hellcats from the 704th TD Battalion. Some M-10 tank destroyers from the 654th TD Battalion (attached to the 35th ID) were also in the area.

Kingsley placed his Shermans into an ambush position behind a slight ridge that offered defilade cover. The spot was incredibly well chosen, as any enemy vehicles coming from the east would have to pass his position, and would probably do so without seeing the American tanks. The firing positions of B Battery of the 94th AFAB were only a few hundred yards away as well. As a precaution, they repositioned their guns to face the direction of the enemy armor, and camouflaged their guns with white sheets.

The lead group of six Mark IV tanks belonged to the 6. Panzerkompanie of the 1st SS Panzer Division. After bypassing Lutrebois to the north, the panzers headed west toward the Arlon-Bastogne highway. They advanced through the throat of the woods, emerged into the wider clearing, and headed for Remoifosse. The Mark IVs reached the Arlon highway at a point just north of Hill 535. It was then that they spotted the four Sherman tanks of C/35 to the north. The German tankers turned in that direction to engage the M4s, and in so doing, unwittingly turned the flanks of their tanks towards Kingsley's Shermans lurking behind the ridge.

The first German tank taken out with a direct shot from B Company was the command tank for the advance guard. The loss of their leader seemed to cause immediate confusion, as the balance of the tanks churned in various directions, apparently not knowing where the deadly shots had come from. Kingsley's six Shermans proceeded to quickly knock out all of the Mark IVs in the German's lead group of tanks.

As the battle progressed, Kingsley maintained an open channel on his FM radio with Delk Oden's headquarters. With each successive Mark IV that was knocked out, Kingsley would announce the score: "Got one ... Got two ... Got three...." And on he went. No sooner had the last of the Mark IVs in the first group been knocked out, when ten more Mark IVs came across the open ground in the same general direction as the first group of panzers. These belonged to the 7. Panzerkompanie.

As Oden received the great news from Kingsley, he in turn radioed the results into CCA's command post. Martha Gellhorn was present to hear that end of the radio chatter as well. "We got ten and two more coming. Just wanted to keep you posted on the German tanks burning up here. It's a beautiful sight, a beautiful sight, over."

Radio communication between the 6th and 7th Panzerkompanies had broken down. Once the tankers of the 7th Panzerkompanie lost visual contact with the 6th, they were figuratively in the dark. In the words of the company historian, this was about to become "the black day of the .7 Panzerkompanie"; perhaps the worst of days, in what had been a long war for the SS unit.

Manfred Thorn was a driver in one of the Mark IVs of .7 Panzerkompanie. He had originally been positioned further back in the column of 10 panzers, but his tank was ordered to the front of the column well before it reached the point of Kingsley's masterful ambush.

As he advanced, he spotted a lone Panther off to his right, standing idle at the end of the forest. Thorn guided his Mark IV out of the forest and onto the open landscape to the west. Ahead, he witnessed the tanks on the tail end of the 6. Panzerkompanie's formation vanish behind a small hill. Thorn raced his engine at high speed, and took off over the open ground toward Remoifosse, following in the wake of the 6. Panzerkompanie. While en route, he was instructed to head in the direction of Marvie, which was further to the north. The 7. Panzerkompanie set out in a wedge formation across the frozen plain.

Just before 3:15 P.M., Thorn's crew realized that some of the Mark IVs trailing behind them in the formation had already been turned into flaming wrecks. He estimated that, in perhaps no more than 10 minutes, the Americans had destroyed eight of the 7. Panzerkompanie's Mark IVs.

Thorn turned his panzer around, and raced back in the direction from whence he had come, passing the burning hulks of the Mark IVs on his way to safety. An increasing volume of enemy shells followed him, but it was his good fortune that they missed. He drove the tank behind the cover of a haystack near a farm located about 150 meters from the edge of the forest. Not knowing exactly where the American tanks had fired from, the shaken panzer crew remained in hiding for two hours; they would wait for sundown, when they could escape under the cover of darkness. In the meantime, they had lost all radio contact with the other tanks. The only intact German tank they had seen after their escape was the lone Panther parked near the edge of the woods. The crews of the destroyed panzers (most of them survived the hits against their tanks) had fled on foot toward the cover of the woods.

Rolf Ehrhardt, the driver of a Mark IV farther back in the column, saw the battle from a different perspective. As his tank rolled into the open terrain, he sensed that the American artillery had strengthened. He then saw the Mark IVs of the 6. Panzerkompanie suddenly move to the left, and at least one of the panzers began firing its cannon. Buried within the sound of the artillery, he recognized the telltale signature of anti-tank fire, which he identified as coming from the west. Two shots fell short in front of his Mark IV, and realizing they were sitting ducks, Ehrhardt gunned the tank in reverse, and tried to make it behind the cover of the tree line from which he had emerged.

Ehrhardt watched another Mark IV take a hit up ahead of him. Finally, it was his tank's turn to be struck. After the impact, his tank continued to run, but he hit the brakes and stopped the motor. His hatch had been ripped from the hull, and the 75mm cannon was torn from the turret.

Ehrhardt could hear the familiar steel ping of machine gun bullets striking the outside of the tank. Fearing that another armor piercing round would strike, he knew that he had to leave the tank and brave the fire of the American machine guns. As he tried to move as fast as he could through the hatch opening, he snagged his clothing, and fell to the ground beside the tank. Three of the other crewmembers were already outside the tank, and only his tank commander, Hauptsturmfuhrer Klingelhofer, remained inside. Ehrhardt climbed on the deck of the tank to see if he was still inside, but before he even had a chance to look inside the crippled Mark IV, Klingelhofer emerged from the loader's hatch.

All five of the crew members darted for the cover of the woods, making sure to keep the disabled tank between them and the apparent direction of the machine gun fire. One of the crew was wounded in the head, but able to walk. On the way to the woods, however, the commander was separated from them. Not knowing his immediate fate (they would find him later at an aid station, having suffered from shrapnel wounds to the chest, and burns on his face), they took off for the east, not knowing what had happened to the rest of their Panzerkompanie.

Another of the Mark IVs had the good fortune of falling far behind the rest of the column when it ran over a tree stump that caused its track to jump off the rollers. The crew reacted quickly, replaced the track, and was soon trying to catch up to the rear of the formation when the crew heard the sharp warning of *"Achtung Panzerfeind"* barked over the radio.

Still trying to catch up to the other tanks, and now out of radio contact, the only clue regarding the direction to follow was the sight of tracks in the snow leading off into the nearby forest. They followed the trail of the other Mark IVs, but they failed to see them. Once they reached a clearing, they decided to cut their engine in order to listen for the sounds of the other panzers. If they could hear them, it might help them determine the direction they needed to go.

The din of the motor was replaced with the cacophony of battle. Clearly, the rest of their friends were engaged in battle. They urgently went to start the engine to continue their pursuit, but were chagrined to find that it wouldn't start. As they struggled with a hand crank in repeated attempts to start the engine, an American fighter plane swooped down, forcing them to dive for cover in front of the tank. The airplane made another pass from a different direction, but failed to hit its target. Finally, the Germans got the engine to turn over. As they continued their advance, American artillery started pounding the area around them.

No sooner had they started out in search of their comrades, than they spotted their battalion commander, Sturmbannfuhrer Poetschke, running amidst the falling shells. The German officer raced toward the tank and joined the crew within the relative safety of their Mark IV. He asked them if they knew where the lone Panther was, to which the crew responded that, not only did they not know the location of the Panther; they had no idea where the entire company was! Poetschke ordered the tank crew to drive him back to his headquarters, where they waited for further instructions.

Of course, the Americans knew exactly where the panzer company was. Kingsley's six Shermans dealt with the second group just as they had the first. As Kingsley's scorecard crossed the double-digit mark, an elated Delk Oden announced over the open channel to Kingsley that he had just earned a battlefield promotion to the rank of Captain. Later, as Kingsley celebrated his success, he said:

> If that German tank company commander isn't dead I wish they would make him a battalion commander. I wish they were all that dumb.

The American tank destroyers were also getting some licks in, as they took on some Jagdpanzer IV/70s that were also on the move. They knocked out three of them, and sent some accompanying grenadiers scurrying for cover. With the already thin compliment of German armor now reduced to a small fraction of what it had been in the pre-dawn hours, the German attack ground to a halt.

The Fourth Armored's three artillery battalions also played a crucial role in throwing back the German attack. They threw a huge volume of shells in support of not only their own division, but also for the 35th Infantry Division and the units beating off the complimentary attack the Germans had launched against the west side of the corridor (an attack which CCA/9 and the newly arrived 11th Armored Division met head-on).

With the 1st SS Panzer Division's armored force decimated, the German attack began to lose steam. Just before noon, the 51st AIB was ordered to begin mopping up the forest whence the German attacks had been launched. The Germans still occupied the woods in strength, however, and the ensuing battle was far from being just a "mopping up" operation. Heavy fighting against the fanatical members of the 2nd SS Panzer Grenadier Regiment continued well into the night.

Overall, the Germans had some limited success pushing back the 35th Infantry Division along the woods east of the Arlon highway. They had inflicted heavy casualties on the infantry division, having overrun the equivalent of a battalion of infantry at Lutrebois and Villers-la-Bonne-Eau. But the timely response of CCA's 35th Tank Battalion and 51st Armored Infantry Battalion had ensured that the German advance toward Assenois would go no further.

Perhaps the greatest testimony to the renewed confidence that the Americans had in their ability to hold the corridor intact was the fact that General Patton drove into

Bastogne that same day. Passing within about one thousand yards of the German posi-
tions, Patton met with Brigadier General McAuliffe to award him the Distinguished
Service Cross for his effort at Bastogne. In his memoir, Patton wrote of the success of
December 30:

> This was probably the biggest co-ordinated counter-attack that troops under my com-
> mand have ever experienced. We were successful at all points.

And once again, the United States Fourth Armored Division had played a decisive role
in dashing the personal ambitions of Adolph Hitler.

23. The Aftermath

Mission Accomplished

The drive to Bastogne had taken its toll on the Fourth Armored Division. After the successful rebuff of the 1st SS Panzer Division on December 30, the Fourth Armored stood tall, but they had less than fifty combat ready Shermans spread out among three tank battalions. Replacement tanks were beginning to come on line (among them, the brand new M4A3E8s), but the tank battalions lacked the crews to man all of the available tanks. The numbers in all of the armored infantry battalions had been reduced to very low levels, and it was clear that the division's ability to continue with offensive operations had been significantly reduced. During the period between December 22 and January 13, the division suffered 1,101 battle casualties (an ironic number, given the unit designation of the men they were sent to rescue). There were 214 men killed in action, 831 wounded, and 56 missing. There was some consolation to be gained from the fact that, en route to Bastogne, they had killed or wounded more than 2,000 members of the 5th FJ Division, and had captured a number almost equal to that.

Fortunately, relief was on the way for the weary Fourth Armored. The 6th Armored Division was shifted from XII Corps to III Corps, and was inserted into the line in place of the Fourth. The Fourth Armored didn't leave the front immediately, however. It was kept nearby as a reserve, supporting the 35th Infantry Division.

Having beaten off the German's latest attempt to capture Bastogne, Millikin's III Corps now prepared to continue its attack against the south flank of the Bulge. The plan called for the 6th Armored Division to carry the main thrust to the northeast, with the support of the 35th ID on its right. The 26th Infantry Division, located to the right of the 35th ID, would also continue attacking in the direction of the Wiltz-Bastogne highway.

The efforts of the Fourth Armored Division to open the highways into Bastogne now paid dividends, as the 6th Armored Division's CCA rolled north along the Arlon-Bastogne highway into positions southeast of Bastogne, while CCB/6 used the Neufchâteau highway (though not without some difficulty, due to a traffic control SNAFU).

Machine gunners in an outpost position with tanks of the 4th Armored Division. January 3, 1945 (National Archives Photograph SC361012).

CCA/6 launched a limited attack on December 31 and had only modest success. Undermining their effort was the fact that CCB/6 had failed to get into position as planned (a direct result of the traffic problems they had encountered). CCB/6 joined the fray on New Year's Day, and the two powerful combat commands launched a coordinated attack toward the northeast (the 6th Armored entered the battle well-rested and virtually at full strength in tanks and men).

After a strong performance during the morning, the attack hit determined German resistance at Arloncourt and the woods southeast of Neffe. Due to a variety of circumstances, both the 101st Airborne (on the left of the 6th AD) and the 35th Infantry Division (on the right) failed to keep up with the advance of the 6th AD, which compelled Millikin to widen the front of the 6th Armored. Grow's division was spread so thin, that he was forced to commit his entire complement of tank and armored infantry battalions.

Despite the length of its front, the 6th AD carried out a determined attack on January 2. Casualties were heavy, as the Germans had reinforced their positions, and had even launched a counterattack against Grow's division, utilizing elements of the 12th SS Panzer Division, 167th VG Division, and 340th VG Division. "Much ground" had been gained by the end of the day, but the price was such that further advance by the 6th AD was very limited during the next seven days. The lack of progress was also attributable to the delays encountered by the 35th Infantry Division and the 101st Airborne Division. Plans for the 101st to attack on the left of the 6th AD were thwarted when the airborne division came under repeated heavy attacks during the first week of 1945.

One Final Thrust

After several days of rest and refitting, the Fourth Armored prepared once again to go on the offensive. After the initial modest success of the 6th Armored Division, the battle north and northeast of Bastogne had developed into something akin to a stalemate, and the Fourth Armored was called upon to break the logjam.

The plan called for the 101st Airborne Division and the Fourth Armored to attack side by side, with the 101st on the left and the Fourth Armored on the right. The 101st would initiate its portion of the attack on January 9, and the Fourth Armored would kick in the following day, commencing at 9 A.M.

Replacements for the 53rd AIB use a destroyed Mark IV tank for target practice with their bazookas. January 5, 1945 (National Archives Photograph SC324561).

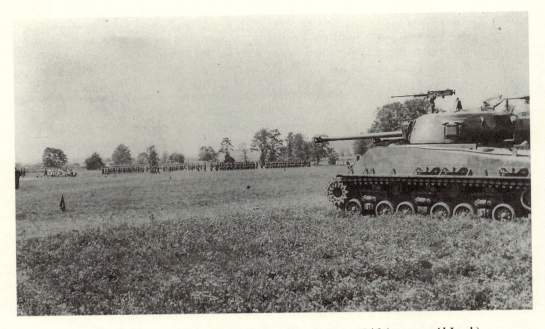

The final assembly of the 8th Tank Battalion, January 1946 (courtesy Al Irzyk).

The Fourth's objective for the first day was the town of Bourcy, located two miles northwest off its jumping off point near Bizory. CCB, which was built around the 37th Tank Battalion and 53rd AIB (C/704 and C/25 were also assigned to Dager's command), would attack on the left. CCA, which included the 35th Tank Battalion and 10th AIB, would strike on the right. The 8th Tank Battalion and 51st Armored Infantry Battalion were assigned to CCR, and remained in reserve.

There were mixed results as the Fourth emerged from the starting blocks. The Germans were still offering incredibly stubborn resistance (primarily from the 340th VG Division). As it advanced, the lead elements of CCB were hit with heavy mortar and artillery fire. A proliferation of machine guns and panzerfaust teams were positioned in the woods, which slowed the tanks down further. Enemy armor and anti-tank guns also cropped up to oppose them; A/37 "encountered one AT gun and three SP guns. The AT gun was destroyed and two of the SPs, the other was damaged."

CCA's 10th AIB and 35th Tank Battalion, which had the initial objective of clearing "the woods on the high ground northeast of Neffe," made good progress during the early part of the day. They had succeeded in clearing half of the woods when "heavy artillery and direct tank fire" forced them to withdraw "back over the crest of the hill to defilade positions."

The attack had not progressed more than 2000 yards when, at 2 P.M., the 37th Tank Battalion received a totally unexpected order. The Fourth Armored's role in the offensive was cancelled. By late that afternoon, every unit of CCA and CCB was so informed, and plans were made for organizing their relief from the front line (the 6th Armored Division would take over their part of the front).

What had happened was that the Allied command had grown nervous in the wake of the German's secondary offensive south of the Ardennes, in the Alsace region. Fearing that the German's might strike a surprise blow toward Luxembourg City, General Bradley ordered Patton to arrange for an armored division to be placed in reserve. With all of his armored divisions committed, Patton chose the Fourth Armored for the assignment.

As the Fourth Armored Division moved out of its positions that day, they were ordered to do something that they had not been called upon to do since the breakout in Normandy: they had to remove their shoulder patches. This was an attempt to keep the move to their new positions in Luxembourg a secret. Radio silence was imposed during the move, and vehicle identification markings were painted over. The division without a nickname was now the division without an identity. If ever the moniker "Name Enough" fit, it was now.

The Bulge in Perspective

Among military history enthusiasts, a frequent debate takes place over the relative importance of the action at Bastogne, as compared to other areas of the Ardennes. There is no doubt that the Drive to Bastogne will always be remembered as the Fourth Armored's most famous mission. But where does it fit in the greater scheme of the entire Battle of the Bulge?

The Bulge was unlike many other engagements, in that it was really defined by a series of small battles at critical points across the Ardennes. This phenomenon was largely a result of the terrain and road network, which produced critical choke points for movement and communications. A strong case can be made for rating several of these engagements among the most crucial to the outcome of the Bulge. Perhaps the one battle within the battle that is elevated to an equal stature with Bastogne, or even placed ahead of it, is the engagement at St. Vith. Certainly, it is easy to see how that case can be made, and it will not be debated here. I think every member of the Fourth Armored Division is proud of what the famous alumnus of the Fourth, Bruce Clarke, accomplished at St. Vith while in command of CCB/7 and, in essence, responsible for the defense of the town. Had Clarke not held as long as he did at St. Vith, events along the north flank of the Bulge would have been very different indeed. The impact would probably have been felt at Bastogne as well.

The German failure to capture Bastogne carried repercussions that were arguably just as devastating to the German cause as their failure to make a timely capture of St. Vith, if not more so. The initial failures at Bastogne were primarily Hitler's responsibility. Having made the mistake of not placing all of his available resources against the capture of Bastogne during the opening days of the offensive, he allowed the 101st Airborne Division, along with its attached units, to win the race to the most important prize east of the Meuse River. He then compounded his mistake by allowing the 101st to hold Bastogne until and beyond its relief by the Fourth Armored Division.

Had adequate resources been allocated at Bastogne, rather than for a premature advance toward the Meuse River, the outcome of the Battle of the Bulge would certainly have been much different. A German salient minus the cancerous cell at Bastogne would have afforded Model many more options for continuing the battle. The ripple effect from an early capture of Bastogne is, for all practical purposes, inestimable.

Just because Hitler failed to take Bastogne during the opening days of the offensive didn't mean that the fate of the German offensive was sealed. No matter how badly the Germans had botched the initial attack against Bastogne, the fact remained that they had it surrounded, and that the American garrison, large though it was, could not hold out indefinitely. The Screaming Eagles were extremely confident of their ability to hold out for as long as would be required of them. But their own top commanders knew that, eventually, someone would have to break through to them if they were to survive the experience. Brigadier General McAuliffe's own well documented day-by-day pre-occupation with the arrival of the Fourth Armored, and his expressions of disappointment over the perceived delay in the relief, stand as the truest barometer of the importance of the Fourth Armored Division's mission during those unforgettable days of December 1944.

Thus, on the morning of December 22, there was perhaps no mission in the Ardennes that was more important than the one assigned to the Fourth Armored Division. If they failed, the fate of the defenders of Bastogne would be in extreme doubt. And if the Fourth succeeded, it meant Bastogne would stay in American hands, and would become the anchor point for reducing the German salient. Though there was still bitter fighting ahead on the north side of the Bulge, the outcome there was never really in doubt after the first week of the battle. The Germans simply didn't have the resources to carry on a successful fight there. But the battle around Bastogne was still anyone's ballgame, and the Fourth Armored played the most critical role in determining the final score.

There had been no denying the men of the Fourth Armored in their drive to Bastogne (and one must certainly include the battalions of the 318th Infantry Regiment in the same breath). Fighting in the spirit and shadow of John Wood, they hammered away in the face of great adversity, until the job of opening and widening the corridor into Bastogne was achieved. But their success had come at a great cost. The Fourth suffered more casualties relieving Bastogne than the defenders of Bastogne suffered themselves. Likewise, the Germans threw down more lives here than anywhere else in the Ardennes. The 5th FJ Division would ultimately suffer more casualties than any other German division that fought in the Bulge. This is a testimony to the effectiveness of the Fourth Armored, but it is also a testimony to the tenacity that the German paratroopers displayed during the battle.

The Opponents

Over the years, the 5th FJ Division has been characterized by some as a weak, untried formation that did not represent itself well during the Battle of the Bulge. Though indeed stocked with its share of inexperienced, green troops, claims that they were weak could not be further from the truth. They were strong not only in numbers, but in courage and resolve. While the German paratroopers did run into some problems during the first few days of the offensive, the fact remains that they were the only

German division to achieve their initial objectives for the offensive. This is a distinction that many historians and students lose sight of.

The men of the Fourth Armored Division provide the best insight into the ability of the 5th FJ Division. "Roosevelt's Butchers," as the Germans liked (or hated) to call them, had fought against some of the toughest units that Hitler could produce. Yet ask the men of the division which unit they remember as giving them the toughest go of it, and many will quickly say the 5th FJ Division. Who better to judge them, than the men who had to go into battle against them?

Nat Frankel, a veteran Sherman tank commander in the 8th Tank Battalion, later summed up his opinion of the paratroopers he faced along the road to Bastogne:

> I want to describe these bastards because some observers have underrated them. They were, to be sure, inexperienced, but I can only know that from a later look at relevant documents. The facts is, they didn't act inexperienced. They were slick, savage, continuously shooting, continuously moving forward, almost sullen in their bloody determination.

But in case that opinion isn't viewed as being objective enough, it is worth pointing out that the Fourth Armored wasn't alone in its impression of the German para-

A column from the 4th AD passes a burning enemy vehicle during the advance through Germany. March 20, 1945 (National Archives Photograph SC203178).

A 4th Armored Division outpost near Bastogne. January 3, 1945 (National Archives Photograph SC364310).

troopers. In the history of 318th Infantry Regiment, which provided the two infantry battalions that fought alongside CCA and CCB against Heilmann's division, the following assessment is offered of the 5th FJ Division:

> Enemy opposition to our troops was identified from prisoners as coming from all elements of the German 5th Parachute Division which had been considerably reinforced by the attachment of the 408th Artillery Corps (6 battalions of artillery). The 5th Parachute Division was fifty percent stronger in infantry manpower than any normal German Volks-grenadier Division which had been encountered during the last few months. Each of the infantry regiments had three battalions and the personnel consisted mostly of the cream of the draft age Hitler Youth with fanatical morale.

The End Draws Near

Of course, the end of the Battle of the Bulge did not mean the end of the war for the men of the Fourth Armored Division. While Hitler's legions were severely weakened by the blow they suffered in the Ardennes, they were still capable of a fanatical defense of their homeland.

The war would continue for another four months, during which time the Fourth Armored would record a growing list of accomplishments, and write the final chapters of their history. Many new members of the division would come aboard after the hard and costly fighting in the Ardennes. More men would become casualties. More medals would be won, cities and towns captured, and rivers crossed with lightning speed. Some of the officers of the Fourth would move on to new commands. Others would move up within the division, and take on new responsibilities. Men that were brand new to the division would find ways to live up to the division's well-earned reputation.

The events after the Bulge are outside the scope of this volume, but they are no less important to the veterans of the division who experienced those closing months of the war. It would be an ambition of mine to write those chapters one day, but for now, we must end on the resounding note of the Fourth Armored Division's greatest deed: the Drive to Bastogne.

Epilogue

The Letter

After the dust of battle settles, and the losses are accounted for, it is a tradition within the United Stated Army that a solemn duty is carried out by the officers in command of those who have fallen. Whenever possible, a personal letter is written to the spouse or closest living relative of those killed in action. This was always a supplement to the standard notification that was sent to the surviving family. The official notification always arrived first, and the more personal reflections of the commanding officer usually trailed by a few weeks.

During my research for this book, James G. Kelly, the son of 1st Lt. Earl J. Kelly (Company A, 10th Armored Infantry Battalion), passed on to me a letter that was written to his father by the widow of one of the men killed at Chaumont: Lt. Charles Gniot. It had fallen on Earl Kelly to write to Lt. Gniot's widow, and she, in turn, felt compelled to share her thoughts with Lt. Kelly regarding her husband. Dated February 26, 1945, the letter reads:

Dear Lt. Kelly,

I hardly know you. I only remember your name through Charlie, who thought his best of you, but today I felt you as a close friend of mine personally, because I received your letter, and I don't find it hard to write to you.

Hope you will accept this letter from me, as little as words can express my deep gratitude to you. I just want you to know I appreciate your taking the time out to let me know your personal feelings towards my beloved Charles, as well as his other friends. I'm forced to believe of his death, but I will never believe he's dead, he's just away.

Allthough years may come before I lose this profound hurt, he lives in my heart forever.

Sympathy doesn't help much at a time like this, it is a great comfort to know others are sharing my sorrow.

He was well liked by all who knew him, but he was loved by me and only I have memories to share in the future. He was a good officer, but he was the best husband.

I get consolation from these words, "We must all die sometime, but we all can not die for a reason worth-while."

But we had such a short marriage, and he wanted so much to come back, he was so determined, it's so hard to believe.

The local American Legion Branch have accepted Gniot for their branch name, so you can imagine his reputation here, although his home town is Milwaukee, Wisc.

There will never be another Charlie, it was too good to be true, and when you own something you've always dreamed of, it never lasts.

My attitude toward life has hardened. I don't want to exist on this war-torn world, but if I must, then God and faith will see me through.

I can understand why you aren't able to tell me more concerning his death, Earl, but I do want to express something that pertains to you.

When you come back, my only hope is that you will try to come visit me and tell me about Charles. I hope my desire isn't asking too much, and I can say a prayer for your speedy & safe return.

I tried to keep my chin up, but I find it a very hard bargain, and I'm not too successful. Time will help, but won't heal.

I respect you for what you've done. I only hope that I can do something for you.

In conclusion of my epistle, I repeat my utmost appreciation to you. Should you find something more to write, please don't hesitate, I beg of you.

Sincerely,

Mrs. Helen Gniot

Yes, Mrs. Gniot, there was something more to write. And my fervent hope is that this book will help extend, to the generations that follow, a sense of the truly great deeds and accomplishments of this wonderful group of men, who sacrificed all, and gave of themselves what no other generation has been asked to give since. Above and beyond that, I truly hope that the survivors and descendents of the members of the Fourth

Lt. Earl Kelly, 10th AIB (right), poses in front of a captured German vehicle, along with Lt. Malloy (courtesy James Kelly).

Armored Division will find traces of their own loved ones' deeds and accomplishments within this volume, if not on an individual level, than as part of the great team built by John Shirley Wood.

I hope that the reader will walk away from this book having drawn the same conclusion that I did many years ago: that the Fourth Armored Division was the greatest armored division to serve during the Second World War.

If General Wood's vision is to be maintained, we must never lose sight of the actions and achievements of the men who comprised the Fourth Armored Division. No matter if the feat was achieved individually or collectively, we must always remember what they *accomplished*, not just the glowing title of "Patton's Best." To that end, I pray that this book, by documenting their actions for posterity, will help ensure that, in the words of their great leader, John Wood, *they shall be known by their deeds alone.*

Appendix A: The Units and Their Commanders

4th Armored Division

Major General John S. Wood
Major General Hugh J. Gaffey
Major General William M. Hoge

Combat Command A

Colonel Bruce C. Clarke
Lieutenant Colonel Creighton W. Abrams
Colonel William P. Withers
Brigadier General Herbert L. Earnest
Colonel Hayden A. Sears

Combat Command B

Brigadier General Holmes E. Dager
Colonel Creighton W. Abrams

Combat Command R

Colonel Louis J. Storck (KIA)
Colonel Walter A. Bigby
Colonel Wendell Blanchard

Division Artillery

Colonel Ernest A. Bixby
Colonel Alexander Graham*
Lietenant Colonel Neil M. Wallace

Division Trains

Colonel David A. Watt, Jr.
Colonel Wendell Blanchard

10th Armored Infantry Battalion

Lieutenant Colonel Graham Kirkpatrick *
Lieutenant Colonel Arthur L. West*
Lieutenant Colonel Harold Cohen

51st Armored Infantry Battalion

Lieutenant Colonel Alfred A. Maybach (KIA)
Major Harry R. Van Arnam*
Lieutenant Colonel Dan C. Alanis

53rd Armored Infantry Battalion

Lieutenant Colonel George L. Jaques

*Relinquished command as a result of wounds received in action

8th Tank Battalion	Lieutenant Colonel Edgar T. Conley, Jr.
	Lieutenant Colonel Henry P. Heid, Jr.
	Major Thomas G. Churchill
	Lieutenant Colonel Albin F. Irzyk
35th Tank Battalion	Lieutenant Colonel Bill A. Bailey
	Lieutenant Colonel Delk M. Oden
37th Tank Battalion	Lieutenant Colonel Creighton W. Abrams
	Major William L. Hunter
	Major Edward Bautz, Jr.
	Captain William A. Dwight
25th Cavalry Rec.Sqd. Mech	Lieutenant Colonel Leslie D. Goodall
22nd Armored Field Artillery Bn	Lieutenant Colonel Arthur C. Peterson
66th Armored Field Artillery Bn	Lieutenant Colonel Neil M. Wallace*
	Lieutenant Colonel F.W. Hasselback
94th Armored Field Artillery Bn	Lieutenant Colonel Alexander Graham
	Lieutenant Colonel Lloyd W. Powers
	Lieutenant Colonel Robert M. Parker, Jr.
24th Armored Engineer Battalion	Lieutenant Colonel Louis E. Roth
	Major Alonzo A. Balcom, Jr.
	Lieutenant Colonel William L. Nungesser*
	Major Donald W. Hatch
126th Arm'd Ordnance Maint. Bn	Lieutenant Colonel Richard B. Fuller
704th Tank Destroyer Battalion	Lieutenant Colonel Delk M. Oden
	Lieutenant Colonel Bill A. Bailey (KIA)
	Lieutenant Colonel Henry P. Heid, Jr.
	Major Dan C. Alanis
	Major Charles I. Kimsey
	Lt. Colonel James W. Bidwell
489th AAA (AW) Bn (SP)	Lieutenant Colonel Allen M. Murphy
46th Armored Medical Battalion	Lieutenant Colonel Robert E. Mailliard
144th Armored Signal Company	Captain Lucien E. Trosclair
Headquarters Company CCA	Captain Otis Strong
	Captain Alfred Ownes
Headquarters Company CCB	Captain Richard R. Irving
Headquarters Company, 4th AD	Captain Nelson D. Warwick
HQ Company, Division Trains	Captain La Rue McCleary

Appendix B: U.S. Armored Division — Organization and Weapons

Tank Battalion (3)   *53 Medium Tanks; 17 Light Tanks, 729 Men*
    Medium Tank Company (3)   *17 Medium Tanks*
    Medium Tank Platoon (3)   *5 Medium Tanks*
    Light Tank Company (1)   *17 Light Tanks*
    Light Tank Platoon (3)   *5 Light Tanks*
    HQ Company (1)   *3 105mm Assault Guns, 3 M21 81mm Mortars*
    Battalion HQ (1)   *2 Medium Tanks*
    Service Company (1)

Armored Infantry Battalion (3)   *1,001 Men*
    Armored Infantry Company (3)   *3 57mm Anti-Tank Guns (towed)*
        Armored Infantry Platoon (3)
            Rifle Squad (3)
            Mortar Squad (1)
            LMG Squad (1)
    Service Company (1)
    Battalion HQ (1)

Armored Field Artillery Battalion (3)   *18 M7 SP Howitzers, 534 men*
    Armored Field Artillery Battery (3)   *6 M7s*
    HQ Battery (1)   *3 Medium Tanks*
    Service Battery (1)

Armored Engineer Battalion (1)   *693 men*
    Armored Engineer Company (3)
    HQ Company (1)

Cav Reconnaissance Squadron, Mech. (1)   *935 men*
    Reconnaissance Troop (3)   *12 M8 Armored Cars*
    Light Tank Company (1)   *17 M5 Light Tanks*
    Assault Gun Troop (1)   *8 M8 Assault Guns*

ATTACHED UNITS*

Tank Destroyer Battalion (1)   ***36 Tank Destroyers, 669 men***
    Tank Destroyer Company (3)   *12 Tank Destroyers*
        TD Platoon (3)   *4 Tank Destroyers*

Anti-Aircraft Artillery (SP) Battalion   ***32 M15 SP Mounts, 32 M16 SP Mounts***
    AAA (SP) Battery (4)   *8 M15, 8 M16*

*The TD and AAA Battalions typically remained attached to the Division for the duration (in the case of the 704th and 489th, they were considered by all to be de facto integral parts of the division). As noted in the narrative, other units, such as artillery and infantry battalions, would be attached to the division from time to time.

Bibliography

Books

Astor, Gerald. *The Bloody Forest.* Novato, CA: Presidio Press, 2000.

Baldwin, Hanson W. *Tiger Jack.* Ft. Collins, CO: The Old Army Press, 1979.

Blumenson, Martin. *Breakout and Pursuit — United States Army in World War II: The European Theater of Operation.* Washington, D.C.: Office of the Chief of Military History, 1961.

_____. *The Duel for France, 1944.* Da Capo Press, 1963.

_____. *Heroes Never Die.* New York: Cooper Square Press, 2001.

_____. *The Patton Papers 1940–1945.* New York: Houghton Mifflin, 1974.

Bradley, Omar N. *A Soldier's Story.* New York: Henry Holt, 1951.

Buchanan, Richard R., et al., eds. *Men of the 704th — A Pictorial and Spoken History of the 704th Tank Destroyer Battalion in World War II.* Latrobe, PA: Publications of the Saint Vincent College Center for Northern Appalachian Studies, 1998.

Cole, Hugh M. *The Ardennes: Battle of the Bulge — United States Army in World War II: The European Theater of Operations.* Washington D.C.: Office of the Chief of Military History, 1965.

_____. *The Lorraine Campaign — United States Army in World War II: The European Theatre of Operations,* Washington D.C.: Historical Division, Department of the Army, 1950.

Cooper, Belton Y. *Death Traps.* Novato, CA: Presidio Press, 1998.

D'Este, Carlo. *Patton — A Genius for War.* New York: HarperCollins, 1995.

Dupuy, Trevor N. *Hitler's Last Gamble* New York: HarperCollins, 1994.

Eisenhower, Dwight D. *Crusade in Europe.* Garden City, N.Y: Doubleday, 1948.

Eisenhower, John S. D. *The Bitter Woods.* New York: G.P. Putnam's Sons, 1969.

Folkstead, William B. *The View from the Turret.* Shippensburg, PA: Burd Street Press, 2000.

Forty, George. *The Armies of George S. Patton.* London: Arms and Armour Press, 1996.

Gaul, Roland. *The Battle of the Bulge in Luxembourg — Volume II: The Americans.* Atglen, PA: Schiffer, 1995.

Gilbert, Martin. *The Second World War.* New York: Henry Holt, 1989.

Goldstein, Donald M. *Nuts! The Battle of the Bulge — The Story and Photographs.* Brassey's, 1994.

Green, Michael. *Patton and the Battle of the Bulge.* Osceola, WI: MBI, 1999.

Grow, Robert W. *The Ten Lean Years: From the Mechanized Force (1930) to the Armored Force (1940).* N.p., 1969.

Houston, Donald E. *Hell on Wheels — The 2d Armored Division* Novato, CA: Presidio Press, 1977.

Hynes, Samuel, et al. *Reporting World War II: American Journalism 1938–1946.* New York: The Library of America, 1995.

Irzyk, Albin F. *He Rode Up Front for Patton*. Raleigh, NC: Pentland Press, 1996.

Kane, Steve. *The 1st SS Panzer Division in the Battle of the Bulge*. Bennington, VT: Merriam Press, 1997.

Koyen, Kenneth. *The Fourth Armored Division—from the Beach to Bavaria*. 1946.

Lande, D.A. *I Was with Patton—First-Person Accounts of World War II in George S. Patton's Command*. St. Paul, MN: MBI, 2002.

Lee, Ulysses. *The Employment of Negro Troops, U.S. Army in World War II Special Studies*. Washington, D.C.: Center of Military History, U.S. Army, 1966.

Liddell Hart, Basil Henry, Sir. *History of the Second World War*. New York: Putnam, 1971.

Lyons, Stanley. *Pass in Review*. N.p., 1996.

MacDonald, Charles B. *A Time for Trumpets: The Untold Story of the Battle of the Bulge*. New York: William Morrow, 1985.

Macksey, Kenneth. *Tank Versus Tank*. London: Grub Street, 1999.

Marshall, S.L.A. *Bastogne: The First Eight Days*. Washington, D.C.: Infantry Journal Press, 1946.

Mitchell, Ralph M. *The 101st Airborne Division's Defense of Bastogne*. Combat Command Studies Institute, 1986.

Münch, Karlheinz. *Combat History of Schwere Panzerjäger Abteilung 653*. Winnipeg: J.J. Fedorowicz Publishing, 1997.

Parker, Danny S. *Battle of the Bulge: Hitler's Ardennes Offensive, 1944–1945*. Conshohocken, PA: Combined Publishing, 1991.

Patton, George S. *War as I Knew It*. New York: Houghton Mifflin, 1947.

Pergrin, David. *Engineering the Victory*. Atglen, PA: Schiffer Publishing, 1996.

Phillips, Henry Gerard. *The Making of a Professional: Manton S. Eddy, USA*. Westport, CT: Greenwood Press, 2000.

Quarrie, Bruce. *The Ardennes Offensive: US III & XII Corps—Southern Sector*. Oxford, UK: Osprey Publishing, 2001.

_____. *The Ardennes Offensive: I Armee & VII Armee—Southern Sector*. Oxford, UK: Osprey Publishing, 2001.

Rapport, Leonard. *Rendezvous with Destiny*. USA: 101st Airborne Division Association, 1948.

Reynolds, Michael. *The Devil's Adjutant—Jochen Peiper, Panzer Leader*. Staplehurst, UK: Spellmount Limited, 1995.

Shapiro, Milton J. *Tank Command: General George S. Patton's 4th Armored Division*. New York: David McKay, 1979.

Shirer, William L. *The Rise and Fall of the Third Reich*. New York: Simon & Schuster, 1959.

Sorley, Lewis. *Thunderbolt—From the Battle of the Bulge to Vietnam and Beyond: General Creighton Abrams and the Army of His Times*. New York: Simon & Schuster, 1992.

Tiemann, Ralf. *Chronicle of the 7. Panzer-Kompanie 1. SS-Panzer Division "Liebstandarte."* Atglen, PA: Schiffer Publishing, 1998.

Toland, John. *Battle—The Story of the Bulge*. New York: Random House, 1959.

Tolhurst, Michael. *Bastogne*. South Yorkshire, UK: Leo Cooper, 2001.

Weigley, Russell F. *Eisenhower's Lieutenants: The Campaign of France and Germany 1944–1945*. Bloomington: Indiana University Press, 1981.

Zaloga, Steven J. *Lorraine 1944—Patton vs Manteuffel*. Oxford, UK: Osprey Publishing, 2000.

Zijlstra, Gerrit. *Diary of an Air War*. USA: Eakin Press, 1944.

Papers, Reports, Articles

Baldwin, Hanson W. "'P' Wood of the 4th Armored." *Army Magazine*, January 1968.

Gabel, Christopher R, Dr. "The 4th Armored Division in the Encirclement of Nancy."

Hardison, David C. "Data on World War II Tank Engagements Involving the U.S. Third and

Fourth Armored Divisions. BRL Memorandum Report No. 798." Ballistic Research Laboratory, Aberdeen Proving Ground, Maryland, 1954.

Irzyk, Albin F., Brig. Gen. U.S. Army (ret.). "Bastogne: A Fascinating, Obscure Vignette." *Armor Magazine*, March-April 1986.

_____. "8th Tank Battalion's Daring Moselle Crossing." *World War II Magazine*. September 1997.

_____. "Lt. Gen. George S. Patton — Maj. Gen. John S. Wood." (n.p.) 2001.

_____. "The Mystery of 'Tiger Jack.'" *Armor Magazine*, Jan-Feb 1990.

_____. "The 'Name Enough' Division." *Armor Magazine*, July-August 1987.

_____. "Tank vs. Tank. Military Review," January 1946.

Leach, James H., Colonel, U.S. Army (ret.). "Twenty Days in December —1944." Historical presentation for Israel Defense Forces. Oct-Nov 1993.

_____. "Genesis to Greatness 1940–1945." Fourth Armored Division Association, 1982.

"Memoir of a Tank Killer." *Purple Heart Magazine*, May/June 1997. Assorted recollections from members of the 704th TD Battalion.

Seichepine, Jean-Paul. "The Liberation of Valhey — September 14th 1944." Mariie, Bathelemont, France, Jean-Nicolas Stofflet Association, 1999.

"Small Unit Actions — Singling. 4th Armored Division, 6 December 1944." Historical Division — U.S. War Department, 1946.

Subordinate commanders and staff of Combat Command A, 4th Armored Division. "The Nancy Bridgehead." Fort Knox, Kentucky.

Vandergriff, Donald E., Captain, U.S. Army. "The Exploitation from the Dieulouard Bridgehead." *Armor Magazine*, September-October 1995.

Combat Histories, After Action Reports and Interviews

8th Tank Battalion — Relief of Bastogne. Based on interview with Capt. Ezell, Exec O, and Capt. C.J. Stauber, S-2. Covers time period of 22 Dec 44 through 27 Dec 44. Interview conducted 7 Jan 45.

35th Tank Battalion — Relief of Bastogne. Based on interview with Capt. L.J. Ryan, S-3, and Lt. H.B. Lay. Covers period of 22 Dec 44, through 30 Dec 44. Interview conducted 8 Jan 45.

35th Tank Battalion — Relief of Bastogne. Based on group interview with S/Sgt. William Peterson (A/35), 1st Lt. Joseph Horton (B/35), 2nd Lt. Harold Madison (C/35), 1st Lt. Elmore Rounsavall (D/35), Lt. Col. Delk Oden, CO 35th TB. Covers period 21 Dec 44 through 10 Jan 45. Interview conducted 16-17 Feb 45.

188th Engineer Combat Battalion History (n.p.)

299th Engineer Combat Battalion Journal. (n.p.)

299th Engineer Combat Battalion Interviews. Interviews conducted with S/Sgt. Stanley Green, B/299, Sgt. Leon Tobin, B/299, Pfc. Glenn Rolling, B/299, Pvt. Francis Malkovski, B/299.

704th Tank Destroyer Battalion Combat Journal. Excerpt for September 19 & 20.

Account of CCB in the Relief of Bastogne. Based on interview session with Brig. Gen. Holmes Dager and Col. Clay Olbon. Interview conducted 7 Jan 45.

Account of CCR in the Relief of Bastogne. Based on interview session with Col. Blanchard. Interview conducted 6 Jan 45.

Action of the 1st Bn, 318th Regt in the drive toward Bastogne. Based on interview with Major George W. Connaughton and Capt. George Harwood. Interview conducted 29 Jan 45.

Action of the 2nd Bn, 318th Regt, 80th Div, in the Bastogne salient 24-28 December. Based on interview with Lt. Col. Glenn Gardner, CO 2nd Bn, Capt. Prentiss Foreman, Bn S-3, 2nd Lt. John Shuford. Bn S-2. Interview conducted 25 Jan 45.

After Action Report for Unit Citation — Bastogne. 51st Armored Infantry Battalion, 19 Dec 44 to 10 Jan 45.

Notes submitted by James H. Leach to author. August 13 & September 3, 2002.

Battalion Diary: 37th Tank Battalion, 4th Armored Division. By "Unknown Soldier," U.S. Army Command and General Staff College, Fort Leavenworth, Kansas.

Battle History—299th Engineer Combat Battalion from 16 December to 22 December 1944. Prepared by Lt. Col. Milton A. Jewett.

Citation for DSC: Captain Abraham J. Baum, 10th AIB.

Citation for DSC: Lt. Col. Harold Cohen, 10th AIB.

Citation for DSC: Captain Thomas J. Evans, C/704.

Citation for DSC: First Lieutenant William J. Marshall, C/8.

Citation for Medal of Honor: First Lieutenant James H. Fields, 10th AIB.

Citation for Medal of Honor: Private James R. Hendrix C/53.

Citation for Medal of Honor: Sgt. Joseph J. Sadowski, 37th Tank Battalion.

Citation for Medal of Honor: Private Paul J. Wiedorfer, G/31, 80thInf Div.

Citation for Silver Star: Private First Class Barney Verwolf, 35th Tank Battalion.

Combat Diary of the 10th Armored Infantry Battalion. 1944-1945 (n.p.).

Combat Diary of the 51st Armored Infantry Battalion. 1944-1945 (n.p.).

Combat Diary of the 94th Armored Field Artillery Battalion 1944-1945 (n.p.).

Combat History of the 4th Armored Division. 1944-45. U.S. Army Command and General Staff College. Fort Leavenworth, Kansas.

Drive toward Bastogne: 51st Armd Inf Bn. Period 24–31 Dec 44. Based on interview with Lt. Col. Dan Alanis, CO 51st AIB, and Maj. Harry Rockafeller, Ex O, 51st AIB. Interview conducted 16 Feb 45.

Edward Bautz, Rutgers College Class of 1941, Oral History, October 15, 1999.

Events Preceding Entry Into Bastogne. Report by Capt. Dwight regarding CCR action on 25 Dec and 26 Dec 45.

History of the 318th Infantry Regiment. Compiled by Robert T. Murrell, PNC Company M, 318th Infantry, 80th Infantry Division.

Interview with Major Abrams, Asst. G-4, 4th Armored Division. The Bulge period.

Interview with Lt. Donald E. Guild, 94th AFAB. Additional notes (3 pages) on personal action at the battle for Singling.

Interview with Major General Heinz Kokott, CG, 26th VG Division. Interview conducted 21 November 1945.

Interview with Capt. Harold V McCoy, Asst S3, 4th Armored Div Arty Describing Arty support provided by 4th Armored Div Arty, during relief of Bastogne. Interview conducted on 12 Feb 45.

Interview with Lt. Col. Pattison, Exec O, CCA/4. Report on CCA activities from 19 Dec 44 through 30 Dec 44. Interview conducted 13 Jan 45.

Narrative Summary of Operations of 4th Armored Division in the Relief of Bastogne. Prepared by Captain L.B.Clark.

Narrative Summary of CCB's part in the Relief of Bastogne, 20 through 29 Dec 44. Prepared by Captain L.B.Clark.

Radio Journal—37th Tank Battalion—26 December 44. Transcription for time period starting 1621 and ending 1755.

Relief of Bastogne: 4th Armored Division: 20 Dec 44–1 Jan 45. Based on interview of Captain Stedman Seay, Asst. G-3, 4th Armored, conducted 4 Jan 45.

Relief of Bastogne: Division Artillery, 4th Armored Division: 20 Dec 44 to 29 Dec 44. Based on interview with Major E.H. Meyer, S-3 Division Arty, conducted 7 Jan 45.

Relief of Bastogne: 10th Arm Inf Bn, 4th Armd. Div. Period 22 Dec through 29 Dec 45. Based on interview with Capt. Baum, Bn S-3, and Major Cohen, CO. Interview conducted on 8 Jan 45; supplement to this interview conducted with Cohen on 29 April 45.

Relief of Bastogne: 53rd Armored Infantry Battalion. Period 20–29 Dec 44. Based on interview with Maj. Henry Crosby, Exec O, and Lt. Col. George Jaques, CO 53rd AIB. Interview conducted on 8 Jan 45.

Relief of Bastogne: 94th FA Battalion, 4th Armored Division. Based on interview with Major Robert Parker, CO 94th FA Bn. Interview conducted 7 Jan 45.

Relief of Bastogne Pocket—37th Tank Battalion. Based on interview with Lt. Col. Creighton Abrams, CO 37th TB, Maj. Edward Bautz, Ex O 37th TB, Capt. William Dwight, S-3 37th TB, 2nd Lt. John Whitehill, CO A/37. Interview conducted 5 Jan 45.

War Diary—5th Panzer Army. Command and Staff Department. U.S. Army School. Fort Knox, Kentucky.

Correspondence

Letter from Paul Colangelo to Don Fox, July 2001. Responses to questions regarding the 704th TD Battalion.

Letter from Mrs. Helen Gniot to 1st Lt. Earl J. Kelly. Regarding the death of her husband.

Letters from Albin F. Irzyk to Don Fox. Commencing on April 2, 2001, a series of more than twenty letters covering various aspects of the 4th Armored Division, with particular focus on CCB and the 8th Tank Battalion.

Letter from James G. Kelly to Don Fox, July 3, 2001. Regarding Lt. Earl J. Kelly.

Letter from Hal C. Pattison (4th Armdd CCA HQ), to "The Bulge Bugle." August 1997. Subject: Task Force Ezell, and other items relate to the initial advance into the Ardennes.

Letter from Hal C. Pattison to Michael R. Peed. 23 October 1971. Detailed account regarding the circumstances surrounding the relief of General Wood.

Letter from Sam Ridley to Don Fox, June 30, 2001. Reply to submitted questions.

E-Mail Correspondence

Harry Feinberg to Don Fox, June 30, 2001. Recollections from the Bulge period.

Harry Feinberg to Don Fox, July 1, 2001. Recollections from the Bulge period.

Harry Feinberg to Don Fox, July 4, 2001. Recollections from the Bulge period.

Anthony Giallanza to Don Fox, April 4, 2002. Recollections from Bulge period.

Anthony Giallanza to Don Fox, April 6, 2002. Recollections from Bulge period.

Anthony Giallanza to Don Fox, April 7, 2002. Recollections from Bulge period.

James Kelly to Don Fox, June 25, 2001. Forwarding information regarding his father, Lt. Earl J. Kelly (10th AIB, A Company).

Jamie Leach to Don Fox, February 9, 2001. Relaying information on behalf of his father, Colonel James H. Leach (ret).

Jamie Leach to Don Fox, February 12, 2001. Relaying information for his father.

Jamie Leach to Don Fox, February 13, 2001. Relaying information for his father.

Jamie Leach to Don Fox, March 4, 2001. Relaying information for his father.

Jamie Leach to Don Fox, April 19, 2001. Information regarding correspondence between Horst Lange (5th FJ Division) and Colonel Leach.

John A. Whitehill to Don Fox, April 20 & 21, 2001. Reply to questions regarding the 37th during the Bulge.

John S. Wood, Jr., to Don Fox, August 4, 2002. Observations from meeting with his father shortly after his relief.

Military Unit Index

General Index